P9-CNE-918

ISRAEL

GUIDE

BE A TRAVELER - NOT A TOURIST!

Stephanie Gold

OPEN ROAD PUBLISHING

To Mom, Dad, Mary, Beth, & Eric

2nd Edition

TABLE OF CONTENTS

MAPS

SIDEBARS

1. INTRODUCTION

Israel and its neighboring countries are a mix of stability and flux, stubbornness and change. For thousands of years the wadis have twisted through the deserts, and likewise for thousands of years the trade route passes and water sources have attracted people to live, fight, and worship. Three major religions endure, and while some visit the holy sites in Jerusalem — The Western Wall, the Dome of the Rock, the Church of the Holy Sepulchre — that are a tribute to stability, others seek out the archaeological remains of shrines to Gods no longer honored, highlighting the fact that this is also a land of change.

This region is packed more densely than your luggage with pleasures and activities of all sorts, from scholarly to hedonistic, from religious to cultural, but tensions and dangers certainly exist as well, and a healthy mix of patience, care, and attention to the Practical Information sections should see you safely through them all. Be gentle with the guard doing his or her duty at the airport by carefully checking your toothpaste and dental floss, adapt your personal style and dress to religious and cultural sensitivities when necessary, eat some great food, talk to some wonderful people, and have a magnificent trip.

While travelers are drawn to places like Masada that seem to last forever, be aware of the sands that shift and all that might change since when this guide was researched and written to when you actually take the trip. Governments waver, international relations vacillate (the Jordan border crossing regulations, for example, are different every month), new restaurants come and go, and hotel prices rise (and sometimes even fall, depending on tourist demand). This guide will lead you through the places to stay and eat, sightsee and play, but you'll need to leave a window open to the businesses that change hands, and to prices that aren't carved in stone.

I've also prepared special chapters on excursions to Egypt and Jordan, the latter now accessible directly from Israel. Whether you're looking for desert adventure or just want to hang out on a beautiful sun-drenched beach, **Israel Guide** hopes to show you the way. Have a great trip.

2. EXCITING ISRAEL! - OVERVIEW

Israel is trying hard to set the orange metaphor in place, that it's the *Big Orange*, just like, you know, New York is the Big Apple. But while no one but the Israeli tourism board seems to have picked up on the conceit, the analogy is in some ways apt. Get past the tough rind and Israel opens its many segments to you – and yes, there are some pits.

Fruit symbolism aside, Israel has so many different ways to enjoy a vacation it can become overwhelming, even daunting. Despite its tiny size, no matter whether you have a week, a month, or a year, you're not going to be able to do it all and the sooner you make peace with that, the better. Travel isn't a competition, but it's so easy to get sucked into the game. You meet another traveler in a Jerusalem cafe. You drink coffee and you talk.

Then it begins. Did you go to the Dead Sea? Of course I went to the Dead Sea, what do you take me for, an oaf? Did you *do* Masada? Oh yes, we *did* Masada and walked up the snake path. But did you walk up the snake path before dawn to see the sunrise over Masada? Silence. Time to pay for that coffee and get going, because you just lost.

And so you will always do, because there's so much on offer in Israel, and what's one traveler's thrill will make another cringe with boredom. So, set your priorities, choose what will make you happy, and don't worry overmuch about the excavation not seen or the dive not taken.

RELIGIONS OF ISRAEL

Religious Israel is a trip and a half just by itself.

Many come to the Holy Land as pilgrims, and if that's your motivation your course will be fairly well mapped out in advance. Christians will be kept busy seeing the many sacred Jesus-related sites and churches from Bethlehem's **Grotto of the Nativity** where he was born to **Nazareth** where he grew up, from around the Sea of Galilee where he preached and healed, to Jerusalem where he walked the **Via Dolorosa** and was crucified.

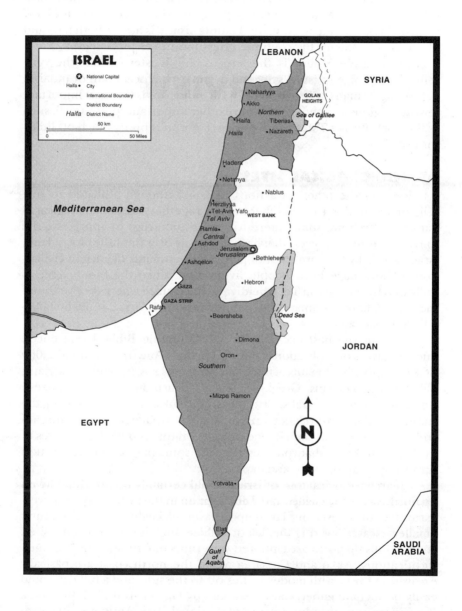

Muslims come to Jerusalem as well to pray at the **Dome of the Rock**, the third Muslim pilgrimage site after Mecca and Medina. Believed to be where Abraham bound Ismael for sacrifice (Muslims believe it was Ismael rather than Isaac who was involved) and the site Mohammed took off from on his journey to heaven, the **Temple Mount** is holy to both Jews and Muslims alike (hence the continued tug-of-war over Jerusalem).

The Temple Mount is the site of the **Western Wall** (the only remaining vestige of Israel's Second Temple, the focal point of Judaism before the Romans destroyed it in 70 CE), and thus is the most important Jewish religious site, though there are other important spots as well, such as the holy cities of **Tsfat** and **Tiberias** (Hebron is pretty much off limits for now).

ARCHAEOLOGICAL SITES

Some of the other attractions in Israel, though affiliated to one religion or another (or a number heaped together) are archaeological in nature and require some interest in excavation digs to appreciate the finds. Given all the powers that have held sway over this little plot of land, Israel is a rocky treasure chest of preserved remnants of ancient civilizations. There have been people living here since the Stone Age, as indicated by the digs on **Tel Ubeidiya** in the Galilee where they've found the earliest known human settlements outside of Africa, some 600,000-800,000 years ago.

Many of the best excavations, substantiating Biblical references, uncover layers of civilizations from the Bronze Age (from around 2,000 BCE) on up, with remnants of the Canaanites, Hyksos, Israelites, Assyrians, Babylonians, Persians, Greeks, Seleucids, Hasmonaeans (Maccabees), Romans, Byzantines, Arabs, Crusaders, Mamluks, and Turks. Among the cultural artifacts are religious relics, ancient synagogues and churches and mosques, usually built by the winners on top of the religious sites of the losers. If this is what you like, there are some magnificent excavation sites to bone up on, visit, and explore.

An archaeological tour of Israel would certainly take in **Beit She'an** up northeast in the Galilee and **Tel Megiddo** in the northwest, both well-excavated sites revealing layer upon layer of civilization and culture. Smaller excavations ring the Sea of Galilee, highlighting religious sites, and the hills up north are cluttered with ruins of Crusader and Mamluk fortifications. Akko and Caesarea along the north coast are basically excavation towns with modern cities off to the side, and a full day could easily be spent at either. **Caesarea**, built by Herod around 22 BCE on a Phoenician port, is a long string of National Park Antiquity sites with especially fine Roman remains in a dazzlingly beautiful setting, while

Akko's ancient city of **Acre** has been excavated underground beneath the Turkish Old City site. Flavored by its modern Arab population living above the old Crusader and Turkish halls and *hammams*, it mixes living culture with past remains.

Jerusalem, of course, among all its other draws, is full of excavations. There's **David's City**, **Hezekiah's Tunnel** (engineered to help withstand an Assyrian siege), the **Cardo** (main street in Roman Jerusalem), and plenty more. In fact it's now more than 3,000 years since Jerusalem was David's City. And to the south along the Dead Sea, **Masada** (the Zealot's mountain stronghold against the Romans) needs a few hours worth of exploration to take in Herod's palaces and the adaptations made by the Zealots as they attempted to weather the siege.

BACK TO NATURE

While tourists are often drawn by Israel's religious and historical treasures, its natural bounties are equally impressive. For a small country Israel has an amazingly diverse array of eco-systems and terrains, and they're all incredibly beautiful, and available for your hiking, biking, swimming, diving, jeeping pleasure.

There are numerous National Parks and Reserves throughout Israel, with tended trails and clean facilities, and **Rosh Hanikra's** white cliffs and water caves up near the border with Lebanon are considered a national natural gem. The **Galilee** and **Golan** regions in the northeast are the Israeli favorites, with verdant hills, icy streams, and fertile fields creating a green paradise in an otherwise arid region.

But the **Judean** and **Negev deserts** to the south are lovely in their own ways, and you don't have to be a geologist to appreciate their rugged charms. There are day or week long treks that guide you into the hills and *wadis* (dry desert river beds), using various means of transportation (feet, bicycle, jeep, or camel) to explore the country up close and physical. This sort of activity not only gives you the leisure to appreciate the appeal of the land, you also gain insights into the history and culture in a more visceral, less academic way. Sure it's athletic and healthy to tromp through the Judean Hills, but climbing up the parched paths to the Judean desert caves where Bar Kokhba and his men hid lets you appreciate that segment of history more keenly than by viewing the cave finds in the air-conditioned haven of the **Israeli Museum Shrine of the Book**.

WATER FUN

But there are other, more refreshing, outdoor amusements available. In and about the deserts, there's a lot of water here. You can go rafting down the Jordan, water-skiing on the Sea of Galilee, swimming and beaching on the Mediterranean, and snorkeling in the Red Sea. The Sea of Galilee, along with its religious appeal, is a vast water park resort in the summer, attracting Israelis and visitors alike to its beautiful shores.

The Mediterranean flanks Israel's west coast, and beach resorts like **Netanya, Herzliya, Nahariya**, and **Ashkelon** are geared toward the easy life of bask and bathe. The **Dead Sea** offers a unique bathing experience, buoyed up to an extreme by the mineral dense waters. Then at the southern tip of Israel, there's **Eilat**. On the Gulf of Aqaba off the Red Sea, Eilat is a resort city dedicated to the hedonistic pleasures of sunbathing, swimming, snorkeling, partying, and getting up to do it again.

MUSEUMS

Then there are the museums and memorials. Between those showcasing archaeological finds, those honoring national triumphs, and those commemorating the dead, there are more museums and memorials than you could shake a stick at, and more importantly, more than you could possibly see in one, two, or three Israel visits. Yet they are all of interest to one taste or another, and it's up to you to decide which sort and how many to take in.

Jerusalem's **Yad Vashem**, a memorial to the victims of the Holocaust, is a special place, sad and moving and unique. Jerusalem's **Israel Museum** is a storehouse of national treasures, and an amazing place to spend a day (or a week). The Israel Museum and East Jerusalem's **Rockefeller Museum** with its archaeological riches house the best that's found throughout Israel, and it's a remarkable collection. And then there are some 20 or so smaller museums, and that's just in Jerusalem alone.

In Tel Aviv you'll find more special spots. The **Diaspora Museum** is an outstanding place devoted to the many facets (facial, musical, genealogical, cultural) of Jewish communities around the world, and the Eretz Israel Museum complex is another interesting collection. The Tel Aviv area hosts lots of nationalist museums as well, telling the story of the War of Independence, the underground struggles under the British Mandate, and the early heroes who led the nation to statehood.

Up north, museums tend to be smaller and more specific, devoted to an individual episode like the Tel Hai massacre, or the archaeological findings a kibbutz dug up as they plowed their fields. And in the south, the most extraordinary collection is in an aquarium. **Coral World** in Eilat is a sophisticated, educational, entertaining venue showing all the fish you'd want to see (but might not actually do so) if you were in the Red Sea with a rubber tube in your mouth. With its underwater observation tank, coral reef room, and electronic guide, it's well worth visiting if you're down around those parts.

KIBBUTZIM

Visiting (or staying, or working on) a kibbutz lets you in on another side of Israel. **Ein Gev** on the Sea of Galilee and **Ein Gedi** on the Dead Sea are famous kibbutzim, and their tourist villages have been in operation for a long time. The Galilee is teeming with kibbutzim that welcome tourists, and there are others scattered throughout Israel as well.

Spending some time on one, relaxing, and talking a bit to the people who live there gives a different view of Israel – their individual histories are interesting, the museum or zoo (they all seem to have a little Archaeological trove or ostrich farm or petting zoo) is usually worthwhile, and many have special facilities set up for tourists (water skiing on the Sea of Galilee, for example) as well.

CULTURE

But while religion, archaeology, museums, and the great outdoors are all important and rewarding, the living, breathing culture of Israel today shouldn't be ignored. There is a wealth of traditions, customs, and foods brought by the many cultures who've settled here, just as vital to understanding Israel as what you'll find in the display cases after you've paid your entrance fee.

The research necessary to understanding it all entails hanging out at cafés, following your nose down alleys to small restaurants, and hobnobbing with the locals at a variety of night spots. Jerusalem offers extraordinary Arabic cuisine, traditional Jewish foods, and Hungarian, Kurdish, and Tunisian as well. And if superior Jewish Italian food is to your liking, Jerusalem has that as well. Jerusalem also has a very active café scene, and you could easily spend hours pursuing sedentary cultural research over some cappuccino and Mozart Cake while reading the *Jerusalem Post* and making conversation with the locals. There's a stimulating nightlife as well, with jazz pubs, historic bars, wee-hour discos, and chamber music and organ recitals.

Tel Aviv, too, has a rollicking nightlife, catering to a young majority that likes music, dance, and a good time. Tel Aviv also has some of the best falafel in Israel, authentic Yemenite and Eastern European Jewish food, as well as classier joints serving haute cuisine to a sophisticated Tel Aviv crowd. Down south in Eilat, hedonism is a way of life. If you want to experience how Israelis live it up when they've finished their tour of army duty, visit the King's Wharf pub strip after 10pm.

Up north, while mountain ridges spread out the clusters of accessible culture, Tiberias offers many of the usual city attractions (though with decidedly touristic overtones), and there are isolated culinary gems such as Vered Hagalil and Ein Camonim with good country fresh food. And to the west, Akko dishes up justly celebrated hummus and baklava. Just remember, it's not only about good eating, it's part of the experience of being in Israel.

EXCURSIONS TO JORDAN & EGYPT

True, Israel is full of a seemingly endless number of ways to enjoy a visit, but that doesn't mean you can't heap your plate a little fuller. Just to the east of Israel is **Jordan**, and now that the borders are open (but before Jordan's tourism industry has advanced any further) it's a terrific time to visit. **Amman** is a multi-tiered and interesting big city to explore, the ruins of **Jerash** are magnificent, the desert castles are exotic, and **Aqaba** offers the underwater wonders of the Red Sea – but **Petra** is the reason most people come to Jordan. And unlike many sites slathered across tourism brochures, Petra is worth the trip. Carved out of the rose colored rock, the Nabatean city of Petra really is an outstanding sight.

And then there's Egypt. The splendors of the pyramids, sphinx, and **Valley of the Kings** are no secret, and they're much closer to you in Israel than they are back home. Soak up the rich traditions and active streetlife of **Cairo**, or enjoy the beauty of the **Sinai** desert. A bus trip takes a long grueling time and a flight may not be in your budget, but it's right there, just next door, and hard to resist.

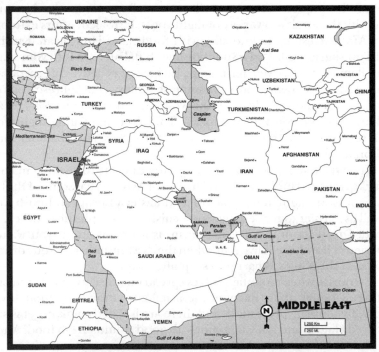

3. SUGGESTED ITINERARIES

To help deal with the vast quantity of possibilities and options, here are some general interest itineraries planned for two week, four week, and six week trips. Mix and match, keep some and chuck the rest, these itineraries map out potential routes for those who want to sample some of all that Israel has to offer, taking in the religious, archaeological, natural and cultural to the best of your time constraints. They move you at a medium to relaxed pace, can be done by car, bus, or a mix of the two, and include some variations and options to accommodate different interests.

Assuming you're flying in and from Ben Gurion Airport, the routes all begin and end in Tel Aviv, the closest city to the airport, though Jerusalem is within easy reach as well. The itineraries can't take into account, however, what day you're arriving, and that complicates matters due to Shabbat restrictions.

If you're driving that eases plans a bit, but if you're going by train or bus, you'll need to stay put for Shabbat or plan for it in advance as the public transport system shuts down, for the most part from Friday sundown to Saturday sundown, and certain sites are shut then as well.

ITINERARY 1
Tel Aviv, the Galilee, the Northwest Coast/Golan Heights, and Jerusalem
• *1a: Tel Aviv - Tiberias - Nahariya or Akko - Haifa - Nazareth or Megiddo - Jerusalem - Dead Sea - Tel Aviv*
• *1b: Tel Aviv - Tiberias - Tsfat - Golan Heights - Jerusalem - Dead Sea - Tel Aviv*
• *Number of days: 14*
• *Transportation: bus or car, though some options need car transport.*

Option 1a: Day One
Assuming you arrive in late afternoon, as many flights do, get settled in your hotel in Tel Aviv, stroll along the promenade by the beach, and

get your bearings. If there's time and it's warm, take a swim, find a cafe to your liking, or wander around HaCarmel shuk (street market) and the old Neve Tzedek neighborhood to stretch the kinks out of your legs.

Day Two
  Take the bus to the Tel Aviv University in Ramat Aviv and go to the Diaspora Museum. When you're done, if you want more good museum time stop off at the Eretz Israel Museum (also in Ramat Aviv) on your way back. Lounge about the beach, find a restaurant to your liking, and take advantage of the Tel Aviv nightlife before heading off to the boonies.

Day Three
  Rent a car or take a bus to Tiberias. Settle into a hotel in Tiberias or at one of the many places around the Sea of Galilee. Explore the open-air Tiberias Archaeological Museum and wander up and around the Promenade. Depending on time and energy, you might want to go the Galilee Experience on the Promenade.

Day Four
  See some of the sights in Tiberias. Get to the tourist office by 9:30 for their free walking tour, or check out the sites that appeal to you. After lunch, head out to Hamat Tiberias followed, maybe, by a soak in the Tiberias Hot Springs across the street. If you have a car, drive up Mount Tabor or to the Horns of Hittin to watch the sun set.

Day Five
  See the religious sights around the lake or do the lower Galilee loop. If you do the loop, you'll have to make some decisions, and how much you see will depend on whether you're going by bus or car, and of course how much time you spend per site. The mosaic at Beit Alpha is one of the best you'll see, Gan HaShlosha is lovely, Beit She'an is worth seeing, and Belvoir Castle is for Crusader ruins fans, while Hammat Gader is for everyone. Hammat Gader is also open at night, and if you ran out of time or cruised the lake sites, going in the evening is another option.

Day Six
  From Tiberias go to Akko if you want a day seeing the ruins or to Nahariya if you want a day on the beach. Explore or hang out, as you prefer. There are more lodging options in Nahariya, so even if you go to Akko for the day you might prefer to stay the night in Nahariya.

Day Seven
  Head north up the coast to the grottos at Rosh Hanikra. On your way

back (and if you have a car) you could detour to see the Montfort Crusader castle, or stop off at Akhziv to see the tide pools and take a swim. Continue on south to Haifa and settle into a hotel.

Day Eight

See the Baha'i Shrine, and more if you're so inclined, then head south, to Nazareth if you've an interest in the Christian sites, or Tel Meggido for an Archaeological treasure, or visit the Druze villages in Carmel. Find a place to stay nearby or on the way to Jerusalem, or push yourself and collapse at night in Jerusalem. Or take the train down to Jerusalem from Haifa.

Day Nine

Head to Jerusalem, get settled, and start taking it all in.

Days Ten-Eleven

See the sites and museums of Jerusalem and environs as per your tastes and interests. You might want to fit in a SPNI hike if you have time (and interest).

Day Twelve

Go climb Masada, swim in the Dead Sea, and visit the Ein Gedi Nature Reserve.

Day Thirteen

Go to Tel Aviv and visit Shuk HaCarmel and Bezelel market for your last wonderful chance at falafel, and visit the Wax Museum in Shalom Tower if you have time.

Option 1b (most practical by car): Day One

Assuming you arrive in late afternoon, as many flights do, get settled in your hotel in Tel Aviv, stroll along the promenade by the beach, and get your bearings. If there's time and it's warm, take a swim, find a cafe to your liking, or wander around HaCarmel shuk (street market) and the old Neve Tzedek neighborhood to stretch the kinks out of your legs.

Day Two

Take the bus to the Tel Aviv University in Ramat Aviv and go to the Diaspora Museum. When you're done, if you want more good museum time stop off at the Eretz Israel Museum (also in Ramat Aviv) on your way back. Lounge about the beach, find a restaurant to your liking, and take advantage of the Tel Aviv nightlife before heading off to the boonies.

Day Three

Rent a car or take a bus to Tiberias. Settle into a hotel in Tiberias or at one of the many places around the Sea of Galilee. Explore the open-air Tiberias Archaeological Museum and wander up and around the Promenade. Depending on time and energy, you might want to go the Galilee Experience on the Promenade.

Day Four

See some of the sights in Tiberias. Get to the tourist office by 9:30 for their free walking tour, or check out the sites that appeal to you. After lunch, head out to Hamat Tiberias followed, maybe, by a soak in the Tiberias Hot Springs across the street. If you have a car, drive up Mount Tabor or to the Horns of Hittin to watch the sun set.

Day Five

See the religious sights around the lake or do the lower Galilee loop. If you do the loop, you'll have to make some decisions, and how much you see will depend on whether you're going by bus or car, and of course how much time you spend per site. The mosaic at Beit Alpha is one of the best you'll see, Gan HaShlosha is lovely, Beit She'an is worth seeing, and Belvoir Castle is for Crusader ruins fans, while Hammat Gader is for everyone. Hammat Gader is also open at night, and if you ran out of time or cruised the lake sites, going in the evening is another option.

Day Six

From Tiberias make your way to Tsfat. Spend the rest of the day and some of the next wandering around the maze like streets.

Day Seven

Spend another day in Tsfat visiting the surrounding sites, or make you way north to see the sights of Hazor and the Hula Valley.

Day Eight

Visit Metulla, Banyas, and Mount Hermon, and figure out where to stay for the night.

Day Nine

Head towards Jerusalem, stopping off at Katzrin and/or Korazim if you're so inclined.

Days Ten-Eleven

See the sites and museums of Jerusalem and environs as per your tastes and interests. You might want to fit in a SPNI hike.

Day Twelve
Go climb Masada, swim in the Dead Sea, and visit the Ein Gedi Nature Reserve.

Day Thirteen
Go to Tel Aviv and visit Shuk HaCarmel and Bezelel market for your last wonderful chance at falafel, and visit the Wax Museum in Shalom Tower if you have time.

ITINERARY 2

Tel Aviv and environs, the Galilee and Golan Heights, the West Coast, Jerusalem, the Dead Sea, the Negev, and Eilat
* *Tel Aviv - Herzliya or Ramla or Rishon le-Zion - Tiberias - Lower Galilee - Tsfat - Golan Heights - Nahariya or Akko - Haifa - Nazareth or Beit Shearim and Megiddo - Jerusalem - Dead Sea - Mitzpe Ramon - Eilat - Tel Aviv*
* *Number of days: 27*
* *Transportation: bus or car, though some options need car transport.*

Days One-Three
Get settled in your hotel in Tel Aviv, stroll along the promenade by the beach, and get your bearings. Take a swim, find a cafe to your liking, or wander around HaCarmel shuk (street market) and the old Neve Tzedek neighborhood to stretch the kinks out of your legs. Visit Jaffa, go to the Diaspora Museum, and maybe the Eretz Israel Museum on your way back. Visit some of the neighboring towns such as Rishon le-Zion, Ramla, Herzliya, or Caesarea. And enjoy the food and nightlife of Tel Aviv.

Days Four-Six
Go to Tiberias and get a hotel there or one of the many options nearby. Take a few days to explore the sights of Tiberias (including Hamat Tiberias and maybe the Hot Springs), around the Sea of Galilee, and the sights in Lower Galilee, including Beit She'an and Hammat Gader.

Days Seven-Nine
Go to Tsfat. Spend a few days getting to know Tsfat and visiting the nearby sites.

Days Ten-Eleven
Drive around the Golan Heights (or go by bus), making you way north to see the sights of Hazor and the Hula Valley. Visit Metulla, Banyas, and Mount Hermon, and figure out where to stay for the night.

Day Twelve-Thirteen

From there go to Akko if you want a day seeing the ruins or to Nahariya if you want a day on the beach. Explore or hang out, as you prefer. There are more lodging options in Nahariya, so even if you go to Akko for the day you might prefer to stay the night in Nahariya. Head north up the coast to the grottos at Rosh Hanikra. On your way back (and if you have a car) you could detour to see the Montfort Crusader castle, or stop off at Akhziv to see the tide pools and take a swim. Continue on south to Haifa and settle into a hotel.

Day Fourteen

See the Baha'i Shrine, and more if you're so inclined, then head south, to Nazareth if you've an interest in the Christian sites, or Beit Shearim and Tel Meggido for Archaeological treasures, or visit the Druze villages in Carmel. Find a place to stay nearby or on the way to Jerusalem, or head back to Haifa so you can take the train down to Jerusalem from Haifa.

Days Fifteen-Eighteen

See the sites and museums of Jerusalem and environs as per your tastes and interests. You might want to fit in a SPNI hike if you have time (and interest).

Day Nineteen

Climb Masada, swim in the Dead Sea, visit Ein Gedi Nature Reserve.

Days Twenty to Twenty-One

Explore the Negev using Mitzpe Ramon as a base.

Days Twenty-Two to Twenty-Five

Go to Eilat, hang out on the beach, see Coral World, and snorkel. See Timna and the Reserve environs, or head back north to Jerusalem (for example) to see places you missed.

Day Twenty-Six

Go to Tel Aviv and visit Shuk HaCarmel and Bezelel market for your last wonderful chance at falafel, and visit the Wax Museum in Shalom Tower if you have time.

ITINERARY 3

Around Tel Aviv, the Galilee and Golan Heights, Jerusalem, the Negev, and Jordan

• *Tel Aviv - Haifa - Nahariya or Akko - Beit Shearim and Megiddo or Nazareth -Tiberias - Tsfat - Golan Heights - Lower Galilee - Jordan - Eilat - Mitzpe Ramon - Dead Sea - Jerusalem - Tel Aviv*

• *Number of days: 34*

• *Transportation: by bus or car, though some options need car transport.*

Days One-Three

Get settled in your hotel in Tel Aviv, stroll along the promenade by the beach, and get your bearings. Take a swim, find a cafe to your liking, or wander around HaCarmel shuk (street market) and the old Neve Tzedek neighborhood to stretch the kinks out of your legs. Visit Jaffa, go to the Diaspora Museum, and maybe the Eretz Israel Museum on your way back. Visit some of the neighboring towns such as Rishon le-Zion, Ramla, Herzliya, or Caesarea. And enjoy the food and nightlife of Tel Aviv.

Day Four

Go to Haifa and see the Baha'i Shrine, some of the rest of Haifa.

Days Five-Seven

From there go to Akko if you want a day seeing the ruins or to Nahariya if you want a day on the beach. Explore or hang out, as you prefer. There are more lodging options in Nahariya, so even if you go to Akko for the day you might prefer to stay the night in Nahariya. Head north up the coast to the grottos at Rosh Hanikra.

On your way back (and if you have a car) you could detour to see the Montfort Crusader castle, or stop off at Akhziv to see the tide pools and take a swim. Continue on east to Tiberias, stopping off at Nazareth if you've an interest in the Christian sites, or Beit Shearim and Tel Meggido for Archaeological treasures.

Days Eight-Nine

Go to Tiberias and get a hotel there or one of the many options nearby. Take a few days to explore the sights of Tiberias (including Hamat Tiberias and maybe the Hot Springs), and around the Sea of Galilee.

Days Ten-Eleven

Go to Tsfat. Spend a couple days getting to know Tsfat and visiting the nearby sites.

Days Twelve-Thirteen
Drive around the Golan Heights (or go by bus), making you way north to see the sights of Hazor and the Hula Valley. Visit Metulla, Banyas, and Mount Hermon, and figure out where to stay for the night.

Days Fourteen-Fifteen
Back to a hotel in Tiberias or around the Sea of Galilee, visit sights in Lower Galilee, including Beit She'an and Hammat Gader.

Day Sixteen
Cross the Jordan River border near Beit She'an into Jordan and spend the night at Irbid, or continue.

Days Seventeen-Twenty
See south in Jordan, stopping off in Jerash or Amman, seeing Petra, and ending up in Aqaba.

Days Twenty-One to Twenty-Five
Go to Eilat, hang out on the beach, see Coral World, and snorkel. See Timna and the Reserve environs, or head back north to Jerusalem (for example) to see places you missed.

Days Twenty-Six to Twenty-Seven
Explore the Negev using Mitzpe Ramon as a base.

Days Twenty-Eight to Thirty-One
See the sites and museums of Jerusalem and environs as per your tastes and interests. You might want to fit in a SPNI hike if you have time (and interest).

Day Thirty-Three
Go climb Masada, swim in the Dead Sea, and visit the Ein Gedi Nature Reserve, and head back to Jerusalem.

Day Thirty-Four
Go to Tel Aviv and visit Shuk HaCarmel and Bezelel market for your last wonderful chance at falafel, and visit the Wax Museum in Shalom Tower if you have time.

ITINERARY 4

Around Tel Aviv, the Galilee and Golan Heights, Jerusalem, Negev, and Egypt

• *Tel Aviv - Tiberias - Lower Galilee - Tsfat - Golan Heights - Nahariya or Akko - Haifa - Tel Aviv - Cairo - Eilat - Mitzpe Ramon - Dead Sea - Jerusalem - Tel Aviv*

• *Number of days: 34*

• *Transportation: bus or car, though some options need car transport, and Egypt requires a plane trip.*

Days One-Two

Get settled in your hotel in Tel Aviv, stroll along the promenade by the beach, and get your bearings. Take a swim, find a cafe to your liking, or wander around HaCarmel shuk (street market) and the old Neve Tzedek neighborhood to stretch the kinks out of your legs.

Visit Jaffa, go to the Diaspora Museum, and maybe the Eretz Israel Museum on your way back. Visit one of the neighboring towns such as Rishon le-Zion, Ramla, Herzliya, or Caesarea. And enjoy the food and nightlife of Tel Aviv.

Days Three-Five

Go to Tiberias and get a hotel there or one of the many options nearby. Take a few days to explore the sights of Tiberias (including Hamat Tiberias and maybe the Hot Springs), around the Sea of Galilee, and the sights in Lower Galilee, including Beit She'an and Hammat Gader.

Days Six-Eight

Go to Tsfat. Spend a few days getting to know Tsfat and visiting the nearby sites.

Days Nine-Ten

Drive around the Golan Heights (or go by bus), making you way north to see the sights of Hazor and the Hula Valley. Visit Metulla, Banyas, and Mount Hermon, and figure out where to stay for the night.

Day Eleven-Twelve

From there go to Akko if you want a day seeing the ruins or to Nahariya if you want a day on the beach. Explore or hang out, as you prefer. There are more lodging options in Nahariya, so even if you go to Akko for the day you might prefer to stay the night in Nahariya. Head north up the coast to the grottos at Rosh Hanikra. On your way back (and if you have a car) you could detour to see the Montfort Crusader castle, or stop off at Akhziv to see the tide pools and take a swim. Continue on south to Haifa and settle into a hotel.

Day Thirteen-Fourteen
See the Baha'i Shrine, and more if you're so inclined, then head south, to Nazareth if you've an interest in the Christian sites, or Beit Shearim and Tel Meggido for Archaeological treasures, or visit the Druze villages in Carmel. Find a place to stay nearby or head back to Haifa or on down to Tel Aviv.

Day Fifteen
Fly down to Cairo and get settled.

Days Sixteen-Twenty
Visit the sites that interest you most in Egypt, given the time. You should be able to see the pyramids, the Egypt Museum, the market, and lots more in five days.

Day Twenty-One
Take the bus up to the Taba border and cross over to Eilat.

Days Twenty-Two to Twenty-Five
Hang out on the beach, see Coral World, snorkel. See Timna and the Reserve environs, or head back north to Jerusalem (for example) to see places you missed.

Days Twenty-Six to Twenty-Seven
Explore the Negev using Mitzpe Ramon as a base.

Days Twenty-Eight to Thirty-One
See the sites and museums of Jerusalem and environs as per your tastes and interests. You might want to fit in a SPNI hike if you have time (and interest).

Day Thirty-Three
Go climb Masada, swim in the Dead Sea, and visit the Ein Gedi Nature Reserve, and head back to Jerusalem.

Day Thirty-Four
Go to Tel Aviv and visit Shuk HaCarmel and Bezelel market for your last wonderful chance at falafel, and visit the Wax Museum in Shalom Tower if you have time.

4. LAND & PEOPLE

LAND

Israel's land stretches for 420 kilometers, from the northern border with Lebanon and Syria in the Golan Heights on down to Eilat, the country's port on the Gulf of Aqaba in the south, while the territory extends inland from the Mediterranean for 100 kilometers, including the occupied West Bank being transferred to the Palestinian Authority, and south to the Rift Valley.

From mountain to valley, river to sea, there are a lot of different land formations and geographic zones in this small country. Arable land makes up 20 percen, and 40 percent of this is irrigated.

Valleys

The **African-Syrian valley** that splits much of the country is a continuation of Africa's Great Rift Valley (the longest valley in the world) and it goes from the **Hula Valley** (Lake Hula was drained in the 1950s) in the north to the Sea of Galilee (696 feet below sea level) and further south along the **Jordan River Valley** to the Dead Sea with the world's lowest land elevation (1,300 feet below sea level).

Further south is the **Arava Valley**, occupying the rift between the Dead Sea and the Red Sea. This Rift Valley is a meeting of tectonic plates, and the region has its fair share of the earthquakes, plus the hot springs that usually accompany such seismic activity. The best soils are alluvial, found in the Hula, Jordan, and Kishon valleys and the Plain of Esdraelon.

Deserts

The southern half of Israel west of the Rift Valley is **Negev** country, mostly desert, somewhat mountainous, and with some of the most beautiful canyons, wadis, and colorful sandstone formations, as well as some well-developed desert agriculture. The **Judean Desert** between Jerusalem and the Dead Sea has its own bleak beauty, with caves (like those that housed the Dead Sea Scrolls), wadis, and oases.

Plains

The principal lowland is a narrow coastal plain just inland from the sandy shores of the Mediterranean Sea, that stretches from Rosh Hanikra in the north to Egypt in the south. North of Haifa it is known as the **Plain of Zebulun**, between Haifa and Tel Aviv it forms the **Plain of Sharon**, and south of Tel Aviv it's called the **Plain of Judea**, but it all translates to a strip that is 40 kilometers at its widest.

The soils of the coastal plain are fertile but sandy, requiring large quantities of water and fertilizer to be productive.

Mountains

The mountain ridges in the Golan Heights and Galilee head south till they slope down into the Jezreel Valley, then pick back up in the Judean Hills and Negev lunar scapes. The highest peak is **Mount Hermon**, rising up north to 9,073 feet. The steeper mountain slopes that cover much of Israel have been severely eroded and are mostly barren.

Water

All along the western border, the **Mediterranean Sea** swells against the shore, providing ports, fishing, and holiday resorts. And on the east runs the **Jordan River**, separating Israel from Jordan, floating inner tubes and rafts, baptizing the faithful, and providing some much sought-after water before it runs into the **Dead Sea**.

While the Dead Sea doesn't provide much in the way of fish or agriculture, it's the region's main source of minerals (potash, salt, bromide, magnesium) as well as mud valued for its healing qualities. The **Sea of Galilee** is the main fresh water lake, irrigating the farm land and yielding lots of fish, there are lots of smaller lakes and rivers up north, and the **Yarkon River** flows near to Tel Aviv.

Climate

Generally speaking, the summers are long, hot, and dry while the winters resemble San Francisco weather, raw and wet with rejuvenating sunny, warm days mixed in. There are many different terrains, however, and you don't have to travel very far to find yourself in a totally different weather zone. You can rely on the coastal areas to be warmer and more humid (i.e. hot and steamy in summer), the hilly regions to be cooler and drier, and the desert zones, not surprisingly, to be more arid, with hot days and chilly nights.

The **rainy season** (with occasional snow on the mountains) is November to April with the heaviest rains falling in December-February. You can get over 1000 millimeters a year on Mount Hermon in the north, 550 millimeters in Jerusalem, and less than 100 millimeters in Eilat in the south.

The hottest areas are those below sea level, such as the Jordan Valley, the Dead Sea, and the Arava Valley. There are also occasional *hamsin*, strong easterly winds that blast hot air during spring and fall. The coolest breezes come from the hill tops, but the desert also gets rather chilly at night.

PEOPLE
The Religions of Israel

Israel has proven a fertile land for religions, and while some like Baalism exist now only in archaeological finds and Biblical references, there are plenty still thriving in the Holy Land.

Freedom of religion is guaranteed by law, and all holy places are to be protected. The national religion of Israel however, is Judaism, and at present, due to current politics, rigid Orthodoxy is the only form of Judaism officially recognized in Israel (in solemnizing marriages, for example), despite the large portion of the population who are secular (a whopping 85% are not Orthodox).

For the **Jewish** population, supreme religious authority is vested in the Chief Rabbinate, made up of a chief rabbi from the Ashkenazim and one from the Sephardim, along with the Supreme Rabbinical Council. Small Jewish minorities that reject the rabbinic tradition and law include the Karaites (near Tel Aviv) and the Samaritans (in Holon and Nablus). Israel's Arab minority is 76 percent **Muslim** and 14 percent **Christian**. Also followers of Islam are the Circassians, a small group brought to the region in the 19th century from the Caucasus and now concentrated in Galilee. The **Druzes** broke away from Islam in the 11th century and practice their own religion, and Israel is also a center of the **Baha'i** faith.

Canaanite Religion (Baalism)

Baal, the storm god and lord of the universe, had a strong following for a long time, way after Joshua led the Israelites into Canaan. Various deities were revered by common folk in the open country at high places on hilltops, beneath sacred trees and at natural springs. According to legend, Baal was killed by monsters but restored to life, and his death and resurrection were celebrated annually as a part of Canaanite fertility rituals.

The cult of Baal (and particularly the human sacrifice and temple prostitution associated with it) was frequently denounced by Old Testament prophets. Another popular deity was Astarte, goddess of fertility, sexual love, and war. Crops, newborn animals, and firstborn children were sacrificed to her to assure fertility (her Babylonian and Greek counterparts were Ishtar and Aphrodite). The Bible refers to Astarte as Ashtoreth, and she was worshipped by the Philistines and, at times, the Israelites.

The Big Three

Judaism, the oldest living religion in the Western world, is practiced (in some manner or other) by over 17 million Jews throughout the world, and is the national religion of Israel. A springboard for both Christianity (with a following of around one billion) and Islam (with around 950 million adherents and growing at a rate of about 25 million a year), the three together claim half the world's population.

A WORD ON HISTORICAL DATES

*In this book, I've used the Jewish system of **BCE** – Before the Common Era – and **CE** – Common Era – rather than the usual BC and AD. BCE corresponds exactly to BC, and CE is the same as AD.*

Judaism

Judaism is a religion, a culture, and a people. True, much of Judaism is based on religious beliefs and practices, but there's a Jewish culture as well, made up of food and humor, legend and lore, perspectives and values, and a sense of peopledom shared by Jews around the world. Generalizations are tricky, verging on the stereotypical as they do, yet some overall flavor of the Jewish people, in all their various ethnicities and forms, holds true.

"Hear O Israel, the Lord our God, the Lord is One," the opening words of the Shema and recited daily, sums up the monotheistic basis of Judaism. According to Genesis (17:5) in the Hebrew Testament, God made a pact with Abraham, the First Patriarch of the Jews, saying "You shall be the ancestor of a multitude of nations," and the religion was on. The covenant signature is the circumcision, called "the seal of God." Known as *brithmilah*, it's performed on eight-day-old sons, and the ritual remains a way that Jews (male ones) continue their covenant with God as prescribed by Genesis (17:10). At the age of 13, a boy is deemed responsible for performing the commandments (**bar mitzvah**). To mark his new status, the bar mitzvah boy takes part in the Bible readings during a synagogue service. (The synagogue service is sometimes popularly referred to as the bar mitzvah.) A similar ceremony for 12-year-old girls (**bat mitzvah**) is a recent innovation. Somewhat older is the confirmation ceremony for both sexes introduced by Reform Judaism; it is usually a class observance on or near Shavuoth.

The Hebrew Testament is full of tales of how Judaism was passed along, tested and established, doubted and renewed. **Isaac**, the Second Patriarch, was Abraham's son, born at long last to the First Matriarch, **Sarah**. According to Jewish tradition Isaac was nearly sacrificed as part of God's test of Abraham's obedience and faith, but spared at the last moment (the Muslims believe it was Ismael, Abraham's son by concubine Haagar, who was spared the knife). Only his deceit made him heir to his father's birthright, instead of twin **Esau**, the favored, hirsute hunter.

But get it he did, and he passed along his faith to **Jacob**, the Third Patriarch. His son **Joseph**, with his many-colored robe, were sold into slavery in Egypt by his jealous brothers, and this was the start of the story of Exodus, how eventually the Jews all moved to Egypt to escape the hardship of famine, how they were pressed into bondage, and how **Moses** led them out of Egypt, through the Sinai, and to the Promised Land.

The **Tanakh** (the Hebrew Bible, also called the Old Testament by Christians) is an acronym for the three categories of books that make it up: *Torah, Neve'im (Prophets)*, and *Ketuvim (Writings)*. It is the primary Jewish religious text. The first five books of Moses (also called the Pentateuch, or *khamesh* in Hebrew, meaning five) comprise the **Torah** (Hebrew for "teaching") and are regarded as Judaism's central document, just as the concept of teaching is central to Judaism, relating to study of the Torah, the whole Tanakh, Judaism in general, and education even more generally. According to religious belief, even God studies torah in heaven, where it's written in black fire upon white fire, and He used it as a blueprint for Creation. The Torah (the Written Law), made up of stories and commandments, is believed to have been dictated to Moses by God around 1220 BCE, shortly after the Exodus from Egypt.

While the final version of the Tanakh was canonized in 90 CE, the religion kept on growing. Not all Jewish sects have agreed through the ages on all facets of Jewish theology, and during the first century CE, the Sadducees differed with the Pharisees on the topic of **Oral Law**. The Pharisees believed that along with the written Torah, God also taught Moses the oral traditions of Judaism, explaining how the commandments were to be carried out, and by which he (and later, other judges and rabbis) could interpret the laws and adapt them to the issues and concerns of the time. The Sadducees (and today's Karaites as well, see *Sects*) rejected the Oral Law, and interpreted quite literally such injunctions as "an eye for an eye."

The Sadducee sect died out, however, and the importance of the Oral Torah continued. Originally viewed as something to be memorized and passed on but not written down, around 200 CE (after the deaths of many of Jewish sages in the Great Revolt and Bar Kokhba rebellion), Judah

HaNassi from Kursi decided to start writing them in a volume called the **Mishna**, expounding on such topics as Shabbat, blessings, marriage, divorce, and so on. In the centuries after HaNassi put together the Mishna, Palestinian rabbis studied and discussed it, commented on and notated it, and around 400 CE they compiled a volume of all this commentary called the Palestinian Talmud.

A century or so later Babylonian rabbis compiled another, more extensive edition of the discussions on the Mishna, and the Babylonian Talmud is now the most authoritative compilation of the Oral Law. The Mishna and the rabbinic discussions (the *Gemara*) make up the **Talmud**, though the terms *Gemara* and Talmud are usually used interchangeably.

SHABBAT

Shabbat (the Jewish Sabbath) is observed by many as a holy day, as per the commandment to remember the Sabbath. Shabbat, from sunset Friday to sunset Saturday, is observed by refraining from work and by attending a synagogue service, and during this time much of Israel, including offices, most stores, and buses, is shut for business. The religious follow a number of rituals as part of the holy day, often starting the day before. On Thursday afternoons the streets are full of women lugging home groceries and flowers. The mother lights two candles Friday evening (having prepared the meal in advance, since no cooking is allowed once the sun sets), and the men go to pray in the synagogue and welcome the Shabbat bride with much dance and song.

After service is Shabbat dinner. The family sings songs, kiddush (a ceremonial blessing affirming the sanctity of the day) is said over a cup of wine, between the hand-washing prayer and the bread-breaking prayer no talking is allowed, and then the meal of traditional foods (and the traditions differ by Ashkenazi and Sephardi background) begins. The end of the Sabbath is marked by parallel ceremonies called havdalah. Similar home ceremonies occur on the festivals.

The religious rationale for observing Shabbat could fill a chapter all on its own, and the individual rationales another, but for here suffice it to say it's an important day for cultural, religious, political, and individual reasons. Some travelers feel inconvenienced by the restrictions, but it offers a good way to experience the country and the people differently than when everything's on. It's a time when family, friends, and strangers are welcomed, and it's easy to get invited to a home to share a Shabbat meal in Jerusalem or Tsfat (see the city chapters of this book).

Asked by a would-be convert to explain the essence of the Torah while standing on one leg (to ensure brevity), the revered rabbi Hillel answered "What is hateful to you do not do to your fellow. The rest is commentary. Now go and study." Though Hebrew Bible stories such as Job ask such basic questions as why a God who is good allows so much evil in the world, much of Judaism focuses more on this world and the rules and regulations by which to lead a virtuous life, rather than on beliefs dealing with the afterlife – though faith in the eventual coming of the Messiah has often flavored Jewish life during hard times, such as the Messianic fervor in the first century, and again in the Middle Ages. The system of law known as **Halakhah** regulates civil and criminal justice, family relationships, personal ethics and manners, social duties as well as worship, and other religious observances.

Along with Shabbat, festivals are observed both in the home and in the **synagogue** (an institution for prayer and instruction that became the model for the church in Christianity and for the mosque in Islam, called *shul* in Yiddish and *beit knesset* in Hebrew). Traditionally, observant Jews wear **tefillin** (Hebrew for "prayer objects" or Aramaic for "ornaments"). Called phylacteries in English (meaning "amulets"), the two black leather boxes containing four biblical passages are attached with leather straps, one to the left arm and the other on the forehead, during morning prayers.

In accordance with biblical law, men wear a fringed shawl (**tallith**) during prayer, and it's important for both men and women to cover their heads. Jews also affix to their doorposts a **mezuzah** (a favorite souvenir from Israel), a little box containing a parchment scroll inscribed with passages of the Torah that emphasize the unity of God, his providence, and the resulting duty of serving him.

The **kosher** (meaning " fit" in Hebrew) dietary laws, or kashrut, started with the Genesis (9:4) law forbidding animal blood to all the seed of Noah, and for over 2,000 years rabbis have been developing and refining an elaborate code of rules to govern slaughtering, preparing, and eating. The only animals that can be eaten are those with cloven hooves that chew their cud (thus ruling out pigs). But to be considered kosher, even these approved beasts have to be slaughtered ritually by a *shokhet* with one quick cut across its throat. If the stroke is delayed, thus needlessly prolonging death, the animal is unkosher and forbidden to Jews.

As for fish, only those with fins and scales are kosher, nixing all shellfish (Leviticus 11:9-12 and Deuteronomy 14:9-10). Sturgeon and swordfish are subjects of controversy, because consensus hasn't been reached (between Orthodox and the more lenient Conservatives) as to whether their scales qualify. And among poultry, birds of prey are not acceptable, but chicken, duck, and turkey are.

And then there's the milk issue. The Torah states "You shall not seethe a kid in its mother's milk" and rabbis spent a lot of time debating the intended meaning. The final ruling was that dairy and meat aren't supposed to be cooked in the same pots or eaten off the same dishes, let alone blended in the same meal. Homes that observe *kashrut*, therefore, have two sets of dishes, cutlery, and pots, one for meat (called *fleishig* in Yiddish) and the other for dairy (or *milchig*).

The neither here-nor-there foods (fish, fruit, vegetables, etc.) are called *pareve*, and can be eaten with either. Jewish law rules that you need to wait for one category of food to digest before adding the other to your stomach, but just how many hours this takes depends on the accepted wisdom of your community. The Dutch thought one hour would do it, the German Jews waited three hours, while in Eastern Europe they felt it took six hours for the meal to properly digest.

Some Jews today observe kashrut in all its minutiae, others keep kosher in a more limited form (maybe they won't eat pork or shellfish, but don't bother with the meat and dairy rules), and some don't keep kosher at all and eat **treif** – the opposite of kosher.

Modern Judaic Divisions

Orthodox Judaism, an umbrella term describing traditionalists who rejected the reforms of the 18th century, distinguishes these Jews from the more modernist Conservative and Reform Jews. The Orthodox, however, can be further divided into the Modern Orthodox (who wear modern clothes and pursue secular education while preserving a strong commitment to halakhic norms) and the Ultra-Orthodox (who reject modern values, wear clothes that were in vogue a few centuries ago, and speak the language – Yiddish – from those days as well).

Hasidim are an Ultra-Orthodox group whose traditions (and clothing styles) hark back to 18th century Poland. While "Hasid" is often used as a synonym for Ultra-Orthodox, the religious movement actually started as a revolutionary and liberal reaction to the Mitnagdim, the status quo Orthodox of the time. One of the best known Hasidic families is the Lubavitchers, many of whom live in Brooklyn, New York, and whose leader Rabbi Schneerson died a couple of years ago. In addition to Brooklyn, there are strong Hasidic communities in Mea She'arim in Jerusalem, Bnei Brak in Tel Aviv, and in Tsfat as well.

The men generally wear long black frock coats and black hats (sometimes trimmed with fur), based on the styles of the 18th century Polish aristocracy, and sport beards and long uncut side curls called *peyot*, while the boys wear shorts and skull caps (*kipah* in Hebrew, *yarmulke* in Yiddish). The women don't dress in 18th century clothes, but they take care to keep their heads covered (sometimes with scarves and sometimes with hats), and most of their body covered as well with long dresses or skirts with modest shirts. And after marriage, Orthodox women shave their heads and wear wigs.

If you go walking in one of these Ultra-Orthodox neighborhoods, you'd do well to keep yourself covered up as well, and respect their traditions by not imposing proximity or conversation on members of the opposite sex. Orthodox Judaism is a patriarchal religion, and religious practices are very gender-conscious. Synagogues are divided into the men's section and a much smaller women's one (prayer is a duty for men, but not for women), the Western Wall is similarly divided, and rights and duties are prescribed according to gender as well. In addition, contraception is frowned on, and large families are the norm.

THE LEADERS OF THE MITNAGDIM & THE HASIDIM

*The **Mitnagdim** were quite proud of their leader, the **Vilna Gaon** (a name that has become synonymous with genius in the same way Einstein has), for the advanced Talmud discourse he delivered while just seven years old, and because he studied 18 hours a day. The **Hasidim**'s leader was **Israel Ba'al Shem Tov** (meaning Master of the Good Name), and he rose from a very poor background to redirect the religion. He veered from the traditional yeshiva (a Talmudic college that focuses on halakhah), focused far more on an individual's personal relationship with God and his fellow man than on the intricacies of Jewish law, and defied the ascetic Mitnagdim by teaching that pleasure and joy were worthy expressions of God's glory.*

*The **Hasidim**, in turn, subdivided still more into various family dynasties, all led by revered Tsaddikim (religious sages).*

Conservative Jews adhere to the halakhah, but believe it should be adapted to the requirements of modern life, a trend also known as Traditional or Mesorati Judaism.

Reform Jews are even more lenient in the application of halakhah, and emphasize the ethical aspects and universals that can be gleaned from the texts.

And then there are the **secular** Jews, who don't attend synagogue or pray, but are strong in their Jewish identity and culture.

Jewish Culture

The Jewish culture, often expressed through humor and food, and is a warm, rich amalgam, with old traditions influenced by host countries during the Diaspora, when Jewish communities existed mainly in Europe and North Africa. While the food will be attended to in the Food and Drink section, some sample anecdotes here can give a taste of Jewish story-telling.

Many jokes celebrate the simpleton or fool (known as the *shlemiel*). One story begins in a little inn in a Russian town, crowded to capacity. The *yeshiva* student who remained overnight was put in the same room with a visiting Rabbi. The student had to catch an early morning train, so he asked the clerk to wake him on time. While getting dressed in the dark the student by mistake put on the Rabbi's long alpaca coat. At the railroad station he passed a mirror and, seeing himself in such unusual garb, muttered angrily: "What a dunce that clerk is! I asked him to wake me up but instead he woke up the Rabbi!"

There are also plenty of jokes about the *moyel*, the man who performs the *brit milah*, or circumcision. In one story, a man is walking down a street and sees an enormous watch hanging over a store window. He brings in his watch to be repaired, but the proprietor tells him he doesn't repair watches, he is a *moyel*. "Why then are you hanging a watch in the window?" asks the man. "What do you suggest, mister, I put in the window?" the *moyel* replies. And there are a zillion more.

Offshoots

A couple other Jewish offshoots, the Samaritans and the Falashas, also have small communities in Israel. The term **Samaritans**, which originally referred to the inhabitants of Samaria, is now generally re-stricted to a sectarian Jewish community that lived in the area. In Jewish tradition the Samaritans are viewed as colonists introduced after the Assyrian conquest of the region (722 BCE) who adopted a distorted form of Judaism, though the Samaritans themselves claimed descent from the tribes of Ephraim and Manasseh and believed that they had preserved the way and will of Yahweh.

The Samaritans held to the Pentateuch as their Scripture and hon-ored Moses as the only prophet. The Jews refused to let them participate in building the Second Temple in Jerusalem because of all the intermar-riage with non-Jews that had gone on during the Babylonian Exile. A small civil war was fought between the two until the walls of Jerusalem were built back up (leading to the parable of the Good Samaritan, Luke 10:25-37, in which Jesus rebuked the Jews for their hostility toward the Samaritans). Small communities of Samaritans still exist today in the north of Israel. The Samaritans believe Mount Gerizim in Nablus is the place where Abraham bound Isaac in sacrificial preparations and also where the original 10 Commandments tablets are buried. Every Passover the Nablus Samaritans sacrifice a lamb up top the mount in honor of Isaac.

JEWISH CALENDAR & HOLIDAYS

*The Hebrew **calendar** in use today begins at the Creation, which is calculated to have occurred 3,760 years before the Christian era. The week has seven days (reckoned from sunset to sunset), ending with the Sabbath, and the year consists of 12 lunar months that start around September: Tishri, Heshvan, Kislev, Tevet, Shevat, Adar, Nisan, Iyar, Sivan, Tammuz, Av, and Elul. Since these lunar months add up to 354 days a year, six times in a 19-year cycle a 13th month (Adar II) is added to keep the festivals on solar track.*

*The holidays prescribed in the Torah are the two "days of awe," **Rosh Hashana** (New Year, ushered in by a blast on the shofar, the ram's horn) and **Yom Kippur** (Day of Atonement, the holiest of holy days, when the devout pray, request forgiveness and fast for 25 hours), and three joyous festivals, **Passover** (or Pesakh, celebrating the Exodus from Egypt with special seder meals during which you recite the story and sing songs), **Shavuot** (Feast of Weeks), and **Sukkot**, the Feast of Tabernacles, a harvest celebration during which people are meant to move to a simple shack structure called a sukkah in which to eat, sleep, and remember their ancestors.*

*Later additions are the festive occasions of **Hanukah** (Festival of Lights, celebrating the Maccabee triumph with menorah lightings, games, and songs), and **Purim** (a holiday commemorating Queen Esther's success over evil Hamman with Halloween-like costumes and parties and games, and the fast of **Tisha B'Av** (the Ninth of Av), commemorating the destruction of the Temple. Other holidays are **Simkhat** Torah (the rejoicing of the torah, when the annual reading of the torah is concluded and scrolls are paraded about before starting again with Genesis), and **Lag B'Omer**, the 33rd day of Omer, which is the anniversary of the second century death of kabbalistic sage Simeon Bar Yochai. It's celebrated with a pilgrimage to his tomb near Tsfat, and is a popular time for weddings.*

The **Falashas** are a group of Ethiopians who claim Jewish origin as descendants of Menelik, the alleged son of King Solomon and the Queen of Sheba, though others believe they stem from a group of converts. Numbering about 30,000, until recently they lived a segregated life in villages north of Lake Tana. The Falashas observe the traditions of Judaism. They obey the biblical laws of purity and circumcision, observe the Sabbath and biblical holidays, recite traditional prayers, and follow biblical dietary customs. In their synagogues they read the Bible in the Geez (an Ethiopian dialect) translation (it includes the Tanakh and some Apocrypha), but they do not know the Talmud.

They call themselves Beta Israel ("House of Israel"); the name Falasha (Amharic for "stranger") was given to them by other Ethiopians. When they lived in Ethiopia they also followed some old Jewish traditions no longer observed by other Jews, such as setting *niddah* (ritually unclean menstruating women) aside in special housing during their periods, but this was dropped upon immigrating to Israel.

The Falashas suffered great hardship in the civil wars and famines that afflicted Ethiopia in the 1970s and 1980s, and many sought refuge in the Sudan. In 1984, 1985, and 1991, almost all of them were airlifted to Israel in a rescue operation sponsored by the Israeli government, and their integration into modern Israel's ways has not been an easy one.

Christianity

Christianity, based on the person and teachings of Jesus Christ, was born with Jesus of Nazareth nearly 2,000 years ago. To Christians, Jesus was and is the Messiah or Christ promised by God in the prophecies of the Old Testament (the Hebrew Bible). By his life, death, and resurrection he freed those who believe in him from their sinful state and made them recipients of God's saving Grace. Many also await the Second Coming of Christ, which they believe will complete God's plan of salvation. The Christian Bible (Holy Scripture) includes the Old Testament and also the New Testament, a collection of early Christian writings proclaiming Jesus as lord and savior. Arising in the Jewish milieu of first-century Palestine, Christianity quickly spread through the Mediterranean world, and in the fourth century became the official religion of the Roman Empire.

Christians have tended to separate into rival groups, but the main body of the Christian Church was united under the Roman emperors. During the Middle Ages when all of Europe became Christianized, this main church was divided into a **Latin** (Western European) and a **Greek** (**Byzantine** or **Orthodox**) branch. The Western church was in turn divided by the **Reformation** of the 16th century into the **Roman Catholic** church and a large number of smaller **Protestant** churches: Lutheran, Reformed (Calvinist), Anglican, and sectarian. These divisions have continued and multiplied, but in the 20th century many Christians joined in the Ecumenical Movement to work for church unity. A stroll through Jerusalem's Old City will illustrate the handiwork of all the various church branches.

Christians are monotheists (believers in one God). The early church, however, developed the characteristic Christian doctrine of the **Trinity** in which God is thought of as Creator (Father), Redeemer (Son), and Sustainer (Holy Spirit), but one God in essence. Certain basic doctrines drawn from Scripture (especially from the Gospels and the letters of Saint Paul), have been accepted by all three of the major traditions. According to this body of teaching, the original human beings rebelled against God, and from that time until the coming of Christ the world was ruled by sin.

The hope of a final reconciliation was kept alive by God's Covenant with the Jews, the chosen people from whom the savior sprang. This savior, Jesus Christ, partly vanquished sin and Satan. Jesus, born of the Virgin Mary by the power of the Holy Spirit, preached the coming of God's Kingdom, and was betrayed by Judas, who delivered him to the Romans to be crucified. On the third day after his death God raised him up again. He appeared to his disciples, commanding them to spread the good news of salvation from sin and death to all people. This, according to Christian belief, is the mission of Christ's church.

Although Christians today tend to emphasize what unites them rather than what divides them, substantial differences in faith exist among the various churches. Those in the Protestant tradition insist on Scripture as the sole source of God's Revelation. The Roman Catholics and Orthodox give greater importance to the tradition of the church in defining the content of faith, believing it to be divinely guided in its understanding of scriptural revelation, and in Roman Catholicism the pope is regarded as the final authority in matters of belief.

Christians also vary widely in worship. Early Christian worship centered on two principal rites or Sacraments: **Baptism**, a ceremonial washing that initiated converts into the church, and the **Eucharist**, a sacred meal preceded by prayers, chants, and Scripture readings, in which the participants were mysteriously united with Christ. As time went on, the Eucharist, or Mass, became surrounded by an increasingly elaborate ritual in the Latin, the Greek, and other Eastern churches, and in the Middle Ages Christians came to venerate saints (especially the Virgin Mary) and holy images.

Early Christian History

The early Christian years extend from Jesus' birth through the fall of the western half of the Roman Empire in the fifth century. After Jesus was crucified, his followers, strengthened by the conviction that he had risen from the dead and that they were filled with the power of the Holy Spirit, formed the first Christian community in Jerusalem. By the middle of the first century, missionaries were spreading the new religion among the peoples of Egypt, Syria, Anatolia, Greece, and Italy.

Chief among these was **Saint Paul**, who laid the foundations of Christian theology and played a key role in the transformation of Christianity from a Jewish sect to a world religion. The original Christians, being Jews, observed the dietary and ritualistic laws of the Torah and required non-Jewish converts to do the same. Paul and others favored eliminating this obligation, thus making Christianity more attractive to

CHRISTIAN HOLIDAYS

*In most Christian churches **Sunday**, the day of Christ's resurrection, is observed as a time of rest and worship. **Lent** is a 40-day penitential period of prayer and fasting that precedes Easter. Observed since the fourth century, in the Western church, Lent begins six and a half weeks prior to Easter (Sundays not included), starting on **Ash Wednesday** right after the hoopla of **Mardigras** (Fat Tuesday), while in the Eastern church the period lasts over seven weeks because both Saturdays and Sundays are excluded. Formerly a severe fast was prescribed where only one full meal a day was allowed, and meat, fish, eggs, and milk products were forbidden.*

*Today, however, prayer and works of charity are emphasized, along with a token denial. Good Friday remembers Christ's crucifixion, while his resurrection is commemorated at **Easter**, a festival in the early spring that has its roots in a pagan spring festival and in the Jewish holiday of Passover. Another major Christian festival is **Christmas**, December 25th, which celebrates Jesus' birth.*

Gentiles. The separation from Judaism was completed by the destruction of the temple of Jerusalem by the Romans during the Jewish Revolt of AD 66-70.

After that Christianity took on a predominantly Gentile character and began to develop in a number of different forms. At first the Christian community looked forward to the imminent return of Christ and the establishment of the Kingdom. This hope carried on in the second century by **Montanism**, an ascetic movement emphasizing the action of the Holy Spirit. **Gnosticism**, which rose to prominence about the same time, also stressed the Spirit, but it disparaged the Old Testament and interpreted the crucifixion and resurrection of Jesus in a spiritual sense. The main body of the church condemned these movements as heretical, and when the Second Coming failed to occur, organized itself as a permanent institution under the leadership of its bishops.

Following the recognition of Christianity by **Emperor Constantine I** in the early fourth century, lengthy controversy about the person of Christ wrestled with the problem of Christian monotheism and the charge that the church also worshipped Christ as Lord and the Holy Spirit of God promised by Christ. In one solution, **Monarchianism**, God the creator was supreme but shared his power with Christ, the Logos or Word. Another (Modalism) held that the three persons of the Trinity were aspects of the same God. These doctrines were rejected, and the Council of Ephesus (431 CE) condemned **Nestorianism**, which denied that Mary was the mother of God, and the Council of Chalcedon (451 CE) repudiated **Monophysitism**, which emphasized the divinity of Christ over his humanity. The condemnation of Monophysitism alienated the churches of Egypt, Syria, Mesopotamia, and Armenia, creating dissension in the Eastern Roman (Byzantine) Empire and lessening its ability to withstand the Islamic invasion in the seventh century.

The **Coptic church** and the **Syrian Orthodox** (also known as Jacobites) are Monophysite branches of Christianity which go back to the fifth century controversies over the identity of Christ. The Coptic church is the major Christian community in Egypt, numbering between six and seven million. The name Coptic is derived from the Greek word for "Egyptian" and reflects the national character of this ancient church. Most Egyptian Christians sided with the Monophysite party, which held that Christ has one nature, a doctrine condemned at the Council of Chalcedon. Coptic is sometimes used improperly to refer to the Ethiopian church because of its unity in faith and close affinity with Christian Egypt. The Ethiopian church, however, declared itself independent of the Coptic patriarch in 1959.

The Copts have had a strong community in Jerusalem since 1236, as evidenced by their churches, their monastery at the back of the Church of the Holy Sepulchre, and their distinctive black garb, and the Syrians have had a bishop there since 1140. The head of the Jacobite church bears the title of Patriarch of Antioch and resides in Homs, Syria, while the Coptic church is headed by the "patriarch and pope of Alexandria, Pentapolis and Ethiopia," who is elected by the entire community of clergy and laity and resides in Cairo. Long discriminated against by the Egyptian government, the Copts have more recently been the target of attacks by Muslim fundamentalists.

The **Armenian church**, also known as the Armenian Apostolic or Gregorian church, is an independent Christian church of about 1,600,000 embracing the majority of the Armenian people. At the end of the third century, the king of Armenia, Tiridates III, was converted to Christianity by Saint Gregory the Illuminator, and since the fifth century the Armenian church, like the Copts and Syrians, has embraced the Monophysite doctrine stating that Christ has a single human and divine nature.

Adherence to Monophysitism has kept the Armenian church separated from other Christian groups, but in other respects, most practices of the Armenian church resemble those of the Orthodox Church. The head of the church is called the supreme catholicos, and his permanent residence is at Echmiadzin in the Republic of Armenia. They have a waning population in Jerusalem, with an Armenian quarter in the Old City, and much of Mount Zion, owned by the Armenians since the 10th century, is graced by their monasteries and churches.

Islam

The **Prophet Mohammed** was born in Mecca in 570 CE. He was orphaned at an early age, raised by his uncle, and had his first revelation from the Angel Gabriel in the month of Ramadan, 610 CE. From those beginnings, Islam has become a major world religion, and dominates in Middle Eastern and North African countries. **Muslims** (sometimes spelled Moslems) are those who believe in Islam, and should not be confused with Arabs, which is a regional rather than a religious designation.

The Arabic word al-islam means the act of committing oneself unreservedly to God, and a Muslim is a person who makes this commitment. Widely used translations such as "resignation," "surrender" and "submission" fail to do justice to the positive aspects of the total commitment for which al-islam stands, a commitment in faith, obedience, and trust to the one and only God (Allah). All of these elements are implied in the name of this religion, which is described in the **Koran** (*Qur'an* in Arabic, the sacred book of Islam) as "the religion of Abraham."

In the Koran, **Abraham** is the patriarch who turned away from idolatry, who "came to his Lord with an undivided heart" (37:84), who responded to God in total obedience when challenged to sacrifice his son (37:102-105), and who served God uncompromisingly. For Muslims, therefore, the proper name of their religion expresses the Koranic insistence that no one but God is to be worshipped. Hence, many Muslims, while recognizing the significance of the Prophet Mohammed, have objected to the terms Muhammedanism and Muhammedans (designations used widely in the West until recently) since they smack of a worship of Mohammed parallel to the worship of Jesus Christ by Christians.

While many Muslims vehemently oppose the assertion that the Prophet Mohammed is the "founder" of Islam (an expression they interpret as an implicit denial of God's initiative and involvement in the history of Islam's origins) none would challenge that Islam dates back to the lifetime (570-632 CE) of the Prophet and the years in which he received the divine revelations recorded in the Koran. Most of them would stress, however, that it is only in a sense that Islam dates back to the seventh century, since they regard their religion not as a seventh-century innovation, but as the restoration of the original religion of Abraham. They further believe that Islam is a timeless religion, not just because of the "eternal truth" that it proclaims but also because it is "every person's religion," the natural religion in which every person is born.

While Islam is a religion, its precepts apply more fully to all aspects of life than those of some other religions. Islam encompasses personal faith and piety, the creed and worship of the community of believers, a way of life, a code of ethics, a culture, a system of laws, an understanding of the function of the state. The revelations Mohammed set down in the Koran provide guidelines and rules for life in all its aspects and dimensions. While Muslims differ on how fixed or adaptable the Sharia (the "way," denoting the sacred law governing the lives of individuals as well as the structures of society) is, the basic notion of Islam's comprehensive character is so intrinsic to Muslim thought and feeling that neither the past history of the Muslim world nor its present situation can be understood without taking this characteristic into consideration.

Mohammed was born in **Mecca**, a trading center in western Arabia. After he received the first of a series of revelations that convinced him that he had been chosen as God's messenger, he began to preach the message entrusted to him, that there is but one God to whom all humankind must commit themselves. The polytheistic Meccans resented Mohammed's attacks on their gods and finally he emigrated with a few followers to **Medina**, an agricultural oasis town. This migration (called the Hegira or Hijrah) took place in 622 and Muslims adopted the beginning of that year as the first year of their lunar calendar (Anno Hegirae, or AH).

At Medina, Mohammed was accepted as a religious and military leader, within a few years he'd gained control of the surrounding region, and in 630 he finally conquered Mecca. There, the **Kaaba**, a shrine that had for some time housed the idols of the pagan Meccans, was rededicated to the worship of Allah, and it became the object of pilgrimage for all Muslims. Before he died in 632, most of the Arab tribes nearby had converted to Islam, and Mohammed had put in place the foundation for a community (*umma*) ruled by the laws of God. The Koran records that Mohammed was the Seal of the Prophets, the last of a line of God's messengers that began with Adam and included Abraham, Noah, Moses, and Jesus.

Islamic doctrines are taught under six headings: God, angels, Scriptures, messengers, the Last Day, and predestination. The Muslims' notion of God (**Allah**) is, in a sense, interrelated with all of these points. There are lots of **angels**, and some play a particularly important role in the daily life of many Muslims. There are the guardian angels, the recording angels (those who write down a person's deeds, for which he or she will have to account on Judgment Day), the angel of death, and the angels who question a person in the tomb. One of those mentioned by name in the Koran is **Jibril** (Gabriel), who transmitted God's revelation to the Prophet.

The promise and threat of the **Last Day**, which occupies an important place in the Koran, continues to play a major role in Muslim thought and piety. On the Last Day (and only God knows the hour) every soul will stand alone and will have to account for its deeds. The last of the six articles, **Predestination**, is also a big issue. Because the divine initiative is all ("had God not guided us, we had surely never been guided," 7:43), some concluded that God is not only responsible for guiding some, but also for not guiding others and allowing them to go astray or even leading them astray. Those opposed to the concept of predestination were concerned less with upholding the notion of human freedom and human dignity than with defending the honor of God, and it's been as fertile a field for Muslim debate as it was for Christians.

Many other theological debates have raged over the unity of Allah and whether the Koran was created, and on some level they boil down to the division between the Shi'ites and the Sunnites. The term **Sunnites** refers to the great majority of the world's Muslims, distinguishing them as the *ahl al-sunna wal-jamaa* ("the people of the sunna and the community") from the Shi'ites. Sunnites are, by this definition, Muslims who strictly follow the sunna (practices) of the Prophet Mohammed and preserve the unity and integrity of the community. Anyone who stands within the mainstream of the Islamic tradition and acts in accordance with generally accepted practices of the community is, therefore, a Sunni.

The **Shi'ites** were those who maintained that only "members of the family" (Hashimites, or, in the more restricted sense, descendants of the Prophet via his daughter, Fatima and her husband Ali) had a right to the caliphate (successors to Mohammed). This power struggle, born of a succession dispute around 660 CE, continues unresolved today. Another group, the **Kharijites** (literally "those who seceded"), broke away from Ali (who was murdered by one of their members) and from the Umayyads. They developed the doctrine that confession, or faith, alone did not make a person a believer and that anyone committing grave sins was a non-believer destined to hell. They applied this argument to the leaders of the community, holding that caliphs who were grave sinners could not claim the allegiance of the faithful.

While the mainstream of Muslims accepted the principle that faith and works must go together, they rejected the Kharijite ideal of establishing here on Earth a pure community of believers, insisting that the ultimate decision on whether a person is a believer or an unbeliever must be left to God. Suspension of the answer until Judgment Day enabled them to recognize anyone accepting the "five pillars" (see below) as a member of the community of believers, and to recognize those Muslims who had political authority over them, even if they objected to some of their practices.

The basic duties of any Muslim, the **"five pillars"** of Islam, are *shahada* (the profession of faith in God and the apostleship of Mohammed), *salat* (the ritual prayer, performed five times a day facing Mecca), *zakat* (almsgiving), *sawm* (abstaining from food and drink during the daylight hours of the month of Ramadan), and *hajj* (the pilgrimage to Mecca, incumbent on every believer who is financially and physically able to undertake it). Muslim worship and devotion, however, are not limited to the precisely prescribed words and gestures of the *salat*. Also important are personal prayers, gathering in the central mosque on Fridays, and celebrating the two main festivals.

The interpretations of *jihad* (literally, "striving" in the way of God), sometimes added as an additional duty, vary from sacred war to striving to fulfill the ethical norms and principles expounded in the Koran. The fundamentalist Muslims have been growing in power in recent years, affecting the governments of Egypt and Israel, among others. Hamas, a Palestinian extremist group, is against any peace talks with Israel, wants to replace the Jewish state with an Islamic fundamentalist one, and has taken the credit for a series of terrorist attacks against Israelis.

ISLAMIC CALENDAR & HOLIDAYS

Muslims begin their calendar at the day and year (July 16, 622 by the Gregorian calendar) when Mohammed fled from Mecca to Medina. The 12 lunar months (alternating 30 and 29 days) make the year only 354 days long, so the months move backward through all the seasons and complete a cycle every 32.5 years. The months are Muharram, Safar, Rabi I, Rabi II, Jumada I, Jumada II, Rajab, Shaban, Ramadan, Shawwal, Zulkadah, and Zulhijjah.

*During **Ramadan** (held holy since it's the month when the Koran was revealed to Mohammed), Muslims must fast during the day (a prohibition which includes food, water, smoking, and sex) but are permitted to partake in any or all of the above between dusk and dawn. This month-long obligation is taxing enough during the winter, but due to the nature of the Islamic calendar, Ramadan sometimes falls during summer months when days are longer and the water restriction is more of a challenge.*

***Id al-Fitr** is the festival that breaks the fast at the end of Ramadan. **Eid al-Adhah**, the festival of the sacrifice, in memory of Abraham's willingness to sacrifice his son, is the occasion of the hajj. The festival of the sacrifice, observed on the 10th day of the month of pilgrimage, is celebrated not only by the participants in the pilgrimage, but also simultaneously by those who've stayed at home. And **Ras as-Sana** (the Islamic New Year) is celebrated on the first of Muharram.*

The Druze

The **Druze**, monotheists with a difference, are an offshoot of the Ismailis, and the religion began in the reign of Fatimid caliph al-Hakim (996-1021). In 1017 there was a public proclamation to the effect that

Hakim was the final manifestation of God, and this remains the central and distinguishing tenet of their belief. Their name comes from al-Darazi, al-Hakim's first missionary. The sect was founded in Egypt, but they fled to Palestine to avoid persecution. The Druze, all 400,000-500,000 of them, live mostly in Syria or Lebanon, but some communities still exist in Israel and Jordan.

Their faith centers on the belief in Hakim as the ultimate *maqam* (location or incarnation) of God. They further believe in the five cosmic emanations: Universal Intelligence, Universal Soul, the Word, the Right Wing, and the Left Wing, as embodied by their five highest ranking disciples. Their community is divided into the *uqqual*, those initiated into the teachings of the *hima*, the religious doctrine, and the *juhhal*, the vast majority who aren't familiar with the religious tenets. They follow seven basic duties, among which truthfulness and mutual support figure strongly. They allow no conversion or intermarriage, and believe community is of great importance.

Baha'i

Baha'i, a religious movement founded in the 19th century by the Persian Bahaullah, claims members in practically every country of the world. Objecting to polygamy, slavery of any kind, religious prejudices, and politicized religion, Baha'is call for world peace and harmony, the ideals of a world federalist government, and a new world language. Recognition of the common ground of all religions is seen as fostering this move toward global unity, so Krishna, Buddha, Moses, Zarathustra, Jesus, and Mohammed are all recognized as divine manifestations, a series of prophets culminating in Bahaullah. Nonresistance, respect for persons, and legal recognition of the equal rights of both sexes constitute additional aspects of Baha'i teaching.

The **Bab** (Siyyid Ali-Muhammad) was the Martyr-Herald of the Baha'i religion. He broke away from Islam in Persia in 1844 declaring his religious mission, was publicly executed in Tabriz in 1850 at the age of 31, and his bones were transferred to Haifa in 1909 to be buried in the gold-domed mausoleum, the Shrine of the Bab. Bahaullah, the founder of the religion, was exiled to Akko in 1868 by the Sultan of Turkey after spending some time in Turkish prisons (following the Shah of Iran's banishment). He then spent some more time in prison in Akko till he died there in 1892. His son Abbas Effendi founded a world palace of justice in Haifa, designed the beautiful gardens, and built the Bab mausoleum and archive temple in 1909.

By the time of Bahaullah's death in 1892, the Baha'i faith had won adherents throughout the Middle East. Under his son Abbas Effendi (or Abdul Baha, 1844-1921), who succeeded him as the movement's leader, it spread to Europe and the United States. Divided into more than 130 national assemblies and more than 26,000 local assemblies, they are estimated to number about two million worldwide. Since the establishment of the Islamic Republic of Iran in 1979, the discrimination to which Baha'is have always been subjected in Iran has escalated into persecution.

The Israeli People
The people who live in Israel are, for the most part, so identified with their religions that their cultures in some ways are part and parcel of those religions, not separate, distinct entities. But even within the religions, people have come from so many countries and cultures (this is especially true of the Jews), that their previous nationalities bear some discussion.

Israel was established in 1948 as a homeland for Jews, and the Jewish population now forms 82 percent of the total population. Immigrants (*olim*) come from many different national backgrounds, including the urbanized societies of Europe and North America and the predominantly Islamic areas of Asia and North Africa, and they are divided into the **Ashkenazim** (those Jews hailing from Europe) and the **Sephardim** (Jews from Middle Eastern, North African, and Mediterranean countries). While the Ashkenazi Jews from Germany and Eastern Europe came speaking Yiddish (a Hebrew-German mix) and eating borsht and chopped liver, the Sephardic Jews often arrive speaking Arabic, French or Ladino (an ancient Spanish language derived from the Spanish of 15th century Spain), and eating couscous and mellawach. Some Ashkenazim emigrated to North and South America and to South Africa as well, and some of Israel's Ashkenazi population has come via those countries.

The Sephardim, descendants of those Jews expelled from Spain in 1492, have come to Israel after centuries spent in Morocco, Algeria and Tunisia, as well as Yemen and Iraq, and the Kurds come from Kurdistan, which is in northern Iraq.

The early Zionist pioneers and government leaders were Ashkenazim, while more than 50% of the Israel's Jewish population is Sephardim, contributing to a rift between the two groups and a feeling of discrimination in Sephardic communities. This situation is much less sensitive than it once was, however, and the younger generation claims it's a non-issue. The radio stations now devote air time to Sephardic melodies (unheard of some 10 years ago), and people seem able to blend ethnic pride (be it Yemenite, Polish, Iraqi, Kurdish, or German) with the predominant Israeli identity.

Some groups that have immigrated lately have attracted controversy. The **Black Hebrews** started coming to Israel in 1969 from the midwestern United States. Now living in Dimona in the Negev, they claim that their slave ancestors were descended from Israelites who were forced to migrate to Western Africa when the Romans closed Jerusalem down in 70 CE. The Israeli government rejected their claims and refused them citizenship unless they converted to Judaism, which they refused to do since they said they were already Jews. But they've reached an agreement, and in 1996 the vegetarian community of some 1,200 members became Israeli citizens.

From 1985-1991 the Ethiopian **Falashas** were airlifted in from their famine-struck country. They've had some rough times adjusting to Israeli society, and there was a bit of a debate over whether their version of Judaism qualified them as Jews, but that situation has been replaced by the more recent mass immigration (starting in 1989) of **Russians**. Amid complaints about their attitude (too entitled, just out for themselves, etc.), what is clear is that this is the largest wave of *olim* in Israeli history (200,000 arrived in 1990 alone) and they are becoming the largest ethnic group in the country. Along with the proliferation of Russian restaurants, some neighborhoods feature signs in Russian as well.

The non-Jewish population of Israel consists mainly of **Arabs**, who make up 13 percent of the total population, and **Druzes**, who account for less than two percent, both of whom are concentrated more in the Galilee. In the lands occupied since 1967 (which are in the process of being transferred to the Palestinian Authority), Arabs constitute by far the majority, although thousands of Jews have settled in the West Bank since 1979.

Language
Modern **Hebrew**, Israel's national language, was created from biblical Hebrew by Eliezer Ben Yehuda in the 1920s. It became the language of choice among Zionists, replacing languages such as Yiddish or Ladino which were viewed by many as relics of oppressed times.

Following Hebrew is **Arabic**, which is a required language in all schools, and can be seen on most road signs. Lots of people speak **English** as well, and it, too, is taught in schools. Most of the people in the tourism (and hotel and restaurant) business speak it fairly well, and people on the street have varying levels of competency. Other languages that are spoken a bit (and that help getting around) are **French** (brought by Tunisian and Algerian *olim*) and **Russian**.

5. A SHORT HISTORY

The area that we today call the Middle East (despite the attempts of political scientists to substitute 'Western Asia' as a new label) has an enormously interesting and complex history. The political boundaries and ruling governments have changed so many times that historians tend to chronicle civilizations and eras rather than countries.

The following condensed history will focus on the area that is now Israel while noting important events in other parts of the Middle East (such as Egypt, for example) as they affect the territories or civilizations under discussion. The development of the major religions will be recounted in more detail in the Religion section of Chapter 4..

Notation of years: the more ancient the history is, the more approximate the dates given. Dates get branded "circa" to indicate approximately, but it all means that the experts just aren't sure about exact dates way back when. And even when dates are known, there are different calendars and various ways of representing the years.

The **Hebrew calendar** follows lunar months and begins at the Creation, calculated at 5755 years ago. The **Muslim calendar** also follows lunar months and started 1375 years ago, when Mohammed moved from Mecca to Medina. The **Gregorian calendar**, commonly accepted in the Western world, is based on the suggestion of a monk (Dionysus Exiguus) to count years in reference to the birth of Christ, with BC for Before Christ and AD for Anno Domini ("the year of the Lord").

The dating system commonly accepted by Jewish historians, with **BCE** for Before Common Era and **CE** for Common Era (corresponding to BC and AD) is used in this book.

PREHISTORY

The years before written records began to document history, prehistory is generally divvied up into eras based on the materials people used for their tools and weapons. Four such ages are Stone (itself subdivided into Paleolithic, Mesolithic, and Neolithic or Old, Middle, and New),

Copper, Bronze, and Iron. One problem with these categories, however, is that while one group may be evolving into the Iron Age, another civilization in another setting may still be using stone, so assigning years to these eras depends on the location of the groups being studied.

The approximate years that follow are for civilizations in the Middle East.

THE STONE AGES - PALEOLITHIC AGE

• **Old Stone Age**: *3,500,000-10,000 BCE*

The earliest known human settlements outside of Africa were in the Galilee (Tel Ubeidiya is where the artifacts were found) some 600,000-800,000 years ago on the shores of a prehistoric lake. During this time people were hunters and gatherers, and tools were made of stone, especially flint. **Mesolithic Age (Middle Stone Age)** and **Neolithic Age (New Stone Age)**: 10,000-4,000 BCE. Stone and bone were used, goats, sheep, and cattle were domesticated, and agriculture began.

COPPER AGE

• **Chalcolithic Age**: *4,000-3,000 BCE*

Copper and brass tools and weapons appeared on the scene, and communities thrived around Israel. Remains of communities from this time can be seen at Tel Megiddo, Beit She'an, and Ein Gedi.

BRONZE AGES

• **Early Bronze**: *3,000-2,000 BCE, Middle Bronze: 2000-1600 BCE, and Late Bronze: 1600-1200 BCE - also known as the Canaanite period.*

During these years, bronze (an alloy of copper and tin) was developed for improved tools and weapons, and the camel was domesticated. Also around 3000-1200 BCE, the **Canaanite** civilization ruled in what is now Israel, Syria, Lebanon, and Jordan, establishing city-states at places like Hazor, Megiddo and Jericho. When archaeological sites such as Megiddo report Canaanite findings, they are talking about Bronze Age artifacts from this time.

When the Israelites, Philistines, and Aramaeans invaded around 1200 BCE, the Canaanites were for the most part absorbed into the new peoples and cultures (with the exception of a group that lasted another few centuries in Phoenicia on the Mediterranean), but some of their religious and cultural advancements contributed significantly to the new civilizations. For one, the Canaanite's Semitic language grew into Hebrew (and Phoenician).

Perhaps more importantly, by 1500 BCE they had developed the alphabet as their system of writing. The Phoenicians, who were great travelers and merchants, brought their alphabet to the Greeks, and it ultimately became the basis for modern Western alphabets. The legacy of Canaanite religion also played a part in the development of the new culture. Icons of and shrines dedicated to Baal, the storm god, and Astarte, the fertility goddess, have been found at many archaeological digs. The development of Judaism is intricately woven with the clash of belief systems between the old Canaanite gods and the Israelites' one god.

As late as circa 850 BCE, Elijah was trying to discredit the formidable belief in Baal. This period of time was important in **Egyptian** history as well. In roughly 2665-2180 BCE the Egyptian Old Kingdom was busy building **pyramids** and developing **papyrus** and writing techniques. In 2000-1700 BCE was the migration into Egypt of the **Hibiru**, a tribe some scholars believe were the ancestors of the Hebrews.

It is postulated that the **Patriarch Abraham** lived somewhere around 1800-1700 BCE, and that the descent of Israel into Egypt, as told in the **Book of Exodus**, took place around 1700-1600 BCE. From 1500-1100 BCE Egypt ruled over parts of Canaan, and under the Hyksos rulers in Egypt in 1400-1370 BCE it's thought that **Joseph** might have lived. Around that time there was a **famine** in Egypt, perhaps the one that moved Joseph's family in Exodus. The **Moses-led Exodus** from Egypt is thought to have happened in 1280 BCE, and their **conquest of Canaan** under Joshua is dated at 1250-1200 BCE.

IRON AGE

• 1200-586 BCE - also known as the Israelite Age

In these years iron was hardened (alloyed) by the addition of carbon, so that it took the place of bronze for tools and weapons. A lot happened in the 600+ years of the Iron Age. From the 1100s-1000 BCE, the **Philistines** ruled much of Palestine. These are also the years of the 5 **Judges** (Deborah, Gideon, Samson, Eli, and Samuel) who ruled in succession. **King Saul** reigned from 1020-1004 BCE, followed by the United Empire of **King David**, who was anointed king over all Israel in 1004 BCE and ruled till 961 BCE. **King Solomon's** rule lasted from 961-922 BCE, and the great **Temple** he had built in Jerusalem was consecrated in 955 BCE. King Solomon died in 922 BCE and his kingdom disintegrated into the **Kingdom of Israel** with its northern capital of **Shekhem** and the Jerusalem-based southern **Kingdom of Judah**.

The next few centuries were filled with weak rulers, civil war, and foreign domination. **King Omri** (887-876) in the north wanted to resist the power and threat from Damascus, and forged a marriage between his son and heir **Ahab**, and **Jezebel**, the daughter of the King of Tyre in Phoenicia. Jezebel (the infamous Jezebel) became queen to King Ahab

(876-855 BCE), and brought her devotion to the Phoenician (old Canaanite) gods Baal (called Melkart in Phoenicia) and Astarte, and a passel of trouble. She wanted temples raised to her gods, and to convert the Jews to her religion. Mosaic priests were persecuted by her, especially the **prophet Elijah** of Tishbi. He denounced Ahab and Jezebel to their faces, and when Ahab called him "a troubler of Israel," he responded with "Not I, but thou and thy father's house are the troublers of Israel," strong words to say to one's king. Israel came under the domination of Assyria in 842 BCE, and Damascus grew in power and became the new overlord.

There was a brief period of peace known as the **Silver Age** when Uzziah ruled as king of Judah (780-740 BCE) and Jeroboam II ruled the northern kingdom of Israel (785-745 BCE), and Damascus and Assyria focused their military attentions elsewhere. Then the Israelites returned to feuds and foreign dominion. While petty, greedy monarchs sat on puppet thrones, prophets such as Amos, Hosea, Isaiah, Micah, Jeremiah, and Ezekiel stepped forward to denounce and warn.

One of the most eloquent of these was **Isaiah**, who lived and preached during the reign of King Ahaz of Judah (735-720 BCE). Ahaz was distressed by the alliance between Pekach (king of the northern Kingdom of Israel) and Rezin, king of Damascus, so Ahaz asked Assyrian King Tiglath-pileser for help against the Israelites in the north. Isaiah was outraged, and warned that this was a very big mistake, a "covenant with death." Isaiah was ignored, but right.

Tiglath-pileser swooped down on Damascus in 734 BCE, killing King Rezin and annexing the country as a province of Assyria, and then came Israel. Tiglath-pileser killed the northern king, Pekach, and took the districts of Galilee and Gilead as additional provinces. He also deported lots of Israelites into Assyria, beginning the strange "disappearance" of the Ten Tribes. King Ahaz of Judah went groveling before Tiglath-pileser with loot plundered from his people and the Temple, trying to avoid total domination. He substituted Assyrian for Hebrew as the official language of Judah, but the Assyrians were not appeased. The remaining northern districts of Israel were taken by the new Assyrian king Sargon in 720 BCE and the kingdom of Israel was renamed **Samaria**.

The Kingdom of Judah limped along a few more generations as a weak dependency of Assyria, with occasional rebellions that kept backfiring. The kings of Judah kept conspiring with other rulers, forging alliances to help break free of Assyria. In 701 BCE, Sargon's successor, Sennacherib sent his forces to punish King Hezekiah of Judah and his Phoenician allies. Sennacherib demolished 46 main cities, for some reason sparing Jerusalem, and 200,000 Judeans were taken into captivity. In anticipation of a prolonged siege in Jerusalem, King Hezekiah had a subterranean tunnel constructed to carry water from the river Gihon to within the city walls. The resulting **Pool of Siloam**, discovered by archaeologists in 1880, was an impressive work of engineering skill, but Hezekiah still failed at his attempted revolt and had to pay the price to Assyrian Sennacherib in humility, humanity, and gold.

While these skirmishes and plots were spinning wheels in Judah, major events and power shifts were happening in nearby Babylon. Babylon, too, had been under Assyrian power for some time, but in 626 BCE Nabopolassar, the Assyrian-appointed governor of Babylon, revolted successfully and founded the Chaldean dynasty. He joined the Medes, and in 612 BCE they destroyed Nineveh, the Assyrian capitol.

Then his son **Nebuchadnezzar** (605-562 BCE) took over. Nebuchadnezzar dispersed the Assyrians, pushed the Egyptians out of Syria, and after taking the throne, turned his attention to the Jews. Judah was positioned smack between the two great powers of the time, Babylon and Egypt, and could remain neither independent nor neutral. **Zedekiah** (597-587 BCE), the last king of Judah, was a weak monarch who ignored the **prophet Jeremiah's** plea to refrain from calamitous rebellions. Zedekiah plotted with the Egyptians against Babylon, and lost.

In 586 BCE Jerusalem was besieged and destroyed, **Solomon's Temple** was demolished, and the Jews were taken off to 50 years of **Babylonian Exile**, along with their King Zedekiah who was taken prisoner, forced to witness the death of his sons, and then led off in chains after having his eyes gouged out (2 Kings 24-25). Nebuchadnezzar is known to many for the "hanging gardens of Babylon," terraced roof gardens the Greeks listed as on of the seven wonders of the world, but in Jewish history he is viewed as one of the most evil of villains, responsible for great cruelty, not to mention the destruction of the sacred Temple.

Events of the last years of Nebuchadnezzar are obscure. Old and senile, he was perhaps dethroned by his own son. The Book of Daniel describes him as eating grass and undergoing a physical transformation. The Dead Sea Scrolls, however, suggest that it was not Nebuchadnezzar, but the last Chaldean king, Nabonidus (556-539 BCE), who was afflicted by some such ailment.

The years of Babylonian Exile are also the years of the prophets Jeremiah, Ezekiel, Isaiah, and Daniel, and include the story of the **Writing on the Wall** (circa 550 BCE), in which Daniel predicts the end of the Chaldean empire.

PERSIAN RULE OVER ISRAELITES
• *538-322 BCE (Achaemenid Dynasty 549-330 BCE)*

Cyrus of Persia founded the Achaemenid dynasty in 549 BCE. In short order he conquered the Persians who opposed him, subdued King Croesus of Lydia (in what is now Turkey) and the Ionian Greek cities on the Aegean. In 539 BCE he overthrew the Babylonian empire (including Syria and Palestine) as well, making him ruler of an empire that stretched from the Mediterranean Sea to India.

A relatively benign monarch, Cyrus made Hebrew Bible history by permitting the Jews in 538 BCE to return to **Jerusalem** and rebuild their **Temple**. Though most Jews elected to remain in Babylon, about 40,000 picked up and returned to what was left of Jerusalem. While the skilled and fit Jews had been marched off to Babylon in 587 BCE, the poor, weak, and ill had remained in Samaria. These Jews intermarried and intermingled with the colonizing Assyrians and Babylonians, and became known as the **Samaritans**.

When the exiled Jews returned 50 years later they rejected the Samaritans and their desire to help rebuild the temple. Zerubbabel, the leader of the second wave to return to Jerusalem, told them "Ye have nothing to do with us to build a house for our God." Despite delays and conflicts with the Samaritans, the **Second Temple** was completed in 515 BCE. While recent returnees dealt with the situation in Jerusalem, many Jews had remained in Babylon. It was during this time that Daniel served as a high official under King Darius (522-486 BCE) and survived his night in the lion's den.

Ezra the Scribe is another Jew who had remained in Babylon, to continue studying religious texts, and in 458 BCE he was named religious head by King Artaxerxes and sent to Jerusalem to officiate. When he got there he was horrified by the widespread intermarriage between the Samaritans and the returned exiles. Ezra declared all Samaritan intermarriages invalid and forced all Samaritans out of the congregation of Israel. Not surprisingly, these harsh decrees didn't go over very well, and civil war resulted. The Persian king sent **Nehemiah** to Jerusalem to pacify and administrate. Nehemiah set about building walls around Jerusalem, a project which took 52 days. Once the walls were up, the threat from the angry Samaritans in the north died down. Ezra, in the meantime, was more concerned with religious fortifications, and he gathered about himself a group of learned scholars and scribes like himself to compile and edit the *Torah* (the Five Books of Moses).

On the first day of Tishri in 444 BCE, some eight centuries after Moses came down from Mount Sinai, the **Torah** was consecrated and accepted by the people of Israel. Ezra is also accredited with introducing the square Hebrew print used in Torah scripture.

HELLENISTIC PERIOD
• *333-63 BCE*

Alexander the Great smashed the Persian Empire, became the new overlord of Palestine, and initiated the Greek empire. Shortly after taking the throne, Alexander occupied Syria, Phoenicia, and Turkey, and was accepted by Egypt as pharaoh. After founding Alexandria in Egypt in 332, he crossed the Eastern Desert and defeated the Persian King Darius III in the autumn of 331 BCE. Alexander went on to occupy Babylon and Persia before setting his sights on India. Alexander III of Macedonia died in June, 323 BCE.

Many of the new Hellenistic cities welcomed and attracted the Jews in Judea, and large Jewish communities grew in Egypt, Syria, and Asia Minor, and in smaller numbers in places as far off as Spain, Morocco, Bulgaria, and Greece. Not only did the Hellenistic culture incite Jews to travel to distant lands, Hellenism was a strong cultural leveler. Greek language, literature, philosophy, art, manners, and dress became shared throughout the Mediterranean world. Jews assimilated to the Greek culture in all ways but religion, and in fact the Hellenistic era was a period of vast numbers of conversions to the Jewish faith.

The synagogues and mosaics uncovered in Israel dating from these years, however, show the strong impact of Hellenistic culture in the excavated statues, Greek inscriptions, and art. All this Hellenistic assimilation, while happily embraced by the upper class, caused tension and conflict among the majority folk of small town Judea.

SELEUCID EMPIRE
• *281-164 BCE*

In the fighting among Alexander's successors, Babylon fell to Seleucus I in 312 BCE. The **Seleucids** established many Greek settlements in the east, and under them Hellenism mixed with local cultures. By 281 BCE the Seleucids controlled most of the Asian provinces of the Macedonian empire—including most of Anatolia, part of Syria-Phoenicia, Babylon, Assyria, and more.

About 198 BC, the Seleucid king Antiochus III conquered Judea (of which Jerusalem was a part), making it tributary to Syria. After the death (163 BCE) of Antiochus IV, the Romans prevented any resurgence of Seleucid power. During this time ancient practices and traditions clashed with "modern" styles and innovations, and it all came to a head during the Seleucid rule of **Antiochus Epiphanes IV** (Epiphanes was the Greek title he chose for himself, meaning "god-manifest") circa 215-163 BCE.

The first two books of Maccabees paints Antiochus as the arch villain. On his way back from a misguided attempt to conquer Egypt, he stopped off in Jerusalem to plunder and sack and pillage, after which he issued the decree that the Jews must not only cease their own religious practices, but were "to profane the Sabbath and feasts and pollute the Sanctuary ... that they should build altars and temples and shrines for idols; and should sacrifice swine's flesh ... and that they should leave their sons uncircumcised." And those who didn't obey, of course, were to be put to death. It was under this oppression that **Hannah** and her seven sons became martyrs. On the 15th day of Kislev, 168 BCE, the Temple was desecrated with a huge statue of Zeus, and lewd bacchanalian revels took place in the courts of prayer. In the ensuing resistance, thousands were killed, and many others took to the hills.

In 167 BCE the resistance grew into a full-scale revolt as the old priest **Mattathias the Hasmonean** from Modi'in (17 miles northeast of Jerusalem) refused to "come forward and do the command of the King." Mattathias killed a weak-willed fellow who started to bow down to the altar of Zeus, saying "Whosoever is zealous for the Law and strives to maintain the covenant, come with me." Mattathias, his five sons, and the other faithful fled to the mountains, and the guerrilla warfare fight was on. When Mattathias neared death, he turned the leadership over to his sons.

Judah Maccabee ("the Hammer") became the military leader, and Simon was put in charge of political affairs. The Maccabeean army was small but impassioned, and led by The Hammer, they prevailed. They took Jerusalem, smashed the statue of Zeus, and chased out the Hellenistic leaders. On the 25th of Kislev (in December, usually), 164 BCE, Judah Maccabee rededicated the Temple in an eight-day festival and lit the lamps of the *menorah*, an event celebrated and remembered in the holiday of **Hanukah**.

MACCABEEAN OR HASMONEAN DYNASTY

• *164-63 BCE*

It took some years before the Hasmonean Dynasty was firmly established. Local Jewish Hellenizers joined with Syrian soldiers to harass the new regime, and in 160 the Syrians returned in force, killed Judah Maccabee, and regained temporary control. Judah's brother Jonathan emerged from the desert two years later and initiated another rebellion, only to be quashed again by the Syrians. Simon was the next brother to lead the fight, and in 142 the Maccabees finally established autonomy. The ensuing years were a time when Judea returned to its Hebrew roots, and the influences of the Greeks began to fade.

The **Great Sanhedrin** (Hebraized from the Greek *synedrion* or "assembly") was the supreme court and state council for legislating and interpreting Jewish religious laws and traditions. The tribunal was composed of 71 members, and was of prime importance during this era. It was also a time of decreasing nobility and ethical leadership from the Maccabees. **King John Hyrcanus** in 125 BCE forced the people he'd conquered in nearby Idumea to covert to Judaism. Simon's grandson,

King Alexander Yannai, executed 800 of his opponents after forcing them first to witness the deaths of their wives and children, while Yannai watched, caroused and hosted a party. The moral and religious slide of the Maccabees led to weakness, civil war, and the Romans.

In 67 BCE, Queen Shlomzion Alexandra died. The kingship should have passed to her eldest son **Hyrcanus II**, but his brother **Aristobulus** fought against him and took the throne. The supporters of the two brothers were soon involved in full-scale civil war. During this time, the **Roman general Pompey** was nearby, conquering and annexing Syria.

The Maccabee brothers decided to submit their conflict to Pompey's arbitration. He ruled in favor of Hyrcanus, and Aristobulus was unable to resist Pompey and his army. Hyrcanus realized that his power depended on Pompey's support, and invited Pompey to occupy Jerusalem. Pompey was happy to comply, and though Jerusalem resisted and was besieged for three months, Pompey entered the city in 63 BCE, killing thousands of priests and defenders, desecrating the Temple's Holy of Holies, and ending the Jewish state's independence. Pompey soon converted the kingdom into a Roman tributary, and Hyrcanus II was given the job of collecting the tributes.

ROMAN PERIOD
63 BCE-324 CE

The **Herod Dynasty** started with **King Herod**, who reigned over Judah from 37-4 BCE. He was put on the throne by the Romans, but his lineage links him to the Maccabeean era. His grandparents were among the people King John Hyrcanus (see above) had conquered, brought to Judea, and forced into Judaism. Herod is notorious for his ruthlessness; scholars cite him as perhaps the most vile Jewish king ever. He started off his regime by murdering 45 of the Sanhedrin, and followed up with many in his family. He murdered his first wife and their two sons, and later murdered his mother-in-law, brother-in-law, and another son from a new wife. Roman emperor Augustus commented: "It is better to be Herod's pig than his son."

When he wasn't doing in his relations, Herod was quite productive. He beautified and expanded the Second Temple (occupying ten thousand laborers and one thousand priests for nine years), rebuilt the walls around Jerusalem, built up theaters, harbors, and fortresses (including Masada) throughout Judea, and founded the city of **Caesarea**. When he died in 4 BCE, emperor Augustus divvied up the kingdom among Herod's surviving sons: Archelaus, Herod Antipas, and Philip.

Despotic **Archelaus** was a real failure; he was banished in 6 CE, and his land, Judea, became a Roman province. **Herod Antipas** (4 BCE-

39CE), was given Galilee and Peraea. His familial habits reflected Herod's upbringing; he divorced his first wife to marry Herodias, previously the wife of his brother Philip, and murdered John the Baptist to please his step-daughter Salome with his head on a platter. Also like his father, Herod Antipas aspired to build, and he founded the city of **Tiberias** around 20 CE before he was finally deposed in 39 CE after seeking the title of king from Emperor Caligula. **Philip** (4 BCE-34 CE), ruled relatively peacefully over the northern third of the kingdom.

After his death that territory as well as the Galilee were governed by Philip's nephew **Agrippa**, (known as Herod Agrippa in the Bible) from 37-44 CE. He was succeeded by his son **Agrippa II**, the last of the Herod dynasty, who ruled until the destruction of the temple in 70 CE, after which he retired to Rome.

RELIGIOUS & REVOLUTIONARY REACTIONS

While the Herod family governed, killed, and built, the people of the land were going through bad economic times. The people were taxed dry to support the ego and glory enriching projects of their rulers, the social and economic class split was accentuated, and assimilation was again an issue. These hard time conditions, as usual, resulted in a variety of extreme reactions.

The **Sadducees** were a priestly sect of Jews who belonged to the aristocratic ruling class. They interpreted the Torah very literally, didn't believe in immortality, collaborated with the Romans, and assimilated to Roman ways. **The Pharisees**, the ancestors of contemporary Jews, disagreed with the strict literal Torah interpretation, believed in the oral traditions of the Torah and in an afterlife, and disapproved mightily of the Sadducee's self-indulgent, luxurious life styles. To them, "Sadducee" took on a derogatory connotation, meaning "heretic." The Pharisees were depicted in a very negative light in the New Testament, and the term came to connote "hypocrite," a development found offensive to Jews.

Another sect were the **Essenes**, pacifists who were big on purity (immersion in the ritual bath was reputedly one of their most important ceremonies). Described by Rabbi Telushkin as "an ascetic and disciplined group of ancient hippies," they left the corrupt cities, eschewed property and material wealth, and set up communities in the countryside to peacefully await the Messiah who would rescue the pure from their evil times. Among other sects living isolated in the desert was the group now known as the **Dead Sea Sect**. The **Dead Sea Scrolls**, found in a cave in Qumran in 1947, indicated that they were an extremist offshoot of the Essenes.

Unlike the Essenes, the **Zealots** were not pacifists. They were a patriotic, militant group who were angry at the Romans and at their own

Jewish oppressors. They drew much of their support from the poor in the cities and the landless in Galilee, the same pocket of poverty from which, not long after, Jesus recruited many of his followers. The Zealots didn't want to wait for the Messiah, they wanted revolution, and they were responsible for the revolts that led to Masada and the destruction of the Temple.

The concept of the **Messiah** was important to more than these reactionary groups. Messianism among Jews was at an all-time high during this time. It was a tradition among Jews that the Messiah (*Mashiach* in Hebrew, *Christos* in Greek) would come during a period of great suffering, when the pain was unbearable. The harsh rule of the Herods made supernatural redemption a popular construct.

Their meaning of the term "Messiah," however, differed a bit from the highly spiritual figure it denotes today. Then, 'Messiah' referred to the military leader who would free the Jews from foreign (Roman) rule and usher in an age of universal peace. Bar-Kokhba, the Zealot military general who led the revolts in 132 BCE, was referred to as a messiah, though no mention was ever made to spiritual greatness. The crucifixion of Jesus under a "King of the Jews" sign supports the view that the Romans, at least, saw him as a political threat.

JESUS
• *Approximately 6 BCE-33 CE*

Jesus of Nazareth, a 1st century Pharisaic Jewish teacher who was crucified by the Romans, is believed by Christians to be the Christ or Messiah. Most knowledge of Jesus comes from the Gospels in the New Testament. From these and a few other 1st and 2nd century sources (such as Roman historian Tacitus), a brief history of his life can be constructed.

His life began in Roman-ruled Palestine during the reign of Augustus (27 BCE-14 CE), just two years before the death of Herod the Great (as best as biblical scholars can tell, making it 6 BCE). Jesus was born in Bethlehem but grew up in the Galilee village of Nazareth. He was a devout Jew and gathered about him a group of disciples attracted by his interpretations of the Torah, and his abilities to heal the sick and perform exorcisms.

According to Luke, his public preaching began in 29 CE after being baptized by John the Baptist. Some of his preachings focused on how God's rule was about to replace human rule, a view that made some Jewish and Roman leaders feel threatened. In 33 CE (again, according to biblical scholar's estimates, since the New Testament doesn't include a lot of dates), Jesus was arrested in Jerusalem, tried and condemned by **Pontius Pilate** (governor of Judea 26-36 CE), and executed according to the

Roman policy that mandated crucifixion for political threats. Jesus' followers then claimed he arose from the dead, and Christianity was born.

The largest section of each of the Gospels is devoted to the final events of the conflict between Jesus and the civil and religious authorities. The last confrontation took place in Jerusalem. Jesus entered the great temple of Jerusalem, denounced the commercial operations that were carried on there, and predicted the destruction of the temple and of Jerusalem. This was to be a sign that God would act in a climactic way to restore and vindicate his true people; meanwhile, however, they must learn to accept suffering, including Jesus' own suffering and death.

The remembrance of that seeming tragedy was to be perpetuated in the community through the meal of the New Covenant, the **Communion** or Eucharist, which Jesus shared as his **Last Supper** with the Apostles. He was betrayed by **Judas Iscariot**, and the others apostles abandoned him when he was seized by the authorities in the **Garden of Gethsemene**. A handful of faithful women remained with him when he died at **Calvary**. The women returned to his tomb on the third day after his death and found it empty, whereafter an angel told them that Jesus was alive.

This day of Jesus' **Resurrection** is celebrated by Christians on Easter Sunday. The Roman emperors Claudius and Nero took actions to suppress Christianity in the middle of the 1st century, and by the end of the century, Jewish authorities in Palestine had adopted policies aimed at sharply differentiating Christians from Jews.

ROMAN PERSECUTION & JEWISH REVOLTS

• *19-70 CE*

Roman rule had a number of practices that stuck in the collective craw of the Judeans. From early in the Common Era, Judea was ruled by Roman procurators, and their main job was to collect and deliver annual taxes for the empire. Whatever they took in above the required amount was theirs for the keeping, so a lot of taxing went on. In addition, Rome handled the Jewish High Priest appointments. This meant, in effect, that they were chosen from the ranks of the Jews who collaborated with Rome (usually the Sadducees), and it further incited hostility among the other groups.

Tiberius, Emperor Augustus' successor, ruled from 14-37 CE. In 19 CE Tiberius expelled all Jews from Rome and began to impose other repressive measures, such as tampering with the powers of the Sanhedrin. Anti-Roman feelings were further exacerbated during the reign of emperor **Caligula** from 37-41 CE. Caligula's name was actually a nickname meaning "little baby boots," his sanity was pretty questionable (he named his horse as high magistrate), and his rule was full of grief for Judea. In 39 CE he declared himself a deity and insisted that his statue be put up in every temple in his empire. The Jews refused to defile their

Temple with Caligula's image and he threatened to destroy the Temple. While his sudden death resolved the conflict, the incident garnered a lot of support for the Zealots' rebellious movement.

After Caligula's death, the provocations continued under emperor **Nero** (54-68 CE). Roman soldiers exposed themselves in the Temple, a Torah scroll was burned, and the financial indignities added to their general woes. In 66 CE Florus (the last Roman procurator) stole huge amounts of silver from the Temple. The resulting outrage sent masses of Jews, led by the Zealots, rioting in the streets of Jerusalem. They wiped out the small Jerusalem garrison, stood off the larger troop sent in from Syria to quell them, and the **Great Revolt** (66-70 CE) was on.

Their initial success was misleading. With the great wisdom of hindsight it's clear they never had a chance, and the Zealots are held accountable by some Jewish historians for the resulting destruction and loss. The Romans returned in force, and led by General **Vespasian**, Roman troops vanquished the Galilee before embarking on the **Siege of Jerusalem**. When Nero died, Vespasian returned to Rome to be crowned the new emperor and his son **Titus** took over as general of the Roman troops.

There was fierce resistance from the Jews who were fighting, but while the Zealots engaged the Romans in the north, the more moderate Jews of Jerusalem remained detached and did not aid the struggle. There was also suspected treachery on the part of **Flavius Josephus.** Josephus was one of the Jewish generals, but he surrendered to Vespasian, and was appointed by him to record the war's progress. Whether he helped out the Romans with his knowledge of Jerusalem and the rebel movement is debated endlessly, but regardless of whether his calls to the besieged to give up and surrender mark him as a traitor or a loyal Jew, he did write an historical account, *The Jewish Wars*, which have provided the best record of the events of the time. Of course he was living under Roman protection so his accounts are skewed a bit to please his patrons and revile the Zealots.

After the Galilee was taken, the survivors of the struggle escaped to Jerusalem and put to death the moderate leaders of the Jewish government. There was terrible squabbling among the factions within the city walls, and hosts of Roman troops outside. Many leaders opposed the revolt, but there were orders out to kill anyone advocating surrender. There's a famous story of **Rabbi Yochanan ben Zakkai** who had his followers smuggle him out of the city disguised as a corpse. Once safe from his countrymen, he surrendered to Vespasian and was granted the right to establish a Jewish seminary in nearby Yavneh.

Eventually the siege machines won out and Jerusalem was taken. The fighters retreated to their Temple, and on the **Ninth of Av**, 70 CE, the

Temple was set on fire and destroyed. What survived was one outer wall from the western side of the Temple's courtyard, and this has remained holy to Jews as the *Kotel ha-Ma'aravi*, the **Western Wall**. Historians believe as many as a million Jews died in the Great Revolt, and many more were led to Rome as slaves. The Ninth of Av marks for the Jews the end of their Temple, their holy city, and their homeland. Since that time it has been a fast day and a day of mourning during which the Book of Lamentations is read to mark the destruction of the First and Second Temples.

MASADA: 73 CE

Though Jerusalem was destroyed, the Temple razed, and the Sanhedrin dissolved, Jewish life limped on. Rabbi Yochanan ben Zakkai's academy at Yavneh thrived, though Zealot survivors viewed him as a traitor. These survivors who had successfully fled Jerusalem took up residence in the fortress of Masada overlooking the Dead Sea. They lasted there for three years while Rome's Tenth Legion proceeded stubbornly with catapults and battering rams.

*When it became clear to their leader **Elazar ben Yair** that the Romans would not go away but would prevail, he proposed mass suicide to avoid capture and enslavement. The only account we have of this episode come from the annals of Flavius Josephus, who witnessed the siege and claimed to have met and interviewed two women and five children who hid during the suicide. From them he recounted Elazer's final speech, in which he said "Let our wives die before they are abused, and our children before they have tasted of slavery, and after we have slain them, let us bestow that glorious benefit upon one another mutually." Though we know of Masada from Josephus, the Talmud omits the story, which highlights its equivocal place in Jewish history.*

While for some, Masada is the greatest symbol of resolution and national defense, others (such as the rabbis compiling the Talmud) viewed the Zealots with resentment for their ill-fated rebellions.

BAR-KOKHBA REBELLION

• *132-135 CE*

In 132 CE, **Simon bar-Kokhba** (*Son of the Star*) led another revolt. Bar-Kokhba was the charismatic military mastermind, but Rabbi Akiva, the leading sage of the age, provided the spiritual encouragement and motivating force by attesting that Bar-Kokhba was the Messiah and the End of Days was near. The specific provocation for this rebellion came from Emperor Hadrian (117-138 CE), who forbade circumcision, forbade

Torah study, and decided to build a shrine to Jupiter on the old site of the Temple in Jerusalem.

As before, initial victories strengthened the conviction that the rebellion was God's will, and as before, the Pharisees and pacifists argued against the wisdom of engaging Rome in battle. Bar-Kokhba managed to drive the Roman legions out of the country and declared the independence of Judea, and minted commemorative coins for the "Redemption of Zion." Hadrian sent Julius Severus to oppose Bar-Kokhba, and one by one he stormed the fortifications. Fifty fortresses and close to a thousand villages were destroyed, and most of Judea lay wasted; Bar-Kokhba died, Rabbi Akiva was burned at the stake, Jerusalem was renamed Aelia Capitolina (after Aelius Hadrian), and the temple to Jupiter was completed on the site of Solomon's Temple.

As with the Great Revolt, the Bar-Kokhba Rebellion was considered a great catastrophe in Jewish history, and the wisdom of the revolt and the heroic vs. foolhardy leadership of bar-Kokhba have remained controversial.

POST-REBELLION ROMAN ERA

Unlike the Great Revolt which started in the Galilee, Bar-Kokhba's Rebellion took place in Judea, and Jewish settlements in the north remained mostly untouched. The overall number of rabbis and scholars had been drastically reduced, however, and in 200 CE Rabbi **Judah ha-Nasi** (*the Prince*) decided to compile the **Mishna**, a written record of the Oral Law.

Ha-Nasi was descended from the esteemed sage **Hillel**, and was regarded as a great rabbinical scholar in his own right. Born in the Galilee town of Kursi, after the failed Rebellion he moved the Sanhedrin to **Tzipori** and later to **Beit She'arim** to work on the Mishna, which was completed after his death by his followers. **Tiberias** was another seat of the Sanhedrin in the 3rd and 4th centuries, and editing work was done there on both the Mishna and the Jerusalem Talmud.

BYZANTINE PERIOD

• *324-640 CE*

Rome's **Emperor Constantine** joined the new Christian religion, thereby redirecting history. Rome became a Christian empire, and the emperor built a new capital in Byzantium (hence our name for the empire, though they still considered it the Roman Empire). He renamed it **Constantinople** after himself, but it's now better known as Istanbul. Under his rule, the Middle East prospered fairly well, and merchants did well on European, Asian, and African trade. Religious tolerance, however, dwindled (and Rome hadn't been all that tolerant before).

Even within Christianity, there were fierce disputes among new sects over the nature of Jesus and whether he was two distinct yet inseparable persons, divine and human (as the Nestorians believed) or alternatively of a single, wholly divine nature (the answer according to the Monophysites, such as the **Copts** who still practice in Egypt). The **Greek Orthodox Church** settled it by declaring Christ to be both perfect God and perfect man, and the Nestorians and Monophysites to be heretics. The disputes turned ugly, heretics were suppressed, resulting in violence such as the Samaritan revolt in 529 CE and the Persian invasion in 614. The dissents eventually paved the way to Islam's success.

Palestine was perhaps more directly affected by the visit of Constantine's mother, **Saint Helena**. She traipsed about identifying holy sites (where Jesus performed miracles, was resurrected, etc.) and commissioning churches to be built, encouraging pilgrimages to the Holy Land. The excavations around the Sea of Galilee, for example, and Bethlehem, are full of Byzantine church ruins or reconstructions (such as the Holy Sepulcher), some with their glorious mosaics still intact.

EARLY ARAB PERIOD
• 640-1099 CE

While the Byzantine Empire lasted until 1453 CE when the Ottomans took over, their reign in the Middle East ended sooner, in 640 CE, with the Arab invasion. **Mohammed** was born in Mecca in 570 CE, had his first revelation from the Angel Gabriel in the month of Ramadan, 610 CE, and by his death in 632 had conquered and converted most of the Arab tribes. They dealt with the power vacuum his death created by finding new leaders who led them quite successfully against the Byzantine and Persian empires.

Abu Bakr became *khalifat rasul Allah* ("successor of the messenger of God"), soon shortened to *khalifah*, or caliph in English. His conquests (from North Africa to the borders of China) were amazingly speedy, taking little more than a decade to tackle some of the greatest powers around. Not all the Arab fighters were zealous Muslims engaged in a *jihad* (holy war). Christian Arabs (Arab denoting regional origin rather than religion) were welcome, and the Byzantine theological conflicts aided the Arab cause. Economic hardship also spurred on the conquests, as looting was an age-old solution to financial woes.

In 638, the Arabs under Caliph Umar took Jerusalem, and in 661 Mu'awiyah established his caliphate there. It was he who made succession hereditary and founded the **Umayyad** dynasty, followed by the **Abbasid**, and Fatimid dynasties. In 688 Abd al-Malik built the **Dome of the Rock** mosque on the Temple Mount, making Jerusalem a third Muslim pilgrimage site after Mecca and Medina, and sending a message to the Christians that Islam was no flash-in-the-pan religion. The **Fatimids** were Shi'ite rather than Sunni Muslims (see Religion section), and despite the great conflict between the two they generally respected the religious freedom of the Christians and Jews they ruled. Caliph al-Hakim (996-1021) persecuted Christians and destroyed their churches. Though his motivations and sanity have been debated, the actions perpetrated against the Christian community are indisputable.

The **Seljuks** were a dynasty in the growing Islamic Turkish civilization. The Seljuk Turks did well for themselves, began to expand their territories, took Jerusalem in 1071, and refused to allow the Christian Pilgrims easy access. It was this restriction (in part) that provoked the Pope to initiate the Crusades.

CRUSADER PERIOD
• *1099-1291 CE*

Promising relief from ecclesiastical penances as an incentive, in 1095 **Pope Urban II** invited all Christians to join a war to retake the Holy Sepulchre in Jerusalem from "the wicked race," responding in part to the plight of the Christian pilgrims (though by '95 that problem had been alleviated by a new ruler), in part to a call for help from the flailing Byzantine Empire, and in part to help solidify the papacy's power (and besides, times were bad and the trade routes over there were pretty good). The term Crusade, derived from the Latin crux ("cross"), refers to the biblical injunction that Christians carry their cross (Matt. 10:38). So, Crusaders wore red cloth crosses sewn on their tunics to show how they were soldiers of Christ.

The Crusades were off and the confrontations between Europe and the Middle East were on. In the First Crusade (1096-99) they took Jerusalem in 1099, slaughtered all the Muslims and most of the Jews, and crowned **Baldwin** King of the Latin Kingdom of Jerusalem. The Second Crusade (1147-49) made it as far as Damascus, but the Third Crusade (1188-92) meant business. By 1187 **Saladin** (Salah al-Din, a brave, shrewd, and magnanimous new caliph) had won the decisive battle at the **Horns of Hittin** and had taken back most of Palestine (including Jerusalem), and the Crusaders weren't pleased.

Led by **Richard the Lionheart**, they weren't terribly successful at reversing things, though they did manage to take Acre and Jaffa. In the Fourth Crusade (1202-04) the concentration was solely on besieging Constantinople and toppling the Byzantine Empire, which is exactly what they did. Many crusades followed in the 13th century, but little changed in the Muslim-Christian balance of power. Acre was the last Crusader stronghold, and it fell to the Mamluk **Sultan Baybars** in 1291. Travel to

Akko (Acre), Belvoir, Montfort, Ceasarea, the Horns of Hittin and plenty sites more to see the ruins and battlefields of those contentious days. The **Mamluks** had an interesting rags-to-riches story. The Muslim dynasties had an age-old tradition of taking Turkish boys (mamluks, or "owned men") as slaves and training them to be soldiers. They rebelled against their Ayyubid masters (Saladin's descendants), killed the new Ayyubid sultan, and established an empire that held sway from the late 13th century up until the Ottoman Empire crashed their party in 1517. During their tenure, not a whole lot of development went on in the Palestinian portion of their kingdom. Baybars (1260-1277) had razed many of the towns he conquered to prevent the fortifications from being used against them, and not much was rebuilt, partly because they were pretty busy defending their regime in Egypt and Syria. Under their rule some Jews began to return from Europe, especially after 1492 when Spain kicked out its Jewish population, and the mystic Kabbalists set up shop in Tsfat.

THE OTTOMAN EMPIRE
• *1517-1918*

The Ottoman Turks under Selim I moved against the Mamluks in 1517 after having humble beginnings in 1280 under **Osman I** and more ambitious successes, such as taking Constantinople in 1453 (looting it for 3 days and turning it into an Ottoman capital), beginning their four century reign over Palestine. Though the Mamluks had gunpowder and used it a tad, the Ottomans really began the gunpowder age in the Middle East. **Suleiman the Magnificent** was the next Sultan and he left his mark by rebuilding the walls around Jerusalem. Other building took place as well during their rule, notably the many fine structures built by Pasha el-Jazzar in Acre in the 1700s.

The Turks had an enormous empire, and they financed it by tax collection. *Multezim* (tax farmers) were assigned sectors to collect from, and so long as they gave a certain amount to the Empire they could keep the rest. Following the same school of thought, officials were authorized to collect fees (*baksheesh*, which has come to mean bribe or handout in common parlance) for services rendered. Later when the treasury needed more money, clerks had to buy their offices, and they would then bleed the public through taxes to recoup their outlay.

This system oiled the works for the next few centuries, and corruption was developed to greater flights of glory than usual. The lower you were on the ladder, the more of the burden you carried. Though religions (Jews, Armenian Christians, Greek Orthodox Christians, and Muslims) were theoretically left to their own devices, law and order were neglected, and the Jews and Christians in the Galilee weren't treated very well. Still, more Jews kept coming from Europe to form settlements because European conditions were even worse. Tsfat continued to establish its Jewish prominence, and Tiberias attracted lots of Jews as well.

To stir things up, **Napoleon Bonaparte** made a cameo appearance. He was sent by France to conquer Egypt (and maybe Syria and Iraq) in 1798. Napoleon occupied Jaffa very briefly in 1799, and then besieged Acre but was thwarted by the British Navy. He went to Haifa and used the Carmelite Monastery as a hospital for his soldiers until the Turks forced his retreat (there is now a monument shaped like a pyramid in memory of his dead).

Corruption, conflict, and the usual afflictions that plague an old empire began to weaken the Turks, and the world began to notice. Britain had a special interest in the region. They had a number of economic motives (their trade route to India involved Ottoman lands, and they had an import treaty with the Ottomans as well), and they didn't care for the expansion going on in Egypt and Syria by France, their arch enemy from the French and Indian War. They opened a British consulate in Jerusalem in 1838, and in 1839 **Sir Moses Montefiore** suggested in London that a Jewish state be established. Britain helped defend Ottoman interests in the Crimean War (1853-1856), and in 1869 the Suez Canal opened, increasing world interest in the area.

In 1908 a revolution led by the **Young Turks** overthrew the Ottoman sultanate. The Young Turk leader (dictator) Enver Pasha entered into World War I (siding with Germany and Austria-Hungary), and put the nails in his empire's coffin. Their defeat led to the breakup and foreign occupation of the Ottoman Empire, and Palestine entered a new era.

BRITISH OCCUPATION & THE BRITISH MANDATE
• 1919-1948

Toward the end of World War I, British troops led by **General Sir Edmund Allenby** invaded Palestine and took Jerusalem in December 1917, ending 400 years of Ottoman sovereignty, and then the waffling began. In 1922 the League of Nations approved a British mandate over Palestine and neighboring **Transjordan**, supposedly to encourage the development of self-governing institutions and, eventually, independence.

The Arab state of Transjordan (later becoming Jordan in 1946) became autonomous in 1923 and was recognized as independent in 1928. The Mandate period was not a happy time: Arabs rioting against Jews and the British trying to stay out of the middle (while keeping their finger on the oil pulse), thereby mucking it up even more. In 1916 the British high commissioner in Cairo had signed an accord with the sharif of Mecca, leading the Arabs to believe the British would support the creation of an independent Arab state that would include Palestine. One year later in 1917, however, the British government issued the **Balfour Declaration**, which promised support for a Zionist nation.

After World War I, a pattern began to emerge from the chaos, but it worsened rather than helped resolve the conflicts. Jewish immigration increased dramatically (the Third and Fourth Aliyahs, spanning 1919-1928, nearly tripled the Jewish population in Palestine), Arab Palestinians reacted with fear and violence, and Jews responded by digging their heels in and increasing immigration - a pattern that has continued in some ways up till today. The international political wheels spun and muddied the waters a bit more, and vague antagonisms became entrenched hostilities. In 1919 (the same year **Dr. Chaim Weizmann** led the Jewish delegation to the Peace Conference in Paris), Damascus demanded independence for a Syrian state that would include Palestine, categorically rejecting the concept of a Jewish national home.

The Third Aliyah began, and anti-Zionist riots broke out among Arab Palestinians in April 1920, followed by even more serious violence in May 1921 after Britain announced that 16,500 Jewish immigrants would be admitted. The **Histradrut** (General Federation of Jewish Labor) and **Haganah** (underground resistance movement) were formed, and the Fourth Aliyah got under way. Haj Amin, Mufti of Jerusalem and Supreme Muslim Council head was probably more responsible for intensifying ill-will than any other one individual. In 1929 there was yet another serious clash at the Western Wall in Jerusalem (instigated by Haj Amin), and that same year the Zionists formed the **Jewish Agency** to help develop quasi-governmental institutions among Palestine's Jews. The Haganah began to retaliate in the absence of British intervention. Also in 1929 the Jewish community of Hebron was slaughtered by Arab extremists, beginning a Hebron tension that hasn't yet begun to heal. **Ze'ev Jabotinsky** and **Menachem Begin** responded by forming the **Irgun Zvai Leumi**, an extreme right-wing underground organization.

The Palestine situation became even more complicated in the 1930s when, in reaction to Nazi persecution of Jews in Europe, Jewish settlement soared (the Jewish population totaled more than 400,000 by 1939, comprising nearly a third of Palestine's inhabitants), triggering the Arab attack reaction. The Mufti was finally arrested, but he escaped and fled to join Hitler in Berlin. Between 1935 and 1939, Britain proposed to stabilize the population with an Arab majority. The only common ground between Arabs and Jews was their displeasure with these plans. During these years, the Zionist struggle was a bit eclipsed by the need to fight WWII, but it wasn't by any means forsaken.

Britain's last serious attempts to reach a compromise were the inconclusive **London Round Table Conference** (1939) and the **White**

Paper of that year, which promised the establishment within ten years of an independent Palestine retaining an Arab majority. The White Paper also limited Jewish immigration to 1,500 per month until 1944, when Jews would no longer be admitted to Palestine. Britain's solution to the racial tensions led to the sad spectacle of boatloads of Holocaust survivors being refused and turned away, and the Zionists responded with Aliyah Bet, the illicit smuggling of refugees (the subject of a book and movie called *The Exodus*). Zionists disillusioned by British waffling (and believing that British influence after the war would wane and be replaced by American policy) focused on gaining US support, with some success.

In May 1942, the **Biltmore Conference** in New York demanded the formation of an independent Jewish commonwealth, a stance strongly endorsed by US political leaders. In addition to smuggling and lobbying, the Zionists also turned to terrorism to further their ends. In one incident, Menachem Begin led the Irgun to hang two British Army sergeants who'd been involved in executing Jews charged with terrorism.

ISRAELI STATEHOOD

By 1947, the British washed their hands of the problem and dumped it in the lap of the United Nations, which voted in November to recommend a split Palestine, with Arab and Jewish states, and an international Jerusalem. The partition (accepted by the Zionists but not by the Arab countries) didn't work out very well. The line was drawn such that houses (and families) were split down the middle, no one was happy, and international Jerusalem streets flowed red.

Fighting quickly spread as Arab guerrillas attacked Jewish settlements to prevent implementation of the UN plan. Jewish forces prevented seizure of most settlements, but Arab guerrillas, supported by the Transjordanian Arab Legion under the command of British officers, besieged Jerusalem. By April, the Haganah went on the offensive, scoring victories against the Arab Liberation Army in northern Palestine, Jaffa, and Jerusalem, and British military forces withdrew to Haifa.

The British got out on May 14, 1948 (months before the UN plan was to supervise the plan), and **David Ben Gurion** (Israel's first prime minister) declared the independent state of Israel. Israel's armed forces were geared for war, and not just defensive action. Based on intelligence reports and Arab incendiary boasts about pushing the Jews out of Palestine and into the sea, they readied to fight tooth and nail. Palestinian Arabs, joined by neighboring Arab allies (though not in anywhere near the numbers promised and expected) engaged in the first in a series of **Arab-Israeli Wars**, Israel's **War of Independence**.

In May of 1949, a UN cease-fire was declared and Israel emerged from the fray with a hard-won victory, new territories, and statehood. More than 700,000 Arab Palestinian refugees left, Israel confiscated the property they vacated (one of the items now sticking in the throats of Palestinians trying to make the peace work), and Palestine ceased to exist as a political entity. Accounts differ, however, over why the Arabs left. The Jews say they just up and vanished, prompted by their higher-ups to set the stage for wiping the Jews out. Arabs, however, say they were forced out by Jewish terrorism. Most of the territory west of the Jordan River that the United Nations had designated as Arab came under the control of Jordan, including the Old City and East Jerusalem, and the Gaza Strip was occupied by Egypt.

Israel was admitted into the United Nations (overcoming a number of objections). During 1949, armistice agreements were signed under UN auspices between Israel and Egypt, Jordan, Syria, and Lebanon. The armistice frontiers were unofficial boundaries until 1967. Since 1950 the Palestinian refugee problem remained unresolved in any way until very recent advances toward a solution acceptable to all parties.

Israel's development boomed, as did immigration. In 1950, the Knesset (Parliament) passed the **Law of Return** granting citizenship to any Jew requesting it, and the 1952 Nationality Law allowed non-Jews to claim citizenship. Kibbutzim and moshavim (collective and co-op farms) sprang up all over the place, and a nation took shape. Aliyah rates remained high, though the nationality of the year depended on who was suffering persecution where and when, with Tunisians and Moroccans flooding in around 1955 and Hungarians coming in 1956.

THE SINAI (SUEZ) WAR OF 1956

Border conflicts between Israel and the Arabs continued despite provisions in the 1949 armistice agreements for peace negotiations. Hundreds of thousands of Palestinian Arabs who had left Israeli-held territory during the first war concentrated in refugee camps along Israel's frontiers and became a major source of friction when they infiltrated back to their homes or attacked Israeli border settlements. A major tension point was the Egyptian-controlled Gaza Strip, from which Arab guerrillas raided southern Israel. Egypt's blockade of Israeli shipping in the Suez Canal and Gulf of Aqaba intensified the hostilities.

These escalating tensions coincided with Egyptian president **Gamal Nasser's** nationalization of the Suez Canal and ensuing the Suez Crisis. Great Britain and France strenuously objected to Nasser's policies, and a joint military campaign was planned against Egypt with the understanding that Israel would take the initiative by seizing the Sinai Peninsula. The war began on Oct. 29, 1956, and Israel's Operation Kadesh, commanded by **Moshe Dayan**, lasted less than a week; its forces reached the eastern bank of the Suez Canal in about 100 hours, seizing the Gaza Strip and nearly all the Sinai Peninsula. The war was halted by a UN cease-fire calling for withdrawal of all occupying forces from Egyptian territory.

No one won in this situation and everyone was condemned for this or that infraction. The facts show that Israel, allied with British, French, and American forces, reacted to Egypt's decision to close the Suez Canal by attacking and occupying Gaza Strip and the Sinai, and after some world pressure Israel gave up that occupation.

The debates go on about whether Israel was looking for reasons to invade, whether Egypt should have been pressured to end its position of war with Israel, and so on. In the next few years Egypt reinstated its Suez closure and more immigrants (from Eastern Europe and North Africa, mostly) arrived in Israel.

THE SIX DAY WAR OF 1967

After some relatively calm years followed by a couple of years with increased terrorism and "push them to the sea" rhetoric, Egypt blockaded the Tiran Straits as they had done in '56, massed their forces in the Sinai, and ordered the UN peace-keepers out of the Sinai. At the end of May, Egypt and Jordan signed a new defense pact placing Jordan's armed forces under Egyptian command. Israel saw the Egyptian forces moving northward with the likely aim of eradicating the still-new Jewish state, and it responded, led by Minister of Defense Moshe Dayan, and Army Chief of Staff **Yitzhak Rabin**.

The Israeli air force struck first and blasted Egyptian, Syrian, Jordanian, and Iraqi airfields on June 5, 1967. Jordan then attacked from the east and Syria from the north, engaging the Israelis on all sides. Six days later after the dust had settled, Israel occupied the Golan Heights, the Sinai Desert, and the West Bank (including Gaza Strip and Jerusalem, Old and East). As with the Sinai War, who planned what, provoked what, and manipulated what is still debated. Raging debates aside, Israeli confidence and developments soared following the brief war. The Jewish quarter of Jerusalem had been destroyed, but following the war it was rebuilt. Tiberias and the Sea of Galilee area were developed for tourism, and all the holy sites in and around Jerusalem became accessible to all, or nearly all.

After the six days, nearly 500,000 Arabs again departed Israel, and those remaining did so under Israeli military occupation, but the addition of more than 1,500,000 Palestinian Arabs to areas under Israeli control threatened internal security.

WAR OF ATTRITION (1969-70) & YOM KIPPUR WAR (1973)

The next war began two years later. Starting in the spring of '69 and going 16 months, Egypt kept up a steady shelling barrage across the Suez Canal border. Jordan made a few forays, terrorism was up, and so it went until the UN and the US brokered a new cease-fire. A tense quiet lasted a few years, and while Israel knew it wouldn't last, and also knew that Egypt was gearing up for a major offensive (supplied by the Soviet Union), the onslaught in '73 took it by surprise.

Egypt refers to it with pride as the **October 6th War** (bridges and such are named after it), other Arab nations call it the **War of Ramadan** (they invaded in the Islamic month of Ramadan) and Israel calls it the **Yom Kippur War** (it was launched on that Day of Atonement holiday). It was initially a military success for Egypt, and nearly the end of Israel. Egypt and Syria (financed by Saudi Arabia's King Faisal) launched a joint offensive on Israel's holiest day of the year, while most of the reserves were in synagogue praying. By the third day, however, Israel's IDF had recovered enough to start its own offensive. Israel pushed the Egyptians back beyond the Sinai and chased the Syrians halfway to Damascus. On October 24th, after 17 days of fighting, the UN again called for a cease-fire, but those 17 days had a severe effect on Israel.

Israel lost lives (more than 2,500), lost face, lost the heady confidence engendered by the Six Day War, lost about $7 million, and ultimately lost Golda Meir as prime minister. Egypt gained a strip of land along the Suez and Syria got a small area in the Golan Heights.

FIRST PEACE

The pursuit for peace became more serious. US Secretary of State **Henry Kissinger** shuttled all over the Middle East. At the Middle East Peace Conference in Geneva, Israel and Egypt reached an agreement, and in May '74 he negotiated a peace between Israel and Syria. In June of 1977 Prime Minister **Menachem Begin** made a call for peace and invited Jordan, Syria, and Egypt to find a solution. The West Bank and Golan settlements that are sticking points still were impediments then as well, and of the three countries, only Egypt took Israel up on the challenge.

Egypt's President **Anwar Sadat** braved the disapproval of the rest of the Arab community, visiting Israel in November 1977, negotiating a peace, and acknowledging Israel's right to exist. Begin visited Egypt a month later, and after 16 months of negotiations in which American President **Jimmy Carter** played an active role, the Camp David **Egypt-Israel Peace Treaty** was signed in March 1979, under which Israel returned the Sinai peninsula to Egypt. Hopes for an expansion of the peace process to include other Arab nations waned, however, when Egypt and Israel were subsequently unable to agree on a formula for Palestinian self-rule in the West Bank and Gaza Strip.

In the 1980s tensions were increased by conflicts between Israeli authorities and Palestinians in the occupied territories, by PLO guerrilla attacks on Israeli settlements in Galilee, and by Israeli retaliatory raids into Lebanon. Israel and Egypt have not become the best of friends, but the peace has held, and the Sinai which Israelis enjoyed during their brief occupation following the Six Day War has remained accessible for desert and Red Sea holidays.

Egypt's President Sadat was assassinated by extremists, at least in part for his Treaty signing, and now Mubarak, his successor, has the difficult job of maintaining the peace while dealing with an ever stronger and more dangerous fundamentalist faction.

WAR WITH LEBANON

On June 6, 1982, Israel launched a full-scale invasion of Lebanon to destroy PLO bases there and to end the attacks across its borders. Israeli commanders pushed northward, reaching the outskirts of Beirut within a week and also tangling a bit with Syrian forces. By the end of June, Israel had captured most of southern Lebanon and besieged PLO and Syrian forces in West Beirut. US mediation ended the fighting in August, when Israel agreed to leave Beirut so long as Syrian and PLO forces also withdrew.

What followed was a mess. On September 15 Lebanese president-elect Bashir Gemayel was assassinated, Israel reoccupied Beirut, and authorized Gemayel's Phalangist militia to "cleanse" Palestinian refugee camps of any remaining PLO fighters. The Phalange massacred hundreds of Palestinians, sparking Israeli antiwar protests. Israel signed an agreement with Lebanon ending the state of war in May 1983, but Lebanon renounced the pact under Syrian pressure in March 1984. Public pressures in Israel led to the withdrawal of Israeli troops by June 1994, leaving 1,000 "security personnel" to assist its Lebanese allies.

PALESTINE LIBERATION ORGANIZATION (THE PLO)

The PLO was formed in 1964 to represent Palestinian Arabs in a struggle to "liberate" their homeland from what they long claimed was an illegitimate Israeli state. In 1974 the PLO was proclaimed the sole legitimate representative of the Palestinian people by the Arab states at the Rabat Conference, and the UN General Assembly recognized the PLO as "the representative of the Palestinian people."

Yasser Arafat became chairman of the PLO in 1969, and remains its head despite serious challenges from without and within. Expelled from Jordan in 1971, PLO guerrillas established a virtual state-within-a-state in Lebanon from which they launched attacks on Israel. They were driven from their Beirut headquarters by the Israeli army in 1982 and scattered throughout the Arab world.

THE INTIFADA

While Israel's borders remained secure, its internal stability was threatened by continued demands for Palestinian autonomy and by an *Intifada* (uprising) in the occupied territories launched in December 1987. It began in the Gaza Strip in December 1987 and spread rapidly to the West Bank and East Jerusalem.

The revolt, which involved throwing stones at Israeli soldiers, commercial strikes, and business boycotts, took both the Israeli government and the Palestine Liberation Organization (PLO) by surprise.

Frustrated and angry, the Palestinians participating in the Intifada raised the costs of occupation and forced the government to take Palestinian nationalism more seriously. The intifada also contributed to Jordan's 1988 decision to sever its link with the West Bank and pushed the PLO to acknowledge Israel's right to exist. Israel's reaction to all this earned international disapproval. Their harsh attempts to suppress the revolt were widely criticized, and their decision in 1980 to name Jerusalem as its official capital was bitterly resented by the Arabs and protested by innumerable terrorist acts.

HAMAS

The **Muslim Brotherhood** is a religious and political organization founded in Egypt in 1928. **Hamas** is the militant Palestinian branch of the Muslim Brotherhood, founded in 1987. They do not recognize the state of Israel, are strongly opposed to Arafat's peace treaties and negotiations, and want to replace the Jewish state with an Islamic fundamentalist one.

As the peace process limps along there have been a number of terrorist suicide bombing attacks against Israel, and Hamas has claimed responsibility for most of them, putting the spotlight on Arafat to see how sincere he is about ending terrorism and how successfully he can control Hamas.

RECENT PEACE ACCORDS & THE PLO

The PLO declared a Palestinian state in November 1988 and conditionally accepted UN Resolution 242, which implicitly recognized Israel. Arafat, who recognized Israel's right to exist and renounced terrorism in December, was appointed president of the Palestinian state in April 1989. Israel and the PLO signed agreements in 1993 and 1994 granting Palestinian Arabs self-rule in the West Bank and Gaza Strip, and Israel and Jordan formally ended their state of war in 1994, raising hopes for a permanent peace between Israel and its Arab neighbors.

Peace treaties were signed, Israeli forces completed their evacuation from the Gaza Strip and Jericho on May 18, 1994, and the two sides began the process of hashing out the details for Palestinian self-rule in the rest of the West Bank (earning the Nobel Peace Prize for Yitzhak Rabin, Shimon Peres, and Yasser Arafat).

In September 1995, Rabin and Arafat signed the 300 page **Interim Agreement** (also known as **Oslo II**) on the West Bank and Gaza Strip, which set forth guidelines on everything from Palestinian elections and Israeli redeployment to security, water allocation, and prisoner release. Much of what was agreed upon has taken place: in January 1996, Palestinian Council elections were held and Yasser Arafat was elected *Ra'ees* (head) of the Authority; the IDF (Israeli Defense Force) evacuated most West Bank cities (with Hebron the notable exception); in April 1996, the Palestinian National Charter was amended to remove the articles that called for the destruction of Israel; and in May Israel and the Palestinian Authority began permanent status negotiations, touching on the touchy subjects of Jerusalem, settlements, and refugees.

YITZHAK RABIN'S DEATH

But between the signing of the Interim Agreement and the implementations above, a major setback and national tragedy occurred. On November 4, 1995, 25-year-old Yigal Amir assassinated Israel's Prime Minister Yitzhak Rabin at a peace rally in Tel Aviv before 100,000 Israelis. Over one million Israelis (both Arabs and Jews) paid respects to Rabin's coffin, and nearly 80 world leaders (including representatives from six Arab states) attended the Jerusalem funeral. Just two months after the Interim Agreement was signed, the Jewish right-wing university student shot Rabin in an effort to derail the peace talks, and while they clearly haven't completely come to a standstill, Rabin's death has had a profound effect on Israeli policy and psychology.

Acting Prime Minister Shimon Peres called for early elections, but by the time the elections were held in May 1996, three Hamas bombs caused 57 deaths and a political backlash; the moderates who'd turned from Likud to Labor after Rabin was murdered renewed their conservative sympathies and peace process distrust. **Benjamin Netanyahu**, the Likud party candidate, defeated Shimon Peres by a razor-thin majority of 50.4%. Netanyahu vowed to continue the peace process, but he's had anything but a light touch.

Nethanyahu appointed one of the most right-wing governments in Israel's history, and his tough-guy stance has elevated the tensions between Israelis and Palestinians, resulting in anger, clashes, and deaths. One of the most explosive incidents took place shortly after he took office.

RECENT TERRORIST ATTACKS

February 25, 1996 - In a suicide bombing of bus No. 18 near the Central Bus Station in Jerusalem, 26 were killed (17 civilians and 9 soldiers).

March 3, 1996 - In a suicide bombing of bus No. 19 on Jaffa Road in Jerusalem, 18 were killed (16 civilians and 3 soldiers).

March 4, 1996 - Outside Dizengoff Center in Tel-Aviv, a suicide bomber detonated a 20-kilogram nail bomb, killing 13 (12 civilians and 1 soldier).

July 30, 1997 - 16 people were killed and 178 wounded in two consecutive suicide bombings in the Mahane Yehuda market in Jerusalem.

September 4, 1997 - Five people were killed and 181 wounded in three suicide bombings on the Ben-Yehuda pedestrian mall in Jerusalem.

When in September 1996 Netanyahu decided to open an archaeological tunnel near Jerusalem's Al Aqsa Mosque (one of Islam's holiest sites), in the dead of night under heavy military security, he stepped on a lot of Palestinian toes. Palestinian forces and rock-hurling Arab youth clashed with Israeli troops in the worst street fighting since the *intifada*, and Israeli tanks were called in for the first time since the 1967 war. Casualties included 44 Palestinians and 11 Israelis dead and more than 740 Palestinians and 50 Israelis wounded.

The US hastily arranged a summit, but only Netanyahu, who stuck to his guns and gave nothing away, was satisfied. Since then, the Palestinians have continued to be angered by Israel's Agreement infractions: continued emphasis on new and expanded settlements and feet-dragging on deployment of troops, humiliations imposed on Palestinians, and border-closings that keep workers from their jobs. Israel has accused the Palestinian Authority of not doing their part to control Hamas and their terrorist activities.

The recriminations go on and on, but some progress has begun again. In January 1997, Netanyahu and Arafat agreed to a partial Israeli military pull-back from Hebron. And though in September 1997 US Secretary of State Madeleine Albright rebuked Netanyahu for his divisive plan to build 300 new homes for settlers, in October 1997 Israel and the Palestinian Authority got together with US Ambassador Dennis Ross to resume the peace process.

Netanyahu has been earning a lot of domestic ire, too. On September 25, 1997, the Israeli press reported that Netanyahu ordered a hit on Hamas political strategist Khalid Mashaal (which was then bungled) without consulting his Cabinet – including his foreign minister, who subsequently threatened to resign. His tendency to act impulsively without advice has lowered his domestic stock, and in November 1997 his government was talking openly of forcing new elections and thereby shoving Netanyahu out of power. Since then, Foreign Minister David Levy resigned in January 1998 (after months of threatening), angered by the go-nowhere peace process and a budget that offers little for social services. Other ministers are thinking of following suit, and talks of new elections are circulating again.

As we go to press, the latest January 1998 attempt by the US to broker peace advances has ended with Netanyahu digging in his heels. Under pressure from his fragile coalition's right-wing hard-liners, Netanyahu said any withdrawals depend on the Palestinian Authority's meeting Israeli conditions – reducing its police force size and cracking down on militants. Of the three withdrawals Netanyahu had promised the Palestinians, he's now willing to carry out just one troop withdrawal from the West Bank, with the rest of the territory to "be handed over as part of the final status agreement" of the future. Netanyahu further defied US interventions and angered Palestinians with a plan to double the number of homes in Jewish settlements over the next two decades with 30,000 new Jewish homes. Some minor progress was made on plans for a Gaza airport and a safe travel route for Palestinians between the Gaza Strip and the West Bank, but frustration is high among Palestinians.

The Palestinians now have full or partial control over 27 percent of the West Bank. They'd hoped for another 60 percent from the promised three withdrawals, but Netanyahu is offering just 10-12 percent instead.

And then there's the situation with Syria. Controversial negotiations had been under discussion in an on-again, off-again sort of way between Syria's **President Assad** and Israel's Rabin and facilitated by US mediation, talking about returning the Golan Heights to Syria in exchange for peace and diplomatic recognition. In December 1995 and January 1996 Peres picked up the ball, and talks continued concerning peace, Israeli withdrawal, and water. They agreed that they'd laid a solid base for further talks, and under Netanyahu that's about where things have remained. It's not a popular topic among Israelis or Syrians.

And up by the border with Lebanon, Israel's and Lebanon's endless fight drags on, occasionally making the news with a missile explosion here or there. In April 1996 the Iranian-backed *Hezbollah* guerrillas upped their Katyusha rocket attacks on Israel's northern settlements (such as Kiryat Shmona). Peres retaliated, southern Lebanese residents fled their homes, and northern Israelis slept in bomb shelters. Then on April 19, Israeli missiles hit a UN refugee camp, killing over 100 Lebanese civilians and provoking international outrage. American Secretary of State Warren Christopher shuttled between Damascus, Beirut, and Jerusalem, and eventually on April 26, 1996, brokered a "document of understanding" between Israel, Syria, and Lebanon. The goal of peace was agreed to, and further talks were indicated, but northern peace relations have yet to bounce back.

AGES & REIGNS

3,500,000-10,000 BCE - Paleolithic
10,000-5000 BCE - Mesolithic
5000-3000 BCE - Neolithic
4000-3000 BCE - Chalcolithic or Copper Age
3000-2000 BCE - Early Bronze Age

2000-1600 BCE - Middle Bronze (Canaanite)

2050-1786 BCE - Egyptian Middle Kingdom
1710-1580 BCE - Hyksos (Egyptian) rule

1600-1200 BCE - Late Bronze

1500-1100 BCE - Egyptian Rule over Canaan

1200-586 BCE - Iron (Israelite) Age
1100s-1000 BCE - Philistine Rule
and Rule of 5 Judges (Deborah,
Gideon, Samson, Eli, Samuel)
1020-1000 BCE - King Saul's rule
1000-961 BCE - United Empire of
David

961-922 BCE - Empire of Solomon

922 BCE - the empire split into
Judah and Israel

724 BCE - Assyrians conquer Israel
587-538 BCE - Nebuchadnezzar destroys
First Temple, Babylonian Exile
538-322 BCE - Persian Rule

333 BCE - Alexander the Great conquers
323 BCE - Ptolomian control

EVENTS

Tel Ubeidiya settlement in Galilee

2665-2180 BCE - in Egypt: pyramids built, papyrus paper made, camels domesticated
2000-1700 BCE - Habiru migration
1800-1700 BCE - Abraham lived
1700-1600 BCE - descent of Israel into Egypt
1300 BCE - Famine forces move to Egypt
1280 BCE - the Exodus, and Torah told to Moses
1250-1200 BCE - Israelites conquer Canaan

1004 BCE - David anointed king over all Israel
955 BCE - Solomon's Temple consecrated

922 BCE - Solomon's death, division of kingdom

537 BCE - King Cyrus permits return of Jews
520-515 BCE - Rebuilding of the Temple

332-63 BCE - Hellenistic Period
198 BCE - Seleucids take over
164 BCE - Maccabees start Hasmonean
  Dynasty

63 BCE-324 CE - Roman Period

324-640 CE - Byzantine Period

640-1099 CE - Early Arab Period
1099-1291 CE - Crusader Period
1250-1517 CE - Mamluk Period
1517-1918 CE - Ottoman Rule
1919-1948 CE - British Mandate
1948 to present - State of Israel

90 BCE - Hebrew Bible
  canonized
66 CE - Jerusalem Revolt
70 CE - Second Temple burned
73 CE - Masada
132 CE - Bar-Kokhba revolts
200s-300s CE - Talmud edited
476 CE - Fall of Roman Empire
570 CE - Mohammed born in Mecca

6. PLANNING YOUR TRIP

BEFORE YOU GO

If you contact the **Israeli Tourism Board**, *Tel. 800/596-1199*, a good few weeks before you go, they'll send you a full packet. Some of the brochures are just useless glossy pictures, but the maps are quite useful, and it's handy to have them before you get there. You can also call the **Royal Jordanian Tour Desk**, *Tel. 800/758-6878*, if you're planning to visit Jordan. For Egypt information, call the **Egyptian Tourism Office**, *Los Angeles, Tel. 213/653-8815*, or *New York, Tel. 212/332-2570*.

If you had a dime for every foreign phrase you intended to learn before taking a trip, you'd probably be living in the lap of luxury, but even if you don't become fluent in Hebrew and Arabic before taking off, familiarizing yourself (i.e. learning) the Hebrew letters will be an enormous help.

Destination signs and such suddenly provide information as they were meant to when the blocky symbols of the Hebrew *Aleph Bayt* become meaningful. And, if you're planning much time in Arab countries, learning the Arabic numbers helps a great deal as well.

INTERNET RESOURCES

The Internet has web sites that provide a wide array of useful and pertinent travel information, from travel advisories to political commentary.
- **US State Department Consular Affairs**
  http://travel.state.gov
- **Israel Tourist Information**
  http://www.infotour.co.il
- **Welcome to Israel**
  http://www.israel-embassy.org.uk/london/web/pages/turisthm.htm

- **Welcome to the Israel Foreign Ministry**
  http://www.israel-mfa.gov.il/index.html
- **Politics – Israeli Culture Net Links**
  http://israeliculture.miningco.msub18.htm
- **Focus on Israel**
  http://www.focusmm.com.au/israel/is_anamn.htm
- **Guide to Mideast Peace Process**
  http://www.israel.org/peace/guide.html
- **Egypt has it all!!**
  http://163.121.10.41/tourism
- **ArabNet**
  http://www.arab.net
- **Akhbar.com**
  http://jordan-online.com

WHEN TO GO

If you have the choice of traveling whenever you want, spring and fall have the nicest weather, neither outrageously hot as it can get in summer nor as wet and cold as it can get in winter. Take note, however, of certain Jewish, Christian, and Muslim holidays, when places can be crowded or shut. **Passover**, typically in March or April, is a time when Israelis travel, hotels charge peak season rates, and reservations need to be made months in advance.

The same is true of the **High Holy days** in September-October. **Christmas** and **Easter** pack the houses in Jerusalem and Nazareth, and during **Ramadan**, Muslim restaurants are often closed during the day but open at night (See *Holidays* below for exact dates).

FAHRENHEIT LOW-HIGH AVERAGES

	December	April	August
Jerusalem	47°-56°	53°-69°	66°-86°
Tel Aviv	47°-66°	54°-72°	72°-66°
Tiberias	53°-68°	56°-80°	75°-99°
Haifa	48°-65°	55°-78°	70°-86°
Eilat	51°-74°	63°-87°	79°-104°
Amman	43°-64°	50°-78°	65°-90°
Cairo	49°-68°	60°-82°	70°-97°

HOLIDAYS

The Jewish religious holidays all start at sundown the evening before the first day, and are called *erev* (evening of), as in Erev Pesakh.

HOLIDAYS OF ALL FAITHS

	1998	1999	Jewish Calendar
Jewish Holidays			
Tu B'Shvat -			
(New Year of Trees)	Feb 11	Feb 1	Shevat 15
Purim (Feast of Lots)	Mar 12	Mar 2	Adar 14 (or Adar II)
Passover (Pesakh)	Apr 10-17	Apr 1-8	Nisan 15-22
Holocaust Memorial Day	Apr 23	Apr 13	Nisan 27
Fighters' Memorial Day	Apr 29	Apr 20	Iyar 3
Israel Independ. Day	Apr 30	Apr 21	Iyar 4
Lag B'Omer	May 14	May 4	Iyar 18
Jerusalem Day	May 24	May 14	Iyar 28
Shavuot	May 31	May 21	Sivan 6
Tisha B'Av	Aug 2	Jul 22	Av 9
Rosh Hashana			
(Jewish New Year)	Sept 21-22	Sept 11-12	Tishri 1-2
Yom Kippur			
(Day of Atonement)	Sept 30	Sept 20	Tishri 10
Sukkot	Oct 5-11	Sept 25-Oct 1	Tishri 15-21
Simkhat Torah	Oct 12	Oct 3	Tishri 23
Hannukah	Dec 14-21	Dec 4-11	Kislev 25-Tevet 2
Christian Holidays	**1998**	**1999**	
Ash Wednesday	Feb 25	Feb 17	
Palm Sunday	Arpil 5	March 28	
Good Friday	April 10	April 2	
Easter	April 12	April 4	
Pentecost	May 31	May 23	
Christmas	Dec 25	Dec 25	
Muslim Holidays	**1998**	**1999**	**Muslim Calendar**
Ramadan	Dec 20	Dec 9	month of Ramadan
Eid al-Fitr	Jan 30	Jan 19	Ramadan 30
Eid al-Adhah			
(hajj to Mecca)	Apr 8	Mar 28	Zulhijjah 9
Ras as-Sana			
(Islamic New Year)	Apr 28	Apr 18	Muharram 1

WHAT TO PACK

It depends on when you go and who you are, but all variables aside, the general rule is as true as ever: take as little as possible without forgoing the important stuff. For **summer** (April-October), pack for heat. Take swimsuits and sandals, and plenty of changes of cotton shirts, socks (if you wear sneakers), and undergarments, as well as shorts or light skirts/dresses, plus a light jacket or sweater for the coolish nights in the hills.

You'll also need a modest outfit for visiting religious sites, which means clothing to cover your legs and shoulders. Israel is fairly casual, but a nice outfit for a splurge meal is a good idea. With the sun in mind, take along a hat, sunglasses, and sunscreen. A water bottle is a good idea, or you can buy a thermal water bottle sling in Israel (which makes a nice souvenir and is easier to pack).

In **winter**, prepare for wet and cold, as well as the occasional warm and dry. Take a thin raincoat (under which you can heap up the sweaters when it's cold), an umbrella, and waterproof boots. Take a swim suit as well, for hot spring visits or Red Sea trips. Clothes that can be layered work best, as you never know in winter.

Clothing and season aside, it's the sundries that make the difference. Hotels generally provide towels, though many hostels don't, but a laundry bag is always useful. No matter when you travel, take a small **first aid kit** with plenty of aspirin, Band-Aids, corn pads, etc. to deal with blisters and pains from lots of walking. It's easy to catch a cold when traveling, and while it's not what you want to think about when packing, your favorite cough drops or cold capsules can be a comfort in the unhappy event. Personal toiletries are available in all the brands you're used to, but they aren't cheap, and earplugs come in very handy in all sorts of otherwise unbearable situations. A small flashlight is useful, as is the all-purpose Swiss army knife, and you may want a small spoon on picnics.

Binoculars come in handy on hikes, and swim goggles can take the place of a snorkel mask in a pinch (and they take less room to pack). Sunscreen is necessary, and you'll need a small day pack as well. And don't forget your driver's license, long distance calling card, and insurance card as well.

MAKING RESERVATIONS

Hotels and hospices appreciate reservations, and it's a good idea during peak seasons (July/August and the Jewish Holidays of Rosh Hashana and Pesakh, as well as Christmas and Easter in some cities). Faxing is probably the most convenient way to reserve (from the US, that is), but the phone will do as well, and the hotel clerks generally speak passable English.

Some hostels take reservations, but for many it's just a matter of showing up right after check-out for the best shot. There's plenty of turnover, and a little walking will get you a room or bed of some sort.

STUDY TOURS/LANGUAGE LEARNING PACKAGES

Ulpan is the place to go to learn Hebrew quickly and well. There are City Ulpan and Kibbutz Ulpan, and their goal is to provide students with a working knowledge of conversational Hebrew, to enable them to read simple Hebrew texts and newspapers, and to build a foundation for further study. The teachers are trained to teach Hebrew as a second language, and most of the students are *Olim* (people immigrating to Israel). Classes usually have 15-25 students, meet for 18-24 hours a week, and last four and a half to five months. For more information, contact the **Ministry of Immigrant Absorption** office, *2 HaKirya Building, Jerusalem, 91006, Tel. 02-675-2760.*

Jewish Agency for Israel, *3 Ben Shatach, Jerusalem, Tel. 02-623-1823,* also has information on less formal study programs for tourists. They're open Sunday, Monday, Wednesday-Thursday 8am-6pm, Tuesday 8am-4pm, and Friday 10am-1pm. Write them at the **Center for Ulpanim and Counseling for Young Adults**, *12 Kaplan, Tel Aviv.*

American Zionist Youth Foundation, *Tel. 800/274-7723 or 212/339-6941, Fax 212/775-4781,* in New York also arranges study, archaeological digs, University, and language programs in Jerusalem, Tel Aviv, Haifa, and Be'er Sheva. Their office is at the *University Student Department, Israel Action Center, 110 E. 59th Street, 3rd floor, New York, NY 10022.*

GETTING TO ISRAEL

By Air

Ben Gurion International Airport, *Lod, near Tel Aviv, Tel. 03-971-0000 or Tel. 03-971-0111, Fax 03-972-1217,* is the main airport in Israel, with scheduled flights from 24 international airlines. To get to and from Ben Gurion, there are shuttles, buses, and taxis to/from the city of your choice in the Arrivals & Departures section. The transport section of your destination city has the details.

A few European flights also land at **Ovda**, *Tel. 07-637-5880/1,* and **Eilat International Airports**, *Tel. 07-636-3838,* in the south as well. Confirm your departing flight at least 72 hours before you're scheduled to take off (don't neglect this – people have been bumped from international flights and their seats assigned to others). You'll need to check in at Ben Gurion two hours before you're scheduled to depart (El Al offers advanced check-in the night before in Jerusalem, Tel Aviv, Haifa, and Eilat, and other airlines may start soon – ask the airline for specifics).

The **departure taxes**, usually already added into the price of your ticket, are $13 from Ben Gurion, $7 from Jerusalem airport, $11 if you're going to Egypt, and zero from Eilat's airport. Due to the nature of the politics of the region, security is a serious issue at Ben Gurion (and other Israeli entry points). In-depth security checks are normal and necessary, and if you are selected for the experience, just take it in stride.

By Sea

A number of ships and ferries sail to Haifa, and pleasure craft can enter Israel through Israel's various ports. Less expensive in low season, from the **Port of Haifa Passengers Terminal**, *Tel. 04-851-8111, Fax 04-867-4853*, it's possible to get to Cyprus for $80-$176 one way ($240-$292 round trip), to Rhodes in Greece for $123-$297 one way ($248-$561 round trip), and to Piraeus for $273-$345 one way ($436-$552 round trip) by ferry. From Patras in Greece you can hop a ferry to Bari in Italy for $41-$85, depending on season and type of seat or cabin, and while there's no longer a direct route to Turkey, it's possible to arrange Turkey-bound transport from Rhodes (though it's probably easier and cheaper to fly). **Port tax** is $25, animals and bicycles ride free, and cars cost extra. From Haifa, call **Caspi**, *76 Ha'atzmaut, Tel. 04-867-4444;* **Mano**, *2 Palmer, Tel. 04-866-7711;* or **Dolphin**, *Tel. 04-855-3278*, for more information, or contact Caspi, *1 Ben Yehuda, Tel Aviv, Tel. 03-510-7423, Fax 03-516-0989*, or *3 Yanai, Jerusalem, Tel. 02-624-4266, Fax 02-623-4262*. In addition to transportation, they also offer cruises.

To enter Israel by pleasure craft, you can sail into **Atarim**, *Tel Aviv Tel. 03-527-2596, Fax 03-527-2466*, **Eilat**, *Tel. 07-635-8333, Fax 07-635-8311*, and **Haifa**, *Tel. 04-851-8111, Fax 04-867-4853*.

Jaffa, *Tel. 03-683-2255, Fax 03-683-1337*, and **Akko**, *Tel. 04-991-9287, Fax 04-825-8382*, also have ports, but they are not international.

By Land

For now you can pass back and forth between Israeli and **Palestinian Authority** lands with just your passport without needing extra visas, but this may change so check for the latest updates. You can also now cross, legally and relatively hassle free, from Israel to Egypt and Jordan and back again, thanks to the peace treaties of the last few years.

You can enter Israel from **Egypt** at two control points: at **Rafiah** and **Taba**, while Israel and **Jordan** share three border crossings: **Allenby Bridge**, the **Jordan River Crossing**, and **Eilat's Arava**. Travelers wishing the most up-to-date border crossing information should contact the US Embassy in Tel Aviv or the US Consulate General in Jerusalem.

For further entry information, contact the **Embassy of Israel**, *3514 International Dr., NW, Washington, DC 20008, Tel. 202-364-5500*, or the nearest **Israeli Consulate General** in San Francisco, Miami, Atlanta, Chicago, New Orleans, Boston, Los Angeles, New York, Philadelphia, or Houston, or the US Consulate in Tel Aviv, email: acs.amcit-telaviv@dos.us-state.gov.

Israel-Egypt By Air

Flights on **Air Sinai**, *1 Ben Yehuda, Tel. 03-510-2481*, go to **Cairo** for $143 one way (plus $11 tax) Sunday, Thursday, Friday at 11:45am. **El Al**, *32 Ben Yehuda, Tel. 03-526-1222*, also goes to **Cairo** for $143 at 8pm Sunday-Thursday.

Israel-Egypt By Bus

There are two border crossings with Egypt, and they're open all year round, seven days a week, except for Yom Kippur and the first day of the Muslim feast of Eid al-Adhah. If you're only going into the Sinai you can get a two-week Sinai-Only visa at the border. To go further into Egypt or stay for longer, you'll need to get a regular one month Egyptian visa, but you can now get them at the border. Through April 1998, visas will be issued free of charge, but in May 1998 the fee will revert back to $15. Private cars are allowed to cross the border, but not rentals. Also, the border bank commission is a bit steep, so it's a good idea to change money elsewhere, if possible.

Rafiah, *Tel. 07-673-4080*, 50 kilometers southwest of Ashkelon and open 24 hours, is the main point of entry, with a number of bus companies routed to Cairo from Tel Aviv and Jerusalem. From Israel to Egypt entails a **departure tax** of NIS 92, while going the other way from Egypt the departure tax to Israel is E£21 (from Egypt to anywhere other than Israel there's no departure tax). Going through BTC costs $40 for the bus from Jerusalem to Cairo ($60 round trip), plus the departure tax, and it takes about 10 hours.

Coming back, buses from Israel and Egypt stay in their own countries and don't cross the border (though a deal is in the process of being worked out), so if you take the Jerusalem or Tel Aviv bus to Cairo, you spend around three hours at the border doing Israel exit and Egypt entrance activities before shlepping to the Egypt bus waiting at the other side, and vice versa. If you come to Rafiah by Cairo bus and plan to transfer on your own to an Israeli connection, get here in the morning if you can, but definitely by early afternoon when the last buses leave for Israel.

Taba, *Tel. 07-637-3110*, a few kilometers and a short NIS 3.9 bus ride south of Eilat, is the point of entry into the Sinai and it's open 24 hours a day. From Israel there's a departure tax of NIS 18 (unless you're just going to the Taba Hilton, in which case you need only present your passport), and coming into Israel from Egypt there's a tax of E£21.

There is bus transport from there into the Sinai and on to Cairo (six-seven hours) with the East Delta Company for E£70 at 2pm. Coming back, the 8am from Cairo costs E£45, the 7:30am is E£51, the 10pm costs E£78, and the 11pm is E£70. Noon-1pm is a very busy time there, and you could wait quite a while for your Israeli security interview and baggage x-ray check.

Nizana, *near Be'er Sheva and 45 kilometers southeast of Rafiah*, is a third crossing into the Sinai, but it's only open for transportation of good, no travelers allowed.

Israel-Jordan By Bus or Taxi

There are three land crossings between Israel and Jordan, evenly dispersed from north to south. From Israel to Jordan the **departure tax** is NIS 53 or NIS 103 (depending on where you cross), while Jordan's overland departure tax is JD4 or JD5, depending on where you cross (as compared to JD6 by sea and JD10 by air). There are buses and taxis to and from the crossings, but private cars are not allowed across. To enter Jordan from Israel you need a Jordanian visa. You can obtain one at the Arava and Beit She'an crossings (JD15 for US, JD31 for Canada, JD23 for UK, JD5 for Ireland, JD4 for New Zealand, Australia and South Africa go free), but to enter via Allenby Bridge you'll need the visa in advance. You can get one at a Jordanian consulate before you leave home, or in Tel Aviv from its Jordanian Consulate, *14 Aba Hillel, Ramat Gan, Tel. 03-751-7722*.

The Allenby Bridge, *near Jericho and just 40 kilometers east of Jerusalem, Tel. 02-994-2302*, is the central and most regulated crossing between the two countries, with tons of security measures and steps, and an Israeli departure tax of NIS 103 (or Jordanian departure tax of JD5). The bridge is open Sunday-Thursday 8am-midnight, Friday, Saturday 8:00am-3:00pm, but it's better to get there as early as you can to make the transport hookups (the Jett bus is finished by 1:30pm, though taxis still wait for late arrivals) and straggle through customs. Unlike in Eilat, *you can not get a Jordan visa at the Allenby Bridge*. If you wish to use this crossing, get your visa in the US, Tel Aviv, or in Egypt.

Just to get there is a hassle. You can take an Egged bus (NIS 17) as far as the junction outside Jericho, from which point you'll need to hunt up a taxi. Special taxis cost a bundle. The best way to get there is via the American Colony taxi, *Tel. 02-628-5171*, for $30, but you need to call the day ahead and set it up.

Close to the border things start to get confused. The taxi may be stopped at the document checkpoint a few kilometers from the bridge, leaving you to board the Arab bus to customs for a few more shekels. Your best bet is to make certain in advance that your taxi is authorized to go all the way to the bridge. At the Allenby Bridge Terminal you get your passport stamped and get directed to the NIS 10 (or $3 or JD1.5) tourist minibus (separated from the Arabs in transit who get to board a local bus) to cross the bridge. On the mini-journey, the driver collects passports and you're off to Jordan's passport control, where you stand around and wait, and wait some more.

The Jordanian JETT buses are gone by 1:30pm or so, but there are other buses for JD1.5, and you can take a taxi to Abduli Bus Station in Amman for JD2 per person. Going to the bridge from Amman, the JETT buses leave daily at 6:30am, cost JD6, and take one hour.

Arava (Wadi al-'Arabah) **border**, *south near Eilat, Tel. 07-633-6815, Fax 07-633-6844*, is the most lenient crossing. The border is open Sunday-Thursday 6:30am-10pm and Friday-Saturday 8am-8pm, closed, Yom Kippur and Eid al-Adhah, and departure tax here is NIS 53. You can get a visa here if you need to (JD15 for US, JD31 for Canada, JD23 for UK, JD5 for Ireland, JD4 for New Zealand, Australia and South Africa go free), and the tension isn't as pronounced. Taxis from the border to and from Aqaba cost JD5. Taxis to and from Eilat cost NIS 20.

Jordan River (Sheikh Husseini Bridge) crossing, *north near Beit She'an, Tel. 06-658-6448, Fax 06-658-6421*. Here too the border is open Sunday-Thursday 6:30am-10pm and Friday-Saturday 8am-8pm. Departure tax here is NIS 53, and you can get your visas here. Beit She'an city bus #16 leaves 8:15am, 9:20am, and 2:15pm for the border. This petite, Ottoman-built bridge holds a lot of traffic, so leave half a day for the ordeal. You can exchange money on the Jordanian side, then take a bus or share taxi to nearby Shona. From there you can catch a minibus to Irbid.

Jordan-Egypt By Air

There are flights between Amman and Cairo on **Royal Jordanian Air**, *US toll-free Tel. 800/223-0470*, for $180 one way, $359 round trip.

Jordan-Egypt By Ferry

The **ferry** across the Gulf of Aqaba to the Sinai sounds like a fun way to travel, but it's not. Passport control and customs at the port involve an elaborate game of tourist football, sending you hither and thither for stamps and checks and processing of all sorts. It's supposed to leave Aqaba Port somewhere between 10am-noon and again at 4pm, take 3.5 hours to cross, and be met by a bus which will take you the six-seven hours to Cairo. But don't count on it. It is just as likely to leave a few hours late, then dawdle about on the water for 11 hours waiting for a breathless calm before docking in Nuweibe.

Once there and once through the mobbed customs scene, you could easily wait a few hours more before being allowed the privilege of a smoky, crowded bus through the Sinai. These same buses, the ones that won't leave till they're good and full, are quite apt to break down in the middle of the icy cold desert in the dead of night, subjecting you to another four hour wait before depositing you in a filthy heap in Cairo. If you decide to chance it, coach class costs $19 (or take a cabin for the trip – you may need it), along with the JD6 departure tax at the port (after the JD3 taxi to the port).

You can also prepay for a Hebton Tours bus to Cairo for an additional JD5.5, but it's not a good idea. It's better to be free to hop the first bus ready to leave the Nuweibe port (for around E£35) than to have to hang around waiting for one particular bus to get ready to leave. Or, you can pay Jett Bus $50, which covers the ferry and connecting Jett bus to Cairo.

There's also a **speedboat** that plies the Gulf of Aqaba waters. It departs Aqaba at 10:30am and 2:30pm, takes an hour, and costs $32 (plus JD4 departure tax). It's less crowded, more punctual, and altogether the easiest and most hassle-free alternative. You can get tickets at any Aqaba travel agency.

You need a visa for Egypt, and can get one at an Egyptian consulate in Israel, Jordan, at home before you leave, or at the border. If you're only going into the Sinai you can get a two-week Sinai-Only visa at the border. To go further into Egypt or stay for longer, you'll need to get a regular one month Egyptian visa. Through April 1998, visas will be issued free of charge, but in May 1998 the fee will revert back to $15.

Jordan-Egypt By Bus

JETT buses go from Amman to Cairo, departing Monday, Tuesday, Thursday, and Saturday at 7:30am and taking close to 24 hours, for JD48.

Jordan-Egypt By Taxi, Via Israel

Another option is to take the **taxi** (JD5) from Aqaba to the Eilat border (open Sunday-Thursday 6:30am-8pm and Friday-Saturday 8am-6pm. departure tax JD4) and NIS 20 for a taxi from the border to Eilat, then proceed from Eilat across the Taba border (see Israel-Egypt section above).

CUSTOMS & ENTRANCE REQUIREMENTS

You need a valid passport, and when you enter Israel you'll receive a three month visitor's visa free of charge (you can ask not to have your passport stamped if you so wish), and you can extend your visa for a nominal fee at any of the Ministry of the Interior offices in any of the main cities in Israel, the same place to apply if you want to work in Israel.

Israel's airports and the Rafiah Terminal have a **customs** clearance system featuring the Green channel (if you have no goods to declare) and the Red channel (if you do). You needn't declare any of the following items (and can therefore go **Green**): personal clothing, alcoholic drinks (up to two liters wine or one liter spirits for individuals 17 or older), perfumes (up to .25 liters per person), tobacco products (up to 250 cigarettes or grams for individuals 17 or older), and gifts, so long as they don't exceed the above limits or $150 in total value. You are also allowed items such as radios, tape recorders, musical instruments, and other such travel needs.

You must line up at the **Red** channel, however, if you possess any items to declare, such as a camcorder, personal computer, diving equipment, etc. For these and similar items, you'll have to pay a deposit for duties and taxes which will be refunded when you bring them back out of the country.

GETTING AROUND ISRAEL
By Car
There are lots of car rental agencies all over Israel, making for convenient (though not cheap) transportation, offering an ever-changing variety of deals and packages. Sometimes good deals can be arranged from the US before you go, but there's not much difference. If you leave it until Israel, shop around and pay attention to the ads in the tourist offices, but be aware that many of the touted prices don't include insurance fees. Winter rates are lower than summer, week-long rentals work out better than day-to-day, and unlimited mileage is worth the extra cost.

Rentals average around $40-$60 a day and $200-$300 a week for economy cars rented in Israel, and $25 (plus 25¢-55¢ a mile) to $33 (unlimited mileage) a day and $196-$420 a week if arranged from the US, plus insurance. To rent a car you need to be over 21 years old, have a US driver's license or an international driver's license, and have a major credit card.

Rules of the road: you drive on the right side of the road, there are lots of one-way streets, and when driving in the winter, keep your lights on, even during the day (required by law).

Parking zones: red & white means no parking ever; blue & white means you need a parking ticket 8am-7pm (they can be bought in most grocery stores or lottery kiosks); white lines mean free parking 8am-5pm; red & yellow indicates a bus stop and taxi station.

By Bus
Egged (pronounced with two syllables) is the main intercity bus company in Israel, and except in Tel Aviv where **Dan Company** reigns supreme, they operate most of the intracity buses as well. Egged sells

Israbus passes (available to tourists but not to locals) which give you unlimited bus use for the duration of the pass. Be warned, however, that they don't work on Dan buses, so they aren't such a hot idea if you're going to be based in Tel Aviv.

They cost NIS 249 for 7 days; NIS 399 for 14 days; NIS 499 for 21 days; for more information, call Egged, *Tel. 03-527-1212*. Otherwise, transport costs within a city run you NIS 4 for each trip, and between cities it depends: Jerusalem to Tel Aviv costs NIS 17, to Haifa it costs NIS 34, and the five-hour jaunt to Eilat is NIS 54 (and student discounts are always available). Most buses don't run on Shabbat, and up-to-date information is available (after a patient wait) from *Tel. 03-537-5555* or *Tel. 04-854-9555* or *Tel. 02-530-4704*.

United Bus, *Tel. 03-639-4444*, runs the 222 shuttle between Tel Aviv and Ben Gurion airport for NIS 10.5. They run 4:30am-midnight roughly every 45 minutes, and the last bus Friday is 7:15, first bus on Saturday is 12:30pm. See the *Tel Aviv Arrivals* section for more details.

By Train

Israel's train line runs from Jerusalem to Tel Aviv and Tel Aviv to northern points such as Netanya, Haifa, Akko, and Nahariya. They are a little bit cheaper and slower than the buses, but the routes (especially up the coast to Haifa) are more scenic than the bus trip. They schedule fewer departures than the buses, however (especially the Tel Aviv -Jerusalem trip).

For the latest fares and information, call 03-693-7515 in Tel Aviv or 04-856-4154 in Haifa.

By Sherut Taxi

A sherut taxi is a shared taxi service that operates at a fixed rate between cities and on some urban routes as well. The ride can be more comfortable than buses, and the rates are competitive.

By Private Taxi

Known as *special* taxis in Israel, they run on meters (insist on this) with 25% higher fares 9pm-5:30am, Shabbat, and holidays. There is also a fare surcharge for pick-up arranged by phone. Taxi-related complaints can be addressed to the **Controller of Road Transport**,*Tel. 03-532-1351 for Tel Aviv and the south, Tel. 02-531-9550 for Jerusalem, and Tel. 04-853-6711 for Haifa and the north.*

By Air

Arkia Air, *11 Frishman, Tel Aviv , Tel. 177-022-5123, Fax 03-690-0525*, operates domestic flights from **Tel Aviv** to Rosh Pina ($46), Eilat ($80),

Kiryat Shemona ($46), and Haifa ($20). Flights also go from **Jerusalem** to Rosh Pina ($46) and Eilat ($20). From **Haifa** there are flights to Tel Aviv and Eilat ($94). From **Eilat** you can fly to Jerusalem, Tel Aviv, and Haifa. And from **Masada** you can go to Tel Aviv. In addition to the Tel Aviv branch, there are offices in all the cities they fly to.

Isra Air, *Tel. 03-613-6564, Fax 03-751-9430*, flies from Tel Aviv to Eilat as well, usually for less than Arkia.

7. BASIC INFORMATION

BAR/BAT MITZVAHS

Bar and Bat Mitzvahs in Israel are big business, as arranged by a number of US based agencies. At the Western Wall in Jerusalem or amid the stone ruins of the Zealot Synagogue on Masada, thousands of adolescents make the journey with families and friends in tow.

Tova Gilead, *983 Port Washington Blvd., Port Washington, NY 11050, Tel. 800/242-8682, Fax 516-883-8383* arranges ceremonies at Masada for $2,200-$3,050 per person, including round-trip El Al air fare NY-Tel Aviv, 5-star hotel accommodations with some meals, and sightseeing trips of 8-15 days. **Travelcare**, *97-77 Queens Blvd., Rego Park, NY 11374, Tel. 800/233-1336 or 718/997-0090*, also features Masada or Wall ceremonies and 14 days of sightseeing for package deals from $4,900 (two adults and one child per room) to $7,000 (two adults, four children, two rooms), plus airfare.

If you want to do it on your own, contact the **Jerusalem Regional Office**, *Ministry of Tourism, PO Box 1018, Jerusalem, Tel. 02-675-4877, Fax 02-675-4974*, for an application form. A bar/bat mitzvah at the Western Wall is free (though donations are accepted). You can bring along your own rabbi or contact the Western Wall rabbi (*Rabbi Nahum, c/o Tzvi Hoffman, Hechal Shlomo, Moreshet Hotel, 58 King George St., Jerusalem, Tel. 02-624-7112 Fax 02-623-3620*. Note, however, that Western Wall services are all orthodox, so a bat mitzvah girl can't read from the Torah. Instead, her father or other male relative can read from the Torah during morning services.

Services for both genders can be arranged at **Masada**, Ms. Nava Granitz, *Tel. 07-658-4207, Fax 07-658-4464*, the **Neot Kedumim Biblical Landscape Reserve**, *Tel. 08-977-0770, Fax 08-977-0775*, or another synagogue of your choice.

BUSINESS HOURS

Stores are generally open Sunday-Thursday 9am-7pm, though some opt for mid-day breaks between 1-4pm. Stores usually close early Fridays and eves of Jewish Holidays. Muslim shops are closed on Fridays and Christian-owned stores close for Sunday.

COST OF LIVING & TRAVEL

Israel isn't cheap, but neither do you have to drop a pile of money; it depends on your budget and the level of luxury you want and are willing to pay for. Lodgings typically start at $7-$10 for dorm beds, you can get cheapish hotel rooms for $50-$80, and for 5 star luxury you should expect to pay $200-$400 (depending on the season and the city). Most hotels have different prices for the different travel seasons, with Low Season in mid-winter, Regular Season, and High or Peak Season including July-August and the Passover holidays.

For food there's more of a range. You can live very well for very little if you have a taste for falafel, hummus, and bagel, spending no more than $1-$2 for a snack or lunch, while local meat dishes (shishlik, shwarma) are a little more but still not what you'd call expensive at $4-$5 a pop. Full meals of local cuisine (Yemenite, Russian, etc.) start around $6, while if you yearn for fish or European cuisines you start paying bigger bucks at fancier restaurants, spending $20-$30 a meal.

Travel is cheaper by bus and train ($1 for city transit and $4-$9 between most cities), more expensive by rental car, which average around $40-$60 a day and $200-$300 a week for economy cars, and more expensive still by organized tours, typically $250 or so for a 3 day trip.

ELECTRICITY

Israel's electric current is 220 volts AC, 50 Hertz. Most Israel sockets accommodate their triangular three-pronged plugs, but they'll generally take the European round two-prong just fine. Electric shavers and such will need adapters, and you can buy these at any hardware store. Some of the finer hotels, however, have adapters built in to the bathrooms.

HEALTH CONCERNS

There are no vaccination requirements for entering Israel, though the usual precautions of hepatitis shots, polio boosters, and diarrhea pills are always advised. The most common health concerns typically involve reactions to heat and all that walking. Israeli camping supply stores sell nifty thermal slings just the right size for mineral water bottles, or bring your own favorite water bottles to take on all your hikes.

Call **101** anywhere in the country at any time for **emergency first aid** provided by Magen David Adom (the Red Star of David, Israel's version of Red Cross). The *Jerusalem Post* lists daily rosters of emergency hospitals, dental clinics, and all-night pharmacies.

Most US medical insurance isn't accepted right off the bat in Israeli hospitals. You generally need to pay them, and then get reimbursed later. **INS-CARE**, *9 Ben Yehuda, Tel Aviv, postal address POB 26136, IL 61261, Tel Aviv, Tel./Fax 03-517-1613*, offers services for insured tourists, meaning tourists who have taken medical insurance with them at the rate of $1.50 a day for a minimum of three months. For this fee you get an INS-CARE card providing access to their clinics (open 24 hours) and affiliated hospitals throughout the country. They offer a lot, including ambulance service, dental clinics, and specialist doctors such as internal, gynecological, and orthopedic.

In 1983, the Knesset banned **smoking** in public places such as buses, taxis, etc. A recent amendment bans smoking in all work places (except for closed, well-ventilated smoking rooms). It's not well adhered to, so if the smoke is bothering you, you can try saying something, or complain to the Ministry of Health, *Ben Tabai St. #2, Jerusalem, Attention: Occupational Health Service, Tel. 02-670-5705*.

Other Medical Services

Intensive care ambulances can be found in Tel Aviv, *Tel. 03-546-0111*, in Jerusalem, *Tel. 02-562-3133*, and in Haifa, *Tel. 04-851-2233*.

• **Shahal**, *Tel. 03-562-5555 or 177-022-1818*, is a private intensive care service for heart patients.

• **Eran Mental Health Hotline** can be reached in Tel Aviv, *Tel. 74-546-1111*, Jerusalem, *Tel. 02-561-0303, Haifa, Tel. 04-867-2222, or Tel. 1201* anywhere in Israel.

• **Psagot Emergency Psychiatric and Neurological Care** is available in *Tel Aviv, Tel. 03-574-1858, or Tel. 05-252-3696*.

• **Rape Crisis Line**: *Tel. 1202*.

For more medical services, check the Practical Information sections of the individual cities.

MONEY & BANKING

Israeli currency is the **New Israeli Shekel** (NIS), and its exchange rate hovers fairly steadily around 3.5 shekels to the American dollar, making each shekel worth about 29¢. The shekel contains 100 smaller units called *agorot*.

The **Jordanian dinar** (JD) is worth about $1.41. Smaller denominations are **fils**, and there are 1000 fils to the dinar. 10 fils equals one **piaster**

GETTING MARRIED

*It is possible for non-Israelis to tie the knot in Israel, but it's neither simple nor easy. Not only must you be committed to one another, you need a strong desire to say your vows in Eretz Yisrael to persevere. First thing is to contact the **Marriage Rabbinut**. While there is such an office in all the major cities (in Tel Aviv contact the Tel Aviv Marriage Rabbinut, 33 King David St., Tel. 03-696-4181) most folks want to do the honors in Jerusalem.*

Step 1: Beit Hadin, 9 Koresh (a small street off Shlomtsion Hamalka), Tel. 02-623-3696, Fax 02-623-2396, open Sunday-Thursday 8:30am-1:30pm) is the Rabbinical Court, and this is where you both go to prove you are Jewish and single. Bring passport with valid visa, a letter from your home Jewish community rabbi attesting to your Jewish and single status, and if possible, a copy of your mother's ketubah (Jewish wedding certificate). Fill out a form and open a file (NIS 170 each). You also need to go to the Chief Rabbinate, Yirmeyahu Street, corner of Hamem-gimel Street, to get a stamp of approval that your rabbi is recognized. You must then bring that approval paper back to Beit Hadin, 9 Koresh, to get a court date (generally two-three weeks unless it's urgent).

Step 2: Attend the court date (back at Beit Hadin), bringing two witnesses to swear you are single and Jewish. The witnesses should be relatives or friends – male, if possible (there have been cases where a female witness was not accepted). A few days later you should receive a letter attesting to your single Jewish status.

Step 3: Take your letter to the Rabbinut Moatza Datit, 12 Hachavatzelet, off Jaffa, Tel. 02-625-6811, Fax 02-625-0600, open Sunday-Thursday 8am-12:30pm. There you open a file to get married (for NIS 500, but only NIS 250 if you're making Aliya). Bring your passport, the letter, and three pictures each.

Step 4: They will give the woman a date to meet a counselor (Rabbinit) to set possible dates for marriage, depending on days of "purity".

All these steps take time and should be done way in advance so you have time to plan the actual wedding.

(pt), however, and prices may be labeled or referred to either way, so 500 fils = 50 piasters. There are silver coins for 250, 100, 50, and 25 fils, copper ones for 10 and 5. The bills come in JD 20, 10, 5, 1 and 500 fils, but all the currency is marked with Arabic numbers; while the Jordanians are a pretty honest lot, it still behooves you to learn the numerals.

The **Egyptian pound** (**E£**) is worth about 29¢, roughly the same exchange as an Israeli shekel. The pound breaks down into 100 **piasters**, and while there are, theoretically, even smaller denominations of millims, it's not a factor in daily life, as it would translate to around 3¢.

American Express (in Tel Aviv and Jerusalem) exchanges travelers' cheques with no commission or fee, whether you're a member or no. Banks change money, but many of them do so at usurious rates or with astounding commissions attached. And hotels change money, often at poor rates. Of the main banks (First International, Leumi Bank, Israeli Discount Bank, Mitzahi Bank, and Hapoalim Bank) Israeli Discount and Hapoalim generally give fair rates, but it changes dramatically from city to city.

Travelers' Cheques are the safest way to carry currency, but it's advisable to bring some hard US cash as well, $100-$200 in denominations of mostly 20s with a few 10s, 5s, and 1s. The cash is useful when banks are closed and you just need a few shekels to see you through. It's especially handy if you're traveling to Jordan and/or Egypt as well, and sometimes gets you a discount. It is illegal to change money on the street with individuals, though police look the other way. Still, it is a risk and you are likely to be ripped off.

Credit cards (Visa, Mastercard, Diners Club, and in some places American Express as well) are widely accepted by all major hotels, restaurants, shops, and car rentals. Plastic is a good alternative to coming laden with checks.

To have money sent, call **Western Union**, *Tel. 02-629-0447, or 177-022-2131, a toll-free number.*

POST OFFICE

You can mail letters, cards, and parcels from any postal branch around the country. Most are open all Sunday-Thursday 7am-7pm and Friday 7am-noon, but some of the branches close for a mid-day break.

The main city GPOs have **Poste Restante** sections (mail should be addressed to you, c/o Poste Restante, followed by GPO, the city, and Israel), and American Express (in Tel Aviv and Jerusalem, open Sunday-Thursday 9am-5pm, Friday 9am-1pm) holds mail (marked Hold for Client) for American Express card holders. See individual city sections for more details.

RETIRING IN ISRAEL & MAKING ALIYAH

There are an number of good resources for those wishing to **retire** in Israel. **A.A.C.I.** (Association of Americans and Canadians in Israel), *6 Mane, Jerusalem, mailing address: POB 30017, Jerusalem 93341, Tel. 02-561-7151, and 22 Mazeh, Tel Aviv, Tel. 03-629-9799,* has a wealth of resources for North Americans moving to Israel, including seminars and info on personal financial planning and staying current with Social Security from abroad, doing business in Israel, finances and investment, and more. Membership (NIS 75 a year) entitles you to travel bargains, financial assistance, health insurance discounts, and social, educational, cultural, and employment information. You can also contact the **Ministry of Immigrant Absorption**, *2 Hakirya Building, 91006 Jerusalem, Tel. 02-624-1121*, for more information.

Making **Aliyah**, meaning literally to ascend and figuratively to leave your homeland and emigrate to Israel, is an age-old tradition among Jews, and one encouraged and supported by the Israeli government. In the Zionist pursuit of Jews returning to their homeland, the government will help sponsor it all, with Absorption Centers to help set you up and pick up part of the tab for moving, studying, and living.

The *Aliyah Pocket Guide* answers all the questions about customs, health care, employment, and more. To get the goods, contact the main **Israel Aliya Center** in New York, *110 E. 59th, New York, NY 10022, Tel. 212/339-6000, Fax 212/832-2597* or in Boston, *20 Park Plaza, Statler Building, Room 1020, Boston, MA 02116, Tel. 617/423-0868, Fax 617/423-0468*.

SHOPPING

You have your urban department stores, your regular small stores, airport duty-free shops, and shuks (street markets, bazaars), all with their own protocol and etiquette. The **department stores** are big and modern, and follow the same norms established 'round the world. Credit cards are accepted, they are usually open from morning to night with no mid-day break, and bargaining is absolutely not the done thing.

Smaller stores, especially those selling souvenirs, are often flexible on their pricing. If you're shopping for antiques or Judaica, you should definitely haggle over price. In the **shuks**, bartering is the game, to be entered into with good humor and a sense of humor. You shouldn't buy if the price isn't what you think it's worth, but nor should you enter into the bartering fray if you're not really interested in the item in the first place. In fact, there is a Jewish law stating you must not go into a shop and ask the proprietor how much an item costs if you know you really have no intention of buying, thus saving him from getting his hopes up unnecessarily.

Antiques, by law, are man-made objects from before 1700 CE; they may not be taken out of Israel without written approval from the Director of the Antiquities Authority, and are subject to an export fee of 10% of the purchase price. For more info you can contact the **Antiquities Authority**, *the Rockefeller Museum, Tel. 02-628-2251, Fax 02-560-2628*.

STAYING OUT OF TROUBLE

It is easy to have a worry-free holiday in Israel, but in a country with as many sensitive political and religious issues as Israel has, you would do well to tread with care and avoid what dangers you can. Argument may be one of the Israeli national past-times, but people have lost friends and family, and emotions may run high. Some things are beyond your control, but there are a few precautions you can take.

• Make a photo copy of the first page of your passport and keep it separate.
• Call Washington, *Tel. 202/364-5500*, for up-to-date information on the political situation before leaving the US.
• Don't go hiking on uncharted trails in the Golan Heights as there are still unexploded land mines up there, and don't go into orthodox neighborhoods dressed immodestly, as assaults have been known to take place.
• The best advice from embassy officials is to avoid power struggles with 18-year-olds carrying guns. Good advice in general, but in a country on edge from terrorism and war, arguing with youths in power isn't advisable. Remember this when some official is giving you the business in the airport, and keep cool.
• Recent advice from embassy folks in the know warned against travel in Gaza and Hebron. In Gaza there's a poor economy and it's getting worse, resulting in a hostile and frustrated populace. The West Bank is pretty calm and Jericho is open and anxious for tourists, but Hebron is still tense, and certain strike dates and anniversaries were observed such as the 23rd (anniversary of the Baruch Goldstein massacre), as well as the 9th and 17th. Wadi Kelt, a popular oasis near Jerusalem, has also been deemed unsafe lately. If you're taking an organized tour, the companies keep tabs on where not to go. If you're setting off on your own, contact the embassy in Jerusalem for the latest scoop, and if you're planning to go into occupied territory, it's a good idea to let the nearest embassy or consulate know.
• According to the Security Advisor in the Jerusalem Consulate, East Jerusalem, Bethlehem, Jericho are all fine to visit, but it's not a great idea to wander around at night, not so much because of trouble but because things close up after dark so you stand out on the streets. They also advised tourists to veer clear of Arab bus lines because they are more prone to break downs and reckless driving.
• While the nature of terrorism is such that you never know where and when it's going to hit, a number of the recent suicide bombings have targeted public buses carrying soldiers returning to duty or leaving base for the weekend.

• If you get in difficulties (jail, lost passport, etc.) while in Israel, call the US Embassy, *Tel. 03-517-4338*, during business hours, *Tel. 03-517-4347*, after hours.

The police stress keeping an eye on your belongings, not accepting gifts from strangers, making use of hotel safes, and all the usual common sense precautions. In Israel, an unattended bag is considered a potential terrorist bomb, and the authorities don't fool around on this issue.

Anywhere in the country, **100** will reach the **police** and **102** will get you the **fire** department.

TAXES

There is a $17 departure tax, but it's usually included in your ticket. If you're not sure, ask your airline.

Israel's 17% **VAT (Value Added Tax)** is levied on all goods and services, but if you (the foreign tourist) pay in foreign currency you are exempt from paying VAT on hotels, tours, car rentals, domestic flights, and hotel meals. You'll often see store signs boasting the VAT reduction for foreign currency purchases. In addition, if you pay with foreign currency for an item worth $50 or more (when shopping at Ministry of Tourism recommended stores – you'll see the seal of approval), you're entitled to a 5% discount and a VAT refund when you leave the country.

Not applicable to tobacco, electrical or photographic purchases, your item must remain in its sealed see-through bag so you can show it to officials in Bank Leumi (in Ben Gurion Airport or Haifa Port) and get your money back. If you leave from another port, customs officials will stamp your invoice and the refund will be mailed to you back home.

TELEGRAMS

Central telegraph offices are open 24 hours a day in Tel Aviv, 7 *Mikve Israel*, Jerusalem, *23 Jaffa*, Haifa, *22 Hanevi'im*, and Be'er Sheva, *9 Hanesi'im* (only open 7:30am-7pm), providing telegraph, telex, and fax services. **Solan Telecom** (see below) also sends telegrams and is open 24 hours.

TELEPHONES

• **Phoning/faxing Israel and the Palestinian Authority from the US**: *dial 011-972*, the city code (just the single digit, no "0"), then the number.
• **Phoning/faxing Jordan from the US**: *dial 011-962*, the city code (just the single digit, no "0"), then the number.
• **Phoning/faxing Egypt from the US**: *dial 011-20*, the city code (just the single digit, no "0"), then the number.

• **Phoning/faxing direct to the US from Israel**: *dial 001 or 013 or 012*, and the area code and number; to charge the call to your long-distance **MCI** account, *dial 177-150-2727*, **AT&T** *is 177-100-2727*, and **Sprint** *is 177-102-2727* (don't give up, it may take a long time to get through). Or, go to one of the **Solan Telecom Centers** in Tel Aviv or Jerusalem (see Practical Information section of the city). They are open 24 hours a day, every day, and place discount international telephone calls. They also can send faxes and provide modem hookups.

• **Phoning/faxing within Israel**: use the two-digit city code (0_) and the phone number if you're phoning another district; use just the phone number without the two-digit area code if phoning within the district. The prefix "050" indicates the number belongs to a cell phone.

Public phones, available in post offices, on the street (often quite noisy), and in many hotel lobbies (generally the quietest place to make a call) operate by tokens sold at the post office, by shekel, and most convenient of all, by phone card (sold at post offices, Solan Offices, and vendors).

The **phone cards** are sold in denominations of 20 (NIS 10.5), 50 (NIS 23), and 120 units (NIS 52), and they make long-distance (within Israel) calls much easier. The cost of a call varies greatly by time of day, with one unit lasting 72 seconds from the 8am-1pm slot, 144 seconds from 1pm-8pm, and 15 minutes from 10pm-7am.

TELEVISION & RADIO
• **English TV news**: Channel 1 at 6:15pm except on Shabbat, and at 4:30pm Erev Shabbat.
• **English Radio news**: Kol Yisrael 927 kh in north, 954 in Jerusalem and central, 7am, 5pm, 8pm.
• **BBC Radio news**: 130 AM with hourly news reports and other English programs

TIME
Given relative to Greenwich Mean Time (GMT) and US time zones: Israel, Jordan, and Egypt are two hours ahead of GMT, 7 hours ahead of Eastern Standard Time, and 10 hours ahead of Pacific Standard Time. So in the summer when it's 7pm in Israel it's 5pm in London, noon in New York, 11am in Chicago, 10am in Denver, and 9am in San Francisco.

TIPPING
Ten to fifteen percent in general is expected in nice restaurants. Side street nooks and market restaurants aren't as sophisticated. Look at the tables around you to get a sense of what the locals are doing.

FOR MORE INFORMATION...

Call **Israeli Tourism**, *Tel. 800-596-1199*, for maps and a general tourist packet, but good luck getting more specific help.

Jewish Literacy by Rabbi Joseph Telushkin is a magnificent source of insight into the Jewish religion and culture.

Dictionary of Jewish Lore and Legend, compiled by Alan Unterman, further explains Jewish terms, traditions, and practices.

The Joys of Yiddish by Leo Rosten may not provide practical daily vocabulary, but it's most amusing, and the Jewish culture really comes through the definitions and anecdotes.

A Concise History of the Middle East by Arthur Goldschmidt does an excellent job explaining the history and growth of Islam as well as the political and cultural shifts through the ages in the Middle East.

Jerusalem Walks by Nitza Rosovsky details a variety of Jerusalem routes.

Israel, a Phaidon Art and Architecture Guide by Prentice Hall Press is full of architectural and Archaeological details about sites throughout Israel.

The Source, a fictional historical novel by James Michener, provides an entertaining introduction to archaeology and the region's history.

Islamic Monuments in Cairo - A Practical Guide by Richard Parker does a good job with Cairo.

Khul-Khad - Five Egyptian Women Tell Their Stories by Nayra Atiya is well written and is an in to the flavor of Egyptian culture.

Nine Parts of Desire: the Hidden World of Islamic Women by Geraldine Brooks takes a personal, personable, and provocative look behind the Middle East's back door.

WEIGHTS & MEASURES
Israel uses the metric system.

inches to centimeters	*x 2.54*	*Centigrade to Fahr.*	*x 1.8 plus 32*
centimeters to inches	*x 0.39*	*Fahr. to Centigrade*	*minus 32 then x.55*
feet to meters	*x 0.30*	*meters to feet*	*x 3.28*
ounces to grams	*x 28.35*	*grams to ounces*	*x 0.035*
yards to meters	*x 0.91*		
meters to yards	*x 1.09*	*kg to pounds*	*x 2.21*
miles to kilometers	*x 1.61*	*pounds to kg*	*x 0.45*
kilometers to miles	*x 0.62*	*US tons to kg*	*x 907*
acres to hectares	*x 0.40*	*British tons to kg*	*x 1016*
hectares	*x 2.47*	*British tons are 2240 lbs*	
		US tons are 2000 lbs	
gallons to liters	*x 3.79*		
liters to gallons	*x 0.26*		

8. SPORTS & RECREATION

Combine ingenuity with an energetic love of the land, and you get a country where every type of terrain sparks some kind of sport or outdoor recreation. This is a place that turns its lemons to lemonade, and even the Dead Sea, hot and unable to sustain any but the simplest organisms, supports a thriving industry of mud-slathering and Dead Sea-bathing.

ON THE BEACH

The **Mediterranean Sea** abuts the entire western coast, and all sorts of beach fun are in vogue. Swimming and sunbathing, of course, are the mainstays, but there's also an active surfing community (though they complain bitterly about the mediocre quality of the swells), as well as windsurfing, sailing, and sailboarding in the water, and the ubiquitous paddle ball game called *matkot* on the beach.

THE GALILEE & GOLAN

Up north, the rivers and **Sea of Galilee** are packed in the summer with all manner of fresh water activities. Waterskiers and motorized bananas zip around the more sedate swimmers, windsurfing and parascending are available, and water amusement parks with devil water slides dot the lake. Fishing is popular, while rafting, canoeing, kayaking and inner-tubing rule the rivers.

A typical river rafting experience (with **Jordan River Rafting**, off route 918, and you must book ahead) involves four-six people per raft (ages 16 and up, and in good physical condition), plus a skilled guide, goes two hours to all day, and promises lots of water, noise, speed, surge and adrenaline, teamwork and exercise, all resulting in the big "We made it."

Along with the water, the north has hills, providing a fantastic setting for hiking and bicycling, horseback and donkey riding, jeep and mini-tractor tours. It's a fine place for bird-watching and paragliding as well, and in winter you can ice-skate, and or ski from **Mount Hermon's summit**.

IN THE DESERT

It may seem barren compared to the lush vegetation up north, but it's not in the least devoid of recreational activities. Guided tours are popular with Israelis and visitors alike. **SPNI**, Society for the Protection of Nature, offers wonderful desert treks. There are nature reserves with paths for hiking, there's rock climbing, there's bird watching, and in Eilat there is terrific snorkeling and scuba diving as well (and scuba schools where you can get certified).

THE SINAI

There are lots of desert safari trips possible in the **Sinai**. **Neot Hakikar**, *Tel. 02-623-6262, Fax 02-623-6161,* specializes here, with a variety of options including hiking, camel riding, snorkeling, and jeep tours.

9. TAKING THE KIDS

The Israeli people welcome kids; theirs is a society that values children and provides for their needs. The weather, however, isn't always ideal for toting youngsters about, and the sites that move and excite adults don't always do it for the young. It's not hard to organize a family trip with components that please all, so long as you keep some points in mind.

Plan your visit, if possible, with seasons and climate in mind. You know your kids, you know which conditions will more likely cause problems. If you come in summer (and often with kids, there's no other option) there are more outdoor kids-oriented activities available than during the winter. And, there's air-conditioning. Don't drive through the desert without it.

Pools are often children-pleasers, and many hotels have them (years ago, my five-year-old sister's favorite part of a family trip to Israel was the hotel pool). Then there's the beach, lake-side water amusement parks on the Sea of Galilee, and for older kids, a whole host of water activities. Sunburn can be a real drag at any time, but especially on vacation, so make sure children take proper hat and sunscreen precautions.

As for sightseeing, a lot depends on your children's personalities and ages. Some kids will enjoy a good museum or excavation as much as an adult, but others need something more. Places like **Hamat Gader** in the Galilee, or the **Diaspora Museum** and **Wax Museum** in Tel Aviv are especially geared toward keeping children as well as adults interested. What families often find is that compromise and variation keep everyone reasonably happy. If you spend the morning seeing religious sites around the Sea of Galilee, maybe you spend the afternoon swimming, and so on.

The other thing to keep in mind is that most hotels have family plans and family rooms, even if they aren't listed, and they're accommodating to family needs. A number of the better hotels are even set up with babysitting services, doctors, and special kids' activity clubs. Israeli families frequently take vacations together, and even the hostels are set up with family facilities. Kibbutzim are especially geared towards families, and unlike in regular hotels, there's space for children to run around, play with the kibbutz animals, etc.

As far as food goes, once again it all depends. Some kids love the new spices and adventurous eating, others may require a daily diet of pizza and burgers. The cities all have standard American fare. You may run into fewer eating options in smaller towns and might do well to pack a snack along.

CAMP

If the family trip just isn't going to work, but you all want to go to Israel, consider letting your kids join a camp there while you tour around. The **Tapuz Foundation** operates a summer camp for Jewish children from the US and other countries.

Held at **Kibbutz Regavim** near Mount Carmel, they offer a Junior Program for ages 6-12, a Senior Program for ages 12-14, the I.S.A Travelers for the 14-17 group, and a more adventurous, challenging program called Scouts for ages 15-18. Lasting five weeks, the programs cost $2460 and include registration fee, room and board, and laundry services, while $3615 includes air fare from New York as well. The second child from a family gets a $50 discount, and for medical insurance, add $2 per day per child.

In New York, contact **Camp Tapuz**, *POB 234577, Great Neck, NY 11023, Tel. 516/482-3934, Fax 516/482-3934*, in Los Angeles, *POB 15743, Beverly Hills, CA 90209, Tel. 310/276-5183, Fax 310/276-1353*, and in Israel, contact Camp Tapuz, *POB 78, Givat Ada 37808, Tel. 06-638-0394, Fax 06-638-0395.*

10. ECO-TOURISM & TRAVEL ALTERNATIVES

NATURE TOURS

SPNI (Society for Protection of Nature), *3 Hashfela, Tel Aviv, Tel. 03-638-8674, Fax 03-688-3940 and 13 Helene Ha'Malka, Jerusalem, 02-625-2357*, leads excellently guided tours to all over the countryside. They offer a wealth of knowledge about Israel's history, botany, legend and lore. Usually including hiking and nature exploration, they're a great way to experience the country without windows between you and desert, hills, and springs. Bring hiking boots (sneakers are allowed if that's all you have, but they don't protect against sprains) or nature sandals (depending on what hike you're going on). Water (three liter minimum in summer) and a hat are necessary. Also bring clothes for cool and warm (in winter) and lunch (for a day hike).

Neot Hakikar, *67 Ben Yehuda, Tel Aviv, Tel. 03-520-5858, Fax 03-522-10206 Shlomzion HaMalka, Jerusalem, Tel. 02-236-262, Khan Amiel Center, Eilat, Tel. 07-632-6281, Fax 07-632-6297*, specializes in guided tours in the Sinai, in fact they were the first company in Israel to organize trips there.

JORDAN & EGYPT TOURS

ABC-BTC, *1 Hasoreg, off Jaffa near Shlomzion, Jerusalem, Tel. 02-623-3990, Fax 02-625-7827*, is open Sunday-Thursday 9:30am-5:30pm, Friday 9am-1pm. Their initials stand for Better Travel Consultants, and they offer tours and tickets for less, advice for free, and specialize in bus trips to Cairo and Petra/Jordash trips.

BIG BUS TOURS

Egged Tours, *59 Ben Yehuda, Tel Aviv, Tel. 03-527-1212, Fax 03-527-1229, 224 Jaffa, Jerusalem, Tel. 02-625-4198, Fax 02-624-2150*, does tours all over Israel in large buses. It's the largest tour agency in Israel, but not necessarily the best, and certainly not the most personal or the most friendly.

United Tours, *57 Ben Yehuda, Tel Aviv, Tel. 03-693-3412, King David Street just near the King David Hotel, Jerusalem, Tel. 02-625-2187, fax 02-625-5013*, has offices throughout Israel. The staff is friendly and the tour guides knowledgeable, if you don't mind the nature of a big bus tour.

LOCAL LAWS & CUSTOMS ON CAMPING & HIKING

There are campsites around the country, though perhaps not as many as you might wish for. Tourists with tents or sleeping bags yearly set up on their own on the beaches along the coast, but this isn't a safe thing to do, and asks for thefts and worse.

Official campsites have full sanitary facilities (toilets and showers), electric current, first aid and postal services, small markets and/or cafeterias, picnic and campfire areas, and 24-hour security.

KIBBUTZ & MOSHAV STAYS

Kibbutzim and moshavim offer different experiences. The **kibbutz** is a community of people and you do rotation work, one week in the laundry, one week in the cafeteria, etc. You live in the volunteer house with all the other volunteers, and you get free food but no pay. The **moshav** is a community of families; you work with one family and live in its own volunteer house. Though the moshav usually has, in total, more volunteers than a kibbutz, you live with just the volunteers of one family. You are responsible for buying and preparing your own food, and the work is usually harder agricultural work than on a kibbutz, but you get paid NIS 1200 a month minimum, plus bonuses (NIS 150 every two months) and overtime (7.50 an hour extra).

Meira's Volunteers For Kibbutz/Moshav, *73 Ben Yehuda, 1st floor (the entrance to the building is behind the restaurant), Tel Aviv 63435, Tel. 03-523-7369/03-523-8073, Fax 03-524-1604*, open Sunday-Thursday 9am-3:30pm, is one office that sets you up at a kibbutz or moshav. Generally speaking, the minimum stay is two months, though a few will accept a one month stay. To apply, come in to Meira's office with your passport, four passport pictures, driver's license if you have one, and some money (take bus 4 from the central bus station, or 10 from the train station). You'll need to pay a NIS 160 handling fee and NIS 220 for insurance, but you'll get back NIS 160 after one month's work. Meira will find a spot for you, and is very adept at matching the right moshav or kibbutz to your temperament and needs.

Project 67 LTD, *94 Ben Yehuda, Tel Aviv, Tel. 03-523-0140, Fax 03-524-7474*, is another such agency. Their registration fee is NIS 150, and insurance costs NIS 170. The insurance can be waived if you have your own that accepts collect calls. They also offer mail-collection services, and will hold your bags for a few days for you, if you wish. Open Sunday-Thursday 9am-4pm, Friday 9am-noon, Mr. Gat is a nice man who'll do his best for you.

Kibbutz Program Center, *18 Frishman, Tel Aviv, Tel. 03-524-6156, Fax 03-523-9966, or Kibbutz Aliya Desk, 110 East 59th Street, New York, NY 10022, Tel. 212/318-6130*, is the non-profit agency funded and operated by the kibbutzim. They accept individuals between the ages of 18-32 (but this is not hard and fast) and in good health, and advise September-May for best placements.

To register, come to their office (open Sunday-Thursday 8am-2pm) with your passport, medical certificate, airline ticket, at least $250 (you keep it, they just want to see it), two passport photos, and $110 for the registration fee plus $50-$145 for insurance.

VOLUNTEERING WITH THE ISRAELI ARMY

Sar El, *111 Jerusalem Street, Jaffa, Tel. 03-681-4108, Fax 03-681-2353*, or in the USA, Volunteers for Israel, *330 W 42nd Street, Suite 1318, New York, NY 10036, Tel. 212/643-4848*, runs a volunteer program whereby Jews can sign up for three weeks (extendible to more three-week segments) to live with, work with, and hobnob with the Israeli Army. Dressed in army garb and eating army grub, you can see some sides of Israel left off most tour itineraries while doing your bit to help out.

You can apply from the states or in Israel, but either way when you go to your interview you'll need a medical form (from a general physical) and two letters of recommendation from Israelis, (ideally a rabbi or university, not friends and family), plus $100 for registration (waived for students).

ARCHAEOLOGICAL DIGS

In general, these involve lots of hours spent hunched in the sun digging or hauling from 5am till dusk with few history-making finds but among an interesting crew. You pay for transport to the site, and usually for lodgings and food as well for the experience.

• **Biblical Archaeology Review**, *3000 Connecticut Avenue NW 300, Washington, DC 20008, Tel. 202-387-8888, Fax 202-483-4323*. Contact them for dig information.

• **Archaeological Institute of America**, *675 Commonwealth Avenue, Boston, MA 02215, Tel. 617-353-9361*, puts out the annual Archaeological Fieldwork Opportunities Bulletin listing over 250 opportunities.

• **Israel Antiquities Authority**, *Rockefeller Museum (PO Box 586, Jerusalem 91004), Jerusalem, Tel. 02-560-2627, Fax 02-560-2628*, compiles a February listing of summer digs.
• **Archaeological Seminars, Inc.**, *PO Box 14002, Jaffa Gate, Jerusalem 91140, Tel. 02-627-3515, Fax 02-627-2660*, arranges digs year round.

THE PALESTINE CENTER FOR RAPPROCHEMENT BETWEEN PEOPLE

The **Alternative Tourism Program** in Beit Sahour is setting up a program to offer a Palestinian experience in lieu of (or along side) the normal sight-seeing trip. Beit Sahour, a small Palestinian village just outside of Jerusalem, will organize things so you can visit and see the town, meet the people, and even volunteer in the community.

They'll have lectures on topics such as Christian-Islamic Coexistence, Liberation Theology, and the ever popular Taxation. They're also setting up a Bed and Breakfast network. For more info, call Dr. Majed Nassar at the Medical Clinic or Mr. Ghassan Andoni at the Palestinian Center for Rapprochement (call information for phone numbers – they're changing).

11. FOOD & DRINK

FOOD
The cuisine of Israel is one of the major pleasures of a trip here, or it can be if you venture away from the hotel dining room and sample some of what the locals eat. If you're looking for American style food, however, you'll probably be disappointed. It exists, but the quality is nowhere near what you can find in the foods people have been making here for centuries.

There are lots of ethnic cuisines to choose from, and they've got some exquisite specialties to offer. Arabic (aka oriental or Mediterranean) food predominates with its falafel and hummus, but there's also Moroccan and Tunisian, Yemenite, Russian, Kurdish, Hungarian, and what's loosely called Jewish food, which is really Ashkenazi Jewish cuisine. Most of the restaurants are kosher (see kosher under Religion section), some are glatt kosher (again, see above), and a few aren't kosher at all.

Arabic or Oriental Cuisine
The **falafel** reigns supreme; it's good, nourishing, cheap food, and when it's done just right it can be sublime (but done poorly it's a mushy, boring affair). Made of mashed chick peas and spices and then deep-fried, it's the staple food stall snack stuffed in a pita with a variety of salad toppings (note: Israelis define "salads" much more broadly than do Americans or Europeans).

Hummus, a dip made from chick peas and olive oil, is another standard, and restaurants in Jerusalem war over who has the best (see the Jerusalem section for the answers). Served with a basket of pita bread (unleavened disk-shaped bread that can be opened to form a pocket) it can make a light lunch by itself, but it's also used to line the pita for falafel and other pita pocket sandwiches. **Tehina**, another favorite falafel sandwich addition, is a dip made from sesame paste and olive oil, and **baba ghanoush** is a smoky eggplant-based dip with tehina mixed in.

BUILD YOUR OWN FALAFEL PITA

Common Salad Bar Ingredients:
sliced radishes - lefet (large ones) or tznonit (smaller ones)
pickled cabbage - kruv kavoosh or kruv khamutz
eggplant - khatzilim
pink cabbage - kruv varod
pickled beets - selek
sesame seed sauce - tehina
hot sauce, red or green (pretty hot) - kharif
yellow sauce (curry & mango) - amba

Amba *is either loved or abhorred by Israelis, though it tends to be a Sephardi favorite. It stays with you for days, on your breath (and maybe your clothes) and sweated out your pores.*

The Steps to Build a Falafel Pita:

1) Get hummus-chips-salád - said like it's one word, this is the falafel foundation.

2) Put amba/tehina in first and spread it around so the goodness permeates the whole sandwich (warning: the risk in this is if the pita isn't high quality it is more likely to fall apart. To counter this risk, eat pita smeared side up to minimize soggy/spongy factor).

3) If there are lots of salads you want to try, order half a pita (khatzi manah), put in some salads and eat, then order another khatzi manah and do the other salads.

4) Don't mix two hot sauces, but amba can go with everything.

5) If you order manah (a whole pita), you can ask for just three falafels in first, then take the pita and add some salads, return to the falafel man for the remaining falafels, then add your final salad choice and toppings, with a dribble of tehina on top (warning: not every falafel man will have patience for this procedure).

Fuul (pronounced fool, and sometimes spelled that way, too) is made from fava beans, sometimes mashed with garlic and lemon, sometimes whole. Also in the snack or quick meal department is the ubiquitous **shwarma**, a sandwich of sliced grilled meat (carved off a rotating, grilling chunk that's meant to be lamb but is usually turkey, packed like pressboard with old meat ends). The meat goes in a pita (or a larger flat bread rolled like a burrito) and filled with all the same salad options as the falafel.

Labane, a goat cheese and olive oil dip, is another light lunch or dinner appetizer option. Order a **mezza** and you'll get a whole plate with tastes of salads, **dolma** (stuffed grape leaves) and pita. **Majadera** is a rice and lentils side dish, and **kubbeh** is ground spiced meat stuffed in a cracked wheat casing and deep fried. For more substantial meals, there are a variety of grilled meats such as **shishlik** (meat chunks grilled on skewers), and **kebab** (spiced minced meat, also grilled on skewers). They can both be very tasty, but kids tend to distrust the kebabs because they're not familiar with the spices.

And for dessert, there's honey-sweet **baklava**, a flaky pastry with honey and a variety of possible extras like pistachio nuts, for example, that can be heavenly, or just sweet and viscous.

While this food can be found all over Israel, not to mention Egypt and Jordan, it's worth it to seek out a truly fine restaurant (try East Jerusalem) at least once to see what this cuisine is like at its very best.

FALAFEL RECIPE

1/2 kilo chick peas (a little more than 1 lb)
2 medium onions
5-8 cloves garlic
1-2 parsley sprigs
2-4 red hot peppers
1-2 tsp cumin
salt & pepper to taste
1 Tbs baking powder
1/4 tsp baking soda

1) Wash chick peas several times and soak over night.

2) Drain then grind together with onions, garlic, peppers, parsley. If you use a food processor, process once, otherwise grind twice.

3) Add spices and powders. Mix and knead well, and set aside for 30 minutes.

4) Add baking soda last minute before frying. Make balls or croquets and deep fry till golden brown.

The Three Precautions for Eating Falafel with as much Dignity as Possible:

1) Eat with your body at 60° so you don't wear your sandwich.

2) Get extra napkins to hold on the bottom: if you are given two, take five; if you are given six, take ten.

3) Look for a falafel stand with a sink to wash your hands afterwards.

*The same rules apply for **shwarma** eating, but there are no half pitas, and it can't be built in segments.*

Eastern European Cuisine

The standard Ashkenazi appetizers are **chopped liver**, **gefilte fish**, and **stuffed cabbage** (or other vegetables, they're stuffed with a mix of meat, rice, nuts and spices). Not everyone's cup of tea but no less authentic is **pickled herring**, **patcha** (jellied calf foot), and **kishke** (stuffed stomach lining).

Soup is the specialty of this cuisine, starring **chicken soup**, **kneidlach** or **kreplach soup** with dumplings (some filled with meat), as well as **borsht** (beet soup, hot with meat and cabbage or cold and meatless), and a **goulash soup** that changes shape from venue to venue. **Schnitzel** is a popular main dish, a bit lacking in pizzazz though perfectly adequate as a meal. Other sturdy but zipless meals include roast or boiled chicken and pot roast.

Tcholent is a ground up heavy meaty stew, usually including some innards, and traditional for Shabbat. Other organ meals include hot potted **tongue**, **pupiks** (chicken gizzards, *pupik* means belly button), **spleen**, or **lungs** in gravy. At dairy restaurants (kosher and with no meat) **blintzes** are popular, stuffed with either cheese or fruit.

Yemenite Cuisine

A delicious and often overlooked cuisine, many of the dishes are similar to other Arabic standards. Hummus, tehina, and baba ghanoush are all available, though the hummus with egg is a different treat. **Mellawach** is unique, however. It's a kind of baked unleavened bread (different than pita) that is either covered with a sauce or filled with meat or vegetables, and it's a traditional Yemenite dish.

Also traditional, though not always found at restaurants that cater to tourists, are the **soups**. **Lung** soup, **brain** soup, **testicle** soup, and **stomach** soup, all are exceptionally delicious if your appetite overrides your trained cerebral reactions. They also have a **rice and okra** (*bamya*) dish that's very tasty and filling, and lots more.

North African Cuisine

The best known North African food is **couscous**, a tender small grain served with a variety of sauces and meats or vegetables. There is also a stew called **tagine** that can be quite tasty. The appetizers and soups that accompany can vary from place to place, but lemon flavored soups are common, as are **cigars** (a deep-fried tube of spicy ground meat, common in Yemenite restaurants as well).

Mint tea is a regional treat, and the platters of gooey flaky **baklava** go without saying.

Vegetarian

Israel's a fairly easy place to be vegetarian. Falafel stands are everywhere, dairy restaurants are guaranteed by kosher law to serve no meat, and the Black Hebrew restaurants (one in Tel Aviv and one in Dimona) are vegan with a vengeance, serving no animal products, meat, or dairy.

There are also lots of markets with a plenitude of fresh fruit, vegetables, yogurt, and a variety of cheeses. **Hummus** can be purchased at street markets, along with pita, for a fine picnic.

Fast Foods & Snacks

Burekas are flaky pastries stuffed with a variety of fillings, though white cheese or potato are the most common. Cheap (around NIS 3) and tasty (though not a diet item), they make an easy snack if you're on the move, and are available in bakeries and supermarkets. **Arabic style pizzas**, usually topped with egg or olive oil and za'atar (ground thyme) are filling snacks. There are also **American style pizza** slices, mediocre but edible, and poor quality burgers from the **Burger Ranch** chain.

And then there are **bagels**. They're different from what Americans are used to, but once you accept this, they're quite good and a cheap snack that's not dripping with oil. The Israeli bagel is round, soft, and studded with sesame seeds, and the Arab version, larger and oval, is always available on the streets of the Old City in Jerusalem, where they sell them with little folded packets of za'atar (ground thyme-based spice) to dip it in. **Seeds** and **nuts** are very popular, and lots of little shops sell nothing but paper bags of these treats. **Pickles** are also an Israeli specialty, and any deli or market will have a full selection of half sour, full sour, pickled cabbage, pickled eggplant, and pickled et cetera.

Desserts & Sweets

Baklava, as described above, is a buttery, flaky pastry (or toasted shredded wheat) with or without pistachios, and soaked in honey – Akko has some fine examples. **Katayeef** and **kanafe** are more oriental sweets with cheese in a flaky pastry and sugar syrup over all (it can actually be quite good if the proportions are right).

Halvah, a traditional dessert, is a dense, sweet loaf made from sesame seeds ground fine and crumbly. It can round off a meal nicely, but just a little bit will do you. If it's **ice cream** you're after there's good old Ben & Jerry's as well as the local Dr. Lek chain, all very good. And all the **cafes** dish up sublime cake, pastry, and pie concoctions that'll bust your bank and diet, but might be worth it anyway.

Other Cuisines

There are other cuisines to chose from as well, especially in the larger cities like Jerusalem, Tel Aviv, and Eilat. El Gauchos is an **Argentinean** steak chain that's beloved by those pining for a big slab of meat. There are plenty of Italian and French restaurants, and some of them are quite good. With Kurdish food and Hungarian, Chinese, Thai, and Indian, there's not the dearth of cuisines people used to complain about.

Israeli Breakfast

A concept popular with (and created by) hotels and kibbutzim, it's a big buffet of cheeses, cereals, salads and eggs, and whatever else the establishment cares to throw in. Ask your average Joe (or Shlomo) on the street what an Israeli Breakfast is, however, and you'll get a blank look. Some of these spreads really are magnificent, others are just some Laughing Cow cheese triangles and bug juice, so when a hotel promises the world and a "full Israeli Breakfast" you might want to ask what exactly theirs has.

DRINKS

Israeli Beer

Israel brews its own beer, with **Maccabee** and **Goldstar** being the two local brands you see most often. They're both okay, though Goldstar is a little darker and more flavorful, and generally more popular with travelers. You can also purchase imported brands, but you'll pay a lot more for them.

Israeli Wines & Spirits

Israel isn't known for boozing, but they do have a booming wine business and any self-respecting Israeli prides himself on knowing the best Yarden, Carmel, and Gamla vintages, even if he doesn't drink the stuff himself.

There are lots of decent wines put out by Israel's three main vintners, but the following are very fine, good for a picnic, gift, or souvenir: Note: prices greatly subject to change.

- **Yarden Blonde Blanc** - a good champagne
- **Yarden Brut** - around NIS 64
- **Gamla Chardannay** and **Cabernet Sauvignon** - NIS 37
- **Yarden Chardannay** and **Cabernet Sauvignon** - NIS 46
- **Yarden Mt. Hermon** red and white - NIS 32
- **Barkan Cabernet Sauvignon Reserved '88**
- **Yarden Cabernet Sauvignon '89**

The local brandies and other spirits are not remarkable other than for the hangovers suffered by unwary travelers, but the orange and chocolate flavored liqueur **Sabra** is special. Not only does it come in a bottle that looks like it might contain a genie, it's a tasty liqueur and unique to Israel. A small bottle is NIS 24 and a 750 ml bottle is NIS 39.

Non-Alcoholic Drinks

Israeli tap water is safe to drink, but if you've a sensitive stomach it might be a good idea to get bottled water (available everywhere), as foreign microbes aren't always welcomed wholeheartedly by your stomach.

Coffee is an extremely popular drink, and the quality isn't bad. Most cafes have espresso and cappuccino, European Nescafe and the Israel concoction called *café hafukh* which is espresso and milk and quite good. Asking for it will not only earn you the respect of the coffee maker, it'll net you a fine and relatively inexpensive cup of coffee as well.

Soft drinks are ubiquitous here, as they are worldwide.

12. TEL AVIV

Tel Aviv is a big, modern city (Israel's largest after Jerusalem), and some visitors can't figure why they should bother with it. So many bus routes and busy streets, so many highrises and new buildings – why go to Israel to see all that? Akin to the *Sabra* cactus symbolizing the Israeli attitude (prickly on the outside but warm and sweet within), Tel Aviv's appeal isn't immediately evident, but a little effort reaps big rewards – the city grows on you.

Tel Aviv reveals the essence of Israel, the core without the artifacts and shrines. Want insight into Israeli culture? Spend some time hanging out on the beach, in restaurants and cafés, in theaters and clubs, and don't think of it as hedonism – it's anthropological research of the best sort, and it can always be supplemented by their fine museums. And if you still manage to get bored, ask residents why they prefer Tel Aviv to Jerusalem, then sit back and enjoy the earful.

Tel Aviv (*Hill of Spring*) started quite recently, by Israeli standards, as a Jewish suburb of Arab Jaffa in 1909. The **Balfour Declaration** in 1917, the anti-Jewish Jaffa riots of 1921, and the advent of Nazism in Germany all encouraged development of the empty sand dunes. When Israel declared independence in 1948, Tel Aviv became home to the provisional government, and its population grew by 60%.

The municipality (including **Jaffa**) has a population of 357,400 while the larger metropolitan area (known as the Tel Aviv District) spreads over 170 square kilometers and has a population of over one million individuals. Though Jerusalem was named as the country's capital in 1980, Tel Aviv still serves as the headquarters for the Israeli Ministry of Defense, Histadrut, and some foreign embassies including the US Embassy.

While Tel Aviv is home to roughly 50% of the country's industrial plants (such as diamond polishing) as well as the Stock Exchange, it's also the hub of Israeli education and culture (Jerusalem residents would, of course, disagree), with Tel Aviv and Bar-Ilan Universities, the Israeli

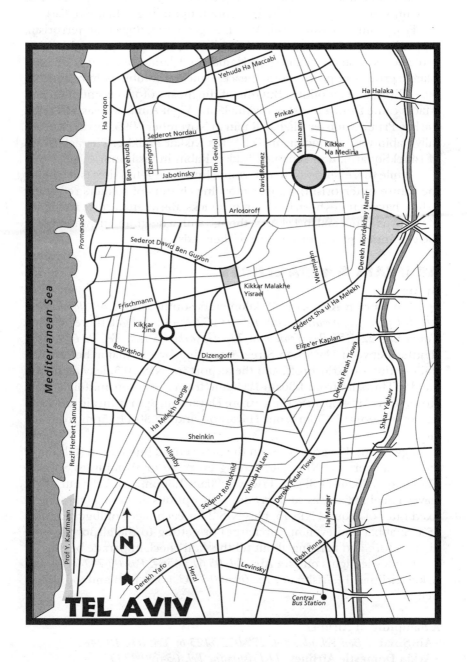

Philharmonic and national theater (Habima), as well as a plethora of museums (the Museum of the Diaspora topping the exhaustive list).

From time to time, Tel Aviv has been the object of terrorism, especially as the Israeli-Palestinian peace negotiations approach critical agreements. Usually claimed by Hamas or Islamic Jihad (two militant Islamic groups opposed to the peace), suicide bombings have torn up buses, lives, and emotions. But one of the most notorious and injurious attacks came from a Jewish individual, one Yigal Amir, who assassinated the late Prime Minister Yitzhak Rabin in November 1995, during a peace rally Rabin was conducting in Tel Aviv's Kikkar Malkhei Y'Israel (Kings of Israel Square), now renamed Kikkar Rabin in his honor.

While there is no way to determine future targeted sites (such being the nature of terrorism), Sunday morning clusters of soldiers returning to base have at times been the focus of attacks. Between the rare incidents, life returns to normal in Tel Aviv, though with a heightened awareness of the continued precarious nature of their existence.

ARRIVALS & DEPARTURES

By Air

Ben Gurion Airport is 18 kilometers southeast in **Lod** *(for English recorded flight information, call Tel. 03-972-3344).* To get there, **United Tours** bus 222, *57 Ben Yehuda or 113 Hayarkon Street, Tel. 03-639-4444,* shuttles between Hayarkon Street (stopping by the major hotels), the train station on Arlozoroff, and the airport for NIS 10.5, leaving hourly Sunday-Thursday from 4:30am-12:45am (from Hayarkon, midnight from airport), Friday 4:30am-7:15pm (from Hayarkon, 8pm from airport), and Saturday noon-12:45pm from Hayarkon and 12:30-11:15pm from the airport.

Egged bus 475 goes between the new central bus station (6th floor) and the airport for NIS 5.70, leaving every 20 or so minutes Sunday-Thursday 5:20am-11:35pm, Friday 5:20am-1:30pm. And if your flight leaves Israel at 6am, as so many do, your options are a taxi (running at fixed rates of around NIS 75, plus NIS 2 for each piece of luggage and a 25% Shabbat and evening surcharge) or getting to the airport late the night before and hanging about till the 4am check-in parade begins.

Domestic flights on **Isra Air,** *Tel. 03-613-6564, Fax 03-751-9430,* and **Arkia Airlines,** 11 Frishman, *Tel. 03-690-3333,* go to Eilat and to Haifa as well.

A Sampling of Airlines

• **Air Sinai,** *1 Ben Yehuda, Tel. 177-022-5123 or Tel. 03-510-2481*
• **Arkia Domestic Airlines,** *11 Frishman, Tel. 03-690-3333*

• **American Airlines**, *1 Ben Yehuda, Tel. 03-510-4322*
• **Delta Airlines**, *29 Allenby, Tel. 03-620-1101*
• **El Al**, *32 Ben Yehuda, Tel. 03-526-1222*
• **KLM**, *124 Ibn Gvirol, Tel. 03-521-9999*
• **Isra Air**, *Tel. 03-613-6564*
• **TWA**, *74 Hayarkon, Tel. 03-517-4266*
• **Tower Air**, *78 Hayarkon, Tel. 03-517-1212*
• **United Air**, *41 Ben Yehuda, Tel. 03-527-9551*

Flights To Cairo
Flights on **Air Sinai**, *1 Ben Yehuda, Tel. 03-510-2481*, go to Cairo for $143 one way (plus $11 tax) Thursday, Friday, Sunday at 11:45am. El Al, *32 Ben Yehuda, Tel. 03-510-2481 or 03-526-1222*, also goes to **Cairo** for $143 at 8pm Sunday-Thursday.

By Bus
The **New Central Bus Station**, *108 Levinsky, Tel. 03-510-2481, 03-526-1222, 03-638-4040, or Egged Info 03-537-5555*, is enormous. Swelled with pride, folks boast how it's bigger than New York's Port Authority, and how former Mayor Ed Koch came to attend the opening. It's also cleaner and safer, and along with the Egged and Dan company inter- and intra-city buses and platforms, there are shops (1,400) and cafes, amusements and facilities, and happily, the **tourist information office**, *Tel. 03-639-5660, Fax 03-639-5659*, is now located there as well, on the 6th floor near platform 630.

Unfortunately, the station's far from downtown, so you need to bus there to bus away (bus 4 from Ben Yehuda and Allenby or bus 5 from Dizengoff). There's a smaller station in **Reading**, and there's also the **Arlozoroff station** in Ramat Gan by the train station where fares are sometimes slightly cheaper for northerly destinations. You can get to anywhere in Israel from here. The 405 double decker goes direct from/ to Jerusalem for NIS 17, and the 900 connects direct with Haifa for NIS 20. And for the five-hour trip to Eilat, take the 394 for NIS 59, and reserve ahead.

By Train
The **train station**, *Arlozoroff Street near Haifa Road, Tel. 03-693-7515*, is open 6am-8pm, and buses 62 and 64 from Ben Yehuda go there. Trains (all air-conditioned) go to Jerusalem at 8:35am for NIS 17 (NIS 12.75 for students) and take two hours. Trains head north for a scenic trip to Haifa for NIS 19 (NIS 15.5 for students), stopping at Netanya, and continuing on to Akko and Nahariya.

BEST OF TEL AVIV
HOTELS

• *THE ALEXANDER*, 3 Habakook, Tel. 03-546-2222, Fax 03-546-9346, has single suites for $190-$225, doubles are $225-$260, and a 4-person suite is $300. This suites-only place has elegant rooms with a luxurious feel.

• *GRAND BEACH HOTEL*, 250 HaYarkon, Tel. 03-543-3333, Fax 03-546-6589, costs $98-$105 for singles and $154 for doubles + 15% service charge, and including a big buffet breakfast. They have a pool and are big, friendly, quiet, and across the street from the beach.

• *AMBASSADOR*, 56 Herbert Samuel Esplanade, Tel. 03-510-3993, Fax 03-517-6308, costs $65-85 for singles and $90-100 for doubles, full Israeli breakfast included. The Ambassador is a charming, very friendly 3-star place right on the beach.

• *GORDON INN*, 17 Gordon, Tel. 03-523-8239, Fax 03-523-7419, costs $16 for dorm beds, $50 for private rooms. This hostel is meticulously neat and attractive.

BEST FOOD & DRINK

• *CAMELOT*, 16 Shalom Aleichem, Tel. 03-528-5222, offers nice tables, good music, and a suave, interesting crowd who do a good job of compensating for the somewhat steep prices.

• *ELIMELAKH*, 35 Wolfson (close to Shalom Tower, a block from Ha'aliya), Tel. 03-518-2978) offers traditional Jewish foods in a warm, friendly, old neighborhood establishment.

• *ASRAF*, 86 King George (not far from City Hall), Tel. 03-622-6685, has great home-cooked Moroccan/Tunisian food, tasty and innovative.

• *THE SHAKESPEARE*, 140 Hayarkon (near Gordon), Tel. 03-522-2194, is a pleasant cafe in the British Council with English newspapers for free.

• *ESPRESSO MERSAND*, 70 Ben Yehuda, Tel. 03-523-4318, may not be chic, but they're the best coffee you can find in the city for less than NIS 5.

• *BETZAL EL MARKET*, down Beit Lechem, off King George at #3, is the best falafel stand in the city. Huge salad selection, and build-your-own-pita for NIS 7.

BEST SIGHTS

• *BETH HATEFUTSOTH* – The Museum of the Diaspora, Tel Aviv University campus, Tel. 03-646-2020, is one of the best museums in Israel, with fascinating genealogy databases as well as music, culture, and artifacts from Jewish communities around the world.

BEST HOTSPOTS

• *CAMELOT*, 16 Shalom Aleichem, Tel. 03-528-5222, features live music, (usually rock, jazz, or blues) in The Back Room and is the most popular Tel Aviv spot for the local music scene.

• *LOGOS*, 8 Hashomer, Tel. 03-516-1176, is off 14 Nahalat Binyamin, but the sign isn't in English. A friendly hang-out cafe with live music (jazz and blues) nightly and Friday afternoons.

• *SHANBO* and *JOSEPHINE*, 25 Lillenbloom, Tel. 03-510-6739, are beautifully decorated new discos (upstairs and down for posh or funky) for dancing and an interesting crowd without that meat market feel.

The trains leave a number of times daily, but the schedule changes frequently, so call for up-to-date info.

By Taxi

Allenby, *Ha-Moshavot Square,* has taxis going to most major cities and aren't that much more than buses. For private inter-city taxis, there's **Balfour Taxi**, *57 Balfour, Tel. 03-560-4545.*

ORIENTATION

On the Mediterranean coast, about 55 kilometers northwest of Jerusalem, 354 kilometers from the southern tip of Eilat, and 137 kilometers from Rosh Hanikra in the north, Tel Aviv lies on what used to be sandy dunes. Hot and humid in summer and at times wet and raw in winter, the weather is always a good bit warmer than in nearby, lofty Jerusalem.

Downtown Tel Aviv is a rectangle of streets snuggled up against the sea, its length stretching 6 kilometers north-south along the coast, with the suburbs of **Ramat Gan**, **Ramat Aviv**, **Bnei Brak**, and **Petah Tikva** flung eastward, as well as further north and south. Street numbers run west to east and south to north, with many buildings often sharing one number.

Hayarkon is the first street just east of the beach **Promenade**, and it's the hotel and car rental strip, with the posher luxury lodgings and cafes to the north and some low-life hostels to the south; it's also the route of the 222 airport shuttle. **Ben Yehuda** to the east of Hayarkon (mostly parallel before it angles eastward to the south) is a busy downtown street full of shops, cafes, supermarkets, and important bus routes. **Frishman** runs east-west and while it's the site of some very fine restaurants and the Solan international phone office, it's most frequently used as a connector between Hayarkon and Ben Yehuda in the west and Dizengoff further east.

Dizengoff is the central boulevard, full of stores and cafes, pubs and theaters, window-shoppers and commuters, and it leads to **Dizengoff Square**, with its fountain and the Dizengoff Center mall. It's also a confusing street, running south till Dizengoff Square before veering eastward to intersect King George (look at a map before navigating by Dizengoff).

King George (*George Hamelekh* in Hebrew), east of Dizengoff Square, runs south to intersect with Allenby and Ben Yehuda, and has some museums, a good book store, bakery, and Tunisian restaurant. And still farther east is **Ibn Gvirol**, a noisy thoroughfare with supermarkets, theaters, some consulate and airline offices, and a big mall. To the north of the downtown area, **Arlozorov** and **Ben Gurion** (the next street to the south) connect Ibn Gvirol to Dizengoff, Ben Yehuda, and Hayarkon. At the end of Ben Gurion is Kikkar Atarim and the Tel Aviv marina. South of Ben Gurion is **Gordon**, not a major street but with a number of hostels and pubs; follow it to Gordon beach.

Kikkar Magen David is the intersection where King George, Ben Yehuda, Sheinkin and Allenby meet. **Sheinkin**, heading east from there, is a newly trendy street with cafes galore. **Allenby**, once the heart of Tel Aviv, is now a somewhat shunned street. It does have some raunchy elements (by Israeli standards, still a bit cleaner than some US neighborhoods) and the start of Allenby (veering west to the beach and Tel Aviv's red light district) is decidedly crummy.

The portion of Allenby that heads south, however, has shops selling Judaica, some nice restaurants, some cheap *falafel* and *shwarma* fast food joints (of so-so quality), and a number of cheaper hotels. It's also the route to a number of Tel Aviv's museums, street markets, and interesting old neighborhoods.

GETTING AROUND TOWN
By Bus

Dan Company, *Tel. 03-639-4444*, operates most of the intra-city buses (though **Egged** does run a few), and a trip costs NIS 3.9 (though month passes exist and are worthwhile if you plan a longish stay). If you're going to spend more than a few days in Tel Aviv, buying a Dan bus map is a good investment. These are some of the major city routes (note - the last buses on Fridays leave at 6:45pm, earlier in winter):

• **Bus 4** (every five minutes from 6am-midnight) goes from the central bus station to the northern Reading terminal via Petach-Tikva, Allenby, Ben Yehuda, and Dizengoff.
• **Bus 5** (every five minutes from 4:50am-midnight) goes from the central bus station to Pinkas via Petach-Tichva, Allenby, Rothschild, Tarsat, Dizengoff, Nordau, and Ibn Gvirol.
• **Bus 10** (every 15 minutes from 5:20am-midnight) goes from the Arlozorov railway station to Bat Yam via Arlozorov, Ben Yehuda, Allenby, Herbert Samuel, Kaufman, Balfour, Herzl, and Rothschild.
• **Bus 18** (every 5-10 minutes from 6:30am-midnight) goes from the railway station to Bat Yam via Petach Tikva, Sha'ul Hamelech, Ben Yehuda, Allenby, Aliya, and Yerushalayim.
• **Bus 25** (every 15 minutes from 5:15am-midnight) goes from Tel Aviv University to the Carmelit bus terminal via Klatzkin, Klausner, Levanon, Einstein, Brodetzky, Reading, Namir, Yehuda Hamaccabi, De Haas, Pinkas, Ibn Gvirol, Arlozoroff, Shlomo Hamelech, Frishman, King George, Allenby, Montefiore, Hashachar, Yavetz, Carmel, Tzhak Elhanan (and on to Bat Yam till 9:30pm).

Car Rentals (prices subject to change, negotiating often worthwhile)
• **Chai**, *27 Achimeir, Ramat Gan, Tel. 03-751-7682*, offers 1 week $325 unlimited mileage.
• **Europcar**, *126 Hayarkon, Tel. 03-524-8181*, has 1 day $76-$91 for 200km, 1 week $364-$469 unlimited mileage.
• **Gindy**, *132 Hayarkon, Tel. 03-527-8344*, has 1 day $60 for 150km, 1 week $350 unlimited mileage.
• **Omer**, *138 Hayarkon, Tel. 03-522-1611*, has rates of 1 day $48 for 100km, 1 week $330 unlimited mileage.
• **Perry**, 112 Hayarkon, *Tel.* 03-523-1111, has 1 day $80 (incl. ins.), 1 week $340 unlimited mileage.
• **Traffic**, *130 Hayarkon, Tel. 03-524-9187*, has rates of 1 day $70 for 250 km, 1 week $350 unlimited mileage.

By Taxi

Sherut taxis run along some of the bus routes and charge comparable bus fares (look for the cars with number signs on the roof). **Special** or **private taxis** use meters (make sure they are on), and charge 25% extra at night from 9pm-5:30am. Along with flagging one down on the street, you can call *03-524-9090, or 03-527-1999* at night.

WHERE TO STAY

HOLIDAY INN, *145 Hayarkon, Tel. 03-520-1111, Fax 03-520-1122, has 239 rooms, with singles $246-$431, doubles $276-$461, and suites from $375 (15% included but usually no breakfast).*

The rooms come with enormous beds but small balconies, and the hotel has a new health club ($12 entrance), sauna, and a swimming pool (inside in winter and open in summer). In addition, they have a business floor with its own check-in.

TEL AVIV HILTON, *Independence Park, Tel. 03-520-2222, Fax 03-522-6111, has 582 rooms with singles for $290-$385 and doubles for $315-$385. There are also the business and executive floors that run from $335 a single to $390 a double, as well as suites starting at $380.*

This is a fully equipped hotel with the works: restaurants (there's a Sushi Bar open 6pm-11pm) and shops, health club, tennis courts, big outdoor pool, and beach. The Superior Room sports executive style hard wood and desk, and from the balcony there's a lovely view of the park and the sea, all the way to Jaffa. There is an emphasis here on accommodating the business guest, and they offer special Japanese services as well.

YAMIT PARK PLAZA, *79 Hayarkon, Tel. 03-519-7111, Fax 03-517-4719, has 40 executive rooms (B&B) at $197 a single and $161 a double, plus 36 suites (breakfast not included), $232 for 1BR and $348 for 2BR, with a high season supplement of $15 an executive room and $45-$65 for suites.*

The room number plates have red roses on them, and the rooms all have phone, alarm clock, TV, pants press, coffee/tea (on the house), mini bars, and bathrooms with marble sinks (the suites have balconies and kitchens). Breakfast buffet is 7am-10am, while the Rainbow Lounge is open 9am-6pm. There's a pleasant lobby with sofas, rugs, and a great view of the sea, while outside there's a deck and small pool.

SHERATON TEL AVIV, *115 Hayarkon, Tel 03-521-1111, Fax 03-523-3322, has 346 rooms priced by season at $232-$335 for singles and $252-$360 for doubles (no breakfast and plus 15% service).*

Open since 1977, they offer a wide variety of services, especially for business people. They have voice mail in each otherwise unremarkable room as well as messages and fax service. Why the Sheraton? Really nice staff and emphasis on hospitable, so says the staff. They have a new health club gym and sauna with massage, while outside is a swimming pool with deck and cafe. In addition, the communication center is being renovated into a business center and the Tango Club (catering to 40-somethings) rocks on weekends from 10pm on with music of the 60s & 70s.

RADISSON MORIAH PLAZA TEL AVIV, *155 Hayarkon, Tel. 03-527-1515, Fax 03-521-6666, has 355 rooms with singles for $160-$220 and doubles for $190-$290, all including 15% service and breakfast.*

Pretty rooms with nice balconies, and a swimming pool with direct access to the beach, but the physical plant isn't as spiffy as some of the big beach hotels, so they stress personal attention and good service to compensate. A popular hotel with a nice lobby, it's often full. There is an executive floor as well.

DAN TEL AVIV, *99 Hayarkon, Tel. 03-520-2525, Fax 03-524-9755, has 285 rooms for $206-$266 a single and $226-$286 a double, with additional peak period and weekend surcharges and 15% service charge added to all. There are also a variety of suites from $332.*

Some rooms face the sea, others face the city, and the lowest priced face nothing at all. Many rooms have fax hook ups (if not you can request one). It's an Israeli luxury hotel (not an American chain) with a European feel, the first in Tel Aviv (40 years old), and it caters to business people. There's a sun deck with snack bar in summer, indoor pool, Jacuzzi, masseurs, changing rooms, two pools and (children's and adult) outside, plus a health club/gym as well. For Deluxe and Sea View suites, there is a deluxe lounge free of charge with free food/drinks, as well as butler service and a business center with fax & computers.

ALEXANDER, *3 Havakook, Tel. 03-546-2222, Fax 03-546-9346, is a suites-only hotel with 48 suites. Rates for a single range from $190-$225, doubles run $225-$260, and a four-person suite is $300 (all including 15% service, but in high season there's a $35 supplement).*

This place has truly lovely rooms with a luxury feel. You get a morning newspaper, three phones per suite, a three-speed massage shower, and silk sheets on request. And the Superior room lives up to its name. The suites have bathroom, bedroom, living room and kitchen, and there's a Shabbat elevator. There is parking downstairs and a fitness room, plus a pool on the roof for summer and winter use. Full of businessmen in the diamond business, there are 25% discount for stays longer than a month.

THE CARLTON TEL AVIV, *10 Eliezer Peri, Tel. 03-520-1818, Fax 03-527-1043, has 281 rooms, offering singles for $160-$216 and doubles for $190-$224, with suites beginning at $220, including service charge and breakfast (there are extra peak surcharges during busy seasons).*

The hotel has an outdoor swimming pool, a sauna (but no health club), a synagogue and a Melodies bar, as well as fresh roses in the rooms, and tiny balconies overlooking the sea.

RAMADA CONTINENTAL, *121 Hayarkon, Tel. 03-521-5555, Fax 03-521-5588, has 340 rooms with singles for $160-$205 and doubles for $170-$215, plus 15% service (check for low season specials).*

The rooms are okay, with balconies overlooking the water and all the usual amenities. From the outside it looks like stacked leggo blocks, but inside are lots of restaurants, a health club (7am-9pm), sauna, pool, and massage. The daily piano bar goes 6pm-10pm, and an Israeli singer performs Thursday and Friday 10:30pm-2ish, plus a folk concert once a month. And the business club with fax/telex is open daily 7am-10pm.

OLYMPIA HOTEL, *164 Hayarkon, Tel. 03-524-2184, Fax 03-524-7278, charges $100 for singles, $215 for doubles, including 15% service charge and breakfast.*

The Olympia is the new reincarnation of the Florida, just recently opened. The rooms are pleasant, and there are tiny balconies overlooking Hayarkon and the sea.

DAN PANORAMA, *Charles Clore Park (near Jaffa), Tel. 03-519-0190, Fax 03-517-1777, has 500 rooms with singles for $132-$172 and doubles for $152-$192, including breakfast, with additional peak period and weekend surcharges, and 15% service charge added to all.*

Nice views, but it's just not as luxurious as the Dan in central Tel Aviv.

GRAND BEACH HOTEL, *250 Hayarkon, Tel. 03-543-3333, Fax 03-546-6589, has singles for $98-$105 and doubles for $154 (all rooms are doubles, price depends on occupancy), plus 15% service charge, and including a big buffet breakfast.*

This 3-star hotel is big, friendly, quiet, and across the street from the beach (regular and religious) and Ha Atzmaut park (gay hang-out park). The rooms are cheery if not deluxe, and all have the standard TV, phone, air conditioning, and bathroom as well as fridge and room service. With its business/fax center on the 7th floor, prayer or conference room near the lobby, Sabbath elevator, kosher restaurant, and rooftop swimming pool, this is a good middle range option.

TAL HOTEL, *287 Hayarkon, Tel. 03-546-8126, Fax 03-546-7687, near little Tel Aviv, has 120 rooms with singles for $113 and doubles for $141 (plus 15% service), with reductions for children in the room.*

Not very special for a luxury hotel.

BASEL HOTEL, *156 Hayarkon, Tel. 03-524-4161, has 120 rooms with singles for $89-$103, doubles for $110-$140, (plus 15% service, breakfast included), reductions for children in the room.*

Not the most helpful staff, nor the most impressive rooms.

PRIMA ASTOR, *105 Hayarkon, Tel 03-522-3141, Fax 03-523-7247, has 67 rooms for $70-$105 a single, and $105-$140 a double, breakfast included.*

The rates vary by size (standard with shower and large with bath), view (sea view or other), and season (high, regular, and low). The singles are very basic and small, the doubles larger, and some have nice views.

CITY HOTEL, *9 Mapu, Tel. 03-524-6253, Fax 03-524-6250, email: atlashot@netvision.net.il, has 96 rooms at $81-$93 a single and $98-$122 a double (plus 15% service), with reductions for children in the room.*

They have a central location, a friendly staff, and a homelike atmosphere.

SHALOM HOTEL, *216 Hayarkon, Tel. 03-524-3277, Fax 03-523-5895, has 48 rooms for $60 a single and $85-$105 a double, including 15% service and full Israeli breakfast.*

The superior rooms have sea views and balconies while the standard rooms face the Hilton and are without balconies, but all the rooms are spacious and clean with nubbly blankets and old carpets. The lobby sets the tone with comfy chairs but no fancy fountains or ocean views.

AMBASSADOR, *56 Herbert Samuel Esplanade, Tel. 03-510-3993, Fax 03-517-6308, has 50 rooms with singles for $60-$85, doubles for $90-$100 (same rooms, price depends on occupancy), triples at $110, and quads for $120, including service charge and full Israeli breakfast buffet (15% discount for week long stays, 20% student discount with card).*

A charming, friendly three-star place right on the beach in front of New Opera Tower. The rooms are fully equipped with bathrooms, phones, and air conditioning but no TV (which may be a plus). The decor isn't exciting, but some rooms have fine balconies and views.

MAXIM HOTEL, *86 Hayarkon, Tel. 03-517-3721, Fax 03-517-3726, has 60 rooms with singles for $58-$72, doubles for $91-$95, including 15% service charge and Israeli breakfast.*

There are pleasant rooms with all the amenities plus art work over the bed. In additions, there's a 24-hour cafe with light meals.

AMI HOTEL, *152 Hayarkon, Tel. 03-524-9141, Fax 03-523-1151, has singles for $70-$75, doubles for $86-$92, and triples for $105, all including continental breakfast.*

The singles are small and tidy, the doubles nicer, squat gray chairs are placed randomly in the hallways, and the TV lounge is newly renovated.

HOTEL MOSS, *6 Ness Ziona, Tel./Fax 03-517-1655, has 70 rooms with singles for $80, and doubles $90 (breakfast included).*

If you stay for a week, the seventh day is free. It is quiet with clean, plain little rooms furnished with TV, phone, bath, air conditioning, and coffee, and cold drinks are available.

TOP HOTEL, *35 Ben Yehuda, Tel. 03-517-0941, Fax 03-517-1322, with 64 rooms has singles for $69, and doubles for $88 (higher in summer).*

All rooms are fully equipped with air conditioning, direct dial phones, bath/shower, and cable TV, and come with full Israeli breakfast. This hotel has no discomfort, no dirt, no charm, and no personality.

CENTER HOTEL, *2 Zamenhoff, Tel. 03-629-6181, Fax 03-629-6751, has 56 rooms and is part of the Atlas Hotel chain. They have singles for $64-$69 and doubles for $76-$88, with higher rates in summer.*

This is a fully appointed, professionally set up hotel, very clean and safe. All rooms come with shower/toilet, phone, air conditioning, and cable TV. It is attractive and cozy for an impersonal chain.

HOTEL ADIV, *5 Mendele, Tel. 03-522-9141, Fax 03-522-9144, with 71 rooms, charges $56-$62 a single, $77-$85 a double, and $104 for junior suites, (including 15% service and Israeli breakfast).*

On a relatively quiet street in downtown, there's an underground parking lot for those with cars. In addition, there are clean, modern rooms, and the shower curtains sport cheery penguins.

ARMON HAYARKON, *268 Hayarkon, Tel. 03-605-5272, Fax 03-605-8485, has 24 rooms with singles for $50-65 and doubles for $60-80, breakfast included.*

Just okay, with plain, worn rooms and a roof terrace.

IMPERIAL HOTEL, *66 Hayarkon, Tel. 03-517-7002, Fax 03-517-8314, with 46 rooms. Singles are $50, doubles are $68. Breakfast (included) is served 7am-10am.*

This is a plain, clean hotel with a working lift, and all rooms come with the standard air conditioning/TV/phone/shower.

HOTEL EILAT, *58 Hayarkon, Tel. 03-510-2453, has singles for $50 and doubles for $60.*

They have pleasant, neat rooms with double beds, toilet and shower, air conditioning, and a slight musty smell.

HOSTEL MIAMI, *8 Allenby, Tel. 03-510-3868, charges $50 a single and $60 a double, breakfast included.*

They are unwilling to show their rooms unless you commit to book for the night. There appears to be no good reason to stay there.

HOTEL AVIV, *88 Hayarkon, Tel. 03-510-2784, Fax 03-523-9450, costs $30-$40 a single and $50-$55 a double.*

Some rooms have ocean views and all save the one cheap single have toilet & shower. There's an eatery downstairs, Cafe Picasso, that's great for people and wave watching but has pricy and not overly exciting food.

HOTEL NES ZIONA, *10 Nes Tziona (off Ben Yehuda), Tel. 03-510-3404, has singles for $25-$40 (shared toilet/shower), and doubles for $40-$45.*

The rooms are very clean and airy, but small, and some of them have balconies. There's a kitchen, and a TV lobby with coffee for NIS 3. The staff is helpful, in a nervous sort of way.

MONOPOL, *4 Allenby, 03-517-5906, has singles for NIS 90, doubles for NIS 140, and breakfast for $6, all credit cards accepted.*

This is a ratty-tatty hotel with unfriendly staff, but some of the rooms have a view of the Opera Towers fountain and the sea, if that makes it worth your while.

HOTEL EUROPE, *42 Allenby, Tel. 03-517-7912, Fax 03-510-3964, costs NIS 130 for a single with shower.*

Clean and decent looking, though with no real personality; all rooms come with shower and phone.

NORDAU HOTEL, *27 Nahalat Binyamin, Tel. 03-560-6612, has rooms costing NIS 70-100.*

The desk help speak limited English and some German. No reservations taken, they say to just show up.

HAGALIL HOTEL, *23 Beyt Yosuf, Tel 03-517-5036, is off an alley between Allenby 54-56. Singles cost $25. They'll take reservations over the phone in English, no credit number required.*

An old hotel in the red light district, you can get your own room for relatively few shekels, giving you more privacy than a hostel, though you'll have to contend with the verbose hotel manager. It's run down but has touches of personality, like old oriental rugs by the army style beds. The toilet and shower are shared, there's no heat and no air conditioning, but there are fans and plenty of blankets. It is quiet inside, noisy out, and tatty all over.

HOTEL GALIM, *9 Allenby, Tel. 03-517-5703, costs NIS 100 for singles, and NIS 40 for a dorm bed, with group discounts.*

Advertised for students and young travelers, it is fairly clean and not far from the sea, but not cozy.

Hostels

BNEI DAN YOUTH HOSTEL, *36 Bnei Dan, Tel. 03-544-1748, Fax 03-544-103, is accessible via bus #5, #24, #25, or #222. Dorm beds are $20 in the old wing, while the new wing has singles for $36, doubles for $52, triples for $65, and quads for $85 for non-members ($1.50 per person discount for members); all prices include full breakfast, and all credit cards accepted.*

There are over 200 beds, and they're spotlessly clean and safe, with heat and air conditioning, and bath/toilet in each room (the rooms in the new wing are very impressive), but way out of the way. There are conference rooms and a TV room, as well as sitting areas, and the dining room is very large and glatt kosher. The hostel is across the street from a park, and was built as a gift by the Germans in memory of the Olympic athletes killed in 1972.

GORDON INN, *17 Gordon, Tel. 03-523-8239, Fax 03-523-7419, is a newish, up-scale hostel. Dorm room rates start at $16 and go up as high as $50 for large private room with shower, and there's every option in between.*

The staff is very helpful and efficient and the hostel is meticulously neat and attractive. If you want to spend less than the hotels charge for private rooms but the hostels seem too grimy and risky, take a look at this place. They serve a full continental breakfast, and downstairs is a cafe with pasties and light meals that's open 8:30 am-1 am daily.

SEA & SUN HOSTEL, *62 Hayarkon, Tel. 03-517-3313, Fax 03-517-3562, has dorm beds for NIS 35.*

Sea & Sun has a reputation as a good place to be if you want to find work, but otherwise it's a good place to avoid. It has a prime location by the beach, but the management may be too busy listening to music to attend to your needs, and it's not got the safest reputation for belongings. They keep your passport till you check out and they assign you a bed, an irritating voice booms over intercom, and young questionables hang about, loitering everywhere.

DIZENGOFF SQUARE HOSTEL, *11 Dizengoff Square, Tel. 03-522-5184, Fax 03-522-5181, is across from the cinema. They have dorm beds for NIS 35 (long term NIS 33) and doubles for $39-$49.*

Continental breakfast is included in the price, as is free coffee any time, and the kitchen is available for use 24 hours. It costs NIS 7 for the washer, NIS 7 for the dryer, there's a free, secure safe for small valuables, and it's NIS 5 for a locker. The hostel is closed daily from 10:30-2:30, but it isn't strictly enforced; they won't kick you out of bed. Most dorms are coed, though there is one all-girl dorm. There are currently 100 beds, but a rooftop pyramid room is under construction for year-round use, while the roof top bar and lounge area are popular in summer. Drinks (alcoholic and non) are on sale behind reception, and there's a TV lounge with cable downstairs.

There's no curfew, and the place has a friendly feel. Gaining in popularity for people looking for work, reservations are recommended. The dorms look well lived in, and some have balconies; it's a nice place to stay.

NO. 1 HOSTEL, *84 Ben Yehuda, Tel. 03-523-7807, Fax 03-523-3521, has dorm beds for NIS 33 (less for long term), private rooms for $35, and they take Visa/Mastercard, (travelers cheques are okay, but they charge an additional NIS 7). Continental breakfast consisting of toast and jam is included.*

New bright yellow paint leads the way to the reception desk, indicating a place that is well-taken care of, bus such is not the case. The reception desk is so far removed (and the desk person so wrapped up in TV) that anyone could wander around without being noticed, leading to rather questionable security. There are lockers for NIS 3.5, use of washer/dryer (NIS 4 each), a TV bar, and a kitchen that's open till 10:30 pm. The hostel is closed daily 11 am-2 pm.

THE GREENHOUSE HOSTEL, *201 Dizengoff, Tel. 03-523-5994, has dorm beds for NIS 33, private room s with two single beds for NIS 80, and a private room for NIS 72.*

You get pleasant ambiance for the extra shekels, with comfy sofas in the TV living room (off limits after midnight). The dorms have cots, no bunks. Laundry service is NIS 18 for wash/dry, and it's NIS 5 for a locker. The kitchen is open for limited hours, and has free coffee. The phone takes phone cards, and the roof bar is open in summer. There's no curfew, and you use a code to open the door. Closed 10-3 daily for cleaning.

GORDON HOSTEL, *2 Gordon, Tel. 03-522-9870, Fax 03-523-3521, charges NIS 30 a dorm bed, with no private rooms.*

Not a very appealing place, though it is near the beach, the dorm rooms are claustrophobic, and a lethargic air permeates. They do have a kitchen, and there's a laundromat downstairs that charges NIS 10 per wash and per dry. There is also a cafe downstairs with loud music.

HOTEL JOSEF, *15 Bugrashov, Tel. 03- 528-0955, has dorm beds for NIS 28-35 and a private room for NIS 140.*

Each dorm has four beds and its own toilet and shower, and in the summer people sleep on the roof. The dorms are coed and single sex, by preference and availability. The bar is a happy, friendly place – good for meeting people and getting information, especially since there is no TV to absorb all the focus.

MOMO'S HOSTEL, *28 Ben Yehuda, Tel. 03-528-7471, has dorm beds for NIS 28, doubles for NIS 100-120, rooftop beds in summer for NIS 25, and they don't take reservations.*

Most of the people staying here are students interested in saving money and partying. Momo's has been an institution for decades, with its Snake Bar serving cheap food and beer, and its graffiti-covered walls decor. Described by one traveler as a place of yobs and hooligans, it has a strong, loud personality, and you will either feel immediately at home or want to run away. If you stay, take care with your belongings.

THE TRAVELLER'S HOSTEL, *47 Ben Yehuda, Tel. 03-524-3083, Fax 03-523-7281, has dorm beds for NIS 25, and doubles for NIS 140.*

They have an information board, message board, open kitchen with free coffee/tea, cable TV lounge, bar, and provide information on travel, money changing, and jobs.

PHILADELPHIA HOSTEL, *28 Allenby, Tel. 03-517-1620, has dorm beds for NIS 25 and private rooms for NIS 75.*

If you can't find a bed anywhere else, can't afford a fancier hotel, and are desperate, then this place will do. Otherwise, don't bother. It's dingy and dirty and the cluster of sleazy looking men in the 'lounge' look up and stop talking when you enter as though you were interrupting illicit business. Spare yourself the experience.

HOME HOSTEL, *20 Alsheich, Tel. 03-517-6736, is down the alley by 56 Allenby – hang a left, then take your next right. They offers dorm beds for NIS 25, and private rooms for NIS 50.*

It's very basic, the clientele is pretty young, and the price is the lowest in town.

Long-Term Stays
TEL AVIV UNIVERSITY STUDENT UNION, *Tel. 03-642-2549, Fax 03-524-0815.*

The Student Union has lists of flats and rooms for rent, ranging from $300 to $900 a month, with lists changing and updated weekly.

THE HOME, *106 Hayarkon (corner of Frishman), office #16.*

Rates vary by season and size, ranging from $300-$500 a week, discounts available for stays of a month or longer.

ROOMS TO RENT, *Becky Greller, 7 HaShomer St, Ramat Gan, Israel, 52394, 03-570-5911. Becky lives in a private house in Ramat Gan with rooms for $325 a single, one month minimum. Call to see if one of her three rooms are available, or write.*

Becky is a friendly, motherly type, the house is flawlessly clean, the bathroom is shared by the three tenants upstairs, and you can use the kitchen.

WHERE TO EAT
Downtown Restaurants & Cafes
KETON, *145 Dizengoff, Tel. 03-523-3679*, open Sunday-Thursday noon-9pm and serves traditional Jewish food in a homey small dining room with appealing ink and water color pictures on the walls. Some of their offerings include: cholent and kishke (NIS 23), borscht (NIS 6), tripe

(NIS 23), cow jelly (NIS 8.5), kreplech soup (NIS 9), and gefülte fish (NIS 8.5), and they do a nice basket of rye bread too. Quiet and pleasant inside, it's a nice respite from the noise of Dizengoff.

BATIA, *197 Dizengoff, Tel. 03-522-1335*, open Sunday-Thursday 11am-9pm, is a pleasant, attractive place to sip a cup of strong coffee (NIS 6) or sample some traditional Jewish foods like latkes (NIS 10), borsht (NIS 8), or cholent & kishkes (NIS 25). With indoor and outdoor seating, nice wood tables and chairs, and a young clientele, it's a good spot for lunch.

KASSIT RESTAURANT, *117 Dizengoff, Tel. 03-522-3855*, is open Sunday-Thursday 9am-1am and a great place to hang out and watch for famous people. The walls are full of photos of artists and politicians who have favored this place with their patronage (Frank Sinatra and Harry Belafonte are just two of many). There are also interesting paintings to look at, and the green-checked tables are nicely set for a somewhat pricy repast. Breakfasts go for NIS 18-27, salads are NIS 15-25, and entrees are 20-55, while a lowly cup of coffee will set you back NIS 6.

CHIMNEY, *2 Mendele, Tel. 03-523-3141*, opposite the Dan Hotel, is open daily noon-3am (Friday/Saturday till 4am). In the winter they have a warm and cozy fire going under their namesake chimney, just adding to the already warm and pleasant ambiance of wood tables, blue bar stools and easy-on-the-eyes decor. They have a special cocktail menu that's as long as the food counterpart, and its cover depicts elephants hunkering up to the bar and having a good time.

The drink list (NIS 20) is extensive, from classics like Rusty Nails and Singapore Slings to ice cream-based drinks (the Charlie Brown – a concoction with kahlua, peanut butter, and chocolate ice cream – might help explain a lot) and specials like A Loving Kiss (no more explanation forthcoming). And there's food, too. You can accompany your drinks with sandwiches or stuffed potatoes (NIS 17-23) or heartier food like chicken/veal dishes or pasta (NIS 24-50). If you want to splurge on a nice meal out, this is a good option.

CAMELOT, *16 Shalom Aleichem, Tel. 03-528-5222*, is a very cool place and it's open Sunday-Thursday 11am-5pm and 8pm-dawn, and from 5:30pm on Friday. An Israeli restaurant/bistro, they serve baguette sandwiches and salads (NIS 20-30) as well as coffees, beer on tap, and a full bar. Nice tables, good music, and a suave, interesting crowd do a good job of compensating for the somewhat steep prices. They also feature live music in the Back Room (see Entertainment section). Swing by and see who's playing.

CHIN CHIN, *42 Frishman, Tel. 03-522-2134*, is a Chinese Take Away, no credit cards accepted. With a quiet interior and tasteful pictures, it's a popular place for Chinese food. Soups will run you NIS 7, entrees are NIS 22, and the food is okay as a change from hummus.

ETERNITY, *60 Ben Yehuda, Tel. 03-620-3151*, is open Monday-Thursday 9am-11pm, Friday 9am-3pm, and Sunday after sundown to 11pm. It's been run by Black Hebrews for 12 years, and everything on the menu is vegen (no meat, no dairy, no eggs included), with most entries around NIS 9. Clean white plastic tables, a menu in yellow sunburst design, yellow & white plastic wall panels, and tables outside add to the airy feel despite its small space. Veggie shwarma is made of wheat glutin but tastes very much like turkey and is a popular dish. Lentil soup is wholesome and fresh and very boring. And then there's the wheat glutin Bar-B-Que twist that looks like something Fido left behind the sofa and tastes like a BBQ flavored lufah sponge. After your meal there is a selection of desserts such as tofu cream pie or banana split (soymilk based).

Next door people are smoking cigarettes, swilling down meat and grease, and showing their age, while in Eternity the workers look 10 years younger than they are, but is it really worth it? They say it all goes back to the Torah, where folks were supposed to eat seeds and fruit (and wheat glutin?).

ESPRESSO MERSAND, *70 Ben Yehuda, Tel. 03-523-4318*, is open Sunday-Thursday 8am-8pm, Friday 8am-4pm, and has the best coffee you can find in the city for less than NIS 5. It is a self-service cafe with dreary inside decor and the omnipresent white plastic tables outside, but their good, cheap coffee (NIS 4.5) and central location makes an indispensable hang-out.

FOREL, *10 Frishman, Tel. 03-522-2664*, is open daily noon till midnight. It is an attractive, modern looking restaurant with clean lines and softly lit ochre walls. Eli the chef/owner claims that his fish soup is perhaps the best in the world and at NIS 27 one would hope so, but its taste really lives up to the claim. Forel ("Trout" in Hebrew) is the most popular dish, grilled over charcoal for NIS 48, and the charming manager can advise on specials and wine. It's a good choice for a nice meal out, reservations recommended.

SHANGRILA, *Astor Hotel, 105 Hayarkon, Tel. 03-523-8913*, is a Thai restaurant open 12:30pm-12am daily, all credit cards accepted and reservations recommended. Soups run NIS 17-21, salads NIS 16-35, and entrees NIS 29-65. There is a nice view of the sea, fresh flowers, and not surprisingly, a Thai decor.

ACAPULCO, *105 Dizengoff, Tel. 03-523-7552*, is a cafe right in the center of things. Open daily 10am-midnight, they serve breakfast for NIS 18, appetizers for NIS 7-21, and entrees NIS 20-48. There are tables inside and out, and it is a popular hang out spot.

ETSTEKA, *82 Hayarkon, Tel. 03-517-3638*, is open daily noon-1am, sometimes longer, and all credit cards are accepted. This relatively new place serves Mexican food in a casual setting. Appetizers cost NIS 10-20, and entrees are NIS 30-62.

REGATA CAFE, *87 Hayarkon, Tel. 03-527-8666*, serves Italian food daily 4am-midnight. They have salads, pasta, focaccia and other sandwiches NIS 15-30. The room with a sea view has a yachty theme, modern colorful trendy decor, and a full bar in same building as the Dan, connected by an inside walkway.

THE SHAKESPEARE, *140 Hayarkon (near Gordon), Tel. 03-552-2194*, is a pleasant cafe in the British Council. Open Sunday-Thursday 8am-8pm, Friday 8am-12:30pm, they serve breakfasts, soups, salads, sandwiches for NIS 8.5-19 and you can read the English newspapers for free.

NAMELESS LUNCH PLACE, *109 Hayarkon (next to the Astor hotel)*, is open 8am-5pm daily and offers good cheap food (hummus plate NIS 6, soup 8) served by friendly waiters. If you are caught hungry in expensive hotel row and want a reasonable meal, this is the place. There's not much atmosphere, but there are tables inside and out, and the food's not bad.

HARD ROCK CAFE, *Dizengoff Center, Tel. 03-525-1336*, is open Sunday-Thursday 12am-1am, Friday 12-3pm, and Saturday 11:30am-1am. It's a mall eatery with expensive meals (burgers start NIS 26, and the burger with avocado and cheese is the best) and lots of rock memorabilia. Tourists throng during the week, while the weekends belong to teenagers. If you want to see Elvis' suit from '75 or Eric Clapton's blue shoes (circa 1970) while you eat, this is your place.

REMI, *King David Tower, 87 Hayarkon, Tel. 03-527-8444, Fax 03-524-8696*, prepares excellent Italian food for an elegant meal overlooking the sea. Business lunch costs NIS 69, a la carte lunch (pasta) is NIS 28-45 (half portions NIS 20), and entrees are NIS 42-85 (for dinner, figure NIS 65-100 for full meal).

SEZAN RESTAURANT, *215 Dizengoff, Tel. 03-527-8147*, is a new French restaurant. This used to be Edan Caffe Shop, but it's now moved up in the world to dish out French cuisine.

ASRAF, *86 King George (not far from City Hall), Tel. 03-622-6685*, is open Sunday-Thursday 9am-6pm, but food is served 11am-5:30pm. Though the sign's not in English, this small kosher Morrocan/Tunisian style restaurant is worth finding. Look for the white porch and roof, and inside you'll get some of the best home-cooked Moroccan food ever. The exact menu changes daily, but there will be some vegetarian couscous (NIS 16) or couscous with veggies and meat (NIS 28). Meat goulashes (stomach goulash is surprisingly tasty) run NIS 20-27 and include rice or potatoes. Stuffed vegetables (try the stuffed prune – despite its awful appearance it may be one of the best things you eat in Israel) are NIS 9. Spicy salads and sauces come with all entrees, as does a cookie with your bill. Eat in or take away, but no credit cards accepted.

BEN & JERRY'S, *93 and 284 Dizengoff*, serve up the flavors you left behind as well as a few Israeli specials for NIS 4.5 a scoop.

DR. LEK, *239 Ben Yehuda, Tel. 03-604-5454*, is an Israeli ice cream chain, and it's quite good, open daily 10am-midnight.

YIN YANG, *64 Rothchild Blvd., Tel. 03-560-4121*, serves very good, expensive Chinese food, but for this you came to Israel?

TNUVA SHELANU, *41 Frishman, Tel. 03-522-0297*, on the corner with Dizengoff, is a nice dairy cafe with enormous desserts. It's not cheap, but you can't beat its location, and the no-smoking section is a pleasant change.

Ha-Carmel Area

ZION RESTAURANT, *28 Peduyim, Tel. 03-517-8714*, the 5th right off Ha-Carmel from Allenby, dishes up kosher Yemenite foods 10am-midnight every day but shabbat. After maneuvering over the piles of trash from Carmel Market, this cozy restaurant is a real pleasure. The red table cloths, key-shaped arches, and Yemenite paintings on the wall create a warm atmosphere in which to enjoy traditional dishes. Try a soup (lungs, bones, or leg) for NIS 10-16, an appetizer of fried Cigar (a filo dough and meat creation, tobacco not included) for NIS 7, or grilled meats for NIS 19-40. If you've been hankering after ox testicles, this is definitely the place to visit. It's popular with locals, and friendly to tourists. One hint: if you get lost on your way there and ask directions, make sure to pronounce Zion "Tzeeon" as Zion with a long "I" is an obscenity in Hebrew and won't win you any friends, let alone directions.

SHAUL'S INN, *11 Eliashiv off Harav Kook, Tel. 03-517-3303, Fax 03-517-7619*, open Sunday-Thursday noon-12:30pm and Saturdays after Shabbat, is also known for its Yemenite cuisine, though it's fancier, more expensive, and more geared towards tourists.

BIG MAMMA, *22 Rabbi Akiva, Tel. 03-517-5096/03-604-3838*, the 2nd right off Ha-Carmel from Allenby, serves fine Israeli pizza amid a happy Hebrew yammer. Though open nightly 8pm-4am, from 9-11pm it's the happening place. You go down a dingy, deserted Ha-Carmel alley, empty but for cats feeding on garbage, you turn at the Big Mamma sign and enter another world full of life and good smells and people waiting to be seated. NIS 20-35 gets you a big plate of pizza with a super-thin crust, or fresh pasta for the same price, and then there are desserts like panna cotta and tartufo, incredibly delicious and worth saving room for.

Dinner for two, with wine and dessert, costs around NIS 90, and visa is accepted. Good food and a lively atmosphere make it worth the trip, or you can sacrifice the scene and have it delivered.

Allenby & Sheinkin
CAFE KAZÉ, *19 Sheinkin, Tel. 03-293-756*, is open daily 8am-midnight. You walk into a cozy interior where lots of people are drinking coffee and reading the paper or animatedly discussing the world. White walls and varnished wood furniture set the tone, while breakfast is NIS 18, and lunches cost from NIS 14 (soup) to NIS 45 (smoked trout).

Newe Tzedek & Kerem Ha-Temanim
ELIMELAKH, *35 Wolfson, Tel. 03-814-545*, close to Shalom Tower and a block from Ha'aliya, is open Sunday-Thursday noon-12:30pm, open Friday until Shabbat, and open Saturday after Shabbat till 2am. A wonderful, authentic little hole-in-the-wall, a great place to have traditional Jewish foods like chopped liver (NIS 17), gefilte fish (NIS 9.5), and cholent (Fridays only, NIS 16) while soaking in the warmth and friendliness of old-timer regulars. Two small yellow-walled rooms, one mostly for eating, the other more for a pint of Goldstar and a nosh. Established in 1936, there are old Hebrew newspapers framed on walls and laminated on tables, and lots of old codgers drinking and gabbing just before shabbat. Busy Thursday and Friday afternoons, otherwise it does mostly a lunch trade. Set in the heart of Newe Tzedek, it's worth the trek off Dizengoff to enjoy the food surrounded by local color. Recommended items: goulash (NIS 23) washed down by a pint of foamy-headed Goldstar from the tap.

ZCHARYA, *22 Ha-Koveshim*, open Sunday-Thursday 10am-11pm, Friday 10am-4ish, is a Yemenite culinary diamond in the rough just around the corner from Harov Kook, one block up and parallel to Hayarkon. The name's not written in English, but find the street number and a bunch of people sopping up bowls of luscious grub and you've found the right spot. While it's not big on decor, the chef is friendly and the authentic cooking is worth the detour. There's the usual hummus (or "cheak bean salad" as the menu entertainingly calls it), ful, and tehina for NIS 8, but the soups (NIS 15) are the main specialty. In the little kitchen in back big pots simmer full of a variety of rich broths.

There's stomach (kishke), brain (rosh), oxtail (zanov), lung, goulash, and testicle soups, yummy okra (bamya) on rice, and skewers of chicken livers, lamb, and the ever popular (and surprising succulent) cow tit. Everything is fresh and well seasoned, but the favorites were the brain, cow tit, stomach, oxtail, and okra. Zcharya will reward you for your adventurous palate.

Ramat Aviv
GREEN VILLA, *24 George Weis, Tel. 03-641-8295*, is open daily noon-3pm. They serve French food that's worth the splurge, along with

consommé lighter than water and especially fine beef tartare, plus goose liver in balsamic vinegar and beef fillet in herb crust.

Fast Food & Snacks

HA-CARMEL MARKET, *off Allenby*, is not only a great place to wander around, it has good, fresh, inexpensive produce, bread, hummus, and deli items.

BEST FALAFEL STAND, *Betzal El Market*, is down Beit Lechem, which is off King George at #3. Past stalls that hawk the same crappy clothes as Ha-Carmel, the main draw is the falafel. There are two competing stands – look at their salad selections and take your pick. Both have fresh and very tasty falafel and build-your-own-pita for NIS 7.

BAKERY, *7 King George*, has very good bagel, and fresh croissants.

SHASHLIK HOUSE, *91 Dizengoff*, the middle shwarma joint of the three in a row, is open 9am-2am and has shwarma/shashlik (turkey or lamb) for NIS 10 and falafel for NIS 7. There are tables inside and out, and a good salad topping selection. If you're hungry on Dizengoff it's an okay place to go. Though it isn't the finest shwarma in Israel, it's a favored fast-food spot of individuals who live and work in the area.

SEEING THE SIGHTS
Great Walks

Tel Aviv tourism has recently set up the **Orange Routes**, do-it-yourself walking tours of Tel Aviv and Jaffa, arranged by districts and themes. Get the Tel Aviv Tourism booklet from the tourist office for a full description of the routes and all their sights. Here are some of my favorites:

The Promenade is the long walkway by the beach, just past Hayarkon. It's pleasant to stroll and observe, at least when the wind's not kicking up.

Dizengoff on Shabbat is mostly closed to traffic. People saunter and hang out, kids rollerblade, families play, and old men and women sit and *bebitz* (chitchat) around the fountain.

Spiegel Park, donated by Abraham and Edita of Beverly Hills in 1989, is adjacent to the Hilton and nice for a stretch.

Shuk Ha-Carmel, at the intersection of Allenby and King George, shouldn't be missed. It's a boisterous, colorful, aromatic great market, full of magnificent fruit and vegetable displays (very cheap and very fresh), bins of marinated olives, stalls of glaring hocks of meat, barrels of live fish swimming about (the fishmonger bonks it on the head to kill it just after the sale, it's that fresh), hangers full of chintzy buyer-beware clothes, and some of the best cheese, hummus, and falafel around. The cobbled streets of nearby pedestrian walkway **Nahalat Binyamin** offer respite from the chaos with cheery, homey cafes and outdoor tables. On Tuesdays and

Fridays from 10am-4pm it's less peaceful but more entertaining, as it becomes the site for a street fair, with lots of unusual hand-crafted wares. **Gan Me'ir** is a park between King George and Tchernachovsky. It's pretty boring by day, but comes alive at night as a gay hang-out.

Old Neighborhoods (take buses 22, 40, 42, 44, 46)
Northwest of Allenby and near Shuk Ha-Carmel is **Kerem Ha-Temanim**, the old Yemenite Quarter. This community still feels very different from the hubbub of downtown, and there is wonderful gustatory experiences to be had here in small restaurants unfamiliar with English and tourists but very familiar with good food (see *Where to Eat*). **Newe Tzedek**, west of Herzl and Ahad Ha'Ain, is a great neighborhood to wander around. It was the first Jewish neighborhood built up outside of Jaffa and the stone houses and narrow streets have become attractive to the Tel Aviv yuppy community to renovate and gentrify.

While there you can visit the **Rokach House**, *36 Shimon Rokach, Tel. 03-516-2531*. Built in 1887, Shimon Rokach's house inaugurated this new neighborhood. It's a beautiful house with a golden cupola and was used as the Town Hall in the early years. Now it displays a collection of sculptures by Lea Majaro-Mintz, the man who restored the house. Open Saturday 10am-2pm, you can make arrangements to see it during the week by calling ahead.

Ben Gurion House, *17 Ben Gurion, Tel. 03-522-1010*, is open Sunday, Tuesday, Wednesday, Thursday 8am-3pm, Monday 8am-5pm, Friday 8am-1pm. It's free, but a waste of 10 precious minutes. There are pictures of Ben Gurion with . . ., the kitchen as was, the library as was, the study as was, lots of books, and quotes from Ben Gurion on "moral rectitude."

Tel Aviv Aquarium, *1 Kaufman, Tel. 03-510-6670*, by the Dolphinarium and south of the city along the coast, is open Sunday-Thursday 9am-6pm and Friday 9am-3pm, and costs NIS 10. The English descriptions are good enough, but some are amusingly mislabelled, like the "Parrotfish" that was actually a Nile crocodile. It's too dark to read about or see the butterfly display, and the halls and waters are murky. There is an impressive room of snakes (especially the African Python), and the little white rabbit in a cage outside is a nice touch.

Etzel Museum, *38 King George, Tel. 03-528-4001*, is open Sunday-Thursday 8:30am-4pm, and costs NIS 6 per adult, NIS 3 for students. This is yet another museum devoted to the I.Z.L., the Jewish underground organization active in Palestine from 1931-1948. The two floors of this museum provide a detailed history of the organization from the founding of the underground during WWI and the establishment of the Irgun under Avraham Tehomi in 1931, up until Nov. 29, 1947, when the Jaffa museum takes over. There are weapons, news clips, photographs, and models of clandestine immigration ships, detention camps in Africa, and gallows in Jerusalem and Acre. Of interest to a select set of visitors.

In the same building is the **Jabotinsky Institute**, *Tel. 03-528-7320*, displaying works relating to the life and times of Zeev Jabotinsky, an organizer in the Jewish resistance who was arrested with other Haganah members in 1920 and served time in the Acre prison after responding to Arab attacks in the Old City of Jerusalem. Open Sunday-Thursday 8am-4pm, and costs NIS 6, NIS 3 for students, but can be seen on the Etzel Museum ticket.

Museum of the I.Z.L., *Charles Clore Garden (on the way to Jaffa), Tel. 03-517-2044*, is devoted to the memory of Jaffa's liberation. Open Sunday-Thursday 8:30-4, adults pay NIS 10, children/students/seniors pay NIS 5, while soldiers and police enter free. This museum picks up where the Etzel Museum on King George leaves off. It covers the 1947-1948 years with a well-organized and one-sided presentation of the campaign to conquer Jaffa.

Haganah (Defense) Museum, *23 Rothschild, Tel. 03-560-0809*, is open Sunday-Thursday 8am-4pm, and admission is NIS 6 for adults, NIS 3 for children, students, seniors. Set up next to the old home of Eliahu Golomb (one of the founders of the Haganah), this museum is devoted to the history of the Haganah. Starting as far back as 1878, the museum follows the development of the Defense organizations, the people who led them, and the related activities of arms purchasing, training, and fighting.

The first floor is devoted to the early history from 1878 to 1939, the second floor deals with responses to the "White Paper" of 1939 that forbade Jewish immigration and promised Arab self-rule, and continues on through to "Black Saturday" in 1946, while the third floor focuses on the illegal immigration ships of WWII years through 1948 when Israel became a state and the Haganah emerged from the underground and became official. Though charged with the fervor of propaganda, the museum does a very good job of explaining the role and activities of the Haganah through the early pre-statehood days, complete with period pictures and dressed-up mannequins.

This is not a museum for everyone, however. You should come with a healthy interest in the topic and without small children. They also publish and hand out an informative pamphlet that explains the exhibits, a good thing since most of the picture legends are in Hebrew. It's neither as interesting as Independence Hall, nor as well organized.

Independence Hall, *16 Rothschild, Tel. 03-517-3942*, is open Sunday-Thursday 9am-2pm, Fridays by prior arrangement, and costs NIS 8 an adult, NIS 4 for soldiers, students, children, seniors. Once Meir Dizengoff's home and donated by him to the community to be used as an art museum in 1930 when his wife died, this house was chosen to be the site for the declaration of the establishment of the State of Israel on May 14th, 1948. In 1978, Independence Hall was opened to the public with the hall restored to its 1948 condition and lots of pictures to commemorate the event. Two other rooms document the founding of Tel Aviv, six months of bloodshed preceding the declaration, and the events immediately following the declaration.

It's interesting to see the stages of development as Tel Aviv grew from barren sand dunes to Israel's largest city, and the Independence documentation is also worth viewing for history buffs. They have pamphlets with the Declaration as well as Hatikva, the national anthem of Israel. You can ask for the recording to be played of the actual declaration (it's in Hebrew, but it gives a feel), and you also hear the rabbi bless and the anthem played. And that's not all. There is a 15 minute movie about the building of Tel Aviv that isn't bad.

Next door is the **Bible House**, *16 Rothschild, Tel. 03-517-7760*, open Sunday-Thursday 9:30am-1pm, housing a permanent collection of enamel paintings by Albert Dov Digal. **Founder's Monument** is near Independence Hall, and you'll see it as you walk toward Allenby.

Tel Aviv Museum of Art, *27 Shaul Hamelech, Tel. 03-696-1297*, is open Sunday-Monday, Wednesday-Thursday 10am-6pm, Tuesday 10am-10pm, Friday-Saturday 10am-2pm, and costs NIS 20 for adults, NIS 10 for children/soldiers, and NIS 15 for students/seniors. The large modern building is a full culture center. It houses permanent art exhibits such as 16th-19th Century European art, Impressionism and Post-Impressionism, an Edvard Munch collection, Modern Masters and more, as well as changing temporary exhibits. There is also a sculpture garden, the **Helena Rubenstein Pavilion for Contemporary Art**, *6 Tarsat, Tel. 03-528-7196*, which comes with the price of admission and exhibits international and Israeli works of art. In addition the museum hosts concerts, films, and lectures. The tourist office should have their monthly schedule, or call the museum office for details.

Bialik House, *22 Bialik, Tel. 03-525-4530*, is open Sunday-Thursday 9am-5pm, Saturday 11am-2pm, and admission is free. Chaim Nachman Bialik, 1873-1934, was a revered Hebrew poet. The museum was once Bialik's house; he lived there from 1925 until the end of 1933. After his death, his widow gave the house and its contents to the city of Tel Aviv, and they opened it to the public as a museum in 1937. It's a lovely house and it gives a strong feeling of times past. Wonderful pictures on the wall by Reuvin Rubin and Pinchas Litvinovsky, but unless you read Hebrew you won't get the full benefit of a visit as most of the exhibits are Bialik's original documents, written in Hebrew and untranslated. The museum does, however, hand out a pamphlet guide which describes the various exhibits and it helps a bit.

The **Rubin House**, *14 Bialik, Tel. 03-525-5961, Fax 03-525-4260*, is open Sunday-Monday, Wednesday-Thursday 10am-2pm, Tuesday 10am-1pm, 4-8pm, Saturday 11am-2pm. This museum, also free, showcases Rubin's life and his beautiful artwork.

The **Great Synagogue**, *Har-Sinai and Allenby*, is an enormous stucco structure outside, while inside is a lofty ceiling, stained glass windows, and not much decoration. It's a place of worship, not a place to go out of your way for casual sight-seeing.

Not too far away is the **Shalom Tower**, *1 Herzl and Ahad Ha'Am, Tel. 03-517-7304*. An enormous building, it's topped by an **observation tower** on the 34th floor (open Sunday-Thursday 10am-6:30pm, Friday 10am-2pm for NIS 7, or NIS 6 for students) which lets you see the whole bulky sky-scraper sprawl of modern Tel Aviv

Also there and worth a visit for kids and adults is the **Wax Museum**, *Tel 03-517-7304*, open Sunday-Thursday 10am-6:30pm, Friday 10am-1:30pm, and Saturday 11am-4pm, it costs NIS 15 for adults and NIS 12 for students, while the combo ticket for the two attractions costs NIS 19 for adults and NIS 14 for students. Past the cheesy arcade with remote control bumper cars and Hillbilly Moonshine Shooting Gallery (tokens for these delights cost NIS 2) is the wax museum, full of truly bad wax jobs of early pioneer Sarah Aaronson's suicide with blood running down her head, Rothschild tasting wine, Meir Dizengoff on what's meant to be a donkey, parasol pertly shading him from the sun, and, Topol pulling a cart singing "If I were a rich man...."

For lovers of camp, these sincerely intended tableaux of courage and pain top the charts.

Eretz Israel Museum

Eretz Israel Museum, *2 Haim Levanon, near Tel Aviv University, Tel. 03-641-5244*, is an enormous collection of small museums, pavilions, exhibits, and a planetarium attractively set on a big sweep of green lawns. The Museum Complex is open Sunday-Thursday 9am-2pm, Wednesday 9am-7pm, Saturday 10am-2pm. The Tel Qasile Pavilion is open Sunday-Thursday 9am-12pm, Wednesday 9am-12:30pm, and the Library is open Sunday-Thursday 9am-3:30pm. The entrance ticket can be purchased for the museum complex with or without planetarium admission, as follows: adults are NIS 25, students, handicapped are NIS 15, plus NIS 15 with planetarium. There are guided family tours available running 2-3 hours or a longer, more comprehensive tour. Call for details.

Tel Qasile Pavilion and Excavations, circa 12th century BCE, hold Israel's first archaeological dig (begun 1949) showing what was once a part of the Kingdoms of David and Solomon. There are clay-colored foundations, a reconstructed Dwelling House, and picnic tables. As the name indicates ("tel" meaning "hill") it's a slight climb to this one. The **Ethnography and Folklore Pavilion** is a worthwhile display with an engraved 18th century shofar, Polish cantor cup, and eastern European 18th and 19th century menorahs, dreydles, etc. There are Torah scrolls from around the world, items for various holiday functions, and elaborate marriage ketubahs from Italy and Iran.

This museum has a fine collection of some of Judaism's otherwise lost treasures. **Man and His Works**, open Sunday-Thursday 9:30am-1pm, Wednesday 9:30am-5pm, Saturday 10:15am-1:45pm has half hourly shows with men and women demonstrating ancient crafts. Especially interesting is the glassblower who does his stuff over a hot forge, turning molten glass into blue vases and such that can be purchased in the gift shop.

The **Holy Land Landscapes Park** has a flour mill, olive oil extraction plant, Garden of Jotham's Parable, Roads and Railways Site, and Sundial Square – not the most scintillating of exhibits, you might consider skipping it if you're running out of time. **Mosaic Square** has Byzantine 6th century CE mosaics. **Ceramics Pavilion** displays the history of pottery as well as exhibits like Neolithic hunting weapons, agricultural tools and Sumerian cuneiform clay tablets, plus two anthropoid coffins from Gaza and some interesting Chalcolithic Period ossuaries, and they have an English pamphlet that explains all. **Hunting Among the Dunes** focuses on prehistoric man and his weapons, especially the flints and arrowheads found by Felix Burian and Erich Friedmann in their research in the Western Negev.

Postal Philatetic Pavilion Kadman Numismatics Pavilion covers coins from medieval times through the modern era. If you're interested in coins, this display does a much better job of it than the museum in Jaffa. **Eretz Israel Library** has a large collection of English books on archaeology in Israel, Greece, Rome, Egypt, and Jordan; they're mostly in English and Hebrew though there are some in German and French. It's a peaceful, cool, quiet place to do extended reading on the Ancient Near East.

The **Lasky Planetarium**, *Tel. 03-641-3217*, is the only one in Israel, but right now the shows are only in Hebrew and Arabic. There are plans to start an English program, however, so ask about it before purchasing your tickets. The shows, one about UFOs and the other a simulated flight between the stars and planets, last 40 minutes. There are astronomy displays inside, also soon to be labeled in English.

Elsewhere in Ramat Aviv

Beth Hatefutsoth, the Museum of the Diaspora, *Tel Aviv University campus, Tel. 03-646-2020*, is open Sunday-Tuesday, Thursday 10am-4pm, Wednesday 10am-6pm, Friday 9am-1pm, and costs NIS 18 for adults, NIS

13 for children, students, seniors. This is an amazing place. One wing is devoted to temporary exhibits and the rest of the museum houses their permanent stuff: the study areas, films, and Genealogy center.

It's a wonderful museum, one of the best in Israel. There's an impressive display of Jewish Faces, "portraits from the four corners of the world," that shows changing slides of Jewish *punim* , all ages, expressions, and countries. As you walk through, these lit-up faces emphasize the world community. There are other interesting exhibits as well, such as circumcisions and their implements, prayer and holiday artifacts and customs (with excellent photos), and a video of Jewish weddings and their music from around the world. In the video rooms people sit with hearing horns cupped to ears (an entertaining sight in itself) watching films on Jews in Fez, Salonika, or Eastern Europe. In addition, there are study areas with private video booths. You can view short films (15-30 minutes) on Jewish life for NIS 5 a viewing token, or access the computer data banks for history of specific Jewish communities (2,500 on file) and origins and meanings of various Jewish family names (18,000 on file).

The **Genealogy Department** (open till 4pm) performs a variety of services for a variety of fees. You can get into their files for NIS 5, or you can enter your own family tree for $1 a name, minimum of 50 names (that's $50), and family tree software can be bought as well. And there's more. There's an extensive Jewish music center where you can listen to any of the selections, and a video library of ethnic music and customs you can watch.

Come early and full of energy because there's a lot to see and do, and it's presented more impressively than at most museums. It is also a fairly accessible and entertaining museum for children, more so than most. Guided 90 minute tours for groups (up to eight people) are available for NIS 60. Dan buses 49, 45, 27, 25, 24, 14 and Egged buses 572, 274, 86, 79, 74 all go there.

Tel Aviv University, with its pleasant campus, is a nicer setting for a green stroll than nearby **Hayarkon Park**, though the park does have a **Tropical Garden** and **Bird Safari**, *Tel. 03-642-2888*. For more verdant walks, the campus has its **Botanical Gardens**, *Tel. 03-545-0111*. **Apropo Cafe** has tables inside and out, and a selection of cheap snacks and meals. You can eat, refuel, and rest between museums for NIS 10 or so while hobnobbing with young intellectuals. See Diaspora Museum above for buses.

Ramat Gan

Harry Oppenheimer Diamond Museum, *Diamond Exchange, 1 Jabotinsky, Ramat Gan, Tel. 03-576-0219*, is open Sunday, Monday, Wednesday, Thursday 10am-4pm, and the entrance is around the back. Admission is NIS 10 for adults, NIS 5 for children, and NIS 6 for students, soldiers, seniors.

The museum shows mining photos and tools of the trade as well as jewelry and gems. While it might not sound that fascinating, a good tour guide makes for a much more interesting visit. The interactive section is only explained in Hebrew, another reason to get on a tour for this museum. The diamond cutting computer and robot technology, top in its field, is worth a visit. The **IDC** (**Israel Diamond Center**) offers free transport and tours of Jaffa and Ramat Gan, as well as their diamond jewelry retail outlet. *Call 03-575-7979 for details*, or call the museum and set up one of their tours.

Ramat Gan National Park, *Geah Road, next to the African Park*, is beautiful and green (at least in winter) with a pond, boats, tables for picnics, and paths on which to stroll.

African Park/Zoological Center, Geah Road, Ramat Gan, Tel. 03-631-2181, has hours that change with the seasons, open Saturday-Thursday 9am-2:30pm spring and autumn, 9am-5pm in summer, 9am-3pm in winter, and 9am-1pm Fridays and holiday evenings, and admission is NIS 22-27. You can visit for two hours after the entrance gate closes, but the lion area closes one hour after the gate closes. Located on a 250 acre site just next to the Ramat Gan National Park, there is an African drive-through area as well as an enclosed zoo that houses some 700 animals.

The African safari section is stocked with lions, hippos, white rhinos and an assortment of antlered, hoofed animals. In addition, the zoo has a monkey path, a birds of prey section, and a petting zoo for children. There is a shuttle bus for visitors, as well as a restaurant and snack bar near the lake. Come during the cooler hours for maximum animal viewing, as they rest during the heat of the day. You can get to the center on buses 30, 34, 35, 55, or 67. It's a bit out of the way for casual touring from Tel Aviv, but it makes a nice outing for kids.

To the northeast of Ramat Gan is the suburb city of **Bnei Brak**, not a stop on most tour itineraries, but an interesting neighborhood all the same. A smaller version of Jerusalem's Mea She'arim, Bnei Brak is a highly orthodox community, filled with large families following the religious, sartorial, and cultural traditions they brought from the Old World of Eastern Europe.

NIGHTLIFE & ENTERTAINMENT
Music & Discos
HA-KOSSIT, *5 Kikkar Rabin (off Frishmann and King George), Tel. 03-522-3244*, is a little tough to find since the name doesn't appear in English, but it's the only cafe at #5. Go upstairs for the blues and jazz, full bar, food

menu and smoky authentic atmosphere. The music quality varies, but it's a popular place with the casually trendy set. The music starts at 10pm, there's no cover charge, but the drinks are fairly pricy.

HOUSE ON 26, *26 Allenby, Tel. 03-517-7497*, charges NIS 30 admission Sunday-Wednesday, while Thursday-Saturday it's NIS 35. The music varies from alternative music, jazz, soul, to rap. It's a popular place, the lines start forming around midnight, and it gets going very late and stays going even later. Nearby is the **Lemon Pub**, *17 HaNagarim, Tel. 03-681-3313*, which is popular with a young crowd, has loud music and a gay night.

LOGOS, *8 Hashomer, Tel. 03-516-1176*, is off 14 Nahalat Binyamin, but the sign isn't in English. It's a friendly hang-out cafe with live music (jazz and blues) nightly and Friday afternoons. At night the music starts at 11pm and ends by 12:30am, so you need to be prompt to hear it, while on Fridays it starts at 3:30pm. This pub is held in high repute by Tel Aviv folk, and their bands are of good local repute.

SOWETO CLUB, *6 Frishman, corner of Hayarkon, Tel. 03-516-0222*, features reggae and African disco 6pm-4am Monday-Saturday, and in the summer, Sunday too. Cover is NIS 25-30. Inside it looks like a big multi-ethnic college party, with youths eyeing one another and dancing, and large colorful murals of Bob Marley and Peter Tosh looming up on the walls.

THE COLISEUM, *intersection of Ben Gurion and Hayarkon at Atarim Square, Tel. 03-527-1177*, is a round frisbee of a building where women enter for free, but men must pay NIS 30 for the privilege. There are white cushion benches to sit on and check out the huddled, horny bunches of men and women. With a slightly older crowd than other discos (late 20s and 30s), women jockey for position by mirrored platforms for dancing and posing. Upstairs, there are benches for sprawling, tables for tete-a-tetes, and a rail for the voyeurs from which to observe all the exhibitionists, pounding music, and people on the make below.

SHANBO and **JOSEPHINE**, *25 Lillenbloom, Tel. 03-510-6739*, are two discos, one downstairs and the other above. These two fairly new and much appreciated additions to the disco scene are open Thursday-Saturday 11pm-4am as well as 4pm-9pm Friday, and the cover is NIS 30-40. Shanbo on the ground floor plays rock music under muted colored lights. Murals and abstract Mexicans motifs on the walls add to the ambiance, while cement floors, rough walls, and funky design give it a different appeal than the posher upper level. Upstairs, Josephine plays House music in a more polished setting, with wood floors and carefully designed lighting, plus the same agreeable style of murals and paint. It's clear that a lot of thought and care were put into the design, the lights, and the decor, and it looks great. These discos cater to the 23 and older crowd.

While Lillenbloom isn't smack in the middle of downtown Tel Aviv, it's worth visiting if you want a dancing night out with the in-crowd.

CAMELOT, *16 Shalom Aleichem, Tel. 03-528-5222*, has the Back Room featuring live music, (usually rock, jazz, or blues) for roughly NIS 25 (depending on who's playing) from 9:30pm nightly. All the music lovers of Tel Aviv know to check the schedule (they're printed in Hebrew but the staff is happy to translate), and for the hottest performances it's a good idea to get there early to make sure you get a decent seat. The music room, downstairs from the bistro, is pretty small and gets clogged early with locals and their smoke.

Bars & Pubs

BAR YEHUDA, *90 Ben Yehuda, Tel. 03-527-3394*, is open Sunday-Friday 8:30am-2:30am, Saturday 11:30am-2:30am. They play mixed music, and serve very good roast beef and seafood.

LESSEL PUB, *113 Ben Yehuda, Tel. 03-523-7244*, is open daily 7pm-5am. Taking the place of what used to be "Cats," Lessel has reasonable prices, pleasant service, and laudable hummus and malawach.

LOT'S WIFE, *226 Ben Yehuda, Tel. 03-605-0896*, is open Sunday-Friday 11am until the last client leaves. They play the music of Stevie Wonder and such, and serve excellent goose liver paté.

MASH, *275 Dizengoff, Tel. 03-605-1007*, is open daily noon-4am. The acronym stands for More Alcohol Served Here, but they dish up a lot of burgers (NIS 17) and breakfasts (NIS 23 for the special), too. Popular with tourists, expats, and young Israelis, it's a cozy pub with a lot of dark wood, and good music that doesn't drown out your conversation. Happy hour 5pm-10pm takes 20% off already moderate drink prices, and credit cards are accepted.

SMOKING DOG, *138 Dizengoff*, has no English sign, but the weird picture of a dog smoking in the window is a dead giveaway. It's in with the moneyed, dreadlocks crowd, black leather jacket and lots of angst are de rigueur. It doesn't open till 10pm but stays open till 6am nightly, and draft beers cost NIS 8 for small and 11 for large. So cool it's palpable, the clientele sport scraggly hair, motorcycle helmets, and sullen intellectual looks while the high funk decor features exposed pipes and wires on the wall, crystal chandelier on the ceiling, and cigarette butts by the bucketful.

SHANBO PUB, *25 Lillenbloom*, has rock & roll Friday afternoon parties starting around 4pm. See description under Music section above.

Culture

There's more to Tel Aviv at night, however, than just rock & roll and booze. *Tel Aviv Today* (available at the Tourist Info office) has listings.

WHERE TO GET TICKETS

Tickets to many concerts and plays can be purchased at Castel, 153 Ibn Gvirol, Tel. 03-604-4725, Hadran, 90 Ibn Gvirol, Tel. 03-527-9797, Le'an, 101 Dizengoff, Tel. 03-524-7373, and Rokoko, 93 Dizengoff, Tel. 03-527-6677.

Dance

Ramada Continental, *121 Hayarkon, Tel. 03-521-5555, Fax 03-527-2576*, features folk songs and dance once a month at 8:30. There's **Israeli Folk Dancing**, *Ben & Jerry's, on the Promenade under the Ramada Continental Hotel*, Saturdays from 11am-3pm.

Mishan, *20 Mendele*, has ballroom dancing for senior citizens Tuesday, Thursday, and Saturday 6pm-8pm for NIS 12 per person. There's not a lot of decor, but everyone seems to have a great time. **Bikurei Ha'Etim Cellar**, *6 Heftman, Tel. 03-691-9510*, teaches folk dance Monday-Tuesday, Thursday-Friday at 9pm.

Theater & Music

Cameri Theater, *101 Dizengoff off Frishman, Tel. 03-524-5211*, provides simultaneous English translations for NIS 7 on Tuesdays. **Habima Theater**, *Habima Square, Tel. 03-526-6666*, is the site of Israel's national theater.

ZOA House, *1 Daniel Frisch, Tel. 03-695-9341*, puts on productions by the Yiddish Theater. **Israel Conservatory of Music**, *19 Strieker, Tel. 03-546-6228*, can advise on classical music options. **Beit Leissen**, *34 Weizman, Tel. 03-694-1111*, often has jazz, blues, and classical concerts.

The **Mann Auditorium**, *1 Huberman, Tel. 03-528-9163*, hosts the Israel Philharmonic Orchestra as well as musical troupes visiting from abroad. You can also call the Philharmonic's office, *Tel. 03-525-1502*. **Immanuel Church**, *9 Be'er Hofman, Tel. 03-682-0654*, often has classical music recitals.

The **Suzanne Dellal Center for Dance and Theater**, *Neve Tzedek Complex, 5 Yehieli, Tel. 03-510-5656*, hosts the Inbal and Bat Sheva dance companies for some extraordinary shows. **The Tel Aviv Performing Arts Center**, *28 Leonardo da Vinci, Tel. 03-692-7777*, houses the controversial new **Opera House**. **Tel Aviv Museum**, *27 Shaul Hamelech, Tel. 03-696-1297*, sponsors a variety of concerts, theater, and lectures.

The **Wohl Amphitheater**, *Yehoshua Gardens, Yarkon Park, Tel. 03-692-0487*, is an acoustic shell. They host performances of world famous artists as well as annual visits by the Israel Philharmonic Orchestra while the audience sprawls on the grass.

Tzavta Theater, *30 Ibn Gvirol, Tel. 03-695-0156*, has a Saturday morning Shacharit, their classical morning concert at 11:11am.

Movies
Dizengoff Center, *off Dizengoff and King George, Tel. 03-620-0485*, has seven movie theaters, and the **Opera Tower**, *1 Allenby, Tel. 03-510-2674*, has five cinemas.

SHOPPING

Tabak Oz, *6 King George, Tel. 03-528-1495*, in addition to the usual assortment of cigarettes and tobacco items, there is an amazing collection of tarot cards from around the world and dice too, interesting to look at, novel for souvenirs.

Nahalat Binyamin, *a block off Allenby*, has a street fair Tuesdays and Fridays from 10am-4pm , selling lots of unusual hand-crafted wares like jewelry, pictures, and Judaica.

Dizengoff Center, *off Dizengoff and King George*, is a big, modern mall with all the sorts of stores usually found in such establishments, and can be reached by buses 5, 61, 99. Tel Aviv chic is not cheap, so bring your credit card if you plan to shop. Along with the shops there are cafes, restaurants, and seven movie theaters.

Gan Ha'Ir, *71 Ibn Gvirol near Frishman, Tel. 03-527-9111*, is a new mall, a little less frenetic than Dizengoff, served by buses 8, 10, 24, 26, 29, and 32. It's got greenery, fountains, nifty elevators, air conditioning, and tons of stores in its City Garden Shopping Center.

There are a number of **Judaica** stores downtown selling menorahs, jewelry, mezuzzahs, and such, with prices and qualities varying. If you shop in them, it's a good idea to bargain. The **Opera Tower**, *1 Allenby, Tel. 03-510-7496*, also has three floors of shops, many selling jewelry, Judaica, and ceramics. In addition to the shops, they have cafes, restaurants, and five cinemas.

If you're looking for **oriental carpets**, northern Ben Yehuda (north of Ben Gurion) is the district. **Shuk Ha-Carmel**, *off Allenby*, is a lively street market full of inexpensive, fresh foodstuffs and cheap (in all senses) clothes. It can be reached by bus 4.

Bezalel Market, *near the corner of King George and Allenby*, is notable for its superb falafel stands (see Where to Eat section), and is also accessible from bus 4. Further south on the bus 4 route is the less touristed **Levinsky Market**, *near the central bus station*. Here are vast quantities of food – fresh, dried, and pickled.

SPORTS & RECREATION

The **beach** is where it's at in Tel Aviv on a hot summer day. *Hof* in Hebrew, the beach is full of shapely young and sagging old, picnicking families and ogling singles, all tanning, swimming, and playing the omnipresent paddle ball on a warm weekend. Most beaches have life-guards on duty till 7pm, but the flag system tells you what's what with the swimming: white means all is safe, red is a danger warning, and black means swimming is forbidden.

The most accessible (therefore most crowded) beach is just down from the Promenade. Starting at the seamy end of Allenby and getting posher as you head north to the beaches at the end of Frishman and Gordon, then further still to the Hilton and Sheraton beaches, they all have toilets, sand and sea, and are free. Further north beyond the city limits and towards Herzliya the beaches are cleaner and more sparsely populated, and that's where those with cars head.

Easier to get to but still more serene than in mid-city Tel Aviv are the beaches to the south. Bat Yam, a resort wanna-be, has clean beaches and less of a packed-out feel, and it's easily available on bus 10. Take care, however, with your belongings wherever you swim, as theft on the beach is brazen and frequent. From south to north, the following beaches all have lifeguards, First Aid stations, showers, and toilets: Givat Aliyah, Yerushalyim, Charles Clore, Frishman, Bograshov, Gordon, Hilton, Nordau, and Chof Hatzuk.

Gordon Swimming Pool, *Tel. 03-527-1555*, is a public pool next to Moriah costing $15 for a one-day pass.

Levian Club, *Herbert Samuel, Tel. 03-522-4079*, across from Rehov Daniel and next to the aquarium, is a wind surfing and sailing club on Dolphin Beach that rents equipment for NIS 45 per hour. They sell a card worth 10 hours for NIS 360.

Tel Aviv Marina, *Atarim Square, Tel. 03-524-9776*, has sail boards, wind surf equipment, and yachts for hire.

In addition there's **rowing** and **kayaking** on the Yarkon River, *Ussishkin Street, Tel. 03-642-0541*, from 9:30-6pm. Open daily 7am-7:30pm, they charge NIS 45-55 for rowing or pedal boats, NIS 65 per half hour for motor boats.

Sportek, *Rokach, Tel. 03-699-0307*, is at the northern end of the city. Admission is free to their sports fields, amenities, and jogging track. Nearby in the Hadar Yosef suburb are **tennis courts**, *69 Rokach, Tel. 03-641-7301*.

EXCURSIONS & DAY TRIPS

Tours

Free daily tours, *Tel 03-576-0211*, of Tel Aviv, Old Jaffa, and Ramat Gan are sponsored by **The Israeli Diamond Exchange Center**, leaving 10am-1pm or 2pm-5:30pm, they will pick you up from and drop you off at your hotel, show you the sights, and give you an opportunity to buy some diamonds. Ask you hotel reception or call to reserve.

Free Wednesday walking tours of Old City of **Jaffa** and its Flea Market meet at the Jaffa Clock Tower (bus 10 goes there) at 9:30.

SPNI, *3 Hashfela, Tel. 03-638-8674, Fax 03-688-3940*, is near the old central bus station and off Derech Petah Tikvah, between Harakevet and Hanegev streets – your first challenge and adventure is finding the office. SPNI offers wonderful nature hikes led by knowledgeable, personable guides all over Israel. Tuesdays they start a three-day Galilee and Golan tour for moderate-to-good hikers that costs $298, on Mondays (if the political situation permits) there's a wonderful day trip to Wadi Kelt Oasis and the Monastery of Saint George for $51. There are plenty more, and they're well worth the fees. Visit or call to arrange.

Neot Hakikar, *67 Ben Yehuda (down the walkway at the Neot Hakikar sign), Tel. 03-520-5858, Fax 03-522-1020*, specializes in Sinai tours (they were the first group to organize tours there), though they also go to Egypt (beyond the Sinai) and Jordan. You can arrange for a short trip (from Eilat) that in one day takes in St. Catherine Monastery (difficult to get to on your own) and Mount Sinai as well on the two-day jaunt (costing $55 for 1 day, $125 for two days, or $165 overnight in a hotel).

If you have the time and money, however, the four day trip lets the Sinai soak in (to your hair, your clothes, and your psyche) as you camp, jeep, and hike your way around St. Catherine's, Mt. Sinai, Colored Canyon, Dahab, and snorkel at the Blue Hole for $290 with an Israeli and an Arab guide leading the way. Or go for the Camel Safari (two days for $140) and learn more than you ever wanted to know about life aboard the desert ship. The tours are for the adventurous, those who like some organization but enjoy camping out in the desert under the stars.

Rent-A-Guide, *3 Hata'arucha Street, Tel. 03-605-8281, Fax 03-605-8606*, offers guided tours for small groups, taking in trips such as Jerusalem, Bethlehem and a kibbutz for $70, or Masada and the Dead Sea for $85.

Egged Tours, *59 Ben Yehuda, Tel. 03-527-1212, Fax 03-527-1229*, does big bus tours all over Israel, fueled by the attitude that since they're the biggest company in Israel, why be nice. They go everywhere and their prices are competitive with the other companies (it's government regulated), but their attitude (not regulated) is less attentive. They do schedule trips with greater frequency, however, so they might have what you want.

United Tours, *57 Ben Yehuda, Tel. 03-693-3412*, is another big bus line, but they're friendly and try to please. They do half-day Tel Aviv tours ($25) and trips to Jerusalem, Bethlehem, and Yad Vashem for $44, as well as other trips throughout Israel.

Travel Agents
International Student Travel Service - ISTS, *128 Ben Yehuda, Tel. 03-521-0555*, is open Sunday-Thursday 9am-7pm, Friday 8:30am-1pm. They issue student cards for NIS 55.
Mona Tours, *45 Ben Yehuda, Tel. 03-523-7103, Fax 03-523-2106*, is open Sunday-Thursday 9am-6pm, Friday 9am-1pm, and specializes in low airfares to Europe.

PRACTICAL INFORMATION
• **AACI: Association of Americans and Canadians**, *22 Mazeh, Tel. 03-629-9799*, are a good English-speaking resource to know about. Open 8:30am-4:30pm, they're set up for North Americans moving to Israel, interested in jobs and retirement. They also organize tours of Israel, social groups from scrabble to single mothers, list the cultural events of the city, and have an information bulletin board.
• **Books: Bibliophile**, *44 Ge'ula (near corner with Allenby)*, is open Sunday-Thursday 7am-6pm, Friday 7am-3pm (later in summer). Any paperback NIS 5, five books for NIS 20, or swap a book and get one for NIS 2.5. Surrounded by porno mags, it's not the best selection of books and they aren't in the best condition, but you can find some good literature if you take the time to search the seedy shelves. **Book Boutique**, *190 Ben Yehuda (near Arlozorov), Tel. 03-527-4527*, has a good selection, and a cheap clearance box. Open Sunday-Thursday 10am-7pm, Friday 10am-3pm, the books are in alphabetical order (a nice plus), and cost NIS 5-15, with half back when returned. **Books**, *48 Allenby (just down the street from Bibliophile)*, is open Sunday-Thursday 6am-6pm, Friday 6am-3pm (later in summer). Not a huge selection, they cost around NIS 4-7. **Katzman Gallery**, *152 Dizengoff, Tel. 03-523-5243*, has a large selection of used English books NIS 10-15, open 8am-8pm daily (sometimes closed at noon), and they will buy books for NIS 2-5. **Pollak's Used Books**, *36 King George, Tel. 03-528-8613*, has been buying and selling for over a century. They're open Sunday-Friday 9am-1:30pm, Tuesday 4-7pm. **Steimatzky**, *103 Allenby*, is open Sunday-Thursday 8:30am-8pm, Friday 8:30am-2pm and has new English books downstairs for lots of shekels.
• **Camping:** Supplies can be purchased at **Maslool Travellers' Equipment and Information Center**, *36 Ben Yehuda, Tel. 03-528-8418*, open Sunday-Thursday 7:30am-7:30pm, Friday 8am-3pm. **LaMetayel**,

Dizengoff Center, Gate 3, Tel. 03-528-6894, has the largest camping store in the area and is open Sunday-Thursday 9:30am-8pm, Friday 9:30am-2pm. **SPNI**, *3 Hashfela, Tel. 03-638-8729, Fax 03-383-940*, is near the old central bus station, off Derech Petah Tikvah, between Harakevet and Hanegev streets. They sell camping equipment and are a good source of camping advice as well.

- **Consulates: Australia**, *37 King Saul, 4th floor, European House, Tel. 03-695-0451*, is open Monday-Thursday 8-11am. **Canada**, *3 Nirim Yad Eliahu, Tel. 03-636-3300*, is open Monday-Friday 8am-noon or by phone 1:30-4pm. **Egypt**, *54 Basel, off Ibn Gvirol, Tel. 03-546-4151, Fax 03-544-1615*, is open Sunday-Thursday 9-11am. To apply for a visa, bring passport, and photo. Visas to the Sinai and to Egypt proper are now both free (but in May 1998 the visa may cost $15). **Jordan**, *14 Aba Hillel, Ramat Gan, Tel. 03-751-7722*, provides visas for crossing into Jordan via the Allenby Bridge. **South Africa**, *Top Tower, 16th floor, Dizengoff Center, Gate 3, Tel. 03-525-2566*, is open Monday-Friday 9-11:30am and Wednesday 2-3 pm. **UK** and **New Zealand**, *1 Ben Yehuda, Migdalor Building, 6th floor, Tel. 03-510-0166 for passports, Tel. 03-510-0497 for visas, Fax 03-510-1167*, is open Monday-Friday 8-11am. **US Embassy**, *71 Hayarkon, Tel. 03-519-7725, or after hours Tel. 03-517-4347, email: acs.amcit-telaviv@dos.us-state.gov*, open Monday-Friday 8-11am, mainly processes US visas and replaces lost passports, but you can also get up-to-date advice on political situations and safety.

- **Currency Exchange: Banks** are generally open Sunday-Friday 8:30am-12:30pm and an additional 4-5:30pm Sunday, Tuesday, and Thursday. There are banks all over, and especially on Ben Yehuda, but they all charge varying commissions and fees. Of the banks, **Hapoalim**, *104 Hayarkon*, and **Israel Discount**, *27 Yehuda HaLevi*, have the fairest rates, while **First International**, **Mitzahi**, and **Leumi** charge outlandish fees. **American Express**, *112 Hayarkon, Tel. 03-524-2211, Fax 03-523-1030*, open Sunday-Thursday 9am-5pm, Friday 9am-1pm, remains the best money exchange deal, charging no commissions on travel checks or cash. They also sell US cash for a 3% fee, arrange tours, and provide reliable mail service for AmEx card holders as well. For evening money needs, hotels change currency at night, though for higher commissions.

- **English-language News: Israel Radio**, 576 and 1458 kHz at 7am, 1pm, 5pm, and 8pm. **BBC**, 1323 kHz is on 2:15pm, 3pm, 6pm GMT. **Voice of America**, 1260, 15205, 15260, 9700 kHz is on 6am, 7am, 5pm, 5:30pm, and 6pm. **TV channel 1** airs news Sunday-Thursday 6:15pm, Friday 4:30pm and Saturday 5:30pm.

• **Ferries**: **Caspi**, *1 Ben Yehuda, Migdalor Building, Tel. 03-517-5749*, books ferries to Cyprus, and Rhodes for $53-$116, one way, leaving from Haifa.

• **Fire**: *Call Tel. 102* in case of emergency.

• **Help Lines in English**: **Drug Counseling**, *Tel. 03-683-6251*, is open 24 hours a day. **Eran Mental Health Hotline**, *Tel. 1201 or Tel. 03-546-1111*. **Gay and Lesbian Hotline**, *Tel. 03-629-2797*, is open Sunday, Tuesday-Thursday 7:30am-11:30pm, and Monday 7pm-11pm. **Rape Crisis Lines**, *Tel. 03-685-0041, or Tel. 1202 for emergencies*, are open 24 hours a day.

• **Jewish National Fund**: This prominent fund, *96 Hayarkon, Tel. 03-523-4449 or 177-022-3484*, is where to go if you want to have a hand in reforesting Israel, or want to plant a memorial tree. For $10 you can plant a tree at one of the planting centers, and in addition to the experience you'll receive a tree certificate and a lapel pin.

• **Laundry**: **Bu'ot**, *49 Sheinkin, Tel.03-629-2094*, will pick up, wash and dry, and deliver 6kg for NIS 24, folding NIS 4 extra, and ironing NIS 6 more. **Nikita**, *98 Ben Yehuda*, has NIS 8 coin-op machines for a 7kg wash, dryers for NIS 1 per 4 minutes, and detergent for NIS 2. And **Orly**, *81 Ben Yehuda, Tel. 03-522-5440*, is open Saturday-Thursday 8am-1am, closing a little earlier on Fridays. They have coin-op washers for NIS 10, dryers at NIS 10 for a half hour, and detergent for NIS 1.

• **Libraries**: **American Culture Center and Library**, *1 Ben Yehuda, Midgalor Building, 5th floor, Tel. 03-510-6935*, is open Monday-Thursday 8am-4:30pm, and closed all American and Israeli holidays. They have books on the US as well as out-of date American newspapers (New York Times, Washington Post, Wall Street Journal), journals, and a good selection of informational and literary videotapes for on-sight access. People with Israeli identity cards or immigrant documentation can get a library card (no charge) and check out up to four books. **British Council Library**, *140 Hayarkon near Gordon, Tel. 03-522-2194*, is open Monday-Thursday 10am-1pm, 4pm-7pm, and Friday 10am-1pm. Anyone may use the library but only council members can take books out. **Shaar Zion Public Library**, *near Tel Aviv Museum, Tel. 03-691-0141*, is open Sunday-Thursday 10am-7:45pm. There's a small selection of English books on Israel/Judaism topics upstairs and to the right in the Maimonides room. They also have a CD section.

• **Medical Aid**: In case of emergency, *call Tel. 101* for **Magen David Adom** (**First Aid**). For other medical help, *call toll-free Tel. 177-022-9110* or **SOS Doctors** *at Tel. 177-022-5005*. **INS Care**, *3A Nes Ziona, up from Hayarkon, Tel. 03-517-7222*, is open Sunday-Thursday 2pm-8pm,

Friday 10am-2pm and is a clinic to serve tourists. **Emergency dental,** *49 Bar Kokhba Street,* treatment is available on weekends and holidays.
• **Pharmacies: HaGalil Pharmacy,** *80 Ben Yehuda, Tel. 03-522-3358,* open Sunday-Friday 8:30am-8pm, specializes in homeopathic herbs and cures. **Merkaz Ha-tsafon,** *200 Ben Yehuda, Tel. 03-546-1684,* is open daily 8am-8pm,closing at 4pm on Fridays. **Superpharm,** *Dizengoff Center, Tel. 03-620-0975,* has more standard pharmacy products, and there are plenty more pharmacy branches scattered around Tel Aviv.
• **Newspapers:** *The Jerusalem Post* comes out daily, while *The Jerusalem Report* is published as a biweekly magazine.
• **Police:** *Call Tel. 100* in an emergency, or **Lost & Found,** *14 Ha-rakevet, Tel. 03-681-8107.*
• **Post Office:** The main branch, *7 Mikveh Yisrael, toll free number Tel. 177-022-2121, or 03-564-3651,* is two blocks east of Allenby, the south end, and is open Sunday-Thursday 7am-9:30pm, Friday 7am-noon. Here are poste restante services, *Tel. 03-564-3660,* as well as fax, telegram, and telex (open Sunday-Thursday 8am-10pm, Friday 8am-2pm). There are many branches throughout the city, and the one at *61 Hayarkon* does **Western Union** money transfers Sunday-Thursday 8am-6pm, Friday 8am-noon. Many other postal branches (*do'ar* in Hebrew) have fax and telegram services, though some close for a mid-day break. If you're an American Express card holder, their 112 Hayarkon office is more convenient and reliable as a mail drop.
• **Supermarkets: Supersol,** *79 Ben Yehuda,* is open Tuesday-Saturday 24 hours, on Sunday and Monday it closes at midnight **Supersol,** *Ibn Gvirol and Nordau,* is another. **The Co-op,** *basement of Ha-Mashbir department store, Dizengoff Center,* is open 7am-8pm. And there's another **Co-op,** *Ibn Gvirol,* near King Saul.
• **Telephone: Solan Communications,** *13 Frishman, Tel. 03-522-9424, Fax 03-522-9449,* is the most convenient and inexpensive way to make international calls in private booths. They're a discount service and are open 24 hours daily (after midnight the rates drop considerably and the people back home might be awake). **Directory Assistance,** call *Tel. 144,* and for changed numbers, call *Tel. 146.*
• **Tourist Information:** The new **tourist information office,** *New Central Bus Station, 108 Levinsky, Tel. 03-639-5660, Fax 03-639-5659,* is on the 6th floor near platform 630, and it's open Sunday-Thursday 9am-5pm, Friday 9am-1pm. To get there from downtown, take bus 4 from Ben Yehuda and Allenby or bus 5 from Dizengoff, heading south.

13. SOUTH OF TEL AVIV

JAFFA

Jaffa, or **Yafo** as it's known in Hebrew, was the original city of the Tel Aviv–Jaffa metropolis, the Arab community that spawned the suburb Tel Aviv in 1909. Now the roles have switched, and Jaffa is the small adjunct to modern Tel Aviv. It hasn't been engulfed, however, and one of the refreshing things about visiting Jaffa is that it really has a different feel from its big sister big city neighbor. The **Old City** is where most visitors head, and the reconstructed Kedumim Square is charming with its old houses, blue waters, and cobbled lanes.

Some say Jaffa was named after Japhet, Noah's son, who built it after the flood, while others hold out for the Hebrew *Yofi* (beauty) derivative. Originally a Phoenician city, Jaffa has had an active and productive port since 2000 BCE. The Egyptian Hyksos took over in 1472 and made Jaffa a provincial capital, but during the reign of Ramses II (1290–1224 BCE) the Philistines took possession. Joshua assigned the city to the tribe of Dan, but they weren't able to take control, and moved up north to Galilee instead. Meanwhile Jaffa remained in Philistine hands during the reign of King Jeroboam II (787–747 BCE), as reported by Jonah the Prophet, who is said to have boarded a Phoenician ship in Jaffa in order to escape to Tarshish.

In the 4th century Alexander the Great conquered, followed by Seleucid rule, but the Hasmonaeans weren't able to take it till 144 BCE. Roman Pompey captured Jaffa in 63, and its importance waned when the port of Caesarea came to be. Saint Peter spent some time here, but in 68 CE Jaffa was destroyed by Roman emperor Vespasian.

The Arabs conquered in 636 CE, and during Crusader times it was a main pilgrim port. Muslims captured it in 1268, and it was the site of many Muslim–Crusader battles. The Ottomans took control in the 1500s, the port regained its status, and it remained in Muslim hands (aside from a brief Napoleon occupation in 1799) till Allenby took it from the Turks in

1917. Conflicts intensified between the Arabs and the Jewish immigrants who had started arriving in the mid 1800s, and there were nasty anti-Jewish riots in 1929, 1936, and 1939. There was fierce fighting in the War of Independence in 1947–1948, and when the blood and dust settled on the Irgun victory, most of the Arabs fled town.

In 1950, Jaffa and its modern Jewish suburb Tel Aviv were incorporated into one city. And today, Jaffa now earns much of its keep from the tourist trade, both international and Israeli.

ORIENTATION

Just south of Tel Aviv and down the coast, **Herbert Samuel** merges with **David Razi'el** and becomes **Yefet**, Jaffa's central road, just before Jaffa's **Clock Tower**. Veering off Yefet towards the coast, **Mifraz Shelomo** takes you to the Old City with its sights and restaurants, and the Old Port south of that.

Further south on Yefet takes you to the Arab neighborhoods, with stores that are open on Shabbat.

ARRIVALS & DEPARTURES

By Bus

From the Clock Tower, the 46 bus goes to Bat Yam and the central Tel Aviv bus station. The 10, also from the Clock Tower, goes to Tel Aviv's City Hall. The 90 goes from the Dan Panorama Hotel northward towards Herzliya. Bus 25 also goes to Tel Aviv from the Flea Market, but it doesn't run after 9:30pm.

By Taxi

Taxis are easy to find around the Clock Tower.

By Foot

Instead of taking a bus you could take a long walk down Herbert Samuel south to Jaffa, and see the Aquarium and the Museum of the I.Z.L. along the way.

GETTING AROUND TOWN

By foot is really the best way to explore Old Jaffa.

WHERE TO STAY

OLD JAFFA HOSTEL, *8 Oley Tzion, Tel. 03-682-2370/03-682-2316; hard to find. Turn right on Omi'ad at the sign and go about 30 meters to the brass sign plate set in the ground outside the entrance. Dorm beds cost NIS 25, and private rooms are NIS 80-150.*

It's a lovely old building with nice old tile floors, fine views, and many extras. There's a cafe with funky, lumpy old couches upon which folks with messy hair write journals or play backgammon, a balcony overlooking the flea market, and happy hour from 6pm-11pm. The staff is friendly and there's no curfew.

WHERE TO EAT

SAID ABOU ELAFIA & SONS, *7 Yefet*, a block behind the Jaffa Clock Tower, is open 24 hours Monday–Saturday, and thronged with tourists clamoring for the legendary baked goods, especially the Arabic version of the pizza, with eggs baked on pita bread, plus extras. The style has caught on big-time, and now you see Elafia-alikes all over Israel. Jaffa's first bakery in 1880, it's still run by the same family (four generations later) dishing up pizzas, za'atar breads (a delicious middle eastern spice concoction baked with olive oil), and cheese or potato filled zambuska. Prices start around NIS 6.

HAZON RESTAURANT, Mifraz Shomo, serves grilled goods, shishkebab with salad and hummus for NIS 14. Or have some stuffed spleen gladly served by the French speaking owners from Morocco. For an off-the-track authentic meal, try the **NO-NAME STALLS** of wonderful, cheap food. *Turn down Mifraz Shlomo toward the water and turn left into the alley.* There old men are drinking coffee, playing backgammon, and solving the world's problems, past the sign for Hazan Restaurant to the end of the alley and turn left again for the stall of the French–speaking woman with simmering pots of goodness and fresh salads. There's rice with lentils, lamb stew, or turkey in sauce, with salad of radishes, cucumbers and spicy tomatoes (or whatever else has been cooked up that day) and all of it delicious.

DR. SHAKSHUKA, *Bet Eshel*, 03-682-2842, is just before Mifraz Shomo and away from the water to the east. It has good, inexpensive Libyan food for NIS 13-35. There's shakshuka, its namesake tomato and egg dish, and various couscouses. You can look at the pots and choose what you want, and after your meal, the almond tea is especially good as well.

ALADIN RESTAURANT, *5 Mifratz Shlomo Street, Old Jaffa, Tel. 03-682-6766*, is open daily 11am-midnight. In operation 20 years in this 800-year-old building that used to be a Turkish bath, and with a great view over the harbor, they are reasonably priced considering their location, with salads and savory pies NIS 11-24 and full entrees NIS 28-60.

LE RELAIS JAFFA, *13 Hadolpin, Tel. 03-681-0637*, is a fine French restaurant (not kosher) in a lovely 19th century building. Open for dinner Sunday-Thursday 7pm-midnight and Saturday 8pm-midnight, their appetizers cost around NIS 16–26, their entrees NIS 35–75, and their amazing desserts NIS 14-25. To get there from the Clock Tower, go down Yefet till you get to number 56 and turn right on Shaarey Nicanor, then turn right again on HaDolphin.

MARGARITE TIYAR has very, very good fish, and there are plenty of other fine places to eat, from hummus stand to French bistro, depending on how much you care to spend.

For ice cream, **DR. LECK** has a store *just before the Clock Tower.*

SEEING THE SIGHTS

Museum of the I.Z.L. in 1947-1948, *Charles Clore Garden, Tel. 03–517-2044,* on the way to Jaffa from Tel Aviv, is open Sunday–Tuesday 8:30am–4pm, and costs NIS 6 (adults), NIS 3 (children, student, seniors), soldiers and police free. The Irgun Zva'i Leumi (I.Z.L.) – The National Military Organization – was a Jewish underground organization from 1931-1948 that struggled against British policy and Arab terrorism before Israel declared independence as a state. In memory of Jaffa's Liberation, this museum is a well-organized and one-sided presentation of the campaign to conquer Jaffa during the War of Independence from November 29, 1947 to June 1, 1948, when the I.Z.L. was integrated into the I.D.F. (Israel Defense Forces). History of the I.Z.L. in its pre-1947 days can be seen in the I.Z.L. Museum at 38 King George, Tel Aviv.

The **Clock Tower** was built by the Ottomans in 1906 and it juts picturesquely from the northern entrance to the city, just past the end of Herbert Samuel Esplenade, making a useful navigational landmark. The free tour of Old Jaffa leaving Wednesdays at 9am meets here. Nearby is the **Al Mahmudiyya Mosque,** built in 1812 and open to Muslims only, it points to Mifratz Shomo, the street leading to the Old City.

Down from the mosque is **The Antiquities Museum of Tel Aviv– Jaffa,** *10 Mifratz Shlomo, Old Jaffa, Tel. 03–682-5375,* is open Sunday– Tuesday and Thursday 9am-2pm, Wednesday 9am-7pm, Saturday 10am-2pm, and is NIS 10 per adult, NIS 5 per student. This small museum exhibits items unearthed in local excavations, such as a 6,000 year-old skeleton, but devotes itself to coins. If you are interested in numismatics, don't miss this museum. From the Persian Period in 539 BCE, through Hellenistic and Herodian rule, Crusader coins to 19th century minting, the history of Jaffa is reflected in its coins.

In front of the museum are the **HaMidron Gardens,** a nice enough swatch of green with a view of Tel Aviv, though no big thrill. Behind the museum is **HaPisgah Gardens** with its small **amphitheater** and archaeological site featuring an excavation of an 18th century **Hyksos town.** The white statue is meant to show the fall of Jericho, the binding of Isaac, and Jacob's dream.

From the gardens a wood footbridge leads to **Kedumim Square** (*Kikkar Kedumim*), the reconstructed center of Old Jaffa, with winding stone alleys, restaurants, and clubs. In 1840 Jews opened a hostel with two mikvot (ritual baths) and a synagogue. The synagogue, *Mazal Dagim Street*, has recently been reopened by Libyan Jews. There's also an archaeological site with remains of 3rd century catacombs. Formerly Arab homes before the 1948 war, the stone houses became part of an artists' colony with lots of studios and galleries.

Within this complex are some religious buildings as well: the Greek Orthodox **Church of Saint Michael**, the Roman Catholic **Monastery of Saint Peter**, and the house of **Simon the Tanner**, *8 Shimon HaBurski*, the traditional site where the Apostle Peter was said to stay when he was instructed to preach to non-Jews (Acts 9:32–43). The house is at the bottom of an alley near the southern steps of the square. Out in the water near the lighthouse you can see **Andromeda's Rock**. This is supposedly where the Greek princess was rescued by Perseus, but it looks rather like a rock jutting out of the water.

Jaffa's **Shuk HaPishpeshim** or Flea Market, *southeast of the clock tower*, is justly famed, with alleys teeming full of stuff old and new, brass and rugs, music instruments and cheesy clothes, waterpipes, antiques, and you name it. It's a great place to wander about and maybe to buy, but you'll be dealing with some experienced bargainers.

Jaffa Port, *south of Ha'Aliy HaShuiya*, costs NIS 1 to see the fishermen mending their nets or setting sail as the sun sets. This port has been in business since Phoenician times, though it's been run by Egyptian, Philistine, Jewish, Hellenistic, and Roman hands since then.

And by the coast, the **Sea Mosque** is picturesque against the blue sky and sea, with its crumbling walls and flocks of seagulls.

NIGHTLIFE & ENTERTAINMENT
Discos & Oriental Music

Old Jaffa is pretty lively at night, though the venues keep changing. Try the **Caravan Club**, *Kedumim Square, Tel. 03-578-2811*, for their live bands and dancing. The **Metal Zone**, *Kedumim Square*, features heavy metal, and **Omar Khayyam** has live oriental music. **15 Yefet Street** has some discos as well that stay open late with modern and Turkish music.

Hazan Haltadash and **Kazerosa** are busy spots at night, and **Tuta**, *behind the police station west of the Clock Tower*, is hopping in summer. But what's hot one summer is old falafel the next, so trust the locals to point you to the happening scenes.

Theater

Hasimta Theater, *8 Mazal Dagim, Tel. 03-682-8729*, has shows and solo performances in a Cafe-Theater style. **Noga Theater**, *9 Jerusalem Blvd., Tel. 03-681-6433*, has classical music concerts and hosts the Israel Chamber Orchestra. **Immanuel Church**, *9 Beer-Hofman, Tel. 03-682-0654*, has **classical music** concerts.

SHOPPING

Yefet Street, *near the corner of Mifratz Shlomo*, has some very skilled **leather workers**, and the Old City is full of art galleries, jewelry, and Judaica.

For antiques, rugs, and the like, the **Flea Market** (see *Sights*) can be very rewarding.

PRACTICAL INFORMATION

- **First Aid**, *call 101.*
- **Fire Department** emergency number *is 102.*
- **Hot Line** for Jaffa City is *Tel. 03-523-8888.*
- **Lost and Found**, *24 Kibbutz Galuyot, call Tel. 03-681-8107.*
- **Police Station**, *Clock Tower Square, call Tel. 100.*
- **Tourism Office** can be reached at *Tel. 03-639-5660.*

BAT YAM

Just 5.5 kilometers south from Tel Aviv and Jaffa, **Bat Yam** is the butt of Tel Aviv folks' sneering jokes, similar to the condescension New Jersey enjoys from New Yorkers. The tourist office (yes, there is one) in Bat Yam will of course tell you differently. Is it a quiet, pleasant, uncrowded white beach alternative to hectic Tel Aviv, or is it typified by gold chain-wearing, shallow, conspicuous consumers? You can visit, play at being Solomon, and be the judge.

Bat Yam (meaning *Daughter of the Sea*) is a real sun and sand town, with a new promenade along the sea. The main strip is **Ben Gurion Boulevard**, running north and south along the Mediterranean, and that's where you'll find the bus stops, tourist office, hotels, and what there is to experience in the ever-changing nightlife scene.

ARRIVALS & DEPARTURES

By Bus

To Tel Aviv, bus 10 goes every 15 minutes from 5:20am-midnight while bus 18 goes every 5-10 minutes from 6:30am-midnight. To Jerusalem, bus 404 or 406 go hourly from 6am.

By Car

It's fairly easy to find on-street parking in Bat Yam.

By Taxi

Tel Aviv is only 5.5 kilometers away, and taxis aren't that expensive an option.

GETTING AROUND TOWN

The main strip by the beach is easily navigated by foot, bus, or car. There's not much travel that needs to happen between beach and hotel or beach and bus.

WHERE TO STAY

COLONY BEACH RESORT, *138 Ben Gurion, Tel. 03-555 1555, has 350 apartments for $70-$110 a studio and $90-$160 a two-room apartment.*

The apartments sleep two-to-four people, with double beds, mini kitchen, and phone with private number. There's also a health club, squash courts, pool (heated in winter), mini-market, post office, and more. Right on the beach, it's a self-contained holiday complex.

SUN HOTEL, *136 Ben Gurion, Tel. 03-553-2553, Fax 03-552-7796, charges $90 for singles and $110 for doubles, breakfast included, 15% higher in summer.*

A 12-story building with 280 rooms right on the beach, all have the full set of air conditioning, TV, and phone, and the hotel has a sports and spa facilities as well with a health club, sauna, swimming pool, tennis and basketball courts. In addition there is private parking and a shuttle to downtown Tel Aviv. It's a family-oriented hotel with activities for children, and the rooms are comfortable but have no balconies. There's a view of the sea, but it's no big thrill and you could just as well stay in Jaffa or Tel Aviv.

ARMON YAM, *95 Ben Gurion, Tel. 03-552-2424, Fax 03-552-2430, has singles for $57 and doubles for $67, including breakfast.*

Not the cleanest lobby in the world, the rooms are adequate but without balconies. It's not a luxury place, but all 66 rooms face the sea and have TV, phone, and air conditioning. There's a swimming pool across from the hotel.

HOTEL SHENHAV, *2 Yerushalayim at the corner of Ben Gurion, Tel. 03-507-5231, has 20 rooms with phone but no TV, for $50 a double.*

Spacious but spartan, and a little shabby, the rooms come with toilet and hand-held shower in the tub. Not the friendliest management, not much English spoken, and no credit cards accepted.

WHERE TO EAT

There are restaurants on Ben Gurion near the tourist office but they change hands and names frequently, and sometimes close up for the winter. There's Turkish food to be had, but the venues often change.

SEEING THE SIGHTS

The museums are open Sunday-Tuesday, 10am-1pm and 4pm-7pm, Friday 9am-1pm, Saturday closed.

Ben Ari Museum, *2 Ramat-Yosuf, Struma Street, Tel. 03-659-1140*, is an art museum with ever-changing painting exhibitions and no entrance fee.

Ryback Museum, *Ramat-Yosuf, Hadadi Street, Tel. 03-506-8645*, is smaller than Ben Ari, and its exhibits focus on Judaica, also for free.

Shalom Ash Museum, *48 Arlozorov, Tel. 03-506-4536*, is a memorial to and houses a collection of the novelist, and admission is free.

NIGHTLIFE & ENTERTAINMENT

As with the eateries, there are night spots open on Ben Gurion in the summer, but they change frequently and you'll just have to stroll the strip and see if they appeal. Or else hop a bus to Jaffa or Tel Aviv.

SPORTS & RECREATION

Model Beach, *off the promenade*, has lounge chairs (for hire) and changing rooms, showers and lifeguards (during summer). Adjacent to the beach is a large swimming pool (open during summer only) with three wading pools for children. There is also hang-gliding, and surf boards can be rented.

Country Club And Sports Center, Derekh Hakomemiut, Tel. 03-551-1246, Tel. 03-551-9561, is open 9:30am-6pm and has tennis courts as well as a sauna and massage room. There's a swimming pool, *Tel. 03-552-4316*, right on the beach but only open during the summer (it's part of the country club).

Holiday On Ice, *Derekh Hakomemiut, Tel. 03-552-6655*, is an ice skating rink that's open all year round.

PRACTICAL INFORMATION

Bat Yam Tourist Office, *43 Ben Gurion, Tel. 03-507-2777, Fax 03-659-6666*, is open Sunday-Tuesday 8am-3:30pm, Tuesday 8am-2pm and 4pm-7pm, closed Friday and Saturday.

RISHON LE-ZION

Site of the First Aliya to Israel and home to Baron Edmund de Rothschild's Carmel Winery, **Rishon Le-Zion** (meaning *First to Zion*) can hardly contain how proud it is of itself. Seventeen Russian and Rumanian families first pitched their tents on what is now Founders' Square on the eve of Tu Ba'av in 1882, and the community has grown to a city of some 200,000. If you follow their yellow-path walking self-tour, you pass a lot of Firsts.

The civic pride expresses itself in more than just a lot of plaques and memorials; this city is clean, the park is big and green, the *midrahov* (pedestrian walkway) is charming, and the city seems to welcome tourists out of more than just greed.

ORIENTATION

Southeast some eight kilometers and about 20-30 minutes from Tel Aviv, Rishon Le-Zion is now just part of the highway network and suburb sprawl surrounding the big city. **Herzl** is the main commercial town boulevard, with the **bus station** and the stores and the traffic.

From Herzl, **Rothschild** Street becomes a **midrahov** (pedestrian walkway) that goes up past the **City Park** through the heart of historic Rishon Le-Zion, ending at **Founder's Square** on what is **Pinsker** to the left and **Ahad Ha'Am** to the right. One block right of Rothschild is **HaCarmel**, running between Ahad Ha'Am and Herzl, is where the **Winery** is located (just near the corner with Herzl).

ARRIVALS & DEPARTURES

By Bus

The Dan 19 drops you on Herzl and Rothschild while the Egged 200 from Tel Aviv leaves every 20 minutes or so and stops at the bus station further down on Herzl.

By Car

You'll want to ditch your car once you get to the city, and parking isn't easy to find. There's a good, free municipal parking lot on the left–hand side of HaCarmel, just across from the Winery's old red buildings.

GETTING AROUND TOWN

To get around the center and see all the sites, going by feet is not only easy but necessary.

WHERE TO STAY

This is a day trip from Tel Aviv, so Tel Aviv or Jaffa is your best bet for accommodations.

WHERE TO EAT

The Rothschild **midrahov** has lots of cafes, and up above the walkway there are pizza slices, *burekas*, and shwarma fast food joints.

Perhaps the most popular in town is **KIOSK MADAR**, unmarked by any English sign but unmistakable thanks to the impatient queue of locals, *corner of Rothschild and Mohliever*. They serve good fresh falafel in a pita (with a little greenery and sauce but no choice of salads) for NIS 6, and they close around 1pm.

For a more special meal, go to **ROTHSCHILD'S RESTAURANT**, *Rothschild Street*, down four or so blocks from Herzl and on the left, next to the Burger Ranch; open daily 9am–midnight (closed 4–7pm), Friday–Saturday till 2am. It's the new, in spot in Rishon le-Zion, and the food is superb and very creative. The menu's in Hebrew but the staff speaks English, and there are lots of specials daily. Ostrich in blueberry sauce, smoked goose, Thai rabbit, or whatever other fancy the chef whips together is served in style in this small, cozy dining room with its green flowery tablecloths. There is, of course, quite a wine list, and the salads and desserts are outstanding. They aren't kosher, though no pork is served. The business lunch special is NIS 22–48, while dinners will run around NIS 100 with wine and all.

There's also a **BEN & JERRY'S**, *75 Herzl*, one block south of the bus station, open daily from 10am–midnight.

SEEING THE SIGHTS

The **Carmel Winery**, *25 HaCarmel near Herzl, Tel. 03-965-3662*, gives tours at 9am, 11am, 1pm and 3pm for NIS 12 per adult, NIS 10 for seniors, students or youth. The 17 minute audio visual show that comes with the tour is seen through 3D glasses, with grapes just leaping off the screen, in a cavernous room with old wood tables, stone walls, and a pleasant wine smell. If you come in harvest season (August-October) you can actually see the presses working. You get shown all the relevant wine-making rooms and get to sample all the wares.

The **Museum Rishon Le-Zion**, *24 Ahad Ha'am at Rothschild, Tel. 03-964-1621*, is working jointly with the Winery, and an entrance ticket from one gets you admittance to the other. The museum is open Sunday, Tuesday-Thursday 9am-2pm, Monday 9am-1pm and 4-8pm, and the first Saturday of the month from 10am-2pm it's not only open but free as well. Otherwise, it costs NIS 8, or NIS 6 for students and youth.

And then there's the **Freedom Trail**. Starting up at Founders' Square and taking you up, down, and around the sights following a painted yellow trail, you end up back at the Museum at Founders' Square. Along the way you see the **Great Synagogue**, built in 1885 after a permit was granted from the Turks through a bribe and a lie (the building permit was for a "warehous"). There's the **Village Well**, funded by the Baron Rothschild (and now a swank cafe), the home of **Zeev Abramovitch** and the first Flag of Israel, the **Hatikva House** (where Naftali Herz Imber wrote the National Anthem), and many more stops.

NIGHTLIFE & ENTERTAINMENT

The **Annual Wine Festival** takes place during the holiday of Sukkot (usually in September), with lots of wine (of course), dancing, music, and performances throughout the town and in the streets.

SHOPPING

The souvenir of choice here is wine, available at the **Winery** or at **Sokolik**, *across the street,* Tel. *03-964-1343.*

SPORTS & RECREATION

There's an **amusement park** not far from here, out on the sand dunes between Rishon le-Zion and Bat Yam, called **Superland** that is open in summer and very popular with kids.

PRACTICAL INFORMATION

There's no Tourist Information as such, but the folks at the **Museum**, *24 Ahad Ha'am at Rothschild,* Tel. *03-964-1621,* can answer most questions you have about the city.

RAMLA

With a population barcly over 50,000, Ramla's a one-horse town with a nice combination of small-town dusty charm, good food, and walkable sights. The only town in Israel founded and developed by Arabs, Ramla lay on an important trade junction, a meeting point between Egypt, Baghdad, and Damascus, with roads converging from Jaffa, Jerusalem, Haifa and Be'er Sheva.

Founded in 716 by Umayyad Caliph Suleiman ibn Abd el-Malik, Ramla replaced nearby Lod as the capital of Filistin (Palestine) with magnificent palaces and mosques. In the 8th century Ramla attracted a lot of Sunni and Shi'ite Muslims and Karaite and Rabbinical Jews. The party ended with nasty earthquakes in 1033 and 1067, and when the Crusaders arrived in 1099 they found a lot of ruins. They built a church of Saint John (now the **Great Mosque**) as well as the **Monastery of Nicodemus**, after which pilgrims stopped off on their journeys from Jaffa to Jerusalem, and a small community of Christians has remained.

Divided into Muslim and Christian sectors by a treaty between Richard the Lionhearted and Saladin, the Franks ruled until 1268 when Sultan Baybars conquered. The Mamluks built a mosque (the **White Tower**) on the site of Caliph Suleiman's old palace. Christian monks came back in the 14th century, and by the 17th century the town began to decay. After Israel won independence in 1948, most of the Arab community was replaced by Jewish immigrants.

Today it's an attractive small town, if lacking in the grandeur it must once have had, with parks and eucalyptus trees, old stone buildings and fine baklavah, and a festive Thursday market.

ORIENTATION

Ramla lies southeast of Tel Aviv along route 44. **Rehov Herzl**, running north–south, is the main street in this small town. The northern end is where you exit to Tel Aviv, Ashdod, etc., and at the opposite end is the **bus station**. Heading north from the bus station you'll pass shwarma stands on your right across the street from the **Great mosque** and a **park** with nice trees and benches.

Further north past the park and heading west is **Ze'ev Z'abutinski**, the **market** (*shuk*) street that is blocked to traffic till 7pm, and one block north of that is **Kehlat Detroit**, home of Chalil Restaurant and further west across the street, Calypso Dance Hall.

Back on Herzl heading north, a mosque (closed) is on your left and past that a church (corner of Bialik). Go north another street and you come to Danny Moss street, which you can follow west to the tower. And north another block on Herzl but on your right is **Haganah**, where you'll find a park, the **Pool of Saint Helena**, and the end of town.

ARRIVALS & DEPARTURES

By Bus

Egged 411, 451, 452, and 455 all take you from Tel Aviv to Ramla and drop you at the bus station on the southern end of Herzl 35-40 minutes later.

By Car

Ramla is a straight shot southeast on route 44 from Tel Aviv. You'll enter town from the south on Herzl, and should park on the street anywhere past Danny Moss so you can explore on foot.

WHERE TO STAY

This is a day trip from Tel Aviv, so Tel Aviv or Jaffa is your best bet for accommodations.

WHERE TO EAT

Grazing up and down the *shuk* is my advice, but if you want to sit down or don't find yourself here during market hours, **CHALIL RESTAU-RANT**, *Kehilat Detroit*, open 8am-8pm, is another option. There's mounds of hummus for NIS 8, a kebab for NIS 18, shishlik for NIS10, or fish for NIS 30. It's one street over (and parallel) to the market by the yellow sign of a leaping dolphin, before the Calypso Dance Hall. Inside is a plain room with tables and good, simple arabic food.

Back along the *shuk*, there are stores selling dripping good baklavah for dessert.

SEEING THE SIGHTS

The *shuk* is one of best reasons to come to Ramla on Thursday (the big market day), especially if you come with a healthy appetite. All sorts of good food is for sale for practically nothing. 3 NIS gets you a small cup of ful beans with spices sprinkled on top. A terrific cheese burekas with a hard-boiled egg added is sold for NIS 3.5, and fresh made lemonade is ladled using a bottle with a hole in its bottom for NIS 2. And all the friendly conversation, besides, for free.

The **Great Mosque**, *Tel. 08-922-5081*, open Sunday-Tuesday 8am-11am, also known as El Jami'a el-Kabir, was once the Crusader Cathedral of St. John. To the west of the bus station off Shlomo Hamelekh (near the market), the white minaret makes a good landmark. The mosque is one of the better preserved examples of medieval architecture, with vaulted arches and more, and donations are appreciated.

The **Church and Hospice of Saint Nicodemus and Saint Joseph Arimathea**, *fronting Herzl and Bialik, with the entrance off Bialik*, is a big square stone complex. Ring the bell to get a monk to let you in. Christians believe Ramla was ancient Arimathea, home of Joseph who arranged with Nicodemus for Jesus' burial. The church was built in the 1500s, though it was refinished in 1902. Napoleon stayed, and the monks are generally happy to show you where he slept. The church is open Monday–Saturday from 8am–11:30 and admission is free.

The **Tower of the 40 Martyrs**, *end of Danny Moss on the left*, was built in 1318 as the minaret for the 8th century Jami'a el Abyad Mosque, since destroyed. It was built by the Sultan Baybars on the site of the Caliph Suleiman's old palace, but all that's left now is the tower and some crumbling walls. Sometimes called the **White Tower**, it is majestic by daylight and eerie by moonlight. The gate around back is open so you can stroll around the tower and the old, cracked walls. There's meant to be a guard who can let you climb up for the view, but the tower gates are all locked solid, and the safety of the old stairs is in question.

Further north, on the eastern side of Herzl, is Haganah, the road leading to a park and gardens and the **Pool of Saint Helena**. These underground pools, called the 'goat pools' by the Arabs and 'lake of the arcades' by the Jews, were started by Suleiman and finished in 789 by Caliph Harun el–Rashid, better known from *A Thousand and One Nights*. Christian pilgrims in the Middle Ages renamed them St. Helena after Byzantine emperor Constantine's mother.

Two kilometers to the east of Ramla is a **British War Cemetery** for those who died battling the Turks.

NIGHTLIFE & ENTERTAINMENT

On Thursdays the **market** is entertainment enough until it shuts down around 7pm. If you're adventurous and dressed up you could join the frolic in the **Calypso Dance Hall** , *Kehilet Detroit*, down on the right side. If you're with someone special, take a walk down Danny Moss and snoop about the **Tower of the 40 Martyrs**. Or hop a bus or car back to Tel Aviv.

EXCURSIONS & DAY TRIPS
LOD

Lod, just northeast of Ramla, is best known as the home of **Ben Gurion Airport**, but it did exist before airplanes. In fact, it goes back to biblical times and was allotted to the Tribe of Benjamin when the Israelites occupied the land. Aside from the airport, the main draw here is the Church and burial site of St. George (the dragon slayer and patron saint of England). After a checkered past involving the usual smatter of Assyrians, Greeks, Hasmonaeans (under whom it was the seat of the Sanhedrin for a while), it became the capital of the Roman toparchy in 67 BCE, known as Diospolis, and later became Georgopolis under the Byzantines, who went along with the legend that the saint was born here.

The **Tomb of Saint George** has been displayed here since the 5th century, and the Church of St. George was rebuilt in 1870 on the 6th century Byzantine church foundations. Not usually open, you'll need to find a caretaker to let you in. Between two Frankish columns inside is a staircase leading down to the crypt with St. George's sarcophagus, which was restored in 1871 and depicts St. George on the lid.

Two kilometers north on Lod's main street takes you to the country's oldest bridge still in use. On your way there you'll go through an industrial section, past a gas station on your left and a turn-off for Yagel and Zetan. Follow the road as it turns right across the Ayalon River and you've reached the **stone bridge** built in 1273 by Mamluk Sultan Baybars on Roman foundations from Crusader church stones. The two lions (Baybars' heraldic animal) are copies of those found on the Lion Gate in Jerusalem, and frame an Arab inscription blessing Allah and the "great Sultan el Malek ed-Dahar Ruh ed-Din Baybars" who ordered the bridge be built. If you're traveling by bus, you can catch one here to Tel Aviv.

REHOVOT

It's a specialty sort of destination, but a mid-day visit to Rehovot's **Weizmann Institute** can be an interesting side trip. Rehovot itself (the names means *expanses* and comes from Genesis 26:22), a town of over 90,000, was established 1890 by Polish Jews, but it's the Institute people come for; that and the lovely gardens.

ORIENTATION

Southeast of Tel Aviv and just a bit further south than Rishon Le-Zion, the Weizmann Institute is at the north end of **Herzl**, the city's main avenue, a 20 minute walk from the **bus station** on Bilou.

ARRIVALS & DEPARTURES

By Bus
The 200 and 201 from Tel Aviv (or from Rishon Le–Zion) leave every 20 minutes or so for NIS 9.5 and stop just 30 meters from the Weizmann Institute Gate.

By Car
About a 40 minute drive from Tel Aviv, it's just a bit south of Rishon Le-Zion.

WHERE TO STAY

THE MARGOA, *11 Moskowitz, Tel. 08-945-1303, Fax 08-945-1236, has 17 rooms for $45 a single and $55 a double, breakfast included.*

WHERE TO EAT

Herzl is where you'll find the falafel stalls and, further south away from the Institute, a bunch of spicy Yemenite restaurants, while the fruit and vegetable market is on Bilou. There's also a decent self-service place near the Weizmann House.

SEEING THE SIGHTS

The **Weizmann Institute of Science**, *Tel. 61-009-6111 (toll-free)*, and Weizmann House are open Sunday-Tuesday 9am-3pm for NIS 10 with half-hourly tours, and the special documentary film at the **Wix Auditorium** is shown Sunday-Tuesday 11am-2pm. The **Visitors' Section** in the Stone Administration Building on the left from the main gate has maps as well as brochures on the ongoing institute projects, such as cancer, aging, and the environment. Dr. Chaim Weizmann was Israel's first president as well as a research chemist, and he sparked the development of a fine scientific institute. He found a new way to produce acetone during WWI, greatly aiding the British war effort, and helping to influence Balfour's 1917 Declaration promoting a Jewish National homeland.

The grounds are gloriously landscaped and irrigated, encompassing the institute as well as **Weizmann's House**, *08-934-3230*, in which he lived from 1937 and during his presidential years. He's buried near the house, and by the main institute entrance are the **Weizmann Archives**, with his papers and letters.

The **Ayalon Institute**, *Givat Hakibbutzim, Kiryat Hamada, Tel. 08-940-6552*, was the largest munitions factory supplying clandestine military activities from 1945-1948. Underground literally as well as figuratively, the openings were camouflaged by a bakery and laundry while over two million bullets for the Sten sub–machine gun were manufactured below Kibbutz Hill. Now a museum, it's open daily 8:30am-4pm, and costs NIS 14 for adults, NIS 7 for children, and NIS 8 for seniors and students. Guided tours leave every hour on the hour.

ASHDOD

South about 40 kilometers from Tel Aviv, **Ashdod** is Israel's newest port set near one of Israel's ancient cities. With a huge industrial complex, a busy beach, and excavations of past glories, Ashdod has attractions to offer but isn't everybody's cup of tea.

Whatever you think of its present condition, it had a powerful past. Joshua never conquered Ashdod, and it was to Ashdod that the Philistines ran off with the Holy Ark. Along with Gath, Gaza, Ekron, and Ashkelon, this was one of the five great Philistine cities.

The whale spat Jonah out near here, and the Fatamids built a mighty fortress. But now the city gets power from other sources, producing half of Israel's electricity. The modern industrial city was established in 1957, and its newly refurbished port steals business from Haifa, and ruined the port in Tel Aviv. With a population close to 90,000 and growing, Ashdod is one of the major Jewish immigration absorption centers.

ARRIVALS & DEPARTURES
By Bus
From Tel Aviv, the 312 and 314 leave every 10-30 minutes till 9:50pm. From Ashkelon, take the 15, leaving every hour or so.

WHERE TO STAY
MIAMI HOTEL, *12 Nordau, Tel. 08-852-2085, Fax 08-856-0573, has 24 rooms, all with air conditioning, heat, radio, and phone, costing $50 a single and $70 a double (breakfast included).*
The hotel features parking and a disco.
ORLY HOTEL, *22 Nordau, Tel. 08-856-5380, Fax 08-856-5382, is your other option. They have 42 rooms with air conditioning, heat, and phone that cost $60 a single and $80 a double, with breakfast.*

Unofficially, you can also sleep on the beach if you care to. There are showers and no one says you can't.

WHERE TO EAT
There are a number of falafel stands around, and a stretch of bars and cafes along Lido Beach, but nothing to get worked up about.

SEEING THE SIGHTS
Mehov Ashdod Reserve sits at the northeastern entrance to the city. The white acacia trees give a semblance of Africa, but the wildlife (rabbits, turtles, and deer) wont make your heart skip.

The **Ashdod Yam Fortress**, built in the 6th century, was part of Azotos Paralos. Making its mark on the ancient Madaba map as an unfortified city, it had its moment in the sun during the Byzantine-Muslim era, and the remains of the Fatamid fortress are part of a slew of Muslim fortresses. Arab documents tell of Byzantine ships that used to pull in to port to sell back Muslim prisoners to their families. As boats were spotted, the fortress would send up smoke signals so the people could start gathering their goods to pay for their return. Bus 5 will take you south to the entrance to the fortress.

Southeast of the city is **Tel Ashdod**, the site of the ancient city, with 23 levels of standard looking rubble and ruin. Excavations go on, but right now if you're not an archaeologist there's not that much to see. At the end of Ya'ir Street and next to the lighthouse in the northern part of the city is **Giv'at Yona**. This, according to Muslims, is the place where Jonah was delivered from the whale's maw. It also provides a swell view of the city.

NIGHTLIFE & ENTERTAINMENT

There is a beach, **Hof Lido**, but its Mediterranean pleasures are dwarfed by the ship cargo industry that surrounds it. Every Saturday there's Israeli **folk dancing** from 5-8pm at Lido Beach.

SHOPPING

Lido Beach has a **Flea Market** every Wednesday from sunrise to sunset, with the usual interesting mix of junk and gems.

PRACTICAL INFORMATION

Next to the bus station, **Tourist Information**, *the Municipal Building, Tel. 08-854-5481*, will be happy to give you one of their whale-sized maps of the city.

There's a **Steimatsky book store** next to the bus station, too. The **post office** is on the main street, *Shavei Tzion*, as are some falafel stalls.

ASHKELON

Beloved by Israelis for its sandy beaches, there's plenty to visit and like here, but few lodging options. And if you just want beaches, the ones up north are more accessible. There's interesting history here, however, and lots of excavations, and if you want a place to combine archaeology with beach bumming, **Ashklelon** fits the bill.

As with much of this country, Ashkelon changed hands frequently, playing musical conqueror. It was one of the big five Philistine cities, their hero Goliath is said to have been born not far away, and the conflicts between Philistines and Israelites were incessant. It was an important caravan stop on the Via Maris trade route between Syria and Egypt, and as such had a guaranteed income and was a desirable location.

The Romans built many buildings, as was their wont, during their period of control. Believed to be the birthplace of Herod the Great, he put a lot of effort into embellishing the town. The Muslims valued the town as well, calling it The Bride of the East, and before Sultan Baybars destroyed all in 1270 there were many Crusader versus Muslim battles.

Now a city of some 75,000 Israelis (the Arabs from before the war having become refugees in nearby Gaza), Ashkelon is a modern city with a strip of shiny sand and lots of excavations highlighting the past.

ORIENTATION

Located 56 kilometers south of Tel Aviv but only 15 kilometers south of Ashdod, Ashkelon has a lot of spread out neighborhoods for a relatively small city. The bus station is in the new commercial center of **Afridar**, as is the tourist office and **Zephaniah Square**.

Migdal, east of Afridar, is the old Arab neighborhood. It's less polished and more interesting, with the fruit and vegetable shuk and falafel stalls off **Herzl**, and clothes and jewelry stores as well.

Hatayasim is the coastal road, not far east from the beach promenade, and the location of one of Ashkelon's hotels. **Ben Gurion**, another main road running east-west, has the bus station and municipal building, and is south of Afridar. And the **National Park**, with camping and ruins, is way to the south on the beach.

ARRIVALS & DEPARTURES
By Bus
The bus station, *Ben Gurion, Tel. 07-675-0221*, is about 25 minutes walk from the beach. The information booth shuts down for rests Sunday-Tuesday 9-9:30am and 5:30-6pm, Friday 9-9:30am and 12:30-1pm, but the electronic bulletin board needs no such breaks. To go to (or from) Tel Aviv, take bus 300, 311, or 362, leaving every 20 minutes till 10:30 and costing NIS 18. For Jerusalem, take the 437, leaving every hour till 8:30pm and costing NIS 21, and for Be'er Sheva the 363 or 364 will take you hourly till 9:15pm for NIS 20.5.

By Sherut
Sherut taxis, *Tel. 07-675-0334*, to Tel Aviv (NIS 13) are operated by Yael Daroma on Tzahal in Midal.

By Car
Plan a drive of 45 minutes to an hour, depending on traffic.

GETTING AROUND TOWN
By Bus
City bus 5 goes downtown to Zephaniah Square in the business center of Afridar and to the midrahov in the Migdal area, bus 6 (and 13 in the summer) goes to the entrance of the National Parks, the beaches, and on to Midgal, and buses 4 and 7 go to Midgal as well.

WHERE TO STAY
SHULAMIT GARDENS, *Tel. 07-671-1261, Fax 07-671-0066, is a big complex with 260 rooms, all graced with phone, TV, radio, air conditioning and bath, costing $145–$195 a single and $170–$220 a double.*

The hotel has a synagogue, pool, tennis courts, and disco.

SAMSON'S GARDENS, *38 Hatamar, Afridar, Tel. 07-673-4666, Fax 07-673-9615, has 26 rooms, all with phone, radio and air conditioning, which cost $40–$50 a single and $50–$60 a double, breakfast included, but 15% service charges.*

There's free **camping** elsewhere in Ashkelon National Park, that is if you have your own tent and don't need toilets or showers. Camping on the beach is very risky and not recommended. There have been a lot of sad stories of thefts and worse from beach campers.

The Tourist Office can arrange rooms in **private homes**, usually for about NIS 55–65, no meals included.

WHERE TO EAT

In Afridar there are plenty of cafes overlooking the green at Zephaniah Square, but Midgal is the best place for cheap good food; look for the unmarked small Moroccan restaurants.

There's an outdoor *shuk* on Remez in Migdal (open Monday 6am–1pm, Wednesday 6am–9pm, Thursday 5:30am–9pm) between the Migdal stop the mosque. There are some tasty falafel snacks there as well for pittance.

CASSE CROUTE TUNISIEN, *31 Herzl*, on the midrahov serves Tunisian baguettes stuffed with tuna, capers, spicy sauces and salads, lemon, and olives, making a fine meal. **NITZAHON**, *on Herzl, across from the post office*, is an Ashkelon standby for grilled meat and stuffed cabbage.

There's a snack bar and some restaurants in Ashkelon National Park with shishlik and the like for NIS 13.

SEEING THE SIGHTS

The **National Park**, *Tel. 07-673-6444*, open daily 6am–9pm in summer but closing at 4pm in winter (and an hour earlier on Fridays), charges NIS 15 per car, and you'll get a good map with your ticket. Often quite crowded on weekends thanks to its beachside location, you'll find here excavations of the remains of all the civilizations that have held sway here over the years, starting with the Canaanites 4000 years ago within the 12th century Crusader city walls. In the southwest the Tower of Virgins and Tower of Blood have collapsed onto the beach despite their elegant names.

At the bottom of the cliffs you can still see parts of the old sea walls. The oldest section is between the two parking lots, with layers of civilizations etched in the cliff from the Middle Bronze Age 4000 years ago on up to the Romans, and it can be seen well from the beach. The quadrangle in the center of the park has Roman columns and some wonderful **pillar reliefs** of Nike (the winged victory goddess) and the goddess Isis with child-god Horus. Made of Italian marble, they were carved sometime between 200 BCE-100 CE.

Outside to the north of the park is a **Roman tomb** for a rich Hellenistic 3rd century family, and inside are some well-preserved Greek mythology **frescoes**. It's open Sunday-Friday 9am-1pm, Saturday 10am-2pm, admission free.

In Migdal is **Kikkar Ha'Atzma'ut** (Independence Square) where Israel's declaration of independence was first read out in 1948. The **Ashkelon Museum**, *Tel. 07-672-7002*, is open Sunday-Tuesday 9am-12:45pm and 4-6pm, Friday 9am-12:45pm, Saturday 10am-12:45pm, and admission is free. It shows the history of Ashkelon, including a picture of the historic declaration reading. In back of the museum is the now closed **Khan mosque** and a courtyard.

In Afridar, the **Antiquities Courtyard** houses two old Roman sarcophagi. It's open Sunday-Friday 9am-2p, and admission is free.

The **Byzantine Church** ruins in Afridar on Zui Segal are from the 5th or 6th century. There's a **mosaic floor** nearby from the same period, and some marble pillars on the ground.

NIGHTLIFE & ENTERTAINMENT

Bustan Ha–Zeitim campground in the National Park has the **Tough Wood** cafe and disco in a huge tent over a marble dance floor. Open Thursday-Saturday 10pm-late.

In Afridar, try **Signon Pub**, a local favorite. Open nightly 7:30pm-2am, they've live music Tuesdays and Thursdays and karaoke on Wednesdays. Also on Zephaniah Square is **Ha-Sha'on Pub**. Open nightly 8pm-2am, they dish up good music and cheap beer.

And in Migdal, the **Kaphiterion Pub**, *Khan building, Ha'Atzma'ut Square*, is open weekends 9pm-whenever.

EXCURSIONS & DAY TRIPS

South a few kilometers along route 4 is **Yad Mordekhai**, a kibbutz that withstood an attack May 19-May 24, 1948 against Egyptians troops of 2500. Named after Mordekhai Anielewicz, leader of the Warsaw Ghetto uprising, the kibbutz has a model of the battle and a **museum**, *Tel. 07-672-0529*, telling the story of the Jewish resistance. Open daily 8am-4pm, it costs NIS 8 to get in, NIS 6 for students, NIS 4.5 for children. Bus 19 goes here from Ashkelon at noon and 6:05 (4:15 on Friday) and buses return to Tel Aviv at 3:10pm (12:40pm on Friday).

Kiryat Gat lies 22 kilometers east of Ashkelon and comprises a number of villages established in 1954. Named after the Biblical town of Gat, which is believed to have been nearby, it was the birthplace of Goliath. You can get there by bus from Ashkelon (bus 25 goes every half hour for NIS 8), from Jerusalem (bus 446 goes every half hour or so for NIS 18), and from Tel Aviv on bus 369, every 20 minutes, for NIS 14.

Beit Guvrin is a modern kibbutz built in 1949 on an Arab village destroyed after 1948. The ancient town of Beit Guvrin was an important town in Roman and Talmudic times, and the Crusaders were here in the 12th century. Ruins of a 3rd century synagogue was found here, and Greek and Crusader artifacts found here are at the Rockefeller Museum in Jerusalem. The area is graced by cacti, fig trees, and thousands of limestone **caves**. Some were eroded naturally by water, others were carved out by the Byzantines as they gathered materials for their Ashkelon port, and they later served as shelters for wandering hermits. Saint John is know to have stayed here a while, and Sylvester Stallone was here as well, but to film Rambo III, not to ponder the world from a cave. There are lots of trails, and entrance is free. If you're going by bus, get the up-to-date schedule before leaving for Kiryat Gat, because there aren't many buses to make the connections.

Tel Sandahanna nearby has excavations revealing superb Byzantine mosaics, beautifully preserved, of birds and flowers. This was the floor of a Byzantine church, but not much more than the mosaics remain. There is also a Roman mosaic floor, and some burial caves. Ask at Beit Guvrin down the hill for some directions, because the tel is large and unmarked. **Tel Maresha**, two kilometers from Beit Guvrin, has the easiest caves to explore. There are staircases with intricate banisters leading down into the holes, and burial tombs to the east, built by Sidonians in the 2nd or 3rd centuries BCE, are there as well.

Tel Lakhish is between Beit Guvrin and Kiryat Gat. Less visually stunning but more archaeologically significant than the other tels, Lakhish was a fortified city before Joshua's conquest. It sat at the intersection between Egypt and the road to Jerusalem, and its strategic location led to its being a hotly contested and much fought-over site. Nine levels of settlements have been uncovered here, but most of the good stuff has been carted off to museums in Jerusalem and London, so there isn't much to see. If you want to come anyway and look around it's best to have a car. The nearest bus drop is two kilometers away on the Beit Guvrin road.

SPORTS & RECREATION

Ashkelon is full of beaches. The **National Park beach** is at the southern limits of town and features a grassy lawn and ruins to boot. **Delilah Beach** faces three little islands you can wade or swim to, and **Barnea Beach** caters to the city's swell crowd. For nude bathing, go to **North Beach**. The undertow is strong all up and down the coast, so take care no matter what your state of dress. South of Ashkelon, **Kibbutz Zikim** has a beach, but it's not far from where the tankers unload oil and it's not that pleasant.

The new **Ashkeluna Water Park**, *near Delilah Beach, Tel. 07-673-9970*, is the biggest water park in the Middle East. Open daily 9am–5pm, it costs NIS 40 for a day's worth, and is free for children under three.

PRACTICAL INFORMATION

- **Bus Station**, *Ben Gurion, Tel. 07-675-0221*, is about 25 minutes walk from the beach.
- **Currency Exchange**: There are banks in **Zephaniah Square**, as well as on Ben Gurion just west of the bus station, and in Migdal and Samson as well.
- **Fire**, call *102*.
- **First aid**, call *101* in emergency or *Tel. 07-672-3333*.
- **Groceries**: The **HyperCoOp Supermarket**, *4 Ben Gurion, Tel. 07-673-9509*, just south of the bus station, is open Sunday–Tuesday 8:30am–8:30pm and Friday 8am–2pm.
- **Laundromat**: *Herzl, in Migdal*.
- **Pharmacy**: *on the square*, is open Sunday–Monday and Wednesday–Thursday 8:30am–1pm and 4:30–7pm, Tuesday 8:30am–1pm, and Friday 8:30am–1:30pm.
- **Police station**, *corner of HaNassi and Eli Cohen, Tel. 07-677-1490, or 100 in emergencies*.
- **Post office**: the central post office, *18 Herzl, Migdal*, has poste restante and is open Sunday-Tuesday, Thursday 8am-12:30pm and 3:30-7pm, Wednesday and Friday 8am-noon.
- **Tourist Information Office**: *Zephaniah Square, Tel. 07-693-2412*, is in a small building opposite the green. It's open Sunday, Tuesday 8:30-1pm, Monday, Wednesday-Thursday 8:30am-12:30pm, and Friday 8:30am-1:30pm. Here you can get maps, schedules, and pamphlets.

14. FROM TEL AVIV TO HAIFA

HERZLIYA

The turnoff to **Herzliya** is under the benevolent gaze of the likeness of Theodore Herzl himself, smiling down from on high near the freeway. Just 15 kilometers north of Tel Aviv, Herzliya was established in 1924 as an agricultural settlement and named after Theodore Herzl, founder of modern Zionism.

Now it's a wealthy community of 90,000 and a resort town that attracts those with an eye for beauty and a pocket of money, such as flush tourists, foreign diplomats, and retirees. The luxury hotels, beautiful beaches, and pristine setting entice those, for the most part, who want to live, work, or play the well-to-do way.

ORIENTATION

Herzliya Pituah is the resort area near the sea, and it's where all the tourist facilities are. **Ramat Yam** is the street that runs north-south along the coast with all the better hotels. **Kikkar de Shalit** (**De Shalit Square**), half a block east of Ramat Yam, has restaurants and a supermarket. And the beaches, the reason you've come, are just steps away.

Downtown Herzliya is to the east, and **Ben Gurion** is the main north-south street, site of the central **bus station** and Beit Yad Labanim. Since there's no tourist office as such, the major hotel receptions are your best bet for information, maps, and the like.

ARRIVALS & DEPARTURES

By Car

Drive along Route 2 and take the Herzliya turnoff under the figure of Herzl.

By Bus

It's an easy 40 minute ride from Tel Aviv. Egged bus 501 or 502 will get you to De Shalit Square for NIS 4.4. The United Tours bus 90 also goes there, leaving from in front of the Dan Panorama Hotel in Tel Aviv, even on Saturdays.

GETTING AROUND TOWN

It's easy to walk around the main tourist center of Herzliya Pituah, getting from hotel to restaurant to beach without working up too much of a sweat. Traveling between Herzliya and Herzliya Pituah is easier with a car, though there are local buses, and there are always taxis.

WHERE TO STAY

HOLIDAY INN CROWNE PLAZA, *Ramat Yam, Herzlia On Sea, Tel. 09-952-8282, Fax 09-952-8280, offers rates which vary greatly by season, room grade, and a vast array of family plans, include Israeli breakfast and service charge. Their prices range from $220-$270 a single, and $195-$245 per double.*

Of the big fancy monolith genre, The Holiday Inn is one of the spiffier ones. It's got an elaborate, sparkling lobby with fountain and marble staircase, a beach front location and all the amenities. There's the piano bar and kosher Chinese restaurant, synagogue, health and beauty spas with indoor and outdoor pools, fitness room and sauna, tennis courts and sun terrace. If you can foot the bill and want some pampering and relaxation, this is a good choice. The Superior rooms (the cheapest category) are okay, but not nearly as nice as the Deluxe, which come with luxurious bathrooms, balconies, and the works.

DAN ACCADIA, *further down the street from the Holiday Inn, Tel. 09-959-7070, Fax 09-959-7090, has rates that vary by season and room grade and average $208 a single, and $268 per double, including breakfast but not the 15% service charge.*

The rooms are nice enough, though they don't stand out. The hotel offers the usual array of bars, restaurants, pool, and tennis courts, but they also have Danyland, an activity program for children.

THE SHARON, *further on Ramat Yam, Tel. 09-952-5777, Fax 09-957-2448, has 165 rooms and parking. Low season rates start at $100 a Standard single and $120 a double (including balcony), and $120 and $135 for the Superior, (all including breakfast but not the 15% service charge).*

The rooms are agreeable and the whole place has a pleasant feel, though it's not as splashy as the Holiday Inn. Along with the usual luxury hotel facilities, The Sharon has a large outdoor seawater swimming pool (heated in winter) as well as direct beach access to the real thing (the sea). There's a health club with gym, indoor heated pool, mineral baths and saunas. They've a great beach (free for hotel guests, NIS 8 for visitors).

Children have their own pool and playground, and in summer supervised children's activities. Other recreational options include tennis, windsurfing, and ping-pong. They also offer full business services with computers, fax and mailing facilities, and secretarial service for those taking a little work on vacation. With two restaurants, snack bars, piano bar with happy hour and disco, you needn't ever leave the hotel, but they are right near De Shalit Square if you want to venture forth.

TADMOOR HOTEL, *38 Basel, Tel. 09-957-2321, Fax 09-957-5124, has 58 rooms with bathroom, air conditioning, and phone that vary in cost by season and room grade, and range from $59 a single and $70 a double to $82 and $105, including breakfast but not the 15% service charge.*

Five minutes from the beach, the rooms are nice, with little balconies (on some), but small bathrooms. The hotel has a pool as well as bar, TV and video room, and a pleasant, friendly feel. It's a good mid-budget alternative to the luxury beach hotels.

ESHEL INN, *3 Ramat Yam, Tel. 09-956-8208, Fax 09-956-8797, singles cost $40-$54, doubles are $55-$80.*

Crummy rooms with air conditioning, bath, and phone but no TV. And the manager is cranky.

MITTELMANN GUESTHOUSE, *13 Basel, Tel/Fax 09-957-6322, has six rooms to rent for $30 a single and $40 a double.*

Rooms have a fridge and shower, and there's a shared kitchen available. No credit cards accepted, but reservations will be taken over the phone.

WHERE TO EAT

De Shalit Square is the hub of the food scene. There's fast food available on the square from Burger Ranch, a pizza place, and a Chinese take-away, plus the supermarket with picnic goods. And there are some restaurants as well.

CROCODILE RESTAURANT, *De Shalit Square, Tel. 09-451-4446*, is open 12-12 daily. They've a salad bar (NIS 28) with lots of fresh and interesting items, and entrees run NIS 37-64.

CAVEMAN'S CAFÉ, *on the beach*, is a couple kilometers north of De Shalit Square (see Sights section). In summer they serve hummus, sandwiches, and fuul with eggs, all home-made, and priced NIS 8-13. The tables are outside, right by the beach.

NIGHTLIFE & ENTERTAINMENT

The **Herzliya Chamber Orchestra**, *corner of Habanim and Ben Gurion, Tel. 09-954-7175*, plays in the amphitheater in the Labanim Memorial Center. The major luxury hotels along the beach all offer piano bars and disco.

SEEING THE SIGHTS

The **Sydna Ali Mosque** attracts Muslim tourists from all over, and some non-Muslims as well. It was built by Saladin himself some 800 years ago. The shrine holds the tomb of Sydna Ali (*our Master Ali*), an Islamic saint who fell in the fight against the Crusaders. Dress respectfully, and if you're female, bring a head scarf, or you won't be allowed in. A 15-minute walk along the beach from the Sharon will get you just below the mosque, or take bus 29, or drive up Wingate to Golda Meir, and take the dirt turn-off toward the mosque.

A walk along the beach near the mosque would be beautiful and rewarding all by itself, even if it didn't lead to the unique home built by Nissim Kakhalon, the man known as **Caveman**. Twenty-five years ago this burly, idiosyncratic man built an amazing home in the cliffs by the beach, constructed from flotsam and jetsam, from scavenged bottles and plates, tiles and stones, all held together by a pebble/sand/water mix he dug from the mountain and beach.

Not only is his place made up of discarded items, Caveman is an artist and an original designer. He first built his home to look like a dinosaur, but three years ago he took offense at an article written without his permission about his dinosaur abode, so he took chisel to stone and lopped off the head and tail of his house, a dinosaur no longer. Caveman continues to tinker and make improvements, and he's come a long way from his early pioneer privations and authority antagonisms. Now he has indoor plumbing, and colorful dune flowers (planted by him, of course) festoon his garden.

He's building a museum for his fantastic sculptures and whatever else he wants to include, and in summer he operates a pleasant café, with tables outside right by the water. He serves home-made hummus, sandwiches, and fuul with eggs for NIS 8-13. It's a nice change from up-scale Herzliya, in a gorgeous setting, and if you're lucky Nissim might sit with you and tell some of his tales or give you a tour of his architectural gems. A famous local character, known for his iconoclastic ways and prickly temper, but he's also a fine human being with a generous way, and a good eye for art.

To get there, walk along the beach north from the hotels (about 15 minutes), past the mosque. If driving, go up Wingate to Golda Meir, take the dirt turn-off toward the mosque, park in the dirt lot (not the mosque's) and take the stone path on the right down to the beach. Bus 29 from the central bus station will take you near there as well.

From there, you can walk an additional 400 meters north along the beach to a small **fishermen's village** that has a very different milieu from Herzliya.

Above the beach on the cliffs of **Tel Arshaf** are the negligible ruins of the Canaanite town of Arshaf, Assyrian Rishpona, the Greek port of **Apollonia**, Byzantine Sozusa, Arab Arsuf, and the Crusader-fortified Arsur. Despite all this history, there's little to see. A Roman amphitheater and Crusader fortifications have been uncovered so far, but they aren't in the best condition.

Museums

Herzliya also has a few of the more traditional tourist sights, including the **Herzliya Museum of Art,** *Habanim, Tel. 09-955-1011,* on the corner of Ben Gurion, down the street from the central bus station. It's open Sunday-Thursday 4-8pm, Friday-Saturday 10am-2pm, and admission is free. In the same complex (the **Labanim Memorial Center**) is the **Israeli Center for Propaganda Research**, *Tel. 09-955-1011,* with samples of same. Also in the Memorial Center is an **amphitheater** used for concerts, and surrounding it is a **Sculpture Garden** with works by Israeli artists.

The **Founders' Museum,** *8 Hanadiv, Tel. 09-950-4270,* is in **Beit Rishonim** (First Settlers' House) and it tells the story of the establishment of Herzliya on up to present times. Open Sunday, Monday, Thursday, Friday 8:30am-12:30pm, and an additional 4:30-6:30pm on Monday. Admission is NIS 5.

SPORTS & RECREATION

The main sport here, aside from lolling and relaxing, is swimming and sunning on the beach. The luxury hotels have their own beaches, and the **Sharon's beach**, *09-952-5777,* is generally held to be the best. Visitors are welcome for NIS 10. A short walk north is **Sidna Ali Beach,** *below the mosque,* which is free, and right by Caveman's home and café.

Hof Nof Yam, a little past the Sidney Ali Mosque, is a beautiful beach, and it's usually uncluttered by other tourists. Bus 29 form the central bus station takes you to the dirt road leading up the hill to the fence gate.

To the south of the Accadia Hotel is a **religious beach** where men and women bathe separately. It's a 10 minute walk along the beach.

The **Herzliya Marina** is a project to be completed soon. When done, the marina will stretch south from the Accadia Hotel. It'll feature an 800-boat jetty, tourist and recreation facilities, sea sports clubs, and a luxury apartment hotel.

EXCURSIONS & DAY TRIPS

Tel Aviv is just 15 kilometers south. Some people prefer to stay in peaceful Herzliya and venture into Tel Aviv from there.

PRACTICAL INFORMATION

- **Central bus station**, *Ben Gurion*, is in downtown Herzliya.
- **Fire** department, *Tel. 09-958-8222*, or *Tel. 102* in emergencies.
- **First Aid**, *Tel. 101*, is Magen David Adom in Hebrew.
- **Police**, *Tel. 09-955-5555*, or *Tel. 100* in an emergency.
- **Public Health Center**, *Tel. 959-2555*.
- **Supermarket**, *42 Wingate on the square*, is open Sunday-Thursday 7am-6pm. It's a good place for picnic supplies.

There is no official Tourist Information office, so try the major hotel receptions instead. They know the area, and sometimes have maps.

NETANYA

Located in the Sharon Plain overlooking the Mediterranean Sea, **Netanya** is 29 kilometers north of Tel Aviv. Known for its sandy beaches and relatively quiet atmosphere, the square and beach areas are just a small fraction of Netanya. At first glance, it doesn't seem like an appealing seaside resort. The capital of the Sharon district, Netanya looms large and citified as you approach, with ugly highrises clumped together and smoke stacks ruling the sky. The business action is based on the diamond industry, citrus-packaging, and Israel's one beer brewery, profitable ventures for the city. Once you hit the resort district however, you need never venture into Netanya proper.

The town was named after Nathan Strauss, an American philanthropist 1929. Established as a citrus center on the sand dunes of the Sharon Plain, the diamond-cutting industry was initiated in the late 1930s by immigrants from Antwerp and South Africa, and it soon developed as a holiday resort as well. In the 1940s the British used Netanya for convalescing Allied soldiers. Not much of a budget-holiday locale, Netanya attracts Israelis and Europeans (mostly German and French) who have a few bucks to spend, many of whom are retirees, though there's a smaller growing segment of young visitors as well.

ORIENTATION

Kikkar Ha'Atzmaut (Independence Square) on the sea is the hub of the resort area. Most of the restaurants and hotels are either on the midrahov of the square or within walking distance. At the end of the square are steps leading down to the beach. Netanya is just off the Tel Aviv-Haifa coastal highway, and **Herzl**, Netanya's main east-west boulevard, leads straight to the sea, sand, and square.

Gad Machnes and **David Hamelech** are the two streets that branch off to the north and south, and they contain most of the hotels in the area.

ARRIVALS & DEPARTURES

By Car
Drive up (or down) the coastal Tel Aviv-Haifa highway, turn west on Herzl, and keep going till you hit the square. It takes around 30 minutes to drive from Tel Aviv.

By Bus
The bus station, *Herzl, Tel. 09-860-6202*, is at the intersection with Weizmann and Benyamin. Head west to Ha'Atzmaut Square for the hotels and tourist information. Buses shuttle every 10 minutes or so between Netanya and Tel Aviv, with service from (and to) Haifa, Jerusalem, and Ben-Gurion airport every half hour. There are even infrequent buses to Beersheba and Eilat. For Caesarea or Tiberias, you need to bus to Hadera and transfer.

By Train
The train station is on Harakavet, a long block south of Herzl, one block east of the Tel Aviv-Haifa highway. It's a long walk from the station to the resort area, so you might want to take a taxi or bus.

By Taxi Sherut
There are sheruts from Herzl near Zion Square leaving for Tel Aviv and Haifa.

GETTING AROUND TOWN

By Foot
The resort area is easily negotiable by foot.

By Bicycle
Bicycles, a nice transport option, can be rented from a stand outside the tourist information office for NIS 12 an hour, NIS 40 per day. Open daily 8:30 till dark, and the prices are subject to bargaining. **La Promenade Hotel**, *Tel 09-862-6450*, also rents bikes, as does **Blue Bay Hotel**, *Tel. 09-860-3603*.

By Car
Hertz, *Tel. 09-882-8890*, **Tamir-Rent-a Car**, *Tel. 09-833-1831*, and **Budget**, *Tel. 09-860-3603*, are all on Herzl near Ha'Atzmaut.

By Taxi
Call **Hasharon**, *Tel. 09-882-2323*, **Hashahar**, *09-882-2222*, **Chen**, *09-833-3333*, or **Netanya**, *09-834-4443*.

WHERE TO STAY

All of the hotels accept credit cards, unless otherwise stated.

KING SOLOMON HOTEL, *18 Hama'apilim, Tel. 09-833-8444, Fax 09-861-1397. Prices vary by season. A single in winter is $45 and in summer $87, while a double in low season is $57 and in summer it's $120, breakfast included.*

A luxury hotel inside, despite its leggo block outside looks. Their 95 rooms all overlook the sea and come equipped with bath, phone, and air conditioning. They've got a swimming pool, sauna and gym, as well as the usual bar and lounge.

ORLY NETANYA, *20 Hama'apilim, Tel. 09-833-3091, Fax 09-862-5453, has 66 rooms. In winter a single costs $50, a double $65, while in summer a single is $105 and a double is $120, breakfast included. Reservations can be made with SeaGull Hotels and Resorts, Fax 09-699-7922.*

In a big red building facing the sea, the Orly's rooms are nice enough, with small bath and phone. Sixty percent of the rooms face the sea, and some have small balconies. The hotel has a sun deck on the room, a Finnish sauna, and a kosher restaurant.

PARK HOTEL, *7 David Hamelech, Tel. 09-862-3344, Fax 09-862-4029, is right on the beach. Rates vary by season and meal plan – a low season single with breakfast is $54, and in high season $112, a double in low is $65 and in high it's $150, with regular season prices in-between.*

This hotel has 90 rooms and six suites with air conditioning, bath, phone, TV, video, and balcony overlooking the sea. There are adult and children swimming pools, as well as a piano bar and restaurant overlooking the sea.

GINOT YAM HOTEL, *9 David Hamelech, Tel. 09-834-1007, Fax 09-861-5722, charges $40 a single in winter, and $50 a double, breakfast included. Prices goes up in summer, peaking in August at $80 a single, $90 a double.*

A moderate-sized hotel, it has 54 basic and clean rooms, all with air conditioning, bath or shower, phone, and radio, but without view or personality. The hotel has a small bar and restaurant, and a sun terrace overlooking the sea.

MAXIM HOTEL, *8 David Hamelech, Tel. 09-862-1062, Fax 09-862-0190, varies in cost by season and meal plan. A B&B winter single costs $60 and a double $80, while in summer they go for $100 and $140 (special discounts available for UN personnel).*

They have 90 rooms, all with air conditioning, phone, bath, and TV, some have a balcony, and some view the sea. The hotel has an outdoor pool, a Friday night disco, and bingo.

LA PROMENADE, *6 Gad Machnes, Tel/Fax 09-862-6450, has studios ranging from $80-$120 and suites from $100-$160, depending on the season, breakfast included. Prices go up in August, but they have reduced monthly rates (without breakfast) for $1,500-$2,100.*

A fairly new apartment hotel, with 23 studios and suites, all of which have air conditioning, phone, TV, a kitchenette, and a balcony facing the sea. Not far from Atzmaut Square, this 10-story hotel has an indoor swimming pool (heated in winter), jacuzzi, a washer and dryer, synagogue, and shabbat elevator, as well as the usual restaurant, café, bar, and parking garage. They also have bicycles available for rent.

MARGOA HOTEL, *9 Gad Machnes, Tel. 09-862-4434, Fax 09-862-3430, they charge $52 a single and $62 a double in winter (breakfast included), more in summer.*

Their 64 rooms have air conditioning, bath, phone, and TV. Half the rooms face the sea and the other half have balconies. The hotel has a restaurant, and a good pub.

HOTEL JEREMY, *11 Gad Machnes, Tel. 09-862-2652, Fax 09-862-2450, charges by season and meal plan. With breakfast, singles range from $45-$80 and doubles from $55-$94.*

They have 48 rooms, all with air conditioning, phone, radio, and shower or bath, while half the rooms face the sea. The staff at the Jeremy is very nice, and roughly 80% of their clientele is French.

GRAND YAHALOM, *15 Gad Machnes, Tel. 09-862-4888, Fax 09-862-4890, is two doors down. Prices include breakfast and vary by season. In low season, singles are $50, doubles $72, while in high season singles are $66 and doubles $94, all plus 15% service charge.*

Their 48 rooms are pleasanter than usual, and all have air conditioning, phone, TV, bath/shower and small couch. Across from some gardens and 50 yards from the beach, half the rooms face the sea.

RESIDENCE BEACH HOTEL, *16 Gad Machnes, Tel. 09-862-3777, Fax 09-862-3711, charges $62 a studio on a winter weekend, and $150 in summer, while a suite is $106 in winter and $204 in summer (weekday prices are a good 30% less).*

An apartment hotel right above the beach, they have studios and suites, and both include kitchenette, phone, air conditioning, TV, bath, and sea-facing balcony, but the suite has an extra bedroom. The suites aren't exactly luxury, but they're more than adequate. The hotel, with its bar, cafeteria, mini-market, laundromat, and free passes to the Galil's pool, is a good choice for a family.

RESIDENCE HOTEL, *18 Gad Machnes, Tel. 09-862-3777, Fax 09-862-3711, is under the same management. A single on a winter weekend (breakfast included) is $44, and $100 in summer, while a double in winter is $60, and $132* *in summer. Babies stay for free, dogs are $4 a day, and children 2-12 have reduced rates.*

They have 96 cheerful rooms, all with air conditioning, balcony, bathroom, phone, TV, and sea view. They have passes to the Galil pool and will arrange for tours to nearby sights.

METROPOLE GRAND HOTEL, *17 Gad Machnes, Tel 09-862-4777, Fax 09-861-1556, is across the street from Residence Hotel. A single in winter (breakfast included) is $50, and $75 in summer, while a double is $60 in winter and $100 in summer .*

It's a big, boxy hotel with 64 rooms, each with bath or shower, balcony, phone, air conditioning, and TV, and half face the sea. The hotel has a piano bar, parking, and swimming pool. They will arrange tours to nearby sights, but the staff isn't the friendliest.

SIRONIT HOTEL, *19 Gad Machnes, Tel. 09-884-0688, Fax 09-862-3139, is run by the same people who own the Gulilil and Residence. Rates vary by season, weekday, and meal plan. A single in winter on the weekend (breakfast included) is $46, and $100 in summer, while a double is $54 in winter and $120 in summer. No extra charge for babies, other children at reduced rates.*

Another modern block building, the Sironit has 60 basic rooms, all with bath or shower, air conditioning, phone, and small TV. This used to be an immigrant hotel but was opened for tourists in August '94. Right by the sea, the hotel issues free passes to the pool in Galil Hotel.

HOTEL PALACE, *33 Gad Machnes, Tel. 09-862-0222, Fax 09-620-8224, charges winter prices of singles for $40 and doubles for $50, and in summer singles are $70 and doubles $85. Prices include continental breakfast, and there are discounts for month-long stays.*

This hotel has 68 rooms across the street from the sea. The rooms, all with air conditioning, shower or bath, TV, and phone, are a bit plain but quite adequate. The lounge has a fussball game, and the hotel has a nice sun deck with tables and lounge chairs.

KING KORESH HOTEL, *6 Harav Kook, Tel. 09-861-3555, Fax 09-861-3444, costs $53-$75 a single and $65-$100 for doubles.*

A small hotel right near the beach, they've 29 rooms with air conditioning, shower, TV, and phone.

GALIL HOTEL, *26 Nice Blvd., Tel. 09-862-4455, Fax 09-862-4456, has many pricing plans, depending on season, day of week, age of children, breakfast or half board. A weekend single with breakfast averages $64 in winter, $150 in summer, and a double is $80 in winter, $180 in summer, no additional charge for babies, but $10 for the dog.*

Galil offers the full assortment of resort hotel facilities. Their 84 rooms, though a bit plain, all overlook the sea, and all have air conditioning, nice bathrooms, phone, and TV. The hotel, an ugly monolith on the beach, has a swimming pool and terrace, piano bar and disco, snack bar and kosher restaurant. The people who run the hotel are warm and helpful, and the hotel has an hourly minibus shuttle to and from town except for shabbat.

ORIT HOTEL, *21 Chen, Tel/Fax 09-861-6818, just off 13 Jabotinsky, charges $30 a single and $45 a double (breakfast included).*

A warm, welcoming and homey place, even if you're not Swedish, their 7 rooms are extremely pleasant, with shower, balcony, colorful rugs and other nice touches. The hotel is a cheerful, lovely place, and on Monday evenings at 6:30pm they host an open house with singing and Swedish coffee. Call for reservations, as this gem is no secret.

HOTEL MIZPE YAM, *4 Karllbach, Tel/Fax 09-862-3730, is just off Jabotinsky. Rates vary by season. Singles range from $36-$68, and doubles range from $48-$86, breakfast included.*

A smallish hotel not far from the beach, the building has no charm in particular, but the 32 rooms all have private bath or shower, air conditioning, phone, and radio, and are comfortable. There's a sun terrace on the roof, parking, and a kosher restaurant.

HOF HOTEL, *9 Kikkar Ha'Atzmaut, Tel. 09-862-4422, has singles for $50-$60, doubles for $70-$80, and a remarkably unhelpful staff.*

HOTEL GOLDAR, *1 Ussishkin, Tel. 09-833-8188, Fax 09-862-0680, charges $60 a single, $80 a double (breakfast included; 25% more in summer).*

There are 148 rooms in a big cement block of a building. The rooms, functional and okay, all have air conditioning, bath, phone, and TV. The hotel has a swimming pool, sun deck, and parking, as well as the standard lounge, bar, and kosher restaurant.

HOSTEL ATZMAUT, *2 Ussishkin, Tel. 09-862-1315, Fax 09-882-2562), is across the street. Dorm beds (four-eight a room) cost $10-$15, but their are private rooms as well. A single in winter costs $15-20, and double is $30. In summer a single goes for $30, and a double for $50.*

Fairly new and quite a deal, this is the most inexpensive lodgings in town, and the only hostel. All rooms have air conditioning, bath or shower, and a fridge. It's a clean and worthy establishment.

GALEY HASHARON HOTEL, *42 Ussishkin, Tel. 09-834-1946, Fax 09-833-8128, has singles for $32, doubles for $42, and triples for $50.*

It's a small hotel with 24 fairly standard rooms. Each floor has its own sitting area, and each room is equipped with TV, phone, and bath.

THE SEASONS HOTEL, *Nice Blvd., Tel. 09-860-1555, Fax 09-862-3022, is right on the beach. Prices vary by season and type of room (garden room, studio, suite, and penthouse), breakfasts included. In winter, the rates range from $93-$175 a single, $130-$260 a double, in summer singles are $198-$325, and doubles $240-$420.*

The big bulky building contains 88 plush rooms, each with enormous bathroom, air conditioning, phone, cable TV, fridge, mini-bar, and a large balcony. For this kind of money you get a hotel fully equipped with recreational activities. There's an indoor (heated) and outdoor swimming pool, tennis courts, a playground for kids, a health club, and sports facility. They also have private parking and a synagogue. If you want the extra mile of comfort and facilities and don't mind paying the extra dollar for it, this is a good choice.

BLUE BAY HOTEL, *37 Hamelachim, Tel. 09-860-3603, Fax 09-833-7475, is out of town a few kilometers. Singles in winter are $76 and doubles are $90, while in summer a single is $102-$125 and double are $117-$162, full breakfast included.*

The seven-story modern structure has 200 rooms, 49 of which are family rooms, all with air conditioning, direct-dial phone, cable TV, bath, and balcony. The hotel has recreational activities organized for children, a swimming pool (covered and heated in winter), a health club with gym, jacuzzi and sauna, tennis and volley ball courts, a terrace by the ocean, and a free shuttle service to and from town.

ROOMS FOR RENT, *28 Ussishkin, has basic rooms costing NIS 90 a double.*

The office is in back, the rooms are shabby, and credit cards are not accepted.

NATANYA MOTEL, *3 Jabotinsky, Tel. 09-882-2634, charges NIS 100 a single and NIS 120 a double, no breakfast included.*

There are 10 rooms, some with their own toilets, while others use the one in the hall, but all the rooms are pretty decrepit, with peeling paint and no air conditioning. Credit cards not accepted.

LIVING ON THE BEACH, *15 David Hamelech, Tel. 09-882-2253.*

Rooms to rent for long-term stays. Call for more information.

WHERE TO EAT

There are lots of restaurants on the square catering to the resort crowd, though there are a few other options as well for picnic supplies or more adventurous forays into the industrial zone.

The **street market** near the bus station on Zangwill has the least expensive food and supplies in town. And there are fine **falafel stands** on Sha'ar HaGai, which branches southeast off of Zion Square on Herzl.

Then there are the eateries on the square. Most of the restaurants are set up and priced for the tourist trade, Though there is some cheap food on the square as well. Slices of pizza can be had for around NIS 5, but it's pretty mediocre.

SCOTS MAN PUB RESTAURANT, *7 Kikkar Ha'Atzmaut, Tel. 09-862-4546,* is open 9am-4am daily. They serve hummus type starters for NIS 8-10, omelette, pizza, and pasta for around NIS 22, and meat dishes for NIS 21-62.

CREPARIS, *southeast corner of Kikkar Ha'Atzmaut*, is open 7:30am-midnight daily, they serve dairy like blintzes (NIS 15-22) and sandwiches (NIS14-18) as well as yogurt and ice cream. They also do breakfasts for NIS 12, major credit cards accepted.

YOTVETA DAIRY RESTAURANT, *Kikkar Ha'Atzmaut, Tel. 09-862-7576*, is open daily 8am-4am. Run by a kibbutz, they get fresh dairy and produce from the farm. They do a big breakfast for NIS 16-20, and also serve blintzes and pasta dishes for NIS 28-30.

BISTROT JACKY, *2 Ussishkin, Tel. 09-834-4559*, open 8am-2am daily, serves the finest cheap food in Netanya. Jacky dishes up some of the best baguette sandwiches this side of Paris (especially the schnitzel), but that's not all. Though you can get your baguettes (NIS 13) to go, eating at Bistrot Jacky is a fun experience, attracting an interesting mix, from backpacking travelers to local fishermen and business types. They go for a frothy mug of draught beer (NIS 7), nosh on the free-flowing accompanying munchies of salads and nuts, and hang out. If you want a change from the resort feel of Netanya, it's a good place to belly up to the bar and talk to some of the locals, or relax at the outdoor tables and watch the world go by.

PUNDAK HAYAM, *1 Harav Kook, Tel. 09-861-5780*, does a thriving tourist business. They serve starters like hummus and tehina for NIS 6-8, fish dishes for NIS 38-48, and other meat entrees for NIS 17-25, all served with rice or spaghetti. The outdoor seating is popular and festive, but be aware it there's a 10% extra charge there. It's a bustling scene of dining families and folks cooling off with beer.

SEEING THE SIGHTS

The **Promenade and beach gardens** run along the limestone cliffs above the gold-hued beach. During the summer there is free entertainment at the amphitheater facing the sea.

For a change from the beach scene, the **Diamond Cutting Factory**, *90 Herzl, Tel. 09-862-4770*, and **Imbar Diamond Center**, *1 Ussishkin, Tel. 09-882-2233*, offer guided tours of their factories that lead straight to the retail jewelry shops.

There's also the **citrus-packing plants** in Kiryat Eliezer. They're open to the public Sunday-Thursday 8am-4pm, Friday 8am-1pm, closed April-November. **Village Tour**, *Tel. 09-796-7146*, will arrange orange picking at Beit Harishonim.

For a culture break, try the **Association for Society and Culture** Yemenite cultural museum and folklore center, *11 Ha'Atzmaut Square, Tel. 09-833-1325*, open Sunday-Thursday 8am-4pm, admission NIS 5.

Hasharon Museum Emek Hefer, *Tel. 09-898-8644*, open Sunday-Thursday 8:30am-2pm, Saturday 10am-2pm, is a museum of archaeology, nature, and art. It details some of the Mesolithic, Neolithic, and Roman artifacts found in and around Netanya.

Near the southern exit of Netanya on Ben Gurion Blvd. is Israel's largest **Iris Nature Reserve**, located one kilometer past Beit Goldmintz on the right side. On the other side of the reserve is **Winter Pond**, home to a bevy of waterfowl. The SPNI office, *Tel. 09-833-3527*, can help with information.

A few kilometers south of Netanya, facing the Wingate Institute, is the **Yakum Reserve and Tel Poleg**, a wildflower reserve with regional native plants. The lake in the center has paddle boats for rent.

NIGHTLIFE & ENTERTAINMENT

In the summer, the **Netanya Orchestra**, *Ha'Atzmaut Square*, plays free concerts every Tuesday evening. Tuesday night also sees dancing to the music of the 60's in Joel Hall of the Park Hotel, *Tel. 09-862-3344*, starting around 9:30pm.

For **classical music** on Monday afternoons from noon-1pm, go to Beit Israel Congregation, *11 Ha'Atzmaut Square*.

Friday evening entertainment of **Israeli songs** can be heard in the lobby of the Park Hotel, *Tel. 09-862-3344*. And Friday nights The Galil Hotel, *Tel. 09-862-4455*, hosts a night club.

For Saturday evenings of **Israeli folklore** and dances of the 60's, try the Park Hotel, *Tel. 09-862-3344*, or check the Pub Terminal, *off Kikkar Ha'Atzmaut down the walkway past the Burger King*, starting around 10pm.

Sunday nights feature **oriental food**, **dance**, **and song** at **Beit Harishonim**, *Tel. 09-866-3176*, at 7pm.

The **Netanya Cultural Center**, *4 Raziel, Tel. 09-860-3392*, presents concerts, theater, folklore, films and permanent galleries.

Films can be seen at the cinema on Hasharon.

La Promenade Hotel often has dance groups or chamber music Saturday nights.

There are also organized activities (bridge, chess, lawn bowling, bingo) set up with older visitors in mind.

SPORTS & RECREATION

There are 11 kilometers of free sandy beaches with eight official, life-guarded beach stations open May-October up and down the coast. The undertow can be strong, so swimming near the lifeguards is advised. **Sironit Beach**, right near the square, is a convenient spot for bathing and sunning. **Qiryat Sanz Beach** in the north is set aside for religious Jews, with separate bathing times for men and women. Other beaches to the north are lovely and less crowded.

For **chess**, Friday mornings at Herzl Pedestrian Mall is the place to be. People play chess using large chess pieces on a huge board, weather permitting. National Chess Championships are held here in June.

The Ranch, *2 Havazelet Hasharon, Tel. 09-866-3525*, two kilometers south of the Blue Bay Hotel, offers guided **horseback riding** tours among the dunes and hills from 8am till dark. An hour's guided ride is NIS 60, and they do half-day and night trips as well, price negotiable. The horses, mixed arab and quarter horse, are well-tended, and during your hour you get many chances to let your horse run. Bus 29 or 17 will take you to Havazelet.

Cactus Ranch, *intersection of Itamar Ben-Avi and Jabotinsky, Tel. 09-865-1239*, is another place that does horseback rides. It's open daily 8am-sunset, charges NIS 60 per hour, and bus 7 goes there.

Jeep tours, *Tel. 09-866-3053*, lasting three hours can be arranged.

Ariba, *Tel. 08-884-8010*, offers **paragliding** for NIS 250, no experience required).

Paintball, Yishuv B'nai Dior, Tel. 09-748-3868, is also available nearby for NIS 41. There's a large games area for adults aged 17-120, as well as a children's target range.

The more sedate recreation of **petanque** (lawn bowling), *4 Ichilov*, is open daily.

There's **bowling**, *16 Chechterman, Tel. 09-862-5514*, daily from 10am-2am.

The Elizur Sports Center, *Tel. 09-865-2931*, has squash, tennis, and a heated swimming pool. And there are tennis courts available at **Maccabi Tennis Courts**, *Tel. 09-882-4054*, as well.

The Wingate Institute, *Tel. 09-863-9550*, a few kilometers south of Netanya, has squash and a heated swimming pool.

PRACTICAL INFORMATION

• There are **banks** *on Herzl and on Ha'Atzmaut Square*.
• Egged **central bus station**, *Tel. 09-833-7052*.
• **Fire**: *Tel. 102 for emergency or Tel. 08-862-2224*.
• **First Aid**: *Tel. 101 for emergency or Tel. 09-862-3333*.
• **Lanaido Hospital**, *Tel. 09-860-4666*.
• **Pharmacies**, try Trufa, *2 Herzl, Tel. 09-882-8656*, open Sunday-Monday and Wednesday-Thursday 8am-7:30pm, Tuesday 8am-1pm, Friday 8am-2pm. There are others on Herzl, Weizmann, and Sh'ar Ha-Gai. They take turns keeping one open for emergencies.
• **Police**: *Tel. 100 for emergency, or Tel. 09-860-4444*.
• **Post office**, *15 Herzl, Tel. 09-862-7868*, has a poste restante counter. Another branch is located at *2 Herzl, Tel. 09-862-7797*.

- **SPNI field school**, *6 Shmouel Hanatsiv, Tel. 09-833-3527*.
- **Train station**: *Tel. 09-882-3470*.
- **Tourist Information**, *southwest corner of Kikkar Ha'Atzmaut, Tel. 09-882-7286*, is near the beach. Open Sunday-Thursday 8am-7pm, Friday 9am-noon, they have lists of local activities and events. Anther branch, *15 Herzl, 09-833-0583, Fax 09-860-3122*, is open the same hours.

CAESAREA (QISARYA)

Caesarea lies 55 kilometers north of Tel Aviv on the Mediterranean coast, a jewel of a city amid sand dunes, ruins, and resorts. Originally a Phoenician port built by the Sidonian king Abdashtart (*Strato* in Greek) during Alexander the Great's rule around 300 BCE, it was called Stratonas Pyrgos (Strato's Tower). In 90 BCE, Pyrgos was sold to Alexander Jannaeus the Hasmonaean. When the Romans under Pompey conquered the Hasmonaeans in 63 BCE, they annexed the coastal area to their territory in Syria.

In 31 BCE, after Roman Emperor Ceasar Augustus defeated Marc Antony at Actium, he gave the Stratonos Pyrgos area to Herod, who spent 12 years (22-10 BCE) building the town he then named Caesarea Maritima after his emperor. What he had constructed was a stellar Graeco-Roman town, a port city so impressively designed as to make modern scholars wonder. In addition to the port, Herod built an amphitheater, a theater, and a hippodrome. He also had constructed an intricate drainage system with underground channels running to the sea to keep the city clean.

In 6 CE, Caesarea became the seat of the Roman governor of Judea, and it figured prominently in early church history. Pontius Pilate lived here, Philip started a good sized Christian community, Peter baptized the Roman captain Cornelius, and Paul passed through on his way to Jerusalem. Caesarea was the residence of the archbishop of Palestine from the late 2nd century onwards.

Jews were a minority here from day one, and conflicts increased in the early decades CE. In 60 CE procurator Felix put down a protest, and in 66 CE the desecration of the synagogue here and the resulting slaughter of 20,000 Jews was a major catalyst spurring the Great Revolt and the ensuing destruction of Jerusalem and the Temple. After Jerusalem was destroyed by Titus in 70 CE, Titus marched through Caesarea (on his way to Rome) with his booty and prisoners of war. He celebrated his victory in the amphitheater with lion gladiator games during which some 2,500 Jewish prisoners died. And following the Bar Kochba revolts of 132 CE, 10 sages (including Rabbi Akiva) were tortured to death in the same amphitheater. Caesarea experienced a real boom in the following couple of centuries, during which many academies and synagogues were built, and by the 6th century its population is thought to have reached 100,000. The Arabs sacked the city in 639 CE, however, and as the harbor silted up, Caesarea's prominence began to fade.

The Crusaders under King Baldwin I took the site in 1101, razed much of the town, killed the residents, and made off with what was believed to be the Holy Grail, a green glass bowl thought to be the vessel Jesus drank from at the Last Supper (now preserved in Lorenzo, Genoa). Sultan Salid captured Caesarea in 1187 and destroyed the fortifications. Four years later Richard the Lionheart occupied the deserted town, and in 1218 the Frankish castle was rebuilt. Sultan al-Malik al-Mu'azzam conquered in 1220, King Louis IX of France reconquered in 1251, and the town surrendered to Mamluk Sultan Baybars after a seven-day siege in 1265.

After this, Caesarea was truly trashed, and it remained fairly well abandoned until 1878 when Muslim refugees from Bosnia were settled there by the Turks, forming a village that lasted until the War of Independence in 1948. Old Caesarea today is a mix of remnants from all these eras. There's an aqueduct and theater still standing from Herod's rule, and excavations have uncovered Crusader fortifications, a Pontius Pilate inscription, and what's left of the harbor. New Caesarea has followed Herod's style of luxury and opulence, with a wealthy residential community, resort center, and golf course.

ORIENTATION

The approach to Caesarea, after the shooting range club, is full of beautiful white sand dunes and dune shrubs – very peaceful, pretty, and nicely landscaped. From the Caesarea exit off the Coastal Tel Aviv-Haifa highway, signs in Hebrew and English clearly direct you to major sites.

The Dan Caesarea Hotel, Golf Club, and Caesarea Center lie to the north, while the beach, Old City, and Roman Theater are west by the sea. Frequent signs ask drivers to drive carefully and keep Caesarea clean, and the civic concern pays off with sparkling clean grounds, flowers, landscaping, and no litter to mar the scene.

ARRIVALS & DEPARTURES

By Car
The signs directing you to Caesarea from the Tel Aviv-Haifa Highway are clearly marked in English, and the drive in is pretty.

By Bus
Take any coastal bus from Haifa, Tel Aviv or Netanya going in the direction of Hadera and get off at the Caesarea intersection. From there

the 76 from Hadera makes a circuit to the Dan Hotel and nearby sites every two hours, or you can walk the 3.5 kilometers to the harbor excavations, but take plenty of water because Caesarea is hot.

By Taxi
You can take a taxi from Hadera for around NIS 33.

GETTING AROUND TOWN

It's easiest to get around by car, but there are other ways. The 76 bus from Hadera makes a circuit every two hours, stopping at the Dan Hotel, the Golf Course, and the National Park Old City site. You can also cover some of the area by foot; it's 3.5 kilometers to the Old City from the highway intersection. And taxis can be called as well.

WHERE TO STAY

DAN CAESAREA HOTEL, *Tel 06-626-9111, Fax 06-626-9122, right next to the golf course, offers singles for $60-$110, and doubles for $85-$125.*

Beautiful green lawns greet you at this five-star luxury hotel, but you'd want a car to get there. Inside there are lots of nice touches, including flowers on the landings. The reception desk has maps and brochures of the area. They have regular rooms (nice, with a balcony), superior (a little bigger with a nicer view), and deluxe (fancier bathroom). The #76 bus from Hadera comes to the hotel every two hours, or you can take a taxi from Hadera (NIS 33). Taxis to nearby restaurants cost about NIS 20.

SDOT YAM, *south end of town, Tel. 06-636-4470, Fax 06-636-2211, is near the Roman Theater (the last stop on bus 76 from Hadera). Their holiday apartments in summer rent for $49.50 a single and $61 for a couple. The hostel dorms (6 beds per room) cost $16 per bed, with meals available for $6 for breakfast, $9.50 for lunch, and $7 for dinner.*

A kibbutz established in 1940, along with a big plane on the front lawn, they've got apartments, dorm beds, a museum, and a variety of jeep and boat tours and activities. The rooms are nice, with a bedroom, sitting room, and flowery-patterned, homey decor. They're fully equipped with bathroom, air conditioning, TV, phone, fridge, coffee/tea bar, and a porch with table outside.

In addition to lodgings and meals, Kef Yam offers 45 minute speed boat tours of the harbor in their glass bottom boat for NIS 30, Kibbutz tours for NIS 10, and one hour Jeep trips for NIS 190 per jeep (seven people maximum). They also have *Kisry*, their motor sail boat, for day cruises, costing $450 per day for the boat, 17 people max, food not included. They also do longer cruises, such as a six-day trip to Cyprus, 12-

14 days to Turkey, and 18 days up the Israeli coast to the Greek isles. Also on the kibbutz is an archaeology museum (open 10am-4pm, $2 admission), and the Hannah Senesh Memorial.

HOF HACARMEL FIELD SCHOOL HOSTEL, *10 kilometers north of town, Ma'agan Michael, Tel. 06-636-2266, Fax 06-639-4166, is a hostel with family rooms set in a beautiful reserve area.* See entry for "Near Ceasarea".

WHERE TO EAT

Caesarea Center, just down the street from the Dan Caesarea and the Golf Club, has the only low-price food option in town, the **MINI-MARKET**. Open Tuesday-Sunday 7am-8pm, Monday 7am-3pm, the market has excellent baguette sandwiches for NIS 8 and rolls for NIS 5, filled with your choice of salads and meats. Dining overlooking the harbor in the picturesque but pricey restaurants is your other option, so you might want to picnic on mini-market goods. The Center also has the **CAESAREA RESTAURANT**, open noon-3pm and 7-10pm, closed Wednesday and Saturday nights.

SDOT YAM CAFETERIA on the kibbutz is another option. They serve all-you-can lunches for NIS 27.

The Harbor in the Old City is the other main food locale, offering lofty harbor views at equally steep prices.

HEROD'S PALACE CAFE, *Harbor, Tel. 06-636-1103*, in the hall of King Herod's palace, overlooks ruins and the sea. Open 9am-7pm in winter, 8am-1am in summer, but closed Shabbat, they serve fish dishes for around NIS 55, schnitzel for NIS 31, and hummus, etc., for NIS 9-13.

CHARLEY'S RESTAURANT, *Harbor, Tel. 06-636-3050*, is open 10am-midnight, and looks out right over the sea. In summer you can sit on the open terrace (closed in winter) and watch the seagulls and the crashing waves. They've been in business for 22 years despite the expensive seafood prices. On Friday evenings in summer they have dance music and sing-alongs.

CRUSADER'S INN, *Harbor, Tel. 06-636-1931*, open 11am-midnight, has the standard pricey fish, and a salad buffet for NIS 18 with a main course, or NIS 29 if ordered alone. They also have Friday night dance and sing-alongs in the summer.

THE HARBOR CITADEL RESTAURANT, *Harbor, Tel. 06-636-1679*, is open daily, 9:30am-1am. Situated in an old stone building overlooking the sea, they offer a self-service luncheon buffet for NIS 31, as well as the usual fare.

The **Aladin Treasure Store**, *Harbor, Tel. 06-636-0862*, with its **CAFFÉ ESPRESSO SHOP**, is the one place on the harbor for a reasonably priced snack. Just east of Yael Artsi, they're open 8:30am-6pm, later in summer. The Caffé (self-service to little tables on the sidewalk) offers pita made fresh each Saturday morning for NIS 4, with labane for NIS 8. Cheese toasts are NIS 7, as are little pizzas. They serve very good coffee (and tea) for NIS 6-8, and there's a chips/candy/gift shop inside for your sweet tooth. Nor do they ignore your spiritual needs; they offer information on free meditation courses as well.

NIGHTLIFE & ENTERTAINMENT
There isn't much. The only real action is in the Old City, and the fun mostly consists of shelling out money for food and drink at the Harbor restaurants. The old Crusader buildings and the crash of the waves are pretty romantic, however, especially by moonlight. **Charley's Restaurant**, *Tel. 06-636-3050*, and **Crusader's Inn**, *Tel. 06-636-1931*, have dance music and sing-alongs on summer Friday nights.

For more cultural fare in the summer, check out if the **Roman Theater** is presenting any ballet, opera, or theater.

SEEING THE SIGHTS
The primary attraction here is **Caesarea National Park**, with its **Crusader City**, reconstructed gate house, Roman Theater, and old harbor, plus a mix of Roman, Arab, Byzantine, and Crusader ruins. The sites are open 8am-4pm, and they charge NIS 12 an adult, NIS 6 for youth (keep your ticket for admission to the Crusader City and the Roman Theater). There is also a 14-day National Park pass available for NIS 47. The outer gate is open all night for access to the restaurants on the harbor, but you pay an entrance fee only till nightfall (4-6pm).

The **Crusaders' town** was excavated in 1960. The entrance in the east is through a vaulted gate. Nearby is the bridge that led to it, and the ruins of what was once a nine-meter high watchtower. The rampart walls rise dramatically from the ditches, and used to surround the town, punctuated by the three town gates. To the left of the eastern town gate stands a vaulted passageway which used to cover the street. The moat built by Louis IX used to run nine meters wide and 13.5 meters deep, and contributed strongly (but not successfully) to the fortification. The Crusaders began but never completed a cathedral of St. Paul, built on the foundations of the large mosque which was itself built above a Byzantine church. The remains, some apses and buttresses, are in the south of the Crusader town.

The **old harbor** was a state-of-the-art port for the time, in fact the reputedly sophisticated engineering of this long-since destroyed and submerged harbor made many doubt the reports until recent archaeology dives began corroborating what history told us. Herod's innovative architecture included two breakwaters – the first in the country – which made Caesarea one of the prime port cities of the eastern Mediterranean. The city, circa 80 CE, was described in full detail by Flavius Josephus. According to Flavius, in its glory days, two enormous towers flanked the harbor entrance, there was an elevated temple of Augustus with two colossal statues (one of Augustus and one a personification of Rome), and six more large statues rose from the harbor entrance. There was an oil-fueled lighthouse as well. Diving expeditions are now substantiating all these claims to grandeur and fame. The pedestal of one of the statues was discovered in 1961, and coins and pottery have been found as well. The breakwater that can be seen now is the breakwater the Crusaders built on the Roman and Byzantine foundations.

The **Roman Theater** to the south of the Old City was built by Herod and is the oldest to be found so far in the country. It was reconstructed in 1970 and is now used from May-September for concerts, plays, ballets and opera. It's a grand setting in which to enjoy these events. Remnants of Herod's **Hippodrome** (an arena for racing horses and chariots) can be seen northeast of the Theater. There is a rectangular block of red granite, about 7.5 feet long, near the bottom of the hill, which is thought to be the remains of a taraxippos, an object meant to frighten the horses and make them run faster.

Across the road from the National Park's gate is **Statues Park**, where you can wander about free of charge and see the excavated Byzantine road. The street, 425 feet long, is paved with marble slabs taken from Roman palaces and with white mosaics as well. There are also two enormous, headless Roman statues which were taken here by Flavius Strategius from some 2nd or 3rd century temples in 6th century CE. The white marble statue remains unidentified, but the red Egyptian porphyry statue depicts an emperor who is probably Hadrian. The Roman statues and mosaics are surrounded by a mesh fence, so you can't get the same up-close view seen in photos on display in the Harbor gift shops.

To reach the **aqueduct**, take the turn off toward the sea from Rothchild Boulevard (not far south of Caesarea Center) and follow it out to the sea. About one kilometer north of the Crusaders' road, these are remains of Herod's conduit system which carried water from the springs in lower Carmel some 16 kilometers away. You can climb the aqueduct and stroll on it, and it's a fine place for a picnic if the wind isn't kicking up sand. The beach is pretty, but no swimming allowed. It's not a big enough architectural excitement if you don't have a car – it might feel like a let down if you have to hike in – but it's an easy drive.

North of the Crusader fortress (near and easily accessible from the aqueduct) is an excavated **synagogue**, circa 3rd or 4th century CE. It was built on foundations that may be Herodian, but was destroyed in the 4th century. Another synagogue was built on this site in 450 CE, and the

Greek inscription on the white mosaic pavement reads: *Beryllus Archisynagogus and Leiter, the son of Justus, made this mosaic with his money.*

Museums
Sdot Yam, the kibbutz you pass on the way in from the highway, has an **archaeology museum**, *Tel. 06-636-4470*. It's open 10am-4pm, $3 admission, with statuary and archaeological finds from the kibbutz grounds. They also have a **Hannah Senesh Memorial**, *Tel. 06-636-4453*. Hannah Senesh, one of the original settlers of the kibbutz in 1940, went on to become a national hero and martyr with her behind-enemy-lines activities in Europe during WWII and her expressive journals. The audio-video presentation isn't the most advanced technology, but the story is very moving and well worth seeing and hearing.

Across the street from Caesarea Center is the **Ralli Museum**, *Tel. 06-636-0588*. The museum is open every day except Sunday/Wednesday in summer, and only on weekends in winter, from 10:30am-3pm. It features a private collection of Latin American art, as well as plastic arts and a Herod's Dream exhibition, and admission is free.

SHOPPING
Art & Antiques in the Old City
The Citadel Gallery, *Harbor, Tel. 06-636-2950*, is open 9am-5pm in winter, 8am-10pm in summer, and has genuine, certificated artifacts for sale, such as Phoneician glass ($50 and up), Roman glass (less rare and less expensive), and other antiques. They also have an interesting reconstruction of the ancient Herodian Port on display.

Yael Artsi Sculptors, *Harbor, Tel. 06-636-0666*, features Israeli sculpture for viewing and for sale.

Leon Bronstein Gallery, *Harbor, Tel. 06-626-0198*, is an art and sculpture gallery.

EXCURSIONS & DAY TRIPS
North of Caesarea is **Amat HaTaninim**, *old coastal road, Tel. 06-636-3903*, a moshav that offers cart, donkey, and bicycle tours, and has a restaurant and bar. Just outside Amat HaTaninim (whose name means Alligator's Canal) are two well-preserved **Roman aqueducts** believed to have carried water down from the Shuni springs to the old city of Caesarea. North of the moshav are excavations in progress at **Tel Mevorah**, and so far some important Roman artifacts have been unearthed. The marble sarcophagi discovered there is on display at the Rockefeller Museum in Jerusalem.

A little further north is **Kibbutz Ma'agan Michael** and **Nahal Taninim Nature Reserve**. It's an exceptionally beautiful kibbutz, complete with an aviary, wildlife reserve, a small museum of archaeological finds made on kibbutz land, and a hostel. The dam Herod built in the stream as part of the waterworks system is still visible.

Near the stream is the **Bird Reserve**, open to the public November-March, free of charge. For guided tours, call the Hof Harcarmel Field School, *Tel. 06-639-9655*.

SPORTS & RECREATION

The **Caesarea Golf Club**, *down the street from the Dan Caesarea Hotel, Tel. 06-636-1174, Fax 06-636-1173*, is open daily 8am-nightfall. This 18-hole, par 73 golf course is unlike any other. Founded by the Rothchild family some 36 years ago, the golf course (the only one in Israel) is beautifully set among the ruins of ancient Caesarea, with scattered relics of Roman times forming an integral part of the course. The clubhouse has a restaurant, locker rooms, a fleet of electric golf carts, and three qualified senior teaching pros. Weekday green fees for one day cost $90 ($85 for Dan Hotel guests), and $105 a day on weekends ($90 for Dan guests) and there are discount deals for five days, 10 days, 15 days, and a month. The club fee is $30 and you can rent the electric carts for $30 for nine holes and $40 for 18 holes.

There's a big **swimming pool**, *Caesarea Center Country Club*. Open Sunday-Thursday 6am-9pm, Friday/Saturday 6am-6pm in winter, an hour later in summer, entrance tickets (NIS 44 per adult, NIS 34 per child during the week, NIS 12 more on the weekend) can be purchased downstairs in the office through the glass doors.

The Diving Center, *Caesarea Maritima*, is open 9am-4pm, and a day's dive costs NIS 150. It's a great place to go diving because of the underwater archaeological findings of the old harbor of Caesarea Maritima, such as the pedestal of one of the harbor statues, discovered during a diving expedition in 1961.

Beaches

Caesarea Beach Club, *old city, Tel. 06-636-1441*, is a licensed bathing beach and water sports center. They have sunbathing rafts, glass-bottom boats, and a bar at the shore front.

The Partridge Club Shooting Center, *Tel. 06-636-0017*, on the way in to Caesarea from the Haifa-Tel Aviv road, is open Sunday-Thursday 7:30am-2:30pm and Friday 7:30am-4pm, and costs NIS 70-125. If you've been wanting to practice your clay-pigeon shooting skills, here you go.

Herod's Stables, *across from Caesarea Center, 06-636-1181*, is a riding club and school. Open daily (except Wednesdays) from 8am-7pm. It has been amenable to tourists who wanted to ride, but there's been talk of limiting their activities to riding lessons only. Give a call for current news.

Beit Hananya, *north of Caesarea, Tel. 06-636-3903*, is a moshav that offers **cart, donkey**, and **bicycle tours** along the ancient aqueduct leading to Caesarea. It's open 9am-5pm daily.

PRACTICAL INFORMATION

Caesarea Center is down the street from the Dan Caesarea and the Golf Club. This is the hub of the town, with the **post office, Center Club**, and **mini-market**. Equally important, there are public **rest rooms** downstairs as well.

CARMEL

However you spell it – **Karmel** or **Carmel** – the name means *Orchard* and the area is beautiful. The slopes are dotted with gardens, villas, and caves yielding traces of human settlements from the paleolithic period on. The mountain is important in Biblical history, and is sacred to Christians, Jews, Muslims, and Bahai.

Back in the days of Joshua, Mount Carmel formed the northern border to the territory of the tribe of Asher (Joshua 19:26). The prophets made frequent reference to the fertility of the region. It was on Mount Carmel that the prophet Elijah and the priests of Baal had their contest over whose prayers would be heard by God – Elijah's were victorious, the 450 priests of Baal were put to death in the stream Kishon, and the people got their drought-breaking rain. Christians have made pilgrimages to Mount Carmel since the 4th century, and it has been the site of monasteries since the 6th.

Today, Carmel is a place where you can soak up the religious aura, visit Druze villages, and enjoy the area's natural wealth on foot or horseback, by jeep or mini-tractor, or from your car. And when you tire of the rolling hills, some of Israel's best beaches are just a few miles away.

ORIENTATION

The **Carmel ridge** rises up from Haifa and runs 26 kilometers southeast, spanning 10 kilometers at its widest, and jutting up to 1790 feet high. It divides the **Yizre'el plain** in the east from the **Sharon plain** on the west, with the **Mediterranean coast** a little west of that. The sights, for the most part, are bordered by Haifa in the north, Caesarea to the south, the Kishon River in the east, and in the west, the Mediterranean Sea.

ARRIVALS & DEPARTURES

To get to **Isfiya** from Haifa by public transport, take bus 192 or a sherut taxi. If your visit to the Druze villages is a day trip and you have no car, be aware that the last Egged bus back to Haifa leaves around 3pm; there are sheruts till around 8pm, but they start to get scarce after 5pm. Bus transport to **Ein Hod** is on the 202 or 921 from Haifa. It's a two-kilometer uphill hike from the Ein Hod junction where you get off. To get to **Zikhron Ya'akov** by public transport, take bus 202 or 222 from Haifa, 707 or 708 from Netanya, or bus 872, 876, or 877 from Tel Aviv.

To visit **Megiddo** by public transport, there are a number of buses that will drop you at that junction, and a 10-15 minute walk will take you to the site. Buses from Haifa, Nazareth, Afula, Tel Aviv, and Tiberias all pass Megiddo Junction. By car, turn north on Route 66 at the junction with Route 65, and a sign will point you up to the parking lot.

Lots of buses from Haifa go near **Beit She'arim**, but the 301 is most convenient. If driving, the site is off Route 75, nearly equidistant between Haifa and Nazareth, and the parking lot is next to the museum.

To **Dor Beach** by bus, take the 921 from Haifa or Tel Aviv and ask the driver to let you off at Dor. If driving, it's right off the coastal highway, halfway between Caesarea and Atlit Castle.

GETTING AROUND TOWN

There are buses to the major sites, but this area is best traversed by car. If you're just going to focus on one or two locales and plan to do a lot of hiking from home base, a car becomes less important.

To get from village to dig, beach to winery, however, will begin to soak up much of your time if you do it all by Egged.

WHERE TO STAY

STELLA CARMEL HOSPICE, *POB 7045, Haifa 31070, Tel. 04-839-1692, is located in the Druze village of Isfiya. Dorm beds cost $12, and doubles are $45, breakfast included.*

Run by the Anglican Church, this converted lovely old Arab villa with antique Persian rugs is open to everyone. There's a 10:30pm curfew, and unmarried couples don't get doubles. Reservations suggested. From Haifa by public transport, take bus 192 or a sherut taxi.

BEIT OREN, *Carmel, Tel. 04-822-2111, Fax 04-823-1443), is a kibbutz guest house in the heart of the pine forest mountains of Carmel, 10 kilometers south of Haifa. 66 rooms with air conditioning, TV, and private bath or shower cost $93 a double, breakfast included.*

The hotel offers use of their swimming pool (seasonal), tennis courts, and children's playroom. There's horseback riding as well. It's a beautiful location, and near to the Druze villages and Ein Hod, as well as hiking in Park Hacarmel.

NIR ETZION, *Carmel mountains, Tel. 04-984-2542, Fax 04-984-3344, is a kibbutz guest house with a synagogue, traditional observation of shabbat, and a Glatt Kosher kitchen. With 74 rooms with air conditioning, TV, phone, and private bath or shower, they charge $93 for half-board and $104 for full-board.* The facility has a swimming pool (seasonal) and horseback riding, and it's very near Ein Hod and the Druze villages.

BEIT MAIMON, *4 Zahal Street, Zikhron Ya'akov, Tel. 06-639-0212, Fax 06-639-6547, charges $62-$79 a single and $67-$84 a double, breakfast included. There's a 10% discount if you stay more than three nights.*

The hotel has 23 rooms with air conditioning, TV, phones, and private bath. They also have a jacuzzi and sauna, as well as a restaurant and bar.

HAVAT HABARON, *Zikhron Ya'akov, Tel. 06-630-0333, Fax 06-630-0313), is on the slopes of Carmel. A single is $132-$180 while a double costs $165-$220.*

Their 96 rooms come equipped with air conditioning, TV, phone, and private bath. This hotel has a mini-market and music room, as well as a health club, heated swimming pool, children's playground, and great views of the sea. In addition, they can arrange car rentals and baby sitting.

DOR MOSHAV CAMPSITE, *Dor Beach, Tel. 06-639-7180, is on the coast road about 29 kilometers south of Haifa. There are three-person bungalows for NIS 80, or NIS 30 per person, but prices soar in the summer.*

The campsite is built in the old village of Tantura, and the nearby caves and ruins make for an interesting setting. Tent sites are open May-October. Call ahead to reserve.

NACHSHOLIM GUEST HOUSE, *foot of Tel Dor, opposite Dor Bay, Tel. 06-639-9533, Fax 06-639-7614, has more upscale accommodations. Lodging costs $46-$77 per person.*

They have rooms and holiday chalets surrounded by green lawns. All rooms are air conditioned and have kitchenette, bathroom, and phone, and the facility has tennis courts and a kosher restaurant. In addition there is a children's playground, a sports facility, and a private beach.

NEVE YAM HOLIDAY FLATS, *Tel. 04-984-4808, Fax 04-984-0030, are further north up the coast.*

These holiday huts on the beach, with bedroom sitting room/kitchenette, bathroom, dining area, and patio are available in July, August, and holidays. There are activities for children and evening entertainment for the adults, wide lawns, a cafeteria, and the beautiful seashore.

Neve Yam also has **camping sites**, *Tel. 04-984-4808, Fax 04-984-0030.* There is electricity and running water, toilets and showers, a mini-market and cooking facilities as well as a restaurant, and discounts on the entrance fee to Neve Yam waterpark.

WHERE TO EAT

The places to stay all offer some sort of food plans, and the major sites have some sort of snack bars, and there are the following eateries. Mount. Carmel is not, however, a bustling restaurant scene.

ARTISTS' INN CAFÉ, *Ein Hod, Tel. 04-984-2016*, open 11am-11pm, offers somewhat pricey dairy dishes on a balcony overlooking the sea or inside in wood-lined comfort.

THE SHUNI CITADEL RESTAURANT, *Shuni, Tel. 06-638-0227*, offers French country cuisine.

CASA BARONA RESTAURANT, *Zichron Ya'acov, Tel. 06-639-0212*, on the slopes of Mount Carmel, features great homemade food and a stunning view.

NIR ETZION GUEST HOUSE, *Tel. 04-984-2541*, overlooking the sea and Atlit fort, serves vegetarian meals, glatt kosher.

TANTURA RESTAURANT, *Dor Beach, Tel. 06-639-8869*, is a large restaurant serving Mediterranean food in an air conditioned dining room inside, or outside on the open, shaded balcony.

SEEING THE SIGHTS

There were once 14 **Druze villages** thriving in the hills of Carmel. They were destroyed by an angry Egyptian pasha in 1860 following an attempted rebellion in 1830. In the 1860s the Turks were looking for a buffer zone against the Bedouins and Christians, and they invited the Druze back to the villages of Isfiya and Dalyat el Carmel. Today, around 17,000 Druze live here. The older generation still dresses according to tradition: dark robes and white shawls for the women, white headdresses (*kafiyyehs*) and dark mustaches for the men.

Isfiya, the nearest to Haifa of the two, is 21 kilometers southeast. It was built on the ancient Jewish village of Huseifa, and there are mediocre ruins of a 5th/6th century synagogue here. It has a fine mosaic floor, and there's a nice Catholic church, but people come here mostly to experience a Druze village. The housing is mostly awful concrete, but there are lovely views to be seen from nearby Rosh HaCarmel.

A couple kilometers south of Isfiya is **Dalyat el Carmel**. It's a little larger than Isfiya and the last stop for the buses and sheruts from Haifa. The market is a busy, festive scene on Saturdays, and considered a rip-off by some; the prices are lower (somewhat) during the week and it's easier to spend time talking with the locals. Many of the goods (clothes and jewelry) are imported from India. The local items are wheat stalk baskets, embroidery, and tapestries.

At the end of the main street is **Beit Oliphant**, once the home of Sir Lawrence Oliphant. Sir Lawrence was a Christian Zionist mystic, and one of few non-Druze to develop a close relationship with the sect. He and his wife lived here from 1882-1887 and helped the community build their homes. In the sculpture garden is a cave where they hid Arab and Jewish insurgents from the British authorities. The house, recently renovated, was made into a memorial to the many Druze members of the IDF. Oliphant's secretary was the Hebrew poet Naftali Hertz Imber, and he wrote Israel's national anthem *Ha-Tikva* (The Hope) at this site.

Four kilometers southeast of Dalyat el Carmel is **Mukhraqa**, the **Carmelite Monastery of Saint Elijah**. This is where Elijah is said to have massacred the 450 priests of Ba'al (I Kings 17:19). This is also where Elijah's servant spied the clouds that presaged relief from the drought. The Carmelites saw the clouds as a symbol of the Virgin Mary, and inspired them to build this monastery, which is open Monday-Saturday 8am-1:30pm and 2:30pm-5pm, Sunday 8am-1:30pm. Up on the roof (admission NIS 1) there's a wonderful view of the Jezreel Valley below. No buses come here, so you'll need to drive, take a taxi (NIS 10) or walk. If you go for the hike, make sure you bear left at the signposted junction. The Stella Carmel Hospice in Ifiya sometimes organizes walking tours (pilgrimages) to the site. The Feast of St. Elias (Elijah) is on July 20th, and Christian Arab families celebrate in the park.

Fourteen kilometers south of Haifa is the moshav **Ein Hod** (Hebrew for "Spring of Grandeur"). It was founded by Algerian immigrants in 1949 on the site of the evicted Arab village Ein Houd (Arabic for "Spring of Garden Rows"), and in 1953 Marcel Janco, one of the founders of the Dadaist art movement, turned it into an artists' village. Unless you have a strong interest in art and/or Dadaism, a visit here might not be a worthwhile use of your time. The community center offers courses in painting and sculpture, but there isn't much to see in a casual stroll.

The **Ein Hod Gallery**, however, exhibits the residents' works, and is open daily 9:30am-5pm, entrance NIS 1. There is also a **Janco-Dada Museum**, *Tel. 04-984-2350*, displaying mostly Marcel Janco, though some other contemporary Israeli Dadaist art is included as well. It's open Saturday-Thursday 8:30am-5pm, Friday 9:30am-4pm, admission NIS 8 (NIS 4 for students). A third gallery, **Beit Gertrude**, is next to the restaurant. It was once the home of another colony founder, Gertrude Krause, and contains more local artwork. It's open Saturdays, September to June, from 11am-2pm and admission is free. Most Friday evenings the small restored **Roman amphitheater**, *Tel. 04-984-3377*, holds concerts ranging from rock to classical (call or check local newspaper listings).

The **Carmel Caves**, *Tel. 04-984-1750*, also known as Nahal ha-Ma'arot, Wadi el-Mughara, and Valley of the Tombs, lie two kilometers off Route 4, not far south of Atlit, are open Saturday-Thursday 8am-4pm, Friday and holiday eves 8am-1pm. Starting in 1929, archaeologists began discovering traces of the huntsmen who lived here circa 18,000 BCE. Items such as sickle blades and flint fishing spears were found, indicating the inhabitants belonged to an independent culture, probably part of the Natufium (after Wadi en-Natuf, the first place remnants of these people were discovered) that extended as far as Egypt in the south and mid-Lebanon in the north.

The Natufis buried their dead below their living quarters, and collective burial sites disclosed squatting skeletons and decorative necklaces of shells and teeth. Today, the finds (including the 'Woman of Tabun' skeleton and her headband of stone beads) are on display in the Rockefeller Museum in Jerusalem and the caves are just the caves wherein they were found.

Thirty-eight kilometers southeast of Haifa on the slopes of Mount Carmel is the kibbutz **Zikhron Ya'akov**, renowned for its winery, and one of the first Zionist settlements. The kibbutz was founded by Romanians in 1882 and was named after James (Yakov) de Rothschild, the father of the Baron de Rothschild whose generous donations helped reclaim the land from the swamp it was originally. There is a tourist information office, *Tel. 06-639-8811*, to the left of the bus station, and they have maps, brochures, and schedules of events. They are open Sunday-Thursday 8am-1pm, Friday 9am-noon.

Two blocks to the right of the bus station is **HaMeyasdim Street**. Most of the attractions of the city are on or near this pleasant, cobblestoned street. **Bet Aaronsohn**, *41 HaMeyasdim , Tel. 06-639-0120*, has a small **natural history and NILI museum** open Sunday-Thursday 8:30am-1pm, Friday 9am-noon, and costs NIS 8.5 per adult, NIS 7.5 for students. Aharon Aaronsohn (1876-1917) was a botanist, and the museum houses a rich collection of plants and a botanical library. Aaronsohn and his family were also leaders of the NILI, the network which spied on the Turks in WWI, so this museum also commemorates the role of that early paramilitary intelligence unit. Across the street, *39 HaMeyasdim*, is the **Tut Neyar Paper Mill**, where they hand make paper and lampshades from local plants. Their shop sells their wares of stationary and lampshades, but they will also arrange workshops for you to make your own paper if you set it up in advance.

Most people come here, however, for the **Carmel-Mizrahi Winery**, *Tel. 06-639-1241*, the winery founded by the Baron de Rothschild in 1882. From HaMeyasdim Street, continue down the hill and turn right on HaNadiv Street. The winery is at the bottom of the hill, and is open Sunday-Thursday 8:30am-3:30pm, Friday 8:30am-1pm, and costs NIS 10. Call ahead to make sure of a tasting tour in English. There is another, smaller winery, the **Baron's Winery**, *Tel. 06-638-6434*, and their tours are free. It's open Sunday-Thursday 9am-4pm, Friday 8am-3pm, and it's located right near the Baron's Tomb in Ramat HaNadiv.

The **Rothschild Family Tomb** is just outside of town on the road approaching from the coast. It's a 15-20 minute walk from the bus station or a cheap (NIS 2) sherut taxi ride to the Rothschild estate. Inside the estate is the rock-hewn crypt containing the Baron Edmond de Rothschild and his wife. There are lovely gardens, and magnificent views of the Sharon Plain and nearby mountains. Open Sunday-Thursday 6:30am-4pm, Friday 6:30am-2pm, Saturday 8am-4pm, and entrance is free.

Just west of Zichron Ya'akov is **Kibbutz Ma'yan Zvi**, *Tel. 06-639-5122.* Not only do they have a swimming pool, fishing pools, and a kibbutz tour, they have a museum of local fauna and a collection of archaeological finds from the Carmel caves. They also have a communal dining room and a cafe-bar.

South of Zichron Ya'akov is **Bee World** at Binyamina, *Tel. 06-638-0608*, with demonstrations of the honey process from bee to jar. Call for appointments and reservations. Also by Binyamina is the **Shuni National Historical Site**, *Tel. 06-638-9730*, open daily. Excavations here revealed a Roman theater and oil press. There is also an audio-visual show about the period of time before Israel was established as a state, when this site served as a base for underground activity against the British.

NIGHTLIFE & ENTERTAINMENT

Well, there are sometimes Israeli folk sing-alongs with free wine flowing at the **Carmel Mizrahi Winery Club**, *Tel. 06-639-1241*, and sometimes the **Music Center of Beit Daniel**, *Zichron Ya'akov, Tel. 06-639-7007*, holds chamber music festivals, or you could just go to bed early and get up ready to hike about and see the sights.

SPORTS & RECREATION

Carmel offers a wide range of outdoor activities, including jeep and mini-tractor tours, horseback riding, hiking, and sky jumping. These organizations can help hook you up to the sport of your choice.

Carmel National Park, *Tel. 04-823-1452*, has beautiful routes to traveled by foot or by car, with picnic and rest spots overlooking glorious views of the mountains and the sea.

Allona Park and Hurshan Mountain has marked walking routes, and picnic-rest sites. An abundance of springs and underground shafts here formed part of the water-works system constructed by Herod to convey water to Caesarea.

Hai-Bar Nature Reserve, *Tel. 04-984-1750*, off Route 672 about seven kilometers west of Nesher, is a center for wildlife reproduction in their natural settings. You can tour the animals' pens, or hike on marked trails. Open March-June Sunday-Thursday 8am-4pm, Friday and holiday eves 8am-1pm.

Beit Oren, *Tel. 04-830-7242, Fax 04-823-1443*, is a kibbutz guest house 10 kilometers south of Haifa that has **horseback riding** instruction, riding trails, and **mini-tractor** tours. You can join a trip for an hour, on up to several days.

Mechora Stables, *Kerem Maharal, Tel. 04-984-2735, Fax 08-984-1643*, off Route 4 about eight kilometers north of Zichron Ya'akov, offer **horseback riding** (no experienced required) and **jeep tours** in the hills of Carmel. Trips from an hour to several days. They also have a snack bar and a local farm produce stand.

Bat Shlomo, *Tel. 06-639-0884*, off Route 70 about five kilometers northeast of Zichron Ya'akov, has organized **horseback riding, jeep and mini-tractor tours**, and **mountain bike excursions** in Alona Park, Hurshan Mountain, and the Carmel.

Just west of Zichron Ya'akov is **Kibbutz Ma'yan Zvi**, *Tel. 06-639-1141*, and its **fishing park**. With picnic facilities and a snack bar, the main attraction is the fishponds. They rent and sell fishing gear and tackle, and are open in the summer during daylight hours, and on weekends and by appointment in winter.

On the coast near Atlit Castle is **Neveh Yam Water Park**. **Kibbutz Neveh Yam**, *Tel. 04-984-4870*, has a bathing beach, swimming pools, water slides, bumping boats, and deck chairs set on a shaded green lawn. Open May-September, 9am-5pm, they have shower facilities and a restaurant.

About six kilometers south of Neveh Yam is the **Habonim Nature Reserve**, *Tel. 04-984-1750*. Natural coves show a typical limestone formation habitat, and there's a licensed bathing beach. Entrance is free for hikers; call for information on guided tours. Also at Habonim is the **Israeli Sky-Jumping Center**, *Tel. 04-821-8368*. There are introductory jumps for those with no experience, and facilities for those who've done it before.

Dor Beach (Tantura), *Tel. 06-639-0922*, is one of the most beautiful in the country. Further south on the coast than Habonim, Dor is a great place for a swim, with lifeguard and children's recreational services, showers, and a restaurant.

EXCURSIONS & DAY TRIPS

Atlit Crusader Castle lies 14 kilometers south of Haifa on Route 3, the old coastal road. The fortress is rather picturesque on its peninsula jutting into the Mediterranean, and the history of the site is interesting, but the castle is off limits since it's now a military (naval) base. During the Fifth Crusade, the Knights Templar built a Frankish settlement with a castle here, and called it Castrum Peregrinorum, but the site had a history of many previous occupants and even more names. Joshua 21:34 notes a Sebulonite-Levite of Kartah. When Sidon ruled, the town was called Adarus, the Romans renamed it Certha, and so it remained till the Knights Templar came in with their Latin mouthful, Castrum Peregrinorum (Château Pèlerin in French) around 1200 CE. The Frankish settlement included not only a castle, but a chapel, palace, houses, and stables as well. The Crusaders kept control of this place till the bitter end when the Christian kingdom collapsed in 1291. In fact it was the very last Crusader castle to fall to the Arabs.

During the next few centuries the settlement was not well maintained, but the 1837 earthquake really did major damage to the whole area, and some of the masonry was removed at that time by the Turks to help with repairs in Akko and Jaffa. In 1903, Edmond de Rothschild founded the Jewish village of Atlit one kilometer to the south of the Frankish settlement. The British sponsored archaeological digs in 1930 and uncovered relics from the Crusader period and before.

Dor is further down the coast, some 14 kilometers south from Atlit. On the grounds of Moshav Dor, started in 1949 by Greek Jews, excavations have uncovered ruins from the Biblical Dor and Hellenistic Dora. Joshua 11:1 first mentions the place when Jabin, King of Hazor, led his town of Dor against Joshua around the 13th century BCE. Dor was mentioned in an ancient Egyptian papyrus, became the fourth administrative center under King Solomon, and was fortified in the Hellenistic period. Dor had a small Jewish community under Agrippa (41-44 CE), fell into disrepair in the 4th century, and came back to life when the Crusaders built their castle of Merle. Finds on Tel Dor include a basilica from the fifth or sixth century, a Roman theater, and ancient harbor and fortress ruins.

Nearby is **Tantura Beach**, one of the most serene and lovely in the country. Not only is the beach all that a beach should be, there are also the four bird sanctuary islands that can be explored at low tide. The beach is a magnificent setting to pitch a tent, or there are campsites nearby at Dor Moshav.

Kibbutz Nachsholim, *north of Dor, Tel. 06-639-0950*, houses the **Center of Nautical Regional Archaeology** in a building Baron Rothschild built in 1891 as a glass factory for his wine industry. The museum displays finds from the Tel Dor excavations as well as nautical exhibits that go back thousands of years.

Tel Megiddo, *27 kilometers southeast of Haifa, Tel. 06-652-2167, Fax 06-642-0312*, is a popular archaeological site of religious and historical significance. It's open Sunday-Thursday 8am-4pm, Friday 8am-3pm (an hour later in summer) and costs NIS 18 an adult, NIS 9 per child. Plan about an hour and a half to see the site. This is the biblical site of Armageddon that Christian tradition claims is where the War of the End of Days will take place. The excavation site disclosed layers of settlements, from a Chalcolithic village predating 3500 BCE to 400BCE when settled life here petered out. In between there are remains from its heyday circa 1150-1130 BCE when it was an Egyptian provincial capital, and its eras under King Solomon (965-925 BCE) and King Ahab (871-852 BCE) as chariot cities. Under the Roman Empire this city was known as **Via Maris** (Way of the Sea), and was a strategic military center. After Persian rule (4th century BCE), Megiddo lapsed, but regained its status as prime battle location during WWI and again in the 1948 War of Independence.

Highlights of the dig include Hyksos remains, a Canaanite altar, Temple of Astarte, and King Solomon's underground water tunnel which allowed access to the springs outside town during times of war. Megiddo was situated right on the great trade route between Egypt and Mesopotamia. This accounts for the many battles fought there, and the many times Megiddo was destroyed and rebuilt. Its history makes Megiddo both the interesting archaeological and significant Christian site that it is. Megiddo is mentioned in the hieroglyphics in the Karnak Temple in Luxor, telling of Thutmosis III (1490-1436 BCE) and how he conquered Megiddo in 1468 BCE, in the Armarna epistles (14th century BCE), and in the clay tablets of Taanach. The frequency of devastation led to the Revelation of St. John (Revelation 16:16) which describes the city of Harmageddon (Har Megiddo – Mountain of Megiddo) as the embodiment of the last battle between good and evil. It also led to the many settlements and layers of civilizations found here.

By the ticket counter (where you can get a NIS 3.5 site guide that's helpful in keeping track of what you're looking at) is a small museum. They have a 10 minute informational video in English and well-organized collection of items from the site (though some of the finds are in the Rockefeller Museum in Jerusalem). There's also a buffet/snack room and a collection of jewelry and souvenir shops. Megiddo is an enjoyable site to visit. The history is interesting, there are well-preserved structures set attractively in the hills, and palm trees line the paths along the ruins. You feel more a part of this; it's not as fenced off as other sites like Beit She'an.

The highlight of the site for me was the trip through the water tunnel. Down 183 steps and then 80 steps up, you walk right through it and out the exit (don't venture down until you're done with the site). Unfortunately, unless you are with a tour group that will meet you there with buses, you'll have to schlep back up the hill on your own to retrieve your car. Turn right (despite confusing kibbutz sign) to get to the parking lot. It's a five minute walk to the bus stop and another five to the parking lot and bathrooms.

About 18 kilometers north of Megiddo and 19 kilometers south of Haifa is **Beit She'arim** (House of 100 Gates), *Tel. 04-983-1643*, where fancy sarcophagi of important rabbis are cut into the rocky maze of caves discovered by archaeologists in 1936, open Saturday-Thursday 8am-5pm, Friday 8am-4pm, admission NIS 15 per adult, NIS 12 per student, and NIS 1.5 for a map). Beit She'arim's first known history starts at the end of Second Temple times (sixth century BCE) as a fortified town belonging to Berenice, daughter of Agrippa I and sister of Agrippa II.

After the Bar-Kochba rebellion failed in 132 CE, Judah ha-Nasi moved the Sanhedrin (the Supreme Rabbinical Council) to this site and drew up the final edition of the Mishna. Perhaps because of this, and also because Hadrian closed the area around Jerusalem in 135 CE, making it impossible for the Jews to bury their dead on Mount of Olives, this became the fashionable burial place for revered and wealthy Jews in the 3rd and 4th centuries CE. Sarcophagus inscriptions in Greek, Hebrew, and Aramaic tell the tale of leading rabbis from as far away as Palmyra, Beirut, and Sidon making Beit She'arim their final resting place. The town was destroyed by Gallus Caesar during the Jewish revolt of 351 CE, though it continued for a while as a small Jewish settlement.

In the catacombs there are over 200 sarcophagi, some of individuals and some family tombs. Most of the tombs contain coffins of wood, lead, clay or stone, though some just have bare skeletons. This site drew a lot of wealthy families, and some of the mausoleums are ornately decorated with floor mosaics. The earth embankments of catacombs 1-4 have reliefs and some paintings in the style of Jewish art in Roman times. There was a marble sarcophagus whose sides showed the myths of Meleager and Leda, but this is on display in the Rockefeller Museum in Jerusalem. In addition to the wonderfully dark atmosphere inspired by the catacombs, there are remains of a third century synagogue (once one of largest in the country, it was destroyed by the Romans 350 CE as punishment for rebellion), a basilica, an oil press, and a museum housed in a former cistern.

The **museum** features a large collection of sarcophagi, sgraffiti, a model of the synagogue, and a block of reddish glass which weighs eight tons and is one of the largest glass blocks in the world. There is also an equestrian statue up on the hill commemorating Alexander Zaid who discovered the main entrance to the catacombs in 1936. He was killed in a skirmish in 1938.

PRACTICAL INFORMATION
Local guided tours are conducted by the **Hof HaCarmel Field School**, *Tel. 06-639-9655.*

Nature Reserve at Nahal Mearot information center, *Tel. 04-984-1752*, is helpful for hikes and treks.

Carmel Instruction/Guidance Center, *Tel. 04-984-5239, Fax 04-484-1296*, can also provide information on activities in the region.

HAIFA

Haifa, the capital of the north, is a contradictory city. Set in great natural splendor at the southern end of the beautiful blue Bay of Haifa and dominated by Mount Carmel, on whose steep slopes the city is built, Haifa is also Israel's leading seaport, and one of its main industrial areas, specializing in oil refining and chemicals. About 100 kilometers (62 miles) north of Tel Aviv, and with a population of more than 250,000, Haifa is Israel's third largest city.

But Haifa is also a busy tourist destination. The city has scads of museums, the Haifa University and Israel Institute of Technology, and miles of glorious beach and forested hills, as well as being the world headquarters of the Baha'i sect.

Known for the relative harmony in which its inhabitants (Jewish, Muslim, Christian, Druze, Baha'i) live, one still hears plenty of off-handed disparaging comments about "the Arabs," as well as the recent immigrant community of Russians. The impressions you form of the city will depend very much on which faces of this multi-faceted city you see.

History

Given all the natural resources, it's not surprising that people have wanted to live here for a long time; remains indicate settlements going back more than 100,000 years. In ancient times there were two settlements on this site, Shiqmona to the west and Zalmona to the east, but Haifa was first mentioned in the Talmud in the 200s CE. The name is believed to have derived from Ho*f Yafe* meaning "beautiful coast," though the Crusader appellations of *Caife*, *Cayfe* and *Caiphas* may have derived from Caiaphas, the high priest of Jerusalem in Jesus' time who was born in this city.

In the 1300s BCE, a port was built near Abu Huwam on the mouth of the Kishon River, and it lasted 400 years. The Hellenistic-Roman town of Shiqmona (Sycaminium) had no harbor, but the Jewish settlement, as mentioned in the Talmud, was on the sea to the north of the cape. This fishing and glass-blowing town was burned by the Arabs in the 7th century CE, but by the 11th century it was a busy trading community, with a shipbuilding industry and a Talmudic school. Then in July 1100 CE, Haifa was taken by the Crusaders, despite resistance from the city's combined Jewish and Muslim community, who were then slain. The town became the most important port in the Latin kingdom until Acre took precedence in 1104.

In 1155, Berthold of Calabria founded the Carmelite order, but all was destroyed in 1187 after Sultan Saladin defeated the Crusaders at Hittim. The town changed hands frequently for a while: Richard the Lionheart conquered in 1191, fortifications were built up by Louis IX in 1252, and the town was again captured and destroyed by Mamluk Sultan Baybars in 1265. In the 18th century the Bedouin Sheikh Daher el-Omar tore down the old town and built it up anew, and it flourished temporarily with the wheat-export business. Napoleon took up residence in the old Carmelite monastery for a spell in 1799, and the Turks took over in 1840.

The development of the modern city began with the establishment of a colony of German settlers in the 1868, and continued with the arrival of Zionist immigrants after 1900. The Haifa-Damascus railway was built in 1905, and the technical college (Technion) was founded in 1924. Occupied by the British 1918, Haifa became part of mandated Palestine in 1922. Under British rule, the port was constructed in the 1930s, and in the late 30s Haifa was connected to the oil pipe-line from Iraq. Theodor Herzl called Haifa "the town of the future," and it has continued to thrive, growing in population, industry, culture, tourism, pollution, and noise.

ORIENTATION

Haifa is built on three levels – the port area (**Downtown**), the main town (**Hadar**), and the more exclusive **Center Carmel (Carmel Hills)** area.

Center Carmel is the highest tier of the city, with higher prices and higher standards as well. From the Arlozoroff/Balfour intersection, take the **Spinoza Stairs** to the top – a long ascent to mental and physical fitness, into increasingly nicer, quieter, more affluent levels. Turn around to admire the view and catch your breath despite breath-taking view. Up top, the air is fresher, the streets quieter, the prices as steep as the climb, and the food choices fewer. However, on Shabbat you will find there is more action and more open options than elsewhere. The main streets up here are **Yefe Nof** and **HaNassi**; that's where most of the hotels, restaurants, nightclubs, and tourists are to be found.

Hadar HaCarmel (which means Glory of the Carmel, no irony intended), is the middle level of the city, in the heart of the commercial district. The hotels are cheaper and a little seamier, the market rowdier and more festive, and the food cheaper. There is the **Nordau pedestrian mall** in Hadar, however, that's quite chic with some fine restaurants and pubs. **HeHalutz** (near Hanev'im) is one of the main streets in Hadar, with falafel and shashlik and bakeries in abundance. Also set up on the street is a stand with fresh squeezed juices (orange, apple, or grapefruit) for NIS

2 and carrot for NIS 3, doled out by an old man on stool. It's a great street to walk down, especially if you're hungry, though the cars and the honking can get on your nerves. **Herzl**, another Hadar street, is more of a shoes and sweaters boulevard than the fast food and stalls stroll of HeHalutz. On Shabbat, however, all the eateries along HaHalutz shut down.

Downtown is nearest the harbor and the bus stations, where most of the sailor bars and some of the hostels cluster. HaAzmaut and Yafo (Jaffa) are the main streets near the port, and Allenby has a lot of falafel joints, which tend to be shut, however, on Shabbat. **Romema** is a remote suburb of Haifa, near nothing, but with one hotel. And **Carmel Beach**, a beautiful sandy strip south of the city, has hostels and camping sites, but the bus transport is spotty on Shabbat.

BEST OF HAIFA
BEST HOTELS

• *NOF HOTEL, 101 HaNassi, Carmel Center, Tel. 04-835-4311, Fax 04-838-8810, costs $75-$120, breakfast included. The nicest and most reasonable of the luxury hotels.*

• *DVIR HOTEL, 124 Yafe Nof, Carmel Center, Tel. 04-838-9131, Fax 04-838-1068, costs $52 a single and $91 a double, Israeli breakfast included. This training hotel under Dan Hotel management offers all the Dan hotel perks for less money.*

• *BETH SHALOM, 110 HaNassi, Carmel Center, Tel. 04-837-7481, Fax 04-837-2443, costs $70, including full Israeli breakfast. Comfy and warm, but you need to stay for a minimum of three nights.*

• *HOTEL NESHER, 53 Herzl, Hadar, Tel. 04-862-0644, costs $27 a single and $40 a double, breakfast included. Clean and adequate, it's a good price in a city with few options between hostel and big bucks.*

• *BEIT-EL HOSTEL, 40 HaGefen, between Ben Gurion and HaYaroq, Downtown, Tel. 04-852-1110, costs $14 a bed. The staff is friendly, the garden's lovely, and the curfew is 11pm.*

BEST FOOD & DRINK

• *VOILA, 21A Nordau, Hadar, Tel. 04-866-4529, is a real find, with excellent Swiss-French cuisine amid hanging plants everywhere, artful candles on the tables, and a fascinating collection of objects on the walls.*

• *HEHALUTZ STREET near Hanev'im. The street is full of fresh-squeezed juice stands, falafel and shashlik stalls, and a lot of traffic.*

BEST SIGHT

• *BAHA'I SHRINE AND GARDENS, Tel. 04-835-8358, also known as **The Shrine of the Bab**, the gold-domed mausoleum is beautiful and the gardens are lovely.*

ARRIVALS & DEPARTURES

By Air

Most of the major international airlines fly in to Haifa's airport (east of Haifa in the industrial zone), as does Israel's domestic airline, **Arkia**. For domestic air travel to Eilat, Tel Aviv, and Jerusalem, call Arkia Israel Airlines, *80 Ha'atzmaut, Tel. 04-864-3371,* or visit any travel agent.

To get to Ben-Gurion Airport, take a taxi from **A.M.L.**, *Tel. 04-866-2324,* or **Kavei Hagalil**, *Tel. 04-866-4444,* or buses 945 or 947 from the Central Bus Station.

By Car

All the major highways of the region converge on Haifa in a messy web of signs and merging traffic. Familiarize yourself a little with a map of the city before you drive in, know which section you're heading for, and take a deep breath. The signs are well-marked, however, and will direct you to the port, Hadar, or Center Carmel.

By Bus

The **Central Bus Station**, *intersection of Yafo and Rothschild, Bat Galim, Tel. 04-854-9555,* is downtown next to the train station. Buses from Tel Aviv (the 900 or 901) start at 6am and depart hourly, and the last one Friday depends goes at 4 or 4:30pm in winter, 5 or 5:30pm in summer, and takes about an hour. The Jerusalem bus takes two hours and leaves hourly. There are also frequent buses to Akko and Nahariya (the 271).

By Train

The **Train Station**, *intersection of Yafo and Rothschild, Tel. 04-851-5793,* is right next to the bus station. Haifa is the most popular destination on Israel's limited train route, despite the paucity of trains, because the views coming up the coast are so nice. The train to Jerusalem leaves at 7am Sunday-Friday, and there are trains to Tel Aviv almost every hour.

By Ferry

From the Port of Haifa Passengers Terminal, Tel. 04-851-8111, it's possible to get to Rhodes in Greece by ferry. There's no longer a direct route to Turkey, though it's possible from Rhodes to arrange Turkey-bound transport from there. Call **Caspi**, *76 Ha'atzaut, Tel. 04-867-4444,* **Mano**, *2 Palmer, Tel. 04-866-7711,* or **Dolphin**, *Tel. 04-855-3278,* for information.

Inter-City Taxi Service (Sherut)

Most sheruts leave from Eliyahu in Kikkar Paris, though some will pick you up. **Amal**, *Tel. 04-852-2828,* goes to Tel Aviv; **Aviv**, *Tel. 04-866-*

6333, goes to Tel Aviv, Jerusalem, and Tiberias; **Kavei HaGalil**, *Tel. 04-866-4422*, goes to Akko and Nahariya; and **Taxi Carmelit**, *Tel. 04-866-4640*, goes to the Druze villages Isfiya and Daliyat-el-Karmil.

GETTING AROUND TOWN

By Car
It is possible to drive around Haifa; that's what many of the locals do, as evidenced by the swarms of exhaust-spewing cars that clot the intersections and blare their horns at every opportunity. Parking becomes a problem, however, as does navigating the labyrinthine steep streets. For those with cars, driving seems most popular for seeing the remoter sights (like the Carmelite Monastery), for getting around at night, and for Saturday transportation.

By Bus
Egged, *Tel. 04-854-9131*, runs a comprehensive and complicated network of intracity buses, and Intrabus passes are valid on them. The bus stops are marked pretty clearly as to which buses stop where, and the sights all include bus number information. From the central bus station, bus 41 will take you to Downtown, 21, 24, 28, and 37 go to Hadar, and you can take 22 or 25 to Carmel Center. On weekdays, buses run from 5:45am to midnight, on Fridays they stop at 3:30pm, and on Saturday those that do run start at 9am.

There are no Saturday buses from (or to) the bus station. Though some buses do run on Shabbat, they are few and far between, especially those going to remote spots. Most of the Saturday buses start in the Hadar district.

By Subway
The **Carmelit line**, *Tel. 04-837-6861*, the only subway in Israel, is a good way to get from one level of the city to another. It's open Sunday-Thursday 6am-10pm, Friday 6am-3pm, and Saturday it opens half an hour after sundown. It starts at the bottom of the city at Kikkar Paris (its entrance is under the yellow awning) and runs all the way up to Gan Ha-Em in Carmel Center, stopping at Solel Boneh, HaNevi'im, Masada, and Golomb on the way.

By Taxi
Kavei Hagalil, *11 Berwald*, *Tel. 04-866-4444*; **Carmel Ahuza**, *4 Mahanayim*, *Tel. 04-838-2727*; and **Merkaz Mitzpe**, *7 Balfour*, *Tel. 04-866-2525*.

By Foot
The various sections of Haifa are best seen on foot, despite the fact that this is a city that leans too heavily on the horn. The best way to take in the HeHaulutz scene is by walking down the street with a good appetite, the pedestrian mall on Nordau can only be done on foot, and the streets of Center Carmel are worth strolling on as well.

Getting from one tier to another, however, can be time-consuming and sweat-provoking without buses, the Carmelit, or a car – something to keep in mind on Saturdays. The stairs that climb way up to Center Carmel, however, are rewarding with remarkable views and an aerobic workout (if you just want the views, you can always take the stairs down, instead).

There are a number of walking routes mapped out by the tourist information offices and detailed on their free city maps, leading you about the city and its many sets of stairs. The **German Colony** route (1102 stairs) does a circle around the Baha'i sites, the Nuns of Nazareth school, and the German Colony. The **Wadi Nisnas** route (1021 stairs) takes you from below the Haifa Museum, through the stream bed of Wadi Nisnas, down to where the sailors hawk their wares from sidewalk stalls. Both the **Kikkar Paris** route (1025 stairs) and the **Old City** route (1034 stairs) start at the steps by Yefe Nof in Carmel Center, and descend all the way to the bottom tier of the city. Call Tourist Information, *Tel. 04-837-4010*, for more information.

There are also nature walks set up and marked by **SPNI**, *Tel. 04-866-4135*, through wadis, orchards, and historic sites. The **Haifa Ramblers Club**, *Tel. 04-866-4181*, and the **Carmel Field School**, *Tel. 04-866-4159*, can also give advice on nature walks.

WHERE TO STAY
In Center Carmel
DAN PANORAMA, *107 HaNassi, Tel. 04-835-2222, Fax 04-835-2235, has 267 rooms from $126-$180 during regular season, plus 15% service charge and peak period/weekend supplements, including a full Israeli breakfast.*

This is a soaringly tall building, visible from much of Haifa. Nice enough rooms with all standard luxury hotel amenities, and fine views of the city and harbor, the hotel also offers a swimming pool and children's pool, secretarial and telex services, and Chaplins, an in-house disco.

DAN CARMEL, *85-87 HaNassi, Tel. 04-830-6306, Fax 04-838-7504, has 219 rooms for $164-$206 in regular season, not including 15% service charge and supplements, but yes including full Israeli breakfast.*

There's a splashy fountain outside and an elegant lobby within. Nice enough rooms, balcony, views. It's pricier and a little classier than the Panorama.

BETH SHALOM, *110 HaNassi, Tel. 04-837-7481, Fax 04-837-2443, has 30 rooms for $70, including service charge and full Israeli breakfast. No credit cards accepted, three-day minimum stay required.*

Across the street from the Nof, next to Tourist Information, right by the bus stop, it's a nice mid-price alternative to the luxury hotels that dominate Center Carmel. Comfy little rooms are done in warm colors with phone and welcome fruit basket, little sofa/bench, no TV. They offer set lunches for $15 and dinners for $10.

NOF HOTEL, *101 HaNassi, Tel. 04-835-4311, Fax 04-838-8810, has 92 rooms including full Israeli breakfast which go for $75-$120, with half (+$25) and full board (+$50) options, not including 15% service charge and a Passover supplement of $10.*

The rooms are very pleasant, with window seat cushions by bay views, and the suites are beautiful (honeymooner discounts available). The nicest and most reasonable of the luxury hotels, it has an appealing lounge and comfy chairs, and they offer free passes to the Nofar disco next door.

HOTEL SHULAMIT, *15 Kiryat Sefer, Tel. 04-834-2811, Fax 04-825-5206, has 70 rooms for $75-$85 a single and $100-$100 a double in regular season, breakfast included, but not the 15% service charge.*

All the rooms have phone, TV, and bath and are average but nice.

DVIR HOTEL, *124 Yafe Nof, Tel. 04-838-9131, Fax 04-838-1068, has 35 rooms, with singles for $52 and doubles for $91, including service charge and Israeli breakfast.*

This training hotel under Dan Hotel management provides access to all of the HaNassi Dan hotel perks like use of their pools, disco passes, etc. The rooms are okay and some have harbor views, and there's a nice little terrace overlooking the street and the bay.

In Hadar

HOTEL ALIYA, *35 HeHalutz, Tel. 04-862-3918, is priced somewhat randomly, depending on managerial mood. Persistence may lower them, but generally a single is NIS 100, and a double NIS 140.*

Ten dowdy rooms without air conditioning are run by a Russian couple who don't speak much English. The rooms themselves are okay for the price, and shouldn't be ruled out if you don't want a hostel with its dorms and curfews, but it's a noisy and busy place at night, with an odd assortment of guests. Towels and soap are provided, but the share toilets are sticky and foul.

EDEN HOTEL, *8 Shmarjahu Levin, off HeHalutz, Tel. 04-866-4816, has 15 rooms for $30 a single and $45 a double.*

Sordid and run down, this place is hardly paradise. The staff didn't seem eager for business, refused to show a room, and claimed untruth-

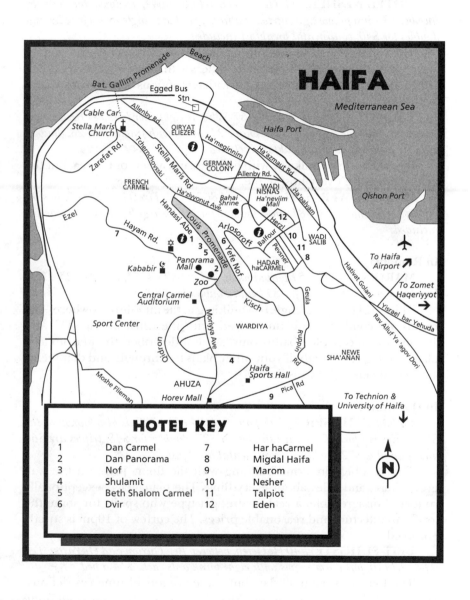

HAIFA

Mediterranean Sea

Bat. Gallim Promenade
Beach
Bat. Gallim Promenade
Egged Bus Stn
Cable Car
Allenby Rd
Stella Maris Church
QIRYAT ELIEZER
Haifa Port
Ha'meginnim
GERMAN COLONY
Zarefat Rd.
Tchernichovski
Stella Maris Rd
Ha'azmaut Rd
Allenby Rd.
FRENCH CARMEL
Ha'ziyyonut Ave.
Bahai Shrine
WADI NISNAS
Ha'neviim Mall
Ha'palyam
Qishon Port
Ezel
Hanassi Abe
Louis Promenade
Arlosoroff
Herzl
12
Balfour
10
11
WADI SALIB
8
To Haifa Airport
Hayam Rd.
7
3 5
6
Yefe Nof
Pevsner
Panorama Mall
2
HADAR haCARMEL
Hativat Golani
To Zomet Haqeriyyot
Kababir
Zoo
Central Carmel Auditorium
Kisch
Geula
Ruppin Rd
Yisrael bar Yehuda
Rav Alluf Ya'agov Dori
Sport Center
Moriyya Ave
WARDIYA
NEWE SHA'ANAN
Qidron
4
Haifa Sports Hall
Moshe Flieman
AHUZA
Horev Mall
9
Pica Rd
To Technion & University of Haifa

HOTEL KEY

1	Dan Carmel	7	Har haCarmel
2	Dan Panorama	8	Migdal Haifa
3	Nof	9	Marom
4	Shulamit	10	Nesher
5	Beth Shalom Carmel	11	Talpiot
6	Dvir	12	Eden

N

fully to be full. I'd take the hint and steer clear unless you are hard up and want to try your luck.

HOTEL NESHER, *53 Herzl, Tel. 04-862-0644, is down the path by number 53 – just follow signs up to the office. They have single rooms for $27 and doubles for $40, continental breakfast included.*

The rooms are clean with phone and little balcony overlooking an alley, some with air conditioning and others with fans. Not a luxury hotel, but adequate and reasonable in a city with few options between hostel and big bucks.

TALPIOT, *61 Herzl, Tel. 04-867-3753, is right over Hamber Restaurant and across from the post office. They have 24 rooms, with singles for $28, doubles for $36, and continental breakfast included.*

It's set on a little walkway with benches and a view of the sea, but the management isn't very hospitable.

HAIFA TOWER, *63 Herzl, Tel. 04-867-7111, Fax 04-862-1863, has 98 rooms, with singles for $81 and doubles for $106, regular season, breakfast included.*

In Romema

MAROM HOTEL, *51 Hapalmach, Tel. 04-825-4355, Fax 04-825-4358, has 45 rooms, with singles for $71 and doubles for $80.*

This is a big ugly rectangle of a building in the middle of nowhere. The rooms are comfortable if uninspired, with the usual phone, TV, and aircon, with nicely tiled bathrooms. A local described the Marom as a place you'd go for a night if your other plans fell through, and that seems an accurate enough assessment.

In Downtown

GERMAN HOSPICE, *105 Yafo, Tel. 04-855-3705, is also known as the St. Charles Hospice. They have singles for $27, doubles for $48, triples are $66 and a quad is $72, including continental breakfast.*

This is a big old stone building with tile floor, Jesus on the wall everywhere, and rules about everything. The manager is exceptionally rude and disagreeable, a real fussbudget type who spoils for some the lovely architecture and reasonable prices. The curfew of 10pm is strictly enforced.

BEIT-EL HOSTEL, *40 HaGefen, between Ben Gurion and HaYaroq, Tel. 04-852-1110, has dorm rooms with eight bunk beds each, $14 a bed.*

The lounge is open all day, but there are lots of time restrictions. Wake up call at 7am, out of the dorm by 9am, registration from 5pm-10pm, and curfew is 11pm. However, there's a luggage room available for drop off before 5pm, the staff is friendly, and there's a lovely garden. You can get continental breakfast for 2 NIS extra, there's a picnic area and a volleyball court, and lots of literature and study resources on Christianity in the lobby.

Further Afield
 CARMEL YOUTH HOSTEL, *Kfar Zamir, Carmel Beach, Tel. 04-853-1944, is four kilometers south of Haifa. Dorm beds (six per room) are NIS 68 for members, NIS 72 for non-members, and private rooms are NIS 140, breakfast included.*
 The location is inconvenient though the beach is nice and there's no curfew. Bus 45 or 43 gets you there, but it's not worth it.
 RAMAT YOHANAN YOUTH HOSTEL, *off Route 70, Tel/Fax 04-844-2976, is 15 kilometers northeast of Haifa. The facility has 180 beds, and there's hiking nearby. If going by public transport, take bus 66 from Haifa.*
 There are also accommodations down the coast (**NEVE YAM** Camping and Holiday Flats) and in the Druze villages (**STELLA CARMEL HOSPICE**), detailed in the Carmel section above.

WHERE TO EAT
In Center Carmel
 CHIN LUNG, *126 HaNassi, Tel. 04-838-1308*, is open daily 12pm-3pm and 6:30pm-12am. Walk down the stairs and around the back to this popular Chinese restaurant in business for 23 years, with meals NIS 27-30. Visa & Mastercard accepted.
 SEA WAVES, *99 Yefe Nof, Tel. 04-838-3025, Fax 04-833-7701*, is open Saturday-Thursday 12pm-3:30pm, 7pm-11:30pm, Friday 12pm-3pm, 7pm-12:15am. This restaurant has an attractive dining room with stone walls, Chinese ornaments, and a harbor view, as well as good Chinese food with entrees starting at NIS 35.
 EL GAUCHO, *120 Yefe Nof, Tel. 04-837-0997*, is an Argentinean meat restaurant, popular with some and thought to be over-rated by others. Steaks go for around NIS 45.
 THE BANK, *119 HaNassi, Tel. 04-838-9623*, is open Sunday-Thursday 8am-1:30am, Friday-Saturday till 2:30ish. With a nice wood deck outside, and big salads, pancakes and breakfasts costing NIS 21-22. It's a popular hang-out and lunch spot, coffee and conversation spot, and watching the crowds walk by outside spot. Inside the tables are a bit close together, and as always, it's smokey, albeit hip.
 PIZZA SPOT, *130 HaNassi*, is open till 1am nightly, NIS 7 a slice, to take away or eat in.
 FRUIT AND ICE CREAM, *131 HaNassi*, is small stand with fresh fruit juice or ice cream for NIS 6.
 KAPULSKY CAFE, *HaNassi*, just next to Dan Towers, is a good place to sit, drink coffee, have dessert, see and be seen, at Carmel Center prices.

In Hadar
    VOILA, *21A Nordau, the midravov, Tel. 04-866-4529*, is open Saturday-Thursday 12pm-12:30am, Friday 12pm-4:30pm, 7:30pm-1:30am. With Swiss-French cuisine, it's very popular with locals, even at midnight. Walls full of interesting hanging objects: scythe, photos, wooden comb, cow bell, sculpture. Soups (including bouillabaisse) cost NIS 18-24, there's a big salad selection (NIS 24-28), and entrees (including fondue) are NIS 36-60. In addition, there are two pages of desserts. Wood bound menu, greenhouse feel, hanging plants everywhere and artful candles on the tables help make this an especially appealing place.
    FALAFEL/SHASHLIK/BAKERIES, *HeHalutz near Hanev'im*. Fresh squeezed juices (orange/grapefruit/apple) for NIS 2 and carrot for NIS 3 doled out by an old man on stool. A great street to walk down, especially if you're hungry, though the cars and the honking can get on your nerves.
    TAKE AWAY PIZZA, *20 Hanevi'im*, is open on Shabbat. And there are lots more cafés and restaurants to browse among on the Nordau midrahov.

In Downtown
    MIXGRILL, *7 Ben Gurion (intersecting with Yafo)*, is a small new restaurant with mixed grill and Oriental salads, a pleasant, reasonably priced place for a meal.,
    There are loads of cheap restaurants on **Ben Gurion** and **Allenby** serving good Arabic food. There's also a **fruit and vegetable market** just west of Kikkar Paris between Nahum and Nathan.

PLANT A TREE IN HAIFA
To plant a tree at a Jewish National Fund center, call their 16 Herzl office at 04-866-4341.

SEEING THE SIGHTS
Center Carmel
    Tikotin Museum of Japanese Art, *89 HaNassi, Tel. 04-838-3554*, is one of the world's premier Japanese Art centers, with large collections of Oriental paintings, graphics, jewelry, and handicrafts in a lovely shoji-screened environment. They're open Sunday, Monday, Wednesday, Thursday 10am-4pm, Tuesday 4-7pm, Friday 10am-1pm, and Saturday 10am-2pm, and admission costs NIS 15 per adult, NIS 12 for children, NIS 7.5 per student or senior. Or you can buy a family ticket for NIS 30. All tickets cover all three museums (Haifa, Japanese Art, and Maritime). Take buses 22, 23, or Carmelit.

Mané Katz Museum, *89 Yefe Nof, Tel. 04-838-3482*, is open Sunday, Monday, Wednesday, Thursday 10am-4pm, Tuesday 2-6pm, Friday 10am-1pm, and Saturday 10am-2pm, and admission is free. The artwork of Mané Katz, the French impressionist painter (1894-1962) who was born in the Ukraine as Emanuel Katz, are exhibited here in his old home. Bus 21, 22, 23, 27, 30, 31 or Carmelit.

Louis Promenade, *all along Yefe Nof in Carmel Center*, is beautiful at night with pretty street lamps and a wonderful view of city and harbor, and it offers some stunning views during the day as well. Take bus 21, 22, 23, 27, 28, 37, or the Carmelit subway.

Gan Ha-Em (Mother's Park), *HaNassi Street, Central Carmel*, is a lovely park. Along with pleasant greenery and walks, the park houses the Zoo and the Museum of Prehistory. In the summer, there are open-air concerts here as well. Take bus 21, 22, 23, 27, 28, 37 or the Carmelit subway.

Haifa Zoo, Zoological and Botanical Gardens, *Gan Ha-Em (see above)*, *Tel. 04-837-2886*, is open Sunday-Thursday 8am-4pm, Friday 8am-1pm, Saturday 9am-4pm, but the hours seem subject to change. Admission is NIS 20 for adults, NIS 16 for children, soldiers and handicapped, and NIS 17 for students. In winter the zoo may close an hour earlier, and in July/August it's open till 6pm. It's an option to consider if traveling with children who are tired of museums and monasteries. The **Stekelis Museum of Prehistory**, *located in the zoo, Tel. 04-837-1833*, is open Sunday-Thursday 8am-3pm, Friday 8am-1pm, Saturday 10am-2pm, and in summer the museum is open till 6pm. They display archaeological artifacts from Carmel and northern Israel, and have dioramas of regional prehistoric life. Take bus 21, 22, 23, 27, 28, 37 or the Carmelit subway.

Baha'i Shrine and Gardens, *Tel. 04-835-8358*, also known as **The Shrine of the Bab**, is open 9am-12pm daily, the gardens are open 8am-5pm, and admission is free. The Bab (Siyyid Ali-Muhammad) was the Martyr-Herald of the Baha'i religion; he broke away from Islam in Persia in 1844 declaring his religious mission, was publicly executed in Tabriz in 1850 at the age of 31, and his bones were transferred to Haifa in 1909 to be buried in this gold-domed mausoleum. You can go inside, but you must dress modestly and remove your shoes to enter the shrine, so wear your good socks.

Baha Ullah, the founder of the religion, was exiled to Akko in 1868 by the Sultan of Turkey after spending some time in Turkish prisons (following the Shah of Iran's banishment). He then spent some more time in prison in Akko till he died there in 1892. His son Abbas Effendi founded a world palace of justice in Haifa, designed the beautiful gardens here, and built the Bab mausoleum and archive temple in 1909 (the shrine, however, wasn't completed till 1953).

Not only of historical interest, the shrine is full of lovely thick Persian carpets to pad on and phenomenal crystal chandeliers. If you look through the lace curtains, you'll see the candelabra (lit only on Baha'i holy days) and still more carpets, as well as the remains of the Bab himself. Buses 22, 23, 25, or 26 will take you there.

Chagall Artist's House, *24 HaZiyyonut, Tel. 04-852-2355*, is open Sunday-Thursday 10am-1pm and 4-7pm, Saturday 10am-1pm. They show exhibits here of contemporary Israeli artists and admission is free. To bus here, take the 10, 12, or 22.

Gan Ha-Pesalim, *opposite 135 HaZiyyonut*, is a sculpture garden with 20 bronze sculptures by Ursula Malbin on grounds overlooking the bay. It's a nice view, a pleasant stroll and place to see, but no thrill. It's available as a Shabbat activity. Buses 22, 23, 25, 26 go there and admission is free.

Hadar

Haifa Museum, *26 Shabbetai Levy, Tel. 04-852-3255*, is open Sunday-Thursday, Saturday 10am-1pm, Tuesday, Thursday, Saturday 6pm-9pm, and has ancient art, modern art, and a music & ethnology section. Admission costs NIS 15 per adult, NIS 12 for children, NIS 7.5 per student or senior. Or you can buy a family ticket for NIS 30. All tickets cover all three museums (Haifa, Japanese Art, and Maritime). Bus 10, 12, 21, 28, 41, and Carmelit all go here.

Beit Hagefen, the Arab-Jewish Cultural Center, *2 Hegefen, Tel. 04-852-5251*, is near the Haifa Museum. The gallery is open Sunday-Thursday 8am-7pm, Friday 8am-1pm, Saturday 10am-1pm, and admission is free. Buses 10, 12, 22, 41, and 42 pass here.

National Museum of Science Design and Technology, *Shmaryahu Levin, Tel. 04-862-8111*, is in the old Technion Building. Open Sunday, Monday, Wednesday, Thursday 9am-5pm, Tuesday 9am-7pm, and Saturday 10am-3pm, this is a science activity center illustrating basic principles and advances in Israeli industry. Take bus 12, 21, 24, 28, or 37.

Binyamin Garden, *off Arlozoroff*, with its fountain and greenery, stone steps and cafés, is a nice and relatively quiet place to rest and read. There's a free public bathroom if you're desperate, but bring your own tissues and hold your nose.

Gan Hazikkaron (Memorial Park), *opposite City Hall*, is a park dedicated to Haifa's fallen heroes. Buses 15, 16, 19, 21, 37, and the Carmelit subway all go there. No biggy, unless you especially want to see the plaque to the Haifa Liberation of 1948.

Grand Synagogue, *60 Herzl*, has on its facade a bas relief of Elijah in his chariot blowing a shofar, the children of Israel following behind bringing the golden menorah to Jerusalem.

Nordau Pedestrian Mall, *parallel to Herzl, center of Hadar*, has a chic collection of restaurants and outdoor cafés. Buses 19 and 37 can drop you there.

Downtown
Maritime-Mediterranean Museum, *198 Allenby, Tel. 04-853-6622*, is near the port. It's open Sunday, Monday, Wednesday, and Thursday 10am-4pm, Tuesday 4-7pm, Friday 10am-1pm, and Saturday 10am-2pm. Admission costs NIS 15 per adult, NIS 12 for children, NIS 7.5 per student or senior. Or you can buy a family ticket for NIS 30. All tickets cover all three museums (Haifa, Japanese Art, and Maritime). Well-marked English signs explain this unexpectedly interesting museum. Upstairs are beautiful ancient Arabic and Chinese compasses, lovely sextants, and a handy pocket sundial.

The scientific instrument section has magnificent pieces, including arabic navigational devices and 17th century astronomy texts. There are also old maps and ship models for those who like that sort of thing. Also good, the fish pendants, figures, and fish hooks from around the world. Downstairs is the Marine Ethnology section, with African art, Ashanti weights, Maori and Luristani sections, and more. If pressed for time, start with the top floor which is the best, then head for the bottom level. The middle level is a bit less scintillating. By bus, take the 3, 5, 43, 44, or 45.

Clandestine Immigration & Naval Museum, *204 Allenby, Tel. 04-853-6249*, is open Sunday-Thursday 9am-4pm, Friday 9am-1pm, and costs NIS 6 for adults, NIS 3 for all others. This museum is devoted to the history of Israel's navy, and the ship *Afalpi* which ran the blockade during the British Mandate period. Buses 3, 5, 43, 44, and 45 go here.

Railway Museum, *Hativat Golani near Feisal Square, Tel. 04-856-4293*, is in the old Haifa-East Railway station. Open Sunday, Tuesday, Thursday 9am-noon, they have a collection of train memorabilia, restored locomotives and such. To get here, take bus 17, 41, or 42.

El Istiklal Mosque, *Feisal Square, Tel. 04-866-7592*, is not far from the Railway Museum. The largest of the three mosques in Haifa, it stands at one end of the former Islamic graveyard.

Elijah's Cave, *corner of HaHagannah and Allenby, Tel. 04-852-7430*, is open Sunday-Thursday 8am-5pm, Friday 8am-1pm and admission is free. The cave is holy to Jews, Christians, Moslems, and Druze as it is believed to have been the center of Elijah's activities as well as the spot where the Holy Family is said to have stayed on their return from Egypt. Buses 3, 5, 43, 44, and 45 go there.

Bat Gallim Promenade, *along the waterfront*, is an area for fishing or just relaxing under the palms. Take bus 3a, 40, 41, or 42.

Dagon Grain Silo & Archaeological Museum, *Plumer Square, Tel. 04-866-4221*, is near the port. Guided tours are held free of charge Sunday-Friday at 9am to learn about grain storage and handling in ancient Israel and the Near East. Take buses 10, 12, 15, 16, 17, 18, or 22.

Israel Industry Oil Museum, *Shemen Oil Factory, Haifa's industrial area, Tel. 04-865-4333*, is for those interested in the oil industry. Open Sunday-Thursday 8:30-3pm, and housed in the original old factory made of stone, this museum exhibits all sorts of ancient and modern items, all oil-related. Bus 2 goes there.

Outlying Areas

The **University of Haifa**, top of Mount Carmel, Tel. 04-824-0097, is on the road to the Druze villages. Free guided tours start at the Main Building Sunday-Thursday 8am-3pm (call to arrange), or you can wander around and see the modern architecture and panoramic views on your own. In the main building is the **Reuben and Edith Hecht Gallery**, *Tel. 04-825-7773*. Open Sunday, Monday, Wednesday, Thursday 10am-4pm, Tuesday 10am-7pm, Friday 10am-1pm, and Saturday 10am-2pm, and free of charge, they show many archaeological items on the theme of The People of Israel in the Land of Israel. **Eshkol Tower** rises 30 stories from the student activities center, and its **observatory**, *Tel. 04-824-0007*, provides magnificently panoramic views. Bus 24, 36, 37, 93, 191, and 192 go there.

The **Cable Car**, *Tel. 04-833-5970*, is fun transport between Stella Maris up on the top of Mount Carmel and Bat Gallim down by the sea. It operates Sunday-Thursday, Saturday 9am-6pm in winter and till 11pm in summer, Friday 9am-2pm, but closes in stormy weather. Up top Stella Maris there's a little coffee shop with great views of the descent. The cable car ride itself is NIS 16 round trip and 10 one way for an adult, NIS 14 and 8 for a child, and for it you get the ride, the views, and a narration of points of interest on your right and left.

The **Carmelite Church and Monastery**, *Derekh Stella Maris, Tel. 04-833-2084*, is open daily 8:30am-1:30pm and 3-6pm, and admission is free. The Carmelites are a religious group affiliated with the Catholic Church, named after Mount Carmel where the Order first got its start. Towards the end of the 12th century some Crusaders who had settled on Mount Carmel decided to emulate Elijah the Prophet by living like hermits in the mountain grottoes. In the early 1200s their Prior, Saint Brocard, incorporated them into the diocese of Jerusalem and initiated the Carmelite Order.

The next 600 years were fairly rocky for the Carmelites. They had to leave the Holy Land in 1291 when Saint Jean of Acre fell. They were back in 1631 and built a small monastery near the lighthouse, but in 1767 Daher el-Omar ordered them to demolish their monastery and leave. So they moved to their present site and built a church and monastery over a grotto where Elijah was said to have lived, first clearing the ruins of a Greek medieval church known as The Abbey of Saint Margaret. Soon after, in 1799, Napoleon showed up and used the monastery as a hospital for his soldiers. When the Turks forced Napoleon to retreat, the church was damaged and the Carmelites were driven out as well. When they were able to return they gave Napoleon's dead an honorable garden burial and put up a pyramid-shaped tomb in their memory.

In 1821, Abdallah Pasha of Acre ordered the ruined church to be totally destroyed. The present church, the Stella Maris, was opened in 1836, and the beautiful paintings on the dome were done by Brother Luigi Poggi in 1924-28. They show Elijah in his Chariot of Fire and King David with his harp, as well as the Saints of the Order, the Prophets Isaiah, Ezekiel, Daniel, and the Holy Family. The stained-glass windows also depict Elijah in the desert and in his Chariot of Fire. The monastery now contains an extension of the International College of Theology of the Carmelites in Rome and a **Pilgrim Hospice**. The church has a small antiquities museum full of ho-hum shards and stone fragments as well as an elaborate creche diorama with running water and moving waves of the Mediterranean Sea. Friars walk about in their brown robes, and the gift shop Brother says an enthusiastic "Bravo" with little provocation. Buses 25, 26, 27, 30, and 31 will all get you there.

Kababir is a small village at the end of Kabbirim Street on Mount. Carmel. It is populated by Moslems of the Ahmadiya sect, and bus 34 from Central Carmel goes there.

Tel Shiqmona, a small hill between the coastal plain and the bay of Haifa, is an excavation of the ancient village site. So far they've found some Hellenistic remains as well as eight Byzantine floor mosaics from a large 6th or 7th century synagogue.

For the **beaches**, there are miles of them, with toilet and shower facilities; take bus 41, 42, 43, 44, 44a, or 45. In summer there are additional buses: 11a 24a, 26a, 33a.

NIGHTLIFE & ENTERTAINMENT

Check the *Events in Haifa* booklet or the *What's Hot in Haifa Hotline, Tel. 04-837-4253*, for more information.

Center Carmel

To find the **Fever Club**, go down the main steps at the entrance to Gan Ha-Em and turn left; it's just behind the Paradise Bar. And right after the Fever Club is the **B-52 Pub**.

The **Back Door Pub**, next to 120 Yefe Nof, open until 3-4am, is an okay place with a deck.

The **Paradise Bar**, *located in the park (Gan Ha-Em)*, is a small smoky place with loud music.

Nofar Nightclub, *just past the 101 HaNassi Nof Hotel entrance, Tel. 04-835-4311*, has a sign pointing down an alley to the club, and is open weekends 11pm-5am or whenever. The oddly lit key hole entrance opens to a disco that gets hopping around 1ish with the 30 something crowd of local professionals. Friday cover is NIS 30, Saturday is NIS 20. They have a band that plays 60's music, old disco, and Israeli folk.

Pub Restaurant, *off Yefe Nof by the Allenby Garden steps*, can be found by their red & white Hebrew sign pointing you down. They've big smoky rooms inside, winning views out on the deck, and snacks/toasts NIS 17-20, draft beer for NIS 8, and lots of fancy drinks with questionable names for NIS 17. If you're bored you can ask the bartender what goes into a "Good Fuck" (answer: Southern Comfort and orange juice).

Bear Pub, *135 HaNassi*. Outside the milling teens overflow from the Joystick arcade, inside it's quiet and dark, and men sit hunched over booze.

Hadar

The **Nordau Pedestrian Mall** (the **midrahov**) has most of the Hadar night action, with outdoor cafes, bars, and occasional outdoor music concerts.

MASH Pub, *on the Nordau midrahov*, is usually overflowing with tourists interested in drinking. Be forewarned, it has ultraviolet light that will make you gleam if you're wearing white.

The **Rodeo Pub**, *23 Balfour Street, Tel. 04-867-4363*, is a woody pub that's been in operation for 20 years and is an appealing place for a drink. With good music, not too loud, there are nice touches like tinted green lamps, and bowls of olives and nuts on the bar. With a mix of people and ages, it's open daily till late, and a beer costs NIS 9/13 (small/large).

Downtown

For port area sleaze, feel free to visit the **London Pride**, *85 Ha'Atzmaut*. Nearby is **The Pub**, *102 Ha'Atzmaut*, for a similarly dark and slightly rough milieu.

Other Entertainment

For a different kind of scene, check out the **Israeli Folkdancing**, *Technion, Beit Hastudent*. Thursdays at 8pm and Saturdays at 10pm there are folkdancing classes, and Sunday at 8:30pm there's folkdancing as well.

Haifa Municipal Theater, *50 Pevsner, Tel. 04-862-0670*, and the Haifa Cinematheque, *142 HaNassi, 04-838-3424*, are worth checking for non-disco entertainment.

Nearby, the Haifa Auditorium, *138 HaNassi, Tel. 04-838-0013*, often features the Haifa Symphony Orchestra. Check with Tourist Information or call the auditorium for a schedule.

SPORTS & RECREATION

SPNI, *8 Menahem, Tel. 04-866-4135*, has lots of information on local nature routes, and they also lead some hikes.

Haifa Ramblers Club, *Tel. 04-866-4181*, and the Carmel Field School *Tel. 04-866-4159*, can also provide information on local hikes.

Haifa Sports Hall, *Romena, Tel. 04-824-1012*, is another information resource.

To go sailing, call Ma'agan Shachaf, *Tel. 04-841-8765*, or Galei-Yam, Tel. *04-864-1744*, both in Kishon port.

Haifa's Squash Center, *Tel. 04-853-9160*, is in Kfar Zamir, and so is the Tennis Center, *Tel. 04-852-2721*.

For bowling, try the Hyperkol Center, *Kiriat Ata junction, Tel. 04-872-0529*, or the bowling alley, *5 Maklef, Check Post junction, Tel. 04-841-4735*.

Ice Skating, *Lev Hamifratz shopping center, Tel. 04-841-5388*, is another option.

There are a few swimming pools in Haifa. Maccabi center, *Bikkurim Street, Tel. 04-838-8341*, in Carmel Central has an outdoor pool for summer, an indoor heated pool for winter use, and admission NIS 25. The Technion Pool, *Tel. 04-823-5944*, also has a sauna, and charges NIS 35 (NIS 25 with ISIC card). There's also the a pool at Neve Sha'anan sport center, *Ya'acov Dori Street, Tel. 04-832-1029*.

For diving, snorkeling and windsurfing, try Yamit Haifa, *Tel. 04-851-2418*, or Shehafit, *Tel. 04-851-4809*, in Bat Galim.

For skiing and gliding, call Rosen & Meents, *105 Hahagannah, Tel. 04-855-5554*.

Beaches provide miles of swimming and tanning joy. Hof Bat Galim is near the central bus station and gets fairly crowded. Hahof Hashaqet is a 10 minute walk from the bus station (or take bus 41) and it costs NIS 5. Hof Hacarmel is free, as are Hof Dado and Hof Zamir, both a little further south, and accessible on bus 44 and 45 lines.

PRACTICAL INFORMATION

Books

Lia's Books, *5 Kiriyat Sefer, Tel. 04-825-5467*, is open Sunday-Thursday 9am-1pm, 4pm-7pm, Friday 9am-1pm. They have a big selection of used English books, (around NIS 12-25) as well as new (discounted 5%)

and French/German/Hebrew. **Hadar's used book store**, *33 Ha-Halutz*, has a good selection of used English books.

And **Steimatzky** has two bus station branches, as well as one downtown at *82 HaAtzma'ut*, at *16 Herzl* in Hadar, and there's one in Carmel Center as well.

Car Rental Agencies
• **Hertz**, *19 Yafo, Tel. 04-852-3239*
• **Avis**, *7 Ben Gurion, Tel. 04-851-3050*
• **Budget**, *46 HaHistadrut, Tel. 04-842-4004*
• **Eldan**, *95 HaNassi, Tel. 04-837-5303*
• **Reliable**, *33 HaHistadrut, Tel. 04-842-2832*
• **Traffic**, *28 Natanzon, Tel. 04-862-1330*

Crisis Lines
Rape Crisis Center, *Tel. 04-866-0111*, and **Emotional First Aid**, *Tel. 04-867-2222*, speak English and are open 24 hours.

Currency Exchange
You'll find plenty of these places on Yafo in downtown and on HaNevi'im in Hadar. The **American Express**, *Meditrad Ltd., 2 Khayat Square, Tel. 04-864-2267*, office is in the port and is open Sunday-Thursday 9am-5pm.

Emergencies
In case of **fire**, call *Tel. 102*. For **First Aid (Magen David Adom)** call *Tel. 101* or go to *10 Yizhaq Sadeh Street*. For the **police**, call *Tel. 100* or go to *28 Yafo Street*.

English News & Programs
Israel TV is on at 6:15pm. **BBC** (1323 KHz) airs at 2:15pm, 3pm, 6pm. **Voice of America** (1260, 15205, 15260, and 9700 KHz) airs at 6am, 7am, 5:30pm, 6pm.

Hospitals
• **Ha-Carmel**, 7 Michal, Tel. 04-825-0211
• **Rambam**, Bat Galim, Tel. 04-854-3111
• **Benei Zion (Rothschild)**, 47 Golomb, Tel. 04-835-9359
• **Haifa Medical Center**, 15 Horev, Tel. 04-830-5222
• **Elisha'**, *Tel. 04-838-9121* or toll-free *Tel. 177-022-8389*

Laundry
Kalujny, *25 Pevsner, Hadar* and *30 Ge'ula*, charges NIS 18 per wash

and dry, and the branch at *2 Liberia* charges NIS 8 per kilo to wash, dry, and fold.

Pharmacies
Shomron, *44 Yafo, downtown, Tel. 04-852-4171*; **HeHalutz**, *12 HeHalutz, Hadar, Tel. 04-866-2962*; **Merkaz**, *130 HaNassi, Carmel Center, Tel. 04-838-1979*.

Post Offices & International Phone Calls
The **main post office**, *19 HaPalyam*, with poste restante and direct dial international phones, is in the port area. There are also direct dial phones at the Hanevi'im branch, *corner of Shabtai Levi, Hadar*, and there's a branch at the *central bus station* as well.

Shopping Centers
Migdal Hanevi'im, *2 Huri, Tel. 04-867-8337*, **Panorama Center**, *109 President Avenue, Tel. 04-837-5011*, **Horev Center**, *Tel. 04-824-6160*, and **Lev Hamifratz**, *55 HaHistadrut, Tel. 04-841-6090*. For English language information on Haifa shopping, call *Tel. 04-837-4253*.

Subway (Carmelit)
Open Sunday-Thursday 6am-10pm, Friday 6am-3pm, Saturday open half an hour after sundown, it goes from near the port on up to Carmel Center, stopping at Kikkar Paris, Solel Boneh, HaNevi'im, Masada, Golomb, and Gan Ha-Em.

Tourist Information Offices
The **Carmel Center** office, *106 HaNassi, Tel. 04-837-4010, Fax 04-837-2953*, is open Sunday-Thursday 8am-6pm, Friday 8am-1pm. There's also the **Hadar** office, *18 Herzl, Tel. 04-866-6521*, and **Downtown** tourist information offices, lower level of the bus station, *Tel. 04-851-2208*, City Hall, *Tel. 04-841-6090*, and in Haifa Port, *Tel. 04-864-5692*. The offices are helpful, and stocked with maps, train schedules, and the bimonthly Events in Haifa booklet. For information in English, call *Tel. 04-837-4253*.
Issta (Israel Student Tour Association), *2 Balfour, 04-867-0222*.

Tours
Egged Tours, *4 Nordau, Tel. 04-862-3131, Central Bus Station, Tel. 04-854-9486*; **United Tours**, *5 Nordau, Tel. 04-866-5656*; **Mitzpa Tours**, *1 Nordau, Tel. 04-867-4341*; **Carmel Touring**, *126 HaNassi, Tel. 04-838-8882*.
The **Haifa Tourism Association** organizes a free guided walking tour Saturdays at 10am, which meets at the corner of Sha'ar HaLevenon and Yefe Nof in Carmel Center.

15. NORTH OF HAIFA

AKKO

Akko (**Acre**) was founded by the Phoenicians on the Bay of Haifa, 19 kilometers north of Haifa. Some visitors come for the beautiful beaches and others for the choice hummus, but most come to take in the Islamic and Crusader City feel of minarets, winding cobbled streets and stone crypts.

The history of this town goes way back. It's been besieged repeatedly over the centuries by Romans, Arabs, Crusaders, Turks, Napoleon, and the British. Joshua assigned the town to the tribe of Asher, but the Israelites were never able to conquer it (Judges 1:31). It was for the most part ruled by Tyre or Egypt until the Assyrians took control circa 700 BCE. Alexander the Great established a mint here in 333 BCE, and with its active port the town was quite important. After Alexander's death the Egyptian Ptolemites redubbed it Ptolemais, and Jonathan the Maccabean was killed here by the Seleucids in 143 BCE.

The Romans ruled for a couple of centuries, though when Caesarea was developed in 22 BCE the importance of Akko's port dwindled. Under the Byzantines (324-640 CE) Akko was a bishop's seat until it was taken by the Arabs in 636 CE. With the decline of Caesarea's port (due to silt), Akko regained prominence as a port city.

In 1067 an earthquake did major damage, followed by the Crusaders under Baldwin I in 1104. Sultan Saladin reconquered in 1187, Richard the Lionheart regained the city in 1191, and for the next century Saint Jean d'Acre (as it was then known) was the capital of the Crusader kingdom of Jerusalem. During those years Akko was an important center for Jewish learning, attracting rabbis from England and France. Other Europeans of note visited as well; both Saint Francis of Assisi and Marco Polo stopped by, and Akko's prominence as a trading port grew.

Then in 1291 al-Malik al-Ashraf put Akko under siege for two months, conquered, and destroyed. The town was deserted for the next few centuries, but came back to life when Druze Emir Fakhr ed-Din decided to rebuild in the early 1600s.

In the 1700s, Pasha el-Jazzar, an Albanian mercenary whose name ("the butcher") was based on character rather than occupation, enlarged the town and built the fine structures people now come to see, such as the outer wall, the Grand Mosque, Hammam, and more. In 1799 Napoleon besieged Akko but was thwarted by the British navy under Sir Sidney Smith. In 1832 the Egyptian army under Ibrahim Pasha took Akko from the Ottoman Turks, and they ruled for eight years until the British intervened in Turkey's favor.

After the fall of the Ottoman Empire, the British made their presence known again, and from 1918-1948 the town was under British Mandate control. The British citadel prison in Acre was the scene of fierce Jewish resistance fighting, and on May 17, 1948 Israeli troops took possession. Since then, Akko has been made up of the Old City as well as a modern Akko which has developed outside the city walls. A large Arab population remains, and it's reflected in the food, the market, el-Jazzar's architecture which continues to dominate the old city, and the need for foreign women to dress modestly.

Akko still gets besieged frequently these days, by tour buses. Early mornings and late evenings are the most peaceful times to take in the special feel of the city. Akko by night is beautiful, with the moon and the sea, the walls lit by the lighthouse flashes, and it's peaceful in the morning before the tour groups arrive, with merchants washing their walks and setting up for the day. Day or night, it's a picturesque city and worth a visit.

ORIENTATION

All the main sites are in the Old City, a small but labyrinthine area to try to get to know. There are a couple of entry points to within the Old City walls. The entrance off **Weizmann Street** puts you right by the Grand Mosque, tourist information office, and Walied's Hostel. There are also entrances off **HaHaganah Street** by the Sea Wall. Entering at the southern Sea Gate (near the lighthouse) puts you right by the Fishing Port, the Acre Youth Hostel, and the Bazaar.

It's possible to navigate the Old City with a map and by asking directions, but it's also fun to just wander about and see where your feet take you. The main Old City streets are **Aj-Jazzar** and **Salah-ed-Din**, **Weizmann Street** connects the old city with the new, and **Ha'Atzma'ut** is the main street in the new city, with the supermarket, central post office, and City Hall.

ARRIVALS & DEPARTURES
By Car
Take the Akko turn off from the coastal highway of route 4, and get on Ben Ami Street. From there, you can follow Ben Ami to the sea and turn left on HaHaganah. Drive along the sea wall till you get to the parking lots near the lighthouse. This is the most convenient place to ditch your car, as it allows you to avoid driving in the Old City (something worth avoiding).

It is possible, however undesirable, to enter the Old City by car. If such is your wish, turn left from Ben Ami onto Weizmann, enter the city near the Grand Mosque, and park in the lot near the bus stand, or on the street if you can find a space.

By Bus
From the bus station, *Ha'Arba'a Road, Tel. 04-991-6333*, in the new city, turn left and walk one block to the traffic lights, where you turn right on Ben Ami. Go four blocks and turn left on Weizmann and you will begin to approach the Old City. There are plenty of #252 buses between Akko and Haifa (even on Saturdays). The 271 goes to Nahariya, and there are half hourly buses to Tzfat as well.

By Train
The train station, *David Remez Street, Tel. 04-991-2350*, is across from the central bus station. The Tel Aviv-Nahariya trains stop in Akko, but there aren't many trains a day.

By Sherut
Sheruts to Haifa leave from the small street off Ha'Arba'a across from the bus station.

By Tour
Egged does a day tour from Haifa that takes you to Akko and Rosh Hanikra.

GETTING AROUND TOWN
The only way to get around the Old City is by foot. You can go on a tour or on your own, but either way it's going to entail walking. For a **taxi** call **Akko Ba'am**, *Tel. 04-991-6666*, or **Riyeh**, *Tel. 04-991-0077*.

WHERE TO STAY
Acre Beach (also known as Purple Beach, or *Hof Argaman* in Hebrew) is slightly south of Akko along the coastal highway, and has the area's two

up-scale hotels. It's a few minutes drive or a ten minute walk from Land Gate along Yonatan HaHoshmonai Street.

PALM BEACH, *Acre Beach, POB 2192, Acre, 24101, Tel. 04-981-5815, Fax 04-991-0434, with 119 rooms facing Haifa Bay, is the one good quality hotel in Acre, with singles for $79 and doubles for $104-$135.*

They are professional and clean, with good service, nice rooms, and fine facilities. Some rooms are bigger and better than others for VIP guests or families, so tell them your needs when you reserve. They have a restaurant, bar, disco, and pool, as well as tennis courts, basketball and soccer courts, ping-pong room and a fitness gym.

ARGAMAN HOTEL, *Acre Beach, POB 153, Acre, 24101, Tel. 04-991-6691, Fax 04-991-6690, has 75 rooms and the usual amenities. Prices range from $55-$60 a single, $70-$90 a double, depending on the season.*

It's not a hostel and the rooms are perfectly suitable, but it's not a hotel to sweep you off your feet with any style or personality.

Hostels in the Old City

If you want to stay right in the Old City (or if you don't have a car) your options are limited to the Akko hostels.

WALIED'S GATE HOSTEL, *Salah ed-Din Street, Old Acre, Tel./Fax 04-981-5530, near Land Gate, has eight rooms with 50 beds, and offers kitchen facilities and a luggage room as well. A bed in a dorm (2-12 per room) costs NIS 25, and a private room is NIS 100-150. The owner will make breakfast for an extra NIS 20.*

The dorms are small, the bunks narrow, though the private rooms boast double beds. Under construction is a cellar restaurant/pub. Walied is eager to please and will accept reservations over the phone. He offers a safe for valuables, tours of the area, and a good information board with maps. There's a midnight curfew, but he won't lock you out.

ACRE YOUTH HOSTEL, *POB 1090, Acre 24110, Old City, Tel./Fax 04-991-1982, is near the lighthouse. With 13 rooms (4-8 beds in each), this stunningly beautiful hostel offers dorm beds for $12 in winter, $14 in summer, breakfast included, reservations suggested. You can rent a locker for NIS 5. Curfew is 10:30pm.*

This hostel stands out among hostels for its magnificent architecture. With stucco walls and stone floors, the sitting room has a view of the water and a bright and spacious feel. Upstairs the lobby is exceptionally beautiful, with cathedral-type stained glass windows overlooking the sea, marble pillars and stone floor. The showers are hot, the toilets clean and airy, and the breakfast filling. You can't get a better value for $12.

NES AMMIM, *the International Christian Village, 04-995-0000, Fax 04-982-2871, is eight kilometers north of Akko and three kilometers from the coast. Rooms cost $74-$94 a single and $96-$136 a double, breakfast included.*

They've 48 rooms, all with air conditioning, radio, and private bath, with 24 specially designed handicapped-accessible rooms. The hotel has a swimming pool (seasonal), botanical gardens, Ecumenical House of Prayer, and a European, non-kosher kitchen.

WHERE TO EAT

Akko is held in high esteem, gastronomically speaking, by Israelis around the country for the fine hummus and baklava in Old Acre, and the reputation is well-deserved. For good, cheap Arabic staples, Akko is your city. You get great quality and large portions anywhere in the Old City, though you pay a little more for a view of the port.

Lots of small restaurants cluster near the **market** in Old Acre, and a good example is **SIMA'AN BROS. RESTAURANT**. They offer a huge bowl of delicious hummus with pita for NIS 10, with grilled meats and such for NIS 22-35. Nearby are stands of fresh-squeezed juice for NIS 3 a glass, stores of spices and Turkish coffee, and grills roasting spicy kebabs. It's a great place to be if you're hungry.

Across from the Tourist Info office are two restaurants with good hummus and other oriental foods: **ABU GEORGE** and **ABU OSAMAH**. Both are reliable, though Abu Osamah is a little cheaper.

ABU CHRISTO, Fishermen's Port, Old Acre, Tel. 04-991-0065, Fax 04-999-1653, has outside dining between the old walls and the sea, and a large indoor dining room overlooking the water. Open daily 10am-midnight, all credit cards accepted, the prices are low and their seafood specialties of consistent good quality.

Nearby, around the corner from the Akko Hostel, is a small **pita bakery** with good, fresh, cheap baked goods.

If you're hungry while in the new city, there are lots of falafel stands around Weizmann and Ben Ami.

SEEING THE SIGHTS

Gates & Walls

To enter the Old City, you must pass within the city walls through one of a number of Crusader gates. From Weizmann Street, the first signs of antiquity are the **wall and moat** that Ahmed el-Jazzar built in 1799 after Napoleon gave up on his siege and retreated, adding to the original Crusader fortifications. The **sea wall**, originally built by the Crusaders in the 12th century, was retouched at the same time, in part with stones taken from the Crusader castle at Atlit.

At the southern end of the peninsula in the middle of the bay is the **Tower of the Flies**. It sits on the site of the original lighthouse, but the connecting fortifications were destroyed in the 1837 earthquake. The **Sea Gate** (near Abu Christo restaurant and the fishing port) and the **Land Gate** (near Salah ed-Din Street and Walied's Hostel) both hail from the 12th century.

El-Jazzar Mosque sticks up like a needle fish from just within the old city walls, with its slender minaret and large green dome. The third largest mosque in Israel, it was completed in 1781 on the site of the Church of Saint John, and is open Saturday-Thursday 8am-12:30pm and 1:30-4pm, Friday 8-11am and 2-4pm, admission NIS 3, modest dress required. When you enter, guides will often offer to tour you around for four shekels extra and their presentations vary in quality. Make it clear if you don't want to be guided to avoid misunderstandings.

Built by Ahmed el-Jazzar, a former slave and captain of the Albanian soldiers, the mosque was constructed in the Turkish rococo style. In its courtyard stands a fine sundial, as well as the tops of underground cisterns which have been attributed to the Crusaders, built against times of siege, and also to el-Jazzar as his answer of what to do with the Crusader church beneath. Also in the courtyard are some lovely Roman columns taken from Caesarea. Inside, the mosque is peaceful and beautiful with Persian carpets, painted tiles and inlaid arabesques. There is also a shrine said to contain hairs of the Prophet's beard, which are displayed annually on the 27th day of Ramadan. To the right of the mosque is a small structure housing the sarcophogi of el-Jazzar and his son.

The **Crusader City**, Akko's most famous attraction, is opposite the Grand Mosque. It's open in summer Sunday-Thursday 8:30am-6:30pm, Friday 8:30am-2:30pm, Saturday 9am-6pm; in winter the hours are Sunday-Thursday 8:30am-5pm, Friday 8:30am-2pm, Saturday 9am-5pm. Tickets, available at the Tourist Information counter, cost NIS 12 an adult, NIS 9 a child/student/senior, and admit you to the museums as well. Forty-five minute guided tours are available for NIS 15 per person, minimum of five people per group. This was all street level in Crusader times, but it's now a subterranean city some eight meters down. There is, no doubt, more to be discovered, but excavations were stopped for fear the existing town of Akko would collapse.

Knight's Hall is a room with rubble and vaulted ceilings. The room is all that remains of the 13th century administrative quarters of the Order of Saint John of Jerusalem, and used to be known as the Hospitaller's Quarter. The *fleur-de-lys* are among the earliest known examples of the French imperial insignia, and the abstract designs are from the Ottoman period.

Connected by a narrow tunnel are the underground vaults and pillars of **Saint John's Crypt** (or Refectory). The halls of the original Crusader complex are now used in July for concerts by the Haifa Symphony Orchestra, as well as for the Fringe Theater Festival in the fall. Next to the Crypt is a staircase leading to a long underground passageway that takes you to six rooms which open to a central courtyard. It's conjectured that this was dug by Crusaders as a hiding place in case of attack, or alternatively as a sewage system. El-Jazzar restored it as a means of escape in case Napoleon made it inside the city walls.

Down el-Jazzar Street through the souq, and a little more visually interesting, is the **Hamam** or **Turkish Bath** (also known as the Municipal Museum). Built by el-Jazzar around 1780 based on the central baths of Cairo, they were still in use until shortly before Israel's 1948 War of Independence. The bath is good condition, with colorful tiles, marble, and glass in the ceiling that captured the sun's rays to heat the steam room in winter. Replacing the bath towels and attendants, the hamam now features artifacts of regional archaeology such as Canaanite period finds, and items relating to Arab and Druze ethnology.

To enter the **Khan el-Umdan** (Caravansary of the Pillars), go through the arched gateway topped by a five-storied **clock tower** (one of the Old City's better navigational landmarks), which was built in 1906 and named after Sultan Abdul Hamid II. The Khan, built by el-Jazzar for Turkish merchants toward the end of the 1700s, it was constructed on a former monastery site. The second floor housed the hostel, and the lower floor served as stables for the camels that came through bringing grain from the southern Golan to the port. The pillars of the title were stolen from nearby Caesarea, as were the pillars in the el-Jazzar Mosque. Near the Khan is the **Isnan Basha Mosque**, and the **Arab market**. The market is full of great smells and good, cheap food, and is worth strolling through. Also nearby in the southeast is the **fishing harbor** and marina, which has recently been built up for tourists with restaurants and sitting areas.

Museum of the Prisoners of the Underground, *10 Hahagana, Tel 049-918-264*, is in the Citadel. It's open Sunday-Thursday 8am-5pm and the admission is free. Baha Ullah the Persian, founder of the Bahai religion, was held prisoner here from 1868-1892. From 1920 onwards it was used by the British as a prison for Jewish resistance fighters such as Ze'ev Jabotinsky. The museum is dedicated to the Jewish underground who were imprisoned and executed here during British Mandate times. Across the street from the Prison Museum is the **Burj al-Kuraim**, the Fortress of the Vineyards.

You can climb the steps where Weizmann Street meets the wall to gain the heights of **Burj al-Kommander** (Commander's Fortress) for spectacular views. Near the Citadel are the **Gardens of the Citadel**, lovely and green, with ficus and palm trees and flowers. It's a refreshing spot after a tour of Crusader stones and prison walls.

Okashi Museum, *1 Weizman, Tel. 04-991-2171, Fax 04-991-9418*, is located in the late artist's renovated studio in the Old City. It now serves as a permanent exhibit for the works of Israeli artist Avshalom Okashi, 1916-1980.

NIGHTLIFE & ENTERTAINMENT

The **Borge Club**, *Old Acre, Tel. 04-991-7857*, is the disco spot. For drinks, you can try **Makom al HaHof**, *Argaman Beach, Tel. 04-991-1762*, or sip wine or beer outdoors at the one of the Fishing Port restaurants while enjoying the sounds of the surf and the evening breeze.

In July, the **Haifa Symphony Orchestra** performs concerts in the Crusader complex.

SPORTS & RECREATION

Every year during Succot (in autumn) Akko hosts the four-day **Fringe Theater Festival**, with lots of original Israeli productions and street theater. The underground halls provide an appropriate setting for the festival, and some of the performances are in English.

The main sun spot is **Argaman Beach** or **Purple Beach**, as it's known in English, *Tel. 04-991-1530*. The name comes from the dye made from snails found here in ancient times, but the pleasure of a good beach on the Mediterranean is timeless. The beach entrance fee is NIS 6 (NIS 5 for students). There used to be a free beach just past the Palm Beach, but plans were being made to close it. Check with Tourist Information, or Walied (at Walied's Hostel) who keeps abreast of these sorts of issues. **Akko Marina**, *near the Khan al-Umdan*, is the place for scuba diving. **Ramy's Diving Center**, *inside the Khan al-Umdan, Tel. 04-991-8990*, rents diving gear and organizes dives.

The **Princess of Akko** or **Galim**, *Tel 04-991-2042*, give 25 minute boat rides to the sea walls for NIS 15, departing on a when-the-boat-is-filled schedule. In the summer, private boat captains are happy to take you out for a view of the city from the water; just set a price in advance that seems reasonable, bearing in mind that the asking price will be outlandish till you barter it down.

EXCURSIONS & DAY TRIPS

Baha'i Gardens, *Tel. 04-981-2763*, are just one kilometer north on the Akko-Nahariya road. Like the ones in Haifa, these are beautifully landscaped and tended. They were planted from 1952-1956, and they house the villa and shrine of Baha'u'llah, the founder of the Baha'i faith. The shrine is open Monday and Friday-Sunday 9am-noon; the gardens are open daily 9am-4pm, and admission is free. The gate to the garden and shrine is just north of the sign for Shomrat Kibbutz.

Lohamei HaGeta'ot is a kibbutz three kilometers to the north. The 'Fighters of the Ghetto' kibbutz was founded by concentration camp survivors in 1949, six years after the Warsaw Uprising. Their **museum**, *Tel. 04-995-8080*, displays texts, photos, and art work documenting life in the ghettos and the camps, as well as Jewish resistance efforts in Poland and the former Soviet Union, and poetry and artwork by prisoners and survivors. The museum is open Sunday-Thursday 9am-4pm, Friday 9am-1pm, and Saturday 10am-5pm; a small donation is requested. The kibbutz also has a fairly well-preserved **aqueduct** just outside the museum. This one isn't Roman, however; it was built by el-Jazzar in 1780 to bring water to Akko from the Kabri springs. By bus, take the 271 (operating on Saturday as well) toward Nahariya (not the express).

To the east of the Akko-Nahariya road you'll find long stretches of the old **Roman aqueduct.**

PRACTICAL INFORMATION

Acre Department of Tourism, *El-Jazzar Street (opposite the mosque)*, *Tel. 04-983-1643, or toll-free Tel. 177-022-7764*, is open Sunday-Thursday 8:30am-4:45pm, Friday 8:30am-1:45pm, Saturday 9am-4:45pm. They aren't extraordinarily helpful, and mainly sell maps (NIS 4.5) of the city and tickets for the Crusader City complex (NIS12).

The central **post office**, *11 HaAtzmaut, new city*, has poste restante and international phones, open Sunday-Thursday 8am-3pm, Friday 8-11:45 am. There is a more convenient **post office branch**, however, right by the Tourist Information office. For **banks** go to Weizmann or Ben Ami.

For **Egged bus** information, call *Tel. 04-991-6333*. For **train** info, call *Tel. 04-991-2350.*

Emergency numbers: The **police station**, 16 Hahaganah, Tel. 04-991-1865, or Tel. 100 in an emergency. **First Aid** (Hagen David Adom), *1 Haavodah, Tel. 04-991-2333 or Tel. 101* in an emergency.

The **Canada-Akko Library**, *13 Weizman, Tel. 04-991-0860*, is open Sunday-Thursday 9-11:45am and 3-6:45pm. It's an air-conditioned, book-lined haven near the Old City.

Pharmacies: **Akko Pharmacy**, *35 Ben Ami Street, Tel. 04-991-2021*, and **Merkaz**, *27 Ben Ami, Tel. 04-991-0527.*

NAHARIYA

Nahariya is a small resort town, focused on sun, sand, and spending money in mediocre cafés. The beach is where the action is during the day, and in the evening tourists (Israeli and otherwise) hang out on the Promenade.

The history of Nahariya goes back to 1933 when Joseph Levy, an engineer from Germany, founded the Nahariya Young Settlers Association Ltd. With his partners Dr. Zelig Susskin and Shimon Reich, they set up an agricultural settlement of German immigrants and called it Nahariya after the river (*nahar* in Hebrew) Ga'aton. The farming paid off somewhat, as did some local factory enterprises, but the beach and holiday village venture was more successful.

In the 1960s Nahariya was practically the only northern vacation spot, but its popularity has fluctuated with hostilities from nearby Lebanon. A number of hotels have in recent years closed down, though there are still more than enough accommodations in business. Since the Lebanese War in 1982 Nahariya has been getting back on its tourism feet, though there is now a good deal of anxiety over proposed Golan land exchanges with Syria. Nahariya is popular with Jewish honeymooners during the *Lag B'Omer* festival in spring, and this relatively quiet resort is nearby Rosh Hanikra, Akhziv, Akko, and the Crusader castles of Montfort and Peqi'in.

ORIENTATION

HaGa'aton Boulevard is the main street in town. Two lanes with a stream down the middle, it runs east-west, starting with the bus and train stations and ending at the sea. This is where the restaurant and café promenade is, as well as the tourist office, shops, banks, etc. The further west (seaward) you get, the more tourist-oriented spots and services you'll find.

ARRIVALS & DEPARTURES

By Car

Turn west off the coast highway (route 4) at the two-way street marked with flags. This is HaGa'aton and will take you to the hotels and beach area.

By Bus

The bus station is at 3 HaGa'aton. When you get off the bus, head west on HaGa'aton to get to Tourist Information, the Promenade, and the hotels.

By Train

The train station is at 1 HaGa'aton, one block east of the bus station. Trains go to (and from) Akko, Haifa, Netanya, and Tel Aviv.

GETTING AROUND TOWN

Nahariya is small. You can walk along the main shop and café-filled **Promedade**. If you want more romantic luxury, horse-drawn carriages will trot you around HaGa'aton Boulevard for NIS 35 for a half hour.

There are also a number of organized and private tour operators available to guide you around Nahariya and the surrounding area. **Egged Tours**, *3 HaGa'aton, Tel.* 04-992-2656, has a number of itineraries around Nahariya, Haifa, Tiberias, and the Galilee. **Aharon Efrat**, *Tel.* 04-992-0966, has his own minibus and also gives tours.

If you have your own vehicle, there are a number of individuals who can be hired as guides. Call Chaim Malach, *Tel.* 04-992-0606, Leah Ron, *Tel.* 04-992-1925, Mendel, *Tel.* 04-992-0963, or Yosef Avi Tzedek, *Tel.* 04-992-2032.

WHERE TO STAY

CARLTON HOTEL, *23 HaGa'aton, Tel. 04-992-2211, Fax 04-982-3771, has 190 rooms and six deluxe suites, all with air conditioning, phone, TV and video. Rooms with breakfast are $81-$108 in winter, while in summer they climb to $163-$218.*

The hotel offers a swimming pool with poolside bar and cafe, jacuzzi, and a variety of sports arrangements such as sailing, windsurfing, snorkeling, tennis, bicycling, and horseback riding. They have special children services that include the Katkaton room with toys, arts & crafts, and children's movies, as well as youth disco parties and dinners graced by the Carlton Clown. For those in search of more adult recreation, there's a piano bar, and a disco on the weekends. The Carlton also accommodates business needs with fax and secretarial services.

ROSENBLATT HOTEL, *59 Weizman, Tel. 04-982-0070, Fax 04-992-8121, is five minutes from the sea and the promenade. In low season rates are $60-$70 and in summer it's $70-$90, breakfast included and credit cards accepted.*

There's no elevator, but their 35 rooms, with air conditioning, radio, bath, and phone, are clean and nice enough. The bathrooms are enormous, with bidets. They've a swimming pool and garden, a friendly, warm staff, and a dining room that serves European cuisine, Israeli breakfasts, and vegetarian meals.

HOTEL KALMAN, *27 Jabotinsky, Tel. 04-992-0355, Fax 04-992-6539, is 100 meters from the beach. The 16 air conditioned rooms with TV and shower or bath cost $55 for a double with breakfast, but the owner Miron Teichner will give a special price of $40 to bearers of this Open Road guide.*

The rooms are nice, with some big enough for families. Other amenities include his collection of famous autographs, a small but pleasant dining room, a luggage storage room, and a shaded garden out back. August gets busy, so call ahead and expect the August rates to be higher by 20%. It's a friendly place, and the owner will give tips about tours, reduction vouchers for restaurants, and unlimited helpful advice.

ERNA HOTEL, *29 Jabotinsky, Tel. 04-992-2832, Fax 04-992-8917, is right next to Kalman. Erna has 26 nice rooms, all with phone, TV, and big bathrooms. In low season rooms with breakfast are $46-$65, and in high season $55-$75.*

The rooms are clean, and some are big enough for families.

HOTEL ASTAR, *27 HaGa'aton, Tel./Fax 04-992-3431, is five minutes from the beach. Low season rates are $50-$58, rising to $63-$76 in summer.*

There are 26 rooms, all with air conditioning, cable TV, and small baths. They are okay but nothing special. Their Cafe Lachmi serves breakfast and light vegetarian meals.

DAYS INN HOTEL, *4 HaAliya, Tel. 04-992-0278, has 50 rooms, with air conditioning, TV, phone, and private bath. They cost $55 a single, $75 a double, breakfast included.*

The rooms are okay and comfortable, but the cinderblock halls smell musty and it feels like a motel. They have a new swimming pool with jacuzzi, a shaded garden, and are block away from the beach.

Rooms for Rent

MOTEL CHARLY, *34 Hamaapilim, Tel./Fax 04-992-8132, has 15 rooms with toilets and air conditioning, common kitchen, and costs NIS 200-240 a double.*

MOTEL ARIELI, *1 Jabotinsky, Tel. 04-992-1076, has eight rooms with toilets and air conditioning, common kitchen, for NIS 180, less in low season.*

No TV or phone, but the rooms are clean and cheery.

GOLDFARM HOUSE, *36 Hamaapilim, Tel. 04-992-9103, has eight rooms with toilets and air conditioning and a common kitchen for NIS 180 in summer, NIS 140 in winter.*

The rooms have TVs but are not remarkable.

For other *Tzimerrim* (rooms to rent), the **Office of Tourism**, *Tel. 04-987-9800*, keeps an updated list.

WHERE TO EAT

HaGa'aton Boulevard near the beach is lined with restaurants, cafés, and falafel stands, but the food tends toward mediocre and the prices vary between slightly over-priced and outrageous. Picnic food, on the other hand, is available at the supermarket, and the beach awaits you.

SINGAPORE CHINESE GARDEN, *17 Jabotinsky, corner of Mayasdim, Tel. 04-992-4952, provides a little variation on the HaGa'aton fare.*

SEEING THE SIGHTS

There are remains of a **Byzantine Church**, *Bielefeld Street, Tel. 04-987-9863*, costing NIS 4 to enter. It has some mosaics and the remnants of a 4,000 year old Canaanite Temple to Astarte (goddess of fertility) on a hill near the shore, 20 minutes south along the beach. Unless you're in it for the walk and keep your sights set low, you might feel underwhelmed.

The lowered threshold of expectation comes in handy for the **Municipal Museum**, *Municipal Building of Nahariya, HaGa'aton, Tel. 04-987-9863*, open Sunday-Thursday 10am-noon, Sunday and Wednesday 4pm-6pm, admission free. Within the Municipal Museum is a **Museum of Modern Art** (5th floor), **History of Nahariya Exhibit** (7th floor), **Archaeology** Exhibit (6th floor), and **Seashell Exhibit** (6th floor). From the roof of City Hall you can see all of Nahariya and the surrounding area.

If you are interested in local industry, Andreus Meir gives tours of the **Nahariya Glass Factory**, *Tel. 04-992-0066.*

NIGHTLIFE & ENTERTAINMENT

The **Municipal Amphitheater** has folk dancing in June, July, and August on Tuesdays (7pm-9pm) and Thursdays (7:30-9:15).

The **Hod Cinema**, *Herzl, Tel. 04-992-0502*, and the **Hekhal Ha-Tarbout**, *Ha'Atzma'ut*, sometimes show English films.

On the disco scene, the reveling starts fairly late on Friday and Saturday nights.

Carlton's La Scala Disco, *Tel. 04-992-6539*, claims to be "famous in the country," with lasers and the works. Friday is the big night (10pm-3am), and the cover is NIS 30-40. Your other option is the bar scene. The **BK Pub**, *2 HaGa'aton, Tel. 04-992-4334*, across from the bus station, is a popular local hangout. Closer to the sea are **Makom Batayelet**, *Tel. 04-992-5801*, and **Mul Ha-Yam**, *Tel. 04-992-5803*, both slightly south of HaGa'aton by the beach (Hof Hayam). Also by the beach is **Hapanas**, *Tel. 04-992-0373.*

SPORTS & RECREATION

The free **public beach** is adjacent to the Seashore Promenade, north and south of Galei Galil, and is open to all during the summer season. **Galei Galil Beach**, *Tel. 04-987-9872*, has swimming pools, *Tel. 04-982-9866*, (heated and unheated) and an amusement park as well as the beach, and it costs NIS 16. The **municipal swimming pool**, *Ma'apilim, just right of HaGa'aton, Tel. 04-987-9866*, is heated, swimming lessons available. Open Sunday-Thursday 6am-3pm and 7-10pm, Friday 6am-3pm, Saturday 6am-4pm and 6-10pm, an entry ticket costs NIS 24 and is good for the day.

Trak-Yam, *Tel. 04-982-3671, Fax 04-982-0146*, offers Jeep Tours, Diving, and Rubber Rafting.

There's also the **Amusement Park** on Galei Galil Beach, with Dodge 'Em Cars and Boats, Giant Inflatable Mattresses, etc.

Municipal Tennis Courts, *Rabbi Akiva Street, Tel. 04-982-6181*, are in the Katznelson neighborhood.

PRACTICAL INFORMATION

Co-op supermarket, *intersection of Herzl and HaGa'aton, Tel. 04-992-7210.*

First Aid (Magen David Adom), *Tel. 04-992-0344 or Tel. 101 in an emergency.*

Ministry of Tourism, *lobby of City Hall, Tel. 04-987-9800, Fax 04-992-2303*, is off HaGa'aton at Herzl Benjamin Ze'ev, and open Sunday-Friday 8am-1pm and Sunday-Thursday 4pm-7pm. A half block east of the Carlton Hotel is a green with trees and flowers. City Hall is at the end, with Tourist Information and museums.

Nahariya Hospital, *Ben Tzvi, Tel. Tel. 04-985-0505.*

Police station, *5 Ben Tzvi, Tel. 04-992-800, or Tel. 100 in an emergency, is just near HaGa'aton.*

Post office, *40 HaGa'aton, near Jabotinsky, Tel. 04-992-0180*, is open Sunday, Monday, Wednesday, Thursday 7:45am-12:30pm and 3:30-6pm, Tuesday 7:45am-2pm, and Friday 7:45am-1pm.

Steimatzky books, *32 HaGa'aton, Tel. 04-992-1079*, is open Sunday-Thursday 9:30am-2pm, 4pm-7pm, Friday 7am-2pm and carries The Herald Times and The European (as well as books).

Szabo Pharmacy, *3 HaGa'aton, Tel. 04-992-1197*, is near the bus station. Open Sunday-Thursday 8am-1pm and 4-7pm, Friday 8am-2pm.

NORTH OF NAHARIYA - THE COAST

From Nahariya up to the border with Lebanon, a distance of ten kilometers, the Mediterranean coast is a relatively undeveloped strip of sandy beaches, craggy rocks, and great beauty.

Akhziv is one popular location, since it combines archaeological sites, beach recreations, and places to stay. **Rosh Hanikra** in the north is the other major destination, popular for its grottos and cliffs. The 70 meter high white cliff is the base of a chalk mountain range with a top layer composed of hard chalk rock and dolomites, a middle of soft chalk, and a bottom of hard chalk. The caves and grottos that people come to explore were carved by thousands of years of sea waves pounding the soft middle layer, while the hard lower level is for the most part underwater and seen only by divers and fish.

March-May and October-November are the nicest months, when the weather is neither storming nor blistering and the Narcissus and Squill bloom. In the winter you can luck out with delightful days, or bad weather can force the cable cars to shut down. It gets very crowded during the summer and holidays, but if you have to come during then, plan to come as early as possible to beat the heat and the bus loads of tour groups. One attraction of early summer is the possibility of seeing the loggerhead turtle clamber up to dig pits in the rough sand in which to lay her eggs. Some weeks later hundreds of little turtles stream out to sea at night under a full moon.

ORIENTATION

Heading about five kilometers north from Nahariya, **Akhziv National Park** is the first spot you'll come to with tourist facilities. To the south of the park is **Club Med**, to the north is controversial **Akhzivland**, and nearby are places to stay and places to play. Continue north another five kilometers or so and you'll get to **Rosh Hanikra**, the other coastal location with accommodations and major appeal.

ARRIVALS & DEPARTURES

By Car

Both Akhziv and Rosh Hanikra are an easy drive on the coastal highway of route 4, and there are parking lots at both sites.

To Mont**fort** by car, drive east from Nahariya on route 89. This will take you to the turn off for the fortress.

To drive to **Yehi'am**, take the same route 89 but turn off earlier to the south by the Yehi'am sign onto the back road leading to the fortress.

For **Peki'in**, continue on route 89 past the fortresses to **Ma'alot**, where the highway turns into a smaller road heading southeast to Peki'in.

By Bus

From Nahariya to **Akhziv**, take bus 22, 26, or 28. There are buses every half hour or so, they take 10 minutes, and stop at the beach, field school, hostel, and campground.

To **Rosh Hanikra**, take bus 20 or 22; they leave at 9:15am, 11:30am, and 2:30pm, take about 15 minutes, and return half an hour later. Other Nahariya buses go to the junction, leaving you with a three kilometer uphill climb.

To **Montfort** by bus, the trip entails more walking. You can bus from Nahariya to Goren, from where you have a one and a half hour walk to Montfort. Alternatively (more interesting, more time, and more sweat), you can take the bus going to Ma'alot, and get off at the Arab Christian village of Mi'ilyah. Walk through toward the small Jewish village of Hila, bearing left at road forks. Signs will point you to a dirt path up and up some more till you reach the summit. Buses 39 and 42 leave infrequently from Nahariya, but they let you off right by the fortress of **Yehi'am**.

To reach the village and holy cave of **Peki'in**, the 44 out of Nahariya takes about 45 minutes to the old village of Peki'in Atika, which is your stop. If you're more interested in a visit to a Druze village, however, and don't really care about the holy cave, stay on the bus past Peki'in and go to **Beit Jann**. To get to Beit Jann, get off the bus three kilometers further past Peki'in at Beit Jann junction, after which you have a two and a half kilometer walk to the village.

By Sherut
Sometimes you can find a taxi sherut going from Nahirya to Akhziv or Rosh Hanikra for around NIS 5 (a fraction less than the bus).

By Taxi
You can take a taxi to Akhziv for around NIS 7, and to Rosh Hanikra for around NIS 13.

GETTING AROUND
It's easiest to get from around by car, but there are buses to both Akhziv and Rosh Hanikra. Once at either spot, it's easy to get travel by foot.

WHERE TO STAY
AKHZIVLAND, *Tel. 04-982-3250, has a camping area which costs NIS 50, dorm beds for NIS 50-60, and Eli's new guest rooms which go for NIS 150, all inclusive of parking, beach, and Eli's Museum entrance.*

Eli Aviv's self-proclaimed state provides somewhat disagreeable accommodations, and lots of attitude. (See *Seeing the Sights*, below.)

AKHZIV CAMPGROUND, *Tel. 04 982 5054, has tent sites costing NIS 40 per person while two and four person bungalows are NIS 250-480. Cabins with air conditioning, private bath, and breakfast included are NIS 235 for doubles and NIS 355 a quad, but prices come down some 15% in low season.*

Just a hop up the road from Akhzivland, this is a big place with 250 sites, as well as a kitchen, pool, and mini-market.

YAD LE YAD YOUTH HOSTEL, *Tel. 04-982-3345, has 40 air conditioned rooms, two-four beds each, with bathroom. Caravan doubles cost NIS 230, breakfast included.*

It is another option, a half kilometer up the road, but this place isn't nearly as nice as the Rosh Hanikra guest house. There's an available kitchen, or you can buy meals at the snack bar.

SPNI AKHZIV FIELD SCHOOL, *Tel. 04-982-3762, private double rooms rent for NIS 245, breakfast included, and NIS 44 extra per additional child.*

Across and up the street from Yad Le Yad Hostel by some 200 meters, they not only know a lot about the outdoor recreational opportunities in the area, they are frequently full with groups taking classes at the school.

SHLOMI YOUTH HOSTEL & GUEST HOUSE, *POB 2120 Shlomi, Tel. 04-980-8975, Fax 04-980-9163, between Shlomi and Hanita, is not far from the Mediterranean Sea. There are 100 four-person air conditioned rooms, all with toilet and shower, costing NIS 364 for youth hostel members, NIS 374 for non-members, breakfast included.*

Set in the hills of Hanita forest, this is a good base for nature activities such as rock and mountain climbing, glider flights, bike trips, and jeep tours, as well as visits to Montfort or Yehi'am Fortress. The rooms are nicely furnished. The hostel sports a game room, TV room, and even a disco. Take bus 22, 23 from Nahariya.

ROSH HANIKRA GUEST HOUSE, *POB 3067 Nahariya, Tel./Fax 04-982-3112, has 50 air conditioned rooms. With breakfast, a double costs NIS 410.*

The rooms are beautiful, with a toilet, shower, and nice decor, and there are family rooms large enough to accommodate a group of five. With a flower-filled garden and a big swimming pool, and just a 20 minute walk from the grottos, reservations are usually essential. Take the 20 bus from Nahariya.

WHERE TO EAT

There's a restaurant on the beach at **Akhziv National Park**, but most folks bring picnic goods and eat on the lawn. There's a cafe with so-so food but a swell view over the cliffs of Rosh Hanikra. And the hostels and guest houses all have food available as well.

Peki'in is a great place to sample *labeneh* or *pitta-eem leben*. It's a simple dish of soft goat cheese mixed with olive oil and zatar spice served up with pita, and it's simply magnificent when prepared well.

There are two cafés with similar quality for you to chose from. One is the **JEWISH COMMUNITY RESTAURANT** which is owned by Arabs, the name notwithstanding, and is across from the bus stop. The **DRUZE RESTAURANT**, a block east of the bus stop, is in fact Druze-owned and operated. Both serve labeneh, as well as hummus and good coffee.

SEEING THE SIGHTS

The hub of the area is **Akhziv National Park**, *Tel. 04-982-3263*, is open daily 8am-7pm, with an entrance fee of NIS 16, or NIS 12 for students. Built on the remnants of an 8th century Phoenician port town, green lawns roll down to tide pools and a small beach with changing rooms and showers. Scattered on the lawns are remains of settlements since Canaanite times, Israelite rock-hewn caves, and the walls of a Crusader fortress. There's also a **museum** exhibiting artifacts from the area. The park is very popular with local families, which means the grounds are pretty full of picnickers on a nice day.

In 1952, Eli Aviv took up residence in an old Arab house by the beach and declared his land the independent state of **Akhzivland**. On this land is **Eli's Museum**, *Tel. 04-982-3250*, entrance fee of NIS 10, NIS 7 for students) with his collection of Phoenician, Roman, and Byzantine artifacts. Eli also provides a variety of accommodations, including camping, and guest rooms. People tend to form strong opinions about Eli and his eccentric ways. Some visitors are charmed by the anti-authoritarian approach and love their Akhzivland passport stamps. Customs officials are definitely not so charmed by the stamp, and locals think he's a nutty blowhard. Your call.

Just north of the Diving Center is **Gesher HaZiv**, *Tel. 04-982-5715*, a kibbutz and restaurant on one of eleven sites targeted in "The Night of the Bridges," a bridge-exploding protest on June 16th, 1946 in response to the British decision to close off Palestine ports to Jewish refugees. Fourteen Haganah soldiers were killed trying to blow up the railway bridges in an attempt to cut British communication, and the **Yad Le Yad Memorial** honors them.

Rosh Hanikra, *Tel. 04-985-7108*, one of the most beautiful sights in Israel, is open Sunday-Thursday 8:30am-4pm in winter, 9am-6pm in spring/autumn, until 10pm in summer, and closes one hour earlier Fridays and holidays. On the border with Lebanon, Rosh Hanikra is the site of magnificent grottos in the sea that you descend to by cable car, NIS 27 per adult, NIS 22 per child. The grottos were originally carved out of the soft chalk rock by the sea waves and used to be accessible only by boat until, in 1968, a tunnel was constructed to make the grottos available to the public. The cable cars take you down (about a one minute ride) so you can wander around the tunnels and get splashed by breaking waves at your leisure. It's an interesting and beautiful site, and worth the trip if you are in the area.

Most people go for the natural beauty of the place (and the cable ride, of course), with white cliffs to rival Dover. But there are also historical, geological, and botanical aspects to explore. Whatever your interests, the white cliffs against the blue sea are stunning, and the grottos are spectacular, with water frothing against rocks and glimpses of sun and blue sky visible through the cracks. It is reassuring to know that the occasional loud booms are from water meeting rock and not artillery from the border. Also worth noting, when they say the rocks get slippery when wet, they're not kidding. Take care and wear rubber-soled shoes.

The site has been an important border and passage way between the north (Syria and Lebanon) and the south (Israel, Egypt, and Africa) since biblical times. The Book of Joshua (13:6) refers to *Misraphot Mayim*, a spot south of Rosh Hanikra, as the border of the Israelite tribes of the time, and the cliff was referred to as "The Ladder of Tyre." The Arabs renamed the site A-Nawakir (the grottos) after they conquered the region, and the present name of Rosh Hanikra is a hebraicized version of Ras-A-Nakura, a later variation. In 323 BCE Alexander the Great is thought to have carved out a tunnel to make a passageway for his army after the Siege of Tyre, and caravans passed through to trade.

During WWI, the British built a road, making the passage accessible to cars, and during WWII they dug a 250 meter tunnel to accommodate a train between Haifa and Beirut, facilitating army cargo shipments from Egypt to the north. After the war during the British Mandate, a road was paved and a border station and duty office set up. After the British forces withdrew the area came under Israeli control. As the Lebanese border is only two kilometers north of Rosh Hanikra, the Palmach blew up the railway bridges during the Independence War to hinder Lebanese attack.

In addition to the cable car ride and the grottos, there is a cheesy 3D narrated **slide show** down near the tunnels for your edification and amusement. If you want to put on the 3D glasses and hear about waves caressing rock blah blah blah, details about the geography of the region and the war lore of 1948, take a seat in the audio video cave. They post the times of the next show as well as which language will be heard, but don't provide popcorn.

NIGHTLIFE & ENTERTAINMENT
Nothin doin'.

SPORTS & RECREATION
Akhziv Beach, *Tel. 04-982-8201*, is a stretch of coast starting about four kilometers north of Nahariya on the way to Rosh Hanikra. It's a nice beach, with changing rooms, showers, and a little restaurant. Open 8am-7pm, entrance is NIS 12 (NIS 10 for students, and NIS 6 for children). Across the road from Akhzivland is the **Akhziv Diving Center**, *Tel. 04-982-3671*. You can rent snorkeling equipment for NIS 45 or take diving classes for a mere NIS 1070.

North a little ways is the **SPNI Akhziv Field School**, *Tel. 04-982-3762*. They rent private rooms and can provide information about nearby outdoor recreation.

The **Montfort fortress** stands high above the Kziv river and the **Nahal Kziv Nature Reserve**. There are hiking trails along the river, and remains of old dams and water mills. From the parking lot in Hila there are signs pointing the way. Further northwest is **Nahal Betzet Reserve**.

Nearby, **Shlomi Youth Hostel**, *Tel. 04-980-8975, Fax 04-980-9163*, has information on hiking, mountain climbing, rock snapling, glider flights, bike trips, and jeep tours.

EXCURSIONS & DAY TRIPS

Head east from the coast to see the Crusader fortresses of **Montfort** and **Yehi'am**, the Druze villages of **Peki'in** and **Beit Jann**, and the holy cave of **Rabbi Simeon bar Yohai**. Seeing these sights involves more work than picking around a tide pool at Akhziv, but they also offer more perspective the religious and political history that shaped this region.

Montfort is about 15 kilometers east northeast of Nahariya, and **Yehi'am** is a few kilometers south of Montfort. About 13 kilometers southeast of Yehi'am Fortress is **Peki'in**, and **Beit Jann** is about five kilometers past that. This is hilly country, and once you climb the heights to the fortresses, the views make it clear why these sites were so desirable to all concerned.

You can walk around each site once you get there, though traveling from one to another is much easier by car than by bus. But car or bus, Montfort entails more walking than the fortress of Yehi'am. To get around the local villages, you'll take in a lot more of the flavor traveling on foot than looking through the windows of an air conditioned car, but you'll sweat a lot more, too.

The Crusader fortress **Montfort** was built by the French Courtenay family in the 12th century for pilgrims. When they sold to Teutonic Hermann von Salza in 1228, the name changed from Montfort (Strong Mountain) to Starkenburg (Strong Castle). The Teutonic Order expanded it, and Montfort became the Order's main fortress, archive and treasury until 1271 when it was captured by Baibars. The Muslims then destroyed the fortress while the Crusaders retreated to Akko. The stony remains of tower and hall are set picturesquely on a steep bushy slope, and the walk up is very beautiful (and, well, steep), but there's not a lot there. If you're looking for a great hike and picnic in a scenic spot, Montfort's for you, but if you want restored Crusader grandeur, other fortress ruins would be a better bet. It's open Saturday-Thursday 8am-5pm, Friday 8am-4pm, and admission is NIS 8 for adults, NIS 6 for students.

Yehi'am (Judin) Fortress, *Tel. 04-985-6004*, stands on the grounds of kibbutz Yehi'am, which was started in 1946 by a group who set up in the deserted castle. The kibbutz name (and now the fortress as well) are in honor of Yehi'am Weitz who fell at the "Night of the Bridges" battle. The original name of Judin Fortress comes from the Arabic "Kala'at Judin," meaning "Heroes Fortress". This Crusader fortress was built in the 12th century by the Templars, destroyed in the Muslim conquest of 1265, and partly rebuilt by Bedouin ruler Dahar el 'Amr in 1738. Considering the commanding views from the tower, it's no surprise this strategic spot was fought over in Crusader times, and more recently during the War of Independence when Yehi'am was under siege. Admission is NIS 5.

About 13 kilometers southeast of Yehi'am Fortress is **Peki'in**, the site where tradition has it that **Rabbi Simeon bar Yohai** and his son Eliezer spent 13 years holed up in a cave after fleeing in defiance of the Roman decree prohibiting Torah study. During these years, the prophet Elijah reputedly visited the two for frequent enlightened discussions, and a carob tree and water spring miraculously appeared to enable their survival. Father and son used to sit buried in sand during the day to prevent wear and tear on their clothes while studying Torah and discussing matters of import with Elijah. The *Zohar*, the main Kabbalistic text, is ascribed to the followers of Simeon who recorded the mystic secrets he learned during his years in hiding. Simeon bar Yohai and his son Eliezar are believed to be buried in Meron (just west of Tsfat), the procession site of the holiday Lag Ba'omer. Despite all this interesting lore, the cave itself is a modest place up on the slope of the mountain above the spring.

To reach the holy cave, take the road going up from the bus stop to the top of the village. When you see a blue-and-white sign on your right, take the path down the stairs. The cave is 10 feet to the right of the stairs. The village of Peki'in is believed to have started as a Jewish community since the destruction of the Second Temple in 587 BCE, continuing on through the Arabs conquest around 1000 CE, the Crusaders in the 12th century, and the Druze settlement in the 1700s. In 1936 the Jewish community was forced out, and only a small contingent returned after independence in 1948.

Peki'im is now predominantly Druze, with small segments of Jewish and Arab communities as well. The Druze cafe next to the bus stop has maps of the town which will help if you're intent on visiting the old Jewish cemetery, old flour mill, and oil presses. In the village is a relatively new **synagogue**, built in 1873, and local tradition claims it was constructed with stones from the Second Temple. There is also a **Greek Orthodox Church**. Built in the 19th century, it contains some beautiful icons. This Druze community is far less touristed than the villages near Haifa, and the countryside is exceptionally lovely.

PRACTICAL INFORMATION

Nahariya is the nearest city, and your best bet for medical attention if you need it.

16. GALILEE & THE GOLAN HEIGHTS

Galilee and Golan, the vast verdant northern chunk of Israel, have been the subjects of contention and clashing arms for a long time. An important trade route in ancient times between Egypt and Syria, and an oasis of farm fertility in an arid land, the region has also nurtured many religions (Judaism, Christianity, Islam, and Druze), all adding to its great richness and its equally immense conflict potential.

Today the Galilee has settled happily under its dual hats of farming and tourism, with kibbutzim every which way plowing and irrigating and setting up guest houses, while pilgrims and nature lovers from around Israel and around the world flock to its abundant religious and recreational treasures. The Golan region, while attracting skiers and hikers with its heights and beauty, has also been the focus of continued political sparring between Syria and Israel, and it is the major pawn in their land-for-peace debate.

History

Galilee was the northern province of ancient Palestine, but the Golan Heights has been a site for human settlements since the Stone Age. Bronze Age communities lived in spots like Hazor as early as 2600 BCE, and the Baal-worshipping Canaanites lived here around 1800-1200 BCE (part of which time, from 1500-1200, was spent under the rule of the Hyksos Egyptians) before Joshua and the Israelites came a-conquering and the Tribe of Dan moved in—giving rise to the Old Testament phrase "from Dan to Beersheba" to denote the breadth of the kingdom.

In the 900s BCE Solomon enlarged on small Israelite settlements such as Hazor, but after King Solomon's death around 922 BCE, his kingdom was divided into the two states. Jeroboam ruled the northern kingdom of Israel, and remnants of his reign have been found at Tel Dan.

In the 800s BCE, King Ahab and his notorious Queen Jezebel ruled, but the Assyrians took over in 842 BCE, followed soon after by Damascan rule. From 785-745 Israel experienced its peaceful Silver Age and Jeroboam II ruled the northern kingdom of Israel, then the Assyrians looked south again and in 732 King Tiglath-pileser swarmed all over, annexed Galilee and Gilead to his growing empire, and substituted Assyrian for Hebrew as the language of the land. His successor was King Sargon, and in 720 BCE Sargon took the remaining northern districts of Israel and renamed the region Samaria. In 586 **Nebuchadnezzar** came in, deporting the Jews to Babylon, and 50 years later King Cyrus of Persia allowed them to return. They who had been in exile rejected the Samaritans (those who lived in Samaria) for their faithless intermarriages, and excluded them from the new Temple in Jerusalem, and from the religion.

Alexander the Great came in 333 BCE and the Hellenistic culture dominated, as is reflected in synagogues found here from that period. The Greeks made Golan the administrative district of Gaulantinus. The north was part of Phoenicia, while the south belonged to Galaaditis. The Seleucids took over in 198 (placing all of Golan under the eparchy of Gilead), followed by the Jewish rebel Maccabee Hasmonaeans in 164 BCE. In 83-80 BCE Alexander Jannaeus the Hasmonaean ruled and forced all the inhabitants to convert to Judaism. Then in 63 BCE the Roman legions descended. Though there were some Jewish settlements here in second century BCE, the area wasn't really developed, with roads and a water system, until the Roman and Byzantine periods.

In 20 BCE, Augustus gave the province to **King Herod**, and after his death Herod Antipas (Herod's son) was given the Galilee to rule from 4BCE-39CE, during which time he murdered John the Baptist to please his step-daughter Salome and also built Tiberias to honor his emperor. From 4BCE to 34CE Golan was ruled by Philippus, who made the capital Caesarea Philippi and turned Golan into a major Greek cultural center. After his death, Golan became a part of Syria, and when Gamla fell in 67CE, the Jewish settlement of Golan ceased for a long time. Jesus, known as "the Galilean" (Matthew 26:69), was raised in Nazareth under the rule of Herod Antipas, and spent most of his life there.

Many important sites from the New Testament are located in the shrine and church filled Galilean hills. After the fall of Jerusalem in 70 CE, Golan and Galilee, especially the city of Tiberias (the Mishna was codified and the Talmud was produced there) became the center of rabbinic learning, and many first century ruins of Galilean synagogues have since been excavated. In Byzantine times (324-640 CE) the Galilee saw lots of church construction, as Saint Helena, Constantine's mother, went around identifying where Jesus performed various miracles. And then, in 640, a new period of fun began.

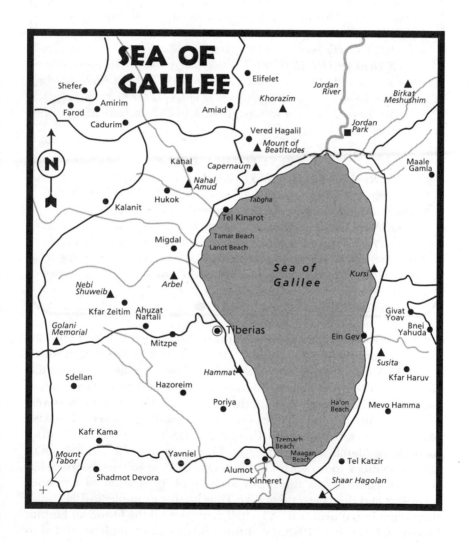

BEST OF THE GALILEE
BEST HOTELS

• *VERED HAGALIL GUEST FARM, off Route 90, four miles north of the Sea of Galilee, Tel. 06-693-5785, Fax 06-693-4964. Cost: $66-$80 for singles, $89-$105 for doubles, depending on type of room. This is a Galilee gem, with cottages of stone and wood, great home cooking, and a stable full of healthy, well-attended horses.*

• *KAREI DESHE HOSTEL, Ten kilometers north of Tiberias on the western shore of the Sea of Galilee, Tel. 06-672-0601, Fax 06-672-4818. Cost: from $25-$33, depending on number of people per room, including breakfast. Karei Deshe is a stunningly beautiful, clean place with palm trees, lawns, and its own beach.*

BEST FOOD & DRINK

• *VERED HAGALIL GUEST FARM, off Route 90, four miles north of the Sea of Galilee, Tel. 06-935-785, Fax 06-934-964. Rustic and pleasant, the food is unpretentious, homemade, and superb.*

• *EIN CAMONIM, off Route 85 about two miles east of the Hananya (Route 89) Junction, Tel. 06-698-9894. Perhaps the best restaurant in Israel, they dish up a feast of traditional and homemade items such as goat cheese, olive oil, vegetables, good wine, and bread in a homey, relaxed setting.*

From 640-1517 the Galilee saw lots of blood shed between Muslims and Christians battling for control. The Early Arab period began with a win at the Yarmuk in 636, and Arabs ruled till the Crusaders started their conquests in 1099 (and made Tiberias the capital of their Galilee). Sultan Saladin won the strategic fight for the Horns of Hittin (six kilometers west of Tiberias) in July of 1187, one of the most serious blows to the Frankish Crusader forces, but not all the Crusader castles fell, and the battles wore on until the Mamluks, a group of Turkish slaves imported by Saladin to train as soldiers, took control in 1250. One of their sultans, Baybars, left a trail of ruins across the north as he took possession of Crusader fortresses and destroyed them (like Tiberias, for example, in 1247), and their reign lasted over two and a half centuries till the Ottoman Empire kicked in. From 1517-1918 the Ottomans ruled, and the Jews started to return from Europe.

In the 1800s, **Golan** was part of the conflict of interests between colonial powers, and it fell to Syria after WWI. Following the Jewish exile from Spain in 1942, Tsfat became the center for the kabbalist mystic scholars, and by 1904 the Zionist movement was a reality in the Galilee, with Tiberias the Jewish settlement headquarters. Fighting was intense between Jews and Arabs from after WWII until independence was declared in 1948 (and some after that), and there are many sites honoring the dead resulting from the War of Independence and beyond.

Syria lost the Golan Heights to Israel in the 1967 Six Day War, and it was annexed to Israel in 1981. And now, controversial negotiations are under discussion in an on-again, off-again sort of way, between Syria's Assad and Israel's Netanyahu, talking about returning the Golan Heights to Syria in exchange for peace and diplomatic recognition. And up by the border with Lebanon, Israel's and Lebanon's 30 year fight drags on, occasionally making the news with a missile explosion here or there.

NAZARETH

Along with Jerusalem, Bethlehem, and the Sea of Galilee, **Nazareth** is one of the most important Christian sites, and the city is visited yearly by bus loads of devout pilgrims as well as curious infidels. Set in the hills of the Galilee, this is where Jesus grew up, but what should be holy air in the center of town is colored more by the hustle and heckle of locals making shekels off its sacred status. The sites themselves can be quite lovely and solemn, and the pilgrim hostels in the hills are all that they should be, but if you are short of time and don't have a special feeling about the spot where the Angel Gabriel visited Mary, you might think twice about making the winding, twisty trip here.

This is the city of **Joseph and Mary**, and though settlements have lived here since Bronze Age times, it's first mentioned in the New Testament when the Angel Gabriel appeared before Mary and announced the Virgin Birth. Some years after Jesus was born in Bethlehem the family returned to Nazareth, and Jesus is believed to have spent his childhood there. Around the time that the country was wrapped up in turmoil and revolt, Jesus was thrown out of Nazareth for what was considered blasphemy in the synagogue.

In Byzantine times, attention focused on Bethlehem once again. In 326 CE Emperor Constantine fulfilled his mother Queen Helena's request by building the first church in Nazareth, a basilica over the traditional site of Mary's home. In 614 the Persians destroyed the city, and that's how it stayed till the Crusaders rebuilt in the 12th century. In 1254, the Mamluk Sultan came on the scene, and did his best to destroy the Crusader churches and the Christian population. A Christian community was re-established in the 1600s when Franciscan monks were allowed in. Churches and monasteries were built, and in 1814 a mosque was added to the places of worship.

Nowadays, modern Nazareth is the largest Arab city in Israel, with a population of 60,000, the Christian half living in harmony with the Muslim half. It's a city of church spires and the smells of oriental food. And there's a fairly new Jewish community, mostly immigrants from Eastern Europe and North Africa, that has developed up in the nearby hills of Nazarat Illit. If you do visit, dress modestly (no shorts or bare midriffs) when visiting the religious sights.

ORIENTATION

Located 30 kilometers southwest of Tiberias, you drive up and up some more in the beautiful hills and winding roads until the drab buildings and settlements welcome you to Nazareth. If you're driving from **Afula** or **Haifa** you'll enter from the southwest on **Paulus VI Street**, the main thoroughfare of the city. If you stick on Paulus VI you'll eventually exit to the northwest, headed towards **Tiberias**. If you come by bus it'll drop you on Paulus VI in town center.

From the bus stop (not really a station as such), go west three blocks to Casa Nova, and you're right at the **tourist office** (with plenty of maps), near the restaurants and just a couple blocks from the first of the sights, with the **Basilica of the Annunciation** on Casa Nova your right, the **market** (*shuk*) to your left, and **St. Joseph's Church** just a bit further north. Once you deviate from the beaten track of Casa Nova Street and Paulus VI, however, good luck. Even armed with a map and addresses, it's a matter of hunt and ask. Most of the streets have numbers for names, but a street sign is a rare thing.

ARRIVALS & DEPARTURES
By Bus

Bus 431 goes to Haifa every 20-60 minutes and takes around 30 minutes, and the same 431 goes east to Tiberias and likewise takes around 30 minutes. Buses 355, 357, 823, 824 go to nearby Afula from where you can transfer to almost anywhere, and 823, 824 continue on to Tel Aviv. There's no baggage storage here, but the Taxi stand north of Tourist Information will store bags for NIS 5 a piece.

By Sherut Taxi

You can leave by sherut taxi as well. Stand in front of the Hamishbir Department store on Paulus VI for sherut taxis to Tiberias, and go to the street next to the Paz gas station for sherut taxis to Haifa and Tel Aviv.

GETTING AROUND TOWN

Town Center is the focus for most visitors, and the only way to get around is on your feet. Driving around the small one-way streets can make you nuts.

WHERE TO STAY

NAZARETH GARDENS HOTEL, *one-half kilometer from Nazareth center, Tel. 06-656-6007, Fax 06-657-3008, is on your approach from Afula in Nazareth Ilit. There are 120 rooms for $92-$138 a single and $103-$105 a double, breakfast included.*

It was built in 1962 and recently acquired by Moriah Hotels. Some of the rooms have terraces, all have air conditioning, TV, and private bath, and none have phones. The hotel has a swimming pool, basketball and handball courts, fitness equipment, and children's play area, and there are lawns and gardens, fish ponds and landscaped paths.

SAINT GABRIEL HOTEL, *Salesian Street, Tel. 06-657-2133, Fax 06-655-4071, has 62 very charming rooms for $60-$80 a single and $82-$100 a double, breakfast (such as it is) included.*

Built in 1953 to be a Franciscan monastery, it was converted to a Catholic church in the 1980s, and opened as a hotel in 1994. The Saffoury family now operates the hotel, and it's a very beautiful place, with lobby tables of inlaid mother-of-pearl, and very good Turkish coffee. The rooms are lovely, with stone walls and views of all Nazareth.

It's not seamless, however. Some bathrooms are a bit cramped, with doors unable to swing open all the way, but with all new fixtures, and very clean. There's a nice view from the breakfast room, but breakfast was a packet of instant coffee, a buffet of salami and cheese, blah white bread, hard boiled eggs, and bug juice. For overall charm, views, good value and good will, this is my choice, especially if you have a car. Also, they have their own church with a bell tower.

GRAND NEW HOTEL, *Hamotran, Tel. 06-657-3325, Fax 06-657-6281, has 92 rooms at $55 a single and $92 a double, breakfast included, but 10%-15% more in the high season.*

At the first junction from Afula Road, turn left, then right after 100 meters, and up the hill. This is the largest and most established of the Nazareth hotels but they are neither terribly friendly nor terribly helpful.

HOTEL HAGALIL, *Paulus VI, Tel. 06-657-1311, Fax 06-655-6627, is a five minutes walk from Casa Nova, with 93 rooms at $50 a single and $80 a double, visa and mastercard accepted.*

Rooms are okay, clean if somewhat dull, with air conditioning and bathroom (some with baths, most with showers) but no TV or phone.

NAZARETH HOTEL, *Paulus VI, Tel. 06-657-7777, Fax 06-657-8511, has singles for $48 and doubles for $62, breakfast included.* Closed in winter.

Christian Hospices

FRERE DE BETHERRAM, *Tel. 06-657-0046, is a Catholic Hospice with 56 beds for pilgrims only. It's easy to get here by car (but difficult otherwise), just drive up from Paulus IV by the Sol gas station. It costs $32 a person, which includes breakfast, lunch, and dinner.*

This is not a tourist hostel. It's a beautiful building of stone floors and arched ceilings, dark wood doors and little oriental rugs by the beds. There's a dorm of five beds and two twin bedrooms. There is also a chapel from 1912 that was converted from stables.

SISTERS OF SAINT CHARLES BORROMAEUS, *#12 on 316th Street, Tel. 06-655-4435, has five rooms for NIS 70, breakfast included (with reductions for students). No credit cards accepted.*

They've cozy rooms with tables and a homey feel, but they're all different, some with big double bed, some single, and one big room with four beds. You get a key, there's no curfew, and there's a garden in summer. To get there take the stairs up to 316 Street. Call or write for reservations.

CASA NOVA FRANCISCAN HOSPICE, *across from Annunciation Basilica on Casa Nova, Tel. 06-645-6660, Fax 06-657-9630, has 67 rooms, 150 beds, costing $21 per person half board, with a $9 single supplement. Open 5:45am-11pm.*

Very clean, spare rooms—no phone, no TV—but the bathroom has a bidet. There's a nice garden and good espresso in the coffee bar.

SISTERS OF NAZARETH, *POB 274, Nazareth 16223, Tel. 06-655-4304, is off Casa Nova. The dorms are single-sex with 8-10 cots in rows costing NIS 18 a bed, also private rooms with private bathrooms for $21 a single and $36 a double; breakfast costs $3. Reception opens at 4pm, and passports are required. Closed 10am-4pm, and curfew is 9pm.*

Up Casa Nova, left after the Casa Nova Hospice, and you'll see it on your right. These are the cheapest beds in town, and they have the most rules and regulations attached to them by the unsmiling head sister who means every word she says. With nice stone walls, very clean bathrooms, a kitchen and living room (co-ed) across the hall, and a lovely courtyard. It's often busy with pilgrims, despite the stickler sister, so reservations are advised.

SACRED HEART, *POB 22, Nazareth 16100, Tel./Fax 06-657-0046, (they prefer letter to Fax for reservations) has 24 rooms with 54 beds at $20 per person, breakfast included, $5 extra for each additional meal taken there, $5 supplement for single, for pilgrims only.*

If on foot, walk past the Sisters of Nazareth hospice and go up the Christ Church stairs. Turn left onto a road, walk through a cemetery, and turn right up the street, and Sacred Heart is on your left.

WHERE TO EAT

There is good food to be had in Nazareth, good, that is, if you like *shwarma* and bakery treats. It's not a real gourmet hot-spot, however. People come here more to feed their souls than to please their bellies, and probably the best food is to be had in half board deals at the Christian hospices.

Paulus VI Street is lined with falafel joints, while Nazareth is re-nowned throughout Israel for its oriental sweets (I know a woman in Tel Aviv who routinely goes up to Nazareth for baklavah every time she's making a party). **MAHROUM BAKERY**, just left of intersection of Casa Nova and Paulus VI has excellent zatar pizza and good pastry. This intersection is crowded with good restaurants such as the **ASTORIA** and **AL-AMAL** that serve middle eastern fare. Good *shwarma* (NIS 10) and roast chicken (NIS 15 a half) can be obtained on Paulus IV, next to Bank Leumi.

Especially good falafel can be had at **SAINT JOSEPH MEETING**, just near the Basilica.

SEEING THE SIGHTS

Go past the line of shlock stands to see the churches here. The most important pilgrimage spot of the city is the **Basilica of the Annunciation Church**, not so much for the fairly modern church (constructed from 1959-1969) as for the Holy Grotto within, where it is believed that the Annunciation took place. The newly built place of worship, crowned by a copper-covered cupola, incorporates the grotto of the Annunciation, believed to be the remains of Mary's home, and restored parts of older churches.

In fact, archaeological research done by the Franciscan Biblical Institute of the Flagellation has discovered that the Basilica is built on the ruins of Judeo-Christian, Byzantine, and Crusader churches. In 356CE, Empress Helena had a small church built here, based on the design of the third century synagogue church, on the foundations of an earlier and smaller church in the center of the Jewish community, just above the spot where it was believed the Angel Gabriel announced to Mary that she would give birth to Jesus. After the Byzantine church was destroyed, Tancred the Crusader King built a large church in the 1100s. It was destroyed by an earthquake in 1170, rebuilt, and destroyed again (except for the grotto) by the Mamluk Sultan Baybars in 1263. In 1620 the emir

Fakhr ed-Kin gave the site to the Franciscans, and they maintain the site still. The church today consists of an upstairs and downstairs, connected by spiral staircases.

Downstairs is the **Holy Grotto**, with the restored Byzantine apse and pre-Constantine baptistry. The two pillars to the right of the passageway to the Chapel are thought to have belonged to the old synagogue church. The north pillar is 'Mary's pillar' and the southern one is 'the pillar of Gabriel'. Tradition has it that they mark the respective spots where those two stood during the Annunciation. There are preserved fifth century Byzantine mosaics by the grotto (the acoustics are lovely when people sing there).

Excavations under the mosaic revealed an earlier mosaic with a cross, dating it before the time of Emperor Theodosius (408-450 CE) who banned the use of crosses in floor decorations. An especially valued find is an example of some third century graffiti; *Chaire Maria* (meaning "Hail Mary") is the oldest known inscription featuring Mary's name. Upstairs are colorful stained-glass windows, murals depicting religious scenes, and some grand mosaics. Above is a bright dome, 190 feet high, meant to resemble the open bloom of a lily, a symbol for the Virgin Mary. Mass is held in different languages many times daily. *Call 06-657-2501 if you have a group and want to reserve a Mass.*

THE STORY OF THE ANNUNCIATION

*St. Luke (26:38) tells of the Annunciation: "In the sixth month the angel **Gabriel** was sent by God to a town in Galilee called Nazareth, to a virgin betrothed to a man named Joseph, of the House of David; and the virgin's name was Mary...the angel said to her, 'Mary, do not be afraid; you have won God's favor. Listen! You are to conceive and bear a son, and you must name him Jesus. He will be great and will be called Son of the Most High.'...'But how can this come about, since I am a virgin?' 'The Holy Spirit will come upon you' the angel answered 'and so the child will be holy and will be called Son of God.'...'I am the handmaid of the Lord,' said Mary "let what you have said be done to me.' And the angel left her."*

North of the Basilica, past the curio and information shop and the big rubber tree, is the **Church of Saint Joseph**. A pretty church, it was built in 1914 on Byzantine and Crusader church foundations. The church, which in Byzantine times was known as Church of the Nutrition is now sometimes called the Church of the Holy Family. Tradition, supported by archaeological finds, has it that here stood the house and carpentry shop of Joseph and the Holy Family.

In the Byzantine baptistry is a baptismal basin (circa 1120 BCE) inlaid with white mosaics around black basalt stones. Next to the font are rough-hewn stairs leading down a narrow passage to a crypt. Bell-shaped grain storage silos from pre-Byzantine times can be seen sunk below the surface (the origin of the Church of Nutrition name?). Since the 1600s this area has been designated as Joseph's workshop. Excavation reveals that it was inhabited as early as the Stone Age and must have been part of the very oldest, underground settlement here. The flattened stone is supposed to have been used by the Holy Family as a table for their meals

Just up the hill and to the left, The Greek Orthodox Church of the Annunciation is known as the **Church of Saint Gabriel** (also the House of Mary, or Beit Mariam in Arabic). Crusaders built a church here on the site of an earlier Byzantine one which had been erected in 670 CE (according to Gaulish Bishop Arnulf) over in the middle of town over Mary's spring. The Frankish church was destroyed in 1263, and in 1741 Greek Orthodox monks were given permission to build the present church. In the crypt bubbles the spring that feeds Mary's Well. It is theorized that this would have been the only water source in Mary's time, and that therefore she (along with the other women) would have come here frequently to draw water.

This is also the site, according to the Greek Orthodox (and in conflict with Saint Helena's opinion, where the Angel Gabriel is believed to have greeted Mary, with "Hail Mary full of grace..." and made the Annunciation. Nearby is what remains of **Mary's Well**, also known as **Fountain of Mary**, and **Virgin's Fountain**. It's now just a faucet, but some hold that the water that issues forth is holy.

Just down the street from the Basilica at the end of the left fork of the shuk (from the end of Casa Nova) is **The Greek Catholic Synagogue Church**, marking the site of the ancient synagogue where Jesus is believed to have regularly prayed (Luke 4:15-30). He also read the prophesy of Isaiah foretelling the coming of the Messiah (Isaiah 61:1-2), implying that he was the Messiah which was construed as blasphemy. Jewish symbols and inscriptions have been discoed here.

About 200 meters north of the Synagogue Church on Al Batris Square, up a steep street through the market, is **Mensa Christi**, a block of limestone that tradition says was a table for Jesus and his disciples after the Resurrection. It's in a chapel dating from around 1800, and contracted around that is a small, domed Franciscan church built n 1861. Right next door is the **Maronite Church**, which was built in 1774 and is also known as the Church of Saint Anthony.

Monastery of Our Lady of the Fright (Notre-Dame de l'Effroi), one kilometer south of the city, is where Mary is believed to have been overcome with terror as she waited to see her son Jesus be cast into the abyss as his punishment for blasphemy in the synagogue (Luke 4:29-30) before he made his escape. The nearby summit is known as The Leap of the Lord.

Salesian Church of Jesus as an Adolescent, on Salesian Street, is northeast of the Basilica at the peak of the hill. Built in 1918 in 13th century style, it's a fine example of Gothic architecture. Not only is the stone building exceedingly lovely, there is a Bogino marble statue of Jesus the Adolescent to see, as well as some stunning views of the city below.

Other Sights

Other churches include the **Anglican Church** (east of Sisters of Nazareth Convent), built at the request of British sailors and completed in 1871, and the **Coptic Church** (off Paulus VI on 718 Street, not far from El Salam Mosque), which was built by the small Coptic community in 1952.

At the edge of the market on El Wadi Street (off 607 Street) is **The White Mosque** (El Abyad), built in 1812 and the first mosque in Nazareth. **Terra Sanca Monastery**, near St. Joseph's Church, is a Franciscan college with a small Crusader art museum.

NIGHTLIFE & ENTERTAINMENT

Not in Nazareth. The **Saint Gabriel Hotel**, *on Salesian Street, Tel. 06-657-2133, Fax 06-655-4071*, has a bar and can be quite festive at night, with grand views of the city below.

SHOPPING

The **marketplace** is a lively Arab street *shuk* at the top of Casa Nova, not far from the Annunciation churches. It's abuzz with fruits and vegetables, cheap clothes and chintzy olive wood crèches.

If you stray off the main thoroughfares it's a more peaceful, interesting place to wander about and get lost. You'll see a different Nazareth in the steep and narrow guttered lanes than what you see in Basilica plaza.

EXCURSIONS & DAY TRIPS

Kafr Kana is a small Arab village seven kilometers northeast of Nazareth on Route 754, where Jesus is believed to have performed the miracle of turning water into wine (John 2:1-11). When a Franciscan church was built in the center of town in 1883 to commemorate the event, a 200-300 CE synagogue foundation and older church remains were discovered underneath.

The Franciscans found columns, capitals, and a mosaic Aramaic inscription relating to the building's Jewish synagogue foundation. The church is built on the traditional site of the miracle, and displays an old jar similar to the one that contained the water. To the right of the Franciscan Church is a Greek Orthodox Church, red-domed like the Franciscan church, with paintings to represent the holy marriage where Jesus worked his first miracle, as well as vats some believe were used in the wedding. If you're not traveling by car, there are frequent arab buses leaving from near Mary's Well in Nazareth, or take the Egged 431 as it heads to Tiberias.

Two kilometers southwest on Route 75 is **Yafa**, which used to be Japhia and was mentioned in the Old Testament (Joshua:9) as a town belonging to the tribe of Zebulun. Titus conquered here in 57 CE. There are ruins of a synagogue from the third century and it's decorated with mosaics, the best of which are now in Jerusalem. West of Yafa a couple kilometers is the pine-filled **Balfour Forest**, planted in honor of Arthur Balfour who penned the Balfour Declaration which promised the Jews the nation of Eretz Yisrael.

Five kilometers northwest off Route 79 are the recently reopened excavations of **Tzipori**, *Tel. 06-656-8273, open daily 8am-7pm in summer and 8am-4pm in winter.* High on the summit of a 800-foot hill are the remains of the former capital of the Roman province of Galilee. The Hasmonaeans knew it as **Sepphoris**, and it was probably their administrative center as well. During the first Jewish rebellion, the inhabitants surrendered their town to Vespasian and Hadrian replaced the Jewish administration with a Gentile one, renaming it Diocaesarea. During the third century, however, this place was the seat of the Sanhedrin, as well as one of the places where Rabbi Judah HaNassi gathered learned scholars to help compile the Mishna. The Crusaders held the town (called Le Sephorie), and built a fortress.

What remains of the Crusader castle of Saphoriesinos were incorporated into the **Turkish fortress** built in 1745 by Daher el-'Amr. Sephoris was supposed to be the birthplace of Saint Anne (Mary's mother), and the Crusaders built a church here to commemorate her. The church was destroyed by Baybars, but the modern **Saint Anne's Church**, built in 1860, has been found to contain some of the Byzantine mosaics. When the Crusader church was excavated in 1909, they found **synagogue** mosaic remains (now housed in the Crusader church), including an inscription which originally read 'To the memory of Rabbi Judas bar Tan chum bar Buta, who endowed this tablet. Blessings be on him.' In addition, a Roman theater, big enough to hold some four to five thousand spectators, was excavated in 1931. To get there by bus is a little tricky. The 16 goes from Nazareth at 1:10pm, no return. The 343 goes by the junction frequently, but it's a three kilometers walk to the site.

Tel Megiddo, *23 kilometers southwest, Tel. 06-652-2167, Fax 06-642-0312*, is a popular archaeological site of religious and historical significance on Route 66 (just north of the Megiddo Junction with Route 65). It's open Sunday-Thursday 8am-4pm, Friday 8am-3pm (an hour later in summer) and costs NIS 18 an adult, NIS 9 per child. Plan about an hour and a half to see the site. It's best known for the Christian tradition that claims this is the biblical site of Armageddon where the war of the End of the Days will take place (Revelations 16:16).

The name comes from the Hebrew *Har Megiddo* (Mount of Megiddo). The excavation site shows sections of what was one of King Solomon's and later Ahab's chariot cities. There's a Canaanite altar and Solomonic water tunnel, as well as a museum and film. (For more on Megiddo, see Chapter 14, *Carmel*).

PRACTICAL INFORMATION

• Buses: The **bus stop**, *Paulus VI, Tel. 06-657-0040*, is not really a station bus just a glorified drop-off, three blocks east of Casa Nova Street and Tourist Information. **Egged information**, *Paulus VI*, is across from Bank HaPoalim, and open Sunday-Thursday 4am-7pm, Friday 4am-3pm.

• **Car Rental: Europcar**, *Tel. 06-655-4129*, **Hertz**, *Tel. 06-657-5313*.

• **Currency Exchange: Bank HaPoalim** and **Leumi** are on Paulus VI and are open Sunday-Thursday 8:30am-12:30pm, Sunday, Tuesday, Thursday 4pm-6pm, and Friday 8:30-noon.

• **First Aid** (Magen David Adom): call *Tel. 101*.

• **Hospitals: Nazareth Hospital**, *Wadi el Juwwani Street, Tel. 06-657-1501*, is up in the hills near Freres de Betharram Monastery; **Italian Holy Family Hospital**, *off El Hanuq Street, 06-657-4535*, is a good bit out of town ; **French Hospital**, *off Wadi el Juwwani Street, Tel. 06-657-4530*, is southwest of town center.

• **Market** (Shuk) is open Monday-Saturday about 8am to about 6pm.

• **Pharmacy: Farah Pharmacy**, *Paulus VI, Tel. 06-655-4018*, is next to Egged Information and is open Monday, Tuesday, Thursday, Friday 8:30am-1:30pm, 3:30pm-7pm, and Wednesday, Saturday 8am-2pm.

• **Police**: 100 or 06-574-444, the station is near Mary's Well.

• **Post Office**, *907 Street, Tel. 06-655-4019*, is the main branch. To get there go north on Paulus VI to Mary's Well and turn left a block up the hill. They have Poste Restante and an International Calls section, and are open Monday-Friday 8am-12:30pm, Monday, Tuesday, Thursday, Friday 3:30pm-6pm, and Saturday 8:30am-noon. Another post office branch, Paulus VI, is way in the other direction, just before the Nazarene Church.

• **Tourist Information**, *1601 Casa Nova, Tel. 06-657-3333, Fax 06-657-5279*, near Paulus VI is open Monday-Friday 8:30am-5pm, Saturday 8:30-2pm.

TIBERIAS

For a small city, **Tiberias** (or *Teverya* in Hebrew) has been the hub of many cultures and religions since Herod Antipas, son of Herod the Great, decided to continue in the building footsteps of his notorious father and founded it in 19 CE in honor of Roman Emperor Tiberius. It's changed hands many times since then (and before, as the Torah records how the town of Hammat, believed to be here by the springs, was conquered by Egyptians in the 13th century BCE), but seems to have taken quite nicely to its most recent reincarnation of tourist magnet.

With the same warm clime, black basalt stones, hot mineral spring luxury, and stunning lake and hillside scenery that first caught Herod's eye still exist today, and coupled with the added draw of Judaic holy city status and proximity to important Christian sites, tourism is booming. On warm summer nights Israeli and international tourists stroll the promenade, music and flirting youth fill the pubs, while during the day pilgrims throng the sites, hikers head for the hills, and revelers laze on the beaches shoring up energy for the coming night.

Jesus and most other Jews of the time avoided Tiberias because it was considered unclean, due to the graves disturbed in construction, but in the second century Rabbi Shimon Bar Yohai declared it ritually clean, and following the destruction of Jerusalem in 135 CE Tiberias became one of the great Jewish scholarly centers and the seat of the Sanhedrin. In the third and fourth centuries CE the Mishna and Talmud were written and compiled here, and vowels were added to the Hebrew alphabet. For all this Tiberias is considered one of the four holy cities (alongside Tsfat, Jerusalem, and Hebron). In the sixth century, Tiberias continued as a Jewish spiritual center and there were 13 synagogues.

Persians conquered in 614, followed in 636 CE by the Arabs, then from 1099 to 1187 Tiberias was part of the Frankish Crusader kingdom, the capital of their Galilee region (and many of the structures date from that time), despite 150 years of fierce fighting with the Muslims. Sultan Baybars prevailed, destroying the town in 1247, and it wasn't resettled until 1517. In 1562, Don Joseph Naxi (the Jewish adventurer from Spain) and his aunt Donna Gracia Mendes acquired Tiberias from the Sultan Suleiman the Magnificent and tried to re-establish Tiberias as a Jewish community under the Ottoman rule. It failed, however, and the town was mostly deserted until it was rebuilt in 1738 by the Bedouin Sheik Daher el-Omar and his son, who walled it and built a fortress, but Tiberias was severely damaged by the earthquake of 1837.

In 1904 Jewish settlement activities began in earnest, and Tiberias was its administrative center. And by WWI, the tourism business was already going strong, what with the Sea of Galilee, the religious sites, and the hot springs. The 4000 Muslims and 5000 Jews living here before 1948 had good relations, but the Muslim right wing replaced the friendly Muslim head, relations soured, and there was a good bit of fighting between Jews and Arabs in the War for Independence.

You'll find the memorial garden to soldiers killed since '48 in the old Jewish quarter of Tiberias, with flowing water to symbolize blood and life, and a list of names. As for what happened next, accounts differ. Jewish history records that after the war, Arabs were offered to stay under Jewish authority, but they all left and didn't return, but the Arab version says otherwise. Now a Jewish community of 35,000, the Arabs you find here commute, for the most part, from nearby villages to share in the tourist industry profits.

ORIENTATION

Midway down the western shore of the Sea of Galilee, Tiberias' placement on the Syrian-African Rift, an area of great seismic activity, has made it subject to devastating earthquakes, but is also responsible for its much lauded hot springs and black basalt stones. Its climate is warm. The coldest months (December-March) average 50°-72°F while in summer (May-August) the temps rise to 89°-99°F, and humidity (thanks to its 200 meters below sea level status) tends to be high.

The **Old City** by the water is the main tourist focus. The **Promenade** (built in 1934) is chock full of fish restaurants and pubs, and the **midrahov** (pedestrian walkway) leading from the Promenade to HaGalil is similarly endowed. The bus station is up on **Hayarden**, a street that continues down past falafel stands to intersect with Hagalil and HaBanim and end up at the Promenade by the lake. **Hayarkon**, one block south of Hayardon, eventually runs into the midrahov. **Hagalil** runs parallel to the coast till it ends in the south on the coastal road of **Eliezer Kaplan**, and is the central street for stores and traffic. **HaBanim**, one block down, is another central road, this one ending in the north in **Elhadeff**, the street leading up to the new city of **Kiryat Shmuel**.

Tiberias is a city that doesn't use street addresses much. Many addresses are given just using the street name, and those that give the number aren't always of great help as not all buildings indicate numbers. Cross streets and landmarks are by far more helpful directors.

ARRIVALS & DEPARTURES

By Bus

The **central bus station**, *up on Hayarden, Tel. 06-679-1080*, has buses to all over. There are buses to Tel Aviv (the 836, 830, or 831 for NIS 29.5, last Friday bus 4pm); to Jerusalem (961 or 963 for NIS 35.5); to Nazareth (431), to Haifa (431 or 431 for NIS 20.5); for Afula (830 or 831); for Kiryat Shemona (541, 841, or 963); and to Tsfat (the 459).

For more local transit to the **southwest** Sea of Galilee you can take 17, 18, 19, 20, 21, while the 22 goes up the **eastern** side.

By Ferry (in July and August on the Sea of Galilee)
- Tiberias-Ginnosar: *departs 8:30am*
- Tiberias-Ein Gev: *departs 10:30am, 12pm, 1:30 pm (and costs NIS 25 one way, NIS 40 round trip)*
- Ein Gev-Tiberias: *departs 12:15pm, 1:15pm, 3pm, 4pm*

Kinneret Sailing, *Tel. 06-657-8007*; **Lido Sailing**, *Tel. 06-672-6488*; **Holyland Sailing** , *Tel. 06-672-3006*, takes groups only.

By Taxi

For 24-Hour Service to Ben-Gurion Airport for NIS 350, call Benny Dahan, *Tel. 06-672-2234*. **Aviv**, *Elhadef, Tel. 06-672-0098*, near the post office, has regular service to Tel Aviv for NIS 24.30 (but not on Shabbat) and you need to arrange it the day before.

GETTING AROUND TOWN

By Foot

The downtown section of the city is easily manageable by foot, but you might want to investigate another form of transportation for the sites scattered further afield. Tiberias walking is made more pleasant through the innovation of crosswalks which give the right of way to pedestrians. Enjoy it while you're here as it is perhaps the only place with this sort of civilized street ethic in Israel.

By Bicycle

Bikes are a fine alternative for getting to places nearby like the Hot Springs or the Tombs, and some people like to make a day of it peddling around the lake as well.

Hotel Aviv, *14 HaGalil, Tel. 06-672-3510*, rents a wide range of bikes, including new 18 gear mountain bikes, for NIS 45 a day, and some other hostels have a few bikes to rent as well.

By Bus
There are local buses in and about the town. The 1 and 5 go south towards Tiberias Hot Springs, and bus 4 goes to the Tomb of Akiva. There is, however, no public transport in Tiberias on Shabbat.

By Taxi
Sherut and private cabs wait in front of the bus station, or you can call Tiberius Taxi, *Tel. 06-672-0444.*

WHERE TO STAY

RADISSON MORIAH PLAZA TOWERS, *Habanim, Tel. 06-679-2233, Fax 06-679-2320, by the sea has 232 rooms and suites priced at $168-$268 a single and $200-$305 a double. North American reservations toll free is Tel. 800/221-0203.*

An enormous structure towering over central Tiberias, rooms all have cable TV, video, air conditioning, bathrooms, and direct-dial phones. There's a pool and health club with sauna and jacuzzi, as well as shops, ping-pong, video games, a Texas restaurant, and free parking. Not as classy as Galei Kinnereth, it's got with more services and more centrally located.

GAI BEACH HOTEL, *Derech Hamerchatzaot, Tel. 06-679-0790, Fax 06-679-2776, has 120 rooms for $178-$256 a single and $182-$269 a double, plus 15% service charge, breakfast included.*

A five minute walk from town, this place attends to comfort and recreation, with soft leather chairs in the lobby, a very green lawn, pleasant verandah, and a private beach and Luna Beach water park (in season) with two kamikaze water slides. They also run a disco during high season, and offer a 50% reduction for children under 12.

CAESAR HOTEL, *103 The Promenade, Tel. 06-672-3333, Fax 06-679-1013, has 227 rooms for $173-$216 a single and $204-$255 a double, breakfast included.*

The Caesar sees itself as "a modern luxury resort hotel" with health club, indoor/outdoor pools, book store, restaurant, coffee shop, and piano bar. Thursday and Friday nights there's a disco, they have a Children's Club (weekends and peak seasons), an aerobics studio in the summer, as well as a synagogue, and underground parking. Very centrally located, they also provide a shuttle to Tiberias Hot Springs.

GALEI KINNERETH, *1 Eliezer Daplan, Tel. 06-672-8888, Fax 06-679-0260, toll free in Israel Tel. 177-022-8686, has 123 rooms at $161-$236 a single and $186-$258 a double, plus 15% service charge, but breakfast included.*

Open since 1947, this was Ben Gurion's favorite hotel. There's a heated swimming pool, massage, fitness room, ping-pong, boat rental, kayak and speed banana (three people on a balloon behind a motor boat), and some activities for children, depending on occupancy. With more prestige and more class, it's less showy than the other luxury hotels, but has a quiet elegance, and a car park.

CARMEL JORDAN RIVER HOTEL, *Habanim, Tel. 06-671-4444, Fax 06-672-2111, has 400 rooms that cost $130-$160 a double, breakfast included.*

An enormous and not overly attractive structure on the outside, inside it's a full-service resort, with swimming pool, sauna, and health club, synagogue, babysitters and physician on call. There's a piano bar, a disco (Friday night is Israeli folk night), and there's children's entertainment (Saturday morning activities and Friday night teenager disco 9-11pm on weekends).

PANORAMA, *HaGalil, Tel. 06-672-0963, Fax 06-679-0146, has 47 rooms. A single with breakfast is $36-$65 and a double is $54-$79.*

To the South and Kiriat Shemuel, up the hill to the North
HOLIDAY INN, *Habanim, Tel. 06-672-8555, Fax 06-672-4443, is a little south of town. With 246 rooms and plenty of parking, prices run $159-$179 a single and $213-$223 a double.*

A large complex, this Holiday Inn is a little outside of Tiberias but right next door to the hot springs, so expect a fair number of guests taking the cure. All rooms have air conditioning, direct-dial phones, and TV, and they have special facilities for disabled. They are also within a short walk of a private beach, tennis courts, synagogue, and a horseback riding farm.

GALILEE HOTEL, *Elhadef, Tel. 06-679-1166, Fax 06-672-2994, just before Kolton, is a tall block-like building with 93 rooms for NIS 295 a single and NIS 370 a double.*

Just renovated, they've clean, nice rooms.

KOLTON INN, *2 Ohel Ya'acov, Tel. 06-679-1641, Fax 06-672-0633, has 78 rooms for $75-$94 a single and $100-$129 a double, Israeli breakfast included.*

With a nice coffee shop, in what used to be Pe'er Hotel, it's a pleasant place. They've a disco on when people request, whatever kind of music they want, and it closes when hotel guests retire for the evening.

HOTEL EDEN, *4 Ohel Ya'acov, Tel. 06-679-0070, Fax 06-672-2461, has 103 rooms that cost $70-$85 for a single and $85-$110 for doubles.*

It has your basic lobby, dining room, pub/cafe, and a disco at the request of hotel groups.

HOTEL ASTORIA, *13 Ohel Ya'acov, Tel. 06-672-2351, Fax 06-672-5108, has the entrance around the back. Singles cost $62-$88 and doubles are $78-$110, breakfast included, but the management is offering a 15% discount to guests bearing this Open Road Guide.*

There's a swimming pool outside with a cafe, the rooms are pleasant, and a small park and municipal tennis courts are nearby.

HARTMAN, *3 Ahad Ha'am, Tel. 06-679-1555, Fax 06-679-1556, has 63 rooms costing $61-$79 a single and $79-$105 a double, breakfast included.*

Despite the large, ugly block edifice, the hotel has nice amenities such as the rooftop swimming pool and sauna, and the terrace with its view of the lake.

HOTEL TIBERIAS, *19 Ohel Ya'acov, Tel. 06-679-2270, Fax 06-679-2211, has 68 somewhat nondescript rooms costing $70 a single and $90 a double, breakfast included.*

There's a pool and jacuzzi in summer, and plenty of parking.

RON HOTEL, *12 Ehad Ha'am, Tel. 06-679-0829, Fax 06-679-1117, next to Yeshivah Ohel Yacov, has 50 rooms for NIS 180-220 a single and NIS 210-250 a double, breakfast included.*

Newly renovated, it's high up over the water, has good views, but is far from the center of town.

HOTEL TIBERIAS GARDEN, *Bruria, Tel. 06-672-6736, Fax 06-679-0780, costs NIS 80-150 a single and NIS 80-200 a double, breakfast included.*

The entrance is round the back, the small rooms are a bit run down but basically okay, with TV, fridge, air conditioning, but no phone, and gardens and municipal tennis courts are right nearby.

CONTINENTAL, *Elhadef, Tel. 06-672-0018, Fax 06-679-1870, has 25 rooms, all with air conditioning and radio, for $45 a single and $60 a double, including Israeli breakfast.*

Comfy and clean though not luxurious, there's a lounge and TV room, and patio overlooking the freeway.

BEIH BERGER, *25 Neiberg, Tel. 06-672-0850, Fax 06-679-1514, rents 45 rooms for $30-$60, depending.*

The rooms have cable TV and air conditioning, and there's access to a kitchen, with coffee and tea free.

Hostels & Guest Houses

MEYOUHAS YOUTH HOSTEL, *2 Jordan, Tel. 06-672-1775, Fax 06-672-0372, just off Hayarkon, has two sturdy wood bunk beds per room, one of which costs NIS 95 with sink, shower, toilet in the room, NIS 88 without, or stay in a three-bunk room for NIS 63 with toilet, NIS 53 without, and a private double is NIS 198. All prices include breakfast in their cafeteria room, complete with fussball and video games.*

It's clean, it's pleasant, and it's quiet. The kosher kitchen also provides half board for NIS 30. From the bus station go straight down Hayarkon till you see the youth hostel sign on your left.

NAHUM, *Tabor, Tel. 06-672-1505, charges $10-$15 for dorm beds (six to a room) and has private rooms $40.*

There's air conditioning, hot showers, and a toilet in each dorm room. There's also a deck and bar on the roof, and bicycles for rent. From the bus station, walk down to Hagalil, turn right, and turn right again on Tabor. Walk up the hill and you're there.

AVIV HOTEL, *Hagalil, Tel. 06-672-0007, has dorm beds (four-five per room) for NIS 30 in winter, 45 in summer, and double rooms with fridge, bath, and air conditioning for NIS 90 in winter, 130 in summer (some rooms even have TV).*

There are balconies, a terrace, free use of kitchen, it's near the sea, and they rent bikes for NIS 45 a day. From the bus station, go right on Hayarkon and right again on Hagalil. Keep going past HaQishon, and it'll be on your right hand side.

ADLER HOSTEL, *14 Hagalil, Tel. 06-672-0031, is right in the center of the old city. A dorm bed is NIS 40 with shower and toilet, and a private double is NIS 80.*

There's a kitchen, TV lounge, bar, and balcony, a sun roof and bicycles for rent. From the bus station, go down Hayarkon and turn right on Hagalil.

MAMAN HOSTEL, *Atzmon, Tel. Tel. 06-679-2986, has dorm beds (eight to a room) for NIS 30 in winter, NIS 40 in summer and private rooms for NIS 80 in winter, NIS 140 in summer.*

You get keys for dorm and hostel, which is a good thing because it's often hard to find the manager. There's no communal area, but out back is a garden and small pool. The Moroccan restaurant in front offers breakfasts for NIS 14. To get there from the bus station turn right on Hagalil, bear right again on Tabor, and your next right takes you up to Maman.

CHURCH OF SCOTLAND HOSTEL, *Tel. 06-672-3769, Fax 06-679-0145, is on the corner of HaYarden and Gedud Barak–the road heading north out of Tiberias. Hostel dorms, are $8 a bed (two-eight beds per room) while Guest House rates run $40-$45 per person, breakfast included, plus $15 for half board. There are $5 supplements for single occupancy and rooms with views, but children 6-12 are half price, ages 4-5 are $4, and under 3 are free. All credit cards accepted except American Express.*

This place features both a hostel and a guest house set on beautiful grounds, with lofty, airy, comfortable, clean rooms, and a gorgeous garden. Patios overlook the sea and garden, and the Garden Cafe is lovely. While affiliated with the Church of Scotland, they make a point of welcoming Jews, Christians, and Muslims equally. This is a fine place for the price.

MEZUMAN HOUSE, *Hayarkon, is between Hagalil and Habanim. The 11 rooms cost NIS 50 for a single and NIS 80 a double, while dorm beds (four per room) go for NIS 30.*

There's a verandah with a view of the bank, a washing machine and free use of kitchen, free nescafe and tea, parking, and an owner who speaks French.

ADINA, *15 HaShiloah, Tel. 06-672-2507, offers dorm beds for NIS 30 in winter and doubles with fridge and bathroom for NIS 120, though prices rise in summer.*

WHERE TO EAT

Snacks & Fast Food

There are loads of falafel shacks lining Hayarden between the bus station and HaBanim, though they're closed on Shabbat.

SHWARMA SHOP, *1 Elhadef Street*, one door down from City Rent-A-Car, is open till 5am Friday night, 10am-2am other days and sells a baguette full of good stuff for NIS 12. It's not bad any time, but it's especially good to keep in mind for Shabbat.

On the Promenade there's good ice cream at the sign of **FROZEN YOGURT**, *opposite Fish & Grill.*

BAKERY, *way up on Elhadeff just a little before Continental Hotel*, has a good, inexpensive, tasty selection. For supermarket picnic supplies, see *Practical Information* below.

Promenade Restaurants

KARAMBA, *Promenade, Tel. 06-672-4505*, is open daily 11:30am-midnight, credit cards accepted. They serve vegetarian dishes for NIS 15-25.

BIG BEN PUB & RESTAURANT, *cobbled midrahov path next to Pirate Pub, Tel. 06-672-2248*, serves decent pub grub in a pleasant site.

KOREAN RESTAURANT, *Waterfront Marina, 2nd floor, Tel. 06-679-2017, near Galilee Experience, is open daily featuring Korean food for a change of pace.*

There are plenty of fish-mongering restaurants along the strip, but none stand out. They all buy from the same catch, cook the same styles, and charge the same prices, so chose the setting that most appeals, or have your fish meal elsewhere on the lake.

Downtown Restaurants

ARCHES RESTAURANT, *56 Galilee, Tel./Fax 06-679-0146, and is next to Panorama Hotel. They're open daily (including Shabbat) and serve oriental foods and fish.*

GUY RESTAURANT, *HaGalil, back from the street a little, next to Panorama Hotel, Tel. 06-672-3036*, has a nice blend of atmosphere and moderate prices. You can order lung and spleen as well as oriental standbys like shishlik, schnitzel, or eggplant, but avoid the stuffed broccoli at all cost. A full dinner with appetizer, dinner, and wine costs around NIS 30 per person.

EAT AS MUCH AS YOU CAN, *corner of Hayarkon and Hagalil*, offers what it claims for fish, salads, and chips at NIS 27.

SEEING THE SIGHTS

In Tiberias, an introduction to the area and its history can be spoon fed to you through the audiovisual production of the **Galilee Experience**, *up the stairs by the sign on the Promenade, Tel. 06-672-3620*, is open Sunday-Thursday 8am-9:15pm, Friday 8am-4pm, and costs $8 an adult, $5 students and seniors (credit cards accepted). The show can be aired in most languages, depending on the language spoken by the majority of the given group, but they have headsets in many languages for everyone else. It takes about 36 minutes and covers everything from the prophets of Baal to Elijah, the naming of Tiberias to the development of Zionism. It is most popular (and crowded) from 4-6pm when people are just drifting back from more active sightseeing.

The ancient **walls of Tiberias** to the south near the Galei Kinneret Hotel, built of local black basalt, are left over from Crusader times. In 1564 Donna Grazia repaired the ramparts while trying to impart new life in the town, and in 1738 they were rebuilt again by Daher el-Amar. Daher's son Chulabi added the **northern citadel** (where the Donna Gracia complex of restaurants and art galleries is now house) off Habanim. In 1833 Egyptian Pasha Ibrahim repaired the walls one more time, but the earthquake of 1837 did them serious damage.

Tiberias Archaeological Park, HaBanim, Tel. 06-672-3788, between the Plaza and the Jordan River hotels, is open daily and admission is free. It shows an excavation that came of digging foundations for another hotel when they stumbled upon ruins of a sixth century synagogue and the Crusader structure built on top. There are colorful mosaics, arched Crusader stones, a modern open theater with 300 seats, and a restored Crusader building that houses the Tourist Office.

Tiberias is known for its **Tombs of Tzaddikim** (the Righteous): **The Tomb of Maimonides** or **RAMBAM**, (1136-1204) on Ben Zakkai above Hatanaim is under the tall red modernistic structure. The seven black marble columns each represent one chapter of Maimonides' book *Yad Hazaka* (Strong Hand). Get your cardboard yarmulke at the entrance, pass the candles and oil cans lit in memory, and then go see the tomb. Outside there is also the tomb of **Rabbi Ben Zakkai**. Is this for you? Some go there to reflect, pray, and even weep. The casual visitor might find the tombs a let-down.

For the tomb of **Rabbi Akiva**, take bus 4 and look for the blue dome. It's here that Rabbi Akiva was said to have hid during the Great Revolt, and according to tradition, 24,000 learned men are buried next to him.

Nearby are the tombs of **Rabbi Moshe Hayyim Luzzatto** (The Ramhal) and **Rabbi Hiya** and sons. Near Tiberias Hot Springs is the tomb of **Rabbi Meir B'al Ha'ness**, the Miracle Worker (take bus 5 or 1). **The Tomb of the Matriarchs** is on HaShomer, near the Kinneret Rest Home (take bus 5). According to tradition, Moses' sister Miriam, his mother Yochevet, wife Zipporah, and Aaron's wife Elisheva, as well as the matriarchs Bilhah and Zilpah, are buried there.

The **Franciscan church of Saint Peter** or **Terra Sancta Church**, *Tel. 06-672-0516*, was built on top of foundations from a Crusader church built in the 12th century to commemorate Saint Peter, and is open daily 8-11:45am and 2-5pm. The Franciscans bought the ruins in 1847 and restored it to its present grandeur. It now has a beautiful cloister, while the triangular apse is meant to recall the prow of Peter's fishing boat. In 1942-1945 Polish troops were stationed in the church, and they are to be thanked for the Virgin Mary statue in the courtyard, as well as the memorial for Polish soldiers who died in WWII.

The mosques in the city, reminiscent of different times, are all boarded up, though the small Arab population wants to open them again. The **Grand Mosque of El Omri**, *off Habanim and Hayarden*, was built in the 18th century by Daher al Omar, the same Bedouin ruler who built up the city walls. At the southern end of the Promenade is the **el-Bahri mosque**. Also known as the White mosque, is was built on Crusader church ruins and on the basalt lintel of the door you can still see the cross decorations. The Ottomans built a small hostel near it (now in ruins) and fishermen used to dock under the arches for easy prayer access, back when it fronted on the water before the Promenade was built.

Tiberias Hot Springs, *Habanim Street, Tel. 06-672-8500, Fax 06-672-1288*, is a couple kilometers south of town (take bus 5 or 1) and is open Sunday, Monday, Wednesday, Saturday 8am-8pm, Tuesday, Thursday 8am-11pm, Friday 8am-6pm. This hot springs spa will relax you and your wallet at the same time. The springs go back some 2,000 years, though this particular facility has been in business for only 11. They have two buildings, one devoted to recreational treatments such as mud, mineral baths, and massage, while the health building specializes in arthritis, back pain, and amputation healing. The medical building (Tiberias Old Mineral Hot Springs) assumes you'll be staying a minimum of one week with three treatments a day including check-up and doctor's visit.

The recreational center (Tiberias Young Mineral Hot Springs) is more informal. Entrance to the mineral pool complex costs $15 an adult, $10 a child. A mineral bubble bath, ethereal bubble bath, cosmetic mud pack, and massage cost around $30 each. These services cost more on weekends and holidays, and there are extras you can pay for like robe rental, Saint Peters fish lunch, etc. The communal mineral pool complex, indoor and out, all coed, are 32°-37°C (90°-99°F). Free shuttle service is provided between the Hot Springs Spa and major hotels in Tiberias from 8am-4pm.

Across the street from the spa is **Hamat Tiberias**, *Tel. 06-672-5287*, the ancient version. The National Park is open 8am-4pm daily and costs NIS 7 an adult, 5.25 for students. There's the **Lehmann Museum**, detailing the hot springs history, the **synagogue ruins**, up at the top of the path, and the **ancient Jewish baths**, which lie near the road. This area was renowned for its hot springs before Joshua led the Jews into Canaan, and the popularity of the waters never waned. The tribe of Naphtali fortified a town here. Later, the Romans build a fancy spa facility that drew visitors from all over, even before Herod Antipas built Tiberias in 20 CE.

After the Romans, the Byzantines and Omayyads resided here, and more spas were constructed in the 1700's-1800's CE as well. Now in ruins, parts of the ancient spa still remain. Stone stoops sit in hot sulfurous waters behind the wire fence through which you can view the lake and the cars zipping down the freeway. Pools nearby are cold, shallow, and muddy, but hot, hot water bubbles down ancient stone channels. You can dip your tired toes for a second, but soaking will parboil you.

When Nachum Slouschz excavated the site (after a group paving the Tiberias-Zemach road stumbled on the Hamat Tiberias ruins in 1920), he found a small synagogue (circa 200's-400's CE). Forty years later further excavations under Moshe Dothan revealed more synagogues, circa 100's-700's CE, built one on top of the other.

The **Severus Synagogue** (Severus was one of the synagogue founders and had close ties to the Tiberias Sanhedrin) was built in the 300's CE and destroyed in the 400's. This synagogue has wonderfully preserved mosaics, especially the zodiac, lions, and menorah; they are well worth the climb.

Near the entrance to the Hamat Tiberias National Park is the **Ernest Lehman Museum**, open Sunday-Thursday 8am-4pm, covering the history of Tiberias Hot Springs (admission included in the Hammas ticket).

Just north (towards Tiberias) of Tiberias Hot Springs is **Sironit Beach**, and at the southern tip of the parking lot are remains of a **Roman basilica**. It served as a municipal courthouse, and in Byzantine times was turned into a church. Taking the dirt road southwest from the basilica leads to more ruins. There's a section of the **Cardo**, the main street of the Roman town, once flanked by granite pillars. Paved in basalt, it probably was built when the town was first constructed in 18 CE. There's also a **bathhouse**, and a **covered marketplace** from after the Arab conquest.

From the northern end of the Cardo excavation site is a dirt path leading past the water treatment plant at the foot of Mount Berenice to the remains of a **Roman theater**, commanding a swell view of the Cardo and bathhouse below. About 150 meters south are **wall ruins** from what was once conjectured to be a large reservoir from the Early Arab period. Further south and up the hill sits a well-preserved section of the **Berenice Aqueduct**. Back to the road and across Eliezer Kaplan (the lake highway) is what's left of the **ancient harbor**, at the northern end of which is a section of the Byzantine city wall. If you thirst for more of a hike and more ruins, trek up or drive to the top of Mount Berenice to see the recently discovered remains of a **Byzantine church**, and a stupendous view.

Museums & Art Galleries

Rifka's Art Gallery, *Crusader Castle, Donna Gracia Street, Tel. 06-672-1375*, is open Sunday-Thursday 10am-1pm, 4pm-7pm, Saturday 10am-1pm, and is worth a visit. Rifka Ganun charges NIS 8 admission to wander the tower and see her work.

Yad La'Banim, Tiberias War of Independence Museum, *4 HaGdud Ha'Ivri, Tel. 06-73-9580*, with paintings and sculpture exhibits, is open Sunday-Thursday 4pm-7:30pm and bus 5 and 1 both go there.

NIGHTLIFE & ENTERTAINMENT

Cultural Events

Yad Shitrit, *Bialik, Tel. 06-672-4237*, the culture and art center, houses the **central library**, an art and photo exhibit (open Sunday-Thursday 8am-noon and 4-7pm), a **cinema**, and, and a **theater**.

Classical music concerts are played at Hemdat Yamim Saturdays at 11:30am.

"Jerusalem's Holy Temple" film is shown Sunday-Thursday at 9pm in the Heritage Expo Gallery for free.

Dancing

Jordan River Hotel and **Moriah Plaza Hotel** have live bands on Sunday, Tuesday from 8pm, Monday from 8:30pm, Wednesday-Thursday from 9pm, and Friday from 10pm.

Caesar Hotel has live music on Thursday-Saturday from 9:30pm.

Kibbutz Beit Zera, *Tel. 06-675-7624*, has folkdancing on Tuesdays.

Kibbutz Ginnosar, *Tel. 06-679-2161*, has dancing on Thursdays from 10pm (but call to check on the schedule).

The Petra Pub (see below) has disco as well on Wednesday evenings from 10pm.

There's folkdancing at **Lido Beach** from 9:30pm on Saturdays.

Or check out the **Lipstick Club**, *Hehuda Halevi*, in the industrial zone, with a different program every night of the week.

Pubs

La Pirate Pub, *Caesar Hotel, the Promenade, Tel. 06-672-3333*, is open daily from noon-4am.

Big Ben Pub, *up the cobble stone path next to Pirate Pub and past the synagogue, Tel. 06-672-2248*, stays open nightly till 3am and is a more appealing place than La Pirate. Locals and tourists hang out and mix, and it's a very happening spot on a Friday night, with a nice marble bar and table tops, though the music is can get too loud, and it's NIS 12 or more a beer. There's good lighting and free pretzels and olives inside, and outdoor tables under the trees. Credit cards are accepted.

Pub Carlsberg, *buttressing the Promenade on the northern end*, has occasional live music and is open Thursday-Saturday 10pm-4am.

Festivals

The **Sea of Galilee Festival** takes place during the second week of July and Tiberias fills with international folk troupes. **Ein Gev's Passover Music Festival** (April 11-17 in 1998, April 2-8 in 1999) is just across the lake.

And nearby **Tzemah** hosts its annual **Tu be'Av Love Fest** in August for rock & roll.

SHOPPING

Shopping centers you may want to visit include:

Lev Ha'Ir shopping mall, *corner of HaShiloah and Bilbas*, is between the city park and the central bus station, and has lots of shops. Donna Gracia Street to the north hosts local artists and their galleries.

The **vegetable and fish street market**, *HaPrahim off HaYarden and HaGilboa*, is near town center. And the **Caprice diamond factory** has showrooms at their plant on Tabor.

SPORTS & RECREATION

The beaches of Tiberias afford access to the water but leave a bit to be desired. It's all quite beautiful, depending on whether you look at the rocks of Galilee, the sunlit brown western shore backed by verdant green hills, or the garbage everywhere.

The Tiberias Municipal Beach, *Derch Hamehatzaot, Tel. 06-672-0254*, is open 9am-7pm and costs NIS 10. With lifeguard and first aid services, there's a green swath of grass, a beach area for games, umbrellas by the water, a cafeteria, restaurant, toilets and showers.

Gai Beach, *Derech Hamerchatzaot, Tel. 06-670-0700*, run by Gai Beach Hotel, one kilometer south of the city is a water park with kamikaze water slides. Open 9am-5pm (summer only), it costs NIS 50 to get in.

Luna Gal, *eastern shore, Tel. 06-673-1750*, however, is the real McCoy water park, with a genuine beach, bumper boats, slides, pools, waterfalls, and more, open in summer Sunday-Saturday 8am-5pm, and costing NIS 45.

Sironit Beach, *just next door, Tel. 06-672-1449*, is open 9am-5pm daily and costing NIS 15. They have slides too, but not as many or as grand.

For **horseback riding**, check with the **Holiday Inn**, *Habanim near the Hot Springs, Tel. 06-679-2890, Fax 06-672-4443*. Or better yet, visit **Vered HaGalil** north of the lake (see Western Shore of Galilee for all the details).

There are **bicycles** to be rented all over Tiberias, providing fine exercise as well a convenient form of locomotion. See *Getting Around Town* for details

The **Tiberias Bowling Club**, *Lev Ha'Ir mall, corner of HaShiloah and Bilbas*, is open daily 10am-1pm and features a spiffy bowling alley scene, NIS 15 a game and NIS 3 to rent the shoes.

The **Center of Water Sports**, *Kaplan, Tel. 06-679-0677*, is open Sunday-Friday 9am-5pm, and arranges kayaking, rowing, and sailing.

In and around the Galilee are loads of outdoor recreational options, including kayaks, white water rafting, hiking, donkey rides, and jeep tours. See the Recreation section in the Golan and Galilee.

EXCURSIONS & DAY TRIPS

The **Horns of Hittin**, *above the road to Nazareth*, are situated six kilometers west of Tiberias. This horn-pronged hill is where Saladin defeated the Crusader Franks on July 4th, 1187 CE, one of most important battles in those Crusader War years. Up top there's nothing much more than a great view, but at the foot is the traditional site of the Tomb of Jethro, father-in-law of Moses and patron of the Druze, who make an annual pilgrimage here April 25th. Also nearby is **Arbel**, with ruins of an ancient Jewish city in Roman times, and **Kibbutz Lavi**, *10 kilometers west of Tiberias on Route 77*, a modern Jewish orthodox kibbutz with accommodations.

Golan Brigade Museum, *Golani Junction, Tel. 06-676-7215*, is further west on Route 77 and is open Sunday-Thursday 9am-4pm, Friday 9am-1pm, Saturday 9am-5pm. They've a collection of maps, documents, and photos in memory of Golani Brigade soldiers. By bus take the 830, 841 to Golani Junction. Call in advance for an English guide.

To see Beit She'an, Gan HaShlosha, and the mosaics at Beit Alpha Synagogue, see The Lower Galilee section. To see the sights on the lake, see Around the Sea of Galilee.

PRACTICAL INFORMATION

- **Books**: **Salon Des Judith**, *94 Shuv Pa'am*; **Steimatzky**, *3 Hagalil, Tel. 06-679-5758*, is open Sunday-Thursday 8am-1pm and 4-7pm, Friday 8am-2pm, visa accepted.
- **Car Rentals**: **Reliable**, *Tel. 06-672-3464*; **Eldan**, *Tel. 06-672-2831*; **Europcar**, *Tel. 06-672-2777*; **Hertz**, *Tel. 06-672-1804*; **Avis**, *Tel. 06-672-2766*; **City Car**, *Tel. 06-679-2766*.
- **Currency Exchange**: **Bank Ha-Poalim**, *HaBanim between Hayarden and Hayarkon, Tel. 06-679-8411*, and **Bank Leumi**, *corner of Hayarden and HaBanim, Tel. 06-672-7111*, are the main options. Both are open Sunday-Thursday 8:30am-12:30pm, Sunday, Tuesday, Thursday 4-6pm, and Friday 8:30am-noon.
- **English News**: **Israel Radio** (576 and 1458 KHz) at 7am, 1pm, 5pm, 8pm; **Voice of America** (1260, 15205, 15260, 9700 KHz) at 6am, 7am, 5pm, 5:30pm, 6pm; **BBC** (1323 KHz) at 2:15pm, 3pm, 6pm GMT; **Israel TV**, daily at 5:30pm.
- **Fire**: call *Tel. 102* in an emergency, or *Tel. 06-679-1222* otherwise.
- **Laundromats**: **Panorama**, *HaGalil south of HaKishon, Tel. 06-672-4324*, does wash, dry and fold, costing NIS 35 for 7kg.
- **Medical Aid**: **First Aid** (Magen David Adom), *corner of HaBanim and Hakishon, across the street from Jordan River Hotel, Tel. 101 in emergencies or Tel. 06-679-0111 for an ambulance; it's open 24 hours*. **The Poriya Hospital**, *southwestern side of the Sea of Galilee, Tel. 06-673-8211*. **Tiberias Medical Center**, *Lev HaGalil Center, 2nd floor, Tel. 06-672-3077*.
- **Pharmacy**: **Center Pharmacy**, *corner of Bibas and Hagalil, Tel. 06-679-0613*, is open Sunday-Thursday 8am-8pm, Friday 8am-3pm; **Schwartz Pharmacy**, *HaGalil, Tel. 06-672-0994*, is near the park and open Sunday-Thursday 8am-7pm, Friday 8am-2:30pm.
- **Police**: call *Tel. 100* in emergencies or *Tel. 06-679-2444* otherwise.
- **Post Office main branch**, *Hayarden near Elhadef, Tel. 06-679-0432*, is open Sunday-Tuesday, Thursday 8am-12:30pm and 3:30-6pm, Wednesday 8am-1:30pm, Friday 8am-12:30pm and has poste restante. **Another branch**, *Bialik and Ehrlich, Tel. 06-672-0894*, is in Kiryat Shmuel.
- **Religious Services**: There are a number of **synagogues** (local Rabbinate, *Tel. 06-672-0993*, in Tiberias. The **Great Synagogue Ohel Nachum** (Ashkenazi) is on Herzl; **Gur Arye** (Sephardi) is on HaMaginim; **Great Synagogue Ohel Ya'acov** (Ashkenazi) is on Ohel Ya'acacov; **Karlin Synagogue** (Ashkenazi) is in town center; **Senior Synagogue** (Sephardi) is on the old city seashore; **Kibbutz Lavi Synagogue** (Ashkenazi) can be reached at *Tel. 06-679-9450*. There are also plenty of churches. **Saint Peter's Church**, *Tel. 06-672-0516*, on the seashore

has services Saturday 7pm, Sunday 8:30am, Monday-Thursday, Saturday 7am, Friday 5:30pm, (Catholic, Franciscan Terra Sancta); **Saint Andrew's Church**, *Tel. 06-672-1001*, on the north end of the Promenade has services Sunday 7:30am, 6pm, Monday-Saturday 7:45am, (Church of Scotland Centre).

• **Supermarkets**: A **Co-op supermarket**, *Great Mosque Plaza across from Meyouhas Hostel*, is open Sunday-Tuesday 7am-7pm, Wednesday-Thursday 7am-8pm, and Friday 7am-2pm. Another supermarket, *HaGalil near Hayarkon, across from Bank Hapolim*, is open Saturday-Thursday 8:30am-8pm, Friday 8:30am-2pm.

• **Tourist Information Office**, *Tiberias Archaeological Park, HaBanim Street, Tel. 06-672-5666, Fax 06-672-5062*, next to Jordan River and Moriah-Plaza hotels, is open Sunday-Thursday 8:30am-5pm, Friday 8:30am-2pm and has maps and pamphlets. **Tourist Information**, *Tzemach, Tel. 06-675-2056*.

• **Tours**: Sunday-Friday is a **free walking tour** from the Tourist Office at 9:30am. **Free Tiberias tours** leave Saturdays at 10am from the Moriah Tower lobby, though the language the tour is conducted in depends on group composition. Saturdays there's a free **Scottish Centre tour** at 11am. **SPNI**, *Tel. 03-658-8674*, leaves Tuesdays from Tiberias Tourist Information office at 10:30am for a magnificent three day hiking and driving tour for moderately good hikers. If you want to explore the stunning natural beauty of this region, SPNI excels. Call ahead to reserve. **Egged Tours**, Tel. 06-672-0474, takes big bus trips of the area Tuesday and Saturday (and Thursday in summer), leaving 8:30am and returning 6pm for $37, with discounts for students, seniors, soldiers. For **private tour guides**, call to arrange details: Max Bullhorn, *Tel. 06-679-3588*; Moshe Cohen, *Tel. 06-672-1608*; Imanuel Eliad, *Tel. 06-672-0250*; Yisrael Shalem, *Tel. 06-697-1870*; Yehuda Gavish, *Tel. 06-672-0553*; Eli Halewa, *Tel. 06-672-0842*; Oded Geva, *Tel. 06-674-5171*.

AROUND THE SEA OF GALILEE

The **Sea of Galilee** (or **Lake Tiberias**—*Yam Kinneret* in Hebrew or *Bahr Tabariya* in Arabic) has been doing its thing for a long time, irrigating farms, supplying fish, and attracting scads of tourists. Agriculturally, a huge body of fresh water in Israel is a marvelous boon, and the lands surrounding the lake have been tilled for ages, while today its waters irrigate by tunnel and canal as far as the Negev. A source of water in the Middle East is always where the action's to be found, so it's not surprising that settlements, civilizations, and religions have been equally nourished by its waters (and fish).

While Greek and Roman cultures flourished here, **Herod Antipas** built Tiberias here, and synagogues ringed the lake in the third and fourth centuries, it's the Galilean activities of Jesus from nearby Nazareth that today flavor the area. It's here that the miracle of the Fishes and Loaves took place, and here that **Simon Peter** was said to have lived. And so since Byzantine times pilgrims have stormed the shores of the Sea of Galilee to visit all the New Testament sites and see the waters that Jesus walked.

But it's not just the religious who bus, fly, and drive to this lake up north. Tourists multiply as the loaves and fishes once did, supplying a magnificent source of income to the lakeside guest houses and resorts. And who can blame them. It's beautiful and peaceful, with the blue waters, green hills, and clean air. There are water parks and horseback riding farms, hiking trails and jeep tours. Combine the glorious setting with the religious shrines and archaeological finds, and there's something for every persuasion and temperament, with a hopping nightlife in Tiberias and serene solitude in the hills, romantic hide-a-ways, and family packages.

ORIENTATION

The Sea of Galilee is a large lake some 150 kilometers northeast of Jerusalem and 57 kilometers east of Akko, fed mostly by the Jordan River. Its position smack on the African-Syrian Rift gives it nasty earthquakes, lovely hot springs, and black basalt ridges, while its altitude (or lack thereof – it's 670 feet below sea level) accounts for the warm and humid weather. Wet in winter, it gets as cold as 40°F in January and as warm as 100°F or so in July.

The lake is much longer than it is wide, and its sights and attractions lie for the most part on its eastern and western sides. **Route 90** serves the west before heading north toward the Lebanese border and south toward Beit She'an, while the eastern shore's **Route 92** starts at the southern tip of the lake and ends near Tel Bethsaida in the north where it intersects with Route 87. **Route 87** covers the short north shore stretch and intersects up with Route 90 at Tabgha, making the circle complete.

ARRIVALS & DEPARTURES

By Car

This area is most easily seen with the convenience of a car, but you can take the bus here and rent cars in Tiberias.

By Bus

The main bus terminal on the lake is in **Tiberias** (*the central bus station, Hayarden, Tel. 06-679-1080*), and it has buses to Tel Aviv (the 836, 830, or

831 for NIS 29.5, last Friday bus 4pm); to Jerusalem (961 or 963 for NIS 35.5); to Nazareth (431), to Haifa (431 or 431 for NIS 20.5); for Afula (830 or 831); for Kiryat Shemona (541, 841, or 963); and to Tsfat (the 459).

By Ferry (in July and August on the Sea of Galilee)
• Tiberias-Ginnosar: *departs 8:30am*
• Tiberias-Ein Gev: *departs 10:30am, 12pm, 1:30 pm, costs NIS 25 one way, NIS 40 round trip*
• Ein Gev-Tiberias: *departs 12:15pm, 1:15pm, 3pm, 4pm*

Kinneret Sailing, *Tel. 06-675-8007*; **Lido Sailing**, *Tel. 06-672-4488*; **Holyland Sailing**, *Tel. 06-672-3006*, takes groups only.

By Taxi
For 24-Hour Service to Ben-Gurion Airport, NIS 350, call Benny Dahan *Tel. 06-672-2234*. **Aviv**, *Elhadef near the post office, Tel. 06-672-0098*, has regular service to Tel Aviv for NIS 24.30 (but not on Shabbat) and you need to arrange it the day before.

GETTING AROUND
By Bus
Buses 17, 18, 19, 20, and 21 ply the **southwest coast**, while the 22 goes up the **eastern side**.

By Bicycle
Biking around is a popular alternative. **Hotel Aviv**, *14 HaGalil, Tiberias, Tel. 06-672-3510*, rents a wide range of bikes, including new 18 gear mountain bikes, for NIS 45 a day.

By Car
You can rent a car in Tiberias from **Reliable**, *Tel. 06-672-3464*, **Eldan**, *Tel. 06-672-2831*, **Europcar**, *Tel. 06-672-2777*, **Hertz**, *Tel. 06-672-1804*, **Avis**, *Tel. 06-672-2766*, **City Car**, *Tel. 06-679-2766*.

WHERE TO STAY
On the Western Shore of Galilee
NOF GINOSAR HOTEL, *Kibbutz Ginosar, Tel. 06-679-2161, Fax 06-679-2170, is eight kilometers north of Tiberias on the lake. Their 170 fairly basic air conditioned rooms with TV, phone, and private bathroom, cost $100-$126 a single and $126-$156 a double, breakfast and service charge included (+10% during Passover and Rosh Hashana).*

Nof Ginosar does have a beach, a swimming pool, kosher dairy and meat restaurants, and a synagogue, as well as kayaks, pedal boats, windsurfing, and tennis courts, but what you get doesn't seem worth what they charge. Next to the hotel is the **Yigal Alon "Man in Galilee" Museum**, which showcases an ancient boat found nearby.

RON BEACH HOTEL, *Gdud Barak Street, just north of Tiberias, Tel. 06-6791-350, Fax 06-679-1351, is right on the sea. They've 74 rooms, with singles for $90-$110 and doubles for $100-$140, breakfast included.*

The rooms here are much nicer than the local competition. Roomy, comfortable rooms come with views of the lake, and the staff is friendly and helpful as well. They have beach access and a swimming pool, and are a 10 minute walk from Tiberias. Their dining room overlooks the lake, and they strive for attentive service (see *Where to Eat* section).

KIBBUTZ LAVI, *off Route 77, 10 kilometers west of Tiberias, Tel. 06-679-9450, Fax 06-679-9399, Lavi offers 124 air conditioned rooms, some with shower, some with bath, all with TV and phone. Singles cost $64-$126 and doubles $72-$170, depending on the season and room size, breakfast included.*

They have a pool (closed Saturday) with separate and coed swim times, they are Glatt Kosher, and there's a special Shabbat atmosphere.

VERED HAGALIL GUEST FARM, *off Route 90, about four miles north of the lake, just before the intersection with Route 85, Tel. 06-693-5785, Fax 06-693-4964, the prices vary by type of accommodation (bunkhouse, cabin, studio, or cottage, in ascending luxury) and day of week. Singles are $66-$80 and doubles are $29-$105, plus $22 for each additional person, breakfast included.*

A real gem, Vered Hagalil has beautiful stone and wood cabins and cottages, a rustic restaurant with gourmet cooking, a stable of healthy, well-attended horses (arabians, quarter horses, and others) for trail-riding, a pool, and magnificent views of the lake and the hills of the Golan. Peaceful and romantic for a couple wanting to get away, it's also a great choice for a family, as each cabin sleeps four, and there are lots of possible activities. In addition to the horseback riding (one hour $20, half day $55, and full day with lunch $95), they also arrange jeep trips, water and snow skiing, biking, rafting, and tubing on the Jordan River (around NIS 680 for a half day's jeep tour, NIS 60 for a day of kayaking).

If you have the time, this place is well worth the visit. The cottages, studios, and cabins are especially lovely with the wood and stone construction and stupendous views. They opened in 1960 as a family operation, and the owners are always looking for ways to improve. They sell a Galilee touring map, their own creation, that is better than any you'll find elsewhere. This place is no secret to Israelis and if you want to visit in July-August or Passover you'll need to reserve months in advance. It's easiest to get here by car, but if traveling by bus, get off at Korazim Junction.

GINNOSAR INN, *just north of Ginosar Hotel, Tel. 06-679-8762, has 43 rooms with two-four beds, a sink and fridge, and air conditioning. The rooms cost*

NIS 170 a single, NIS 265 a double, and NIS 360 a triple, all with breakfast included.

The rooms aren't particularly special, but the rates are comparatively moderate, and they have their own beach.

DAYS INN PLAZA, *Mifratz Amnon, Tel. 06-679-2013, Fax 06-672-0147, is currently closed for renovation. Call to see if they're open and for rates.*

This hotel is a sort of a village, in that it comes with its own map, car park, beach, and lots of little bungalows set up on mini streets. In the summer you can kayak and water ski.

KAREI DESHE HOSTEL, *Doar-Na Korazim, western shore of the lake, Tel. 06-672-0601, Fax 06-672-4818, is about three kilometers north of Kibbutz Ginnosar and 10 kilometers north of Tiberias. Take bus 841 from Tel Aviv, or 459/841 from Tiberias, get off at Atar Sapir junction and walk in one kilometer. The rates vary for their 300 beds (74 air conditioning rooms with two-six beds per) depending on the number of people per room. One person is $33, two are $29 each, and so on up to six people at $25 each, including breakfast (IYHF members get a $1.50 nightly discount), and in summer, prices go up 15%.*

One of the most magnificent hostels ever, it's built in the form of a khan, with a beautiful courtyard and terrace, palm trees and green lawns. No mere stunning structure, Karei Deshe is meticulously clean, and is set on its own beach on the lake, supervised in summer by a lifeguard. The reception office is open 7am-9pm, and check-in is from 3pm (no lock-out, no curfew). There is also a TV and video room, ping-pong, a cafeteria with $11 meals, and Friday night folk dancing on the balcony in the summer.

PORIA TAIBER HOSTEL, *Route 7677, opposite Barniki Beach, four kilometers south of Tiberias, Tel. 06-675-0050, Fax 06-675-1628, has 149 beds (three-six beds per dorm) in heated/air conditioned rooms with shower for $24, or dorms without shower or air conditioning for $18.*

Overlooking the Sea of Galilee, surrounded by flowers, and with the Golan Heights in the background, it's a lovely spot, well-maintained, and a three kilometer hike up from the road. They have family rooms, and a guest house. Meals are served, and there's a TV lounge, sports facility, and park.

Eastern Shore of Galilee

MA'AGAN HOLIDAY VILLAGE, *southeastern tip of the lake off Route 92, Tel. 06-675-3753, Fax 06-675-3707, has 124 air conditioned holiday homes, all outfitted with kitchenette and bathroom. Prices range from $94-$115 in low season to $115-$147 in high, and suites are $158-$250, large buffet breakfast included.*

They've a private beach and water sports (including a surfing club), and there's a tour of the kibbutz for the history of the kibbutz from their

Transylvanian Zionist Youth Movement origins up to today, and including a visit to their mini zoo to see the peacocks, ponies, monkeys, and deer. The staff is warm and friendly, and the suites comfortable and spacious. They are spread out, giving a sense of privacy, and there are generous lawns for kids to play on. The atmosphere is more casual than at a hotel, and nice for a family. The buffet breakfast is generous and delicious, and you can get good dinners there as well.

RAMOT RESORT-HOTEL, *in the hills above the northern end of the lake, near Luna-Gal water park, Tel. 06-673-2732, Fax 06-679-3590, they charge $80-$95 a single, and $95-$120 for doubles, breakfast included.*

They've 80 rooms with air conditioning, TV, phone and fridge, and balcony facing the lake as well as 40 village houses that are more private, with their own gardens instead of TV, phone or radio. They've a restaurant with panoramic view, a verandah, a large swimming pool, and a kiddie pool, and they also offer horseback riding, organized hikes, archery, and Jordan River inner-tubing. The rooms are nicely done, with lovely patios and views. It's quiet and peaceful here, and a convenient place if you want a lot of activities.

KIBBUTZ EIN-GEV, *a little south of midway, across the lake from Tiberias, Tel. 06-675-8027, Fax 06-675-1590, has rates that vary considerably by season and type. Singles range from $53-$95 and doubles $72-$119, and they only book reservations for four in high season.*

Established in 1937, Ein-Gev offers a lot in terms of history and tourist orientation. For accommodations, they have 111 rooms and 33 holiday chalets, all air conditioned with cooking facilities and private toilet/shower, and very, very close together. Of the various types, the Deluxe are the nicest, with patios facing the lake. They also have 120 camping areas with toilets, electric points, refrigeration compartments and cooking areas. But that's just the beginning. There's a little blue and white train that will give you a history tour around the kibbutz for NIS 8. Then there are the ferries, with regular trips to Tiberias and Kfar Nahum (Capernaum) NIS 25 one way and NIS 40 round trip (30% discount for guests) as well as shoreline sailings, disco-boats, etc. Also the kibbutz hosts an annual music festival at Passover. See below for their renowned fish restaurant.

HA'ON HOLIDAY VILLAGE, *Kibbutz Ha'on, just east of the southern tip of the lake, Tel. 06-665-6555, Fax 06-665-6557, and reservations/information can also be obtained in the US at Kibbutz Hotels, c/o Toam, 60 East 42nd Street, New York, 212/697-5116. Ha'on offers a variety of accommodations, with 54 holiday homes (set in a palm grove, they sleep up to six and have air conditioning, kitchenettes, and shower/toilet facilities) for $75-$110 a double, breakfast included. Their rooms on the kibbutz are $75-$88 a double, and they also have camping grounds with picnic tables and electricity points where you can* *pitch a tent (advance reservations suggested in summer), $20 a car and $35 per van.*

The Village has kayaks and pedal boats to rent, a restaurant, mini-market, bar/lounge, and disco. Their special claim to fame, however, is the **Ostrich Farm**. Open daily 9am-4pm (till 6pm in summer), the farm has around 200 birds. You can see them in various stages of development (egg, chick, parent), and entrance is free to Ha'on guests (otherwise it costs NIS 12 per adult, NIS 10 per child/student). There are beautiful flowers on the long driveway in and it's right on the water, but the caravan/bungalows are boxy and claustrophobic with unappealing cots, and they're all made out of ticky tacky and they all look just the same.

AMI TAI, *just up the road from Ramot Resort, Tel. 06-673-2258, offers three guest houses, each with two bedrooms, a kitchen, and a porch with view. The houses (sleeping up to four) go for NIS 350 in low season, and NIS 450 in summer.*

It's quiet and scenic, but you'll need a car. Follow the "Golan rooms" signs, park at the first major parking spot, follow to the end the path heading away from the lake, and ring the bell of the house on the left.

WHERE TO EAT

Almost every restaurant around the Sea of Galilee features the omnipresent Saint Peter's Fish, more scientifically known as *Tilapia Galilea*. Now associated with the fish that multiplied with the loaves (or at least marketed that way), it used to be called Comb Fish (*musht* in Arabic, *amnun* in Hebrew), and for good cause. It's a bony, spiny little number, and though the flesh can be succulent, the real miracle of these fish is how many are ordered daily due to their nominal connection to sainthood.

While all the guest houses serve meals, a few spots really stand out. Tiberias is also close by and has plenty of dining options.

Western Shore

VERED HAGALIL RESTAURANT, *off Route 90, Tel. 06-693-5785, Fax 06-693-4964*, about four miles north of the lake and just before the intersection with Route 85, is open 8am-11pm daily. Rustic and pleasant, with wood tables, a view of the horses, and great food, there are fresh flowers on every table, and friendly dogs wandering about. Cold summer soups (gazpacho, yogurt, borsht) are NIS 16, desserts NIS 11-16, main courses NIS 30-62, and fresh juices wash it all down. There's good onion soup, excellent fresh bread and garlic butter, great pies, and everything is homemade. It's worth the detour for the genuine warmth and fresh, unpretentious food.

RON BEACH HOTEL RESTAURANT, *Gdud Barak Street, Tel. 06-679-1350, Fax 06-679-1351*, is just north of Tiberias and right on the sea, but isn't kosher. They've nice settings with pink linen napkins and lots of cutlery. The set menu for dinner, prix fixe NIS 80, gets you soup, appetizer, entree, salad, dessert, and a basket of unappetizing sliced white bread. They do a beautiful plate of Saint Peter's fish, sliced tomato arranged artistically, everything (lemon, cucumber) scrolled, and quite tasty.

Eastern Shore

KIBBUTZ EIN-GEV, *is a little south of midway, and across the lake from Tiberias, Tel. 06-657-8027, Fax 06-675-1590.* The kibbutz has a guest house, ferry dock, and more, but perhaps the biggest draw here is the **Fish Restaurant**. They've been in business for a long time, and are still churning out the deep-fried Saint Peter's Fish by the bushel. Around lunchtime the place is a madhouse of tours herded in for their fish dinner package. There is indoor seating as well as patio dining by a duck pond, people seem well-pleased with their meals, and the prices are reasonable (hummus NIS 9, chips NIS 8, fish NIS 30-57). The patio is a nice place to sample the fish, but avoid the tour bus times when the restaurant gets a frenetic assembly-line feel.

SEEING THE SIGHTS

One of the nicest activities in the area is to drive (or cycle) around the lake, stopping off here and there at the sites, and enjoying the views of the lake on one side and the green rolling hills on the other.

Western Shore North of Tiberias

Migdal (Tarichea), *off Route 807, is about four miles northwest of Tiberias.* This town is rich in history, though nowadays Migdal is a moshav of about 700 settlers. It was an important Jewish city in Second Temple times, however, specializing in fishing and fish processing, hence the town's name (*Migdal Nunia* means tower of fish in Aramaic). The town was a base for the Zealot navy, was captured by the Romans during the great rebellion of 67CE, and the inhabitants were taken prisoner or killed. Known as Magdala in the Bible, this is also the city from which Mary Magdalene hailed. There is an **excavation site** here with parts of a paved street, remains of a Roman villa and bath, Roman sarcophagi, and a synagogue dating from around first century BCE.

Kibbutz Ginosar, *eight kilometers north of Tiberias, Tel. 06-672-1995, Fax 06-679-2170,* has the **Yigal Alon "Man in Galilee" Museum**, including the 2,000 year old boat recently discovered on the lake bed. The museum is open Saturday-Thursday 8am-5pm, Friday 8am-1pm, and costs NIS 14, NIS 12 for seniors and children. Buses 459, 541, 841, 963 all go here.

Further north is **Tabgha**, an important site in Christian history. The site is open 8am-5pm and admission is free, but no shorts are allowed. The name "Tabgha" comes from the Greek "Heptapegan," which means seven springs, and people flock in on tour buses to see the churches, old and new, which commemorate three important events: the miracle of the Loaves and the Fishes, the coronation of Simon Peter as head of the disciples, and the Sermon on the Mount. The **Church of the Miracle of the Loaves and Fishes** was built in 1982 in the Byzantine style by the German Society of the Holy Land on the site where two earlier churches (the first in the 300s CE and the second in the 400s CE) had stood.

Remains include a block of unhewn limestone that was taken from the first church and was believed by Christians as late as 5th century to have been the lord's table (mensa Christi), and the fine mosaic floor (including the beautiful pattern of fish and loaves, copies of which exist all over Israel on souvenir plates and jewelry). The **Garden of the Seven Springs** is next to the church.

Monastery of the Sermon on the Mount, *325 yards away*, was built in the 300s CE, and the mosaics from the narthex and nave are now in the garden at Kfar Nahum. There is a beautiful tree-lined path leading to the **Chapel of the Primacy**. It's a small, intimate chapel with stone walls and stained glass, and the sound of the waves of the lake against the shore, and was built by the Franciscans in 1933 to commemorate the appearance of the resurrected Christ to the apostles when he thrice gave Peter a last commandment (John 21:15). The rock (known as the **mensa domini**) is supposed to be the table at which Jesus and His disciples ate. Should you visit? You could come for the religious significance, or the peaceful ambiance, or you could drive on by.

Mount of Beatitudes, *on a hill behind Tabgha*, is where Jesus is said to have preached the Sermon on the Mount. **Church of the Sermon on the Mount**, built in 1938 along with the Franciscan hospice, was a replacement for the chapel which had been abandoned in the 600s CE and is made mostly of black basalt and white Nazareth stones; its octagonal shape is meant to symbolize the eight Beatitudes (Matthew 5:3-10). Nearby (two kilometers west) are the partially excavated ruins of **Khirbet el-Minya**, the Palace of the Umayyad Caliph Walid I (705-715 CE). Among the grasses and palm trees you can see the remains of one the earliest mosques in existence, as well as palace boundary walls, the throne hall, and mosaics.

Capernaum (Kfar Nahum), "the town of Jesus," *is on the northwestern tip of the lake on Route 87*. People visit this site (open 8:30am-4:15pm, admission NIS 5) to see the **reconstructed synagogue** that was originally made from carved limestone in the late fourth century CE, and the remains of an octagonal church built on the traditional site of **Saint Peter's house**. The old limestone pillars and steel reinforced walls of the ancient synagogue are beautiful, as are the red domes of the Greek

Orthodox church in the background. Unfortunately, a new, somewhat ugly church (just opened three years ago) has been constructed over the first century church and Peter's house remains.

The name *Kfar Nahum* means "village of the Nahum" in Hebrew. It was probably originally a Herodian foundation, but wasn't destroyed in the first or second centuries CE because it didn't participate in the revolts against Rome. From the New Testament this town is known as the site where Jesus preached and worked miracles (Street. Mark 1:21-34), healing the sick and those possessed by devils. The synagogue where he preached no longer stands, but the White Synagogue was built beside the original synagogue circa 200 CE in the Graeco-Roman style, with symbols and iconography such as menorah, shofar, and the Roman double eagle; and the Star of David is one of the oldest that has been found in Israel. South of the synagogue is the fifth century octagonal church, built on the traditional site of Peter's house, with a mosaic showing a peacock and lotus blossoms.

If you're making a pilgrimage of holy sites, this is an important stop. Otherwise, it's attractive and interesting if you're in the neighborhood, but not necessarily worth going out of your way for. If you do visit, modest dress (no shorts) is expected.

Western Shore South of Tiberias

Near the southern tip of the lake, the **Founders' Farmyard Kinneret Museum**, *Moshavat Kinneret, Tel. 06-675-1170*, is open daily 9am-2pm, and accessible by bus 18, 22, or 26.

Yardenit, *near the southwest tip of the Sea of Galilee just off Route 90*, is **The Place of Baptism**. Often dressed in white gowns, pilgrims from all over come to immerse themselves in the holy Jordan waters. Near Yardenit is **Kibbutz Deganya**, *Tel. 06-675-0040*, the oldest kibbutz in Israel (founded in 1909). Their cemetery contains the graves of Otto Warburg, Joseph Bussel, A.D. Gordon, and Arthur Ruppin. In addition, they have a museum of natural science, the **Beit Gordon Museum**, *Tel. 06-675-0040*, open Sunday-Thursday 8:30am-4pm, Friday 8:30am-12pm, Saturday 9:30am-12pm with agricultural, historical, and archaeological displays. Buses 23, 26, 27, and 29 all go there.

Sha'ar ha'Golan Museum of Prehistory, Kibbutz Sha'ar HaGolan, east of Route 90, Tel. 06-675-7386, near Deganya, is open daily 9am-12pm, but afternoons by advance request only. Take bus 26 to the crossroads and ask the bus driver.

Beit Yerah (also called **Tel Ubeidiya** or **Khirbet al Karak**), *about three kilometers west of Route 90 and south of Kibbutz Deganya*, is a tel mentioned in the Talmud and the site of an excavation that uncovered finds of the oldest human settlement outside Africa, some 600,000-800,000 years old, at the shore of a prehistoric lake. During excavations in the '40s and '50s, a synagogue (one of the largest to be discovered) was uncovered inside a Roman fort, though little of the original mosaic can still be made out.

There is also a church complex from the early fifth century CE which was in use till the late sixth-early seventh century. In addition are the remains of Roman baths (fed from a conduit leading from Wadi Fayyon to Tiberias) and a fortress that was built in the 200s CE and abandoned in the late 300s.

Eastern Shore from North to South

Tel Bethsaida, right near **Jordan River Park** (Park Hayarden—a nature reserve at the point where the Jordan flows into the Sea of Galilee), *off Route 87 and just a few miles east of Capernaum*, is the fisherman's town from which Peter, Andrew, and Philip came. It is another of the towns (along with biblical Khorazin and Capernaum) that Jesus cursed ("Woe unto thee, Bethsaida," Mt.11:21) for their lack of belief. Recent excavations have revealed more of its history. The city of Bethsaida was heavily fortified from 1000-586 BCE, and Flavius Josephus led Israel's troops against the Romans from 66-70 CE. Excavators have uncovered statues of an ancient Egyptian deity, Roman buildings, a fisherman's home circa Jesus' time, and an Iron Age temple and palace (possibly the residence of Talmai—Absalom's father-in-law and Geshur's king). Also uncovered was a pottery shard with a cross inscribed on its side. The shard's been dated at 66 CE, raising questions about just when the cross became a Christian symbol.

For Khorazim National Park, see the *Upper Galilee* section.

Kursi, *further south on the western side of the lake*, features the remains of a Jewish agricultural fishing settlement from the Talmudic period. The site has also been linked with New Testament Gargasa, where Jesus expelled the devils from the body of a sick man and put them instead into a herd of pigs that later drowned in the sea. In fifth century CE a walled monastery was built here to commemorate this miracle. In addition to the beautiful mosaic floors, a holy rock was discovered from which the pigs were said to have slid into the water. In 1981 the church was restored and the site declared a national park. Also of note, Jaqov of Kursi, who taught Juda HaNassi (who compiled the *mishna*) was born here.

Further south, **Susita**, two kilometers east of Kibbutz Ein-Gev, is on top of a steep hill, and was a flourishing town in Hellenistic and Byzantine days. On this site are the ruins of the Greek city Antiochia Hippos. It was conquered by Pompey in 63 BCE, and Augustus gave Susita to Herod in 30 BCE. After Augustus' death in 14 CE, Susita fell to Syria. There was a Jewish community here during Talmudic times and it was a bishop's seat in the Byzantine period, but after the Arabs' victory in the battle on the

Yarmuk (636 CE) the town was abandoned. There are remains of five churches, with magnificent stone pillars that collapsed in an earthquake. And there are other remains: temple, walls, arches, watch towers, and an old conduit system that brought in water from the Golan Heights. There's an unpaved road from the west, off of Route 98, but easier access is on the paved road off Route 92 in the east.

Hammat Gader, *southeast of the Sea of Galilee and on the border with Jordan, Tel. 06-675-1039, Fax 06-675-2745*, is open Monday-Saturday 7am-11pm, Sunday 7am-6:30pm, and costs NIS 37 per person (children under three admitted free), and prices are reduced to NIS 30 after 6pm, and NIS 21 after 9pm. The fun starts before you even enter the gates, thanks to entertaining welcome signs featuring gators dressed in bright red terry robes all along the approach.

There's a wide range of choices and activities here at Hammat Gader, including a stroll in the Alligator Farm, a visit to the Aviary and Mini Zoo, trampolines and waterslides, Roman Bath Ruins, and the Hot Spring Pools. Most people tend to make a beeline for the hot springs, and while the human lizards spend the entirety of their visit lounging in the hot waters, you can have the real lizards (as well as the other entertainment) all to yourself. The parking lots are full of Israeli tour buses that have come from as far away as Tel Aviv, a bus trip to Hammat Gader being perhaps comparable for Israeli senior citizens to a package tour to Atlantic City or Reno for Americans.

Despite the alluring signs, the thrill of the alligators, crocodiles, and cayman really depends on chance. If they're doing their solar recharge statue imitations, the visit can be a bit dull; however, if you catch the caymans when they're opening their big maws and moaning, it's a gruesome and wonderful experience. Nearby is the aviary and **zoo** with ostriches and zebras and peacocks, and while it's not the best zoo, it might be of interest to children. For more animal fun and 3 NIS extra, you can attend their alligator wrestling and performing parrot shows. For active fun, visit the **trampolines** and **water slide**. The slide is slicked with natural thermal water, and is a great ride.

If you keep walking you'll come to the **ruins**. The Roman town of Gadara (now in Jordan) was one of the ten cities of the Decapolis that Jesus is known to have visited, and was a center of Greek culture in Hellenistic times; Hammat Gader was one of its suburbs. Excavated ruins feature a fifth century **synagogue**, a 2,000 seat Roman theater, and Roman baths. The synagogue up on Tel Bani was destroyed by fire, but remains of benches still exist along the walls, and the mosaic floor from this synagogue is now on display at Israel's High Court in Jerusalem. The **Roman theater** is 350 yards east of Tel Bani, had 15 rows of basalt seats, and held 2,000 spectators. Then there are the **baths**. Hammat Gader was the second largest mineral water spa in the Roman Empire, and then as now, the attraction here was the waters. There were seven pools in Roman times (one of which was reserved for lepers at night), and natural mineral water flowed through beautifully sculpted fountains. The ruins are quite picturesque, and you sometimes have them all to yourself.

The big draw, however, are still the **hot mineral water pools**, and they are worth it. There are five pools of varying temperatures. The pool by the antiques is 127°F, too hot to enter. The pool under the shelter area is 113°F, in the jacuzzi area the water is 108°F, the water fall is 98.6°F, and Saint Paul's pool (fresh water) is cool at 79°F. There is, of course, a story as to why it's called Saint Paul's. Apparently when Paul was traveling in these parts they were thirsty but couldn't quench their thirst from the mineral pools. Paul found the one pool that is natural spring water, hence its name. Or, alternatively, the miracle of Saint Paul's cure happened here.

All this you get with your entrance ticket, but there are plenty more ways to spend money here. There are changing rooms and showers at the mineral baths, but it's NIS 6 to rent a towel, and NIS 10 to rent a robe. You can rent a locker for your belongings for NIS 5, or you can leave your bag at the check-in counter for free. Then there are the massages (health and Tai), 30 minutes for NIS 80-100, an hour for NIS 160-180 (credit cards accepted), and the full line of Balzam mineral-based muds and creams and shampoos. On Saturdays there is a mini-train that does a full tour. There are also a variety of restaurants and snack bars throughout the complex. And along with the usual assortment of souvenirs, you can have your picture taken while you hold a real live baby gator. Bus 24 takes you there.

NIGHTLIFE & ENTERTAINMENT

Hammat Gader (see above) can be fun at night, otherwise you're pretty much limited to the goings-on in Tiberias.

SHOPPING

This isn't really the spot for shopping, though Hammat Gader has Balzam mineral-based muds and creams and shampoos as well as a shop of kitschy souvenirs.

SPORTS & RECREATION

There's **horseback riding** at **Kfar Hittin Ranch**, *west of Tiberias, Tel. 06-679-5921*; **Ramot Ranch**, *east of the lake, Tel. 06-673-1112*; and **Vered Hagalil**, *near Korazim, Tel. 06-693-5785*.

Ramot Ranch, *Tel. 06-673-1112*, also arranges jeep trips and Jordan River inner-tubing.

ATV (mini-tractor) **Trips** can be had at Kfar Hittin, *Tel. 06-679-5921*. **Water Parks** (in summer): **Gai Beach**, *Derech Hamerchatzaot, Tel. 06-670-0700*, run by Gai Beach Hotel, one kilometer south of Tiberias, is a water park with kamizaze water slides. Open 9am-5pm (summer only), it costs NIS 50 to get in. **Luna Gal**, *on the eastern shore near Ramot Resort, Tel. 06-673-1750*, is the real thing, with a genuine beach, bumper boats, slides and pools and waterfalls, and more, open in summer daily 8am-5pm, and costing NIS 45.

Boat Rentals/Water Skiing is available at major hotels in Tiberias and Luna Gal.

Windsurfing can be done at *Kibbutz Ma'agan, southern shore of the Kinneret, Tel. 06-675-3753*.

For **Parascending** go to *Luna Gal, Tel. 06-673-1750*.

EXCURSIONS & DAY TRIPS

There are a number of tour options to see the sights in the area.

SPNI, *Tel. 03-537-4425*, leaves Tuesdays from Tiberias Tourist Information office at 10:30am for a magnificent three day hiking and driving tour for moderately good hikers. If you want to explore the stunning natural beauty of this region, SPNI excels. Call ahead to reserve.

Egged Tours, *Tel. 06-672-0474*, takes big bus trips of the area Tuesday and Saturday (and Thursday in summer), leaving 8:30am and returning 6pm for $37, with discounts for students, seniors, soldiers.

And then there are private Tour Guides (call to arrange details): Max Bullhorn, *Tel. 06-679-3588*; Moshe Cohen, *Tel. 06-672-1608*; Imanuel Eliad, *Tel. 06-672-0250*; Yisrael Shalem, *Tel. 06-697-1870*; Yehuda Gavish, *Tel. 06-672-0553*; Eli Halewa, *Tel. 06-672-0842*; Oded Geva, *Tel. 06-674-5171*.

PRACTICAL INFORMATION

For all the comforts of civilization such as banks, books, laundromats, supermarkets, and pharmacies, go to Tiberias. The post office is there too, though most hotels can mail letters for you.

- **English News: Israel Radio** (576 and 1458 KHz) at 7am, 1pm, 5pm, 8pm; **Voice of America** (1260, 15205, 15260, 9700 KHz) at 6am, 7am, 5pm, 5:30pm, 6pm; **BBC** (1323 KHz) at 2:15pm, 3pm, 6pm GMT; **Israel TV**, daily at 5:30pm.
- **Fire**: call *Tel. 102* in an emergency, or *Tel. 06-679-1222* otherwise.
- **Medical Aid: First Aid** (Magen David Adom), *corner of HaBanim and Hakishon, across the street from Jordan River Hotel, Tel. 101 in emergencies or Tel. 06-679-0111* for an ambulance; it's open 24 hours. **The Poriya Hospital**, *southwestern side of the Sea of Galilee, Tel. 06-673-8211*.

Tiberias Medical Center, *Lev HaGalil Center, 2nd floor, Tel. 06-672-3077.*

- **Pharmacy**: **Center Pharmacy**, *corner of Bibas and Hagalil, Tel. 06-679-0613*, is open Sunday-Thursday 8am-8pm, Friday 8am-3pm; **Schwartz Pharmacy**, *HaGalil, Tel. 06-672-0994*, is near the park and open Sunday-Thursday 8am-7pm, Friday 8am-2:30pm.
- **Police**: call *Tel. 100* in emergencies or *Tel. 06-679-2444* otherwise.
- **Supermarkets**: A **Co-op supermarket**, *Great Mosque Plaza across from Meyouhas Hostel*, is open Sunday-Tuesday 7am-7pm, Wednesday-Thursday 7am-8pm, and Friday 7am-2pm. **Another supermarket**, *HaGalil near Hayarkon, across from Bank Hapolim*, is open Saturday-Thursday 8:30am-8pm, Friday 8:30am-2pm.
- **Tourist Information Office**, *Tiberias Archaeological Park, HaBanim Street, Tel. 06-672-5666, Fax 06-672-5062*, next to Jordan River and Moriah-Plaza hotels, is open Sunday-Thursday 8:30am-5pm, Friday 8:30am-2pm and has maps and pamphlets. **Tourist Information**, *Tzemach, Tel. 06-675-2056.*

LOWER GALILEE & VALLEYS

Jordan & Yizre'el Valleys – Galilee to Beit She'an to Afula & Back

This triangle of Galilee is loaded with archaeological treasures, fertile fields, and relics of the years of conflict between Muslims and Crusaders. There's not much in the way of places to stay or eat, but you'll run out of time before you run out of sites to see.

Rent a car, load it with cold water, good food, a bathing suit and towel, and set off early.

ORIENTATION

Heading south from the tip of the Sea of Galilee, **Route 90** is the road that takes you to **Gesher, Belvoir**, and **Beit She'an**. From there, **Route 71** heads west towards **Afula**, passing the exits to **Gan HaShlosha, Beit Alfa Synagogue**, and **Ma'ayan Harod**. From Afula, head back northeast on **Route 65** to **Kfar Tavor** and on back to the Sea of Galilee.

ARRIVALS & DEPARTURES

By Bus

By bus, Afula and Tiberias are the closest transportation hubs. It's also possible to cross the border into **Jordan** down by Beit She'an at the **Sheikh Hussein Bridge** Jordan River crossing (private vehicles not allowed), but see the *International Borders* section for more information.

GETTING AROUND

By Car
A car is highly recommended.

By Bus
Bus transport is possible, if unwieldy. Buses 434, 961, 963, and 964 head down Route 90 from the lake to Beit She'an. Buses 961, 963, 964, and 434 run west from Beit She'an back toward Tiberias.

By Bicycle
Hotel Aviv, *14 HaGalil, Tiberias, Tel. 06-672-3510*, rents a wide range of bikes, including new 18 gear mountain bikes, for NIS 45 a day, and some other hostels have a few bikes to rent as well.

WHERE TO STAY

MA'AYAN HAROD, *Moshav Gide'ona, off highway 71, Tel./Fax 06-653-1660*, is adjacent to Ma'ayan Harod National Park at the foot of Mount Gilboa, near Gideona.

The accommodations are in cabins, some two rooms with four beds, others three rooms with seven beds, all have their own bathrooms and air conditioning for NIS 83-98 for dorm beds and NIS 230 for doubles. Their facilities include a kosher kitchen, a cafeteria, and a playground for children. There is also a discount to the Ma'ayan Harod park and its swimming pool. It's in a beautiful, bucolic setting, and is clean and well-attended. Take bus 412, 402, or 405 from Afula toward Beit She'an and ask the driver for Ma'ayan-Harod, or take the express #35 directly there.

Otherwise, staying at one of the many places on or around the Sea of Galilee is your best bet.

WHERE TO EAT

Bring your own food if you don't feel like eating at tourist site cafeterias. There are, however, the usual assortment of falafel stands and cafes in Beit She'an near the bus station.

SEEING THE SIGHTS

Doctor's House Museum and Menahamiya Historical Museum, *Moshav Menahamiya, Tel. 06-675-1019*, about three kilometers south of the lake and west of Route 90, is open Sunday-Thursday 9am-2pm, Saturday 10am-2pm. The museum shows the history of medicine in Israel from 1900 as well as the history of Menahamiya, the oldest modern Jewish village in the Jordan Valley. There is a picnic area and a playground, as well as a pool (open in summer), and bus 26 will get you there.

Old Gesher and Battle Museum, *Kibbutz Gesher, Tel. 06-675-2685*, shows settlement history and underground life during the war. Take bus 434, 963, or 964 to Gesher entrance, then walk one kilometer to the museum.

Belvoir, *Route 717 about four kilometers west of Route 90, Tel. 06-658-1766*, on the way from Tiberias to Beit She'an, is open Saturday-Thursday 8am-5pm, Friday 8am-4pm (and closing one hour earlier in winter), the site costs NIS 11 to enter. The Crusader castle is way up (1,800 feet) above the Jordan valley, affording swell views ("Belvoir" in French) of the vicinity. The castle started and ended with the Crusaders, but it changed hands many times along the way. In 1168 CE, Ivo Velos sold his small castle to the Hospitallers, who set about rebuilding the fortress and renaming it Belvoir, though it was also referred to as Coquet (from Kaukab el-Hawa, the Arabic rendition of the Hebrew name Kochav HaYarden, the small town near the fortress). Sultan Saladin did quite well for himself in the 1187 battle of Hattin, but the fortress didn't fall to the Muslims till 1189.

Belvoir remained a Muslim stronghold until 1219, at which time Al-Malik al-Mu'azzam, ruler of Damascus, ordered the castle razed to prevent its return to Crusader hands. In 1241 the treaty between the Egyptian ruler Malik es-Salih Ayyub and Richard of Cornwall gave the castle back to the Crusaders. They didn't rebuild it, however, and it remained as was until the early 1800s when the Arabs built the village Kaukab el-Hawa on the castle ruins. The fortress was excavated in 1966, and the National Parks Authority has done some impressive restoration.

Along with the panoramic views and traditional Crusader fortifications, you can see some rare examples of Crusader sculpture. Eight hundred yards southeast was Kokhav HaYarden, a Jewish town that existed from Second Temple times until the fourth century CE. The Crusaders used materials from this settlement to build their castle, including stones from the synagogue with Aramaic and Greek inscriptions. Bus 434, 961, 963, 964 (toward Beit She'an) and ask for Belvoir crossroads, then walk seven kilometers uphill (take water).

Beit She'an

A good 34 kilometers bus trip (bus 961, 963, 964, 434) or drive will take you to **Beit She'an**, *south on Route 90, Tel. 06-658-7189*, an important archaeological site with excavations of more than 20 different settlement strata, from Chalcolithic times (about 3500 BCE) onward. The National Park site is open Saturday-Thursday 8am-4pm, Friday 8am-3pm in winter, and stays open an hour later in summer. To enter it'll cost you NIS 16 an adult, NIS 7 a youth, and NIS 12 for students and seniors.

One of the oldest cities in the region, Beit She'an was well situated. Near water and fertile fields, and also near major crossroads, the city was maintained throughout the years under various rulers. Most of the ruins to be seen now are from Roman and Byzantine times, but the city goes way back. A community lived here when the Egyptians ruled over Canaan from about 1500-1100 BCE, when the oldest temple on the site (circa 1350 BCE) was built in a mix of Canaanite and Egyptian styles. In the late 1000s BCE, the Philistines ruled Beit She'an, and they festively displayed the bodies of King Saul and his sons upon the walls after the Battle of Mount Gilboa.

Later, **King David** conquered the city, which under **King Solomon's** rule became an important administration center. During Hellenistic (332-63 BCE) times the city was known as Scythopolis (City of Scythians), though Nysa was another name associated with this city. Nysa was the nurse of Dionysus (the Greek wine god), and tradition has it that she was buried there. Thriving during Roman (63 BCE-324 CE) and Byzantine times (324-640 CE), the city became a provincial capital around 400 CE, and had a population of between 30,000-40,000 in sixth century CE. In the early 600s the city came under Muslim rule, but was destroyed by a bad earthquake in 749.

During medieval years Beit She'an continued as a small city; a fortress was built during Crusader times, and it remained a small regional center during Ottoman and British Mandate days. Since the establishment of the State of Israel, modern Beit She'an has continued developing and now has a population of around 15,000. The trip from Tiberias to Beit She'an is pleasant, about 40 minutes by bus, surrounded by fertile fields, green hills, rocks and mounds, and impressive irrigation. Watch for cows being herded by horse and motorcycle. There isn't that much to see in the town itself, the real attraction is the National Park ruins.

From the bus stop in Beit She'an, walk through the arcade of shops and food stalls to the street, turn left to Leumi Bank, then turn right and follow signs, past the kids' park to the entrance of Beit She'an. Just past the playground and to the left is the path to the **Municipal Swimming Pool**, open in summer only, and costing about NIS 6. It's a nice option to keep in mind, especially if you're visiting the ruins in the heat of summer.

The major **excavations** are on **Tel el-husn** ("hill of strength"). There are more excavations going on under the auspices of the Israeli Antiquities Authority and Hebrew University, and should be continuing (that is, they have funding for) at least two more years. Some of the ruins are in their original state, while others such as the street and the amphitheater have been reconstructed. The **Roman Theater** is perhaps the largest and best-preserved Roman building in Israel. Built under Emperor Septimius Severus (193-211 CE) to hold up to 8000 spectators, the lower section was cut into the ground while the upper section had nine vomitories (entrances) which led into the interior.

The **Monastery of the Noble Lady Maria**, *north of Tel el-husn*, was probably built no earlier than 567 CE (as indicated by a tombstone in the chapel). It was abandoned after the Persian invasion of 614 CE but the colorful mosaics weren't destroyed. The **Ashtaroth Temple**, used for cultic practices until around 1000 CE, was built by Ramses III. Items from the temple, including a magnificent statue of Ramses III (1184-1153 BCE) are in the Rockefeller Museum in Jerusalem.

There are plenty other sights to see here as well, such as the second century CE **Nymphaeum**, **Roman colonnades**, and **Byzantine baths**. The **Roman Amphitheater** ruins (not the same as the Roman Theater, it was built in second century CE for gladiator events, held only 6000, and only three of its original 10-12 rows of benches remain), **Byzantine Residential Quarter**, and **Crusader Fortress** are to be found about 270 meters south of the main site.

If you're hot and still have a little patience, there's a spot not too far away, nicer than the municipal pool, where you can swim and refresh your body surrounded by luxuriant greenery, rejuvenating your eyes and spirits, and that's **Gan HaShlosha**, *Tel. 06-658-6219*. Also known as **Sachne**, you can get there by bus 434, 961, 963, 964, 829 or 412, or any bus heading toward Tel Aviv—just ask the driver for Gan HaShlosha. The park is open Sunday-Friday 8am-5pm, Saturday 8am-6pm, and costs NIS 29 an adult, NIS 12 a child (discounted in winter and also for groups). And worth every shekel. Truly beautiful and peaceful, with luscious date palm and olive trees, flowers, waterfalls and deep green pools (28°C/82°F year round). It's a lovely place in which to rest, swim, picnic (there are BBQ grills) and revive yourself.

For children, in addition to the water, there's a playground with sandbox, swings, and a slide. Changing rooms with showers are available, and in summer there are lifeguards supervising the pools and waters slides. There's a kosher restaurant that's open in summer as well as some snack kiosks, and an **Archaeological Museum**, open all year Sunday-Thursday 8am-2pm, Saturday 10:30am-1pm, that showcases discoveries in the Beit She'an valley, ancient weaving techniques, Greek and Egyptian art, and Etruscan jewelry.

Continuing back in the direction of Tiberias (bus 961, 963, 964, 434) is the **Bet Alpha Synagogue**, *Heftzi Bah Kibbutz*, adjacent to Kibbutz Beit Alpha, foot of Mount Gilboa, *Tel. 06-653-204*, located one kilometer east of Gan HaShlosha and another one kilometer off from the highway. It is has been partially reconstructed by the National Parks Authority, is open Saturday-Thursday 8am-4pm, Friday 8am-3pm, and costs NIS 8 an adult, NIS 4 for youth.

The **mosaics** here, laid between 517-528 CE (as indicated by inscriptions in the floor that give credit to artists Marianus and his son Chanina in the reign of Emperor Justin) are magnificent and well worth the shlepp getting there. It's in great shape, with vibrant colors—one of the best in Israel.

The synagogue ruins were discovered in 1928 by kibbutz members and excavated the following year by E.L. Sukenik, with further digs exposing still more of the synagogue complex in 1962. The entire area of the synagogue was covered with elaborate mosaics, though the main decoration are in the nave. Jewish ritual objects are represented, such as a Holy Ark flanked by lions, birds and menorot surrounded by animals, fruit, and geometric designs. The central section of the mosaic depicts a zodiac with the sun god Helios in his horse-drawn chariot. Rather than indicating pagan worship, the zodiac was probably used for decorative purposes. In an agricultural society, the progression of months and seasons was noteworthy, further evidenced by the women in the four corners who symbolize the four seasons of the year.

Mount Gilboa Reserve, *Yezre'el Valley*, has hiking trails, and picnic sites. Buses 830 and 831 toward Afula go here, just ask the driver for Gilboa.

Shturman Institute and Mishkan La'omanut (Art Museum), *Kibbutz Ein Harod, Tel. 06-653-1605*, is open Sunday-Thursday 8am-3pm, Saturday 10am-2pm and shows regional studies. There's also a science museum plus contemporary Jewish art. Take bus 830, 831, 841 (to Afula) and ask the driver for Ein Harod.

Museum of Pioneer Agricultural Settlements, *Kibbutz Yifat*, is open Sunday-Thursday 8am-4pm, Friday 10am-3pm with hands-on children's activities. Take bus 830, 831, 840, 841 and ask for Yifat.

Ma'ayan Harod National Park, *Yizre'el Valley, Tel. 06-653-2211*, has natural springs, swimming, picnic areas, and summer camping at the foot of Mount Gilboa. It's very pretty, is open daily 8am-5:45pm, and costs NIS 21 for adults to get in, NIS 12 for children. Take bus 961, 963, 964, 434 toward Beit She'an.

Tabor

Farmer's Yard, **Kfar Tabor Museum**, **and Art Gallery**, *Kfar Tabor, Tel. 06-676-5844*, is open Sunday-Thursday 8am-4pm, Friday 8am-1pm, Saturday 9am-2pm and displays a typical turn-of-the-century farmyard, the history of Kfar Tabor, and an art gallery. Take bus 830 or 841.

Dvorat Hatavor Visitor Center, *Shadmot Devorah, Tel. 06-676-9598*, is open Saturday and holidays 10am-3pm and shows honey and silk production. Next to Kfar Tabor, take bus 830, 841.

Galilee Bedouin Heritage Center, *Kfar Shibli, Mount Tabor, Tel. 06-676-7875*, is open daily 9am-5pm. This museum displays Bedouin lifestyles and traditional hospitality. Take bus 830 or 841 to Kfar Shibli crossroads, then walk two and a half kilometers up Tabor.
Nightlife & Entertainment
There is sometimes something on at the **Roman Amphitheatre**, *Beit She'an, 06-658-7189*, otherwise head to the lake if you want nightlife or entertainment.

SPORTS & RECREATION
SPNI Field School, *Alon Tavor, Tel. 06-676-7798*, can advise about hiking, or go to **Ma'ayan Harod** or **Mount Gilboa Reserve**.
There are **Jeep Trips** at **Hey Ha'Jeep**, *Tel. 06-670-8117*, **Jimmy Jeep**, *Givat Yoav, Tel. 06-676-3406*, and **Yavne'el Jeep Trips**, *Tel. 06-670-8672*.
There's **camping**, *Ma'ayan Harod National Park, Tel. 06-653-2211*.
Refreshing **swimming** is yours at **Gan HaShlosha**, *Tel. 06-658-6219*.

PRACTICAL INFORMATION
• **English News**: **Israel Radio** (576 and 1458 KHz) at 7am, 1pm, 5pm, 8pm; **Voice of America** (1260, 15205, 15260, 9700 KHz) at 6am, 7am, 5pm, 5:30pm, 6pm; **BBC** (1323 KHz) at 2:15pm, 3pm, 6pm GMT; **Israel TV**, daily at 5:30pm.
• **Fire**: *Tel. 102* in an emergency, otherwise *Tel. 06-679-1222*.
• **Medical Aid**: **First Aid** (Magen David Adom), *corner of HaBanim and Hakishon, across the street from Jordan River Hotel, Tel. 101 in emergencies or Tel. 06-679-0111* for an ambulance; it's open 24 hours. **The Poriya Hospital**, *southwestern side of the Sea of Galilee, Tel. 06-673-8211*. **Tiberias Medical Center**, *Lev HaGalil Center, 2nd floor, Tel. 06-672-3077*.
• **Police**: *Tel. 100* in emergencies or *Tel. 06-679-2444* otherwise.
• **Golan and Galilee Touring Information**: *Mahanayim Junction Information Station, Paz Gaz Station, Route 90 north of Rosh Pina, Tel. 06-693-5016*, is open Sunday-Thursday 9am-3pm, Friday 9am-2:30pm, Saturday 8:30am-2:30pm. There's also a **Touring Office**, *Rosh Pina, Tel. 06-693-6751*.

UPPER GALILEE & GOLAN HEIGHTS
The **Upper Galilee** is way in the north of Israel, bordered by the Golan, the Sea of Galilee, and Jordan on the east and the plains of Acre on the west, while the Golan Heights run from the spurs of Mount Hermon in the north to the Yarmuk River in the south. It's a vast and hilly

region with just a few major highways cutting swaths of transportation and sight-seeing routes between the slopes, roughly 60 kilometers from sea to northern border.

From the north of the Sea of Galilee, Route 87 heads northeast up to Katzrin, while Route 90 goes straight up north to Rosh Pina, Tel Hazor, and the beautiful Hula Valley, all the way up past Kiryat Shemona to Metulla on the Lebanese border. From Route 90 at the Mahanayim Junction (where there's a tourist information center), Route 91 veers off northeast past the Gilbon Reserve to the disengagement zone before Syria, at which juncture (Zivan Junction) Route 98 heads up north along the eastern border of Golan, all the way up to the ski lodge at Mount Hermon.

Connecting Routes 98 and 90 near the top is Route 99, going from Birkat Ram in the east past Nimrod's Castle, Banyas, and Tel Dan to Kiryat Shemona in the west. Closer to the Sea of Galilee, Route 89 winds through the hills to Tsfat, and further south still, Route 85 leads you from Vered Hagalil to Ein Kamonim restaurant and on west towards Akko.

ARRIVALS & DEPARTURES

By Car
Have a good map (Vered Hagalil sells a spectacular one for this region), keep your lights on during the winter even in daylight, and don't forget to petrol up when you pass a station.

By Bus
From Tiberias to Kiryat Shemona ride the 541, 841, or 963; and from Haifa to Rosh Pina take bus 500 or 501. Look at the specific sites for the best bus instructions.

By Air
There is an airport for domestic flights (from Tel Aviv and Jerusalem) in Mahanayim, off Route 90, not far from Rosh Pina.

GETTING AROUND

By Car
Given the distances involved and the infrequent public transportation, a rental car is really the way to go, though there are other options.

By Bus
If you go by bus, plan your routes and stop-overs so you don't get stuck desperately hitching in the dark.

By Bus Tour
Another option is to go on an organized tour. These cost money, of course, and limit privacy and autonomy, but they do get you around to a lot of different sites without your having to hassle with the big map blowing in the wind and the twisty hilly roads.

By Adventure Tour
And then there are the organized out-door adventures, like bicycling or hiking with SPNI or horseback riding with Vered Hagalil, letting you experience the region up-close and rugged in an organized sort of way. See *Sports and Recreation* for all the options.

WHERE TO STAY

VERED HAGALIL GUEST FARM, *off Route 90, just before the intersection with Route 85, Tel. 06-693-5785, Fax 06-693-4964, it's about four miles north of the lake. Prices vary by type of accommodation (bunkhouse, cabin, studio, or cottage, in ascending luxury) and day of week. Singles are $66-$89 and double are $89-$105, plus $28 for each additional person, breakfast included.*

Vered HaGalil is listed in the *Sea of Galilee* section above, but it merits a mention for the Upper Galilee as well. A real gem, Vered Hagalil has beautiful stone and wood cabins and cottages, a rustic restaurant with gourmet cooking, a stable full of healthy, well-attended horses for trail-riding, a pool, and magnificent views of the lake and the hills of the Golan. Peaceful and romantic, it's also a great choice for a family, as each cabin, sleeps four, and there are lots of activities. In addition to the horseback riding (one hour $20, half day $55, and full day with lunch $95), they also arrange jeep trips, water and snow skiing, biking, rafting, and tubing on the Jordan River (NIS 680 for a half day's jeep tour, NIS 60 for a day of kayaking). The cottages, studios, and cabins are especially lovely with the wood and stone construction and stupendous views.

They sell a Galilee touring map, their own creation, that is better than any you'll find elsewhere. If you want to visit in July-August or Passover you'll need to reserve months in advance. It's easiest to get here by car, but if traveling by bus, get off at Korazim Junction.

Rosh Pina
MIZPE HAYAMIM, *Route 89 between Tsfat and Rosh Pina, Tel. 06-699-9666, Fax 06-699-9555, has 100 rooms with TV, phones, air conditioning and heat. Rooms cost from $122-$134 a single and $135-$148 a double (depending on weekday or weekend stay), including breakfast and all the special tea and coffee you can drink.*

Mizpe Hayamim, Hebrew for Sea View, is a beautiful and comfortable place, renovated in a rustic European style with lots of flowers, plus amazing views of the sea and the hills, and the focus is on rest and pampering yourself. High in the hills above Rosh Pina on 30 wooded acres, couples and families come to this vegetarian hotel for the health and beauty spa programs, the jacuzzi, and the saunas, wet and dry. A lot of care is given to the vegetarian cuisine, most of the food is grown, baked, or prepared on the premise, and there's a professional staff busy bustling about cleaning and fluffing and plumping pillows. There are nature trails, and guided jeep tours are available as well. More standard Mizpe Hayamim activities include aerobic and yoga classes, massage, reflexology, and Shiatsu treatments. There are warm and cold water pools, herbal mineral baths, a gym, and beauty treatments. Homeopathic medicine and diet plans are available as well.

NATURE FRIENDS YOUTH HOSTEL, *Rehov Ha'Halutzim, Tel. 06-693-7086, has dorm beds for NIS 55 and doubles for NIS 195, breakfast included.*

The hostel is in a beautiful stone building, and the rooms have fridge and fan, and heating in winter. You can take bus 500, 501 from Haifa.

There are also a number of private B&Bs around Rosh Pina, with signs in people's windows.

Hatzor

AYELET HASHAHAR, *near Tel Hatzor, Tel. 06-693-2611, Fax 06-693-4777, charges $72 a single and $88 a double (breakfast included), subject to 15% service charge and high season supplements. You can also make reservations through Alexander Associates in Brooklyn, NY, Tel. 718-253-9400, Fax 718-258-5623.*

This pleasant guest house has 144 rooms with air conditioning and heat, phone and TV, and facilities for handicapped, There's a swimming pool, children's playground, and synagogue. Jeep rides and horseback riding are available as well.

Katzrin

GOLAN FIELD SCHOOL, *Daliyat Street, Tel. 06-696-1234*, is a great source of information and assistance, and also runs the only accommodations in town.

CHENION HA-GOLAN, *Tel. 06-696-1657*, is the Golan Field School Campground, with tent sites for NIS 18 per person, is one option, but they also have bungalows (for up to six people) that cost NIS 180 for two.

Hula Valley

KIBBUTZ HAGOSHERIM, *right off Route 99, Tel. 06-695 6231, Fax 06-695-6234, is about five kilometers east of Kiryat Shemona. They have 120* *guest rooms with singles for $75-$95, and doubles from $96-$136, depending on the season, breakfast included.*

The rooms have TVs and video programs, there is a swimming pool (seasonal), and health club (which is extra). They have tennis courts, kayaking and rafting, and a kosher kitchen. Established in 1948 by Turkish Jews, they've excavated tombs from the mid Bronze Age, Hellenistic pottery, and a fine Byzantine plough.

KFAR BLUM GUEST HOUSE, *Hula Valley, Tel. 06-694-3366, Fax 06-694-8555, is a kibbutz about 12 kilometers southeast of Kiryat Shemona, with 89 air conditioned rooms with TV, radio, phone and bathroom which cost $75-$95 a single, and $96-$136 a double, breakfast included.*

Take Route 90 to Hagome Junction, turn east on small Route 977, and Kfar Blum is north a couple kilometers on a small side road. There is also a swimming pool and sauna, tennis courts, kayaking, a synagogue and kosher kitchen. Set amidst beautiful greenery on the Jordan River, they also host a week-long chamber music festival each summer in July. Tickets (NIS 25 per concert) sell out quickly. Bus 29 from Kiryat Shemona comes here.

KFAR GIL'ADI, *Route 90, Tel. 06-690-0000, Fax 06-690-0069, is just a few kilometers north of Kiryat Shemona. Their guest house has 150 air conditioned rooms with TV, phone, and bathroom, costing $75-$95 a single and $96-$136 a double, breakfast included, no check-out on Saturdays.*

They've a swimming pool (open May-October), dry sauna, tennis courts, basketball courts, and fitness room, as well as the Hashomer Museum, a synagogue, and kosher kitchen. It was settled in 1918 and named after Israel Giladi, one of the HaShomer founders. The stone statue of a roaring lion, made in 1926 by Aharon Melnikov, stands to the south of the kibbutz where Trumpeldor and the other seven died in 1920 defending Tel Hai.

HURSHAT TAL CAMPING GROUND, *Route 99, Tel. 06-694-2360, is about five kilometers east of Kiryat Shimona. There are tent spaces for NIS 36 and bungalows for $45 (three-bed), $58 (four-bed), and $63 (five-bed).*

It's situated right on the banks of the Dan River.

TEL HAI, *off Route 90, Upper Galilee, Tel. 06-694-0043, Fax 06-694-1743, is three kilometers north of Kiryat Shimona. Dorm beds (six per room, some air conditioned) are NIS 59, breakfast included. Accessible by buses 20 and 23 from Kiryat Shimona. Reservations needed in summer.*

The facility overlooks the Galilean Hills, the Golan Heights, and Mount Herman.

Metulla

ARAZIM, *end of Ha-Rishonim, Tel. 06-699-7143, Fax 06-699-7666, has 34 rooms with air conditioning, heat, TV and phone, priced $66-$82 a single and $90-$104 a double, breakfast included.*

They give discounts to the Canada Center, though Arazim has their own outdoor swimming pool and tennis courts.

DAYS INN SHELEG HALEVANON, *Communication Center for Journalists, Tel. 06-699-7111, Fax 06-699-7118, has 49 rooms with air conditioning, heat, TV, and phone. Singles are $78 and doubles $100, breakfast included.*

They, too, offer reduced rate tickets to Canada Center, but have their own health club, outdoor swimming pool, disco, and playground for children. They also feature facilities for disabled.

YAFA PENSION, *Ha-Rishonim, second bus stop, Tel. 06-694-0617, offers doubles for NIS 230-250, breakfast included.*

HAMAVRI, *Ha-Rishonim, Tel. 06-694-0150, has 24 rooms, with singles for $40-$65 and doubles for $45-$75, depending on the season.*

Breakfast is included, and discounts are available to Canada Center.

Mount Hermon

GOLSHEI HAHERMAN, *Sigron Family, Tel. 06-698-1531, offers rooms costing NIS 200-400 a double, NIS 150 a single, continental breakfast included.*

They've two kinds of rooms—those with refrigerators and those without., and rates are highest during winter. They also offer the option of a full Israeli breakfast for NIS 20 extra per person.

GANEI DAFNA, *Kibbutz Dafna, off Route 99, Tel. 06-694-5011, Fax 06-694-5794, near Hurshat Tal, has 22 holiday apartments for up to four people, with rates running from $70 an apartment in low season to $110 in high season, breakfast included.*

WHERE TO EAT

Most guest houses and lodges offer meals, and restaurants unconnected to lodgings are scarce. The following are especially worthy of your time and money, otherwise you can feed yourself wherever you're staying.

VERED HAGALIL RESTAURANT, *Route 90, Tel. 06-693-5785, Fax 06-693-4964*, is about four miles north of the Kinneret, and just before the intersection with Route 85. It's open 8am-11pm daily. Rustic and pleasant, with wood tables, view of the horses, and great food, there are fresh flowers on every table, and friendly dogs wandering about. Cold summer soups (gazpacho, yogurt, borsht) are NIS 16, desserts NIS 11-16, main courses NIS 30-62, and there's fresh juices to wash it all down. There's good onion soup, excellent fresh bread and garlic butter, great pies, and everything is homemade. It's worth the detour for the genuine warmth and fresh food, and unpretentious people.

EIN CAMONIM (Goat Cheese Restaurant), *Route 85, about two miles east of the Hananya (Route 89) Junction, Tel. 06-698-9894*, is open from 11am-8pm in winter, till 9pm in summer, and sometimes till 10 on Fridays. On the north side of the road is a blue and white flag, a blue and white Hebrew sign, and a dirt drive (bear left at the fork) heading up to one of the best restaurants in Israel, if not the world. An extension of their goat farm, this restaurant makes a feast of traditional ingredients of goat cheese, olive oil, vegetables, wine, and amazing bread. All made on their own farm (except the red wine, which comes from a neighboring vineyard), a meal consists of an incredible spread of ten types of goat cheese, homemade bread, garlic butter, olives and salads, coffee/tea, and dessert. It costs NIS 74 per person (NIS 37 for kids) for all you can eat, and you'll want to eat a lot. Not a fast food sort of place, the warm, relaxed atmosphere encourages a leisurely meal. There are long wood tables draped with cheerful table clothes, a wood burning stove in the center to take the chill out of winter evenings, and the couple who own the place serving cheeses and making sure everyone is happy.

MOSHAV AMIRIM, *off Route 866, Tel. 06-698-9788*, up in the hills, is an all-vegetarian community. Many families provide guest house and dining facilities, and you need to call ahead to arrange for a stay or a meal. The Shulabrand House is one of the families in Amirim, and they offer a full dinner of soup, salads, bread, hot main course and dessert for around NIS 70 (wines available as well). There's a lovely patio outside, a fire inside, a view of the lake, and you should plan on two hours for eating. Across the street from Amirim is **Moshav Shefer**. Issak Tavior, a classical pianist, lives here and gives regular Saturday 11am performances for $10, refreshments included. It's a lovely site in which to hear beautiful music. Call first, *Tel. 06-698-9085*, to check and to see about other performance dates.

MIZPE HAYAMIM, *the hills above Rosh Pina, Tel. 06-699-9666, Fax 06-699-9555*, Sea View in Hebrew, is a vegetarian health resort. A lot of care is given to the vegetarian cuisine, and most of the food is grown, baked, or prepared on the premise, they've a bountiful selection of curative teas as well.

SEEING THE SIGHTS

Khorazim National Park, *near Kibbutz Almagor, Tel. 06-693-4982*, is a few miles northeast of Tabgha. Go up Route 90 and turn left (east) at Vered Hagalil—Khorazim is another mile or so on. Jesus cursed this Galilean Jewish town, saying "Woe unto thee, Khorazim," for their failure to follow his teachings (Saint Matthew 11:21).

Built shortly after the Bar-Kochba rebellion on the ruins of an earlier settlement, the town grew in the second century CE. There are no traces of settlements from 700 CE to 1200 CE; the Arab village of Kharazeh (now abandoned) was built in the 1800s CE. Now a national park, there are black basalt ruins of a large synagogue (built in the second/third centuries CE and destroyed in the late fourth century CE) in which was found the carved "Moses' Seat" on which Pharisees and scribes used to sit. The stone seat (now in the Israel Museum in Jerusalem) bears the inscription "In good memory of Judan ben Ishmael who built this stoa and this staircase. May he take his place among the righteous." Near the synagogue is a mikva (ritual bath), a small storeroom, and an oil press. Take bus 459, 541, 841, 963 to crossroads and walk three kilometers to the site.

North of Khorazim about eight kilometers off Route 90 is **Rosh Pina**, the first moshav to be established in the Galilee in 1882. It's a quiet town with some restored cobblestone streets. It's become a center for artists, and is a major crossroads and hub for local bus transportation. Given all that, there's not a whole lot to actually do here. You can visit the local artists and see their stuff, there's a nice garden in The Baron's Park, there's a pleasant local pub for a meal or drink, or you can do the two-hour hike up the steep and winding mountain road to Tsfat.

From Route 90 (the road that heads north to Metulla), head north a few kilometers and you'll hit Machanayim Junction, with its **Machanayim Information Center** that's open all year. Just near the junction is **Hatzor Hagelit** (not to be confused with Tel Hazor), a development town with a dedication site to Honi Hama'agel, the saintly rainmaker. There are picnic sites here, as well as services such as a First Aid station.

A few kilometers north of this is **Tel Hatzor**, one of the largest archaeological sites in Israel, with an Hyksos fortress, Canaanite and Israelite altars, and statues. This 188 acre excavation hill has 21 layers of human settlements, from the Hellenistic period circa 200 BCE to the early Bronze Age circa 2600 BCE, and is cited a number of times in ancient texts. The first mention is in Egyptian execration texts circa 1800 BCE, and The Old Testament refers to Hazor in connection with Joshua's conquests (Joshua 11:10). There was a Canaanite town on this site in the 1600-1700s BCE, and an Israelite settlement, built here around 1000 BCE, was enlarged by King Solomon with gates and walls circa 900 BCE (1 Kings 9:15). King Ahab, who ruled what was then Samaria disastrously with his Queen Jezebel around 860 BCE, built the citadel and large storehouse. Hatzor was destroyed in 732 BCE by the Assyrians (II Kings 15:29). You can wander around the ruins of King Ahab's palace, see Solomon's wide walls and the staircase to underground sources of water, but some of the finer finds now reside at the Israel Museum in Jerusalem.

Across from the excavation site is the **Hatzor Museum**, *Tel. 06-693-4855*, open Sunday-Thursday 8am-5pm and Friday 8am-4pm, NIS 12 for adults, NIS 9 for students. The museum exhibits two pre-Israelite temples and a scale model of ancient Hatzor, as well as some excavation finds. Across from the museum is **Kibbutz Ayelet HaShahar**, *Tel. 06-693-2611, Fax 06-693-4777*, with a swimming pool, art gallery, good restaurant, and accommodations. Another excavation a few kilometers west of the kibbutz is **Meroth**, a recently excavated Jewish town from the 12th century CE with a big synagogue and treasures buried underneath. Bus 541, 841, 963 will take you to Ayelet HaShahar, with just a short walk to the site.

A little north of Tel Hatzor is the **Hula Nature Reserve**, *Tel. 06-694-7069*, open Saturday-Thursday 8am-5pm, Friday 8am-4pm, NIS 15. It's the last remnant of the great swamp which covered an enormous area until it was partly drained to create fertile farm land in the 1950s. Part of the original Hula lake still remains and serves as a sanctuary for the waterfowl who stop off during migrations from as far away as Russia and India, and are especially abundant in winter. In addition to the waterfowl, the reserve was founded to protect the native papyrus reed, white and yellow water lilies, pelican, otters, jungle cats, and more. There's a Visitors' Center with a small flora and fauna museum (open 8am-4pm in summer 8am-3pm in winter, closing an hour earlier on Fridays and holidays) and a bird watching center as well as a picnic area. There are free guided tours Saturday, Sunday, Tuesday, and Thursday 9:30am and 1:30pm. Take bus 541, 840, 841, 963 to the crossroads, then walk three kilometers to the site.

Also north of Tel Hatzor is the **Dubrovin Farm**, *Tel. 06-693-7371*, open Sunday-Thursday 9am-5pm, closing one hour later in summer and one earlier Friday and holidays, admission NIS 6.5 . This is a reconstructed farm demonstrating Jewish settlement life at the turn of the century. There are audiovisual presentations, a restaurant, pottery workshop, and evening entertainment in the summer. It's not convenient by bus, as the nearest stop off the Rosh Pina/Qiryat Shemona bus is four kilometers from the farm. The farm is near the settlement of **Yesod Hama'ala**. The village was originally founded in 1884, and is surrounded by lovely orchards. The street of the founders has been declared a national site for preservation, and at its eastern end are the ruins of a synagogue from 300-500 CE. Take bus 963 or 841 to crossroads.

Kiryat Shemona & Environs

The transportation and administration hub of the Upper Galilee is **Kiryat Shemona** (or Kiryat Shmona), at the junction where north-south Route 90 meets east-west Route 99. The name means "Town of Eight" in memory of Yosef Trumpeldor and the seven others killed in 1920 at Tel Hai. The town was established in 1949 on the ruins of the Arab town Al Khalsa, itself destroyed by the Israelis in 1948. Its political sensitivity hasn't died down that much over the years, thanks to its strategic location near the Lebanon border. Qiryat Shemona was the target of terrorist attacks in the 1970s and retributive attacks after Israel invaded Lebanon in 1982.

If you're traveling by car, there's not much call to visit; the main distinguishing site is the children's playground made of three brightly painted old army tanks. They do have the **Kiryat Shemona Museum**, *Tel. 06-694-0135*, is located in a former mosque on 16 Jordan Street. The museum presents the history of the city, as well as archaeological finds and photos from nearby excavations. If you're getting around by bus, however, Tel Hai Boulevard and its **central bus station** is, *Tel. 06-694-0740*, is the place to be; it's the departure point for Tel Aviv, Tiberias, Tsfat, or anywhere else in the region.

If you get hungry waiting for your bus, **Nargila**, part of the Yemenite food chain, does a good job. There are also falafel and shwarma stands on Tel Hai near Tchernihovsky, and a **Co-op Tzafon** supermarket and **Ha-Mashbir** department store in the shopping center just south of the bus station. And if you're there on Thursday, there's a **street market** (*shuk*) Thursday morning on Tel Hai, north of the bus station. The **post office**, south of the bus station, has international telephones and a poste restante section. Bank Hapoalim is also nearby. The nearest and best accommodations are the hostels in nearby **Tel Hai** or **Rosh Pina**.

Tel Hai Courtyard Museum, *Tel. 06-695-1333, Fax 06-695-1331*, is open Sunday-Thursday 8am-4pm, Friday 8am-1pm, Saturday 10am-5pm, admission NIS 11. The **Sculpture Garden**, *Tel. 06-695-0769*, is open daily 8am-4pm, and the **Museum of Photography**, *Tel. 06-695-0769*, is open Sunday-Thursday 8am-4pm, Saturday 10am-5pm, admission NIS 12 for adults, 8 for students). They're a few kilometers north of Kiryat Shemona off Route 90. **Tel Hai** (Hill of Life), established in 1917 by Yosef Trumpeldor as a shepherds' camp, was one of the first areas to be settled by the Shomer (Watchman) organizations which protected nearby settlements, and the first to be attacked. In 1920, eight settlers were killed defending Tel Hai. Trumpeldor was one of those who died, and his reported last words were "It is good to die for our country."

The museum, in the reconstructed watchtower and stockade, houses a display of agricultural equipment used by Zionist settlers, and there's an audio-visual show in English, shown on request. Outside is a monument to Trumpeldor and the seven others who died. Trumpeldor is a national hero, and his death is seen as symbolic of the best aspects of Zionism. The 11th of Adar is Tel Hai Day, and young Israelis annually visit the graves here to honor those who died. The Sculpture Garden exhibits Israeli works and has films on sculpting. Take bus 541, 841, 963 to Kiryat Shemona and transfer to bus 20 (toward Metulla).

Nearby **Hunin**, 1,650 feet above the Tel Hai valley, are the scant ruins of the **Crusader Chastel Neuf** (Castrum Novum). Built in 1105-1107 on Phoenician walls, it stood on the site of the Biblical Janoah (2 Kings 15;29). It has the usual checkered past: destroyed by Saladin, rebuilt by Onfroi in 1178, possessed by Baldwin IV in 1180, and by Joscelin de Courtenay in 1186. Hunin was one of the last Galilean castles to remain in Crusader hands. Al-Adil, Saladin's brother, took it in 1187. In 1266 the Mamluks took possession and built a small mosque, but an earthquake in 1837 destroyed a lot. Most of what remains are Mamluk additions.

Further north a few kilometers is Kfar Giladi (see *Where to Stay* for more details) is **Beit Hashomer**, *Tel. 06-694-1565*, open Sunday-Thursday 8am-noon and 2pm-4pm, Friday-Saturday 8:30am-noon. It's a museum that focuses on the Hashomer movement during WWI days, with displays of weapons from that time.

Not far from Metulla is the beautiful **Nachal Ayun nature reserve**, *north along Route 90, Tel. 06-695-1519*, and **HaTanur** (the Oven) **falls**. Open Saturday-Thursday 8am-5pm, Friday 8am-4pm, admission is NIS 8.5 in winter, and free in summer when the river is dry. The waterfalls, especially magnificent in winter, are dry in summer. There's also a picnic area, and lovely hiking trails. Migrating birds visit in the winter, followed by a blast of wildflowers in the spring. Bus 20 goes there from Kiryat Shemona.

Just north of the nature reserve is **Metulla**, Israel's northernmost town, and the second oldest in Galilee—a small town on the Lebanese border. Metulla was established in 1986 with a grant from the Rothschild family. The name means "overlooking" in Arabic, and is still apt, considering its position by the fortifications of the Lebanon border. It's not surprising, then, that despite the cool mountain air, attractive stone buildings and relaxed resort pace, the main draw here is **The Good Fence** (Ha-Gader Ga-Tova), the medical clinic whose open policy contrasts with the barbed-wire mentality of the border. The clinic has been a source of medical supplies, aid, and good will for residents of Southern Lebanon since the official opening in 1976, though the passage between the Israel-Lebanon border has been open for medical aid since 1971.

Today, Lebanese Christians and Druze are allowed to pass for free medical services, visits to relatives, and work, and the cross-border activities have expanded to include commercial and agricultural trade as well. From the observation point you can see, on a hill far to the northwest (left), the Crusader fortress of Beaufort which was used by the PLO to shell Israel in the days before the peace accords; you can also see Maronite Christian villages. Metulla boasts one of the best sports facilities in Israel, the **Canada Centre**, *Tel. 06-695-0370*. Bus 20 to Metulla leaves eight times daily from Kiryat Shemona.

Southeast of Metulla and is **Kibbutz Ma'ayan Baruch**, *a few kilometers north of Route 99, Tel. 06-695-4611*. They have their own museum, **The Hula Valley Museum of Prehistory**, *Tel. 06-695-4628*, and **Amnon**, *Tel. 06-695-4796*, cost NIS 10 admission and must be called to arrange in advance. Their exhibits include flints from the Neolithic and Copper ages, clay vessels from the early Bronze Age, plus Roman lamps, glasses, stone mills and oil presses.

A few kilometers east of Ma'ayan Baruch is **Hurshat Tal**, *off Route 99, Tel. 06-694-2360*, a national park with ancient oak trees, grassy meadows, and cold swimming pools diverted from the nearby Dan River. There are even waterfalls, water slides, and fishing ponds. The oak trees, some thought to be 2000 years old, are legendary in Muslim belief. According to the story, Mohammed's messengers were camping here once, just out in the open. Overnight, however, the camel hitching posts they'd pounded into the ground turned into a beautiful oak forest providing shade and shelter. The trees are still lovely, and make a great setting for the (sometimes crowded) picnic facilities. There are also full camping facilities (see *Where To Stay* for camping details). Take buses 25, 26, and 36 from Kiryat Shemona.

About five kilometers west of Banyas, **Tel Dan** and the **Dan Reserve**, *off Route 99, Tel. 06-695-1579*, is open 8am-5pm daily in summer, 8am-4pm in winter, closed one hour earlier on Friday, and admission is NIS 15 for adults, NIS 8 for children. This region was settled by the tribe of Dan in the 1200s BCE. After migrating north from the lands Joshua first gave them near Jaffa (problems with the Philistines forced them out), they destroyed the town of Laish (also known as Leshem in Joshua 19:47), then rebuilt it and named it Dan (Judges 18: 27). Dan was known as the northern parameter of the kingdom, and the expression "from Dan to Beersheba" was a standard Hebrew Testament reference to the north-south spread of the region (Judges 20:1, I Samuel 3:20, II Samuel 3:10). After King Solomon's death around 922 BCE, his kingdom was divided into the two states of Judah and Israel. Jeroboam ruled the northern kingdom of Israel and set up two golden calves in the sanctuaries of Dan and Beth-el. The Assyrian invasion of 732 BCE put an end to this settlement.

The hill of Tel Dan ("Tell el-Qadi" or Hill of the Judge in Arabic) rises above the ancient settlement, and excavation began in 1965. Discoveries so far include middle Bronze Age masonry and remains of the 10th century BCE Gate of Jeroboam. The excavations are situated in the small but lovely nature reserve. In one visit you get cold springs, lush forest, history, and ruins. By bus, go from Kiryat Shemona to Kibbutz Dan, then go up the main road on foot, turn left at the Dan Reserve sign and carry on an additional three kilometers.

While near **Kibbutz Dan**, you can visit their **Beit Ussishkin Natural History Museum**, *Tel. 06-694-1704*, for more information on regional history, geology, flora, and fauna. They also have a birdwatching center. Open Sunday-Thursday 8am-4pm, Friday 8:30am-3:30pm, Saturday 9:30am-4:30pm, admission is NIS 11 per adult, NIS 9.5 per student. Take Bus 541, 840, 841, 963 toward Kiryat Shemona, and ask the driver for Kibbutz Dan.

The Hermon River Reserve (Banyas), *off Route 99, Tel. 06-690-2577*, way in the north and near Kibbutz Snir, costs NIS 15 for adults, NIS 8 for children and offers a little of everything. For one thing, it's a beautiful place. The Hermon River is one of the sources of the Jordan River, and it provides fresh water springs and clear, natural pools galore, as well as a grotto above the source that was a Greek shrine dedicated to Pan, god of springs, and the country's only water-driven mill still in use. There is also **Banyas Waterfall**, one of the largest in the region, and one of the most popular tourist destinations. Open Saturday-Thursday 8am-4pm, Friday 8am-3pm, this area is also full of history.

On the ancient trade route from Acre to Damascus, Banyas may be the site of the Biblical Baal-god (Joshua 13,5). Antiochus the Great fought many battles here, Herod built a temple in honor of Augustus, and Augustus' son Phillipus built the capital of his tetrarchy here, calling it Caesarea Philippi. Jesus and his disciples visited here, according to the New Testament Saint Matthew 16,13. Agrippa II destroyed and then rebuilt the place, renaming it Caesarea-Neronias after the Emperor Nero, but after Agrippa's death, the region was taken over by Syria. In 200 CE Caesarea-Neronias was included in Syrophoenicia, in the 4th century it was a bishop's seat, and during the Crusades it was fought over by Christians and Arabs, eventually going to al-Mu'azzam in the 1200s. Jews lived in the town in the Middle Ages and they called it Dan.

Two kilometers northeast is **Nimrod's Castle** (also known as Subeibe and Qal'at Nimrud). Originally founded by the Arabs, the castle belonged to the Franks from 1129-64 when Saladin conquered it. Qul'at Subeibe, as it was known, was razed during the fifth Crusade (1217-21) but was rebuilt in the 13th century and the Mamluks used it as a prison. Inside is a large vaulted cistern with an Arabic inscription from 1239/40, and there are fine views of the Hula valley.

Mount Hermon, *Tel. 06-698-1337*, is open all year. In the winter there's skiing (beginner to expert, but most slopes require some experience) with ski lifts and rental equipment. The season usually goes from December to April, and the skiing isn't bad. It tends to get jammed on the weekends, so come mid-week if you can, or come early if you plan to rent equipment. In the summer the top of the mount, the highest point in

Israel at 2,244 (some say 2,766) meters, affords a great view and impressive birdwatching.

Near Mount Hermon are the two Druze villages, **Majdal Shams** and **Mas'ada**. These villages have been political hot spots ever since Israel took the Golan Heights in 1967. These Druze live on the Israeli side of the border, but their hearts and political sympathies lie with Syria, and they have made their sentiments known in many protests and violent demonstrations (quelled by Israeli forces) over the years. If you visit you will find very traditional, agricultural villagers dressed in traditional swathes of material and pursuing their livelihoods. They aren't very focused on tourism, but it's always possible to meet people and have a different kind of interaction than you would with ski instructors on Mount Hermon.

Majdal Shams (*Tower of the Sun* in Arabic) lies on Route 98, just about two kilometers below the ski lifts. This farming community of around 8000 is the largest town in Golan, and the residents feel strong connections to their Syrian kin just across the border.

THE DRUZE

*The **Druze**, monotheists with a difference, are an offshoot of the Ismailis, and the religion began in the reign of Fatimid caliph al-Hakim (996-1021). In 1017 there was a public proclamation to the effect that Hakim was the final manifestation of God, and this remains the central and distinguishing tenet of their belief. Their name comes from al-Darazi, al-Hakim's first missionary. The sect was founded in Egypt, but they fled to Palestine to avoid persecution. The Druze, all 400,000-500,000 of them, live mostly in Syria or Lebanon, but some communities still exist in Israel and Jordan.*

Their faith centers on the belief in Hakim as the ultimate maqam (location or incarnation) of God. They further believe in the five cosmic emanations: Universal Intelligence, Universal Soul, the Word, the Right Wing, and the Left Wing, as embodied by their five highest ranking disciples. Their community is divided into the uqqual, those initiated into the teachings of the hima, the religious doctrine, and the juhhal, the vast majority who aren't familiar with the religious tenets. They follow seven basic duties, among which truthfulness and mutual support figure strongly. They allow no conversion or intermarriage, and the community is of great importance.

Mas'ada is five kilometers south on bucolic Route 98, just near the intersection with Route 99 that heads west to Kiryat Shemona. Mas'ada is best known for its lake, **Birket Ram**. Some claim it's a crater lake, but the water actually comes from the underground water table. Whatever the origin of the water, you can paddleboat (NIS 12 per hour) or sailboard it (NIS 19 per half hour), or merely gaze down from the popular **Birket Ram Restaurant**.

Heading south from Mas'ada is kibbutz **Merom Golan**, the first kibbutz to be settled in the Golan after the Six-Day War. West of Merom Golan along Route 959, for the geologists out there, are basalt boulders that show a reversed magnetic field. Further south is the observation point on Mount Avital, from which you can see **Quneitra**, once the capital of Syrian Golan and just 30 kilometers northeast of Damascus. Quneitra was captured by the Israelis, returned to the Syrians under the cease-fire agreement, and is now a buffer zone ghost town.

Modern **Katzrin** (*forts* in Hebrew), near the ancient synagogue, was planned as a regional center for the Golan settlements and is a good hub from which to explore the area. Katzrin's on a side road off Route 91, a few kilometers from Nashut Junction. The **Golan Archaeological Museum**, *Daliyat Street, Tel. 06-696-1350*, and **Golan Winery Visitors Center**, *Daliyat Street, Tel. 06-696-1350*, open Sunday-Thursday 8am-6pm, Friday 8am-3pm, and Saturday 10am-4pm (the Winery is closed Saturday), is right in town. It costs NIS 13 (NIS 7.5 for students), and the ticket also includes admission to Ancient Katzrin Park. The Archaeological Museum is small but interesting. They have local finds from the Golan such as Hebrew inscriptions from ancient synagogues, thousands of coins, a film on the Great Rebellion and martyrdom of Gamla, plus a sound and light show.

Ancient Katzrin (or **Qasrin**) **Park** is just outside the city, features a reconstructed synagogue and village from Talmudic times (third-fourth century CE), including a house set up and furnished in that Talmudic period way. Daliyat is the main street, and on it you will find the **Golan Field School**, *Tel. 06-696-1234*, which has lots of information on the area, as well as the only place to stay.

Next to the Archaeological Museum is a **public pool**, *other end of Daliyat, Tel. 06-696-1655*, that's open daily 8am-6pm and costs NIS 15. There is also a **supermarket** and a couple of **restaurants**. You can get there by bus 55 from Kiryat Shemona (infrequent) or 15, 16, and 19 from Tiberias.

A few kilometers north the road ends on Route 91. Head west eight kilometers and you'll hit **B'not Ya'akov Bridge**, where legend has it that Jacob's daughters predicted the sale of brother Joseph into Egyptian slavery. Go east one kilometer in the direction of Quneitra and you'll come to the turn off to the **Gilbon Nature Reserve**, with its Dvorah waterfalls and hiking trails. Also in the reserve area is **Dabbura**, an

abandoned Arab village in which a few isolated remains of more synagogues still stand.

Two kilometers south of Katzrin is the beautiful **Ya'ar Yehudiyya Nature Reserve**. This stunning reserve stretches all the way down to the Sea of Galilee, and has some of the best hiking in this lush green area as well as some interesting geologic sites. There are trails along the Zavitan River that take you to waterfalls and to Brekhat HaMeshushim, the Hexagon Pond. Here the river forms a basin framed by perfectly formed five and six sided basalt columns, three to five meters high. The rock formations came from rapidly cooling molten rock some three million years ago and are remarkable; they take a good four to five hours to hike.

Gamla, *off Route 808, Tel. 06-696-3721*, 10 kilometers southeast of Katzrin , admission NIS 13, is believed to be the site where the Zealots were besieged by the Romans in 67 CE. The Zealots were a group of Jews in first century CE who combined zealous adherence to Jewish laws with a fierce opposition to Roman rule. Their rebellion led to the destruction of the Temple in 70 CE, and they are even better known for their martyrdom atop Masada in 73 CE. Josephus Flavius, first century histo-rian, records how, during the Great Rebellion of 67, some 9,000 Zealots set up in the religious town of Gamla and were surrounded by the Romans.

They successfully repulsed a first attack, but eventually couldn't hold out against the Roman Legions, and hurled themselves off a cliff, choosing death rather than capture. Though many knew of this ancient town of Gamla, archaeologists didn't identify it until the Golan Heights passed into Israeli hands after the Six-Day War.

This is the spot Shmaryahu Gutman, armed with Flavius' *The Jewish War* descriptions, claims to be ancient Gamla (named after the shape of the escarpment, Gamla means camel in Aramaic), though some historians dispute it. The ruined city contains the remains of an old castle, and nearby to the northeast are **Gamla Falls**, site of a 51 meter waterfall and home of a large vulture colony.

There are a few other interesting sites in the vicinity. A couple kilometers southeast of Gamla is **Gilgal Refa'im** (*Ghost's Circle*), ancient stone circles 156 meters in diameter. And five kilometers southeast of that is **Khasfin**, an abandoned Syrian village built on the ruins of the Jewish town of Hisfiyya. It was mentioned in the Old Testament (1 Maccabees 5:26) as Kaspin, and a church, circa 400 CE, has been found there.

NIGHTLIFE & ENTERTAINMENT

Across the street from Amirim is **Moshav Shefer**. Issak Tavior, a classical pianist, lives here and gives regular Saturday 11am performances for $10, refreshments included. It's a lovely site in which to hear beautiful music. Call *Tel. 06-698-9085*, to check and to see about other performance dates.

There's an annual week-long **Chamber Music Festival**, *Kfar Blum Guest House, Tel. 06-694-3366, Fax 06-694-8555*, in July in the Hula Valley is a kibbutz about 12 kilometers southeast of Kiryat Shemona. Take Route 90 to Hagome Junction, turn east on small Route 977, and Kfar Blum is north a couple kilometers on a small side road. Tickets cost around NIS 100 per concert and sell out quickly. Bus 29 from Kiryat Shemona comes here.

Other than that, stop into Tiberias, Tsfat, or just get a good night sleep in preparation for the next day's activities.

SHOPPING

Not one of the highlights of the Upper Galilee/Golan region, there are always trinkets and souvenirs sold at the shrines and religious and archaeological sites.

SPORTS & RECREATION

Golan and Galilee Touring Information, *Mahanayim Junction Information Station (Paz Gaz Station), Route 90, Tel. 06-693-5016*, is north of Rosh Pina, open daily 8:30am-4:00pm.

Hiking in the Golan Heights must be arranged in advance through an SPNI Field School or Information Station.

SPNI Field Schools in the **Golan Heights** are in **Kazrin**, *Tel. 06-696-1234*, and **Keshet Yonatan**, *Tel. 06-696-2560*; **Hermon** and **Upper Galilee** field schools are in **Hermon**, *Tel. 06-6941-091*, and **Kibbutz Dan's Usisskin Museum**, *Tel. 06-694-1704*.

National Parks and Nature Reserves are open Sunday-Thursday 8am-5pm April through October and 8am-4pm November through March (closing one hour earlier Fridays and Holiday eves).

Bike Rentals are available at **Aviv Hotel**, *HaGalil, Tiberias, Tel. 06-672-0007*.

Horse Back Riding, Jeep trips and Donkey treks in the Upper Galilee are available at **Vered HaGalil**, *Korazim, Tel. 06-693-5785*, **Bat Ya'ar**, *Amuka, Tel. 06-692-1788*, **Ayelet HaShachar**, *Tel Hazor, Tel. 06-693-0733*, and **Baba Yona**, *Tel. 06-693-8773*, just to the north, though there are other options in other regions.

There are more **Donkey Trips** from **Orcha**, *Tel. 06-679-2777*, and **Donkey Tracks**, *Tel. 06-656-5511*.

And more **Jeep Trips** at **Nofei Golan**, *Tel. 06-673-2216*, and **Avi Gavich**, *El-Rom, Tel. 05-025-2269*.

Canada Center, *Metulla, Tel. 06-695-0370*, is quite well equipped. Its entry fee of NIS 36 (NIS 25 for students) gains you admission to an **ice-skating rink**, and includes skate rental as well as us of an elaborate **indoor pool** with slides, jacuzzi, sauna, **squash** and **basketball** courts. The ping-pong tables are NIS 5 for 45 minutes. Open daily 10am-10pm, the Center is just down the hill from the Yafa Pension.

There are **ski slopes**, *Tel. 06-698-1337*, in winter up north on **Mount Hermon**.

Inner Tubing for NIS 35 per person in summer is arranged at **Sde Nechemia Campgrounds**, *near Kiryat Shemona, Tel. 06-694-6010*, and at **Abukayyak**, *Tel. 06-692-2245*.

White-Water adventures are available at **Kfar HaNassi**, *Tel. 06-693-2506*, in catarafts, **Abukayyak**, *Tel. 06-692-2245*, has kayaks, **Kfar Blum**, *Hula Valley, Tel. 06-694-8775*, has kayaks, **Sde Nechemia**, *Hula Valley, Tel. 06-694-6010*, has kayaks, **HaGoshrim**, *Tel. 06-695-6230*, and **Jordan River** by **Kibbutz Gadot**, *near Bnot Ya'akov Bridge, Tel. 06-693-4622, Fax 06-693-8977*, has rafts.

Paragliding is available at the **Upper Galilee Gliding Club**, *Tel. 06-695-2933*.

For **birdwatching** go to **Usisshkin Nature Museum**, *near Banyas, Tel. 06-694-1704*, **Hula Valley Nature Reserve**, *Tel. 06-693-4069*, **Hermon Reserve**, *Tel. 06-698-1337*, **Gamla Reserve**, *Tel. 06-696-3721*, or **Ma'ayan Barach Park**, *Tel. 06-695-4611*.

There's **camping** at **Hurshat Tal Nat'l Park**, *Tel. 06-694-2360*.

EXCURSIONS & DAY TRIPS

SPNI, *Tel. 03-638-8674*, leaves Tuesdays from Tiberias Tourist Information office at 10:30am for a magnificent three day hiking and driving tour for moderately good hikers. If you want to explore the stunning natural beauty of this region, SPNI excels. It costs $298, including lodging and food, call ahead to reserve.

Egged Tours, *Tel. 06-672-0474*, takes big bus trips of the area Tuesday and Saturday (and Thursday in summer), leaving 8:30am and returning 6pm for $35, with discounts for students, seniors, soldiers.

PRACTICAL INFORMATION

• **English News: Israel Radio** (576 and 1458 KHz) at 7am, 1pm, 5pm, 8pm; **Voice of America** (1260, 15205, 15260, 9700 KHz) at 6am, 7am, 5pm, 5:30pm, 6pm; **BBC** (1323 KHz) at 2:15pm, 3pm, 6pm GMT; **Israel TV**, daily at 5:30pm.
• **Fire**: call *Tel. 102* in an emergency.
• **Medical Aid: First Aid** (Magen David Adom), *Tel. 101* in emergencies.

• **Police**: call *Tel. 100* in emergencies.
• **Touring Information**, *Mahanayim Junction Information Station (Paz Gaz Station), Route 90, Tel. 06-693-5016*, is north of Rosh Pina, open Sunday-Thursday 9am-3pm, Friday 9am-2:30pm, Saturday 8:30am-2:30pm.

See *Practical Information* sections for **Tiberias** (page 285) and **Tsfat** (page 338) for fire stations, hospitals, pharmacies, police stations, and post offices.

TSFAT

Also known as **Safed**, **Tzfat**, **Zefat**, and **Zfad**, however you spell it, **Tsfat** is a beautiful place, a special place, and it wants you to stay. People invite you into their lives and lore, they tell stories about why it has been special (i.e. holy) through the ages. The large community of Aliyah-makers from the US attests to its power to draw and hold Still, you can get a tour of a couple hours, see the city and learn some history, or you can stay a day, wander around, and soak in the feeling, then maybe settle in for good. But I suggest you give yourself a couple of days in Tsfat, not only because it's near many other sites but because it is unique in history, beauty, and old Israel atmosphere.

Shabbat is taken seriously here, and it's a good (interesting) time to visit. Businesses close and people's hearts and houses open. If you want to eat on your own Friday night, visit the supermarket before 2pm or make arrangements with a hotel like Rimon Inn. If you want to share in and experience the spirit and life of Tsfat, make arrangements with Ascent for Shabbat dinner (see below under *Nightlife & Entertainment*).

In this fairly Orthodox city, most shops and all restaurants are closed during Shabbat. Even if they claim to be open daily, they assume you understand that this doesn't include Friday afternoon and evening (from an hour or so before sundown) and Saturday day (until after sundown). Tsfat is a city that specializes in mysticism and spirituality. There are mysticism workshops, Kabbal seminars, spiritual city tours, and spas with 12 different varieties of healing teas. In Tiberias locals may care that you learn their history and see their sites; here people are concerned with the state of your soul.

History

One of the four holy cities of the Talmud (along with Hebron, Tiberias, and Jerusalem), Tsfat was an important city for many different periods in history. The Talmud mentions it (though the Bible doesn't), Josephus Flavius fortified it against the Romans, the Crusaders made it an administrative center, and the Mamluk Sultan Baybars captured and ransacked it, then turned Tsfat in 1266 into the headquarters of a 'mamlakah' or province from Galilee to Lebanon. In 1492 Spain expelled their Jews, and many of those found their way to Tsfat, sparking a golden century of learning and mysticism. Joseph Caro (author of *Shulkhan Arukh*), Moses Trani, Isaac Luria, and Hayyim Vital all lived in Tsfat and made it the center of Kabbalist study.

In the 1600s, Tsfat had 18 schools, 21 synagogues, and a large yeshiva with 20 teachers. At that time its population was made up of Ashkenazim, Sephardim, Provençal, and Italian Jews. In 1759 there was a major earthquake followed by a devastating epidemic, and five years later only 60 families still lived in Tsfat. New blood immigrated in 1778 in the form of more than 300 Hassidim, pupils of the Rabbi Israel Eliezer Ba'al Shem Tov, who came with the Rabbi Manahem Mendel from Vitebsk, Russia. In 1810 the disciples of Elijah, the gaon of Vilnius, moved to Tsfat.

The town became strong and healthy again during the reign of Ibrahim Pasha, 1831-1840, but in 1834 the Druze attacked, and in 1836

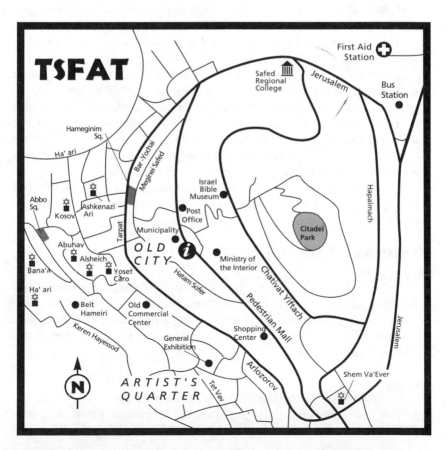

there was another big earthquake; some 4,000 Jews died and many others fled to resettle in Hebron. The population in 1913 was roughly 22,000, half of which was Jewish. In May 1948 during the fight for independence the Palmah captured Tsfat, and it has been an orthodox Jewish community ever since. The new town was built in 1948 around the nucleus of the old one, and the artists set up shop in the old Arab quarter.

ORIENTATION

A giddy 3,330 feet above sea level on the west slope of Mount Canaan, and northwest of the Galilee, Tsfat has many rings of roads winding around on different levels, and it's easy to get lost, especially in a rental car. The main street is **Jerusalem** (or Yerushalayim), and it encircles **Gan Ha-Metzuda** (the Park of the Citadel) on the highest level of the city. The **Tourist Information** office is on Jerusalem #50, the **post office** is nearby, and the southwest section of Jerusalem turns into the **Promenade** (also known as the Pedestrian Mall, or *midrahov* in Hebrew), location of most of Tsfat's restaurants, where people stroll and eat, no cars allowed. Keep following Jerusalem Street. around and it will lead you to the **bus station**.

One level below is the **Artists' Quarter**. If you take enter the shopping center building at the end of the Promenade, take the elevator down to the supermarket, and exit on that level you will find yourself on Arlosoroff Street just minutes from the Artists' Quarter. Dividing the Artists' Quarter from the **Synagogue Quarter** or **Old City** are the stairs of **Ma'alot Olei Hagardom**, built by the British in 1940 to separate and patrol the Jewish and Arab quarters. The name translates to "Those Who Went up On the Gallows," for the seven Irgun who were hung by the British and then taken down these steps on the way to the cemetery.

Once in the Synagogue Quarter it is confusing and easy to get lost, but that's just part of the joy of Tsfat. You might as well give in to the magic, wander the streets and connecting stairs, and enjoy.

ARRIVALS & DEPARTURES
By Car
To leave this town go to the junction by the Egged bus terminal and gas station and take the road with the bus station on your left. When you come to another gas station there are road signs directing you to Akko and Tiberias, and you're on your way. Leaving by bus, go to the central bus station for all transport.

By Bus
The **Central Bus Station**, *Ha'Atzma'ut Square, Tel. 06-692-1122*, has buses to Tiberias (#459) until 7pm, direct to Jerusalem (#964) at 7:30am Sunday-Friday, and to Haifa via Akko (#361, #362) Sunday-Thursday

every 20 minutes 'till 8pm (4pm on Friday, and there's a 9pm bus on Saturday). The bus station won't store bags, but Ascent Institute will for NIS 1.

GETTING AROUND TOWN

By Foot

Get off the bus or park your car, get out your map, and go get lost. It's a small town with little alleys not meant for casual car exploration. It's true the hills are steep, but true appreciation of Tsfat can't take place behind a wheel.

By Bus

There are local buses leaving from the central bus station to the outlying areas.

By Taxi

Call *Tel. 06-697-0707* if you want a cab.

WHERE TO STAY

RIMON INN, *Artists' Colony, Tel. 06-699-4666, Fax 06-692-0456, toll free in Israel Tel. 177-022-7676, has 82 lovely rooms for $80-$153 a single and $102-$175 a double, plus 15% service charge, breakfast included, and there are special family plans available.*

This is without a doubt the most picturesque hotel in one of the loveliest of cities in Israel. If this is within your price range you would be a fool not to stay here. Old stone walls, flowers and oriental carpets, stunning views and antique pottery give a feel of history while the pool, good food, and attention to detail feel like luxury.

CENTRAL HOTEL, *Yerushalayim, Tel. 06-697-2336, Fax 06-697-2366, has 45 rooms with air conditioning and heat as well as TV and phone. Rooms cost NIS 270 a single, NIS 350 a double, breakfast included.*

There's a lobby bar and dance hall, but the rooms are not especially fancy or cozy.

BERINSON HOUSE, *Old City, Tel. 06-697-2555, Fax 06-697-2535, is also called Tel Aviv Hotel. It is across from Ascent in the Old City, and is closed in winter. They've 38 rooms with singles for $70-$80 and doubles for $85-$120, breakfast included.*

RON HOTEL, *Hativat Yiftah, Tel. 06-697-2590, Fax 06-697-2363, has 49 rooms with private facilities, air conditioning and TV. Prices, including breakfast, run $70-$90 a single, $90-$120 a double, and they have a swimming pool.*

RUCKENSTEIN, *Mount Canaan, Tel. 06-692-0060, has 26 rooms with air conditioning, private facilities, and TV. Prices are $60 a single and $75 a double, with coffee and tea in the room.*
HOTEL & PENSION HADAR, *Ridbaz, Tel. 06-692-0068, is off Yerushalayim and has 20 rooms for NIS 150-180, and no breakfast.*
Rooms are pretty basic, with toilet and shower but not much else.
BEIT BINYAMIN YOUTH HOSTEL, *1 Lohamei Ha-geta'ot, Tel. 06-692-1086, Fax 06-697-3514, has 27 rooms (six beds each). Dorm beds cost $11 ($18.50 in summer), private rooms are $56, and all include breakfast.*
The rooms all have their own toilet and shower and are very clean, but get no awards for decor or personality. Bus 6, 7 from the central bus station go there, or you can walk about 20 minutes.
ASCENT INSTITUTE, *2 Ha'Ari, Tel. 06-692-1364, Fax 06-692-1942, is a place of study and a hostel (19 rooms, 75 beds) all in one. The dorms, four to six beds a room and segregated by gender, cost NIS 40 a bed and are available for visiting Jews. There are a few private rooms, for married couples only, NIS 90. You can write to POB 296, Tsfat, Israel 13102.*
Most rooms have their own shower/toilet, though they are otherwise pretty basic, no towels, no cooking, no laundry. You can leave luggage during the day for just NIS 1. It's very safe there, with a security guard at night. Shabbat dinners can be arranged for you and they have a variety of classes (in English) on Judaism and mysticism as well. In fact, so eager are they at Ascent to instruct you on Torah and Jewish lore that they offer a NIS 10 rebate per each class you attend. They pretty much stick to a week's limit for staying there, though it depends on your situation. In addition, they run special seminars on holidays such as Lag Ba'omer, for which you need to make reservations in advance.

There are also lots of rooms to rent in the high season. The Tourist Information office has a list with phone numbers, but if you walk around town you will see the signs in people's windows. If you're carrying luggage people will probably start telling you about their nieces' rooms that are available. The average prices are around NIS 80 per person, but it's good to see the place and good to bargain.
BEIT SHOSHANA, *Tel. 06-697-3939*, has rooms for around NIS 80-100. If she doesn't approach you at the bus station, call.
SARA AND SHLOMI, *Tel. 06-697-2902*, have rooms to rent as well. Call them to see.

Amuka
HOUSE IN THE WOODS, *Birya Forest, Tel. 06-697-3597*, has fully equipped wood cabins, private and peaceful, and run by the Rona family.

WHERE TO EAT

The **Promenade** (a pedestrian walkway on Yerushalayim) is the stretch for restaurants and falafel stands. Also, a street fruit and vegetable **market** is held Wednesdays 6am-2pm next to the bus station.

CAFE RESTAURANT HAMIFGASH, *Pedestrian Mall, Tel. 06-692-0510*, has good kosher oriental food. Open 9am-11pm, closed Shabbat, it's a popular place here, with cheap appetizers of chopped liver, soup, or hummus for NIS 6-9, and main courses NIS 30-33.

PINATI RESTAURANT, *Pedestrian Mall, Tel. 06-692-0855*, is four doors or so down from Hamifgash. Open 9am-midnight, closed Shabbat, the owner likes Elvis very much, so much so that his picture is plastered all around the restaurant, and his music gets more air time than usual. Average prices for their oriental food, appetizers are NIS 8-13, main courses are NIS 26-46, with steaks costing a bit more. This used to be the only restaurant around that was open during Shabbat, but they have gone kosher and now keep the same hours as all the rest.

MI-TZU-YAN, *51 Jerusalem, Tel. 06-697-3245*, is a Chinese kosher restaurant above the Yair Hotel. Open Sunday-Thursday noon-4pm, 6:30pm-12:30am, Friday noon-4pm, it's an attractive place with a Thai chef, good food, and entrees that cost NIS 19-52.

Hakikar Ha-Meganin

This area is in the Synagogue Quarter:

ORGANIC CAFE, *Synagogue Quarter, Tel. 06-692-1866*, open 8am-2pm, 4pm-8pm, closed Shabbat, has soy milk shakes, cereal coffee, waffles, crepes, and pancakes.

HAKIKAR CAFE RESTAURANT, *upstairs on the square*, was in transition, and may or may not be reopening. If it is open, you're in for a treat because the cook is terrific.

Open Shabbat

BAT YA'AR, *Amuka, Tel. 06-692-1788, Fax 06-692-1991*, is accessible only by car. This Country-style ranch has a steak house and pub, and sometimes at night they have jazz.

SEEING THE SIGHTS

Synagogue Quarter (*Qiryat Batei Ha-Knesset*) or **Old City** (*Ha'Ir Ha'Atika*) is a stunningly beautiful and confusing maze of little winding streets, and stairs radiating out from **Kikar HaMeginim** (Defenders' Square) with many old synagogues, all still in active use and with very particular local followings.

Ashkenazi synagogue of HaAri was built a few years after the death of Rabbi Isaac Luria (1533-72). HaAri (The Lion) is an acronym of his name, with the 'A' standing for Adoni or Ashkenazi. The synagogue, just a block or so from Kikar HaMeginim on Gurei Ha'Ari, is simple, with austere arches and vaulting. The windows above the entrance, however, are quite decorative, and there are Kabbalist frescoes on the walls. There are symbols of the 12 tribes as well as various musical instruments and fruit. Above the lintel is an inscription in Hebrew which translates as "How unutterably holy is the Synagogue of the great Master HaAri, blessed be his name." The ark was made of olive wood by an engraver from Colombia, Ukraine in the 19th century, and it's decorated with intricate spirals.

In the back of the synagogue is Kise Eliyahu (Elijah's Chair), carved around the same time as the ark. The story goes that any Jewish couple who put their Jewish rear ends in the chair will have a son within the year, so sit with care. The synagogue was mostly destroyed by an earthquake in 1837, and was later repaired and rebuilt.

RABBI ISAAC LURIA

Luria was a mystic, and the founder of Lurianic Kabbalah. He grew up in Cairo and lived for seven years as a recluse on an island in the Nile studying the Zohar. The prophet Elijah, with whom he was in communication, told him to move to Tsfat. He did so in 1569, studied with the Ramak (Rabbi Moshe Cordeviero), and eventually became the leader of Kabbalistic teaching himself. Though his lessons invariably put Caro to sleep, other students were more attentive, and many of his teachings were recorded by disciples such as Chaim Vital.

Luria introduced new rituals and new forms of mystical prayer. Every Friday evening he would lead his disciples into the fields outside of Tsfat, dressed all in white, to welcome the shabbat bride; the synagogue is built on the site of that field. Luria was believed to be a reincarnation of the soul of Moses. He possessed ruach ha-kodesh (the Holy Spirit) and could tell the state of a person's transmigratory development by looking at his forehead.

Sephardi synagogue of HaAri, *on Hamekubalim* (on the lower slopes of the Old City, just up from the cemeteries) was built originally in the 1600s on the site where Luria prayed, and it is one of the best preserved and restored in Tsfat. Once through the intricate entrance of staircase and courtyard and small door, three windows shed light on a blue hall and allegorical paintings on the wall, plus lovely wrought iron and carved wood. In the back is where the prophet Elijah communed with him over mystical texts. This synagogue also figured prominently during the siege in 1948 and was one of the key positions held by the Jewish defenders.

Issac Abuhav Synagogue, *Abuhav Street,* not far from Alshekh synagogue, was originally built in the time of Rabbi Issac Abuhav, 1433-1493 but was rebuilt after the 1837 earthquake destroyed all but the wall protecting the ark, which remained untouched, according to tradition, thanks to its holy nature. This is the most Kabbalistic of synagogues, structured as it is on the sacred arithmetic of Jewish mysticism. The four pillars around the podium are said to symbolize the four elements and the four holy cities and the four matriarchs. The central dome is decorated with Judaic symbols: the pomegranate, traditionally containing 613 seeds, correlates with the 613 commandments in the Torah, while the 10 windows in the dome represent the 10 commandments. The ark contains the Torah scroll written by Rabbi Abuhav, and they also have two manuscripts done in calligraphy by HaAri himself.

Nearby is **Alshekh Synagogue,** named (predictably) after the Kabbalist Rabbi Yitzhak Alshekh. The synagogue is the only one to have withstood the 1837 earthquake, and is not always open to the public. The blue wall paint represents the color of heaven to protect against the evil eye.

The **Banai Synagogue,** *located on Hamekubalim Street off Yok-alef,* is named after Rabbi Yossi Banai (The Builder). This synagogue contains the Torah scroll which is annually carried to Meron from nearby **Kikkar Abbo** in the festival of Lag B'Omer.

The **Caro Synagogue** is where the Kabbalist Rabbi Yosef Caro studied and taught until his death in 1575. It was destroyed in the 1837 earthquake and rebuilt in 1847. The synagogue ark houses three ancient Torah scrolls: on the right is one from Persia that's around 200 years old, the middle one is from Iraq and goes back about 300 years, and the scroll on the left, from Spain, dates back over 500 years.

Other small synagogues dot the quarter, but are not open to the public.

Other Sites

Citadel comes from Tsfat's Frankish Crusader period around 1100 CE when Hugo of Saint Omer built a small castle which was later enlarged by King Foulques of Anjou in 1140. This castle on HaMetzuda hill was given to the Templars by King Amalric I in 1168, which enabled Tsfat, along with Belvoir and La Fève, to defend the eastern border of the Kingdom of Jerusalem. The castle was taken by Saladin in 1188, destroyed by al-Mu'azzam in 1220, and rebuilt in 1240 to become the strongest Frankish fortress around. **Gan Ha-Metzuda**, a park of cypress, pine, and cedars, looks down on what remains of the old fortifications. It's a popular picnic spot, and also the site of more excavation, resulting from the accidental discovery in 1986 or pottery shards dating to the time of Abraham.

THE RABBI YOSEF CARO STORY

Caro was born in Spain in 1488. After the expulsion of 1492 and 43 subsequent years in Turkey he came to Tsfat in 1535 (he believed, along with many of the Tsfat Kabbalists, that the Messianic Age would dawn in 1540, and that the expulsion from Spain represented 'birth pangs of the Messiah'). He became the chief rabbi here, but is best known for writing the Shulchan Arukh ("The Set Table"), a code of ritual Law that became the most authoritative halakhic (legal decisions of normative practice) text for Sephardim.

Caro was no legal scholar, however. He was guided by a maggid, a heavenly mentor who communicates with men through dreams, visions, or possession. This heavenly guide, the spirit of the Mishna, sometimes took possession of Caro, speaking from Caro's mouth in a strange voice much to the distress of whichever colleagues were there at the time. The maggid also spoke with Caro in private, answered his questions, and lauded his continuing work on Kabbalistic secrets and halakhic decisions. Although he was an important part of the Kabbalist circle of scholars in Tsfat, Caro was unable to study with Isaac Luria (HaAri). Luria told him he wasn't suitable as a pupil, and every time Caro attended one of Luria's lectures he fell asleep.

Near Tourist Information is the **Davidka monument**. The Davidka (the 'ka' suffix is an affectionate diminutive such as are added to names) was a weapon used in the 1948 War. Its main claim to fame was the extreme noise it produced. The fear instilled by the explosion helped make up in effectiveness what was otherwise lacking in its performance and reliability.

The **Jewish Cemeteries** lie west of the synagogue quarter. To get there follow Ha'Ari all the way down, past Ha'Ari Sephardic synagogue, past Ha'Ari Mikve (the men's ritual baths). The oldest one contains the graves of the esteemed 16th century rabbis, many of whom have synagogues named after them, such as Isaac Luria (d. 1572), Moshe Cordevero, the Remak (d. 1570), Ya'akov Beirav (d. 1546) who wanted to re-establish the Sanhedrin in Tsfat in 1538, Joseph Caro (d. 1575), Shelomo Alkavets (d. 1584) who wrote the *Lecha Dodi* hymn, Moshe Alsheikh (d. 1600), and Hayyim Vital (d. 1620) who recorded the teachings of Luria.

The domed tomb was built by the Karaites of Damascus on the site where they believed the body of the prophet Hosea was buried. Hannah and her seven sons, martyred by Antiochus Epiphanes in second century BCE for refusing to eat pork, are also said to be buried here. The fatigue

A MYSTICAL JOURNEY

Abraham Abulafia (1240-1291) was a Spanish mystic and Kabbalist who did a fair bit of traveling in pursuit of his goals. He spent a good while wandering and searching for the Ten Lost Tribes and the Sambatyon River. Unsuccessful in this venture, he studied the Sefer Yetzirah and had visions. He tried to achieve prophecy by meditating on Hebrew letter combinations and on the mystical names of God. What he came up with was that he was the Messiah and went to Rome in 1280 to convert Pope Nicholas III to Judaism. Rather than converting, Pope Nicholas III arrested Abulafia and prepared to burn him at the stake.

Before this was carried out, however, Pope Nicholas died, and Abulafia was released after a short imprisonment. His next stop was Sicily where he proclaimed himself the Messiah, possessor of the Holy Spirit. Abulafia believed the Messianic age would dawn in 1290, but he himself made it to 1291 without seeing it happen.

that overwhelms you as you climb the hill is said not to be because you're out of shape but because you're walking over their graves. More recent graves at the bottom of the hill include seven of the eight Irgun and Lehi who were hanged in Akko Prison by the British.

Beit ha-midrash shel Shem va'Ever, the holy caves where Noah's son Shem and grandson Ever are believed to have studied Torah, are located in the south of Tsfat on the slope of the mountain where the citadel stands, near the bridge off Ha-Palmah where Jerusalem and Arlozorov intersect. The cave is holy to Muslims too; they believe that this is where a messenger told Jacob of the death of his son Joseph. For this reason they call this the "Place of Mourning" and believe the messenger is buried here.

El-Jami'a el-Ahmar (Red Mosque) was built in 1275 by Sultan Baybars during the Mamluk period. **Zawiyat Banat Hamid**, Tomb of the Emir Muzaffer Ed-Din Musa, comes from 1372.

Museums

Hameiri House, Museum of Safed Heritage, *bottom of the Oleh Ha-Gardom steps, Tel. 06-6971-307*, is in a beautifully restored historic building circa 1517). They focus on Jewish life in Tsfat over the past 200 years, and the collection of photos, papers, books, clothes, tools, and religious items do a good job documenting Tsfat's history and heritage. The museum is open Sunday-Thursday 9am-2pm, Friday 9am-1pm. Guided tours of the museum and of the Old City available by prior appointment. Admission is NIS 6 (NIS 5 for students).

Yitzhak Frenkel Museum, *16 Tet-Zayin, Artists' Colony, Tel. 06-692-0235*, is open March-October 11am-6pm, Saturday until 3pm. Frenel was a leading member of the modernist school in the Ecole de Paris. The museum displays his works and tells about his life.

Museum of Hungarian-Speaking Jewry, *Tel. 06-692-3880*, open Sunday-Friday 9am-1pm, has exhibits from the Hungarian community artifacts spanning hundreds of years.

Israel Bible Museum, *Citadel Hill, Tel. 06-699-9972*, is open March-September Sunday-Thursday 10am-4pm, Friday 10am-1pm, Saturday and holidays 10am-2pm; October-November Saturday-Thursday 10am-2pm; December-February Sunday-Friday 10am-2pm, admission is free. This museum features the art of Philip Ratner, a modern American artist with Biblical themes as well as the sculpture of Henoch (Enrico) Glicenstein, 1870-1942. The building is historical too. 125 years old, it was once the home of the Turkish Kaimakam.

The Ts Assaf Printing Museum, *Artists' Colony, Tel. 06-692-3022*, is open only in the summer, Sunday-Thursday 10am-noon, 4pm-6pm, Friday-Saturday 10am-noon. This printing press, which opened in Tsfat in 1563, was established by the Ashkenazi brothers, It was the first printing press to be opened in the Orient, and admission is free.

NIGHTLIFE & ENTERTAINMENT

Beit Yigal Allon, *Tel. 06-697-1990*, is the regional cultural center. They have a cinema and theater, with nightly performances or films. Call for details.

Ascent Institute, *Ha'Ari, Tel. 06-692-1364, Fax 06-692-1942*, or write to POB 296, Tsfat, Israel 13102. The Director Rabbi Shaul Leiter will be happy to arrange seminars and Shabbat dinners with local Jewish families to help you experience a more direct Jewish connection to Tsfat and their community. The lessons are fascinating, regardless of your level of Torah study or religious faith, covering many facets of history, learning, and lore.

The NIS 10 rebate if you're staying with Ascent is the least of the benefits.

Festivals

Tsfat Kleizmer Festival, an annual festival of traditional Jewish music in August, goes for three days of festivities and concerts. The place is mobbed with kleizmer devotees, and there is no parking to be had within the city for love or money.

Lag Ba'omer, in May, features a pilgrimage to Meron. This holiday celebrates the anniversary of the death of Rabbi Shimon Bar Yohai on the

5th day of Av, a month after Passover. Lag ba'omer means "thirty-third day of the Omer period." Since the death of a saint is considered a spiritual 'wedding' it is a popular time for human weddings as well. People make a pilgrimage to the tomb of Rabbi Simeon to study the Zohar, dance around his tomb, and throw hair from the first haircut of young boys into blazing bonfires.

SHOPPING

Safed Candles, *Tel. 06-692-1093, Fax 06-692-2557,* is next to Ashkenazi Ari Synagogue. In the workshop (which happens to have been Tsfat's candle factory 90 years ago as well), Hasidic artisans make a variety of beautiful and original candles from pure beeswax.

GALLERIES IN THE ARTISTS' QUARTER (QIRYAT HA-OMANIM)

General Exhibition, Tel. 06-692-0087, in an ancient mosque is open Sunday-Thursday 9am-6pm in summer, 9am-4pm in winter, Friday 9am-2pm, Saturday 10am-2pm. More than 50 local painters' and sculptors' works are exhibited here in this controversial center. It's a grand display, but some think it's just a bit tacky to have converted a mosque to this end.

Dadon Gallery, Tel. 06-692-1821, open Sunday-Thursday 9am-6pm, Friday 9am-2pm, has original Jewish art with square-letter microcaligraphy, watercolors, and copper art.

Leon Gallery, Beit Yosef, Tel/Fax 06-692-1908, open Sunday-Thursday 9am-6pm, Friday 9am-2pm, has original Jewish art with oil paintings and Biblical texts done in watercolor microcaligraphy.

Shalom Safed Gallery, Beit Yosef, Tel. 06-692-1919, is open Sunday-Thursday 9am-7pm, Friday 9am-2pm. This gallery represents some of Israel's best artists, such as Shalom of Safed, Ben-Avram, Marc Chagall, Shmuel Katz, and more.

Yair Gallery, Tel. 06-692-1752, open Sunday-Thursday 9am-6pm, Friday 9am-2pm, has microcaligraphy (originals and prints), 3-D dioramas, and a shofar center.

And many more – just wander around.

Exhibition of New Olim Painters, *Artists' Quarter, Tel. 06-697-3787,* open Sunday-Thursday 9:30am-5pm, Friday, Saturday 9:30am-2pm, has oil paintings, water colors, and drawings from new immigrant artists.

Bilha, *Tel. 06-692-1636,* is open daily 10am-8pm. They have handicrafts, paintings, and silver jewelry. If the shop's closed, ring the bell and the proprietor will come open up.

Tamar Efrony, *Artists' Quarter, Tel. 06-697-1541*, is open daily 10am-1pm, 4pm-7pm, Fridays 10am-1pm. They feature glazed pottery, ceramic sculpture, ornaments and menorahs.

Daniel Flatauer Safed Craft Pottery, *Artists' Quarter, Tel. 06-697-4970*, is open daily 10am-5pm (closed Shabbat) and has hand-thrown stoneware and porcelain pottery as well as Judaica.

SPORTS & RECREATION

Blue Valley Swimming Pool, *off Ha'Atzma'ut, Tel. 06-692-0217*, is behind the bus station. Open daily in July and August 9am-5pm and costs NIS 17 (NIS 10 for students). There is a half-olympic size pool here.

Heated Swimming Pool, *Tel. 06-697-4294*, is in the southern district of Tsfat (take bus 6 or 7); it's open all year and costs NIS 17 (NIS 10 for students). Half-olympic size pool with sauna and ping-pong.

Bat Ya'ar, *Amuka, Tel. 06-692-1788, Fax 06-692-1991*, a few kilometers northeast of Tsfat, is a country-style ranch with horseback riding, jeep tours, and forest walks as well as a steak house and pub. There's also **hiking** in Amuka and Wadi Amud, and it's very beautiful in both.

Mount Meron Reserve, following Route 89 as it winds north and west for about 15 kilometers towards Baram, is a free and open reserve with picnic tables and marked trails. Set in the wild and wooded mountainside, it's a beautiful area with wildlife and great views of the countryside. At 1208 meters it's the highest mount in Galilee, and on clear days you can see Lebanon, Syria, and the Mediterranean. **Mount Meron Field School**, *Tel. 06-698-0923*, is there as well; they provide information for free and sell trail maps for NIS 54.

EXCURSIONS & DAY TRIPS

Off Route 89, about six kilometers west of Tsfat is the **tomb of Rabbi Simeon Bar Yohai**, spiritual leader of the mystic Kabbalists who took an active part in the Bar-Kochba revolt against Rome on 67 CE. Simeon didn't think much of the Romans, and said "The best of heathens deserves to be put to death." The Romans didn't think much of Simeon either, and to escape them Simeon and his son Eliezer hid in a cave in Peki'in, some 14 kilometers to the west, for 13 years.

The *Zohar*, an important Kabbalistic text, is ascribed to the followers of Simeon who recorded the mystic secrets he learned during his years in hiding. The mausoleum is a stone building with white domes; two domed tombs mark where Simeon bar Yohai and his son Eliezar are said to be buried. On the feast day of Lag Ba'omer each May, the hills are packed with people making the procession from Tsfat to Simeon bar Yohai's tomb to mark the anniversary of his death.

MYSTIC KABBALAH GLOSSARY

Kabbalah: (Hebrew for "received tradition") refers to the mystical teachings that began to emerge in Spain and Southern France in the 13th century. Kabbalistic theosophy concerns the inner workings of the divine and its relationship to man. The Zohar, edited in the 13th century and considered the Bible of the Kabbalists, contains the written account of oral traditions from earlier centuries, based on the mystic revelations of Rabbi Simeon Bar Yochai's teachings in the first century CE.

Tzimtzum: Hebrew for "contraction," tsimtzum refers to a complex process whereby the infinite God could bring the finite world into being through the equally complex process of emanation.

Emanation: the coming into being of the universe through the unfolding of God's essence in a series of stages–Emanation, Creation, Formation, and Action which allows the divine flow to take place. The mystics saw the world as the flame from the divine coal or the garment of God within which divinity itself was contained.

Transmigration of Souls: this is the belief that after death the human soul is reincarnated, sometimes into a human, animal, or inanimate form. Orthodox belief rejects this notion, but it was important to the Kabbalists, who saw one another as possessing elements of the souls of biblical and Talmudic characters. Good deeds led to rebirth as people, but sins led to animals. Pride led to rebirth as bees, adulterers into asses, and cruel people came back as cows.

Dibbuk: Hebrew for "one that cleaves," it's an evil spirit who attaches itself to a living person and takes over. A dibbuk is a 'naked soul' which is not at rest or subject to transmigration therefor has to find an available body to occupy, one made vulnerable through sin. The dibbuk speaks through the person's with a strange voice, and is made to leave by way of the little toe through exorcism.

And if this isn't all perfectly clear, don't worry about it. Kabbalists studied this stuff for a lifetime and still were mystified.

Nearby is **Hillel's Cave**, where first century scholar Hillel the Elder is believed to be buried with his disciples. There are many stories citing the wisdom of Hillel. One of his more famous is his concise summation of the Torah. Asked by a would-be convert to explain the essence of the Torah while standing on one leg (to ensure brevity), Hillel answered "What is hateful to you do not do to your fellow. The rest is commentary. Go and study." Another oft-recited Hillelism is "If I am not for myself, who will be for me, and if I am for myself alone, what am I?"

Up the hill and to the left of the tomb are the remains of the **ancient settlement of Meron**. According to Josephus Flavius (first century CE), Meron used to be a fortified settlement and was well known in the Talmudic period for its olive oil. After the end of the second Jewish War (135 CE) many scholars (such as Simeon bar Yohai and Hillel) settled there. Excavations were begun in 1971 and, along with some doorposts and mikvah remains they found some ruins of a **synagogue** circa 200-300 CE. There's not much to see, just an engraved entrance lintel, hewn from the stone of the mountain, looking over the hills of Tsfat.

Not far north of Mount Meron is **Bar'am**, *Tel. 06-698-9301*, an abandoned Maronite village near the Lebanese border. Bar'am was a big town in Second Temple and Talmudic days and there is a very well-preserved Syrian-Hellenistic period **synagogue** from the third century CE. One of the oldest buildings in the Galilee, this is the only ruined synagogue with a surviving second story. As with most of the synagogues of this period, the entrance faces towards Jerusalem. Outside, some columns remain from the colonnaded hall, and inside on the east-facing window-sill, an inscription gives building credit to El'azar bar Yudan.

On a small hill outside the synagogue is a 19th century **Maronite church**, but the door is walled up. At Kibbutz Bar'am is a **Judaica Museum**, open free every Saturday from 12:30pm-2:30pm, or by previous arrangement with Yoel Nassi, *Tel. 06-698-8237*. Eleven kilometers south of Bar'am is the Maronite and Melchite village of **Jish**. A small village now, Jish (originally Gush Halav or Giscala) was the largest settlement in Upper Galilee in the first few centuries CE. Josephus Flavius mentioned it in his Jewish Wars, recounting how Zealot leader Johanan ben Levi of Giscala defended the last fortifications of the Galilee in 68 CE. Vespasian prevailed, but Jews continued to live there after the destruction of the Second Temple until the 13th century. The remains of two synagogues (one at the highest point of the town, the other 2 kilometers away) are to be found in Jish, as well as a Maronite church from 1886 which stands on the foundations of a third or fourth century synagogue.

There are buses that go to Meron and Bar'am, but they aren't very convenient. Bus 43 goes to Kibbutz Sasa (one kilometers from the Mount Meron Field School) and continues on to Bar'am, but it makes only three trips daily, leaving Tsfat at 7am, 12:30pm, and 5pm, and returning at 7:55am, 1:40pm, and 6:10pm.

PRACTICAL INFORMATION

• **Currency Exchange**: the banks on Jerusalem street (**Leumi, Hapoalim, Israel Discount**, and **First International**) are open Sunday, Tuesday, Thursday 8:30-12:30 and 4-6pm; Monday, Wednesday 8:30-12:30pm, and Friday 8:30-noon.

- **Fire Department**: call *Tel. 102* in an emergency.
- **First Aid** (Magen David Adom): call *Tel. 101*, or *Tel. 06-692-0333* if it's not an emergency.
- **Hospital**: Call *Tel. 06-697-8811* for advice or an appointment.
- **Pharmacies**: There's **Canaan Pharmacy**, *Tel. 06-697-2440, home Tel. 06-697-2713;* **Golan Pharmacy**, *Tel. 06-692-0472*; or **Safed South Pharmacy**, *Tel. 06-697-1777*.
- **Police**: call *Tel. 100*, or *Tel. 06-697-8444* if it's not an emergency.
- **Post Office** main branch, *Ha-Palmah Street, at Aliya Bet, Tel. 06-692-0405*, has poste restante, but the Jerusalem Street Branch is more conveniently located just near the Tourist Information building.
- The **Supermarket**, *end of Pedestrian Mall*, at the end of Jerusalem Street, is connected by elevator to Arlosoroff, the street below. Open Sunday-Thursday until 7pm, on Friday it closes at 2:30pm.
- **Tourist Information**, *50 Jerusalem Street*, *06-692-0961*, in City Hall, is open Sunday-Thursday 8am-6pm, Friday till noon. They have lists of private rooms for rent, and a computer info program.
- **Tours**: **Daily tours**, *Tel. 06-692-0901, Fax 06-697-3116*, are available with Aviva Arlene Minoff, licensed guide. English is her first language, though she speaks Hebrew as well. She gives tours of Tsfat, and beyond, including Christian Pilgrim and Jewish Lore tours. Tours generally leave from Rimon Inn at 10am or 10:30am Monday-Fridays, but call in advance because details are subject to change.

17. JERUSALEM

Jerusalem evokes a swirl of glory, religious splendor, historic battles, and political conflict, and that's before you ever set foot in the city. *Yerushalayim* in Hebrew and *Bayt al-Muqaddas* in Arabic, the city is holy to Jews, Christians, and Muslims alike. Beautiful and hilly, with cool, clean air, and strategically located along an important trade route pass through the Judean Hills, Jerusalem has been desired and fought over for a long time. It's a city that takes traditions seriously; conflict is one of them, and religion is another, though the two often go hand in hand.

For Jews, Jerusalem has been at the core of their religion since David set up the holy Ark of the Covenant there and Solomon built the **First Temple**. Christians revere the city as the place where **Jesus** taught and was crucified. And Muslims count Jerusalem as their third most holy site (after Mecca and Medina) because **Mohammed** is believed to have ascended to heaven from the **Temple Mount**. Out of a total of roughly 550,000 inhabitants, Jews now make up about 72 percent of the Jerusalem population, and Arabs about 26 percent, while the Christian minority continues to dwindle. Both Hebrew and Arabic are spoken, and English is known about as well as elsewhere in the country, which is to say it depends on whom you talk to.

Jerusalem is a magnet that draws people from all over the world and for a wide array of reasons. Religious pilgrims of many denominations have been coming here for centuries to see and worship at the holy sites, students of archaeology come for the excavations and museums, and fans of political history come to see what happens when so many different groups want to honor and possess the same place. The main thing to bear in mind, whether this is your first or your tenth visit, whether you're staying for a day or a month, is that *there is no way you'll see and do it all.*

Don't try, and don't berate yourself for what you didn't get to, that's the rule for a good visit to Jerusalem. Figure out your interests and priorities, and whether you'd get more from a few sights seen in depth or many seen superficially (or some combination thereof), and take it from there.

BEST OF JERUSALEM

BEST HOTELS

· *THE AMERICAN COLONY HOTEL*, Nablus Road, Tel. 02-627-9777, Fax 02-627-9779, 10 minutes up from Damascus Gate. Cost: $115-$230 a single, $175-$275 a double, and suites are $350-$380. Magnificent old Pasha's residence, with style, charm, and attentive service.

· *KINGS HOTEL*, 60 King George, Tel. 02-620-1201, Fax 02-620-1211. Costs: $115 a single and $145 a double, breakfast included, plus 15%. A friendly, helpful place, and very quiet.

· *HOTEL PALATIN*, 4 Agrippas, Tel. 02-623-1141, Fax 02-625-9323, off King George. Cost: $55 a single and $89 a double, including a big breakfast. Family run, feels like a home, and has lovely art.

· *SAINT ANDREW'S*, off King David, Tel. 02-673-2401, Fax 02-673-1711, near the railway station and Bethlehem road. Cost: $43 a single, doubles $65, and triples $83, Scottish breakfast included. Cozy, charming, and beautiful.

· *JERUSALEM INN HOSTEL*, 6 HaHistadrut, Tel. 02-625-1294. Cost: $16 a dorm bed and private rooms are $38 a single, $48 a double. Clean, safe, and centrally located, the manager is exceptionally friendly and helpful.

BEST FOOD & DRINK

· *FINK'S BAR AND RESTAURANT*, 2 HaHistadrut, Tel. 02-623-4523, on the corner with King George. Deemed "One of the best bars in the world" by Newsweek, their goulash is fine, the atmosphere is unique, and the owner is charming and kind.

· *ANGELO*, 9 Horkanos, Tel. 02-623-6095, off Havazelet, parallel to Jaffa. Terrific kosher Italian food in a lovely setting.

· *RAKHMO*, 5 HaEshkol, Tel. 02-623-4595, just off Agrippas. Authentic good oriental food and inexpensive prices.

· *AL-QUDS RESTAURANT*, 23 Sultan Suleiman, Tel. 02-627-2052, a block down from Damascus Gate. Shwarma, kebab, or chicken of excellent quality in festive, busy local restaurant.

· *PHILADELPHIA*, 9 Azzahra, Tel. 02-628-9770, opposite Al-Quds Cinema. Exceptional Arabic food, the best there is.

BEST SPORTS

· *SPNI – Society for Protection of Nature*, 13 Helene Ha'Malka, Tel. 02-625-2357. Leads excellently guided hiking tours all over the countryside.

It's a resplendent and special place to be, with some of the best dining, cafes, and nightlife around to supplement the religious, cultural, and historic points that shout from every corner, hill, and dale. Not surprisingly, Jerusalem is the place where many new immigrants come to establish a new life, and tourism is the city's primary pot of gold. Take a deep breath and enjoy the city on your terms and at your pace.

History

Five thousand years ago, present-day Jerusalem was a **Canaanite** stronghold, and after that the **Jebusites** (a tribe co-existing with the Canaanites in pre-Israelite days) built a citadel here, so for a time this place was called Jebus as well as Jerusalem. The city's Jewish history begins around 1,000 BCE when **David** conquered the city, sending his man Joab into the water system shaft to get inside the fortress walls. David built up his city and made it the capital of his kingdom, but it was vain **Solomon** who taxed his people to the hilt and built the magnificent first Temple to house the Ark of the Covenant, and glorify God (and Solomon) in 955 BCE.

After Solomon's death in 922, the **United Kingdom of Israel** was united no more, and in the aftermath of civil war, Jerusalem was the capital of the southern Kingdom of Judah, governed by Rehoboam (Solomon's son), who ruled over the tribes of Benjamin and Judah, the only two who had remained faithful.

The next few centuries were complicated and eventful, and none of it was good for the Jews. Pharaoh Shishak from Egypt stormed Judah (at the invite of Jeroboam up in the northern Kingdom of Israel), thoroughly looted Solomon's palaces and the Temple, and imposed a fairly heavy annual tribute as well. Judah was an independent kingdom no longer, but existed as a vassal of one dominant force or another for years to come, first to Israel in the north, then to Assyria, and then Damascus.

From 780-740 BCE there was peace in Judah. Uzziah ruled and it was known as the Silver Age, then feuds, greed, and bad foreign policy returned. Prophets such as Isaiah and Jeremiah rebuked and wagged their fingers and warned, but (as is generally the way with prophets) to no avail. In the 700s, King Hezekiah of Judah ran into trouble with the Assyrians (first under Sargon and then with Sennacherib). While Jerusalem escaped the drumming the rest of Judah was subject to (46 main cities were demolished and 200,000 Judeans were taken captive), fear of a siege prompted Hezekiah to reinforce the fortifications, resulting in the underground tunnel and Pool of Siloam that can now be seen near Dung Gate. In 586 BCE Nebuchadnezzar of Babylon stomped in, ending the fun and games, razing Solomon's Temple, and taking the Jews off for 50 years of exile, with their blinded King Zedekiah in tow.

In 537 BCE, **Cyrus the Great** of Persia conquered Babylon and permitted the Jews to return to Jerusalem and rebuild their Temple (a task completed in 515). So began the Second Temple years, first under Persian rule, and in 333 going Greek under Alexander the Great. In 198 BCE, Antiochus III the Seleucid conquered Judah, and Jerusalem came under Macedonian rule. It was against this regime that the Jews revolted in 167 BCE. Antiochus Epiphanes IV (meaning *God-Manifest the Fourth*) was the Seleucid in power at the time, and he plagued the Jews in Jerusalem, plundering and pillaging (favorite kingly pastimes) as well as outlawing religious practices and insisting the Jews profane their Sabbath, worship at pagan temples, and sacrifice swine. The last straw was when he desecrated the Temple in 168 with a huge statue of Zeus and a lewd party. There was resistance, there were deaths, and the revolt led by Mattathias the Hasmonean was on.

After his death, **Judah Maccabee** (the Hammer) led and prevailed. Their small but angry army took Jerusalem, smashed the statue of Zeus, and flushed out the Hellenistic leaders. On the 25th of Kislev (in December, usually), 164 BCE, Judah Maccabee rededicated the Temple in an eight-day festival and lit the lamps of the *menorah*, an event celebrated and remembered in the holiday of Hanukah. By 142 BCE the Hasmoneans had established autonomy and began to return Judah to its Hebrew roots. By 125, however, the Maccabee morals had slid. King Hyrcanus forced Idumeans to convert to Judaism. King Yannai partied while causing 800 opponents to watch their families be killed before being put to death themselves. The kingdom weakened, civil war ensued, and the Romans solved the power squabbles of Hyrcanus II and Aristobulus by sending General Pompey to arbitrate, besiege, and eventually occupy Jerusalem in 63 BCE, killing priests and defenders, desecrating the Temple, and making Judah part of the Roman Empire.

The Romans set up **Herod the Great** to rule most of Palestine. Along with killing a good number of his family and 45 of the Sanhedrin, Herod rebuilt much of Jerusalem, including the Temple, the city walls, and his great Antonia Fortress. The Roman governors retained ultimate control, however, and one of them, **Pontius Pilate**, authorized the crucifixion of Jesus in 33 CE, and a new religion was born. Hard times got harder under 'Caligula, who insisted on putting his statue in the Temple (a conflict solved by Caligula's death in 41 CE). Under Emperor Nero the provocations continued, and in 66 CE Roman procurator Florus stole a great deal of silver from the Temple. The Zealots led rioting in the streets of Jerusalem and the **Great Revolt** was on. The Romans brought in **General Vespasian**, who vanquished the Galilee before embarking on the Siege of Jerusalem. Titus took over when Vespasian was crowned Emperor following Nero's death, and on the Ninth of Av in 70 CE, the Romans took

Jerusalem, set the Temple on fire, and destroyed it, ending the Great Revolt.

In 132 CE what remained of the Jewish community rebelled again, led by **Bar-Kokhba** and in response to Emperor Hadrian's decision to build a shrine to Jupiter on the Temple site. Again the Romans prevailed, and in 135 CE Bar-Kokhba died, Rabbi Akiva was burned at the stake, Jerusalem was renamed Aelia Capitolina (after Aelius Hadrian), the temple to Jupiter was completed on the site of Solomon's Temple and the Jews were banished from Jerusalem.

Under the Byzantine Empire in the fourth century, Christianity flourished under **Constantine's** rule. His mother Helena visited Jerusalem identifying holy sites and funding shrines and churches (such as **The Church of the Holy Sepulchre**), and Jerusalem developed as a center for Christian pilgrimage. Except for a brief period of Persian rule (614-628), the city remained under Byzantine control until 638, when the Muslim Arabs took Jerusalem. In 688, the Arabs built the **Dome of the Rock** mosque on the Temple Mount.

In the 11th century under the Fatimid caliph al-Hakim, Muslim toleration of both Jews and Christians gave way to persecution, and the Seljuks, who took control of Jerusalem in 1071, weren't any more tolerant. Christian Europe responded with the **Crusades**, and in 1099 they gained Jerusalem, but didn't hold it long. In 1187 Saladin cruised in and Jerusalem remained in Muslim hands (under the Ayyubid and Mamluk dynasties till 1517 when the Ottoman Turks took over) for the next few centuries. The walls that now surround the Old City were built by **Suleiman the Magnificent** in 1534-40. Jews began emigrating from Europe to Jerusalem in the 1400s, and have made up a majority of Jerusalem's population since about 1876.

In 1917, the British occupied Jerusalem and the city was ruled by the **British Mandate** from 1923-1948. The Mandate period, not a happy time in Jerusalem's history, was full of Arabs rioting against Jews and British trying to stay out of the middle, thereby mucking it up even more. In 1948 the United Nations partitioned Palestine and designed an internationalized Jerusalem. This did not sit well with the Arabs, who rejected the resolution amid much bloodshed in the Old City streets. In 1949, Jerusalem was divided into Israeli and Jordanian sectors, and it remained' so till the Six Day War in of 1967, when Israel captured the entire city.

The **Old City** was under Jordanian control from 1949 to 1967. During this period the Jewish quarter was destroyed, but it has since been rebuilt. Since then Jerusalem has remained in Israel's hands, and in 1980 Israel named Jerusalem its official capital, an action bitterly resented by Arab nations and protested by innumerable terrorist acts. Starting in 1993, historic strides towards peace have been made between Israel, Jordan, and the PLO. Peace treaties have been signed and the process begun of hashing out the details for self-rule by the Palestinian Authority in the West Bank and the Gaza Strip.

The major sticky question of who gets ultimate control of Jerusalem has not been resolved. As dates get set for Israeli withdrawal from the west bank, new Jewish settlements pop up east of Jerusalem resulting in protests, anger, and more firmly entrenched positions on both sides. Still and all, the process seems to be moving forward, and Jerusalem's status ought to be decided in the near future.

ORIENTATION

Jerusalem is located some 2,440 feet up in the Judean Hills, 59 kilometers southeast of Tel Aviv. Thanks to its lofty elevation, the winters are colder and the summers less glaringly hot than other spots in Israel. The air feels clean, dry, and cool, which is refreshing in summer but less so in winter, when dryness isn't a salient characteristic.

It's a very hilly city, thanks to the Jordan River which has eroded the narrow ridges of **Mount Scopus** (2,684 feet) and **Mount of Olives** (2,652 feet) over the years. Built on light-colored limestone (Jerusalem Stone), the mounts are bisected by the **Tyropoeon Valley** and the valleys of **Bet Seita**, **Kidron**, and **Hinnom**.

BE CAREFUL!

East Jerusalem is considered safe to visit, as are Jericho and Bethlehem, but it's best not to be out on the streets there after dark. It's also a good idea to check the US Travel Advisory for their latest update.

As in Tel Aviv, street numbers include several buildings. Jerusalem is divided into three sections: the **Old City** to the southeast, with its Muslim, Jewish, Christian, and Armenian quarters, **West Jerusalem** (the New City), and **East Jerusalem**.

Most of Jerusalem's religious landmarks are located within the Old City walls: the **Western Wall** (or **Wailing Wall** as it's often known—a remnant of the supporting wall of the Second Temple), the gold-topped **Dome of the Rock** and silver-domed **al-Aqsa** mosques, the **Via Dolorosa** (believed to be the site of the original Stations of the Cross), and the **Church of the Holy Sepulchre**.

David Street is one of the main streets of the Old City, running eastward through the Christian quarter from Jaffa Gate through the shuk toward the Temple Mount. **El Wad** and **Khan ez-Zeit** are other major thoroughfares (in Old City terms this means crowded narrow alleys)

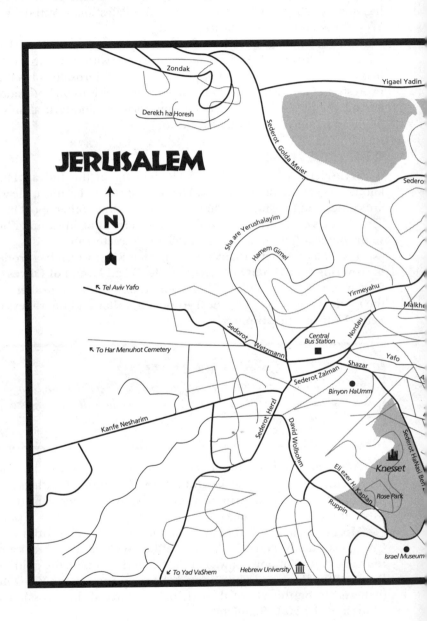

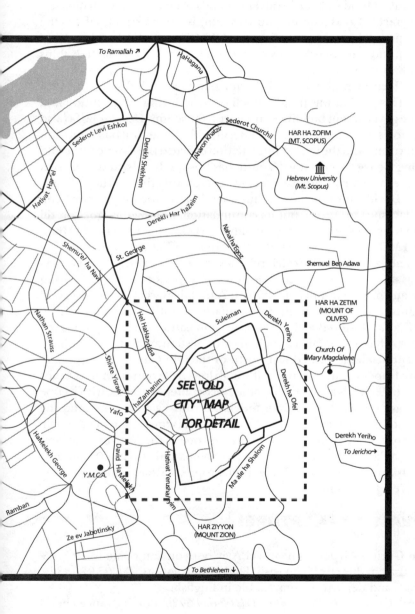

To Ramallah ↗

HaHagana

Sederot Levi Eshkol

Derekh Shekhem

Aharon Khatzir

Sederot Churchil

HAR HA ZOFIM
(MT. SCOPUS)

Hebrew University
(Mt. Scopus)

Hativat Har'el

Derekh i Har hazeim

Nahal ha Egoz

Shemu'el ha Navi

St. George

Shemuel Ben Adava

Nathan Strauss

Hel HaHandasa

Suleiman

Derekh Yeriho

HAR HA ZETIM
(MOUNT OF
OLIVES)

Shivte Yisrael

haZanhanim

Church Of
Mary Magdalene

SEE "OLD
CITY" MAP
FOR DETAIL

Derekh ha Ofel

Yafo

HaMelekh George

David HaMelekh

Hativat Yerushalayim

Derekh Yeriho

To Jericho →

Y.M.C.A.

Ma ale ha Shalom

Ramban

Ze ev Jabotinsky

HAR ZIYYON
(MOUNT ZION)

To Bethlehem ↓

running southward through the Muslim quarter from Damascus Gate, and also full of food stalls and souvenir stands. And in the Jewish quarter, **Jewish Quarter Road** (running north-south) is a main street. Jaffa is the most frequented gate, connecting the Old City to Jaffa Road in West Jerusalem, and Damascus comes next, connecting the Old City to Nablus Road in East Jerusalem.

West Jerusalem, built mostly by Jews, has expanded since the 19th century. This section was under Israeli control during the partition and has all the government buildings and Jewish museums. **Derekh Jaffa** (also called Yafo) is the central downtown street, with the central bus station on the western end and the tourist information office to the east near the Old City. **King George V** cuts north-south, has hostels, hotels, and the Great Synagogue, and turns into Keren Hayesod towards the southern end.

King David runs north from Plummer Square (the intersection with Keren Hayesod) to Agron, but its continuation, **Shlomzion**, goes on till Jaffa. On King David are some major landmarks like the **King David Hotel** and the **YMCA**, as well as most of the car rental offices in town. Off King George and Jaffa is the **Pedestrian Mall** section comprising Ben Yehuda as well as a few smaller streets like Luntz. Agrippas runs north of King George, and has the wonderful **Mahane Yehudah** market and lots of good restaurants. Yoel Salomon off Zion Square is another pedestrian mall, south of Jaffa, cluttered with restaurants and cafes. North of Jaffa is the Horkanos/Heleni HaMalka bunch of cafes, restaurants, and music bars.

East Jerusalem, located just north of the Old City, is the primarily residential modern Arab section, although Jews have outnumbered Arabs there since 1993. It is also the site of the **Rockefeller Museum**, with its fine archaeological collection. **Sultan Suleiman** runs east-west between the Old City and East Jerusalem. And **Nablus Road** is one of the main north-south thoroughfares, site of many hotels and one of the Arab bus stations. To the east, **Salah ed-Din** runs parallel to Nablus and also has restaurants and hotels, and to the west is **HaNevi'im**, Prophets' Road, which connects East to West Jerusalem.

ARRIVALS & DEPARTURES
By Air
Ben Gurion Airport is near Tel Aviv but you can come to or leave from Jerusalem directly if you wish. Flight information, *Tel. 03-972-3344*, on arrivals and departures is available in English.

El Al , *Center 1, 49 Yirmeyahu, Tel. 02-624-6726*, does advance check-in near Jaffa Road in Jerusalem. They're open Sunday-Thursday 1-10pm, Saturday one hour past sunset till 10pm.

By Bus

   Egged Central Bus Station, *Jaffa Road, Tel. 02-530-4704*, is way west of downtown. You'll need to take a city bus (or taxi) to or from your hotel unless you're staying at the Holiday Inn nearby. It's a big station, with buses departing to all over the country (including Ben Gurion Airport). The 405 double decker goes from/to Tel Aviv, direct, for NIS 17. Bus 444 goes to Eilat via the Dead Sea for NIS 54, and bus 392 also goes to Eilat for NIS 47, and transfers in Beersheva.

   Arab Bus Stations serve destinations within the Palestinian Authority. There is one station on Suleiman between Damascus and Herod's Gates for southern routes and another on Nablus serving northern routes. The 22 goes to Bethlehem when politics allows.

By Train

   The **Train Station**, *Remez Square, Tel. 03-693-7515 (Tel Aviv)*, is south of Moshe Yenim and Liberty Bell Park (buses 5, 6, 8, 14, 18, 21, 30, 31, and 48 all go there). Trains go to Tel Aviv Sunday-Thursday at 2:53pm, Friday at 11:56am (arriving two hours later) for NIS 17, continuing one hour more to Haifa for a total of NIS 33.5. Student discount is 25% off, and children 4-10 ride 50% off.

By Taxi (intercity sheruts)

   Nesher, *21 King George, Tel. 02-625-3233/5332*, goes to Ben Gurion for NIS 32, including pick-up at your door and two pieces of luggage. Reserve one day in advance.

GETTING AROUND TOWN

By Foot

   In the Old City you need to get around by foot, there are no other options. In the New City, you can walk around the downtown area if the bus fumes and hills don't get to you.

   There are **midrahov** (pedestrian walkways), and nice walking routes in the valleys and mounts surrounding the city as well.

By Bus

   In West and East Jerusalem there is a vast network of Egged city buses, and there's an invaluable and unwieldy Egged bus map you can buy from the station.

   There are Arab buses going to East Jerusalem destinations as well, but the routes aren't so complicated that a map is required.

By Taxi

There are also taxis, which are a good idea coming and going to/from East Jerusalem at night, but be aware their rates sky-rocket past midnight Sunday-Thursday and when the sun gets ready to set on Friday and the buses stop for Shabbat.

Aside from flagging one down, there are some companies you can call: **Ben-Yehuda Taxi**, *Herbert Samuel, Tel. 02-625-5555*; **David Citadel Taxi**, *Jaffa Gate, Tel. 02-628-4334*; **Ha-Bira**, *239 Jaffa, Tel. 02-538-9999*; **Jerusalem Taxi**, *4 HaHistadrut, Tel. 02-625-5233*; **Kessher-Aviv**, *12 Shammai, Tel. 02-625-7367*, off Yoel Salomon.

WHERE TO STAY
West Jerusalem Hotels

THE KING DAVID, *23 King David, Tel. 02-620-8888, Fax 02-620-8882, has 237 rooms (35 of which are suites), costing $228-$416 for a single and $248-$436 for a double, depending on the season and the type of room. Suites range from $356-$480.*

This is the Dan's best known hotel and the most prestigious in Jerusalem. For elegance and grandeur and all those good things, not to mention superb views and history-soaked ambiance, this is a one-of-a-kind place. The Garden rooms have patios, and are in great demand in summer. The decor was designed in 1931, with Italian marble lights and Victorian study lamps, and an amazing staircase on the fourth floor. While renovated and kept up, the original decor and tradition for the most part has been maintained. The Reading Room is especially lovely. The original parquet floor remains, and its big heavy table was borrowed for the signing of the Jordan/Israel Peace Treaty. Nixon, Ford, and Clinton have all stayed here. Behind the hotel is a lovely garden and terrace, and there is also a good fitness center (with sauna and steam room) that manages to keep the look of Old Jerusalem while incorporating all modern equipment.

Even if you don't stay here, you can take in the special feel with a drink in the dark woody bar room or hang out on the terrace and listen to classical music 5-7pm in summer (starting after Passover).

JERUSALEM HILTON, *7 King David, Tel. 02-621-1111, Fax 02-623-6844, US Tel. 800/445-8667, is a new hotel charging $185-$290 a single and $215-$340 a double, depending on grade of room and time of year.*

This spanking new hotel, just opened in January of 1998, boasts a fine Mamilla location near Yemin Moshe and the Old City, plus all the amenities of outdoor pool (heated in winter), steam room, saunas, jaccuzi, and tennis courts.

LAROMME JERUSALEM HOTEL, *Liberty Bell Park, 3 Jabotinsky, Tel.* *02-675-6666, Fax 02-675-6777, is across from the Jerusalem Theater. Rooms cost* *$131-$271 a single and $148-$288 for doubles, depending on season and type* *of room. Suites start at $265 in low and $385 in peak seasons.*

Their 294 air conditioned rooms all come with private bath, cable TV, phone and phone mail, mini-bar, and breakfast. The Maximum rooms are truly beautiful and elegant, with marble bathrooms, king-sized beds, and lots of nice touches, and the Regulars are luxurious as well. The double windows ensure quiet, the carpets are plush, and the Jerusalem Post is delivered to your room. The hotel provides Shabbat elevators and clocks, a synagogue, dairy and meat restaurants, outdoor pool (heated in winter), sauna and fitness room, and parking.

HOLIDAY INN CROWNE PLAZA, *Givat Ram, Tel. 02-658-8888, Fax* *02-651-4555, across from the central bus station, charges $178-$215 a single and* *$212-$249 a double, breakfast included, 15% service added on.*

The tallest building in Jerusalem is a landmark people negotiate by, though not one of the prettiest. With 21 floors, 397 rooms, 18 suites, and a business center, it makes up in convenience what it lacks in charm, especially if you're attending a function at the Binayanei Hauma Convention Center across the street. The rooms, all air conditioned and with balconies, phone, TV, and bath, are pleasant and have good views. The building has gift shops and hairdressers, car rental, parking, and a bank. There's a pool, sauna, fitness equipment, tennis court, Kids Club, even miniature golf. Among their loads of restaurants, Kohinoor Kosher Indian restaurant attracts most notice. The hotel is about five minutes from City Center (by bus) just across the way from the central bus station, their free shuttle bus goes to and from Jaffa Gate Sunday-Thursday 9am-6pm.

DAN PEARL JERUSALEM, *Zahal Square, Tel. 02-622-6666, Fax 02-* *622-6600, is just 300 meters from Jaffa Gate, facing David's Citadel and Mount* *Zion. The 34 guest rooms cost $144-$200 a single and $164-$220 a double, while* *the suites range from $240-$650, all depending on the month and view, plus 15%* *service charge, breakfast included. Time shares available.*

This luxury extravaganza opened January 1996 with the hottest of locations, where West Jerusalem meets the Old City. Beyond their fully accessorized rooms and suites, the Pearl has an indoor pool, health club, jacuzzi, steam room, sauna and massage. There are a variety of restaurants, coffee shops, and bars, plus room service, a synagogue, a mikveh, laundry and dry cleaning, outlets for taxis, travel agencies, galleries, gift shops, and an underground parking lot with valet service. There's even a multi-purpose amphitheater, and a glass roofed atrium. More a city than a standard hotel, the Pearl sits as close to the Old City as a hotel can get and still be in West Jerusalem.

RADISSON MORIAH PLAZA, *39 Keren Hayesond, Tel. 02-569-5695, Fax 02-623-2411, has 292 rooms and eight suites on 10 floors, costing $140-$200 for a single and $175-$270 a double.* The rooms all have heat/air conditioning, direct-dial phone, cable TV, and are fairly nice and big, but they don't compare with those in the Laromme. The hotel offers parking, a rooftop pool with sun deck, a health club, synagogue, and babysitter and doctor on call.

KING SOLOMON HOTEL, *32 King David, Tel. 02-569-5555, Fax 02-624-1774, charges from $84-$181 a single and $98-$194 a double, based on season and room grade; breakfast is included, but the rates are subject to 15% service charge. In the US, call 800-345-8569 for information or reservations.*

There's an elegant lobby and 150 pleasant rooms, all with air conditioning, cable TV, mini fridge, and direct-dial phone. The restaurants here are all glatt kosher, and the pool (open in summer) overlooks the hills of Judea. Newly renovated, the hotel is quite sedate.

MITZPEH RAMAT RACHEL, *Talpiot district, Tel. 02-670-2555, Fax 02-673-3155, is a kibbutz to south of Jerusalem (bus 7 goes there), with rooms for $152 a single and $174 a double, breakfast included.*

They have 93 rooms, all with air conditioning, radio, phone, TV, and bath. They've many recreational facilities, such as a swimming pool (heated in winter), water slide, sauna, fitness room, and tennis courts. In addition, there's a synagogue, guided tours showing kibbutz life, and a museum with 1948 War exhibits. The guest house closes for one month out of the year for maintenance—check for exact dates.

THE SHERATON, *47 King George, Tel. 02-629-8666, Fax 02-623-1667, is set a bit from the street overlooking the green of Independence Park. They charge $143 a single and $153 a double, breakfast and 15% service included.*

The 300 rooms and suites have all the usual five-star amenities like cable TV and direct-dial phone and the hotel provides restaurants, sauna, and outdoor pool. They're comfortable and large with big balconies, and red roses grace the bathrooms. Next to Henry Wolf Park and across from the Great Synagogue, it's about a 10 minute walk from Jaffa Street.

JERUSALEM TOWER, *23 Hillel, Tel. 02-620-9209, Fax 02-625-2167, charges $100-$115 a single and $120-$150 a double, breakfast included.*

Their 120 rooms with TV and phone are small and tidy, neither crummy nor fancy.

KINGS HOTEL, *60 King George, Tel. 02-620-1201, Fax 02-620-1211, is a big white block of a hotel with cubit balconies on one side. Just next to the Great Synagogue, the Kings Hotel has 217 rooms, all with air conditioning, bath, radio, and phone (TV and mini-bars available for the asking), for $115 a single and $145 for doubles, breakfast included, plus 15% service charge.*

The hotel has a synagogue, Shabbat elevators, and a variety of kosher eateries. It's a friendly, helpful place, and very quiet. Built in '54, opened in '56, and renovated in '88, they clearly try to keep it nice. The rooms are pleasant, but you should specify one with a balcony. There's a piano bar in the lobby (from 7:30pm) and a sun terrace. It's a 15 minute walk to the Old City, and 10 to Jaffa Street.

HOTEL TIRAT BAT-SHEVA, *42 King George, Tel. 02-623-2121, Fax 02-624-0697, has 70 rooms for $66-$110 a single and $88-$144 a double, breakfast and service charge included.*

A hotel for 30 years, there's a pleasant lounge, and the rooms have twin beds, desk, phone, radio, TV, and bath. It's a clean, solid hotel across the street from Rondo Park, in between mid-range and luxury.

THE PARADISE, *4 Wolfson, Tel. 02-655-8888, Fax 02-652-5521, charges $90-$1116 a single and $110-$140 a double.*

The hotel has pleasant, attractive rooms, swimming pools (inside and out), tennis courts and connecting rooms for families. It's a 10 minute walk from the Knesset and the Israel Museum, and 10 minutes by bus from city center.

✗ THE YMCA 3 ARCHES HOTEL, *26 King David, Tel. 02-569-2692, Fax 02-623-5192, has 56 rooms that cost $103 for a single, $126 a double, and $161 a triple, breakfast included.*

Located in one of the more remarkable buildings in Jerusalem, this not your run-of-the-mill YMCA. Across the street from the King David and set off by its magnificent 152 feet high granite tower, the reception area is quite grand, and the rooms are small but beautiful, with marble-topped desks and more. The hotel has a swimming pool, tennis courts, squash courts, and a fitness room, a fine coffee shop and restaurant, and a feel of quiet, simple elegance. They also have occasional evenings of Arab and Jewish Folklore—call *Tel. 02-624-7281* for information.

THE WINDMILL HOTEL, *3 Mendele, Tel. 02-566-3111, Fax 02-561-0964, has 133 rooms with breakfast, with prices for singles $85-$100, and $95-$120 for doubles. During Passover and Sukkot reservations must be made for half-board at $145 a single and $170 a double, 15% service charge added to all rates.*

All the rooms have air conditioning, direct-dial phones, cable TV, and bath or shower. They are adequate but a little dingy and drab. The hotel has parking, a Shabbat elevator, a synagogue, and a sun deck. On a side street off Keren Hayesod, it's fairly quiet while still near Liberty Bell Park. They pride themselves on their traditional religious atmosphere, and offer special Bar Mitzvah packages. They welcome children and have a Family Plan, providing babysitting and a doctor on call.

PARK PLAZA HOTEL, *2 Wolfson, Tel. 02-652-8221, Fax 02-652-8423, is off Herzl. Rooms cost $109 a single and $120 a double, breakfast included, 15% service charge added.*

Another in a series of big modern hotels, their 217 rooms are nice and roomy, with couch and sitting area, phone and TV. The hotel, a 10 minute walk from the Knesset, provides a synagogue, parking, and for families, baby sitting and a doctor on call.

THE HOLYLAND HOTEL, *Bayit Vagan, Tel. 02-643-7777, Fax 02-643-7744, charges $90-$100 a single and $100-$120 a double, breakfast included, plus 15% service charge.*

This hotel is not close to anything except their over-hyped Second Temple replica. There are 115 rooms, with phone and TV. They have tennis courts and a pool, miniature golf and shuffle board, but are a good drive and irregular bus service (#21) away from the city of Jerusalem. There are better, friendlier accommodations available in the city for less money.

THE NOTRE DAME OF JERUSALEM CENTER, *opposite New Gate, Tel. 02-627-9111, Fax 02-627-1995, is in the grand complex by the striking Notre Dame Statue. Rooms cost $79 a single and $98 a double, including breakfast. Special prices and winter discounts sometimes apply.*

Along with the cathedral and the location, this Vatican-owned hospice offers 150 adequate but bland rooms. Built for French pilgrims in 1885, the building incurred heavy damage during the fighting in 1948 and became an Israeli bunker in no-man's land. By 1978 Notre Dame was repaired and opened to the public, and now it functions as a pilgrims' hospice.

HOTEL PALATIN, *4 Agrippas, Tel. 02-623-1141, Fax 02-625-9323, is a family-run hotel one block up from King George, in the center of West Jerusalem; they charge $85 a single and $89 a double year round, including a big breakfast.*

The 28 rooms are cozy, with cable TV, radio, phone, shower, air conditioning, heat, and hairdryer (one room has a balcony as well). The owners run it with care, decorate it with modern art, and maintain a home-like feel. From a Jaffa Street bus you can get off at King George and walk a couple blocks, and the #9 bus comes even closer.

MENORAH HOTEL, *24 King David, Tel. 02-625-3311, Fax 02-624-2860, during regular season the rates are $58 per single and $78 per double, breakfast included.*

The Menorah boasts a "homely atmosphere" and they aren't far off, especially the 64 drab rooms in basic brown (all of which have the standard private bath, phone, and heating). Some of the rooms have air conditioning, and TVs can be hired. It's got a great location however, just across from the King David Hotel and close to the Old City and the Great Synagogue. They've got their own synagogue as well as laundry service, parking and a Shabbat elevator. Credit cards not accepted.

JERUSALEM INN GUEST INN, *7 Horkanos, Tel. 02-625-2757, Fax 02-625-1297, has 22 rooms that are small but with balconies, and marble floors, costing $62-$68 a single and $76 a double (breakfast costs $4 extra). There's also* *a dorm with beds for $14, plus $2 for breakfast for youths aged 28 years and younger.*

Under the same fine management as the Jerusalem Inn Hostel, but is a notch or two higher in quality and price. There's a lovely lounge with white walls and dark wood, with jazz or classical music on Thursdays. Very clean, it's on a quiet street near fine restaurants and nightlife, and seven minutes from the Old City.

RON HOTEL, *44 Jaffa, Tel. 02-622-3122, Fax 02-625-0707, charges $77 a single and $82 a double, breakfast included. There is a 15% service charge added on, but if you present your Open Road guide they will waive it.*

This is a beautiful old building that unfortunately hasn't been kept up. The 22 rooms are up the circular staircase, but they are just okay, with TV, phone, and shower/toilet. Founded by Warshavsky in 1926, Menachem Begin made his first speech after coming out from the Underground from their balcony on March 8, 1948. It's centrally located in West Jerusalem, but the hotel isn't all it could be or all it once was.

HOTEL MERCAZ HABIRA, *4 Havatzelet, Tel. 02-625-5754, Fax 02-623-3513, is across from Zion Square. They have 30 rooms, costing $50 a single, $80 a double with shower, breakfast included.*

This hotel has been newly remodeled, with an entrance of white marble and a new elevator. The quiet rooms are spacious, all have phones, cable TV, private toilets, some with shower and others with bath, and many come with balconies. In addition, up on the roof is a wrap-around patio for lounging and relaxed city viewing.

BEIT SHMUEL, *6 Shama Tel. 02-620-3456, Fax 02-620-3467, is just off King David. The prices depend on the season and number of people per room, all include breakfast, and the maximum stay is two weeks. Singles are $70, doubles $76, and triples $102, single sex only.*

Run by the World Union for Progressive Judaism in the Hebrew Union College complex, most meals cost $13, while Shabbat dinner is $16.

HOUSE 57, *57 Midbar-Sinai, Tel. 02-581-9944, Fax 02-532-2929, are Guest Houses, charging $50 a single, $72 a double, breakfast included.*

This two-story stone building for up to 14 guests with views of Jerusalem and the Judean Hills is in Givat Hamivtar, a residential neighborhood above Ramat Eshkol shopping center, 10 minutes from downtown.

HOTEL ZION, *10 Dorot Rishonim, Tel. 02-625-9511, Fax 02-625-7585, is just next to Rimon Cafe—walk up Luntz off Jaffa and bear right; they've 26 rooms that cost $44-$65 a single and $61-$74 a double, breakfast included.*

Located right on the *midrahav* (pedestrian walkway) and with a pleasant lounge/bar area, but no elevator, the rooms are clean and fresh, and some have balconies overlooking all the cafes below, while all come equipped with TV, phone, and radio, some with showers and some with baths. There's an attractive breakfast room with white arches and windows over the square.

HOTEL GOLDEN JERUSALEM, *40 Jaffa, Tel. 02-623-3074, Fax 02-623-3513, has 21 rooms, at $50 a single and $70 a double ($64 when slow), with continental breakfast.*

Located in the thick of downtown. The rooms are cheery and clean, not fancy but good for the price; all have heat and cable TV, and some have phones, air-conditioning, and balconies. This used to be the offices of marriage and divorce under the Chief Rabbi, but since 1992 the only activities in those departments have been behind closed doors. The location couldn't be more central, but some travelers have complained of noise off the street and from other guests.

SAINT ANDREW'S, *past the foot of King David, Tel. 02-673-2401, Fax 02-673-1711, is near the railway station and Bethlehem Road. Singles are $43, doubles $65 and triples $83, Scottish breakfast included. There are discounts for seven day stays.*

The hospice is a building of exceptional beauty and warmth, with blue tiles, green plants, and all the best of Scottish hospitality. Set on top of the ridge over Hinnom Valley near the British Consulate, Saint Andrew's Scots Memorial Church and Hospice was opened in 1930 in memory of the Scots who died fighting the Turks in WWI. With 14 rooms and 34 beds, the hospice welcomes all and provides comfortable singles, doubles, and family rooms. Every Sunday at 10am the church has service, followed by tea and coffee in the lounge, and there are often vocal concerts, *Tel. 02-561-2342*, held at night. It's centrally heated, has a cozy lounge, and stunning garden. In addition to the concerts, there's Scottish country dancing the first Saturday of every month. Coffee and tea are always available, and credit cards are accepted.

KAPLAN HOTEL, *1 Havatzelet, Tel. 02-625-4591, Fax 02-623-6245, is just off Jaffa in downtown. They have 16 rooms that rent for $50 a single and $60 a double, breakfast not included.*

The rooms are comfy and small, with phone, TV, art on the wall, and clean bathrooms. Some have noisy balconies as well. The hotel is atop a nice old circular stone staircase, has been run by the Kaplan family for three generations, and has a pleasant feel. You can use the washing machine for free, and should make reservations in advance.

ROSARY SISTERS CONVENT GUEST HOUSE, *14 Agron, Tel. 02-625-8529, Fax 02-623-5581, is right next to the US Consulate. They've 22 rooms, at $30 a single and $60 a double, breakfast included.*

Lovely and clean though without frills. They all have phones, rugs, and charm. To gain admittance you have to be buzzed through two large and imposing doors, with the outside bell positioned for the very tall. The Rosary Sisters are dedicated to the education of Arab girls; the mother house was built in 1892 and the church, which holds daily masses for pilgrims and locals, was built in 1937. There's a curfew of 10pm.

GOOD MORNING JERUSALEM, *Binayanei Hauma Convention Center, Tel. 02-623-3459, Fax 02-625-9330*, will set you up in someone's home in a nice neighborhood. The reservation center in the Convention Center is in the behind the central bus station, open Sunday-Thursday 9am-5:30pm, Friday 9am-1pm. For last minute service at night, call *Tel. 05-051-3989*. They'll ask you some questions and match you up, or you can fax them your particulars, including the number of people, grade of accommodations (2-4), dates, and credit card number and expiration date. The houses and locations vary but the prices are set, depending on the grade (2-4) of the place. Singles go for $40-$55 and doubles are $50-$75, plus $13 for an extra bed.

MAMILLA'S VILLAGE – BED & BREAKFAST INN, *4 King David, Tel. 02-625-0075, Fax 02 625-1820, can be reached with bus 6, 13, 18, 20, or 21. There are 10 rooms costing $45 a single, $54 a double, and $153 for a room of six beds, breakfast included.*

The private rooms are pleasant, though their balconies presently overlook a hotel construction site. The hostel room is nicer than most with three wood bunks, heat, a table, bathroom, and balcony. It's a lovely old building with nice tiles, it's close to Jaffa Road, and there's no curfew. Visa/Mastercard accepted.

HOTEL ERETZ ISRAEL, *51 King George, Tel. 02-624-5071, just past Ha-Rav Avid'a–the dilapidated path and signs do in fact lead to this homey little hotel with six rooms that go for $25 a single and $40 a double.*

A small, family-run hotel, you get coffee/tea and cakes in the morning and warm attention and personal loving care from the Barmatz couple round the clock. The rooms are not fancy but they are clean, and though the bathrooms are down the hall, each room has a sink. Eretz Israel, started by Josuf Barmatz' father, has been in the family for 70 years and in its present location for 40. It's a homey place, and since it's off the road there's no traffic noise. Run by an adorable old couple who speak some English as well as Yiddish, Hebrew, Arabic, and German, their sitting room feels like your grandmother's old living room. Midnight curfew.

West Jerusalem Hostels

LOUISE WATERMAN-WISE HOSTEL, *8 Rehov Hapisga, Bayit Vegan, Tel. 02-642-0990, Fax 02-642-3362, is an IYHA off the beaten track. Beds cost $23 for members, and $21 for non-members.*

They have 300 beds, as well as a sports facility, kitchen, and park. You can get there by bus 18, 20, 40, or 39, but once you're there in what's generally considered a fine hostel, you're not near much.

BERNSTEIN YOUTH HOSTEL, *1 Keren Hayesod, Tel. 02-625-8286, Fax 02-624-5875, is a centrally located IYHA in a century-old stone building. Open Sunday-Thursday 7-9am and 3pm-midnight, Friday 7-9am and 2pm-midnight (curfew midnight), the 15 rooms are clean, and some have showers in the room. A bed (five per room) costs $21, big breakfast included.*
There's a cafe, and a TV room, and it's across from a Supersol and King's Hotel. Transport there is easy on buses 7, 8, 9, 14, 31, 32, and 48.

JERUSALEM FOREST HOSTEL, *Mount Herzl, Tel. 02-641-0060, Fax 02-641-3522, has 140 beds for $21 each.*
This IYHA is beautifully situated on the western slopes of Mount Herzl with tremendous views of the Judean Hills. They've a sports facility and swimming pool as well. Not easily reached by bus, you'll need to taxi or drive here.

HADAVIDKA GUEST HOUSE AND YOUTH HOSTEL, *67 Hanevi'im, Tel. 02-538-4555, Fax 02-538-8790, is in Liberty Square. A dorm bed costs $20.50 ($18.50 for members), a single is $40.50, and a quad is $94, breakfast included.*
A new three-story building just near Jaffa and King George streets, with 60 rooms of two-six beds each, all with cupboards, desk, heat/air conditioning, and private bath. There's a cafeteria and rec room with a TV, and no curfew. To bus there, 27, 34, 35, 36, and 39 stop on Hanevi'im and the 3, 18, 20, 21, and 23 stop nearby on Jaffa.

JERUSALEM INN HOSTEL, *6 HaHistadrut, Tel. 02-625-1294, has dorm beds for $16 and private rooms for $38 a single, $48 a double.*
Perhaps the finest hostel in West Jerusalem, it was renovated in 1997, and is safe and quiet with dorms, private rooms, and clean bathrooms. The attentive, friendly, care of the manager makes staying here a special experience. There are heaters and fans, a bulletin board, with a deposit you can have a key, and you can wash or dry laundry for $5 each. It's right near all the cafes and all the bus lines of the new city and just minutes away from the old.

EIN KAREM YOUTH HOSTEL, *Ma'ayan Street, Tel. 02-641-6282, is an IYHA that's away from the center. A dorm bed goes for $11.*
Up in the hills and near Mary's Spring in pretty Ein Kerem, bus 17 gets you there, and it's not far from Yad Vashem. They have 100 beds in a charming old stone building, and there's a TV room as well.

East Jerusalem Hotels
THE AMERICAN COLONY HOTEL, *Nablus Road, Tel. 02-627-9777, Fax 02-627-9779, is a 10 minute walk from Damascus Gate. Superior and Deluxe rooms cost $115-$230 a single and $175-$275 a double, while suites go for $350-$380. Children younger than seven are free, those between seven-twelve*

can stay in their parents' room for $20, while additional adults are $40, breakfast included, and half board available.

The American Colony more than lives up to its reputation for beauty and elegance. The 98 rooms, some modern and some traditional, vary in form and decor depending on their location in the original or added wing. The old wing rooms are wonderful, with Turkish carpets, old stones, and painted ceilings. And the suites in this wing are enormous and lovely and opulent. One of the most fabulous hotels in Jerusalem, this former Pasha palace oozes ambiance and history. From the Cellar Bar done in Mid-East weaves to the verdant oasis of the Palm House Garden, the attention to detail is impressive.

There are the usual room amenities of air-conditioning, direct-dial phones, cable TV, and hotel facilities like parking and a pool. Then there are the unusual pleasures of star-watching (the long list of famous guests includes Ingrid Bergman, T. E. Laurence, Graham Greene, and Joan Baez to name a few) or reading up on the history that started with the Pasha in 1860. If it's in your budget it's worth a stay, and reservations a month ahead are suggested.

HYATT REGENCY, *32 Lehi, Mount Scopus, Tel. 02-533-1234, Fax 02-581-5947, has prices ranging from $126-$212 a single and $139-$235 a double, including breakfast and service charge.*

A remarkable example of modern luxury seven-level architecture high atop Mount Scopus, the hotel is landscaped into the hill and the main entrance and reception is on the sixth floor. Termed a "Conference Resort," it caters to business and tourism alike. There are 501 rooms of differing grades depending on view and luxury. They are pleasant rooms, with writing desk, central heat/air conditioning, and mini-bar, and the private balconies of Deluxe rooms have magnificent views of the Old City. The lounge is outstanding, with leather settees, a fountain, and modern sculpture, and the level of sumptuous luxury and convenience is unsurpassed, especially compared to the prices at the King David.

The restaurants are superb though pricy (Valentino's is well-known for its Italian cuisine, and costs NIS 85 for all-you-can-eat), and the Castel lounge menu features international cuisines from $4.50-$13. The Jerusalem Spa is enormous and state-of-the-art, with fitness machines, trainers, and Dead Sea treatments. There's tennis, a swimming pool, and massage as well. There's a synagogue, Shabbat clock, and elevator. The Orient Express Night Club is a fun disco with a touch of elegance, and free shuttles transverse the route from hotel to Jaffa Gate to King George.

SAINT GEORGE'S CATHEDRAL PILGRIM GUEST HOUSE, *20 Nablus, Tel. 02-627-7232, Fax 02-628-2575, is on the corner of Salah Eddin about eight minutes from Damascus Gate. A single is $120-$135, a double costs $160-$175, and breakfast is included.*

It's a beautiful stone complex of rooms off the old cathedral and courtyard. There are 22 comfy rooms, all with phones and enormous bathrooms, Jerusalem stone walls and floors, in a house that has offered lodgings to travelers since the early 1900s. The Anglican Cathedral, built in 1898 in gothic style, has services daily. The lounge is full of inviting old chairs, the cloistered olive tree garden is especially lovely, and there's a small archaeological museum as well. They recommend you be in by 11pm, but there's no curfew as such.

PILGRIMS PALACE HOTEL, *Sultan Suleiman near Damascus Gate, Tel. 02-627-2135, Fax 02-626-4658, costs $70-$110 a single and $80-$130 for doubles, breakfast included.*

There are 100 spacious air conditioned rooms with private facilities and phone, and TV. The lobby has more comfy couches than you can shake a stick at, plus inexpensive drinks and snacks, and nice views of the old city. The restaurant serves Middle Eastern cuisine, and the gift shop sells local handicrafts.

MERIDIAN HOTEL, *5 Ali Ibn Abitaleb, Tel. 02-656-3175, Fax 02-628-5214, charges $52-$85 for a single, and $74-$125 a double, breakfast included, 15% service charge added.*

Behind the square facade with balconies is a somewhat empty mid-sized hotel. The 72 rooms all have air conditioning, phone, radio and the ubiquitous '50s furniture.

CHRISTMAS HOTEL, *1 Ali Ibn Abitaleb, off Salah Eddin, Tel. 02-628-2588, Fax 02-689-4417, has 24 rooms for $55-$72 a single and $70-$102 a double, no credit cards accepted.*

It's neither fancy nor grotty, and the rooms are small and clean, with phone and shower or bath. They've a pleasant lounge and garden.

HOTEL 7 ARCHES, *Mount of Olives, Tel. 02-627-7555, Fax 02-627-1319, charges $90 for singles and $110 for doubles, breakfast included.*

A stunning hotel with a winning view of the Old City. While the elegant lobby and Bistro are decked out in sumptuous tones, the rooms (200) are a bit drab, though comfortable, with direct-dial phone, air conditioning, and TV. It's close to the Old City, but not an easy walk.

PILGRIMS INN HOTEL, *Rashid, Tel. 02-628-4883, Fax 02-626-4658, is on the street east of and parallel to Salah Eddin, near Herod's Gate. Singles cost $55-$75 and doubles are $65-$110, breakfast included.*

It's a family-oriented hotel with 16 air conditioned rooms done in 50s style decor, but not because it's in vogue. They are open most of the year but are usually closed in January.

AMBASSADOR HOTEL, *Nablus, Tel. 02-582-8515, Fax 02-582-8202, is beyond the American Colony, up the Scopus hill, charging $85 a single and $100 a double, breakfast included and 15% service charge added.*

The rooms are nice enough, with phone, TV, and large clean bathrooms. The lounge has an engaging view, the terrace is pleasant, and there's a restaurant and bar.

CAPITOLINA HOTEL, *29 Nablus, Tel. 02-627-7964, Fax 02-627-6301, rented from the YMCA Jerusalem, has 57 rooms with 113 beds at $69 a single and $92 a double, full breakfast included, and 15% service added on.*

Rooms are comfortable, clean, simple, and small, with phone, radio, heat and air conditioning; some have lovely balconies. The dining room on the fifth floor has a swell view of the city; the YMCA sports facility, Tel. 02-627-1793, with swimming pool, gym, and squash courts, can be used by guests. This big building tends to be used mostly be pilgrims, and there is no curfew.

HOLY LAND HOTEL EAST, *6 Rashid, Tel. 02-628-4846, Fax 02-628-0265, near Herod's Gate, they charge $70 a single and $90 a double, breakfast included, plus 15% service charge.*

Not to be confused with the rip-off Holy Land with the temple model, their 105 rooms have private bath, heat, and phone, and most have balconies. The rooms are a bit chintzy, but adequate and very clean. The hotel provides parking as well as laundry, room service, and a friendly staff.

NATIONAL PALACE HOTEL, *4 Azzahra, Tel. 02-627-3273, Fax 02-628-2139, is on the street at the end of Rashid and Salah Eddin. They charge $65 a single and $90 a double, breakfast included.*

There are 105 small, comfortably pleasant rooms with small clean bathrooms, direct-dial phone, and attractive lamps. Not the promised palace, but they do have marble stairs, nice wall trim, and lots of European groups.

RITZ HOTEL, *corner of Ibn Batuta and Ibn Khaldoun, Tel. 02-627-3233, Fax 02-628-6768, has 103 rooms with heating and air conditioning, for $70 a single and $85 a double.*

For your money you get breakfast, parking, and a snooty attitude.

AZZAHRA HOTEL, *13 Azzahra, Tel. 02-628-2447, Fax 02-628-2415, near the National Palace Hotel, costs $60 a single and $80 a double.*

The fifteen rooms come with phone, heat, air conditioning, and big gorgeous bathrooms with bidet and tub. This century-old stone building is on a quiet side street off Azzahra, with lovely stone walls and steps, and tall ceilings. Three of the rooms have balconies, but no credit cards are accepted.

JERUSALEM HOTEL, *Nablus Road, Tel./Fax 02-628-3282, is on the road across from Damascus Gate, charging $49-$55 a single and $75 a double, rate including breakfast.*

A very lovely place, with 13 rooms, big windows, curved walls, stone and tile floors, and lovely Arabic touches. A lot of care has obviously gone into bringing out the beauty of this old 19th century stone house, and the result is charm, comfort, and ambiance. There is a small Arabic style restaurant with rugs and cushions, and entertainment here Thursday and Saturday nights as well. The only drawback is its proximity to the Arab bus station, with its noise and fumes.

MOUNT SCOPUS HOTEL, *Mount Scopus, Tel. 02-582-8891, Fax 02-582-8825, has singles for $55 and doubles for $74, breakfast included, 15% service charge added.*

This large boxy hotel has 65 comfortable rooms with private bath, phone, TV, patterned spreads and old lamps, and the rooms facing south have great views from the balconies. It's ugly outside but pleasant and friendly within, and you get a lot for your money. Bus #23 stops out front.

NEW REGENT HOTEL, *20 Azzahra, Tel. 02-628-4540, Fax 02-626-4023, has singles that cost $40-$50 and doubles for $50-$70, breakfast included.*

It's a small hotel with 26 sparsely furnished rooms, all with heat, bath, and phone.

RIVOLI HOTEL, *3 Salah Eddin, Tel. 02-628-4871, Fax 02-627-4879, is half a block from Herod's Gate, with rooms for $40 a single and $60 a double.*

Its Persian carpeted lobby appears to be decorated straight out of the 50s. All 31 rooms are nice and spacious, and they've all got private baths and phones.

METROPOLE, *6 Salah Eddin, Tel. 02-628-2507, Fax 02-628-5134, is just up from the Rivoli, with 29 rooms that cost $35 a single and $60 a double, breakfast included.*

The management is rather unfriendly, so this isn't your best bet for a pleasant haven.

NEW METROPOLE, *8 Salah Eddin, Tel. 02-628-3846, Fax 02-627-7485, near Herod's Gate, has 25 rooms that cost $30 a single and $60 a double, breakfast included.*

The rooms are fusty, dusty, and quaint, decorated in old-lady style, and some are graced with bird-dropping bedecked balconies.

East Jerusalem Hostels
THE PALM HOSTEL, *6 HaNevi'im, Tel. 02-627-3189, has dorm beds (4-10 a room) for NIS 18, and private rooms for NIS 80.*

The Palm has a pleasant sitting room and atmosphere despite the atrocious green trim, with old dilapidated sofas, nice stone walls, and tea and coffee (NIS 1). They offer tours to everywhere, have no lockers, but do have a safe. There's a furnace in reception, but that's the only heat in the house. This old building was constructed in the late 1800s and was one of the first built outside the old city walls. Buses 27 and 23 go there from the bus station.

RAMSES HOSTEL, *20 Hanevi'im, Tel. 02-627-1651, is just outside Damascus Gate, the last stop for bus 27. It's got private rooms for NIS 60 a single and NIS 80 a double. The dorm is $10 each but is only for groups of six.*

The Ramses has small basic rooms with high ceilings, very clean and quiet, and beautiful blue tile bathrooms. There's a lounge and TV room, hot showers and central location, laundry service for NIS 10, midnight curfew, and space to park outside.

THE NEW RAGHADAN HOSTEL, *HaNevi'im, Tel. 02-628-3348, opposite Damascus Gate, charges $5 a bed and $17 a private room.*

The prices are cheap, and you get what you pay for.

THE FAISAL HOSTEL, *4 HaNevi'im, Tel. 02-627-2492, near Damascus Gate, costs NIS 15 a bed, or NIS 9-11 in the outside room, and a private is NIS 60.*

The two main dorms have balconies and eight bunks squished together, while the two smaller rooms are roomier, without bunks or balconies. With washing machines, a kitchen with tea and coffee, and a big balcony, the Faisal is seedy, run down, and depressing. Reservations accepted.

THE CAIRO HOSTEL, *21 Nablus, Tel. 02-627-7216, near the American consulate and across from the mosque, is accessible from bus 27. A dorm bed costs NIS 15 and a private room (just a room with beds) is NIS 60.*

The Pink Panther greets you, and their six dorms, with 3-10 beds each, have tile floors and balconies overlooking the street. It's fairly clean, has a nice kitchen, free tea, luggage storage, and movies nightly. They organize trips to Masada, etc., and give travel information as well.

The Old City: Near the Damascus Gate (take bus 23 or 27)

For Old City hostels and hospices: the prices quoted apply for most of the year, but during Christmas the rates skyrocket at most hostels.

ARMENIAN CATHOLIC HOSPICE, *41 Via Dolorosa (third station), Tel. 02-628-4262, Fax 02-627-2123, has reopened. They charge $12 a dorm bed and $45 a private single, no breakfast.*

Inside you'll find beautiful wood furnishings and tile floors, quality mattresses and crisp linens. And all the rooms are properly appointed with TVs, phones, and hair dryers in the pristine bathrooms.

AUSTRIAN HOSPICE, *37 Via Dolorosa, Tel. 02-627-1466/3, Fax 02-627-1472, has dorm beds (8-12 per room, no bunks, one storage unit per bed) for $12, singles for $44, doubles for $68 per, and triples $96, two night minimum required. Prices include breakfast, and half board's available for $5 more. Get* *buzzed in one gate and then another, proceed up the stairs to the Madonna, and continue all the way up for the office. Write to POB 19600, 91194 Jerusalem.*

It's in a beautiful, well-kept building. The rooms are immaculately clean, the bathrooms are beautifully tiled, the ceilings arch loftily and serenely, and the doors shut firmly at 10pm, but keys are available with deposit. There is a lovely garden, and a beautiful view from the terrace. Staffed mostly by volunteers from Austria and Germany, you can apply to volunteer (stay at least one month, be 19 or older, cover your own airfare) for full board, lodging, and pocket money. There are lifts and wheelchair access, and if you want to be met at Lion's Gate to be helped with luggage, phone ahead.

ECCE HOMO CONVENT YOUTH HOSTEL & GUEST HOUSE, *Eastern Via Dolorosa, Tel. 02-622-7292, POB 19056, is just past Ecce Homo Arch, turn left on Via Dolorosa from El Wad coming from Damascus Gate. They've dorm beds for NIS 30 in the Youth Hostel, Guest House cubicles for $18 with breakfast, and private rooms for $30 a single and $55 a double, with breakfast.*

Bang the brass hand and the door mysteriously opens on another world, one of beautiful stone floors, columns, and lofty arching ceilings. The Youth Hostel and Guest House are separate and operate under separate rules, though the facilities look similar. They both have rows of little cubicles complete with bed, wardrobe, and sink, made semi-private with wooden walls and cloth curtains for doors. The Youth Hostel cubbie (for girls only) doesn't include breakfast, has a sitting area and kitchen, and heat in winter, a lockout from 10am-12pm, a curfew of 11pm, a maximum stay of 10 days, and no access to the Guest House section. In the Guest House, the cubicle arrangement (available to both men and women) and charmingly referred to as "boxes," includes breakfast and access to the beautiful terrace, has no lockout, but does share the 11pm curfew.

The Guest House prices do not include the 10% service tax. Reservations taken for Guest House only, no credit cards. Once you get past all these rules and distinctions you are left with a lovely, safe place. In the Jerusalem world of youth hostels, the cubicles give a sense of privacy and let you unpack and spread out a bit without costing much more than the dives. And there are lockers available at no extra cost.

HASHIMI HOSTEL, *73 Khan el-Zeit, Tel. 02-628-4410, is nearly across from Al-Arab. Dorm beds (only four-six beds in room) cost NIS 15, doubles are NIS 50-80, NIS 90 a triple, roof beds are NIS 10, and if you stay seven days, you get the eighth free.*

Each room, including the dorms, has its own toilet/shower, hot water 24 hours, and all appears fresh and quiet. Staying in the dorms, however, is no picnic. The bunk mattresses are on slabs of plywood that tilt and shift if you turn over or sit up, and the dorm toilets aren't the cleanest. There is a kitchen, and from the roof you have a great view of the mosque. Basel, the owner, is aiming at still more improvements to upgrade to two star quality. Right now the prices match the nearby hostels but the aura is different. You'll find it quieter, with lots of friends and family of the management rather than the frenetic college party atmosphere of some nearby hostels.

AL-ARAB HOSTEL, *Khan el-Zeit, Tel. 02-628-3537, has dorm beds (5-15 per room) for NIS 15, small private rooms for NIS 50, and roof mattresses in summer for NIS 11. Enter Damascus Gate, take street on right, and it's about 100 meters on the left.*

This place is chock-a-block with scraggly lounging backpackers. The walls are covered with summer of love style flowers. Entertainment includes hanging out with other travelers, comparing travel war stories, and nightly videos at 9pm. Clean showers, a kitchen, free tea, and a curfew of 1:30am. Tours offered to Masada, refugee camp, and more.

AL-AHRAM YOUTH HOSTEL, *Al-Wad, Tel. 02-628-0926, is left from the Damascus Gate, with dorm beds (five-six a room) for NIS 15 (NIS 18 with heat), and private rooms with shower, toilet, and balcony for NIS 60. Rooftop beds are NIS 10 (you'll need a sleeping bag in winter).*

This place is drab but not disgusting, they offer kitchen use, and have a midnight curfew. Treat it as a back-up if everything else is full.

BLACK HORSE HOSTEL, *28 Aqabat Darwish, Tel. 02-628-0328, has beds for NIS 13 and private rooms with toilet and shower down the hall for NIS 60. It's near Via Dolorosa Street #14, turn left towards Herod's Gate at the Black Horse sign, or better yet enter the city at Herod's Gate and walk 400 meters.*

A relatively new addition to the lodgings scene, with dorm beds 12 to a room, it's close quarters but very clean. There's a bar/coffee shop with beautiful pine tables and a happy hour (7-8:30pm) with Maccabees two for NIS 10. It also has a bedouin tent hang-out popular with the young and groovy crowd, with rugs, pillows, shoes off and hushed tones. It's a neat place to feel with-it and special and compare prices with other travelers. Amazing big, clean bathroom. The private rooms, in a separate building, have many nice touches, and the large bathrooms are spotless. There's no curfew, and there is a washing machine, TV, tours and information.

Inside the Old City: Near the Jaffa Gate (take bus 13, 6, or 20)
GLORIA HOTEL, *33 Latin Patriarchate, Tel. 02-628-2431, Fax 02-628-2401, is left on Latin Patriarch after entering Jaffa Gate. Rooms for $60 a single and $75 a double, breakfast included. No credit cards, no curfew.*

Inside you'll find a clean tile entrance and vaulted faux stained glass windows. Most guests are from France so you can practice your French with them or fall back on English. The rooms are standard.

CHRIST CHURCH GUEST HOUSE, *just inside Jaffa Gate to the right, Tel. 02-627-7727, Fax 02-627-7730, charges $40 a single, $72 a double, $84 a triple, and $96 per quad, less during regular and low season, more during Jewish holidays, breakfast included, credit cards not accepted.*

There's an old wing and new, and both are very nice and very, very clean, with a beautiful dining room, stone arches, and sweeping lines. Tours include Life & World of Jesus, Roots of the Faith, and unmarried couples can't stay together.

LUTHERAN HOSPICE GUEST HOUSE, *Saint Mark's, Tel. 02-628-5105, Fax 02-628-5107, is in the same complex as the Lutheran Youth Hostel, but upscale. They charge $40 a single and $66 a double during peak season, less during regular and low, full breakfast and 5% service charge included, no credit cards accepted.*

The rooms are quite nice, and it's best to book ahead as they are often full.

LARK HOTEL, *8 Latin Patriarchate, Tel. 02-628-3620, is just up the road from the Gloria and next to the Latin Patriarch Church. They charge $30 a single and $60 a double, with bathrooms in each room and continental breakfast included.*

This is a small mediocre place with an 11pm curfew. Downstairs an Armenian Restaurant run by the same family has funky grottoesque decor, chicken soup that tastes Campbells all the way with cinnamon on top, and 17% VAT on top of the low prices.

THE MARONITE CONVENT, *25 Maronite Convent Street, Tel. 02-628-2158, Fax 02-627-2821, has 20 beautiful stone rooms with vaulted ceilings and clean bathrooms for $29 a single and $50 a double, breakfast included.*

The building, purchased in 1893 by the Bishop (and later the Patriarch) Elias Hoyek, had been a hospital before Hoyek took it over. Recently restored, there's the chapel, the Maronite parochial church of Jerusalem, and a section that's been turned into a home for pilgrims. The bedrooms are appealing, the chapel is lovely, and the courtyard through the stone arches gleams in the sun. The only catch is the 10pm curfew.

NEW IMPERIAL HOTEL, *inside Jaffa Gate, Tel. 02-628-2261, Fax 02-627-1530, has singles for $25 and doubles for $40.*

Dingy but clean, with vaulted arches that have seen better days, it's open 6am-midnight, after which ringing the bell will get you in.

LUTHERAN YOUTH HOSTEL, *Saint Mark's, Tel. 02-628-5105, Fax 02-628-5107, not far past Citadel, has dorm beds for NIS 24.*

Though the dorms are large (40 beds in the girls' dorm, 20 in the boys'), they are great all the same, with high vaulted stone ceilings, and private nooks and partitions separating the bunks. There's an age limit of 32, but it's only enforced during crowded peak times. With a nice kitchen, lockers, and pleasant garden, it's spotlessly clean, safe and well-tended.

There is a 9am-noon lockout for cleaning and a curfew of 10:45 (you can get permission to return later, but by no more than a couple of hours).

PETRA HOSTEL, *David Street, Tel. 02-628-6618, is straight into the shuk after entering Jaffa Gate, with dorm beds for NIS 20 and private rooms for NIS 70-120.*

A somewhat dilapidated, once beautiful old building, but each dorm room has a balcony overlooking the square, and there is no curfew.

CITADEL YOUTH HOSTEL, *20 Saint Mark's, Tel./Fax 02-627-4375, has dorm beds (five per room, no bunks) for NIS 20, and private rooms (small) for NIS 75, NIS 90 with views–discounts with week-long stays and students available.*

There's a clean kitchen to use, little sitting/eating areas, a roof, and laundry lines. There's a midnight curfew but no lockout, and you can get a key. This is a likable place with a nice feel to it.

NEW SWEDISH HOSTEL, *29 David Street, Tel. 02-589-4124/02-627-7855, has dorm beds for NIS 15 and private rooms for NIS 40-50, pay six nights in advance, get the seventh free. Roof mattresses (NIS 10) should be in place by summer.*

The dorms rooms are claustrophobic, and as you wend your way through slung towels and back packs you might disturb united couples. The private rooms are, well, more private. The cheap one is very small and its entrance is through the dorm. Those upstairs, however, are cute with curved ceilings and walls, and have their own entrances. The bathrooms are clean, though as of now they are only downstairs. Lockers are NIS 3, laundry NIS 7 a wash or dry, and tea/coffee is free. In winter the curfew is 3am, in summer there's no curfew. They also arrange tours (see Tour section). They take no reservations during peak time—the best time to come by is 10am-1pm.

The Jewish Quarter (take bus 1, 2, or 38)

OLD CITY YOUTH HOSTEL, *3 Dorot Rishonim, Tel. 02-628-8611, is off Saint Mark's, with dorm beds for $13 or NIS 45, including a full Israeli breakfast, spiffy clean toilets/showers, and small, clean dorms with sinks.*

The kosher breakfast is 8-9am, the hostel is closed 9am-4pm (5pm in summer), and curfew is 11pm. There's no heat in the winter, a shame in a big old stone building. The airy, spacious halls, lofty ceilings, and stone floors have been around for a while, starting out as a Protestant Missionary from 1833-1856 and a bikkur holim hospital from 1867-1948 before becoming a hostel. Reservations over the phone may or may not be accepted, and the phone may or may not be answered.

EL-MALAK YOUTH HOSTEL, *18 Jewish Quarter, Tel. 02-628-5362, is between Ararat and El-Malak. A dorm bed costs NIS 30, and a private room is NIS 70.*

You can take bus 1, 2, or 38 to the Jewish quarter or 3, 13, 19, 20, or 30 to Jaffa Gate and walk in from there. There's a TV room and use of the kitchen, as well.

HERITAGE HOUSE, *Men's: 2 Ohr HaChayim, Tel. 02-627-2224, Women's: 7 HaMelakh, Tel. 02-628-1820, has its Heritage office at 90 Habad, Entrance B, Apt. 14, Tel. 02-627-1916, and has dorm beds available for traveling Jews at no charge.*

A Jewish community-sponsored hostel offering free lodging for young traveling Jews interested in their roots (or a bed). There are no strings attached, though Judaism evening lectures (8:30pm, free) and Shabbat programs (including candle lighting, prayer at the Western Wall, and dinner with a local family, lecture, Saturday tour of the city, and final communal meal for NIS 26) are available. They provide a clean, comfortable, warm atmosphere (the women's dorm is especially nice) and though they prefer you not stay longer than a week, the rules can be bent if you're involved in spiritual growth or learning. The hostels are closed from Saturday-Thursday 9am-5pm daily, but you can drop your bags at the Student Center of the hostel. The curfew is 12-1am. The women's dorm, with 28 beds, has a sitting area and a nice kitchen; to get there, go up some stone winding stairs to the cozy charming dorm of comfortable wood bunks, shelves, and curtains.

The men's dorm has 60 beds but no curtains. Clean and spare, but not as cozy, there is also one room for a married couple. They don't accept everyone, depending on how they feel you'll fit in. Though they are funded for and cater to Jewish guests, they won't deny lodging to a non-Jew who's part of a Jewish group. If they can't take you, however, they'll try to place you at a hostel nearby.

To get there, take bus 1, 2, or 38 into Jewish Quarter, or bus 3, 13, 19, or 30 to Jaffa Gate, walk down David, turn right on Armenian Patriarchate and right again on Saint James. The men's dorm is straight ahead (Saint James turns into Ohr HaChayim). Or, keep going straight and turn right on Habad to find the Heritage Office.

WHERE TO EAT
WEST JERUSALEM
Jaffa Street

KIKAR HA'IR, *19 Jaffa, Tel. 02-625-0795*, is a kosher Kurdish restaurant that's open Sunday-Thursday 9am-6pm, serving fast food in pitas or sit-down meals. Snacks and light meals like hummus, mejadarra (rice and lentils) and stuffed vegetables go for NIS 9-16.

MA'ADAN, *35 Jaffa, Tel. 02-625-5631*, specializes in kosher grilled meat and fish. They have tasty goulash for NIS 25, entree platters for NIS 9-15, and fish meals for NIS 25-45.

PIKNIC, *57 Jaffa, Tel. 02-625-4195*, open Sunday-Thursday 8am-7pm, Friday 7am-3pm, has good traditional Jewish food to eat in or to go. Sample prices include soups for NIS 8-15, chopped liver or schnitzel for NIS 15, and a piece gefilte fish is NIS 10.

MISHKENOT SHA'ANANIM, *below the Montefiore Windmill, Tel. 02-625-4424*, is an exclusive French eatery. The elegantly antique neighborhood and splendid views of the Old City enhance the fine French and Moroccan food, and make the lofty prices seem a bit more reasonable. With a bottle of wine from their extensive cellar, a lunch might cost $30 and dinner might start at $40. However, there is also a smaller room (four or five tables) with the same food but much cheaper, within the residence. They're not always open to the public, but it's worth checking.

Yoel Salomon Walkway

PIPO, *16 Yoel Salomon, Tel. 02-624-0468*, down toward the end of the street, is open Monday-Friday 10am-11:30pm, Saturday 11:30am-1am. Serving Argentinian food to occasional Argentinian music, it's a very popular Saturday spot. A friendly place with white walls, lots of stone, and tightly packed tables, they dish up quantities of meat and luscious desserts. Light meals (salads, empanadas) go for NIS 20-35, pastas are NIS 25-35, and the main dishes are NIS 45-65.

OSTERIA PAPAS, *3 Rivlin Street, Tel. 02-625-6738*, is an Italian restaurant. Open Sunday-Friday 9am-midnight, Saturday noon-midnight, it's packed on Shabbat. With a small, cozy dining room, white walls and nice paintings, there are also tables out on the walkway. Focaccio costs NIS 8, soups and salads are NIS 17-24, and main dishes go for NIS 35-49.

Ben Yehuda Pedestrian Mall & Nearby

VILLAGE GREEN, *10 Ben Yehuda, Tel. 02-625-2007*, is a vegetarian restaurant on the Pedestrian Mall. There's another branch at *1 Betsalel, Tel. 02-625-1464*.

FINK'S BAR AND RESTAURANT, *2 HaHistadrut, Tel. 02-623-4523*, is on the corner with King George. Open Saturday-Thursday from 6pm, and it's busiest 8-10pm. Rightly ranked by Newsweek as "One of the best bars in the world," their food is equally noteworthy. The ever-charming Moulli (son-in-law of the late owner Dave Rothschild) runs the joint. With a bar and just six tables, it's big in status and quality alone. If you want to dine at a table, you'd best make reservations (you can call during the day). The chef has been cooking up Moshe Fink's goulash for 40 years, as well as tafelspitz, cordon bleu à la Fink, chopped liver, and a very succulent

A SPECIAL PLACE: FINK'S

Fink's has been called the restaurant equivalent of the Sabra: a plain, unlovely outside belies the warmth and goodness within. Founded in 1933 by Hungarian emigré Moshe Fink, the restaurant/bar served as a hidden arsenal and secret post office for the Haganah. In the pre-war years Fink's was popular with both British Mandate officers and members of the Haganah, creating an interesting dynamic and lots of eavesdropping. Today, Fink's still attracts a mixed bag of diplomats, artists, journalists, Likkud and Labor parliament members, and diverse travelers.

Zubin Mehta, Isaac Stern, and Pablo Casals have bellied up to the polished bar. Golda Meir used to frequent the place as well, but was adamant about wanting no special treatment (in fact she got mad at Rothschild when once he tried to seat her before her turn). Less democratically inclined, when Kissinger wanted to visit in 1973, he had certain conditions: notably that everyone else leave the premises. And here Rothschild didn't play favorites, saying Kissinger was certainly welcome, but no more so than his regular customers. And despite the fancy names and magazine write-ups, it's the regulars who make Fink's. As much a club as a restaurant, it's a place people come back to, it's a family people want to join.

pepper steak, priced NIS 22-63. But you needn't eat. There's fine beer, wine, and more, and even a Fink's Special (aka The Hammer) of gin, vodka, Bacardi, and Triplesec, to melt away your tourist aches and pains.

Other Downtown Restaurants

ANGELO, *9 Horkanos, Tel. 02-623-6095*, is off Havazelet, parallel to Jaffa, and open Sunday-Thursday noon-4pm and 6:30pm-midnight, Saturday from the end of Shabbat. Angelo serves what might be the best kosher Italian food in Jerusalem, in a cozy setting run by a lovely couple. True, you probably didn't come to Israel for pasta, but the authentic Roman cuisine (Angelo's home before emigrating to Israel), rivals the best of New York, San Francisco, and Rome. Business lunches cost NIS 45. There's an innovative anti pasta buffet, and everything is homemade, and the *cecio e pepe* is a real treat. The red wine is good, the espresso is strong, and your bill is sweetened with a complementary glass of dessert wine. There's smoking and non-smoking sections, and they're setting up sidewalk tables as well.

THE TICHO HOUSE CAFE, *7 Harav Kook, Tel. 02-624-4186*, also known as Beit Ticho, is open Sunday-Thursday 10am-midnight, Friday 10am-3pm, Saturday from sundown to midnight, and is a serene, lovely, and popular kosher place to dine. Breakfasts (served 10am-noon) cost NIS 15-25. For lunch or dinner, there are salads (NIS 20-30), soups (NIS 14), entrees (NIS 27-43) and sumptuous desserts (NIS 14-18). The tile tables are decorated with fresh flowers, the cutting boards are laden with fresh brown bread, and the fish soup is delicious. The white walls and vaulted ceilings frame this beautiful little room, and all that's lacking is a non-smoking section. The food is enough of a reason to come here, but the main focus is Anna Ticho's drawing exhibit and Dr. Ticho's menorah lamps.

YEHUDA BISTRO, *Laromme Jerusalem Hotel, Liberty Bell Park, 3 Jabotinsky, Tel. 02-675-6666, Fax 02-675-6777*, provides kosher dinner accompanied by candlelight and classical guitar. Laromme sometimes gives out 10% discount vouchers.

OCEAN, *7 Rivlin, Tel. 02-624-7501*, serves—not surprisingly—fish, and lots of it, generally prepared au Francais. It's not cheap, and you should be prepared to pay NIS 85 for a business lunch and NIS 100 for their fixed dinner menu.

Shuk Mahane Yehuda

HASHLOSHA, *68 Agrippas, Tel. 02-625-3876*, is a reliable Oriental foods standby, open Sunday-Thursday 10am-8pm in winter and 10am-11pm in summer. They sell appetizers like hummus, stuffed veggies, and beans with rice for NIS 8-11, and goulash, fish, and grilled meats for NIS 25-45.

SIMMA, *82 Agrippas, Tel. 02-623-3002*, open Sunday-Thursday 10am-2am, Friday 10am-4:30pm, is well known for its cheap Mediterranean food and good hummus. It's so well known, in fact, that the food it serves is no longer that cheap, and its fame seems to have gone to its head. Simple fare like hummus or shak-shuka are NIS 10, and a main dish will run you NIS 33-50.

RAKHMO, *5 HaEshkol, Tel. 02-623-4595*, serves up a more authentic, inexpensive meal. Open Sunday-Thursday 8:30am-5pm and Friday 8am-1:30pm, an institution in these parts for 42 years. Just off Agrippas, they sell fine, simple foods (self-service) for pittance. Hummus is NIS 7, beans and rice costs the same, and the kubbeh soup is much admired. A light meal will cost you around NIS 7, a full more-than-you-need meal won't run above NIS 20. It's not fancy, but it has its charm, with formica-topped wooden tables surrounded by old men talking politics and eating well.

HASHIPUDIA, *6 Hashikma Street, Tel. 02-254-036*, is open Sunday-Thursday noon-midnight, Saturday from the end of Shabbat until midnight. They serve the usual kebabs, stuffed veggies and salads for NIS 10-20, bull's testicles, fish, and spinal cord for NIS 17-38, and desserts for NIS 6.

Not far past Hashlosha but across the street is a **popular stall** selling grilled innards and meats in a pita (NIS 16-22).

BAGEL BAKERY, *125 Agrippas*, just past the stall , sells fresh, fine bagels hot from the oven.

IMA, *189 Agrippas, Tel. 02-624-6860, Fax 02-625-5693*, open Sunday-Thursday 10am-10pm, Friday 10am-3pm serves up kosher Kurdish food in an old white stone house all the way down Agrippas, past the market and further still. The complimentary pickled cabbage is well-spiced, and a meal here is filling and good. Appetizers of mejadara, hummus, or stuffed veggies are NIS 9-13, main courses run NIS 30-48, and the take-away menu is 10% less. The fried eggplant and stuffed cabbages are especially good, and a big feast can be had in this cozy place for NIS 19. There's smoking and non-smoking sections, and you can rent one of the dining rooms for parties. You can order half portions, and hot sauce is available too, for the asking.

Further Afield

PUNDAK EIN-KAREM, *13 Hama'ayan, Tel. 02-643-1840*, bills itself as a bar-cafe garden restaurant. It's near Yad Vashem, and though you may not have much of an appetite after visiting there, this restaurant has a pleasant garden atmosphere, with colorful paintings and dark wood. The food is moderately priced, with light meals starting at NIS 19.

KOHINOOR, *Holiday Inn Hotel building, Tel. 02-653-6667*, is a kosher Indian restaurant, open Sunday-Thursday noon-4pm and 6pm-midnight. They serve Tandoori cuisine in a classy Indian setting. Appetizers cost NIS 4-11, entrees are NIS 22-32, and the business lunch is NIS 41.

BLUES BROTHERS, *3 Lunz, Tel. 02-258-621*, is open 10am-1am. and specializes in substantial (though not inexpensive) steaks and kebabs.

West Jerusalem Cafés

CAFÉ ATARA, *15 Ben Yehuda, Pedestrian Mall, Tel. 02-625-0141*, has history, good coffee, and incredible desserts. Established in 1938 and long-time hangout of Jerusalem Post (previously Palestinian Post) writers, were closed for a year but have happily reopened. The coffee is good though not cheap, and it's a swell place to sit and sip, people watch, and indulge in their luscious, worth-the-fat-and-shekels desserts. If you like chocolate you shouldn't die without first experiencing the Mozart Chocolate cake with hot chocolate sauce on the side (NIS 14).

Café Atara is more down to earth than many of the abundant cafes in the zone, with marbled floors, plain wood tables, utilitarian chairs. Supposedly a spot for local politicians and intelligentsia, even if you can't recognize any of the patrons you might as well believe you are surrounded by fame, sit back, and enjoy your dessert. They also have lunch/light

WEST JERUSALEM FAST FOOD & SWEETS

TA'AMI, 3 Shammai, Tel. 02-622-5911, off HaHistadrut, serves basic local items to basic local workers, dishing up plates of hummus, rice and macaroni, kebabs, and goulash for NIS 9-20. The decor isn't much to speak of, but around lunch time there are plenty of hungry men slurping up simple, good food. Not as charming or cheap as Rakhmo's, but the same sort of fare. The pita here isn't free (it's 50 agorot each), and the service isn't doting, but the fresh lemonade is great, and it's a fine mid-town option if you tire of the cafe scene.

For good, cheap, fast food there are bakeries all over town.

KHEN BAKERY, 30 Jaffa, not far up from Tourist Information, is open Sunday-Thursday 8am-5pm and has excellent cheesy burekas for just NIS 4.

CHEZ PARIS, 35 Jaffa, open nearly round the clock, is another good bakery, but more western in its outlook and baked goods, with cookies and muffins as well as burekas.

MISEDIT GAZIT, 39 Jaffa, lacks an English sign, but serves a vegetarian omelet in pita (called khavita emerakot in Hebrew or eeja in Arabic) for just NIS 6. Dressed up with hummus and salads, it makes a tasty alternative to the ubiquitous falafel.

AMI PIZZA, Emek Refdim, Tel. 02-563-0469, has serviceable pizza for NIS 6 a slice. Open Sunday-Thursday 9am-midnight, and Saturday after Shabbat till midnight, a slice makes a fine snack.

BEN & JERRY'S, 5 Hillel, Tel. 02-624-2767, is off King George and open Sunday-Thursday 10am-midnight, Friday 10am-2pm, Saturday from the end of Shabbat till midnight. Same good ice cream, at NIS 5 a scoop.

dinner fare, and in the mornings folks sit over coffee and newspapers. The back room is no-smoking.

CAFE TA'AMON, *27 King George, Tel. 02-625-4977*, is open Sunday-Thursday 6am-midnight, Friday 6am-4pm, Saturday 5pm or 6pm to midnight. In operation for 42 years, they're not fancy or charming but they serve a good, relatively inexpensive cup of coffee and draw an interesting crowd. Popular with writers, artists, and retired left-wing scholars, the walls are decorated with pictures painted by the late Abraham Offick; fresh flowers and intently reading, smoking men inhabit the tables. It's not chic, but what it lacks in marble table tops it makes up for in history and integrity.

CAFE RIMON, *Luntz, Tel. 02-624-3712*, is a popular cafe, full of chipper Israelis and travelers in their 20s and 30s, drinking somewhat pricy capuccinos and eating fancy desserts.

OLD CITY
Christian & Muslim Quarters

If you hunger while traipsing the alleys of the Old City, you generally want food without a wait; the heat and crowds of the narrow lanes do something to normally tolerant, patient folk.

If you want a light snack and put off the real meal till later, one of those omnipresent long oval sesame-seeded bagels (*ka'ak*) is a fine choice. It's cheap (3 NIS), and bound to be good. Ask for *za'atar* to go with it and they'll dish up some tasty green spice in a square of newspaper for you to add to your snack (it's very tasty and middle eastern). Generally speaking, the falafels in the Old City are disappointing, especially compared to the fine quality available just blocks away in East Jerusalem.

ABU SEIF, *just inside Jaffa Gate*, has hummus for NIS 9 and falafel for NIS 5. The falafel satisfies your hunger but is boring. If you can, hold out for better fare outside Damascus Gate.

THE COFFEE SHOP, *next to Christian Information near Jaffa Gate, Tel. 02-626-4090*, is a bright and cheery place with nice tile-topped tables, tempting desserts, and lunches for around NIS 15-20.

ABU SHUKRI, *63 Al-Wad, Tel. 02-627-1538*, features Taha's deservedly famous hummus (NIS 9), which is better than the labaneh. He also serves falafel, salads, soda and mint tea (NIS 4) to refresh and refuel you in your Old City wanderings.

ABU ASSAB, *Khan Az-Zeit*, runs a fine juice stand. It's on your right coming from Damascus Gate and has wonderfully refreshing and reasonable fresh squeezed juice (orange/grapefruit/carrot) for NIS 4.

ROTISEREE CHICKEN, *Khan Az-Zeit*, sells half a chicken to go NIS 10 or eat in with salads, pita, and yummy green hot sauce ("felfel" in arabic) for NIS 13. There are lots of chicken joints on the strip, and English signs generally boost the price quite a lot. Make sure to ask how much before ordering.

Shuk Khan ez-Zeit assaults you with trays and trays of gooey flaky treats dripping honey and pistachio nuts that look scrumptious but may be disappointing. **ZALATIMO'S**, *Khan ez-Zeit*, in an exception. Near the Coptic Church and the ninth station of the cross, it makes the real thing. The cheese filled moutabak is their specialty, but there's lots more to choose from if that isn't the treat you yearn for. It's open daily in the morning till 11:30 or whenever the pastry's gone.

Jewish Quarter

QUARTER CAFE, *corner of Tife'eret Yisrael and Ha-Sho'arim, Tel. 02-628-7770,* on the second story, is open Sunday-Thursday 8:30am-6:30pm, Friday 8:30am-3:30pm, with a rooftop terrace and a terrific view. It's self-service, the salads are NIS 9-16 and full meals NIS 38; the food's good, the prices average, and the view of Mount of Olives superb.

Off Cardo Square is food option lane. **HAHOMA RESTAURANT** is a sit-down proper place (credit cards accepted), with salads for NIS 9 and entrees for NIS 33. To the right is a **SHWARMA JOINT** with pita sandwiches for NIS 9-15, and to the left is a hole-in-the-wall **BAKERY** with za'atar pizzas for NIS 5.

Across the lane is **ROMI'S PIZZA** (open Sunday-Thursday 7am-midnight), with regular pizza as well as malawach, soup, spaghetti, and fresh carrot juice, too.

EAST JERUSALEM

AL-QUDS RESTAURANT, *23 Sultan Suleiman, Tel. 02-627-2052,* opposite the post office, across from the Old City, and about a block down from the Damascus Gate, is a self-serve gem. A big shwarma or kebab pita costs just NIS 7. Muscle past all the people in line and pay the cashier, get your ticket and take it to the meat man of your choice (shwarma, kebab, or chicken). Get the pita, help yourself to chips and salad toppings, and enjoy. The roast chicken, NIS 17 for a whole one and NIS 8 for half, are also very tasty. The front of the restaurant is always thronged with locals, attesting to the continuing popularity of this neighborhood place.

PETRA RESTAURANT, *11 Rashid, Tel. 02-628-3655,* Fax 02-628-6008, is open daily noon-midnight. They serve oriental food in one room and sea food in another. The decor is standard, checkered table cloths and such, neither shabby nor dazzling. Prices are reasonable, and NIS 25 gets you a sampler of salads and dips, while NIS 30-40 buys a big spread of meat main dishes.

AL-QUDS, *Azzahra,* around the corner from Rashid, is open daily 7am-6pm. A small cafe with four tables and excellent, inexpensive Arabic food, this isn't the Al-Qud's of shwarma and kebab fame, but the quality is equally fine. The hummus is terrific, better than Abu Shukri's, and only NIS 6 for a plateful (and NIS 3 for a pitaful). The reyani (a spinach-stuffed triangle) is good, as is the falafel (NIS 3) and ojay (an eggs and onion dish). And, if you're willing to be gastronomically adventurous, the brain sandwich (NIS 8) is delicious.

CAFE EUROPE, *9 Azzahra, Tel. 02-628-4313,* jumps out of the pages of colonial decor. Rattan chairs with flowered cushions surround pink table-clothed tables. If you (or the kids) have been yearning for a burger and fries (NIS 18-27) like they make back home or a thick milk shake (NIS

11), this is the place to go. There are chops, steak, and cheeseburgers (this is not a kosher restaurant), and coffee drinks aplenty. This is also a fine spot to hang out over elaborate cocktails—the social hub starts around 5pm.

PHILADELPHIA, *9 Azzahra, Tel. 02-628-9770*, opposite Al-Quds Cinema and open every day from noon-midnight, is an Arabic restaurant of deserved local and international fame. Since 1970, this has been a restaurant that adheres to tradition. The result: food of exceptional quality, service of a standard that is an endangered species, and a stubborn resistance to new-fangled inventions like fax machines and credit cards. And with food this good, who cares how you pay? Certainly not the endless list of famous visitors whose signatures grace the leather-bound guest book. Jimmy Carter ate here, as did Edwin Meese III, Geraldo Rivera, and many more, though most of the guests come from the community—perhaps a greater tribute to its quality. I can honestly say I've never had oriental food as superbly prepared, as delicious, and all the little touches that keep standards high are just honey on the baklavah.

The decor is proper without being ornate, the red table clothes and napkins have been the style since the day they began, and every morning before they open a man rattles an incense pan in all the corners and booths to add to the food aromas the "smell of the Middle East." And with all this, the prices are reasonable. Appetizer salads are NIS 9 each, stuffed foods are NIS 14, and grilled meats are NIS 30-40. $20 will get you a feast so vast and delectable you won't soon forget it, beginning with an enormous spread of 15 dips and salads, kubeh, stuffed veggies, and falafel that enters the category of gourmet, followed by mixed grill and rice pilaf, then assorted baklava, tea or coffee, and fruit. After such a meal, you will waddle out a very happy person, thankful that Philadelphia Restaurant also provides a free shuttle to anywhere in Jerusalem. Reservations are a good idea, especially if you plan to dine at peak times, around 2pm for lunch or 8-9pm for dinner.

KANZAMMAN, *Jerusalem Hotel, Nablus Road, Tel./Fax 02-628-3282*, is a lovely small Arabic subterranean restaurant, awash with rugs and cushions. Cozy and pleasant (with a garden setting in summer), they serve appetizers for NIS 5-7, vegetarian dishes for NIS 10-15, and meat dishes for NIS 20-29. On Saturdays at 8pm there's a special Lebanese buffet, and on Thursdays they have jazz night.

For **sweets**, try one of the bakeries, *HaNevi'im*, near the Old City.

SEEING THE SIGHTS
THE OLD CITY
The Walls & Gates

The walls that now stand were built by **Suleiman the Magnificent** in 1534-40. There had been walls before, but Al Muazzan demolished them in 1219 so the Crusaders wouldn't win a fortified city, and no walls were rebuilt for over 300 years. The Old City walls have eight gates, all with varying names (English, Hebrew, Arabic) and histories; of the six built by Suleiman, only the Jaffa, Zion, and Damascus gates survive in their original form.

Jaffa Gate is one of the old gates to the Old City. There's been one here since 135 CE, but the present gate dates from 1538, though some of the stones in the gate are from Crusader and Mamluk times. The left-hand

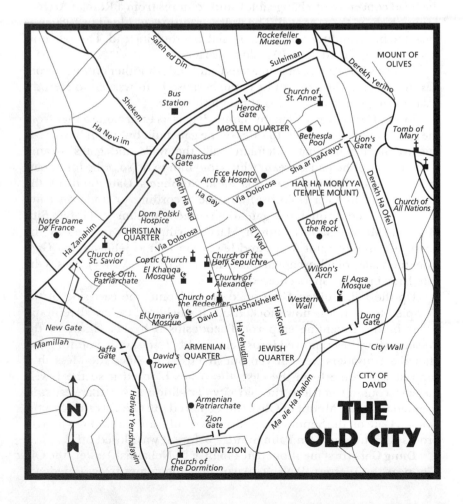

THE OLD CITY

turn you have to make to enter (a mark of an old-time gate) was to deter armed people on horseback from storming the city. It opens into the Christian and Armenian quarters of the city, and stands at the beginning of the former trade route to Jaffa. In '48 the area in front of Jaffa Gate (what used to be a market and industry zone) became no-man's-land. The gate is now the most used entrance to the old city, and many buses (3, 6, 13, 19, or 30) stop here.

New Gate opened in 1889 to ease the way to the Christian Quarter. This gate gave the patriarchs direct access to their Christian Quarter residences.

Damascus Gate, facing East Jerusalem and where the Sultan had his palace, is the largest and grandest of the eight gates. The Cardo Maximus started here, there was a statue of Caesar (the body in permanent bronze, the head conveniently changeable), and columns from a Roman Arch of Triumph stood there as well. The walkway entrance, added in 1980, was meant to be an auditorium, but it is used as a shuk instead. The gate now separates the Christian and Muslim quarters.

Herod's Gate is east of Damascus Gate, and is another entrance from East Jerusalem. The gate got its name because Jesus was led to Herod's palace along the street passing through this gate.

Lion's Gate is a gate of many names. It gets its Lion name either from the two Mamluk lions on both sides of the gate built by Sultan Baybar, or due to the legend that Suleiman built the walls and gates around Jerusalem after he had a dream which told him to do so or be torn apart by lions. The Christians call this **Saint Stephen's Gate** (and it's the beginning of the Via Dolorosa) because according to tradition Saint Stephen was led through this gate to be stoned. Muslims call it **Bab Sitti Maryam** (**Mary's Gate**) to honor Mary's birthplace as marked by the nearby Church of Saint Anne, and Jews refer to it as **Jehoshaphat Gate** from the Valley of Jehoshaphat (also known as Kidron Valley). This is the gate Israeli paratroopers entered in 1967.

Up the hill, **Golden Gate** once opened onto the east side of the Temple Mount but is now blocked up. It's believed to have been built either by the Byzantine emperor Theodosius II in 444 CE or by the Persians after they captured Jerusalem in 614 . It was walled off for good after the Crusaders were driven out in 1187 CE. Since the Messiah is supposed to come from the east, the Arabs blocked it so the Jewish messiah couldn't get into the old city. Tradition has it that Jesus descended from the Mount of Olives and entered the Old City through the Golden Gate on the Sunday preceding his death, and ceremonies used to process through here on Palm Sunday before it was closed off.

Dung Gate (first mentioned in 445 BCE by Nehamiah) enters the Old City near the Western Wall. Its flavorful name comes from a medieval belief that dumping refuse here was a salubrious act. It's been changed a lot over the years, and the lintel shows how small the gate used to be. Buses 1, 3, and 38 enter there into the Jewish Quarter.

Zion Gate connects the Armenian Quarter with Mount Zion. "Zion" as a term first was applied to the Temple mount, and from there it was generalized to Jerusalem, and then to all of Israel. Built in 1540, it was one of the last to be constructed in the old city. Like Jaffa Gate, it has many Crusader stones in its structure, and was really hammered by the pre-independence fighting; the stones are covered with bullet marks.

The **Ramparts Walk**, *Tel. 02-625-4403*, takes you on a path along the top of the Old City walls, providing you with terrific views of Mount Scopus, Mount of Olives, rooftops, and the shiny heads of tourists. Tickets (NIS 8 for adults, NIS 4 for students) are sold at Jaffa Gate, Damascus Gate, and the Citadel, and they grant you unlimited access for two days after purchase. The entrance to the Ramparts at Damascus Gate entails first descending before you enter the gate. Walk under and keep going through the old carriageway to the left of the plaza. It's open Saturday-Thursday 9am-4pm, Friday 9am-2pm—but it's not a good idea for women to walk up there on their own.

At the rampart entrance is also the entrance to the **Roman Square Museum**, and its Aelia Capitolina (second century Roman period) excavations. Open Saturday-Thursday 9am-4pm, Friday 9am-2pm, admission is NIS 2 for adults, NIS 1 for students. In the central plaza is a replica of the 1,400 year old Madaba map, the oldest mosaic map of Jerusalem that shows the Cardo in its glory days. There's a hologram of the 22 meter pillar that used to stand here which gave Damascus Gate its Arabic name of **Bab al Amud** (*Gate of the Pillar*). There are two towers built by Hadrian, and in the eastern one there's a staircase leading up to the Ramparts Walk.

Just inside Jaffa Gate is **Tower of David**, *Tel. 02-627-4111, Fax 02-628-3418*, an important fortress spot from First Temple times, and now a museum of the History of Jerusalem. It was named so by Christian pilgrims even though David's city was on the other end of the Old City. Open Sunday-Thursday 9am-5pm (an hour later in summer), Friday-Saturday 9am-2pm (you can usually stay an hour later before being kicked out), it costs NIS 24 for adults, NIS 17 for students and seniors, and NIS 12 for youth.

In this reconstructed citadel that was first built by Herod 2,000 years ago, history lessons of Jerusalem are portrayed through diaramas, relics, and explanatory texts. The maze-like layout is confusing, but if you don't mind not proceeding chronologically through the ages, you can't go wrong by just wandering around. To help guide you, a number of paths have been set up. Follow the red line, the green line, or the blue line, depending on how much time you set aside (it takes a good two to three hours to "do" the red line) and your interests (some paths focus on archaeology, others on history, etc.).

There is a guided tour in English leaving the main entrance Sunday-Friday at 11am, or there's a headset with recorded lecture you can rent for NIS 5, but they're in the process of improving the system. Soon they'll have a computerized disk that will elaborate on the exhibits as you come to them, rather than requiring you to follow a set path. And on Saturday nights at 9pm there's a special Whodunnit feature that's popular with kids, finding the murderer of the High Priest Aristobulus III. There's also a spring and summer sound and light show in English Monday & Wednesday at 9:30pm and Saturday at 9pm.

The **Shuk** (or *souk*) is the market, the bazaar, the heart of the Old City with the sights, sounds, and smells of the Middle East; it's the gauntlet that frays the nerves and patience of the most saintly. It spans the Muslim, Christian, and Armenian quarters, running principally along David Street, Khan ez-Zeit, and El Wad. For souvenirs, bargaining is the rule, and time, patience, and a sense of humor the tools of the trade. Banter is fine, but don't stand for harassment, sexual or otherwise, and take down the name of the proprietor (or at least the store) if you're subjected to unwarranted nastiness.

The **Old City Police branch**, *Tel. 02-622-6222, ext. 33*, is inside Jaffa Gate to your right, and has a tourist desk. But this isn't to say the shuk is a bad time. It's a wonderful place, especially in the morning when the day, the food, and people's smiles are still fresh.

The Temple Mount

The southwestern corner of the Old City is enormously sacred to Jews, Muslims, and Christians, and that's where nearly all agreement ends. By the **Temple Mount**, called *Har Bayit* in Hebrew and *Al-Haram ash-Sharif* in Arabic, scores of military stand ready to keep the peace among the hordes of the faithful. All agree that this was the biblical **Mount Moriah**, the spot where the Patriarch **Abraham** was called upon by God to sacrifice his son (Isaac according to Jews and Christians, Ishmael according to Muslims). This is the site that **Solomon** chose for his Temple in 950 BCE, and it's here that the **Holy Ark of the Covenant** was given its permanent home.

Destroyed by the Chaldeans under **Nebuchadnezzar** in 587 BCE, the **Second Temple** was built when the Jews returned from Babylon in 538 BCE. In 19 BCE Herod put his two cents in, tearing down the old and putting up a Herodian Temple complex, vast and elaborate, in its place. This, in its turn, was mostly destroyed in 70 CE by Titus following the Great Revolt, and Hadrian ordered the final razing of the Temple in 132 CE after the Bar Kokhba Rebellion. After the Second Temple was destroyed in 132 CE, Hadrian ordered a Temple of Jupiter to be built upon the Temple Mount. Emperor Constantine the Great had this torn down in the third century, and he allowed Jews to pray there once a year on the 10th of Ab in memory of the destroyed Temple. Emperor Julian the Apostate organized the rebuilding of the Temple in 361, but this activity was halted by an earthquake and Julian's death in 363.

In the southwest corner of the Old City, today's Temple Mount is a walled area within the Old City walls and administered by the **Supreme Muslim Council**, with eight entrance gates for Muslims. But while you can exit through any, only two entrances are accessible to non-Muslims: **Moor's Gate** south of the Western Wall and **Chain Gate** at the end of Bab el-Silsila. **Al Haram** and the nearby **Islamic Museum** are open to the public Saturday-Thursday 8am-noon and 1:30-3pm (approximately—the down time is based on the Muslim prayer schedule, which varies from month to month) and 7:30-10am during Ramadan.

While entrance to Al Haram is free, you need to buy a ticket to enter the mosques, and it gains you admission to the Islamic Museum as well. Tickets cost NIS 16 for adults, NIS 10 for students, and the ticket booth is between Al Aqsa Mosque and the museum. To enter the mosques you must be dressed modestly, and you'll have to take off your shoes. The Haram guards have very little sense of humor when it comes to tourists breaking rules. Entrance hours are strictly adhered to, and if areas are marked off-limits, don't test the boundaries. The Western Wall which abuts this complex is under different jurisdiction and has its own entrances and regulations (see below).

The Dome of the Rock (*Qubbet es-Sakhra*) is an extraordinary sight, with its gold dome, marble base, and many thousand tiles; it is also one of the best preserved example of early Islamic architecture. The dome was at one time solid gold, but the caliph's debts had to be paid, and lead replaced gold for a time. In 1958 lead was recapped with aluminum-bronze, but in 1993 the dome received a thin coat of gold. Of the tiles with their Koranic verses, many date back to Suleiman the Magnificent's time, but some were added by Jordan's King Hussein in 1950-1960. Inside it's equally beautiful, all white and gold.

The Holy Rock is associated with **Abraham** and **Ishmael** (Abraham's son by Hagar, whom the Muslims believe was the son to be sacrificed), and also with altars used for burnt offerings in the First and Second Temples. There are also sacred relics with the imprints of prophets' footprints and Angel Gabriel's fingerprints from when he held the rock steady when Mohammed rode into heaven. In the cave below is the "souls' well" where the souls of Elijah, Abraham, David, and Solomon meet twice weekly for prayer.

When the Caliph Omar conquered Jerusalem in 638 CE, he prayed at the rock of Temple Mount and recalled Abraham's call to sacrifice. In 688, Caliph Abd al-Malik had the Dome of the Rock built over the Rock of Abraham, oriented toward Mecca, and Jerusalem became a Muslim pilgrimage site. The Knights Templar took up residence there for a time while the Crusaders held the city, but Sultan Saladin took Jerusalem back in 1187, and the Dome of the Rock has been in Muslim hands ever since. After the Ka'bah in Mecca and the Prophet's tomb in Medina, it is the third holiest Islamic site.

Arab tradition has it that from this rock the **Prophet Mohammed** took off on his horse el-Buraq for his miraculous night journey to heaven, and that this was the motivation for building the mosque. Islamic scholars note, however, that the nearby **Dome of the Ascension** honors that trip, and that the drive to build the Dome of the Rock was far more complicated. It was a message to the Byzantine Empire and Jerusalem's Christians that Islam was there to stay, and a political message directed to Muslims in Mecca and Medina, with a competitive third Holy Shrine.

Between the Dome of the Rock and al Aqsa mosque is **El Kas** (*The Cup*) a fountain where Muslims wash before prayer. Built in 709 CE, the fountain is connected to the vast underground system of cisterns.

Al Aqsa Mosque is domed in silver rather than gold, and is the largest mosque in Jerusalem. Its name (meaning "the farthest") refers to the Koranic verse 17:1 which tells of Mohammed's trip to Heaven from the Holy Rock, "the farthest" point from his journey from Mecca, but to Jews it's known as Midrash Shlomo (the School of King Solomon). Right after the conquest of Jerusalem in 638 CE, Caliph Omar ordered the mosque built, but construction didn't begin until Abd al-Malik initiated it in 710 (probably in wood, and probably on the old site of a sixth century Crusader Church of Saint Mary); it was rebuilt many times after many earthquakes.

It wasn't till 1033 under **Fatimid Caliph az-Zahir** that it took on its present appearance. The last major renovation took place in 1938: The central marble columns were donated by Italian dictator Benito Mussolini, and Egypt's King Farouk funded the ceiling paint job, while the stained-glass and carpets add further color to the interior.

The **Qait-Bey fountain**, built in 1487, was funded by the Egyptian Sultan Qait Bey (but supervised by a Christian constructor), and it's based on cisterns that were there long before. Many of the cisterns on the Temple Mount were at one time routes leading directly to the Temple for priestly access, but were later converted into reservoirs. According to Jewish tradition, the Holy of Holies in the Temple was on the spot now occupied by the Qait-Bey fountain.

Dome of the Chain (*Qubbet es-Silsileh*) is an open pavilion which looks like a smaller version the Dome of the Rock to the west. The Jews refer to is as David's place of Judgment, and Muslims view it as the site where the good will be separated from the evil on the Last Judgment Day by means of a chain hung from Heaven to be grasped by the righteous. It stands in the precise middle of the Temple area, and was probably built by Caliph Abd al-Malik (685-705), who's said to have used the dome to hold his treasure. For a time the Crusaders turned it into a chapel dedicated to Jacobus. Back in Muslim hands, Sultan Suleiman the Magnificent donated the ceramic facing in the 16th century.

Nearby, the **Islamic Museum** admits those with a mosque ticket. Exhibits include architectural designs, textiles, ceramics, manuscripts, coins, and weapons. The so-called **Stables of Solomon** near the al-Aqsa mosque are an enormous underground complex of 13 aisles and 88 pillars holding up the vaults. It is believed that sacrificial animals were housed here in Solomon's day (hence the name), and it's known that some of the structures date to Herod's time. A shell-shaped niche from Roman days is referred to as "Christ's Cradle," and the Virgin Mary is said to have stood here when presenting her child in Temple (Luke 2:22). At times this site is off-limits due to terrorist fears.

The Temple site is also important to Christians in New Testament accounts. Luke tells how John the Baptist's birth was announced there by the Angel Gabriel (1:5-25), how Jesus was consecrated to the Lord there (2:22), and how some years later Jesus stayed behind in Jerusalem and was rediscovered by his parents studying in the temple courts (2:42). Jesus was tempted by the Devil there (4:9) as well. Matthew (21:12-17) tells how Jesus drove from the Temple the wheelers and dealers, calling them robbers.

And John tells of Jesus teaching at the Temple (7:14-53), and (8:2-11) how in the Temple Jesus tells those who have not sinned to cast the first stone. It is also in the Temple that Judas throws down his 30 silver coins (Matthew 27:2-10) and after Jesus dies, Matthew (27:52) recounts that the Temple curtain was torn in two.

But, though it figures in Christian theology, it's not as important a site to them as it is to Jews and Muslims. The major impact of these connections is that when Crusaders held sway here in 1099, they left the Dome of the Rock mostly unaltered because they considered it to have been the place where Jesus taught (hence their renaming of it as *Templum Domini*, or Lord's Temple).

The Western Wall & the Jewish Quarter

All that survives of the Second Temple is the **Western Wall** (*Kotel haMa'aravi*, or just *Kotel* in Hebrew) called the **Wailing Wall** by some due to the grief expressed there mourning the destruction of the Temple. The site is open to all, 24 hours a day, after passing through tight security checks entering from Dung Gate or along El Wad from the Old City. As a relic of that ancient and holy site, the Western Wall is held sacred among Jews.

The cracks between the big old stones brim with wads of paper holding reams of special wishes and prayers. Over the years the scraps pile up, however, and from time to time the notes are removed and buried according to Jewish Law. At night the Wall's spectacularly lit, and it's also wonderful to watch the Orthodox welcome Shabbat with prayer, song, and dance as the sun sets Friday evening.

Not surprisingly, the largest portion of the wall is set aside for the men, rocking and chanting in their black robes and yarmulkas (there are cardboard ones available if you wish to approach the Wall and didn't bring your own), while a lesser section is apportioned to the women, who cover their heads and pray more modestly on their side. Monday and Thursday mornings are popular times for Bar Mitzvahs to be held here, and they are festive events.

Though the area is open to all, certain attitudes of decorum should be respected, such as modest dress (no shorts, no overly exposed flesh). Photographs are okay, but only during the regular week; the praying Hasidim may look photogenic, but it's not appreciated during Shabbat.

FAX-A-PRAYER TO THE WAILING WALL!

*Tradition embraces modern innovation in odd combinations throughout Israel, and a fine example is the service **Bezek** offers. You can fax your message to them at 02-661-2222 and your prayer will be dutifully wedged in.*

Excavations have been done in the vicinity of the Wall, and **Wilson's Arch** is one of the finds. Named after the archaeologist who found it, it's in a large, arched room to the left of the Wall. It used to be part of a water-supply system in the Maccabean period, and spanned Tyropoeon (Cheesemakers') Valley, letting Jewish priests cross to the Temple from their homes. If you look down the shafts you'll get a sense of the wall's original height. The room is open to men only, and just on Sunday, Tuesday, Wednesday 8:30am-3pm, Monday and Thursday 12:30-3pm, and Friday 8:30am-noon. There are tunnels under the Western Wall area, and you can take tours of them from a number of companies (see *Tours*).

The **Yitzhak Ben-Youssef Archaeological Garden/Ophel**, *Tel. 02-625-4403*, named for the complex built on the Ophel Hill in First Temple days, is open Sunday-Thursday 9am-4pm, Friday 9am-2pm and costs NIS

9 for adults, NIS 4.5 for youth. Near Dung Gate and extending from the foot of the Southern Wall to the southern part of the Western Wall, the site contains structures from King Solomon's days in 10th century BCE to the time of Suleiman the Magnificent who built the Old City walls in 16th century CE, including remains such as *mikvaot* (Jewish ritual baths), sections of **Robinson's Arch** (the oldest crossover in the world), and parts of the Caliph's palace. Tours help take it all in, and Archaeological Seminars does a three and a half hour tour on Sunday, Tuesday, Wednesday, and Friday at 9:30am.

In the southeast of the Old City, the **Jewish Quarter** offers sacred sites, Roman ruins, synagogues, history, and tiny winding stone streets. Step off the main plaza, stray from the Cardo complex and the tour groups in full-throated explanation and you can easily find yourself completely lost among old houses, cobbled paths, and Hasidic boys coming back from yeshiva. There are many yeshivas and small synagogues in and about the alleys and courtyards of the quarter, and you are generally welcome to stop in, visit, and learn. This was the ritzy Upper City in Second Temple times, but after Jews were driven from the city in 135 CE, a Jewish community didn't begin to reestablish itself here till the late 1400s (when Jews were kicked out of Spain).

In 1800, the Jewish community held 2,000 people; by 1865 that number had grown to 11,000, and Jews started looking outside the city walls for housing. By British Mandate times, the Jewish Quarter had become an overcrowded slum, a problem soon solved by fierce fighting between Jews and Jordanians. This section of the city was devastated by the fighting, and few of the buildings survived. When the Jordanians took the Old City, the remaining Jews were evacuated. Now, about 650 families live in the fairly pricy Jewish Quarter, mostly Orthodox (and many American in origin). After Israel reclaimed this quarter following the Six Day War of '67, the rubble of destruction was cleared and a lot of building went on, incorporating gracefully what remained of the old, and leaving room for excavations to delve into the older still.

A section of the Roman **Cardo Maximus** (think 'heart' of the city) has been uncovered off David Street near Jewish Quarter Road. The Cardo was Jerusalem's main artery in Roman and Byzantine times, and it appears on the sixth century Madaba mosaic map of the city (a copy of which is on display). You can see part of the original street, flanked by pillar remains, as well as remains of the city walls from First and Second Temple days, though the site is a bit overshadowed by the nearby complex of overpriced boutiques and shops and galleries.

The Cardo is open till 11pm, and illuminated nicely after dark. **One Last Day**, *Tel. 02-628-8141*, is an interesting exhibit in the Cardo complex. It shows a series of photographs taken by John Phillips the day the

Jordanians took the Jewish Quarter in 1948. Open Sunday-Thursday 9am-5pm and Friday 9am-1pm, it costs NIS 5 to get in.

The Hurva and Ramban Synagogues are just off Jewish Quarter Street near the southern end of the Cardo, built over the ruins of the Crusader Church of Saint. Martin. A stored stone arch stands over what's left of the ruins of the **Hurva Synagogue**, recalling the synagogue built by followers of Rabbi Yehudi the Hassid in 1700. It was demolished by Muslims 21 years later, giving the synagogue and surrounding courtyard the name of Hurva (which means "ruins"). This important Ashkenazi community synagogue was rebuilt in 1856, and was destroyed once more by Jordanian explosives in 1948.

Next to Hurva stands **Ramban Synagogue**, named after Rabbi Moshe Ben-Nahman (his acronym formed 'Ramban,' but he was also known as Nachmanides). He was considered a great sage, and inside is the letter he wrote in 1267, the year he arrived from Spain, describing the poor state of the Jewish community he found in Jerusalem. The synagogue is believed to have originally stood on Mount. Zion, but was moved to its present site around 1400. The minaret was built in the 1400s by the mother of someone who converted to Islam after arguing with neighbors. In the 1500s when Jews were forbidden to pray here, the building served as a workshop, and later (during the British Mandate) as a cheese and butter shop. Today it's back to being a synagogue

Next to the synagogues is the **War of Independence Memorial**, paying tribute to those Jews who died in battles here in the 1948 War of Independence.

The **Old Yshuv Court Museum**, *6 Or HaChayim, Tel./Fax 02-628-4636*, is up the steps at the southern end of the Cardo—cross over, and up the other side. The exhibits how things were in the quarter before 1948, with rooms set up to reflect various aspects of Jewish life. Open Sunday-Thursday 9am-2pm, it costs NIS 8, NIS 5 for students.

More city history is available through the **Jerusalem Multi-Media Presentation**, *1 Jewish Quarter Road*, shown Sunday-Thursday at 11am, 2pm, and 5pm in English near the parking lot. The show lasts 35 minutes and costs NIS 12.

Not far from the southern end of Jewish Quarter Road—take a left on HaTuppim, left again, and down the stairs—are the four **Sephardic Synagogues**. The Sephardic community built these synagogues underground in the late 1500s because laws of the time forbade synagogues to be built taller than the surrounding buildings. The large chambers beneath the street allowed a sense of loftiness otherwise unattainable in those times. These synagogues (named Rabbi Yohanan Ben-Zakkai, Elijah the Prophet, the Central, and the Istanbuli Synagogues) were used by the Jordanians as sheep pens, but were restored using remains of WWII damaged Italian synagogues. Still vital to the Sephardic community, services are held twice daily. They are open to viewers Sunday-Thursday 9:30am-12:30pm and additional hours 12:30-4pm Wednesday-Thursday, and admission is free.

Batei Machseh Square was once the quarter's largest square, and in the 19th century this was the site of an independent Jewish neighborhood. The **Shelter Houses** here were built to provide for the poor. During the last 10 days of fighting in 1948, hundreds of Jews hid in the basements, close to the nearby Jewish military headquarters. One such was Rothschild Building A, built in 1871 by the Baron Wolf Rothschild of Frankfurt.

Tife'eret Yisrael Synagogue (*Glory of Israel*) was dedicated in 1872 as the twin brother of the Hurva Synagogue. Its tall frame and dome served as a well-known quarter landmark till it was demolished in 1948. This was once the largest Hassidic center in the Old City. Its ruins stand on Tife'eret Yisrael Road, near the northeast corner of the courtyard behind the Hurva Synagogue.

Burnt House, *east on Tife'eret Yisrael and next to the Quarter Café, Tel. 02-628-7211*, is open Sunday-Thursday 9am-5pm, Friday 9am-1pm, and costs NIS 7.5 for adults, NIS 6 per child and student (the combo ticket, including the Israelite Tower and Wohl Archaeological Museum, costs NIS 16, NIS 13 for students). They have shows every half hour 9am-4:30pm describing how this once luxurious house in the Second Temple era's Upper City was destroyed by the Romans in 70CE following the Great Revolt. They set fire to all of Upper City and killed the inhabitants after first razing the Temple. Excavations of this house gave direct evidence of this, what with the severed bones and carbonized spears they found.

Saint Maria of the Germans, *Misgav Ladakh*, is a 12th century church, hospital, and hospice, just east of the Quarter Café.

The **Wide Wall**, *at the western end of Tife'eret Yisreal and north on Plugat Ha-Kotel*, is what's left of the Israelite wall that once circled the City of David, the Temple Mount, and the Upper City. King Hezekiah built it in 701 BCE, along with his tunnel, to defend his city and its water access against Assyrian attacks.

The **Israelite Tower**, *east of the Cardo on Shonei HaLakhot (corner of Plugat Hakotel)*, is the tower of the northern wall gate from the Babylonian siege when the First Temple was destroyed in 586 BCE. Open Sunday-Thursday 9am-5pm and Friday 9am-1pm, it costs NIS 7.5 for adults, NIS 6 per child and student, or get the combo ticket including the Burnt House and Wohl Archaeological Museum for NIS 16, NIS 13 for students.

The **Rachel Ben-Zvi Center**, *across from the Israelite Tower, Tel. 02-628-6288*, is open Sunday-Thursday 9am-4pm and Fridays by appointment, admission costs NIS 8. This institute focuses its research on the history of

Jewish communities. Of more interest to most visitors is their model of Jerusalem in First Temple days, along with archaeological findings from King David's rule (the water system as shown by the model is pretty elaborate).

New Church was the New Church built by Justinian in 543. Its southern apse sticks outside the city wall, and after the Holy Sepulchre it was once the city's second grandest church. When Justinian extended the Cardo, he did so in all likelihood to connect up with this church.

The Siebenberg House, *35 Misgav Ladakh, corner of HaGittit, Tel. 02-628-2341*, is an archaeological museum. Open Sunday-Thursday 9am-5pm, and costing NIS 10, it features a Hasmonean cistern and aqueduct parts that may once have connected Solomon's Pools to the Temple.

The Wohl Archaeological Museum, *off the Jewish Quarter's main square, Herodian Quarter, Tel. 02-628-3448*, is around the corner the Yeshivat Ha-Kotel and is open Sunday-Thursday 9am-5pm, and Friday 9am-1pm, costing NIS 10 for adults, and NIS 9 for students. A combined ticket with the Israelite Tower and Burnt House costs NIS 16, NIS 13 for students. This vast complex shows renovated mansions built for the Temple's high priests, and illustrates how the wealthy Upper City folk lived in Herod's day. The Cohanim and Temple servants lived quite well, as shown by the frescoes, stucco reliefs, fancy furniture, and floor mosaics on display.

Christian & Muslim Quarters

These two quarters take up the northern portion of the Old City, and within its quadrant are many sites holy to Christians, such as the Church of the Holy Sepulchre and the Via Dolorosa, and Muslims too, as well as densely packed shuk alleys catering to (perceived) tourists' needs.

The **Via Dolorosa** (literally, *The Way of Suffering*) is believed to be the route Jesus took as he carried his cross to Skull Hill. Divided into the Via Dolorosa and Via Dolorosa East (with a turn left then right connecting the two), the street starts from the east in the old Muslim Quarter near Saint Stephen's Gate and ends west in the Church of the Holy Sepulchre. All along the way the **Stations of the Cross** are honored on this route, mounted at intervals on church walls or placed in outdoor shrines, though some are hard to find, and others are mobbed by large flocks of tourists being herded from one to the next.

The 14 Stations of the Cross (eight of which are mentioned in the Gospels) can be seen with tour groups, or on your own with guide book and map. Or you can join the Franciscan Friars' processions (often complete with carried cross) Fridays at 3pm starting at Station 1.

The **1st Station**, *200 meters west of Saint Stephen's Gate*, is near Saint Anne's Church—see the following section of *Other Sites along the Via*

VIA DOLOROSA: THE STATIONS OF THE CROSS

*As with many Christian holy sites, the faith that this **Via Dolorosa** is the path goes back to the Byzantines, who traced Holy Thursday processions from Gethsemane to Cavalry, pretty much along the path now marked out as Via Dolorosa, though minus the official stops. Over the years, the routes taken were changed and argued about. As Christianity became more divided, church locations (they all had their own) complicated procession routes, one saying the Praetorium was on Mount Zion, and another saying that no, it was to the north.*

The idea of the stations emerged during the Middle Ages, when they developed as a devotional substitute for actually following the Via Dolorosa, the route in Jerusalem that Christ followed to Calvary. By the 14th century, the Franciscans mapped out a walk including some of today's stations but starting at the Holy Sepulchre. This became the accepted route for nearly 200 years till the European pilgrims started adding to the eight stations, following more gospel stops, and totaling 14. The Jerusalem Way of the Cross as we know it now came into use in the 1800s, and probably has little in common with historic reality, as best as scholars can figure.

Dolorosa—in the courtyard of **Al Omariyeh College**, *through the door at the top of the ramp east of the Ecce Homo Arch*, and it's closed 1-3pm. *Gabbatha* in Hebrew (meaning elevation) and *Lithostrotos* in Greek (meaning stone pavement), this is where Pilate sat in judgment and condemned Jesus to death on the cross (Saint John 19:13). This building was once Turkish military barracks on the sight of the Herodian Antonia fortress. Aside from historic and religious significance, the main attraction is the view of the Temple Mount.

The **2nd Station**, *marked by a board across from the Omariyeh College*, signifies where Jesus took up the cross. To the right of the station is the **Chapel of Flagellation** where Jesus was scourged by Roman soldiers; open daily 8am-noon and 1-5pm, the dome is decorated with a crown of thorns and the windows depict the witnessing mob. To the left is another Franciscan building, **Condemnation Chapel**, built on the foundations of a Byzantine church.

Continuing along the Via Dolorosa you come to the Ecce Homo Convent, Arch, and archaeological remains (see the following section of *Other Sites along the Via Dolorosa*). The **3rd Station**, where Via Dolorosa intersects with El-Wad, is where Jesus first fell while carrying the cross. A small Polish chapel built in 1947 marks the spot with a relief in the arch above the lintel showing Jesus falling under the weight of the cross.

Just past the Hospice is the **4th Station**, where Jesus saw his mother in the crowd. Commemorated by the Chapel of the Swooning Virgin (built around 1950) and the Armenian Catholic Church of the Virgin Mary's Sorrows (built 1881), this event is not mentioned in the New Testament.

The **5th Station** *requires a right turn on Via Dolorosa* to where Simon the Cyrene (from modern day Libya) helped Jesus carry the cross. A Franciscan chapel built in 1881 with signs on the door mark the spot.

Fifty meters on is the **6th Station** where Veronica wiped Jesus' face with her cloth (*sudarium* in Latin). Neither Veronica nor sudarium is mentioned in the bible, but the holy relic of the cloth, complete with imprint of Jesus' face, is revered by the Catholic Church; it's on display at the Greek Orthodox Patriarchate in the Christian Quarter.

The **7th Station** is for Jesus' second fall, honored by a Fransciscan chapel built in 1875 and by *signs on the wall west of Shuk khan ez-Zeit*. In the first century this marked the edge of the city with a gate, a fact used to substantiate the argument that the Church of the Holy Sepulchre is the true location of Jesus' crucifixion.

The **8th Station** represents where Jesus said to the lamenting women "Weep not for me, but weep for yourselves, and for your children..." (Saint Luke 23:28-30). This is a difficult one to find. Cross Khan ez-Zeit and ascend Aqabatel-Khanqa. *Just past the Greek Orthodox Convent on the left* is the stone with a cross and the inscription IC XC NIKA (Jesus Christ is victorious) to mark the station.

For the **9th Station**, there are remnants of a pillar back on *Khan ez-Zeit by the Coptic Church*, marking the point where Jesus fell for a third time. The remaining stations are all in the Church of the Holy Sepulchre, so retrace your steps back to the main street and head there.

For the **10th Station**, enter the Church of the Holy Sepulchre and climb the steep stairway on your right. The chapel has two naves, and the entrance to the one on the right, the Franciscan one, is where Jesus had his clothes stripped from his body. At the far end of this same chapel is the **11th Station** where Jesus was nailed to the cross. The other nave is the Greek Orthodox Chapel, and in there is the **12th Station** where Jesus was crucified and died. To mark the spot there hangs a life-sized Jesus amid flowers and the flames of oil lamps and candles.

The **13th Station**, between the 11th and 12th, is where Jesus was taken down from the cross and received by Mary, as commemorated by a statue of a bejeweled Mary with a silver dagger stuck in her breast. And lastly the **14th Station**, down in the Holy Sepulchre, is where Jesus was buried. Walk down the stairs past the Greek Orthodox Chapel to the ground floor. In the center of the rotunda is a large marble complex surrounded by candles, the Holy Sepulchre, within which is the actual tomb. Beyond the Chapel of the Angel is the Tomb of Jesus, amid still more candles. Around the back of the Holy Sepulchre is the Coptic Chapel where pilgrims come to kiss the wall of the tomb.

Not the prettiest church, **The Church of the Holy Sepulchre** is definitely one of the most sacred of Christian sites, standing above Cavalry (also known as Golgatha), the spot most agree was where Jesus was crucified, where he died and was entombed, and where he rose again. The church is open daily from 4:30am-8pm in summer and to 7pm in winter, but only to those in suitable modest dress. The guards don't mess around, and hold no truck with bare shoulders, legs, or midriffs. Shorts are not acceptable, even in summer. *The main entrance is in the southern courtyard, accessible from Christian Quarter Road or Dabbaga Road off Shuk Khan ez-Zeit.*

The area around **Cavalry** rock was revered by Christians as early as the first century CE, following the Jewish tradition of the time of praying at the tombs of holy people. When Hadrian kicked the Jews out of Jerusalem following the Bar Kokhba Rebellion of 135 CE, he did his best to suppress the budding Christianity and its significant sites as well. The place of the Crucifixion and Resurrection was targeted, and a temple to Venus was erected in its place.

Nearly two centuries later in 326 CE Helena (Emperor Constantine's mother) visited the Holy Land and went around locating and naming the holy sites. Makarios, the Bishop of Jerusalem, showed her where Jesus had been crucified. She initiated some excavations and came upon a tomb (which she identified as the tomb of Joseph of Arimathea) and three crosses, confirming her belief in the holiness of the spot. Shortly thereafter Constantine issued an order to pull down the Venus temple and in its stead build a basilica. It was consecrated in 335 as Anastasis (the Church of the Resurrection); it was destroyed in 614 by the Persians, and later rebuilt. The Caliph al-Hakim demolished it in 1009, leaving little, and a new church was built by the Crusaders in 1149, the church that is there today, though it's buttressed by some of Constantine's foundations.

Given its religious importance (five of the 14 stations of the cross are located within), all the Christian communities and divisions have angled for as much Church of the Holy Sepulchre terrain as possible. In 1852 the Ottoman Empire passed the **Law of the Status Quo** (and the law still stands today), declaring who got what. So the Church of the Holy Sepulchre, the rotunda, the chapel of the Holy Sepulchre, and the anointment stone all belong jointly to the Greek Orthodox, the Armenian, and the Roman Catholic churches, while the Copts, Syrians, and Ethiopians get only individual chapels. This feuding has injured the church a bit in that it's not kept up as it should be. There were fires in 1808 and 1949 and an earthquake in 1927, but the cooperation hasn't existed to pool resources and funds and make all the necessary restorations.

The church is a conglomeration of chapels and alters and stations of the cross. Once in the church, the **Anointment Stone** is the first holy site you come to. The reddish-brown limestone slab is regarded as the place where the body of Jesus was anointed before he was entombed. Underneath the Golgotha chapel is the Greek Orthodox **Chapel of Adam**, where a skull was found, and the claim is that it's the skull of Adam.

Above the Chapel of Adam is **Golgotha Rock**. Golgotha is interpreted to mean "place of a skull," probably from the Aramaic *gulgulta* meaning skull, whereas Cavalry derives from the Latin *calvaria* which means brain case or skull. The argument in Byzantine times ran that the name was given to the rock because Adam was buried here, but some scholars nowadays figure the most likely interpretation is that Golgotha was a skull-shaped hill outside the walls of Jerusalem which was used as a place of execution and burial. By this definition, both the Holy Sepulchre and the Garden Tomb (see *East Jerusalem Sights*) fit the specifications.

The rotunda's 165 foot high dome spans the **Holy Sepulchre**, and is the primary focus of faith and candle-lit glow. The portico of the chamber is called the **Angel Chapel** because tradition has it that the angels were sitting here when they announced to the women that Christ had risen. The body of Jesus lay in the burial chamber on the bench now faced in marble.

Behind the Holy Sepulchre is the **Chapel of the Copts**, which boasts a part of the rock tomb which can be seen (and kissed) at the alter in back. And to the right of the Sepulchre is the **Chapel of Mary Magdalene**, celebrating where she, along with two others, discovered the empty tomb on Easter morning. She is also believed to be the first to have seen the Risen Christ. The church holds many more chapels to wander through. There's the **Chapel of the Appearance** (where Jesus appeared to his mother), the **Prison of Christ** (where Jesus and other criminals were supposedly held prisoner), the **Seven Arches of the Virgin Mary**, the **Crypt of the Invention of the Cross** (where Helena is said to have found the cross Jesus died on), and more.

The **Ethiopian Monastery**, *up some stairs on Khan ez-Zeit*, is right over part of the Church of the Holy Sepulchre, and since the Ethiopians weren't allotted any of the church itself they value their access to the Holy Sepulchre roof. This pleasant monastery with green doors also has access to the Church of the Holy Sepulchre through the Ethiopian Chapel.

Next to the Holy Sepulchre are two mosques. The **Khanqah Salahiyya** is to the north. Built in the late 1100s but with a minaret added in 1417 during restorations, the Khanqah mosque is on the site of the Crusader Patriarch of Jerusalem's palace. The **Mosque of Omar** to the south was built in 1193, and its minaret was also added later in the 1400s. The mosques are not open to non-Muslims, and the minarets are a puzzle.

Seemingly meant to match (note the design and material), it has also been pointed out by someone good at geometry that the mid-point of an imaginary line drawn between the two minarets would be the entrance to the Tomb of Jesus in the Holy Sepulchre. Merely coincidental? Many think not, though the intent remains mysterious.

In the east of the Christian Quarter is an area called **Muristan** (named for the Persian word for hospice), after a ninth century hospice built here by Charlemagne. Sultan Abdulhamid II in 1896 gave the east section to the German state and the west to the Greek Orthodox. **Saint Alexander's Church**, a block east of the Church of the Holy Sepulchre on Dabbaga, attends to the Russian mission in exile. With its restored triumphal arch dating from Hadrian's times, there is also a part of the pavement from Hadrian's Temple to Venus that replaced the first Church of the Holy Sepulchre. Open for services Thursdays at 7am when prayers are said for Tsar Alexander III, its excavations are open Monday-Saturday 9am-1pm and 3-5pm and cost NIS 2—ring the bell to be let in.

Kaiser Wilhelm II's **Lutheran Church of the Redeemer**, *across the street from Saint Alexander's Church, Tel. 02-627-6111*, is open Monday-Saturday 9am-1pm and 1:30-5pm. To climb the tall white bell tower and feel like Quasimodo, enter on Muristan and climb the spiral staircase to the top. There's also a nice medieval door with zodiac signs.

The Greek Orthodox **Church of John the Baptist**, *Christian Quarter Road*, is nearby. It's the oldest surviving church in Jerusalem, or at least the lower level is. Built by the Byzantines in the fifth century, it serves as a base for the more recent 12th century Crusader addition.

Greek Orthodox Patriarchate Museum, *Greek Orthodox Patriarchate Street, Tel. 02-628-9112*, is open Tuesday-Friday 9am-1pm and 3-5pm, and Saturday 9am-1pm, and costs NIS 1 to get in. It contains gifts from pilgrims and early Patriarchate printings in a reconstructed Crusader building. It also features the imprinted cloth with which Veronica wiped the face of Jesus (see *Station of the Cross #6*).

Other Sites along the Via Dolorosa

Saint Anne's Church by Lion's Gate (also known as Saint Stephen's Gate) is one of the best-preserved Crusader churches in Israel. It is traditionally viewed as the site of Saint Anne, the Virgin Mary's mother. The basilica, built in 1140 on some fifth century ruins, resembles a castle. It was used as a mosque for some 700 years after Saladin captured Jerusalem. Next to the church is the **Pool of Bethesda**, an archaeological excavation of an early Roman pool where Jesus healed a crippled man (Saint John 5:1).

Ecce Homo Convent archaeological remains, *Via Dolorosa, Tel. 02-627-7292*, is open Monday-Saturday 8:30am-12:30pm and 2-5pm, and costs NIS 5 for adults and NIS 3 for students. The excavations here, funded by the Sisters of Sion, showcase the **Struthion Pool**, some Roman pavement, and the **Ecce Homo Triumphal Arch**. The convent is believed to be just north of where Herod's Antonia Fortress stood, surrounded by a moat. Herod had it built in 30 BCE, destroying part of the canal (built by the Hasmoneans in second century BCE to provide water to the Temple Mount cisterns) when the moat was dug. A reservoir (the Struthion Pool, a part of the moat) replaced the canal to serve the fortress. The pool was later vaulted over by Hadrian (second century CE) and turned into a cistern.

Much of the convent is built over the cistern remains. The Roman pavement was laid above the cistern and served as a plaza. Hadrian's triple Truimphal Arch formed a gate to the plaza, and the largest one was known as Ecce Homo Arch. This arch now marks the spot the church remembers for Jesus' trial before Pilate (John 19:5) and his words "Behold the man" (*Ecce Homo* in Latin).

Other Muslim Quarter Sites

The architecture is Ayyubid and Mamluk, the area is the largest, the population is the densest, and the quarter is the least well-explored by travelers. Near the entrance to the Temple Mount is **Bab el-Silsila**, a street built on what used to be part of the Mamluk route over the Tyropoeon (Cheesemaker) Valley and leading to Chain Gate. It eventually becomes David Street deep in the core of the tourist markets and exits out by Jaffa Gate.

Near the beginning of the street is the **Khan as-Sultan**, a well-preserved Crusader caravansary which lodged merchants and donkeys. Farther down and to the right (just past Misgav Ladakh) is the **Tashtamuriya Building**. It holds the tomb of none other than the builder himself, Tashtamuriya (d. 1384), and used to be an Islamic college.

If you follow Bab el-Silsilah to its intersection with HaKotel you'll come to the **Kilaniya Mausoleum** (1352) and its Mamluk half-dome. Further on are the **Tomb of Lady Turkan** (Turba Turkan Khatun, 1352) and **Turba Sadiyya** (1311). And at the end of Bab el-Silsilah on the right is the **Tankiziya Building**, built in 1328 by a Mamluk with a varied career. He started out as a slave, rose to Governor of Damascus, and then fell back down to imprisonment and execution. This building is on the site of what used to be the Sanhedrin, and is now occupied by Israelis for its strategic location near the Western Wall and Temple Mount.

Aqabat et-Takiya is a small street that intersects with El Wad. On it stands the old palace **Serai es-Sitt Tunshuq** (1382) which is now an orphanage. Across the street is the domed tomb **Turbatt es-Sitt Tunshuq**, built by and for the lord of the palace. On the corner with El Wad is an old pilgrim's hospice **Ribat Bayram Jawish**; built in 1540, it's one of the last examples of Mamluk architecture.

Tariq Bab en Nazir is another main route to the Temple Mount, and as with the others, it's named after the gate (*bab*) at the end. The gate has two names: Gate of the Inspector and Gate of the Prison. The former refers to the founder, and the latter to the Turks who used Ribat Mansuri (built in 1282 and once a hospice) as a prison. Nearby is **Ribat Ala ed-din el-Basir** (built in 1267 as a hospice and the first Mamluk building in the city). Next to the gate is the **Supreme Muslim Council** office, the grandly decorated place to plead your case (probably futilely) if you want access to a Muslim site not currently open to tourists.

Tariq Bab el-Hadid leads from El Wad to the Temple Mount's Iron Gate. There is some very nice stone work to see there, as well as a fine view of the Western Wall. **Madrasa Jawhariyya** is on this street. Built in 1440, it was once a college, while the building next door, **Ribat Kurd**, was a hospice built in 1293. Across the street were two more colleges, **Madrasa Arghuniyya** (1358) and **Madrasa Muzhiriyya** (1480). And further still is the **Small Wall**. Also known as the Hidden Wall, it's marked by a sign near the Iron Gate. It's now part of a Muslim house, but it's also part of the very same Western Wall revered by Jews.

Shuk el Qattanin was the Market of Cotton Merchants, and the vaulted passageway was built in the 1200s to provide income for the poor. **Hammam el-Ayn** and **Hammam esh-Shifa**, two Turkish style baths, are also on this street.

On El Wad itself is **Beit Sharon**, home of the Israeli controversial politician and fighter Ariel Sharon. He bought this spot in the middle of the Muslim Quarter, as he did many things, to make a statement about the rights of Jews to live anywhere in Israel.

Armenian Quarter

In the southwest quadrant of the Old City between Jaffa and Zion gates, this quarter manages to maintain its own schools, library, residential section, unique flavor and language. Aramaic, the old biblical language, is still spoken on the street and in the churches. Armenia was the first nation to adopt Christianity in the fourth century, but their kingdom was dissolved later that century, resulting in centuries of exile and persecution, climaxing in the Turkish massacre of 1.5 million in 1915. The exiled community here identifies strongly with their language, culture, and church.

Armenian Compound, *Armenian Patriarchate Road, Tel. 02-628-2331*, lodges around 1,000 Armenians and is closed to tourists, though visits can sometimes be arranged if you call. It used to be a pilgrims' hospice but turned residential to accommodate the refugees after 1915. Go in Jaffa Gate and turn right, skirting the Tower of David.

Saint James Cathedral, *Armenian Patriarchate, just past Saint James Street*, is open for services daily 3-3:30pm. Originally built in the 400s CE, the cathedral honors both Saint James the Greater and the Lesser. Saint James the Greater was the first martyred Apostle. He was beheaded, supposedly on this site, by Herod Agrippas in 44 CE and then delivered to Mary on the wings of angels. Saint James the Lesser lies entombed in the northern chapel. He was the first bishop of Jerusalem but was chased out by Jews who disapproved of his teachings. The cathedral was destroyed by Persians in the seventh century, rebuilt by Armenians in the 11th century, and the Crusaders enlarged it 100 years later. The Armenian touch can be seen in all the beautiful tiles throughout the ornate cathedral, with loads of hanging lamps and censors.

The **Mardigian Museum**, *further along Armenian Patriarchate, Tel. 02628-2331*, is open to all Monday-Saturday 9:30am-4:30pm for NIS 5 (or NIS 3 for students)—follow the Armenian Museum signs or enter from Saint James Cathedral. This museum with nice courtyard and arched colonnades, previously a theological seminary built in 1843, tells the story of Armenia from early Christianity in 46 CE to the Turkish massacre of 1.5 million Armenians in 1915.

The **Convent of the Olive Tree** is down the narrow street near the museum and through the gateway in the wall. Built around 1300 and beautifully, classically Armenian, the best time to visit is 8-9am, though someone from the convent will usually be willing to let you in until noon (admission is free). It's believed that this was the site of the house of high priest Annas, father-in-law to Caiaphas (John 18:13). Some also think that this is where Jesus was imprisoned instead of where the Via Dolorosa stations indicate. And in the 15th century the belief circulated that the olive tree in the courtyard was the very same to which Jesus was tied before being flogged. The stone in the northeast corner is also of theological significance, thought to be the stone Luke (19:40) said would have cried out had not the disciples praised God.

The **Syrian Orthodox Convent** and **Saint Mark's Chapel**, *Ararat*, is the site, according to Syrian church belief, of Saint Mark's house. The Virgin Mary is believed to have been baptized here and that the Last Supper took place here as well—this in contrast to most other Christians who see the Cenacle on Mount Zion as the true locale. Open in the afternoon (ring the bell), the door is marked by a lovely mosaic, and there's an interesting painting, on leather canvas, of the Virgin and Child attributed to Saint Luke. To get there from Armenian Patriarchate Road, turn left on Saint James and again on Ararat, and there you are.

Mount Zion

"Zion" first referred to the fortress on the eastern hill of Jerusalem belonging to the Jebusites (one of the tribes occupying Canaan prior to the Israelites moving in) before David took it over. The southwest hill was where David's city was thought to stand, and since Byzantine times has been known as Mount Zion. You can exit the Old City through Zion Gate to get there or take bus 1 or 38 from Western Jerusalem.

The **Cenacle** (Greek for *supper*) or **Coenaculum** (Latin for *dining hall*) is where the **Last Supper** is generally thought to have occurred (except by the Syrian Orthodox, see above). The Room of the Last Supper through the green door is from a Crusader building, and inside there's an interesting scene depicting a pelican (a Christian symbol for repentance) feeding two young ones blood from his heart.

Below is **King David's tomb**. Tradition has it that it was one of the first synagogue spots. There's a tomb there now in a Crusader niche, with plentiful decorations. It's used sometimes as a synagogue, with a blue tiled niche facing Mecca so Muslims can pray here as well, while the Christians pray upstairs. There is no evidence that David was really buried here, it's too far from his city, but it's a lovely spot and highly revered. Open daily 8am-5pm, admission is free.

MOUNT ZION'S MANY RULERS

This is a favorite place for Christians and Jews to fight about. There was a village of Jews here during First Temple times. Then there was a community of early Christians living here, and during Byzantine rule a church was built here. The Persians destroyed the Byzantine church, and then the Crusaders came, killing Muslims as they went, and they built a huge complex here.

So Jews claimed it as theirs, Christians did the same, and in the 15th century the Turks came in and made it a mosque (the mihrab can still be seen on the southern wall). The bullet holes attest to its popularity among the many religions, but now all religions can pray here, and there's a nice view from the roof, as well. It was an important view for Jews before '67 as it was a place from which they could see the Temple Mount (Israel's president used to climb up here to pray during 1948-1967). From up here you can also see the Kidron Valley leading down toward the Dead Sea, the Hill of Ill Repute, and the Hill of Evil Council, the latter named after Caiaphus.

Diaspora Yeshiva, *below the Cenacle, Tel. 02-671-6841*, is where many Americans study Torah. Outside across the courtyard and across from David's Tomb is the **Chamber of the Holocaust**, *Tel. 02-671-5105*, open Sunday-Thursday 8am-6pm, Friday 8am-2pm, costing NIS 7, and commemorating the victims of WWII. Not as elaborate as Yad Vashem, it's still an effective display.

The **Museum of King David**, *next door*, exhibits modern art that's meant to evoke his life and spirit. And the **Palombo Museum**, *across the street to the left, Tel. 02-673-6640*, exhibits works of the same sculptor who did the Knesset gate and pieces in Yad Vashem.

Dormitsion Church, *off the right fork of the road leading to the Cenacle, Tel. 02-671-9927*, is the big, beautiful basilica commemorating where Mary "fell asleep" (died). Open daily 8am-noon and 2-6pm, admission free, the church stands on the site of the late fourth century Byzantine Haiga Sion, a huge building which was destroyed in 996 and had been described as the 'mother of all churches' because it was believed to be the place where Jesus washed the disciples feet, where the Last Supper took place, where Peter denied Jesus, where Judas betrayed him, and where the disciples were filled with the Holy Spirit and enabled to speak in many tongues. The church here now is relatively new, built in the early 1900's by the Benedictines on land 'given' them by the King of Austria.

It sustained quite a lot of damage during the fighting in 1948 and 1967, and parts of the basilica have never been repaired. Mosaics on the wall and floor of the crypt show Mary in a coffin, gaudy with gold, there's a figure of her stretched out in a restful death position, and the floor is inlaid with figures of the zodiac. Downstairs is an interesting mosaic of Jesus surrounded by Biblical women. The complex has a cafe selling cakes and drinks (including beer).

The **Church of Saint Peter in Gallicantu** (Saint Peter of the Cockcrow) stands on the eastern slope of Mount Zion as you descend toward the Sultan's Pool. Open Monday-Saturday 8-11:45am and 2-5pm and with free admission, it's built on foundations from Herodian and early Christian times, though the building there now was consecrated in 1931. The church is known as the site of Peter's threefold denial of Christ, and the grotto below is supposedly the prison where Caiaphas held Jesus prisoner (though not according to the Church of the Holy Sepulchre). There's a fine view from the church balcony, looking over the City of David, the Arab village of Silwan, and the three valleys below.

The City of David

Southeast of Temple Mount between the Tyropeoen and Kidron valleys is where Jerusalem started back in the 20th century BCE. Excavations began in 1850, but only recently have answers begun to make sense.

Archaeologists agree that the steep hill of **Ophel** (*hump*) is in fact the site of the Jebusite city conquered by King David.

It seems the early walls enclosed an area of some eight acres. It was a strategic location, taking into account the major considerations of war and water. The top of a hill is traditionally easier to defend, and nearby was the water source of Gihon Spring (meaning Spring that Gushes). In peaceful times the townspeople came and went through Water Gate, but for siege conditions, there was a shaft to import water without leaving the safety of the city walls. These features played a role in David's strategy for taking the city, as he sent his soldier Joab down the walls of the shaft.

In 1867 the biblical account (2 Sarmuel 5:8) was confirmed by the long shaft found by archaeologist Warren. In 701 BCE King Hezekiah, fearing an attack from the Assyrians, adapted the system to prevent David's trick from being turned against him. He built a tunnel to bring water from Gihon Spring into the city and into a reservoir (the pool of Shiloah or Siloam), hiding the spring entrance from prying Assyrian eyes. In 1880 after the tunnel was excavated, an inscription (the Siloam Inscription) was found celebrating the completion of the tunnel by Hezekiah's engineers.

To see the **excavations**, go out Dung Gate, turn left, and walk down the hill to the entrance. There's a signposted path leading round the excavations, pointing out the Jebusite citadel and Jerusalem's Upper City where the wealthy lived before Babylon put an end to their high style. The site is open daily 9am-5pm and it's free.

There's a small **museum**, *100 meters down from the City of David entrance, Tel. 02-628-8141*, with photos of the excavation in progress, and **Warren's Shaft** down the spiral staircase. Open Sunday-Thursday 9am-5pm and Friday 9am-1pm and costing NIS 3.5, bring a flashlight to see the walls that Joab scaled.

Downhill from the shaft, **Hezekiah's Tunnel** is open for soggy exploration, but you'd be advised to do so with a guide. The water reaches a few feet high, the trip takes a good half hour before you emerge wet and mucky out the other end, and a flashlight (not to mention shoes that won't be ruined by a little water) are recommended. Enter at the Gihon source on Shiloah Wȧy (off Jericho Road going toward Kidron Valley from Mount of Olives) and take the tunnel to the Pool of Shiloah (*Silwan* in Arabic, or *Siloam* in Hebrew). It's open all day free of charge, but not necessarily free of hassle, and Arab buses run up and down the valley.

Kidron Valley

Kidron Valley (*Valley of the Dark One*) lies between Temple Mount and the Mount of Olives. In the time of the Israelite kings (1020-922 BCE) Kidron formed the eastern city boundary of Jerusalem. It must have had

DAY OF JUDGMENT STORIES

According to Jewish legend, people will be assembled together on the Mount of Olives, across from the Temple Mount and the Judgment Seat. Two bridges will appear across the valley, one of iron and one of paper, and all humanity will have to cross one of them, depending on how they have been judged. The iron bridge will collapse under the weight of the guilty, and those sent across it will die, while the paper bridge will easily bear up under the light consciences of those sent upon it, and they will live eternally.

According to Muslim beliefs, Mohammed will sit in Judgment on a pillar by Golden Gate, and everyone will have to pass over arches. Those weighted down by heavy consciences will sink, while those light with goodness will pass over the hair-thin arch to heaven.

a running river in biblical times, since Aza told the Levites to clean out the desecrating idols and throw them in Kidron Valley, but it doesn't have a source and can only collect rainwater from the surrounding slopes.

The valley winds through Silwan village, out through the Judean wilderness, and down to the Dead Sea. It was used as a burial site for common people, and kings Asa and Josiah burned heathen idols here. The **Valley of Jehoshaphat** (meaning *God judges*) is the part of Kidron Valley between the Mount of Olives and the Temple Mount. Jews, Christians, and Muslims all believe its the place where the 'nations' will be judged on Judgment Day. Thanks to the belief that God would waken the dead to be brought for judgment, Kidron Valley has been a favored burial site, and the tombs to the side of the road are among the best first and second century tomb monuments around. Previously a road that was only suitable for walking, construction is now under way to pave a road to haul in the tours.

Heading south from Ophel on Shiloah Way, the **Tomb of Jehoshaphat** is first. This is a first century tomb on the right, with an interesting frieze above the entrance.

Just in front of Jehoshaphat's is **Absolom's Tomb**, supposedly belonging to the traitorous son of David (II Samuel 15-18), though the fact that it was built in the first century BCE makes this rather unlikely. It's impressive all the same, with its Ionic columns, burial chambers hewn from rock, and cone-like top. It's pock-marked with stone acne thanks to another tradition which calls for parents when they pass the monument with their children to revile the bad son and throw rocks at his tomb.

A dirt path to the left leads to another monument, the **Tomb of B'nei Hesir**. The burial chambers for the Hesir family of priests dates from the late 100s BCE. It's intricately decorated and inscribed, and is impressively carved out of the cliff. According to Christian tradition, James the Just was buried here after his martyrdom.

ABSALOM'S STORY

The story goes that Absalom, who was King David's third son, was renowned for his beauty and graces, and held the love of David and his people. Amnon was David's first-born, and he fell in love with his sister, Tamar. He schemed and lied to get time alone with Tamar, and then raped her. David was angry, but did nothing to punish Amnon, while Tamar went off to live a secluded life in Absalom's home. Two years later, Absalom invited all his brothers to a big sheep-sheering feast, and then he had Amnon killed. Absalom fled to his mother's home in Geshur to escape his father's wrath.

A few years later, after David had cooled down, Absalom came back to Jerusalem, but it took more years yet before he won back his father's favor. When he was firmly back in court life Absalom got himself a small force of men and began to stir things up among his people, instigating resentment against David, and was said to have "stolen the hearts of the people of Israel." After four years of this he went to Hebron with a force of 200, and announced: 'As soon as ye hear the sound of the trumpet, then ye shall say "Absalom reigneth in Hebron." People from all around joined Absalom, and the rebellion was on. They fought, and Absalom's troops were soundly trounced. When Absalom rode his mule under a large oak tree his hair got tangled in the branches and he was stuck. David's general Joab saw him there and, contrary to David's express orders, took the opportunity to kill Absalom, thrusting three darts into Absalom's heart. They tossed his body in a pit, and David was inconsolable when he heard.

Absalom had planned ahead, however, and while still alive had ordered a memorial stone to be set up for him in the king's dale, saying "I have no son to keep my name in remembrance," and he ordered the pillar to be called Absalom's place (2 Samuel 18:18).

The **Tomb of Zechariah** nearby is carved entirely out of the rock, with Ionic columns and pyramid roof. Tradition has it that this first century BCE tomb is the burial site of the prophet Zechariah (II Chronicles 24:21) who advocated rebuilding the Temple to the Jews newly returned from Babylon.

Hinnom Valley

Hinnom Valley (properly **Gei-Ben-Hinnom**, *Valley of Hinnom's Son*, or sometimes Gei-Hinnom, *Valley of Hinnom*) stretches from below Mount Zion to Kidron Valley. *Gehenna*, the Greek and Latin word for Hell, derives from Hinnom, as does the Muslim *Gahannam*, one of their hells.

Perhaps one reason for all this hellish reference is the child sacrifice that used to go on here as part of the Topheth and Molock cult. Though Topheth's form is unknown, the word has been interpreted to mean "place of fire" or "hearth," and it, too, was a name for hell in the Middle Ages. Ahaz (King of Judah in 736-725 BCE) reputedly sacrificed here and burnt his children in the fire (2 Chronicles 28:3, 2 Kings 16:3) though the rite comes from pre-Israelite Ammonite days. After King Josiah (639-609 BCE) ordered the cultic sites be destroyed, the memory of the sacrifices remained linked to the valley of Hinnom and its name took on the strong associations with Hell, associations that began with Jeremiah, who predicted that the valley of Hinnom would one day be called the 'valley of slaughter.'

The Greek Orthodox **Monastery of Saint Onuphrius (Aceldama)** and the so-called **Field of Blood** or **Potter's Field (Hakeldamach)** are on the southern slope of the valley of Hinnom. According to the New Testament (Acts 1:18) after Judas betrayed Jesus, his 30 pieces of silver were used by the head priests to buy a field to which Judas went "and falling headlong, he burst asunder in the midst, and his bowels gushed out." The monastery is named after an Egyptian hermit, known for wearing a long beard and nothing else.

Mount of Olives

Up above is the **Mount of Olives**, a 2,655 foot hill beyond Kidron Valley that's important in Jewish and Christian theology (the Byzantines built 14 churches up there). Named after the many olive trees that thrived here at one time (a few representative trees can still be seen) this is also where the Last Judgment is supposed to take place. According to Jews, the Messiah is to appear on the western slope, and according to Zechariah (14:4) this is where the Lord's feet will stand on the apocalyptic day of the Lord. At that time, presumably, everyone is going to have to travel from their graves get here to be judged, and if you're buried right here, there's that much less to travel.

The valley is replete with cemeteries full of Jewish graves, but Mount of Olives is the oldest and largest Jewish burial site and holds maybe 75,000 graves. In addition, this is said to be the site of an old Israelite shrine, since 2 Samuel tells how King David went up there to mourn Absalom's death. Jesus and his disciples often hung out in the Garden of Gethsemane at the foot of its western slope, and Jesus is said to have ascended into Heaven from the middle peak of Ascension Hill, so the hill is also holy to Christians. There's an Arab village of At Tur (Mount of Olives in Arabic) on the summit, and Arab bus 75 goes there from the bus station on Suleiman. To see the sights, head up in the morning when the churches are open and the sun is still low, then walk down via the churches along the way, or come later in the afternoon when the sights have reopened and the afternoon light imparts a special touch.

North of the terrific vantage point of Seven Arches Hotel are the **Church of the Eleona** and the **Church of the Paternoster**, both behind the same gate, and both founded by Queen Helena in the fourth century. The Church of the Eleona (*elaion* means olives in Greek) was built in the fourth century, destroyed by Persians in 614, and restored in 1927. It's to mark where Jesus revealed his "inscrutable mysteries" concerning the destruction of Jerusalem and the Second Coming to his disciples. The Church of the Paternoster, built in 1875 by French Princess Aurelie de la Tour d'Auvergene, marks where Jesus taught the Lord's Prayer (it's written in 77 languages on the tiled wall). Both are open Monday-Saturday 8:30-11:45am and 3-4:45pm, and entrance is free.

Church of Ascension, *farther north next to Augusta Victoria Hospital, Tel. 02-28-7704,* is open Monday-Saturday for free, but a visit to the tower costs NIS 6). The 45 meter high tower commands amazing views, and the church has nice paintings and mosaics. The **Russian Chapel of the Ascension** boasts the tallest belfry with the best views, but they rarely open their doors to the public.

There is also a **Mosque of the Ascension**, since Islam recognized Jesus as a prophet worthy of veneration. There was a church built here in the fourth century, but the Crusaders renovated it, and when Saladin came in, he authorized some followers to take it over. The stone floor features what's meant to be the footprint Jesus left as he ascended, though bits of it have been chipped away by Byzantine pilgrims seeking holy souvenirs. Ring the bell if the door's closed, and pay NIS 2 to see the sacred footprint within.

Down from the hotel there's a gate on the left leading to two tunnels identified as the **Tombs of the Prophets** Malachi, Haggai, and Zechariah, unlikely given the graves actually date to the fourth century. The tombs consist of 36 niches hewn from the rock; you can visit them Sunday-Friday from 8am-3pm. The orange sign designates the **Common Grave** of those who died in Jewish Quarter fighting in 1948, and next to them is the **National Cemetery**. Further along the path and you come to the **Jewish Graveyard**, the largest Jewish cemetery in the world, dating back to biblical times. Its popularity hinges on the belief that the Mount of Olives is where the Resurrection will take place when the Messiah comes, bringing the Day of Judgment.

Down and to the right is the **Sanctuary of Dominus Flevit** (meaning *The Lord Wept*), built in 1955 to commemorate where medieval pilgrims claimed Jesus wept for Jerusalem. When the present church was built in 1954, a fifth century monastery was discovered and excavated, as well as a large cemetery from 1500 BCE. The cemetery has been covered back up, but some of the tombs are still visible. It's open daily 8am-noon and 2:30-5pm in winter, till 6pm in summer.

Proceeding down the hill you come to the **Russian Church of Mary Magdalene**, *Tel. 02-628-2897*, open Tuesday and Thursday 10-11:30am, but call ahead to make sure, and admission is free. The seven onion-domed golden cupolas provide a gleaming authentic Russian landmark on the hill. Built by Czar Alexander III in 1885, he had it constructed in the 16th century Russian baroque style and he dedicated it to his mother, the Empress Maria Alexandrovna. The body of a Russian Grand Duchess, Elizaveta Fyodorovna (sister of the last Czarina) who died in the Russian Revolution, was smuggled here via Beijing and is buried in the crypt. The church is now a convent and has a terrific choir, as well as some very fine paintings by Vaisly Vereshchagin and Aleksandr Ivanov. It also claims that part of the Garden of Gethsemane is on its grounds.

The Mount of Olives is also where Mary is said to be buried. The **Tomb of the Virgin Mary**, open Monday-Saturday 6:30am-noon and 2-5pm, admission free, marks the spot, and is revered by Christians and Muslims. This was a burial site during the first and second centuries, a Byzantine church stood over Mary's alleged tomb in the fourth century, and then a Crusader church was rebuilt here in 1130, a big church in the shape of a cross. The church flooded regularly, and now there are steps up to avoid the problem. The Crusader queen Melissanda was buried here, as was Joseph. Now an eastern church, the sounds and incense are meant to appeal to the senses. There is also a Muslim *mihrab* facing Mecca for Arab women with fertility or other women's problems to pray.

Gethsemane (or *Getsemani*—Aramaic, the language Jesus spoke, for *oil press*) is the garden at the foot of Mount of Olives where Christ's Agony and subsequent capture took place, and the garden now supports some of the oldest olive trees on the mount. Inside the garden gate is the **Church of all Nations** (also called **The Basilica of the Agony**), facing west toward the Old City. The church is open daily 8:30am-noon and 2:30-6pm (till 5pm in winter), while the grotto down below closes year-round at 5pm, admission free. The spot here has been regarded as holy since the fourth century, but the church here wasn't built till after WWI in 1924, financed by twelve countries. Inside, mosaics illustrate the last days of Jesus' life, and the rocky apses are said to be where Jesus prayed three times. **Betrayal Grotto** is where it's believed Judas betrayed Jesus and where Judas was arrested. The floor of the grotto was decorated with mosaics in early Byzantine days, and the tombs were built here later. **Saint Stephen's Church** is on the south side of the main road. A 'modern Byzantine' church constructed in 1968, this is where the first Christian martyr is said to have been stoned to death. Ring the bell to come in as there are no set visiting hours and no admission fee, and once in you can see the site where Stephen was slain, remains from the old Roman road, and an anonymous tomb cut into the rock.

Mount Scopus

To the south is the **Mount of Umbrage**, also known as the Mountain of Perdition, and to the north is **Mount Scopus**, the start of the same chain of hills that includes the Mount of Olives. From up top there are marvelous views of the city and the Judean Desert, as well as the luxury of the Hyatt Regency Hotel. Given its strategic lookout and location, it's not surprising it's played important roles in centuries of Jerusalem wars. In 70 CE Roman legions under Titus camped here, the Crusaders set up camp in 1099, the British followed suit in 1917, and Arab troops attacked from here in 1948. In addition to war camps, Mount Scopus is a place of learning, hosting universities and hospitals. To get here without doing a lot of up-hill hiking, take Arab bus 75 or Egged bus 4, 4a, 9, 23, or 28.

The Mount Scopus campus of **Hebrew University** was founded here in 1925. The university was relocated to Giv'at Ram after 1948, but the Mount Scopus campus was renovated after the Six Day War of 1967. There are free English guided tours around the modern architecture of the renowned campus Sunday-Thursday at 11am, about an hour. They leave from the Bronfman Visitors' Center in the administration building. Even if you don't take the tour, you can visit the **Hecht Synagogue**, one of the major sites on the tour.

Northwest of Hebrew University is **Hadassah University Hospital** (not to be confused with the Hadassah Hebrew University Medical Center with the Chagall windows in the southeast). The **British WWI Cemetery** east of the hospital holds soldiers from the British Commonwealth forces. Also on Mount Scopus to the south is the American-affiliated **Jerusalem Center for Near East Studies** of Brigham Young University.

EAST JERUSALEM

The **American Colony Hotel**, *Nablus*, is worth visiting if you're in the neighborhood (see *East Jerusalem Hotels* for the full description of this sumptuous pasha palace). The **Tomb of the Kings**, *Nablus*, is just near American Colony. Open Monday-Saturday 8am-12:30pm and 2-5pm, it costs NIS 4 and takes two minutes to see. It's not really worth a special trip.

Tourjeman Post, *4 Cheil HaHandasa, Tel. 02-628-1278*, tells the history of Jerusalem during the dicey years of 1948-1967. Currently closed for renovations (call to see if they've reopened to the public), they're generally open Sunday-Thursday 9am-4pm, Friday 9am-1pm. This museum is in an old Turkish house and costs NIS 8 for adults, NIS 6 for students, and NIS 5 for children. Its theme is 'a divided city reunited' and it presents a somewhat rose-colored view of the time when the city was divided by barbed wire between Israel and Jordan. To get there, continue south on Nablus till you get to the US Consulate and take the fork northwest on Shmuel Hanavi. Tourjeman Post is just off there.

Garden Tomb is a lovely green leafy garden with paths to all the relevant Christian sites. Very friendly English speaking staff proffer literature in many languages, and admittance is free. At the far corner of the garden is a platform from which you can see Skull Hill (*Golgatha* or *Cavalry* from Mark 15:22, both of which mean "Place of the Skull"), the site some believe to be where Christ was crucified. Some also see the craggy hill as resembling a human skull, adding another layer of potential significance. The Tomb, discovered in 1867, is thought to be the one in which Jesus was placed. Though tombs aplenty have been unearthed in Jerusalem, this one seems to match a number of New Testament descriptions (John 19:41-42-, Matt 27:60, Luke 24:1-4): in a garden, hewn from stone, and near Golgotha. The tomb and sights are interesting for devout Christians, and beautiful and peaceful for heretics. Leafy bowers, singing birds, and flowers surround Skull Hill, the Tomb, and its legend which reads "He is not here for he has risen."

King Solomon's Quarry, *across from the Garden Tomb and northeast of Damascus Gate*, is open Saturday-Thursday 9am-4pm, Friday 9am-2pm, and entrance costs NIS 6 for adults and NIS 3 for children. It's also called Zedekiah's Cave, after the sixth century BCE King who was blinded before being led off to Babylonian exile by Nebuchadnezzar after first witnessing the murder of his own sons. Legend has it King Zedekiah used this cave to try to escape to Jericho before Nebuchadnezzar took him captive. According to the Muslims, this was where Korah and his followers were swallowed up by the earth (Numbers 16:32). And it was named King Solomon's Quarry by the Freemasons since Solomon is said to have been one of the first Freemasons, and they believe he hewed stones from here for the First Temple. It is agreed that stones from this quarry were used for buildings in Jerusalem during First Temple times, in Hasmonean times, during Herod's rule, and for the Jaffa Gate clock tower. And, the YMCA got permission to quarry stones from here for their chapel. Whatever you choose to call it, it's deep underground and worth a visit.

The **Rockefeller Museum**, *Sultan Suleiman, Tel. 02-628-2251*, is open Sunday-Thursday 10am-5pm and Friday-Saturday 10am-2pm, and costs

NIS 20 an adult and NIS 12 for students and seniors. Set near the Old City in East Jerusalem, the American Colony convinced Rockefeller to build a museum here to showcase archaeological findings. There are exhibits from all ages of human habitation, starting with Paleolithic and Neolithic times, and going on up through the Bronze and Hellenistic, Roman and Persian, Crusader and Islamic periods. They've got a statue of Ramses III, detail findings at Beit Shean, and the history of crucifixion, including the Crucified Man from Giv'at Ha-mivtar—the world's only archaeological evidence of crucifixion. It's a pleasant and interesting place to stroll through history and pass an hour or so, and the stucco dancing girls between the North and South wings shouldn't be missed. Come early or late in the day to avoid the crowds.

WEST JERUSALEM

Also called the **New City**, West Jerusalem has its own goodly number of sights. There are also all the pleasures of a modern city, including swank cafés, pedestrian walks, and intricate bus routes.

Downtown/Zion Square Area

The **Russian Compound**, *at the foot of Jaffa Street*, was bought by the Russian Church in the mid 1800s (pre-revolution) for their Holyland pilgrims. In their complex the church built a hospital, hospice and a library, while those who couldn't afford the hospice pitched tents. In the British Mandate days (1917-1948) police were stationed here—it's a police station still—and a prison was here as well. The prison is now a museum, the **Hall of Heroism**, *Tel. 02-623-3166*, commemorating Israel's underground movement in the early fight for independence against the British. It's open Sunday-Thursday 8am-4pm and costs NIS 6, or NIS 3 for students.

Parts of Hebrew University moved here after the Mount Scopus campus was given up in '48, and the Supreme Court used to be here as well. The last effort of Mayor Teddy Kolleck, the plaza and with its many palm trees was to be named after him, but was named after the influential Safra family instead.

One of the grand buildings at the foot of Jaffa near the Old City is **Saint Louis Hospital**, a hospital for the terminally ill. During the war for independence, this was no-man's land, site of many incidents. One involved a patient at the hospital who leaned out his window and dropped his false teeth. It took a week of UN intervention for the man to get them back.

Down the hill is **Notre Dame**, not a hospital any longer, but a hospice for pilgrims. This magnificent structure was built by the Roman Catholic Assumpionist Fathers in 1887 for the French Pilgrims, and it came under heavy fire during the War of Independence in 1948, so much so that the south wing facing the Old City became uninhabitable from the bombing and was used as an Israeli bunker instead. In 1970 the Assumpionists sold the building to the Jewish National Fund who turned it into a students' residence for Hebrew University. The Vatican eventually bought the property and from 1973-1978 refurbished it for use as a Catholic hospice.

The **Great Synagogue**, *King George, Tel.* 02-624-7112, is across from the Sheraton and open Sunday-Friday 9am-1pm. It's an enormous though unremarkable synagogue. You should come in modest attire. Next door, in Heichal Shlomo, is the **Wolfson Museum**, *58 King George*, open Sunday-Thursday 9am-1pm, and admission costs NIS 4. The museum displays Judaica and scenes illustrating Jewish history. Heichal Shlomo, meaning Solomon's Mansion, is the seat of the Chief Rabbinate of Israel, and the scales on both sides of the entrance stand for justice.

Museum of Italian Jewish Art and Synagogue, *27 Hillel, Tel.* 02-624-1610, is open Sunday-Thursday 9am-1pm and Wednesday 4-7pm as well, with admission for NIS 4. The 18th century synagogue, brought here from Italy, is the only one outside of Italy where the ancient Italian liturgy is performed.

The **Skirball Museum**, *Hebrew Union College, 13 King David, Tel.* 02-620-3333, is open Sunday-Thursday 10am-4pm and Saturday 10am-2pm. Admission is free but the explanatory brochure costs NIS 5. There are two floors of finds from archaeological excavations, including the "House of David" Stele (the first reference outside of the Bible to mention King David and his dynasty), lots of pottery and funerary offerings, and pictures showing the process of discovery at the ongoing excavation of the ancient cities of Laish/Dan, Gezer, and Aroer. Of special interest to linguists are storage jars from Gezer displaying the earliest alphabet (Proto-Canaanite) known in Israel, dating from the 16th century BCE.

Another fine, small, free museum is the **Anna Ticho House**, *7 Harav Kook, Tel.* 02-624-5068, open Sunday, Monday, Wednesday, Thursday 10am-5pm, Tuesday 10am-10pm, Friday 10am-2pm. Her drawings are interesting, Dr. Ticho's Menorah collection is wonderful, and the cafe is reason enough to stop by. There is a small library there, peaceful and comfortable and lined with books on Jerusalem, art, and literature, and a gift shop as well. The Ticho House was one of the first to be constructed outside the Old City Walls. Built in the late 1800s by an Arab dignitary, and Shapira (a notorious antiquities forger) was one of his first occupants. Dr. Avraham Albert Ticho left his native Moravia in 1912 to open a eye clinic in Jerusalem; his cousin Anna joined and married him that same year. The Tichos bought this house in 1924 and converted the lower portion to an eye clinic, while Anna applied her talents to the Jerusalem landscapes.

Beit Harav Kook, *9 Harav Kook, Tel. 02-623-2560*, is near Zion Square and open Sunday-Thursday 9am-2pm, Friday 9am-noon. It's a tribute to the life, works, and pedagogical achievements of Rabbi Abraham Yitzhak Hacohen Kook, first chief Rabbi of Eretz Yisrael. Built in 1923 and recently restored and opened to the public, there are weekly classes and seminars available as well as tours of the library and exhibits.

Mahane Yehuda, *off Agrippas*, is a street market full of noise and bustle, orthodox Jews and tourists, and tempting smells and great food. It's a wonderful, lively, aromatic scene, and Thursday afternoon is best to see the pre-Shabbat rush. Bountifully-hipped matrons shove about for fruit, vegetables, cheese, pickles, and delectable bakery items in this market whose name means Camp of Judah. Falafel joints dot the corner of HaEgoz and Agrippas, selling pitas for NIS 7 (see *Where to Eat* section for more gustatory options).

Avraham Haba Museum, *43 Hanevi'im, Tel. 02-644-4444*, is temporarily closed and will reopen in April, 1998. Their usual hours are Sunday-Thursday 9am-5pm and they have a large collection of micrography, with the Bible, sacred Jewish texts, and biographies of Jewish leaders.

Artists House, *12 Shmuel Hanagid, Tel. 02-625-3653*, is open Sunday-Thursday 10am-1pm and 4-9pm, Friday 10am-1pm, Saturday 11am-2pm.

Mea She'arim

This neighborhood of the very orthodox is just north of downtown near Ethiopia Street. Its name means *One Hundred Gates*, and is a reference to Genesis 26:12 and Isaac receiving one-hundred fold from his labors. It's interesting to walk around and see a community that has kept intact many of the traditions and life styles that existed in the Eastern Europe of pre-WWII days. What may be fascinating and unique to visitors, however, is everyday life to the residents in this district, so you need to be careful about stepping on their cultural or religious toes, avoid overboard gawking, and dress modestly (which in this community means no shorts for men, no shorts, minis, or bare shoulders for women; public affection between the sexes is also frowned on). As in Mahane Yehuda, the shops and markets really hum Thursday afternoons as people prepare for Shabbat.

Visitors during Shabbat (after sundown Friday to sundown Saturday) should respect the holiday; they should be on foot, and should not include picture-taking (photography of people won't be very popular at any time unless you ask first).

The **Ministry of Education Building**, *Shivtei Y'Israel*, is between HaNevi'im and Mea She'arim streets. It's is grand building in 16th century Italian renaissance style, built in the 1880s to be the Italian Hospital.

Nearby is the **Ethiopian Church**, *Ethiopia Street*, magnificently domed but rarely visited. Built between 1896 and 1904 with an entrance gate carved like the Lion of Judah, the church is open daily 7am-6pm in summer and 8am-5pm in winter, and admission is free. The lions recall Ethiopa's Queen of Sheba and the lion emblem Solomon gave her when she visited. Across from the church is the **Eliezer Ben Yehuda** house, where he lived and worked on reviving the Hebrew language (much to the disapproval of the very orthodox, who felt Hebrew should be saved for prayer).

Nahl'ot and **Zikhronot** are other religious neighborhoods south of Mahane Yehuda, these ones filled with mostly Sephardic Jews from Yemin, Morocco, Turkey, and Iran. It's another interesting place in which to wander and explore the winding narrow alleys and little shops.

Giv'at Ram

Giv'at Ram is served by buses 9, 17, and 24.

Start your visit to this district with a trip to the **Israel Museum**, *Giv'at Ram, Tel. 02-670-8811*, wonderfully large and full of Israel's treasures. It's a place to visit with time and energy to spare. Most days (all but Tuesday) the museum opens at 10am; Saturday, Wednesday, and Thursday the museum closes at 5pm, Friday at 2pm, and Saturday at 4pm; Tuesday it's open 4-10pm. The entrance fee is NIS 30 an adult, NIS 20 for student or senior, and NIS 15 for youth. Save your ticket, because re-admission on another day costs only NIS 10 when you show your stub. And there are free guided tours (1.5 hours) at 3pm (not including Tuesday or Friday).

Their permanent exhibits show the stuff you want to see when you visit sites around the country and read that their best finds are now located at the Israel Museum. You could go here and only here and still get a sense of the history and richness of the country. There are always changing temporary exhibits as well. The **Youth Wing** is very well done; it's interesting for adults but a must for kids. The **Shrine of the Book** where the Dead Sea Scrolls are kept is also fascinating, and there's a free 45 minute tour Sunday, Monday, Wednesday, Thursday at 1:30pm, Tuesday at 3pm and Friday at 12:45pm. The white dome is sculpted to look like the lid of the jars in which the scrolls were found. The scrolls and clothing remnants on view were preserved by the dry desert air so well the text on the parchments and the status-indicating colored stripes on the cloth can still be seen.

The main building houses the most comprehensive collection of Judaica, with Ashkenazi and Sephardi cultures represented. The remnants of the Harb Synagogue, brought over from Germany, are wonderful, as is the 1701 Vittorio Veneto Synagogue, donated in its entirety, from Italy. In the Archaeology wing, get a look at the anthropoid sarcophogai, and the prehistory section as well. And the mosaic from Beit She'an is exceptional. The buildings are arranged around landscaped courtyards, and the **Billy Rose Sculpture Garden** is one of the outdoor exhibits.

Bible Lands Museum, *25 Granot, Tel.* 02-561-1066, is across the street from the Israel Museum, accessible by bus 9, 17, 24, 99, and is open Sunday-Tuesday, Thursday 9:30am-5:30pm, Wednesday 9:30-9:30pm, Friday 10am-2pm, and Saturday 11am-3pm. It has a collection of ancient art portraying scenes and civilizations from the Bible, with Egyptian sculpture, ivories, and ancient seals.

The **Knesset**, *Eliezer Kaplan, Tel.* 02-675-3333, is located across and up from the Israel Museum. Israel's law-making assembly, it has a free tour that leaves Sunday and Thursday at 8:30am and 2:30pm or when a large enough group has gathered, lasts 15 minutes, and isn't worth the bother. You don't need the tour to see Chagall hall and its truly beautiful tapestries. They were designed by Chagall in 1964 and hand-woven in France. The 12 floor mosaics were also designed by Chagall. The open sessions however, even though they are in untranslated Hebrew, are more interesting. The sessions are Monday and Tuesday from 4pm and Wednesday at 11am. They last two hours and you must bring your passport to get in.

The **Supreme Court**, *behind the Knesset, Tel.* 02-675-9666, connected by the Rose Garden walk, is open for visits Sunday-Thursday 8:30am-2:30pm. It's worth a visit, both for the magnificence of the structure (with Israeli marble, copper from Solomon's mines, and Jerusalem Stone) and the interesting content of the free one hour tour that leaves Sunday-Thursday at noon. They explain the beautiful and symbolic architecture, and discuss the Israeli constitution (the one still in the process of being drafted), how a supreme court decides laws without one, and the controversial role of today's court.

Across from the Government Center is the Giv'at Ram **Hebrew University Science Department**. The Visitors' Center, *Sherman Building, Tel.* 02-588-2819, offers tours Sunday-Thursday at 10am.

There too is the new **Bloomfield Science Museum**, *Tel.* 02-561-8128, open Monday, Wednesday, Thursday 10am-6pm, Tuesday 10am-8pm, Friday 10am-2pm, and Saturday 10am-3pm. Admission is NIS 20 for adults, NIS 17 for students, and NIS 14 for children. It's a hands-on, interactive museum, popular with children and adults alike. Also on this campus is the **National Library** with the beautiful **Ardon Window**, of second-largest-stained-glass-window-in-the-world fame. The window gloriously depicts Kabbalistic symbols in mystically dark, rich colors. The library is open Sunday-Thursday 9am-7pm, Friday 9am-1pm, and admission is free.

Ein Kerem & Environs
Yad Vashem, *Tel. 02-675-1611*, is open Sunday-Thursday 9am-5pm, Friday 9am-2pm, and is free. Easily accessible by buses 13, 17, 18, 20, 23, 24, and 27, this extraordinarily moving museum was established in 1953 in memory of the victims of the Holocaust, named "a memorial and a name" from chapter 56 in Isaiah. The **Children's Memorial**, done in 1987, has five flames reflected in countless mirrors. In the dark, names are called out while the flames flicker. The **Garden of Righteous Gentiles** (over 7,000 trees so far) was featured in *Schindler's List* and honors the many gentiles who helped with kindness and bravery. In the Hall of Members Cemetery burns the **Eternal Flame**. Ash brought from Europe was buried here. The pillars symbolize the chimneys and incinerators of the concentration camps. The **Historical Museum** is the main section.

There is so much to see here, you could easily spend hours. Outside are "Last March" and "Resistance to Warsaw Ghetto," sculptures by Naftalee Bezem representing Jews, from the horror of the holocaust to rebirth, full of intriguing symbols like the fish that stand for fertility and the cactus (sabra) for the resilient Israelis. Inside tells the sad story of European Jewry from the restrictions and humiliations of the 30s to WWII's horrors, with documentation, pictures, and films.

Save some time for the **Art Museum** as well. They have a wonderful exhibit on "The Last Ghetto, Life in the Lodz Ghetto" that is interesting and moving. If you can help it, go on your own rather than on a tour to Yad Vashem. It's such a personal experience, time pressures and deadlines don't fit the mood. Also, some of the tour guides tend to shatter private horror and reflection with their intrusive lectures.

The **Military Cemetery**, *Mount Herzl*, has **Herzl's tomb**. Heads of state come here to pay respect, plant a cedar. There's a big Independence Day ceremony here, but unless you feel deeply about the founder of Zionism there isn't much to see here. The **Herzl Museum**, *Tel. 02-651-1108*, open Sunday-Thursday 9am-5pm, Friday 9am-1pm, admission NIS 4.5 and students NIS 3, tells the story of the man who pioneered Zionism up until he died in 1904. **Jerusalem Forest**, *west of Mount Herzl*, a fine spot for a picnic and a cool breeze. Bus 17 can get you there, and bus 19 takes you to Hadassah Medical Center, just 15 minutes walk away.

Ein Kerem (*fountain of vines*) used to be an Arab village and it's said to be where John the Baptist was born. It's a strikingly pretty place, with hills and views and little winding streets. It's now got lots of pottery galleries as well. Along with the churches and hostel, there's a nice garden restaurant (see *Where to Eat* section) as well.

Saint John Ba Harim, *Tel. 02-641-3639*, also known as the **Church of Saint John**, commemorates the spot he was born with a stunning clock tower. Open daily 6am-noon and 2-6pm (2-5pm in winter), there are fine paintings within and ceramic prayer plaques in many different languages outside. There are excavations from early Arab times, and the Grotto of the Nativity below, where you can see a pheasant mosaic from the Byzantine chapel through a grate. The views from the hill are beautiful, and there are pottery galleries nearby.

Across the valley, **Church of the Visitation**, *up Ma'ayan, Tel. 02-641-7291*, also called **Saint Mary's Catholic Holy Church**, has beautiful arches, and a painting of Mary with gold halo and gilt edge. The church celebrates Mary's visit to Elizabeth and has the rock the infant Saint John hid behind when the Romans were looking for babies to kill. The tower is tall, the site peaceful and serene, and there's cool water running in **Mary's Spring**. Open 8-11:45am and 2:30-6pm (2:30-5pm in winter), there's cactus and palm fronds in the garden and another swell view over the terraced hills. There's also a hostel nearby (see *Where to Stay*). The pink tower is part of the **Russian Monastery**, *Tel. 02-625-2565*, and you can visit by appointment.

South of the church complex is the synagogue of **Hadassah Medical Center**, *Tel. 02-677-6271*, not to be confused with the Hadassah Hospital on Mount Scopus. Here are the famed **Chagall Windows**, showing the 12 tribes in stained-glass depiction based on Genesis 49 and Deuteronomy 33. Chagall gave the windows to the hospital in 1962. In '67 four windows were damaged in the war and Chagall was cabled. He replied "You worry about the war, I'll worry about my windows." True to his word, two years later he replaced the damaged panes, though three windows still bear bullet holes from the battle. It's open Sunday-Thursday 8am-1:15pm and 2-3:45pm, Friday 8am-12:30pm, and admission costs NIS 12 per adult and NIS 8 for students. There are free tours in English Sunday-Thursday every half hour from 8:30am-12:30pm and 2:30pm, and Friday every hour 9:30-11:30am.

Holyland Hotel's **Model of the Second Temple**, *Bayit Vagan, Tel. 02-643-7777*, is a two-foot-high big nothing, west of Hadassah. Open 8am-10pm daily, it costs NIS 15 for adults, NIS 12 for children and students, and NIS 60 for a family ticket. Bus 21 will drop you a short walk away, but it'll take you longer to get here than it will to see the sight.

Giv'at Hatahmoshet/Ramat Eshkol

Ammunition Hill, *Sderot Eshkol, Tel. 02-582-8442, Fax 02-582-9132*, is near University Boulevard to the north of city center, and is open Sunday-Thursday 8am-6pm, Friday 8am-2pm. On the crest of the hill is an outdoor museum including plaques listing fallen soldiers, pillboxes, trenches, fields of the Harel Tank Brigade, and an Observation Overlook. The Underground Museum was once the main Jordanian command bunker and weapons depot on the 1948 Jerusalem partition line. They also show videos on the Battle for Jerusalem, Six Days in Jerusalem, If I Forget Thee, and audio presentations of In the Eyes of the Enemy and Battle Reports. Surrounding the museum are public gardens (trees and dirt), picnic tables and public toilets. Buses 4, 9, 28, and 29 go there.

To the west are the **Sanhedrin Tombs**, also called the **Judges' Tombs**. Open Sunday-Thursday 9am to sunset, buses 9, 26, 27 take you there and admission is free. The Sanhedrin was ancient Israel's 71 member supreme court, and in this pleasant park is where they are said to be buried.

Southwest of the Tombs is the new **Biblical Zoo**, *BarHan off HaSanhedrin, Tel. 02-643-0111*. Open in summer Sunday-Thursday 9am-7:30pm, and in winter Sunday-Thursday 9am-5pm, and year-round Friday 9am-3pm, Saturday 10am-5pm, and admission is NIS 25 for adults, NIS 18 for children. The old Biblical Zoo was a disappointment, but this new one is a delight.

Southern Districts

The **Yemin Moshe** area outside Dung Gate was the first settlement to be built up outside of the protection of the city walls in the 1850s. Walls meant security in those times, and building outside of them didn't catch on at first. **Mishkenot Sha'anim** (Tranquil Settlement), Yemin Moshe, was one of these early attempts. Sir Moshe (Moses) Montefury started building there (he even brought the windmill, but it didn't work, and it's now a small **museum**, open Sunday-Thursday 9am-4pm, Friday 9am-1pm, and free).

By 1948 the area had fallen into neglect, and in 1967 Teddy Kolleck sold the property to those rich enough to renovate the insides without changing the old exteriors. Mishkenot Sha'ananim is now a guest house of 10 apartments, used by the government to house visiting artists and writers (though no longer for free), and there's an exclusive French restaurant of the same name as well. Across the street on King David is **Liberty Bell Park (Gan HaPa'amon)** which features a copy of the Liberty Bell in Philadelphia. There are several art galleries lining the expensively quaint alleys of Yemin Moshe.

Herod's Family Tomb is just south of the King David Hotel. Thanks to grave robbers, little was here when archaeologists came upon the scene, and Herod himself isn't here but was buried near Bethlehem instead. Below in the valley is **Sultan's Pool**, named after Suleiman the Magnificent. Not only did he build the Old City walls in the 16th century, he added a dam and fountain to this Second Temple reservoir. These days it's an amphitheater and gets used for open-air concerts.

Rehavia

This beautiful residential triangle between **Derekh Aza** (Gaza) and **Ramban** (southwest of Independence Park) was developed by German Jews fleeing the Nazi regime in the 1930s. Not much of the original high German cultural flavor remains, but the preserved old stone buildings and well-tended gardens make for a pleasant amble away from faster paced, bus-clogged regions.

Jason's Tomb on Alfassi is in the middle of the district. It was built around 100 BCE as the burial site for three generations of a substantial Jewish family in Hasmonean days. Charcoal drawings of ships on the porch wall indicate the Jasons' wealth was financed by ocean trade, but the pyramid on top was a later add-on. Findings of cooking pots and food shed light on notions of an after life, and the dice included in the collection of essentials may speak to their perception of the importance of gambling at the time and in the great beyond.

Further east on the Balfour and Smolenskin corner is the **Prime Minister's house**. And next door on Balfour is **Schocken Library**, designed by Erich Mendelsohn in the late 1930s (his own house was in the windmill on Ramban near Kikkar Tzarfat).

Komemiyut (Talbiye)

This district is accessible by bus 15.

Between the district of Rehavia and the Liberty Bell Garden lies the small and equally elegant neighborhood of Komemiyut (Talbiye). This was a wealthy Arab community before the inhabitants were dispossessed in 1948. Their graceful villas are now popular with Hebrew University profs and other successful professionals.

The official residence of the **Israeli President**, *HaNassi*, is near the **Jerusalem Theater, southeast** *on Chopin*.

To the west, is the **Mayer Institute for Islamic Art**, *2 HaPalmah, Tel. 02-566-1291*. They have a worthwhile collection of Islamic paintings, jewelry, and artifacts, it's open Sunday-Monday, Wednesday-Thursday 10am-5pm, Tuesday 4-8pm, and Friday-Saturday 10am-2pm, and the cost is NIS 10 for adults, NIS 8 for students, and NIS 5 for children (and free on Saturday).

The office of the **AACI**, *6 Mane, Tel. 02-561-7151*, down Balfour past the circle to Disraeli, Mane is opposite 13 Disraeli. Inside the beautiful stone building and its lovely garden is a wealth of material and information meant to ease the process of living in Israel for Americans and Canadians taking the plunge. Even if you're just visiting, you may want a piece of information, be interested in a social group, concert, tour or lecture, or just welcome the North American accent.

The German Colony

South of Komemiyut along Emek Refaim (take King David south till it turns into Bethlehem and keep going past the train station, fork right and you're there) is one of the 19th century communities built by the German Templars. The streets are peaceful and lovely, the gardens lush, and the old Arab and German style stones emanate serene wealth.

Talpiot

Beit Agnon, *161 Joseph Klausner, Talpiot, Tel. 02-671-6498*, can be reached with bus 7. Open Sunday-Thursday 9am-1pm, there are tours and an English film presenting Nobel Laureate S. Y. Agnon, his library and home. It's near **Kibbutz Ramat Rachel**, *Tel. 02-670-2555*, a spot that saw a lot of bloody fighting in 1948. Now a tourist attraction, its name (meaning Height of Rachel) refers to Jacob's wife who's buried in Bethlehem. They have guided tours showing kibbutz life and a museum with 1948 War exhibits that's open daily 8am-noon, and bus 7 will take you there. For information on the guest house, see the *Where to Stay* section.

The **Haas Promenade** has view of the mounts and view of the city, while nearby on the east side of Kidron Valley is the Hill of Evil Counsel. The vistas are nice but it's not a big deal. Tour guides treat it mostly as a photo opportunity, though joggers show up for the sunset run. There is also a self-service restaurant there, with seating inside and out, and reasonable prices. Bus 6 or 6A will get you there and back.

GUIDED TOURS

Egged's Circle Line, *bus station office at 224 Jaffa, or downtown office at 44a Jaffa, Tel. 02-625-4198 or Tel. 02-625-3454*, offers the Circle Line bus #99 to 33 of Jerusalem's main tourist sites. A day pass is NIS 18.5, a two-day pass is NIS 77, including three tourist site tickets. You can look at these places through the windows of your air-conditioning bus, or get off and resume with the next bus two hours later. The bus departs from King David Street every two hours Sunday-Thursday 10am-4pm, Friday 10am-12pm, and the last trip doesn't include Yad Vashem.

Is it worthwhile? If you have to leave Israel the next day and want to get a glimpse of all these spots so you can tell the folks back home that yes, you saw them, go get your ticket. Otherwise you will probably be disappointed. Even if you start with the first bus, you can only disembark and see four places for your money (not counting entrance fees), and the public transport system is just as good for NIS 4 per trip.

Free Walking Tours, every Saturday from 10am-noon, leave from 32 Jaffa. They are informative and enjoyable, and a good way to see some of the Old City, especially if you get in Moosha's group.

Jewish Quarter Tours, *Tel. 02-627-2360*, leave from the Women's Water Fountain in the Jewish Quarter daily (except Wednesday) at 3pm, Saturdays at 5pm, but call first to see if it's on and the exact time (it depends on the season). Jeffrey Seidel charges NIS 15, though it can be waived if you can't afford the fee, and modest dress is required.

Zion Walking Tours, *Jaffa Gate office to the right of David Street, Tel. 02-628-7866 or Tel. 05-030-5552*, has three hour tours ($9 for adults, $7 for students) leaving at 9am, 11am, and 2pm, and include a rampart walk. They also do a 3.5 hour Mount of Olives tour Monday at 9am, Wednesday at 2pm for $20 (students $16) and a 3.5 hour Southern Wall and Herodian tour Monday at 9am and Wednesday at 2pm for the same price.

Archaeological Digs Ltd., *Tel. 02-627-3515*, offers a number of tours, all with a short seminar/slide show introduction, for $13. Meet at 34 Habad above the Cardo at 9:30am. They arrange digs in Beit-Gourim (see below), and do full ($160) and half day ($90) walking tours of the city.

Jaffa Gate unaffiliated entrepreneurs (also know as pests) will try to hook you for a tour of the city. They may start at $20 or higher, drop easily to NIS 50, and can be bargained way down. But you take your chances on quality, and the city offers tours for free.

Rent-A-Guide, *Tel. 02-676-8111*, offers guided tours for small groups, taking in trips such as Jerusalem, Bethlehem and a kibbutz for $70, or Massada and the Dead Sea for $85.

Egged Tours, *224 Jaffa, Tel. 02-625-4198, Fax 02-624-2150*, is open 7am-7pm. They have tours all over Israel and Jerusalem, starting at $22-$24 for half a day in Jerusalem to $320 for three days in Eilat. It's the largest tour agency in Israel, but not necessarily the best, and certainly not the most personal or the friendly.

United, *King David Street just near the King David Hotel, Tel. 02-625-2187, fax 02-625-5013*, with pick ups in East Jerusalem at Notre Dame, American Colony or anywhere in West Jerusalem. They have tours from $20 for half a day in Jerusalem to $275 for 3 days in Eilat. The staff is friendly and the tour guides knowledgeable, if you don't mind the nature of a big bus tour.

Galilee Tours, *Hillel opposite El Al, Tel. 02-625-8866*, is Israel's Grey Line representative. They offer tours around Israel and to Jordan.

Many hostels arrange inexpensive tours, providing transport without a guide. **Swedish Hostel**, *29 David Street, Tel. 02-589-4124/02-627-7855*, is one example, but most hostels provide similar services and prices. The **Old City** tour (NIS 20) starts at Jaffa Gate at 9am and is five hours. For **Masada** (NIS 65) you are picked up at your hostel at 3am to allow you to climb the snake path in time for the sunrise. It also takes in visits to the Dead Sea, Ein Gedi Reserve, Qumran, and Jericho. The **Bethlehem** trip (NIS 25) takes three hours, and the **Galilee** (NIS 100) is a full day.

SEMINARS, LECTURES, & DIGS

• *Hebrew Union College, 13 King David, Tel. 02-620-3333, posts a bulletin board out front listing lectures and concerts.*

•*Jeffrey Seidel's Jewish Student Information Center, 1/15 Hameshoririm, Jewish Quarter, Old City, Tel. 02-627-2360, Fax 02-628-8338, run weekly Torah readings and organize Sabbath Programs, lead Jewish Quarter, Moslem Quarter, and Tunnel Tours, and offer special holiday programs as well. They can also be reached on e-mail at ohel.avrohom@yankel.sprint.com.*

• *Aish HaTorah, Beit Ha-Sho'eva Road, Jewish Quarter, is a mostly American yeshiva. Women should apply to the administrative offices off Shvut Road.*

• *Albright Institute of Archaeological Research, Nablus Road, has irregular hours but has information on archaeological digs.*

• *The Rockefeller Museum Antiquity Department, Tel. 02-560-2607, can help set you up on a dig. Or call Tel. 06-658-5367 to find out about joining the Beit She'an dig.*

• *Archaeological Digs, LTD., Tel. 627-3515, arranges digs in Beit-Gourin every Friday, charging $22 per adult, $17 per child, NIS 16 entrance and transportation not included. For a ride, guide and entrance, it costs $55 an adult, $50 a child.*

• *Archaeological Institute of America, 656 Beacon Street, Boston, MA 02215, Tel. 617/353-9361, Fax 617-353-6550, email: aia@bu.edu, lists over 300 dig sites throughout the world in their Archaeological Fieldwork Opportunities Bulletin, available for $11 from Kendall Hunt Publishing, Tel. 800/228-0810.*

SPNI (Society for Protection of Nature), *13 Helene Ha'Malka, Tel. 02-625-2357*, leads excellently guided tours to all over the countryside, most of them including hiking and nature exploration. They also do some trips in Jerusalem, and all are well worth the time and money. The Wednesday trip to the Judean Hills (and Bar Kokhba's cave, and more) leaves from their office at 8am (get there 15 minutes in advance) and costs $46 (bring your own flashlight, lunch, and water).

The guides are very knowledgeable, not just about the history, but the desert plants and geology as well, and it makes for a wonderful combination of legend, lore, hiking—not strenuous but neither is it for the complete couch potato. Their Monday (9am) Wadi Kelt Oasis and Saint George Monastery tour ($45) is very popular; it's been canceled for the time due to unrest in the Wadi Kelt area, but will be resumed just as soon as political conditions warrant. Visit their offices or call to reserve, or go through BTC (see below) who are authorized to book SPNI tours.

Bring hiking boots (sneakers are allowed if that's all you have, but they don't protect against sprains) or nature sandals (depending on what hike you're going on). Water (three liter minimum in summer) and a hat are necessary, and lunch for a day hike.

Neot HaKikar, *6 Shlomzion HaMalka, Tel. 02-623-6262*, specializes in guided tours in the Sinai.

ABC-BTC, *1 Hasoreg, Tel. 02-623-3990, Fax 02-25-7827*, is off Jaffa near Shlomzion. Open Sunday-Thursday 9am-7pm, Friday 9am-1pm, their initials stand for Better Travel Consultants, and they offer tours and tickets for less, and advice for free. They specialize in bus trips to Cairo and Petra/Jordash trips.

Budget Travel ISSTA, *31 HaNevi'im, Tel. 02-625-7257*, sells ISIC cards for NIS 35 (bring proof of student status and some ID), and book student discounts on flights, car rentals, etc.

NIGHTLIFE & ENTERTAINMENT
Ethnic Music & Folklore
The Khan Club, *David Remez Square, Tel. 02-671-8283, Fax 02-673-3095*, is near the railway station. The nightclub folklore show starts at 9pm and costs $15 or NIS 55, with all the free wine (semi-dry white or rosé) and soda you care to guzzle. You should call to reserve, and in the winter call again before heading over to see if there were enough sign-ups for the show to go on. The theater is a stone cave, dim with oriental carpets, and kind of great. The show, unfortunately, is a tourist group thing, with a "Here's Johnny," lounge act tone. Called a nightclub, there's nothing striptease about it. The show is all folkloric dance and song, a cross between *Fiddler on the Roof* and *Beach Blanket Babylon*—cheesy but not campy—with a singer/comedian type who's a cross between Tom Jones and Soupy Sales. Bus 6, 7, 8, and 30 will drop you at the railway station.

YMCA, *Tel. 02-623-3210 for reservations, Tel. 02-624 7281 for information*, has **Arab and Jewish Folklore** evenings on Mondays, Thursdays, and Saturdays.

The Jerusalem Hotel, *Nablus Road, Tel. 02-628-3282*, features Jazz Night on winter Thursdays and Lebanese Buffet Dinner with Afghani music on Saturdays at 8pm. The ambiance is cozy and Arabic and interesting, and the special evenings are well-attended. Call in advance, however, to make sure it's on and to reserve.

Classical Music
The Jerusalem Symphony, *Tel. 02-561-1498 after 4pm*, performs in the Jerusalem Theater, *David Marcus and Chopin Streets*.

Gerard Bakhar Center, *11 Bezalel, Tel. 02-625-1139*, has concerts of classical, jazz, and Israeli folk music.
Dormitsion Church, *Tel. 02-671-9927*, sometimes has classical organ concerts. **Saint Andrew's** sponsors a Vocal Concert Series, *Tel. 02-673-2401*, at 8pm, with four concerts for NIS 130. **Saint George's Cathedral**, *20 Nablus, Tel. 02-627-7232*, on the corner of Salah Eddin about eight minutes from Damascus Gate, sometimes has free concerts.
Hebrew Union College, *13 King David, Tel. 02-620-3333*, posts a bulletin board out front listing lectures and concerts. And the **Israel Museum**, *Tel. 02-563-6231*, sometimes has concerts, lectures, and dance as well.

Pubs

Heleni HaMalka and Horkenos streets (near the Russian Compound, just off Jaffa) hold loads of neat old stone houses turned trendily into bars for the yuppie crowd.
Glastnost, *15 Heleni Hamalka, Tel. 02-625-6954*, has a palm-tree filled patio, meals (NIS 16-28) and beer (NIS 8-15), and the music ranges from jazz to rock to funk (mostly tapes with the occasional live group). Open 7pm to the wee hours, there's hard liquor too, but it'll cost you as much as a meal.
Sergey, *Heleni Hamalka, Tel. 02-625-8511*, next door to Glastnost, hosts the intelligentsia, dishing up beer (NIS 12), mixed drinks (NIS 22) and Italian food to young intellectuals with money.
Over on the other side of Jaffa are some more options:
Tavern Pub, *16 Rivilin, Tel. 02-624-4541*, is open daily from 2pm-3am. This small, dark, friendly spot has been in business for 33 years, serving mugs of beer and shots of booze for not very much.
The Rock, *11 Yoel Salomon, Tel. 02-625-9170*, is a cafe and bar that caters to the scruffy-haired low-budget travelers who make good use of the daily happy hour deal from 5-9pm that gets you one free beer with each that you buy. With relatively cheap food (mallaweh is NIS 9, blintzes are NIS 15-20), this can be a pleasant place to hang out, but the music can get over loud and sometimes it's just too precious.
And of course there's **Fink's**, *2 HaHistadrut, corner of King George, Tel. 02-623-4523*, deservedly written up by Newsweek as "One of the best bars in the world," and not to be missed for a drink served by Moulli, one of the best bartenders (and owners) in the world, accompanied by a cup of goulash (NIS 19) and an interesting mix of politicos, journalists, and regular locals. See *Where to Eat* for the full picture.

Discos

Arizona Pub and Disco, *37 Jaffa near Zion Square*, has happy hour nightly from 7:50-8:10pm. Drink all the gassy weak beer you want and can for NIS 7, and from 8:10-9pm, buy one drink and get one free. After that, dance the night away till 4am. Western in theme and young in clientele, there's no cover, just a one-drink minimum.

The Underground, *8 Yoel Salomon, Tel. 02-625-1918*, is around the corner. Slightly more popular (for now) and definitely more cave-like, the happy hour and drink minimum deals are the same, and so is the sweaty, gyrating crowd, and so is the pounding disco beat.

Talpiot, *to the south off Hebron Road*, has some bigger dance clubs. The **Opera**, **Pythagoras**, and **Decadence** swing into action on Fridays and Saturdays from 9pm-5am, and charge covers from NIS 20-45 (plus the taxi fare home).

Sultan's Pool (Brekhat Ha-Sultan) amphitheater, *down below Yemin Moshe*, has summer shows featuring British and American rock stars. It's a great setting for a rock concert if you like that sort of thing, and tickets start at around NIS 70.

Folk Dancing

The **International Cultural Center for Youth**, *12a Emek Refa'im, Tel. 02-566-4144*, has folk dancing Sundays at 7:30pm for NIS 12 (bus 4 and 18 will go there). **The House for Hebrew Youth**, *105 HaRav Herzog, Tel. 02-678-8642*, or *Beit Ha'No'ar* in Hebrew, has folk dance classes Thursdays at 8pm. Bus 19 takes you there.

And the **Liberty Bell Gardens** hosts a post-Shabbat outdoors dance jubilee, teaching folk and modern jazz to whomever shows up.

Theater

The **Jerusalem Cinematheque**, *Hebron Road, Tel. 02-672-4131*, in the Hinnom Valley has two screens showing a number of films nightly at 9:30pm (plus 10pm and midnight on Fridays and 4pm on Saturdays) for NIS 16. Southwest of the Old City, bus 5 and 21 go there. In early July they host the **Israeli Film Festival**, with international and local showings listed in the Jerusalem Post or the theater. **Kakao Cafe**, open daily 11:30am-1am, has good albeit pricy food for a pre or post show meal.

The **Palestinian National Theater**, *Nuzuh, near the American Colony Hotel, Tel. 02-628-0957*, puts on plays and musicals, usually political in content and Arabic in language, though English synopses are provided. Al Hakawati in Arabic, from Nablus the theater is on the first right after Salah ad-Din; plays cost NIS 15-20 and tourists are welcome, but call first to make sure a show is on.

SHOPPING

Palestinian Pottery, *14 Nablus, Tel. 02-628-2826*, across from the American Consulate, is open Monday-Saturday 8am-4pm. Run by the Balian family and established in 1922, this is a factory, showcase, and shop of fine, hand-painted pottery. It's not only a swell place to look around and shop, if it's not busy, Mr. Balian can tell you some interesting tales. His Armenian parents were recruited in 1919 to use their craft renovating the Mosque of Omar. Three years later the Balian family started up their own business, and they've been throwing hand-made pots on wheels and painting them ever since. You can buy plates and bowls for NIS 10-200 and vases for NIS 15-300, depending on size and design, but they don't take credit cards and they don't ship.

Palestinian Needlework Shop, *79 Nablus opposite the Ambassador Hotel, Tel. 02-582-8834, Fax 02-582-5823*, is open Monday-Saturday 8am-7pm and sells handcrafted traditional cross-stitch embroidery on locally woven fabrics. A non-profit project of the Minnonites, it aims to supplement the incomes of local (mostly Ramallah and Surif) Palestinian women. Items range from $2 bookmarks to $50 pillow cases and $55 shawls.

Tarshish, *18 King David, corner of Hess, Tel. 02-625-8039*, is a reputable place to shop for antiques, Judaica (beautiful mezuzim), and Yemenite jewelry (nicer than average). Open Sunday-Thursday 10am-1pm and 4-7pm, the owner is honest, and it's a great place to shop for coins. Credit cards accepted.

Galleria David, *near the bottom of King David*, has good art.

Avi Ben's Wine Store, *22 Rivlin, Tel. 02-625-9703*, has a fine selection of Israeli products as well as an espresso counter serving good, strong coffee for NIS 4.5 and glasses of wine for NIS 7-13.

SPORTS & RECREATION

Hiking trips to the Judean Desert (see *Tours* above).

The **Jerusalem Skating Center**, *19 Hillel*, is up above the Croissanteriee. Open Sunday-Thursday 10am-11pm, Friday 10am-2pm, Saturday sun-down-11:30pm, skate rental and access to the silicon "ice" will cost you NIS 20.

Jerusalem Walks - See *Tours*.

Swimming pools: Beit Zayit, *Tel. 02-533-2239*, is the last stop on bus 151 and is open daily 10am-5pm, costing NIS 30 (children NIS 24) and NIS 35 on Friday-Saturday (children 24); **Jerusalem Swimming Pool**, *Emek Refa'am, Tel. 02-563-2092*, by bus 4 or 18, is open daily 6am-8:45pm and costs NIS 35, but you need Shabbat tickets in advance.

EXCURSIONS & DAY TRIPS

According to the U.S. Embassy, travel to Hebron and the Gaza Strip are considered dangerous, though it's a good idea to call the Embassy and check the status when you're planning your trip.

The Arab village of **Abu Ghosh** is 13 kilometers west of Jerusalem, accessible by bus 185 or 186 leaving hourly from the central station and costing NIS 3.9 (sherut taxis to Tel Aviv will drop you two kilometers from the from the town). This place is believed to the original site where the Ark of the Covenant was kept before King David moved it to Jerusalem, and for this it's considered holy by Jews and Christians. The town was the last of a series of caravan stops to Jerusalem in the 18th century, and Sheik Abu Ghosh made some good money off his pilgrim toll.

On top of a hill is where people believe the Ark sat, and in its stead is now Notre **Dame de l'Arche d'Alliance** (Our Lady of the Ark of the Covenant). Open daily 8:30-11:30am and 2:30-6pm, the church was built in the 1920s over the Byzantine mosaic fragments of an otherwise demolished previous church. Below the hill is a lovely garden and in that garden is the preserved Crusader **Church of the Resurrection**. Open Monday-Wednesday and Friday-Saturday 8:30-11am and 2:30-5:30pm, and free, the church was built in 1142. Beneath the church excavations have revealed remains from Neolithic days. Find the minaret of the mosque next door and the church entrance is on your right. For a bite to eat in Abu Ghosh, the **Caravan Inn** on the road to town has hummus and fine views.

Avshalom, 19 kilometers southwest of Jerusalem, has a spectacular stalagmite and stalactite cave, worth seeing despite the hordes who think the same. Open Saturday-Thursday 8:30am-3:30pm, Friday 8:30am-12:30pm admission costs NIS 13 for adults, NIS 7 for children. The ticket includes a slide show and guided tour every day but Friday. Friday is special. Though no tours are arranged, it's the only day when you're allowed to take pictures, since unlimited flash photography would damage the mineral formations. Bus 184 or 413 will take you as far as the village of Nes Harim, but that leaves you seven more kilometers to go. You can hike or find a taxi, or better yet rent a car or join an Egged tour from Jerusalem.

Neot Kedumim, Route 443 off Route 1, near Lod and Ben Gurion Airport, *Tel. 08-977-0777, Fax 08-977-0775* (in the US, *Tel. 914/254-5031, Fax 914-254-4458*, is the **Biblical Landscape Reserve**. Open Sunday-Thursday 8:30am-sunset and Friday 8:30am-1pm (last entrance is two hours before closing), admission is NIS 16 per adult and NIS 11 per senior/student. On their 625 acres you'll find recreated the landscapes of the Ancient Israel, including hundreds of varietals mentioned in the Bible and Talmud. "Discover Your Roots" is their motto, and you can do so by exploring the two to three kilometer trails on your own with a map and guide pamphlet, or by joining one of their two-hour guided tours in English, leaving Tuesdays at 9:30am in winter and 3:30pm in summer of Fridays at 9:30am. Wear good walking shoes and a hat, and bring some water. There are outdoor shaded picnic areas and an indoor kosher dairy dinning room. They also host special events like Bar mitzvah celebrations, Biblical meals, and archaeological excavations.

Special Religious Activities
  Christmas in Bethlehem is a much touted, crowded affair. There are Anglican, Christ Church, Lutheran, and Roman Catholic services all over town, but everyone wants to go to the Grotto of the Nativity in the Franciscan Parish Church of Saint Catherine. However, not everyone can. You need a special free entrance ticket from the Franciscan Pilgrims Office at the **Christian Information Center**, *Jaffa Gate, Jerusalem, Tel. 02-627-2697, Fax 02-627-2692, or write to POB 14308 Jerusalem*. At present, tickets are possible only for certified Roman Catholics. They can be obtained by written request or in person, but the fussbudget Franciscan priest in charge of such matters has added an intimidating load of requirements and obstacles.

  The written requests should be sent from September to November, and must include a letter from your Roman Catholic priest corroborating your Catholic identity, and must have a legible signature and the Parish seal or forget it. If you show up in person at the office, the requirements are the same, but he will stop accepting requests at some undefined point in December unless you had previously sent in a written request. Nothing will move him from this, so don't try.

  There are plenty of other services to be seen, however, as well as the televised version in Manger Square. If that doesn't appeal, you might want to reconsider Bethlehem. People mostly stand around in Manger Square for many hours drinking bad coffee, listening to endless choirs, waiting for midnight. And then? Nothing. Midnight Mass from the Church of the Nativity is broadcast onto a big screen for the viewing pleasure of those who can't get in.

  Transportation: There are buses running from Talpiot Station in Jerusalem to and from Bethlehem from 8am-3am, NIS 9.80 each way. And the Lutheran Church, *Tel. 02-627-6111, Fax 02-627-6222*, will arrange transport for NIS 28. Special buses leave from outside Damascus Gate, as do regular (and much cheaper) Arab buses.

PRACTICAL INFORMATION
• **AACI—Association of Americans and Canadians**, *6 Mane, Tel. 02-561-7151*, is opposite 13 Disraeli. They are a good English-speaking

resource covering a wide range of possibilities. If you want to move (or retire) to Israel, meet the American/Canadian community, get a job or attend lectures, concerts, or mixers, AACI has the information (see Rehavia section of *Sights* for more).

• **American Consulate General**, *27 Nablus Road, East Jerusalem, Tel. 02-625-3288*, bus 23 or 27, is open Monday-Friday 8am-4pm. The Executive, Commercial, and Administrative Sections, however, are located at *18 Agron Road*. They don't accept phone inquiries during the hours they are open; call about visas, and routine passport and citizenship questions from 2-4pm. American citizens with emergencies can call *Tel. 02-625-3201*.

• **American Express**, *40 Jaffa*, is open Sunday-Thursday 9am-5pm and Friday 9am-1pm. They charge no commission to change travelers checks, and you can get US cash for a 3% fee.

• **British Consulate**, *19 Nashashibi, near Sheikh Jarrah, East Jerusalem, Tel. 02-582-8281*, is open Monday-Friday 8am-12:30pm.

• **Buses, Arab** have one station on *Suleiman between Damascus and Herod's Gates* for southern routes and another on *Nablus Road* serving northern routes.

• **Bus Station, Egged Central**, *Jaffa Road, Tel. 02-530-4704*, way west of downtown, has intercity buses, intracity buses, and a baggage check at NIS 4 per item per day.

• **Car Rental: Avis**, *22 King George, Tel. 02-624-9001*; **Budget**, *8 King David, Tel. 02-624-8991*; **Hertz**, *18 King David, the Hyatt, Tel. 02-623-1351*; **Thrifty**, *18 King David, Tel. 02-625-0833*.

• **Christian Information Center**, *the square just inside Jaffa Gate, Tel. 02-627-2695, Fax 02-628-6417*, is open Monday-Friday 8:30am-1pm. They have information on churches, services, and special events like Christmas.

• **Currency Exchange** is possible at hotels and a variety of banks (**Leumi**, *21 Jaffa*, **HaPoalim**, *1 Zion Square and 16 King George*, and **First International**, *10 Hillel*, to name at few) but the best exchange rates without commission is available at American Express (see above).

• **Disabled Services: Yad Sarah Organization**, *43 HaNevi'im, Tel. 02-644-4444*, loans medical equipment for one month (extendable to three months) for free (full deposit required). They're open Sunday-Thursday 9am-7pm, Friday 9am-noon, and are available for emergencies.

• **English Books: The Book Mavin**, *21 Agrippas Tel. Tel. 02-624-5902*, is open Sunday-Thursday 8am-8pm and Friday 8am-2pm. They've a fair selection of used books, buy used books for credit, and offer two for one type specials. **Muffet Books**, off Agrippas just before the Mahane Yehuda Market, Tel. 02-625-9872, sells new and used. They say their address is *2 Kiach*, but the street sign says *Alliance Israe'lite*. **Sefer Ve Sefel**, *2 Yavetz, Tel. 02-624-8237*, in a small walkway off 47 Jaffa, is a pleasant book store whose name means "mug and book". Open Sunday-Thursday 8am-8pm, Friday 8am-2:30pm, there are lots of books (including a large travel section), used and new. **Steimatzky**, *7 Ben Yehuda on the midrahov, Tel. 02-625-5487*, has other branches as well. Open 8:30am-10pm, Friday 8:30am-2:30pm, Saturday 8:30-11pm, they sell new books. **Tmol Shilshom Bookstore Cafe**, *5 Yoel Salomon Street, Tel. 02-623-2758*, has live jazz every Saturday night, a happy hour, milk shakes and cheese schnitzel, and lots of books.

• **Film Developing: Kodak Express**, *25 King George, Tel. 02-625-6557*, does 36 prints for NIS 38. **Photo Ha-Bira**, *91 Jaffa, Tel. 02-623-1915*, at sells rolls for NIS 8, develops at NIS .55 per print and is open Sunday-Thursday 8am-1pm and 4-7pm, Friday 8am-2pm. **Photo Yehezkel**, *47 Jaffa, Tel. 02-625-5590*, sells at NIS 8.9 per roll, develops at NIS .33 per print, and is open Sunday-Thursday 9am-7pm, Friday 9am-2pm.

• **First Aid for Tourists**, *Bikur Holim Hospital, 74 HaNevi'im, Tel. 02-670-1111*, is on the corner of Strauss, which is the east extension of King George, and is available 24 hours a day.

• **Franciscan Pilgrims Office**, *same building as the Christian Information Center, inside Jaffa Gate, Tel. 02-627-2697*, is open Monday-Friday 9am-noon and 3:30-5:30pm, Saturday 9am-noon. They handle reservations for Franciscan sanctuary Masses and sell pilgrimage certificates.

• **Help Lines: Alcoholics Anonymous**, *Tel. 02-563-0524*; **Gay and Lesbian Support Line**, *Tel. 02-624-2853*, is also called **Ozen Kashevet**; **Mental Health Hotline**, *Tel. 02-1201*, is also called **Eran** and is open 8am-11pm but gives an alternate number (in Hebrew) when closed; **Rape Crisis Center**, *Tel. 02-625-5558*, is open 24 hours and will help you to police and through procedures.

• **Jewish Student Information Center**, *5 Beit El, Jewish Quarter, Tel. 02-628-2634, Fax 02-02-628-8338*, across from the Hurva Arch is open Sunday-Thursday 9am-7pm, Friday 9am-sundown.

• **Jewish National Fund**, *1 Keren Kayemet, Tel. 02-563-9650, or the Tannenbaum Center, Hadassah Ein Kerem hospital*, is open Sunday-Thursday 8:30am-3pm, Friday 8:30am-noon. You can plant a tree with them for $10.

• **Laundry: Ha-Merkaz Laundry**, *11 Kakal off Usushkin, Tel. 02-566-4246*, is open Sunday-Thursday 8am-1pm and 3-7pm, Friday 8am-1pm, and do 5kg wash and dry for NIS 25; **Michali Laundry**, *36 Azza Street, Rehavia* and **Suzana Laundry**, *46 Emek Refa'im Street, German Colony*, are open Sunday-Thursday 7:30am-11:30pm, Friday 7:30am-3pm, and Saturday 6pm-11:30pm and charge NIS 16 to wash and dry; **Superclean Laundromat**, *16 Palmah, Tel. 02-566-0367*, is open Sunday-Thursday 7am-7pm, Friday 7am-2pm, and does 6kg wash/dry/ fold for NIS 30 and 10kg for NIS 40; **Tzipor Ha-Nefesh**, *10 Rivlin Street, Tel. 02-624-9890*, has wash and dry facilities (NIS 15 for 5kg), plus a cafe and email center; **Washmatic**, *35 Emek Refa'im, Tel. 02-563-1878*, is open Sunday-Thursday 8am-7pm, Friday 8am-2pm and has small load wash/dry/fold for NIS 45 and large load for NIS 61.

- **Libraries: American Cultural Center Library**, *19 Keren Hayesod, Tel. 02-625-2376, Fax 02-624-2560*, is open Sunday-Thursday 10am-4pm, Friday 9am-noon, answer phone questions from 8am, and are closed all Israeli and American holidays. The library carries American magazines and newspapers (such as five-day-old Herald Tribunes and two-week-old NY Times), as well as books and videotapes on American themes. **Abramov Library**, *Hebrew Union College, 13 King David, Tel. 02-620-3270*, is a quiet, pleasant, cool library with Newsweek and the Jerusalem Post as well as books and journals on Judaica and archaeology. They're open Sunday-Thursday 8am-4:45pm and have a copy machine, 30 agorot a page.

- **Medical Emergencies**, *Tel. 101*, are handled at the sign of the **Magen David Adom** (Israel's Red Cross) *next to the central bus station or inside Dung gate*. **Blue Cross-Blue Shield**, *Hadassah Ein Kerem and Mount Scopus hospitals, Tel. 02-677-6040*, covers members for pre-paid hospitalization.

- **Pharmacies: Iba Pharmacy**, *7 Ben Yehuda, Tel. 02-625-7785*, is open Sunday-Thursday 8am-7pm, Friday 8am-2pm; **Super-Pharm branches**, *4 HaHistadrut off King George, Tel. 02-624-6244*, and *5 Burla, near Hebrew University, Giv'at Ram, Tel. 02-563-9321*, are open Sunday-Thursday 9am-9pm and Saturday from sundown-9pm. There are also pharmacies on Jaffa and around the city.

- **Police**, *Russian Compound off Jaffa, Tel. 100* for emergencies. **Tourist Police**, *30 Jaffa Street, Tel. 02-539-1254*.

- **Post Office**, *23 Jaffa, Tel. 02-629-0647*, is the main branch and is open Sunday-Thursday 7am-7pm, Friday 7am-noon, with poste restante, telegram, and fax services.

- **Supermarkets: Coop Supermarket**, *King George at Ben Yehuda*, is open Sunday-Tuesday 7am-8pm, Wednesday-Thursday 7am-10pm, Friday 7am-2pm. **Supermarket**, *7 Mordechai Ben Hillel off 9 King George*, is open Sunday-Thursday 7:30am-7pm, Friday 7:30am-3pm. **Supermarket**, *Agron near King George*, is open Sunday-Tuesday 7am-midnight, Wednesday 7am-1am, Thursday 24 hours, Friday 7am-Shabbat, and Saturday after Shabbat-midnight.

- **Telephone** service from **Bezek**, *1 Koresh, Tel. 02-624-6196*, is behind the post office. They have booths to facilitate international calls; open Sunday through Thursday 8am-10pm, and Friday 8am-2pm.

SolanTelecommunications, *2 Luntz, Tel. 02-625-8908*, off Ben Yehuda and near Cafe Rimon, does the same for less money and they're open 24 hours a day, seven days a week. After midnight their discount rate is even cheaper.

• **Ticket Agencies**: **Ben Naim**, *Tel. 02-625-4008*; **Bimot**, *8 Shammai, Tel. 02-623-4061*; **Kla'im**, *Tel. 02-625-6869*.

• **Tourist Information**, *17 Jaffa, Tel. 02-628-0382*, is open Sunday-Thursday 8:30am-4:30pm, Friday 8:30am-12:30pm. It's not manned by the warmest of beings, but he'll answer your questions if he can, and there are plenty of brochures and maps. **Computerized information**, *26 King George, corner of Schatz*, is available 24 hours a day. The **Ministry of Tourism**, *26 King George, Tel. 02-675-4910*, are the offices of the bureaucracy, not the place that handles garden variety tourist questions and concerns. For other **Tourist questions**, call *Tel. 02-675-4811*.

18. THE DEAD SEA

The **Dead Sea**, also called **Yam ha-Melah** (Hebrew for *Salt Sea*) and Buhr Lut (Arabic for *Sea of Lot*), boasts a shoreline that is the lowest point on Earth. The sea, divided into two basins by the peninsula of Lisan ('tongue' in Arabic), is part of the five million year old Great Syrian-African Rift Valley, and with the Judean Mountains to the west and the Moab Mountains to the east, Israel on one bank and Jordan on the other, it's a special place.

DEAD SEA VITAL STATISTICS

• *Altitude:* 1,300 feet below sea level (on average)
• *Area:* 405 square miles (1,049 kilometers)
• *Length:* 46 miles (74 kilometers) long
• *Width:* about 10 miles (16 kilometers) wide
• *Depth:* ranging from 1,310 feet in the north to less than nine feet in the south
• *Temperature highs (F°):* Dec-Apr 68°-84°, Sept-Nov 81°-97°, and June-Aug 99°-102°
• *Annual rainfall:* about two inches
• *Evaporation Rate:* about 55 inches annually
• *Rate of Level Change:* the lake is sinking around .4 inches a year
• *Saline Content:* every liter is 30% salt, or 2.5 lbs worth, about seven times as much as the ocean
• *Chemical Content:* chloride, bromide, bicarbonate, sulfate, sodium, potassium, calcium, and magnesium
• *Shore Content:* flanked on east and west by ridges of sandstone and dolomite
• *Source:* Jordan River (diverted for irrigation, reducing flow and lowering its level)
• *Outlet:* none
• *Life Support:* only simple organisms can live in its saline waters

---

The Sea has been cited in works from the Bible to Beckett's *Waiting For Godot*, where Estragon said "I remember the maps of the Holy Land. Coloured they were. Very pretty. The Dead Sea was pale blue. The very look of it made me thirsty. That's where we'll go, I used to say, that's where we'll go for our honeymoon. We'll swim. We'll be happy." Many still want to go there and be happy, with greater success than Estragon.

The area is as rich in remarkable natural and historic diversity as the sea is in minerals. With **Masada**, **Ein Gedi**, and **Qumran** of Dead Sea Scrolls fame, there are stark desert vistas with craggy canyons, hot springs, cool oases with water falls, nature reserves and bird sanctuaries, salt formations, and of course the sea, where you can sit and float far more easily than swim.

One word of caution: the salt-dense sea packs a real wallop to an abrasion or cut. Even a recent shave can sting mightily in the Dead Sea.

THE NORTHERN BASIN

This stretch of Dead Sea coast is alive with some of the most important historical sites and lushest oasis reserves in Israel. **Qumran**, site of the Dead Sea Scrolls is in the north, **Ein Feshka** and **Ein Gedi** beaches are good for a dip in the brine, **Metzoke Drogot** is an entry into the Judean Desert, **Ein Gedi Reserve** refreshes with waterfalls and wildlife, and **Masada**, last stand of the Judeans against the Roman forces, is in the south.

QUMRAN

Khirbet Qumran, *Tel. 02-994-2235*, the ruins of Qumran, is what's left of the site where a community was founded by the Essenes around 150 BCE. Though there were Jewish settlements on this site since the 700s BCE, the Essene community put Qumran on the map thanks to some Bedouin shepherds who stumbled on seven of the ancient scrolls (since labeled **The Dead Sea Scrolls**) in a local cave in 1947. Following excavations revealed additional scrolls, and structures supporting the theory that Qumran had been a center for the Essene sect, who had written and stored the scrolls that were found.

The **Essenes** were a splinter religious sect that formed in the same tumultuous times that gave birth to the Zealots, Christianity, and the Great Revolts. They were pacifists and purists; they emphasized the importance of purity and the ritual bath, de-emphasized property and material wealth, and took off to the countryside to set up pure commu-

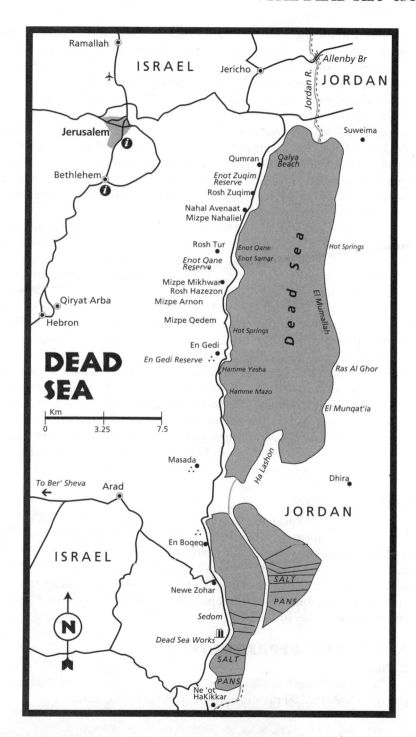

nities and await the Messiah. This Dead Sea Sect was apparently an extremist offshoot of the Essenes. An earthquake in 31 BCE caused the sect to flee the site, but sometime during the rule of Archelaus (Herod's son, who reigned from 4 BCE-6 CE), they returned and rebuilt.

During the Great Jewish Revolt of 68 CE the Romans took Qumran, scattering the Dead Sea Sect. The last known inhabitants were the Romans, who set up a garrison there during the Bar Kokhba Rebellions of 132-135 CE. After that, the place was abandoned and forgotten till the scroll discovery some 1800 years later. After the Six Day War of 1967, Qumran was taken over by the National Parks Authority. Thanks to them, there now is a parking lot, pamphlets with maps, informative signs, snack bar and bathrooms, and an entrance fee.

Slopes pocked with caves rise to the west of the old settlement site. Some of the caves, difficult to access, were used as hiding places for their library when danger threatened. The scrolls were hidden in jars, and the extreme dry climate preserved them for nearly two thousand years. The finds, including copies of the Old Testament, the Apocrypha, and the sect's own works, were written in Hebrew, Aramaic, and Greek on scrolls of leather or papyrus (one was even chiseled on copper) and are now on display at the Shrine of the Book in the Israel Museum in Jerusalem.

To be seen here, along with the now-empty caves, is the excavated settlement, including dining room, scriptorium (presumably where The Scrolls were written), cisterns, tower, and cattle pen. Though the find was extraordinary and the scrolls are fascinating, the actual site is a bit of a let-down. It's a long, hot walk to the caves of fame, and when you get there, they are, well, caves, and no signs indicate which were *the* caves. Open daily 8am-5pm, entrance costs NIS 12 for adults, NIS 6 for youth, and NIS 9 for seniors and students.

ORIENTATION

The National Parks site is west of the Kaliah-Sedom road off the northwestern shore of the Dead Sea, 40 kilometers south of Jerusalem. As you drive along the turn-off, you come to a parking lot busy with private cars and tour buses. To the right is a blessedly air-conditioned building with souvenir shop and snack bar. To the left is the ticket booth that lets onto the excavation site. Marked paths lead to the excavated settlement and off to the caves in the hills.

ARRIVALS & DEPARTURES
By Bus
There are buses from Ein Gedi or Jerusalem. From where the bus lets you off it's about 100 meters up a steep drive to the entrance.

By Tour

Lots of people choose one of many tours operating out of Jerusalem. See *Tours* in the Jerusalem chapter for more details.

WHERE TO STAY

KALIA GUEST HOUSE, *Tel. 02-993-6253,* charges singles NIS 205-250, doubles NIS 250-330. This is the place if you want to stay by Qumran, but most people see this as a day trip from Jerusalem or further south on the Dead Sea.

WHERE TO EAT

There's a **self-serve cafeteria,** *Tel. 02-994-2533,* next to the souvenir shop that stays open until 4pm and will do if you're hungry and don't want to wait for other choices, with sandwiches for NIS 15 and main dishes starting at NIS30.

METZOKEI DRAGOT

*Just an hour's drive from Jerusalem in the heart of the Judean Desert is **Metzokei Dragot International Center for Desert Tourism**, Tel. 02-994-4777, Fax 02-994-4333. The turn-off from the Dead Sea Coast road is roughly halfway between the Ein Feshka and Ein Gedi oases, up into the rocks and wadis of the Judean Hills. You can go for just a day hike (guided or not) or stay for a while.*

The accommodations are not luxurious, but this is a place from which to explore the desert, not a luxury spa. There are 45 air conditioned rooms with private toilet and shower for $49-$59 a single and $70-$84 a double, breakfast and free access to the mineral beach (worth NIS 25-29) included. They lead tours in the Judean Desert and Dead Sea area, with desert safari vehicles, hiking, mountain climbing, rappelling, and camel safari as options. They also have regular desert tours every Tuesday and Saturday from Jerusalem (call to arrange). The Judean Desert can be quite beautiful, and a tour with some desert company is worthwhile if you have the time (see Jerusalem Tours for more options).

SPORTS & RECREATION

Three kilometers south of Qumran is **Ein Feshka,** *Tel. 02-994-2355,* also called **Einot Zukim,** a very pleasant place to recuperate from the heat. Go floating in the Dead Sea on the beach (open daily 8am-5pm, NIS 20 for adults, NIS 10 for children) or splash in the pools from the fresh water springs in the Nature Reserve oasis across the road. There's a lifeguard on the beach, as well as showers, changing rooms, bathrooms, and drinking water. It's a prime Dead Sea mud wallow spot, and folks stroll caked and crusty before attempting to rinse off. Any buses plying the Dead Sea coastal highway can let you off there.

Go north seven kilometers from Qumran to **Attraction Water Park**, *Kalya Beach, Tel. 02-994-2393*, for a fun way to cool off. Open daily March-October 9am-4:45pm, it costs NIS 55 for adults, is free for children under one meter, and is a good option if the kids are beginning to wilt. Any buses heading north along the Dead Sea can drop you there.

And **Lot's Wife**, *Tel. 07-659-4760, Fax 07-658-4137*, runs a **Dead Sea Cruise**. They leave Tuesday and Thursday at 2:30pm, Saturday at 11:30am and 2:30pm, providing guided tours of Ein Gedi on the Dead Sea, and lunch by prior arrangement. They charge NIS 35 for adults and NIS 25 for children.

EIN GEDI

Ein Gedi (*fountain of the goat*) refers both to the Dead Sea beach and the oasis in the nature reserve, to the east and west of the road, respectively. While a dip in the Dead Sea is a unique and not-to-be-missed experience, Ein Gedi may not be where you choose to try it (your bathing plans might better include Ein Feshka or Ein Bokek), but a visit to the nature reserve, steeped in history and cool spring water, is bound to be rewarding.

ORIENTATION

On the eastern edge of the Judean Desert, Ein Gedi is bordered by the HaHaetakim Cliffs to the west, the Dead Sea to the east, mount Yishai Ridge to the north, and Nahal Hever to the south. On the west coast of the Dead Sea, Ein Gedi is 34 kilometers south of Ein Feshka, 15 kilometers north of Masada, and 25 kilometers northeast of Arad.

Entrance to all the sites are easily accessible from the main road, spreading out over a 2.5 kilometers span. From north to south, their order is: the nature reserve, youth hostel, and SPNI field school; then comes the beach, campgrounds, mini-market, restaurant, gas station, and first aid station; and lastly are the thermal baths, resort, and spa.

ARRIVALS & DEPARTURES

By Bus

If Ein Gedi is to be a day trip involving a few sites and getting back before the last bus departs, plan carefully. Buses 486 and 487 go to and from Jerusalem for NIS 26, leaving as early as 7:45am. The last bus back is at 6pm, 1:30pm on Fridays (the 444 goes all the way to Eilat for NIS 45 at 8, 11, 3, and 6). Buses 384 and 385 ply the Arad (NIS 21.80) /Be'er Sheva (NIS 29) route, leaving Ein Gedi at 8, 11:15, 12:30, 3:30, and 5:45. Bus 486 goes to Masada and Ein Bokek at 11, 12:15, and 2:15) for NIS 3.90. To be sure, check with Egged before setting off.

When arriving, be aware that there are three bus stops. From the north, the first is for the nature reserve, youth hostel, and SPNI field school; the next is the beach, campgrounds, mini-market, restaurant, gas station, and first aid station; and the third is for the thermal baths, resort, and spa.

WHERE TO STAY

EIN GEDI "BEIT SARAH" YOUTH HOSTEL, *Tel. 07-658-4165, Fax 07-658-4445, has dorm beds for NIS 35 (NIS 69 for non-members), including a big breakfast. There are also private rooms for NIS 140 per person (less 4 shekels for members).*

Just around the corner from the nature reserve, this is a lovely place. With 208 beds, they offer a variety of lodging options. Dinners cost NIS 35, and they give discounts to the reserve (NIS 2 off) and 20% discounts off the Ein Gedi Spa as well. The bunks are sturdy and most are made of wood, the rooms are pleasant and clean, with air conditioning and wardrobes, and the bathrooms are clean and big. The office is open 7am-7pm, and the cafe is open 6pm to whenever. The terrace is surrounded by trees and very pleasant, overlooking green lawns, flowers, big beautiful palms, and the Dead Sea.

SPNI FIELD SCHOOL, *Tel. 07-658-4288, has dorm rooms with 6 beds for NIS 645 for the room. Doubles are NIS 245, breakfast included.*

The field school is a 10 minute walk uphill from the hostel (buses 384 and 385 go all the way if you ask). All the rooms have air conditioning and private baths. The accommodations are almost always full of school groups and tours, so arrange ahead if you want to stay there. They also have trail maps and a small museum (entrance NIS 6 for visitors, free for SPNI guests) featuring snakes and a 15 minute video on the desert flora and fauna.

EIN GEDI BEACH allows camping for free under the green and yellow awnings. Bring whatever you need; all they provide is the shelter, some bathrooms, and an open-air shower. The kiosk, however, does sell charcoal, flashlights, beer, and sandwiches.

EIN GEDI CAMPING, *Tel. 07-658-4342, Fax 07-658-4455, charges NIS 25 per adult, NIS 13 per child, for camping. Or you can stay in the caravans, for $77 a single, $92 a double, and $15 per each additional person.*

They're located further south, just to the right of the gas station. You bring the tent and sleeping bags, they provide the site, and bathrooms. They have lockers, too, costing NIS 6 per opening. They also offer 23 air conditioned rooms and 42 somewhat claustrophobic air conditioned caravans for up to six people, with kitchenettes and bathrooms. For this, you also get 30% discounts off the thermal mineral Ein Gedi Spa, with its private beach, TV room, and solarium. There's a gas station and first aid station there as well.

EIN GEDI RESORT AND SPA, *Tel. 07-659-4222, Fax 07-658-4328, charges $122-$143 a single and $174-$204 a double, half board included.*

South of Ein Gedi Camping, the Resort has 120 air conditioned rooms, all with TV, radio, phone, and coffee/tea counter. This is the top of the line at Ein Gedi. Here there are palm trees and flowers, swimming pools (indoor and out), natural sulfur pools, mineral mud baths, private Dead Sea beach, tennis courts, and regular shuttle service to the spa.

WHERE TO EAT

The pickings are slim. There's the **KIOSK NAHAL DAVID**, *just outside the nature reserve ticket booth*, with sandwiches, mineral water, and ice cream.

MILKY RESTAURANT, *Ein Gedi free beach*, open 8am-6pm, is air-conditioned, self-serviced, and reasonably priced. The **KIOSK EIN GEDI** outside sells beer and sandwiches to go.

From 6pm on, the **YOUTH HOSTEL CAFE** serves light dinner fare.

For a more comfortable and pricier setting, try the **EIN GEDI RESORT SELF-SERVICE RESTAURANT**.

SEEING THE SIGHTS

Ein Gedi beach is one of the most popular on the Dead Sea; perhaps because of the nature reserve across the street, it's the only name many people know. The 'beach' is free, and you get your money's worth. The bathing area is one little strip of shore, very rocky, and a trip to the water entails a perilous bare-foot journey across sharp stones. Green and yellow awnings provide shade, and you can camp under them free of charge, though it's not the coziest of places. The kiosk sells charcoal along with expensive Dead Sea beauty products, and the bus schedules to Eilat, Jerusalem, and Be'er Sheva are posted there too.

There's a self-serve restaurant that's quite reasonably priced (open 8:30am-5pm), bathrooms and changing rooms, and it's better than nothing but not as nice as the others.

A couple kilometers down the road, the upscale **Ein Gedi Resort and Spa** (owned by the Ein Gedi kibbutz) is a popular destination for many of the organized tours from Jerusalem. A 10 minute walk north takes you to great globs of **Dead Sea mud**, yours for the slathering, and some freshwater springs as well.

Ein Gedi Nature Reserve

Ein Gedi Nature Reserve, *Tel. 07-658-4285*, was an oasis of abundant fertility even in Old Testament times, and the vineyards of Ein Gedi are celebrated in the Song of Solomon (1:14). The oasis also figured in the history of the time; when young David ran from King Saul's wrath, he hid in a cave in "the wilderness of Ein Gedi" (I Samuel 24:1-4). Around 100 BCE, Ein Gedi had a large Jewish community, and it became the administrative center for Idumea, the province forcibly converted to Judaism by John Hyrcanus from which Herod's family came. Perhaps for this reason (or for no reason), Herod the Great later conquered Ein Gedi during his rule (37-4 BCE).

Ein Gedi was plundered during the Great Revolt of 68 CE, and figured again as a refuge during the Bar-Kokhba Rebellion of 132 CE when Simon Bar Kokhba and his men hid in a cave some six kilometers southwest. The settlement here flourished from the fourth-sixth centuries, and was highly valued for its production of balsam, but Ein Gedi began to decline in the Byzantine period, and by the 19th century it was home to just a few Bedouin families living in reed huts by the mouth of Ein Gedi Spring. In 1949 the Israel Defense Force opened a route from the south (Sodom) and Kibbutz Ein Gedi was established.

The reserve, officially declared in 1972, is comprised of 6,750 acres including **Nahal David**, **Nahal Arugot**, and the slopes between. The oasis is fed by four springs: David, Shulamit, Ein Gedi, and Ein Arugot, supplying an abundance of fresh water yearly for the verdant vegetation and healthy wildlife community that thrive there. It's a pleasant jaunt for anyone wanting a green change of pace from the Judean Desert, but it's an especially rewarding site for botanists; the oasis is rare in that Tropical, Desert, Mediterranean, and Steppian plants manage to grow side by side.

The reserve is also home to a goodly collection of ibex, whose mating season in September-October is amazing to watch, as is the April scene of female ibex descending to the lowland springs and streams with their young. Hyrax live there, as do hyenas, fox, and four leopards. Ein Gedi is also a bird refuge—Tristam's starling, the Arabian babbler (the bird), and Griffon vultures are just three of the many species who reside there. During migration season, thousands more fly over; it's a wonderful time to visit.

In addition to the natural wealth, there are archaeological finds here as well, including a synagogue and bathhouse from Talmudic times and a flour (or sugar) mill from the Islamic period, a Roman fortress ruin, an Israeli fortress ruin, and a Chalcolithic temple from 5,000 years ago. There are hiking trails to these sites, and to waterfalls and pools, and loads of caves, ranging from one and a half to six hours, and fairly well marked—the ticket office will give you a useful map when you enter. The short trip takes you to Shulamit Falls, and is one of the most popular destinations for the hot and dusty.

Daily hours are from 8am-3pm in winter and 8am-4pm is summer, closing one hour earlier in Nahal Augot. Entrance costs NIS 15 for adults, NIS 8 for seniors/youth, and Visa & Mastercard are accepted. There's a souvenir shop that also sells water bottles in case you forgot to bring one, and a snack bar sells fast foods.

SHOPPING

Ein Gedi Nature Reserve has a shop selling hiking goods like thermal shoulder slings for mineral water bottles (with the adorable Nature Reserve antelope logo), hats, shorts, and more.

The Kiosk Ein Gedi by the beach and the shop at the Ein Gedi Spa sell Dead Sea mud and other Dead Sea beauty and health products.

SPORTS & RECREATION

Hiking in the nature reserve and bathing in the Dead Sea are the activities of choice. For desert exploration, see Metzokei Dragot.

EXCURSIONS & DAY TRIPS

See Qumran and Masada.

PRACTICAL INFORMATION

There is a gas station and first aid station by the Ein Gedi Camping Site, south of the nature reserve and free beach.

MASADA

Probably one of the most visited sites in Israel, the rock fortress of Masada looms as large in history and in tour itineraries as it does in the Judean Desert hills.

It's a place that actually lives up to its hype; it is awe-inspiring to see the rocky outpost jutting up in the heat above the Dead Sea, with the muted shades of the Judean hills and canyons behind, especially if you can arrange to be there when it isn't aswarm with bus loads of group tours.

The site is officially open 5:20am-6pm, but the times seem flexible. Entrance without cable car tickets costs NIS 14 per adult and NIS 10.5 for students. A cable car ticket one-way is NIS 29 (NIS 18.5 for students) and NIS 40 for return (NIS 22.5 for students).

ORIENTATION

Majestically rising 1,440 feet above the Dead Sea shore, Masada is an isolated mountain plateau among the hills of the **Judean Desert**. It's located near the southern tip of the northern basin of the Dead Sea, off the Arad road, about 15 kilometers south of Ein Gedi and 15 kilometers north of Ein Bokek. From the parking lot you proceed west along the path to the ticket booth and gate, and there you have to choose the Snake Path climb or buy the tickets for the cable car ascent. Either way, once you are atop the rock the excavated remains await you.

You arrive facing southeast (the Snake Path gate is just a little south of the cable car terminal). To your left are a few scattered sites (the Byzantine Cave Dwelling, the Eastern Wall, the Royal Family Residence). If you follow the Eastern Wall 400 meters or so you come to the Water Cistern and nearby Southern Citadel lookout. Southwest from the Snake Path Gate about 200 meters is a cluster of the Southern Villa, the Swimming Pool, Building #11, and the Western Palace.

To the right of the Snake Path and cable car gates you'll find another cluster of sites, with Storehouses, a Villa, the Administration Building, Water Gate, Bath House, and further on, the Northern Palace. And southwest of that, is the Northern Palace Lookout, Synagogue, and Tower, and Roman Ramp.

ARRIVALS & DEPARTURES
By Bus
The 486, 487, and 444 go to and from Jerusalem (the 444 goes south as far as Eilat), and from Be'er Sheva take the 384 or 385. The 421 comes from Tel Aviv once daily at 8:30am.

By Car
Drive up (or down) the Dead Sea coast road and turn west on the road to Arad, following the Masada signs. There's an ample parking lot at the foot of the mountain.

By Foot
Just kidding.

GETTING AROUND TOWN
You have two choices: walking up the Snake Path or riding the cable car. It takes around 40 minutes of fairly steady walking, give or take a rest stop, to reach the top, and 25 minutes going down, and roughly three minutes by cable car.

The **cable car** runs 8am-4pm in winter, 8am-5pm in summer, shutting two hours earlier on Fridays. It leaves every half hour or when 40 people are ready to ride, and takes 3 minutes.

The **Snake Path**, the only way up the mountain before the Romans built their ramp, is rock-strewn and uneven, so climbing in flip flops can result in stubbed toes. If you're going to do the hike, take plenty of water, and save yourself future pain by doing some leg stretches after your climb and/or descent.

Some people choose to hike up in the wee hours of the night to see the sunrise from the top, then cable car down when it's hot. This is a worthwhile plan, and not only because it avoids the heat of the day. The Masada ruins look eerie in the pre-dawn light, and you get to appreciate more of the magic of Masada before loud tour guides and masses of tourists break the spell. If you do this, take a flashlight, wear sneakers or hiking boots, take adequate water, and wear layers that will keep you warm in the cold desert night but can peel down for the heat.

Others, who want the Snake Path experience but don't want to die of heat stroke in the process take the cable car up and casually saunter down.

WHERE TO STAY

TAYLOR YOUTH HOSTEL, *eastern foothills of Masada, Tel. 07-658-4349, Fax 07-658-4650, is to the left of where the bus drops you. They charge $17 per dorm bed, $36 a single, $52 for doubles, and $67 for a triple, less $1.50 for members, breakfast included.*

Overlooking the mountains of Moab and the Dead Sea, this hostel is a pleasant respite from the heat of the sun, the glare of the rocks, and the noise of the countless tour guides. There's a welcome cluster of green trees offering shade and color around an outdoor roofed patio with tables. There are 104 beds, and the dorm rooms are all air-conditioned, with private baths, and six-eight beds. Dinners are available for $8, and there's a kitchen facility as well. Lockers can be rented for NIS 5.

They allow campers to stay for free on the concrete pavilion outside, but there are no facilities for them. No camping is allowed atop Masada.

WHERE TO EAT

Well, there's **TAYLOR HOSTEL DINING ROOM**, *Tel. 07-658-4349*, with dinners for $8, but you need to put your order in by 6pm. There's also a **snack bar** near the lower cable car landing, and a **restaurant** closer to the parking lot. It's not a place that's really geared toward fine dining; just treat yourself to something nice when you get back to Jerusalem.

SEEING THE SIGHTS

The Masada Story

Masada is best known as the site of the **Zealots'** last gasp against the Romans in 73 CE, but there have been people taking shelter there since men lived in caves in Neolithic times (5,000-3,000 BCE). According to the historian Josephus, a fort was first built on the Judean plateau by high priest Jonathan Maccabaeus around 150 BCE. This fortification was enlarged by Johanan Hyrakanus I (134-104 BCE), the high priest and de facto king. In 40 CE, **Herod** escaped with his family from besieged Jerusalem (during his battles with the Parthians and Hasmonaeans) and fled to the old fortress at Masada, where he left the women, food, and a garrison of 800 men, and went on to Petra to get help.

Herod then went to Rome, was appointed king of the Jews, and returned to liberate his relatives. Later, in 36-30 BCE, Herod constructed a new fortress on the site, making it the biggest in his country. According to Josephus Flavius, Masada was intended as a defense against Cleopatra, queen of Egypt, who was strongly suggesting to Marc Antony that Herod be deposed. After Herod's death Masada became a Roman garrison site, but it was taken by the Jews in 66 CE near the start of the Great Revolt. Two years later, following the destruction of the Temple in Jerusalem, the surviving Zealots fled the tatters of Jerusalem and took up residence in the desert fortress. They lasted three years while Rome's Tenth Legion inched forward with catapults and determination.

The Roman legion under **Flavius Silva** couldn't starve them out because they had so much food, so they began to build a ramp of stone, wood, and sand up the western side of the mountain, and advanced with their battering rams. Eventually the Zealots' leader **Elazar ben Yair** had to see that despite their hopes, the Romans were not going to dismiss their band as an insignificant community, and that in fact they weren't going to stop till Masada (and the last remnants of the Great Revolt) was theirs.

He called a meeting (according to accounts of two women and five children who hid and survived) and said "let our wives die before they are abused, and our children before they have tasted of slavery, and after we have slain them, let us bestow that glorious benefit upon one another mutually." In 73 CE, as recorded by Flavius Josephus, the Romans attained the heights of Masada and found the bodies of the Zealots strewn about.

Though we know of Masada from Josephus, the Talmud omits the story, which highlights its equivocal place in Jewish history. For some, Masada is the greatest symbol of resolution and national defense, but others (such as the rabbis compiling the Talmud) viewed the Zealots with resentment for their ill-fated rebellions.

The Excavation Site

The Excavation (begun in 1963 by archaeologists headed by **Yigael Yadin**) have revealed pre-Herodian remains, including Iron Age pottery shards from the 10th-7th centuries BCE and coins from the reign of

THE ZEALOTS' PLIGHT ATOP MASADA

The 960 Zealots on Masada planned the suicide, drawing lots to see who was to kill whom, with women and children killed first. Josephus Flavius wrote describing the scene (according to his interviews with the surviving few who hid from the carnage), saying that after nearly everyone had been killed, the remaining men believed "that they would be wronging those murdered if they survived the latter even for a short time. So they quickly threw all their possessions on to a heap and set it on fire. They then drew lots and selected ten men who were to be the murderers of all the others. Then each one lay down beside his family members, the women and children, who already lay dead, embraced them with their arms, and readily proffered their throats to the men who had to carry out the unhappy task . . . .

But the lonely last man surveyed the crowd of those who lay dead to see whether anyone had remained alive after all the killing and still required his hand. When he realized that they all were dead he lit fires at several points in the palace. Then, having gathered his strength, he thrust the sword right through his body and collapsed beside his family."

Alexander Janneus (103-76 BCE), as well as structures from the Byzantine period like a small church that was built near Herod's western palace. Most of the finds, however, come from Herod's palaces and the Zealots' quarters. Depending on your interest in this sort of thing, you could do a cursory once over or spend hours seeing all. If you are only going to check out a few spots, the most rewarding by far is the Northern Palace frescos. The painted black lines you see on some structures are there to divide the reconstructed add-ons from the original ruins.

To the North
Herod's Northern Palace is an amazing structure, built into the rock on three levels and connected by stone stairs. This was the king's private villa, and the attention to detail indicates the luxury in which he lived. The upper terrace contains the living rooms and a semi-circular balcony. The middle terrace is formed by a colonnaded pavilion. Even if you walked up the Snake Path, it's still worth expending the extra energy to climb down to the lower terrace.

There are still frescos there, brilliantly colorful, protected against the elements (and tourists) by clear sheets of glass that hardly mar their beauty. This courtyard is bordered by a double row of fluted columns, and as further indication of Herod's sumptuous lifestyle, his bathroom floor was heated (though Masada isn't a place one associates with a lack of heat).

While excavating, archaeologists found skeletons of a man, woman, and child, Zealots who met their fate surrounded by their belongings of a prayer shall, arrows, and armor.

On the western side, the **Water Gate**, with its walls of stone and waiting benches, offers a tremendous view over the hills to the north. Down the wall a bit the **Northern Palace Lookout** had fantastic views of Ein Gedi, as well as the slopes leading to the Palace itself. Further south is the **Synagogue**, one of the oldest ever found dating from the time of the Temple. Pillars held up the roof, and still remaining is the base of the wall that divided the large hall. Scrolls were found here, including several books of the Torah now on display at the Israel Museum in Jerusalem, along with silver coins and a prayer shawl.

On the eastern side is the **Bathhouse**, Herod's own, featuring pillars, three tiled rooms ranging from hot to cold with colorful mosaic floors, and a dressing room with wall frescos. South of that the **Snake Path Lookout** near the cable car terminus has a fine view down the path and across to the Dead Sea.

In the middle of the complex, the **Administration Building** was once one of Herod's courtyards. The Zealots built one of their ritual baths here, with rainwater collected in the southern pool. When it reached the right height, it drained through a slit into another pool which was used for the ritual immersions. The Zealots used the smaller pool to the west to wash before embarking on the ritual bath. In keeping with the water motif, it now houses **rest rooms**, and fresh water taps help slake summer thirst.

The **Storehouses** on the eastern side kept hundreds of jars holding years' worth of supplies. The **Villa**, with its courtyard, pillars and large rooms, was partitioned up by the Zealots to accommodate their families. From the **Quarry** nearby came some of the stone used to construct Masada.

Along the Eastern Wall

The **Snake Path Gate**, typical of other Masada gates, has a stone floor with benches, a guardroom, and white plaster walls made to look like marble. The **Eastern Wall**, constructed by Herod's men, shows the original layout that included inner and outer walls connected by partitions and a few towers.

About 100 meters southeast of the Gate, the **Byzantine Dwelling Cave** was built by monks in an existing crater that was probably a quarry for plaster. Further south, the **Royal Family Residence** was once a luxurious villa built by Herod. With an inner courtyard, it had large rooms separated by pillars and decorated by frescos. The Zealots converted the grand design to suit their needs, and partitioned it into smaller residences. Walking east again, the **Southeast Wall** has a tower and small room. Inside there's a little niche with what might be a Roman inscription. About 200 meters along, the **Southern Wall** has a lookout tower and a bakery (the latter probably added by the Zealots).

The ritual baths played an important role in Zealot life. These have a dressing room with clothing 'shelves.' The southern gate led to water cisterns and caves outside the wall. At the southern tip, the **Southern Citadel** helped fortify Masada at a weak spot.

The Southwestern Cluster

Heading due north some 200 meters from the Citadel you'll reach the **Southern Villa**. It was designed by Herod but not completed, and the Zealots made it into more living quarters. One of the rooms has been set up to look like how the Zealots left it, with hearth and kitchen pots. To the east of that is the **Columbarium** that once contained cremation urns, and north is **Building #11**, with its evocative name. This was one of Herod's villas, converted by the Zealots into a water reservoir. West of that is the **Swimming Pool**, another part of the good life Herod wanted included in his desert fortress. Given the weather, it certainly makes sense.

North 100 meters is the **Western Palace**, extending over an area of nearly 43,100 square feet. It had residential and domestic wings, storage and administrative rooms, a kitchen, and underground cisterns. The throne room was magnificent, and mosaics that remain are some of the oldest in Israel. West by the wall is **Tanner's Tower**, probably where the Zealots treated their hides, using the basins in the walls to store the necessary liquids. And a little north, the **Western Stairs and Gate**, built by the Byzantines, is where you would enter coming from the Arad road. To the north of this is the **Tower**. Originally made of sandstone, the Byzantine monks built the wall around it.

The **Byzantine Church**, southeast 100 meters from the Tower, was built in the 400s CE and had a hall, three rooms, a tiled roof, glass windows, and a mosaic floor. Northeast of the Church, the **Officers' Family Quarters** is split into nine apartments, each with two small rooms and a large courtyard. From here, you're just south of the Administrative Building and its public toilets and just west of the Snake Path Gate and Cable Car Terminal heading back down the mountain.

NIGHTLIFE & ENTERTAINMENT

Masada does a **sound and light show**, *Tel. 07-995-8144*, Tuesday and Thursday nights at 9pm from April-October. Tickets cost NIS 30 (NIS 25 for children). On the Arad side of the mountain, the 50 minute show is done in Hebrew, but you can rent earphones (NIS 13) with simultaneous translations in English, French, German, Russian, or Spanish.

No public buses go there, so you either drive yourself, or take one of the round-trip deals (make arrangements from Tourist Information or your hotel) from Arad and Dead Sea spots for NIS 35.

THE SOUTHERN BASIN

Ein Bokek is the main site on the southern segment of the Dead Sea. A resort town, Ein Bokek is frequented mostly by those with money and skin conditions, though some do come just for the fun and the holiday. The community is formed almost exclusively by large boxy resort hotels offering recuperative spa services to primarily German tourists.

ORIENTATION

There's the Dead Sea east of the main road, the desert cliffs to the west, and hotels all around in Ein Bokek. Fifteen kilometers south of Masada and three kilometers north of Hammei Zohar, the Ein Bokek Tourist office is in the white mall complex just north of the bus stop and south of Hotel Lot. The other shopping center is west, near the Hod Hotel.

ARRIVALS & DEPARTURES

The 444 goes north to Jerusalem (1.5 hours, NIS 31) and Masada (15 minutes). If you don't plan to overnight here, be aware the last one leaves at 4:30pm. The same 444 also goes south to Eilat.

GETTING AROUND TOWN

Ein Bokek is a pretty compact resort spot, and there's not much that's hard to get to. For destinations farther than a mild stroll, the hotels generally provide shuttles.

WHERE TO STAY

The hotels in Ein Bokek are all medium high to high priced; there are no budget accommodations here. All take credit cards, all provide breakfast, and most cater to clients seeking relief from skin ailments.

LOT HOTEL, *Tel. 07-658-4321, Fax 07-658-4623, charges $130-$180 for singles and $140-$190 for doubles.*

The Lot has 190 rooms, half of which face the sea (the views are stunning) and the rest looking over the Moab mountains. All the rooms have cable TV and phone, and are nice enough though not special.

Though all are air-conditioned, the rooms on the Masada side are slightly cooler in summertime.

The hotel has a private beach, and an elevator which leads directly to the sea or the swimming pool. And for a little more sun, there's a solarium on the roof. People come here for weeks of treatment when the clinic is open (March-September).

CARLTON GALEI ZOHAR, *Tel. 07-658-4311, Fax 07-658-4503, charges $118-$152 for a single and $148-$190 a double.*

There are two buildings on the hill; the old one is on the right and the new addition on the left combine to offer 250 rooms overlooking the sea, with cable TV, radio, air conditioning, and direct-dial phone. The new wing rooms are nice and large with fridges, while the older rooms, a little cheaper, are a bit smaller with no fridges. The hotel has a synagogue, as well as swimming pools, children's activities, and evening entertainment. The clientele here are mostly for psoriasis treatment, but there's more of a mix of ages.

PARK INN HOTEL, *Tel. 07-659-1666, Fax 07-658-4162, is up on the hill, charging $98-$120 per single, $122-$166 a double.*

Their 102 rooms are all equipped with cable TV, radio, air conditioning, phone, and 220V current, are attractive, and have small balconies. The hotel has a pool with snack bar, tennis court, handball court, solarium, and game rooms. They have a private beach, with free shuttles between hotel and sulfur springs solarium Sunday-Thursday from 7am-5:30pm, Friday-Saturday till 3:15pm. The solarium, their beach on the Dead Sea, has nude sun bathing, with separate sections for men and women, and they've an additional solarium on the roof, plus a very lovely garden. They also provide therapeutic skin treatments at their Hammei Zohar Spa.

RADISSON MORIAH GARDENS DEAD SEA HOTEL, *Tel. 07-658-4351, Fax 07-658-4383, also up on the hill, charges $170-$190 for singles, $205-$230 for doubles.*

This hotel features 196 rooms in their modern monstrosity between the sea and the cliffs. All the rooms have air conditioning, cable TV, direct-dial phone, views of either the Sea or the Moab ridges, are large, and nicer than most. The hotel facilities include a pool with snack bar, a beauty-health center, indoor Dead Sea pool, Jacuzzi and sauna. There's a special toddlers' pool, floodlit tennis court, and a rooftop solarium. And at night there's the disco, and the staff is helpful and friendly.

HOD HOTEL, *Tel. 07-658-4644, Fax 07-658-4606, costs $146-$177 a single, $177-$216 for doubles.*

The Hod has 203 air conditioned rooms, all with cable TV, radio, and direct-dial phone. Right on the beach, with ice cream parlor and snack bar, they also have a sun deck swimming pool and kids' pool, indoor Dead

Sea pool, health club with work-out equipment, pool table and ping-pong, and the glitzy Minus 400 Disco. They sponsor a range of activities for kids and adults, including folk dancing, fashion shows, lectures on subjects from astrology to health & beauty, and bingo or casino evenings. Next door they have a medical clinic. Seventy percent of their guests come from Germany, and most of them are senior citizens. It's a pleasant place with small but comfortable rooms, but what's outstanding about this hotel is the friendly staff, family atmosphere, and attention to personal detail.

TSELL HARIM BEACH RESORT, *Tel. 07-658-4121, Fax 07-658-4666, charges $85-$143 a single and $105-$165 a double.*

The Tsell Harim has 160 rooms, all air conditioned with cable TV, radio and phone. They are private but not really fancy little bungalows with bedroom, bath, and sitting room, and the suites have sun terraces. The resort has its own private stretch of beach, as well as solarium, outdoor pool, toddlers' pool, tennis court, fitness facilities, and massage, and a disco open till late at night. Eighty percent of their guests come for psoriasis care, and the staff doesn't trip over itself in helpfulness.

NIRVANA HOTEL, *further south, Tel. 07-658-4626, Fax 07-658-4345, more isolated and more expensive, has 200 rooms costing $198-$221 a single and $252-$283 a double.*

The rooms all have air conditioning, phone, cable TV, radio, and mini bar. The hotel has a synagogue, private beach, swimming pool, health club, playground for children, and disco for adults.

MORIAH'S PLAZA DEAD SEA, *three kilometers to the south, Hammei Zohar, Tel. 07-659-1591, Fax 07-658-4238, charges $100-$220 a single and $250-$290 a double.*

A separate entity from the Gardens Hotel, there are 220 rooms, all with air conditioning, radio, cable TV, and phone. The hotel has all the amenities: a synagogue, private beach, health club, disco, swimming pool, tennis court, and sports facility.

MOTI, *Tel./Fax 07-652-0143,* rents out rooms, $100 per family per night. You can find him in the Onil Tourist Center, which he also runs.

WHERE TO EAT

The food options in Ein Bokek are all middle to high end, and most are in the rip-off category. If you're here, you are a captive market. Aside from hotel restaurants (and they all have at least one), the cafes are centered in the white complex near the sea between the bus stop and Lot Hotel, or in the Petra Shopping Center near the Hod Hotel, where the prices are a bit lower.

In the mini-mall by the Sea

KAPULSKY CAFE is a self-serve affair, offering pizza for NIS 23, pasta at NIS 29, and desserts from NIS 8-18.

There's a SELF-HELP CAFETERIA that's just a rip-off.

The LOVE & PEACE RESTAURANT has a pleasant seating area with trellises and paper flowers. There are salads from NIS 22, sandwiches for NIS 18, pastas NIS 20-30, and entrees at NIS 35-65. Given the competition, it's not a bad choice.

In the Petra Shopping Center

There is ice cream at the FORUM for NIS 5 a scoop.

BARBIQUE CENTER, *Tel. 07-652-0143*, is open noon-midnight offering Israeli barbecue fare.

Nightlife & Entertainment

The main form of nightlife here the disco. Most of the hotels have them, though the action really depends on the season and the clientele of the moment.

Cleopatra Pub, recently opened, provides the cheapest beer around at NIS 2 a glass, in a Bedouin type atmosphere.

SHOPPING

There's a minimart kiosk in the mini-mall open 9am-9pm, but it has pretty slim pickings. They do have yogurt, cheese, pita, canned goods, and chocolate for a fairly miserly picnic.

The Petra Shopping Center (near Hod Hotel) looks a bit like a flying saucer and has shops and some restaurants.

Ahava Health Products are the favored souvenirs from the Dead Sea, starting at $6 for a bag of mud, and going up from there.

SPORTS & RECREATION

Outside the private hotel beaches, there's one free public beach. This is the best public beach on the Dead Sea.

Hamme Zohar beaches (one free and one with an entrance fee) are nearby, three kilometers to the south. Hamme Zohar Thermal Baths has a private beach and an open-air sulfur pool. Admission is $9. Off the beach, Kupat Holim Hot Springs offers more clinical treatments, with a hot pool, sulfur or air bubble bath, and massage from $12.

Motoric Camel, open 7am-7pm, offers tractors to rent. It's $40 for a self-driven two hour trip, driver's license required.

Health Spas

The spas around the Dead Sea focus the curative powers of the minerals and climate on skin diseases such as psoriasis, neurodermitis, and vitiligo; muscle and joint diseases, especially polyarthritis; respiratory diseases such as sinusitis and emphysema; and physical rehabilitation and psychosomatic ailments.

Galei Zohar Spa, *Tel. 07-658-4422, Fax 07-658-4503*, open Saturday-Thursday 8am-6pm, Friday 8am-3pm, offers Universal gym room, heated pool, Jacuzzi, sauna, mud treatments, and massage.

Hamei Zohar Spa, *Tel. 07-658-4161, Fax 07-658-4159*, offers clinic treatment at NIS 25, medical exam at NIS 110, rheumatologist exam at NIS 170, sulfur pool at NIS 37, sulfur bath or sulfur pearl bath at NIS 69, pelodium at NIS 105, mud package at NIS 94, and sulfur jacuzzi at NIS 56.

EXCURSIONS & DAY TRIPS

Newé Zohar lies 1.5 kilometers south of Hammei Zohar on Route 31. A regional center and local residential quarter, Newé Zohar has a hostel, camping, a store and cafeteria, police, a first aid clinic, and a gas station. Also at Newé Zohar is **Bet HaYotzer Museum**, which deals with Dead Sea research and history. To the west of Newé Zohar is **Nahal Zohar** and **Mezad Zohar**, canyons with ruins of ancient Israelite and Roman strongholds. You can drive there, or view them from the Arad road.

Further afield are a number of sites in the **Sodom** (Sedom) region. 12 kilometers south of Newé Zohar and 78 kilometers southeast of Be'er Sheva, this is the Sodom of Biblical renown, infamous for its profligate ways and God's subsequent fire and brimstone wrath. The story goes that God permitted Lot and his wife to escape before the town and its inhabitants were destroyed, but with the proviso that Lot not look back at his wife. He did look, however, and his wife was turned into a pillar of salt before his eyes. Regardless of how one interprets the tale, this area certainly abounds with salt.

Sodom Mountain, about nine kilometers south of Newé Zohar, is an 11 kilometers mountain range running parallel to the coast, made almost entirely (98%) of salt. The **caves**, formed by water dissolving the salt, are quite beautiful, but the danger of avalanches is very real. East of Mount Sodom is the old camp that used to house employees of the Dead Sea Works, and near the camp is a salt rock formation that has been dubbed "**Lot's Wife**."

A few years ago, some Israeli tourism promoters suggested turning Sodom into a casino/night club/strip joint spot, but the Chief Rabbinate firmly nixed the idea, saying that there was nothing to prevent God from destroying the city a second time.

Further south along the coastal Route 90 at the southern tip of the Dead Sea lies the **Dead Sea Works**, a large industrial complex that takes full advantage of the elements to extract the salt, as well as potash, chlorine, and bromide for profitable export.

Nearby are **Nahal Perazim** and the **Flour Cave**, where water currents have carved weird figures and shapes in the soft limestone canyon. Upstream is the Flour Cave, which got its name due to the powdery fine chalk that lines it.

Kikkar Sodom (*Sodom Plains*) are full of salt marshes and lush vegetation, and the fresh springs are popular watering holes for thirsty local wildlife. It's around 30 kilometers from Newé Zohar, and it takes most of a day to drive, look around, and go back.

PRACTICAL INFORMATION

• **Onil Tourist Center**, *Tel./Fax 07-652-0143*, in the mall complex on the sea, is now a privately run tourist information center run by Moti, a nice man who's lived in the region for 16 years. He also runs rents out rooms, $100 per family per night.

HEALTH TREATMENTS & SUPPOSED BENEFITS OF THE DEAD SEA

• *Bromine:* relaxes the nervous system
• *Magnesium:* tones and refreshes the skin
• *Oxygen-rich air:* lifts spirits and breathing
• *Low altitude:* filters harmful ultra-violet rays while you tan
• *Balneotherapy:* immersion treatment
• *Thalassotherapy:* sea treatment
• *Pelotherapy:* mud treatment
• *Heliotherapy:* sun treatment
• *Climatotherapy:* sun, mud, and sea treatment

19. THE NEGEV

The **Negev** is a desert occupying slightly more than half of Israel in the southern part of the country. A narrow wedge between Egypt and Jordan, it is eight to 130 kilometers wide, about 240 kilometers long, and stretches from **Be'er Sheva** in the north to the **Gulf of Aqaba** in the south. Consisting of sandy loam over limestone, the Negev is a plateau with an average elevation of 457 meters, and less than 10 inches of rain a year.

Hot in the summer and cold in the winter, irrigation makes the northern part highly productive, and wheat, barley, citrus fruits, and vegetables are grown successfully. In addition to its agriculture, the Negev is also rich in copper, phosphates, natural gas, and oil. Fairly populous in ancient times, the area used to be occupied by Semitic peoples who learned to use the sparse winter rains for their agriculture; remnants of their forts and trading posts can still be seen. In the seventh century, Arabs overran the Negev, and in 1948 it was the scene of fierce fighting between Israeli and Egyptian troops.

ARAD

Arad gets left off many Israel itineraries, but it's a convenient spot from which to dabble in the glories of the Negev, the Judean Desert, and the Dead Sea. Just a place to change buses for some, it's also making a name for itself as a the vacation of choice for those with asthma or other respiratory ailments, due to the cool, dry, pollen-free air of the desert plateau.

Founded in 1961 after natural gas was discovered, Arad's population is around 20,000 and growing. The town is fairly attractive, accommodations here are cheaper than in the resorts of Ein Bokek, and the atmosphere is pretty quiet, with all the pros and cons that come with it. If you're looking for asthma therapy or a good base for desert exploration, Arad might suit you perfectly. If you want socializing and nightlife, the Dead Sea area will provide more people to watch and nightlife to enjoy.

ORIENTATION

On the northern edge of the Negev, 48 kilometers from Be'er Sheva and 28 kilometers from the Dead Sea, Arad's situated at the crossroads to Eilat, the Dead Sea, and the Coastal Plain. Arad is high up on a desert plateau, 2,000 feet above sea level (3,200 feet above the Dead Sea), and its weather is the high desert norm: very dry, pretty hot during the day and much cooler at night. The central hub of the city is easy to navigate by foot.

The bus stops on **Yehuda**, a main street running east-west, but the station is more of a stop than a full-fledged station; look for it right next to the police station. To the east of the bus stop, **Yerushalayim** heads north into the commercial district, and a bit further east on Yehuda takes you to **HaPalmach**, which runs south to the Youth Hostel and Arad Hotel.

ARRIVALS & DEPARTURES

By Bus

The **central bus station**, *Yehuda at the corner of Yerushalayim, Tel. 07-995-7393*, is near the hostel and quick food. Bus 389 from Tel Aviv stops in Arad.

To or from Be'er Sheva, buses 384, 385, 386 and 388 leave every 15 minutes and cost NIS 15. There are frequent buses from here to Be'er Sheva (45 minutes), Ein Gedi (one hour), and Masada (45 minutes).

By Car

Many roads converge at Arad. It's easy to drive from and has plenty of parking.

GETTING AROUND TOWN

By Foot

It's easy to walk from bus to hostel to falafel stand, but further afield requires a vehicle. The town was planned with separate pedestrian and vehicular traffic in mind, so there are plenty of pedestrian walkways.

By Car

There's not much traffic, so driving and parking are a breeze, but some places you can't get to by driving.

By Taxi

Call *07-995-0888* or *07-995-9565*.

WHERE TO STAY

MORGOA, *Mo'av, Tel. 07-995-1222, Fax 07-995-7778, has singles that cost $79-$88, while doubles are $133-$126, breakfast included.*

The Morgoa's 167 rooms come with air conditioning, phone, TV, toilet, and private bath or shower. They have a swimming pool and asthma clinic. The Morgoa is across the street from Nof Arad.

NOF ARAD, *Mo'av, Tel. 07-995-7056, Fax 07-995-4053, costs $58-$63 a single, and $80-$92 a double, breakfast included.*

There are 117 rooms here, each equipped with air conditioning, toilet, phone, and bath or shower. The hotel has a swimming pool, a synagogue, and an asthma clinic, and is far from the center of town. To get there from Yehuda (where the bus stop is) turn left on Yerushalayim and then right on Ben Yair. Ben Yair will eventually turn in Mo'av and take you to the hotel.

ARAD HOTEL, *6 HaPalmach, Tel. 07-995-7040, Fax 07-995-7272, is about five minutes walk from the bus station. Singles cost $40, doubles are $60, and breakfast is included.*

The Arad's 45 rooms, with air conditioning and private toilet and shower, are serviceable and clean. The rooms are grouped around lawns and flowers that are pleasant, though all seems coated with a fine layer of desert dust. From the bus station turn right on Yehuda, then right again on HaPalmach. The hotel is on your right.

BLAU WEISS YOUTH HOSTEL, *4 HaAtad, Tel. 07-995-7150, Fax 07-995-5078, just off HaPalmach, charges NIS 55 a dorm bed (four beds to a room), breakfast included.*

In a quiet setting in Arad, it's not far past the Arad Hotel. They've 160 beds, and all the rooms have attached showers and toilets. The hostel has a TV room, a lighted basketball court, and a cheerful rose garden that is a lovely sight in arid Arad. From the bus station, go right on Yehuda and then right again on HaPalmach. Walk a few minutes and the hostel, one of the cleaner, pleasanter places to stay in Arad, will be on your left. No private rooms, but lots of helpful friendly service, not to mention fluency in English. Visa accepted.

WHERE TO EAT

Chen Street, *commercial center*, is the place to go for what few food options Arad has to offer. From the bus station, turn left on Yerushalayim. Your next left is Chen, home of shwarma and falafel stands, supermarkets and cafés.

SEEING THE SIGHTS

Arad's **Visitor Center**, **Cultural Center**, and **Museum**, *Ben Ya'ir*, are a block west of Yerushalayim. The museum costs NIS 11, is open Saturday-Thursday 9am-5pm, Friday 9am-4pm, and reflects the excavations on Tel Arad; there's a sound and light show as well.

The **Artists' Village**, *south of Yehuda off HaMadregot*, such as it is, is east of HaPalmach.

To the west, past the asthma clinic hotels on Mo'av is an **Observation Point** (Mizpe Mo'av).

In mid-July, Arad hosts the **Hebrew Music Festival**, and for four days the town bulges at the seams with rocking Israeli youth. Admission to the folk music concerts and dances is free, while the shows and band concerts cost NIS 40-60. Make reservations for accommodations well in advance, or join the mobs camping out under the stars.

SHOPPING

Canyon Arad, *center of Arad, Tel. 07-995-5595*, is a large mall with fast food, a pharmacy, book store, three cinemas, public parking, tourist information, and plenty more.

The **Market**, *south of the Be'er Sheva road*, is a few blocks west of the central bus station.

EXCURSIONS & DAY TRIPS

Arad Park is west of the city on Route 31. It's a pine and eucalyptus forest, with picnic facilities and a children's playground.

Tel Arad displays the excavations of ancient Arad. Open Sunday-Thursday 8am-4pm, Friday 8am-3pm in winter (and one hour longer is summer) and costing NIS 7 per adult, NIS 3 for students, the tel features a fortress, and a temple dating back to the Bronze Age (circa 2000 BCE), and is one of Israel's best examples of an early Bronze Age city. To drive there, go past Arad Park on Route 31 and turn right just past the Route 80 junction on the left, it's about 10 kilometers west of the city. By bus, take the Be'er Sheva bus and get off at the orange Tel Arad sign (ask the driver) then hike in two kilometers.

Further north on the Tel Arad road is the **Amasa Reserve** and **Yattir Forest**, with trails through the forest, observation points, and picnic sites.

Nahal Zin creates an especially lovely landscape as it drains down from the Negev mountains through lunar craters and eventually flows into Sodom Plain south of Dead Sea Works. The river is a few kilometers southwest of Ha'Arava Junction.

HaMakhtesh HaQatan (*the Small Crater*) is northeast a few kilometers from Nahal Zin in the northern Negev. The elements of water and time on limestone and sandstone has formed a truly beautiful site, exposing many geological strata with colors and interesting formations. **United**, *Tel. 03-522-2008*, runs organized tours every Friday.

North of Hamakhtesh HaQatan on Route 25 is **Mezad Tamar**, an excavated ancient Roman fort that was once a part of Rome's Limes network of military roads and towers.

Hebron and the Hebron Mountains lie to the west of Arad, and as the traditional burial place for the Patriarchs, it's a popular pilgrimage for Jews, Christians, and Muslims. For these same religious reasons, Hebron's not been a safe tourist spot due to high conflict and tensions. Contact the US Embassy for a security update before planning a trip there.

Other destinations, like Sodom, Masada, Ein Bokek, and Ein Gedi are described in the Dead Sea chapter.

PRACTICAL INFORMATION

- **Bus information**, *Tel. 07-995-7393*.
- **First Aid** (Magen David Adom), *off HaPalmach near Yehuda, Tel. 101*.
- **Fire Brigade**, *off HaPalmach near Yehuda, Tel. 102* .
- **Pharmacy**, *Tel. 07-995-7439* or *Tel. 07-995-5173*.
- **Post office**, *Commercial Center on Ben Ya'ir*, is a block west of Yerushalayim.
- **Police**, *off HaPalmach near Yehuda, Tel. 07-995-7044, or Tel. 100* in emergencies, is just next to the First Aid and Fire Brigade.
- **Tourist Information Office**, *Canyon Arad, Tel. 07-995-8144*, is open Sunday-Thursday 8am-7pm, Friday 9am-noon.
- **Visitor Center**, *Ben Ya'ir, Tel. 07-995-4409, Fax 07-995-5866*, is a block west of Yerushalayim. Arad's new visitor center has displays and a new information center.

DIMONA

Established fairly recently in 1955, **Dimona** is named after the biblical town of the Tribe of Judah (Joshua 15:22). It started as a residential quarter for employees of the Dead Sea Works, though the town now has expanded to glass-making, ceramics, textiles, and a much down-played nuclear reactor.

Dimona is also home to the **Black Hebrew settlement**, *Tel. 07-655-5400*, an interesting group of immigrants from the United States midwest who believe their roots lead back to Israel, and whose dietary laws are stricter than kosher. It is possible (and rewarding) to visit them, but you should call to set it up in advance; a surprise drop-in might not be welcomed. It's about a 10 minute walk from the bus station–turn left on Herzl and keep on till you see the green hedges announce the beginning of the village.

ARRIVALS & DEPARTURES

There are frequent buses to Dimona from Be'er Sheva (about 15 kilometers northwest, NIS 12), Mitzpe Ramon (about 25 kilometers southwest), and Arad (about 20 kilometers northeast). There are less frequent buses from Tel Aviv (NIS 30) and Eilat (NIS 44) as well.

WHERE TO STAY

The **BLACK HEBREWS GUEST HOUSE**, *Tel. 07-655-5400, will put you up for $20, with advance notice, including breakfast and dinner.*
DRACHIM YOUTH HOSTEL AND GUEST HOUSE, *1 HaNassi, Tel. 07-655-6811, has dorm beds (six per room) for $25 or NIS 85.*

If you want to stay in Dimona proper, this relatively new 323 bed facility has air conditioning and private baths in each room. In addition, the hostel has a sauna, jacuzzi, and heated pool.
MAMSHIT CAMEL FARM, *one kilometers from the archaeology site, Tel. 07-655-4012, Fax 07-655-0965, lets guests stay in a Bedouin tent of goat hair and wool and enjoy Bedouin hospitality for around $15 a day, goat hair tent, food, and activities included.*

They are a Bedouin center that can arrange for a camel safari, desert jeep tour, rappelling, or hiking. It's difficult to get here without a car, however, as no buses currently come close.

WHERE TO EAT

BLACK HEBREWS' RESTAURANT is open Sunday-Thursday 11am-11pm, Friday 10am-2pm and prepared food according to their veganesque dietary laws.
DRACHIM YOUTH HOSTEL serves kosher meals in their dining room.

NIGHTLIFE & ENTERTAINMENT

The Black Hebrew community has its own **Academy for the Performing and Fine Arts**, and there are frequently concerts at night.

SHOPPING

The community also makes it own clothes and jewelry in accordance with their religious beliefs that require pure, natural fabrics. Their **boutique** is open Sunday-Thursday 10:30am-1:30pm, and 4-9pm and has some unique and beautiful items.

EXCURSIONS & DAY TRIPS

Six kilometers southeast of Dimona is **Mamshit**, *Tel. 07-655-6478*, a Nabatean town from the third century BCE. Excavated and reconstructed by the National Parks Authority, it's open Sunday-Thursday 8am-4pm, Friday 8am-3pm in winter, and an hour later in summer. Admission is NIS 7, with students/children for NIS 4. It's the biggest Nabatean city ever discovered (meaning bigger than Petra in Jordan), and there are Roman and Byzantine ruins as well. Mamshit isn't on most tourist itineraries, and to lure you there the Parks Authority is making the excavation more like a theme park, with folks dressed like ancient Nabateans busily engaged in Nabatean tasks and skills.

To get there without a car, take any bus heading toward Eilat and ask to be dropped at the sign-posted turn-off for the two kilometers walk. Or take bus 5 from Dimona's central bus station, leaving hourly for NIS 8. Call Egged, *Tel. 07-627-8558*, or the Mamshit Tourism Authority, *Tel. 07-655-6478*, for more information.

Mamshit Camel Farm, *one kilometers from the archaeology site, Tel. 07-655-4012, Fax 07-655-0965*, is a Bedouin center where you can sip coffee or tea in a Bedouin tent or arrange for a camel safari, desert jeep tour, rappelling, or hiking. Guests stay in a Bedouin tent of goat hair and wool and enjoy Bedouin hospitality for around $15 a day (goat hair tent, food, and activities all included). It's tough to get here without a car, however, as no buses currently come close, but how often do you get to stay at a place called "Mamshit?"

For trips to the crater **Ha-Makhtesh Ha-Katan**, see the *Arad Excursions* section.

BE'ER SHEVA

Be'er Sheva (also known as **Beersheba**), capital of the Southern District of Israel, is a hot, drab, dusty town, a long drive or bus ride from anywhere. Named in biblical times, Be'er Sheva is interpreted to mean "well of the pledge" or "well of the seven," referring to a well supposedly dug there by Abraham some 4,000 years ago.

Be'er Sheva was ancient Israel's southernmost city, and as it was on a major caravan route, it was an important hub; it also figured as a sanctuary for Jacob and Elijah. There are very few remains from Roman and Byzantine times, and from the 600s CE onward, Be'er Sheva wasn't much more than a Bedouin caravansarai with a market and a few wells. The Turks built a town here in the early 1900s, serving as an administrative center for the Negev Bedouins. Then, in 1917, General Allenby led the British to victory over the Turks here as his troops moved northwards.

The UN Partition Plan placed Be'er Sheva in the Palestinian Zone, and the Egyptian Army took control at the start of the 1948 War of Independence, but the Israelis took it back on October 21st in 'Operation Ten Plagues.' Old Be'er Sheva had a reputation as an untamed 'frontier town,' but modern Be'er Sheva is calm–some would say boring.

Along with its old Turkish district and more recent Jewish sectors, there's an artists' colony and a resettlement center for immigrant Russian Jews. Still affected and shaped by the Negev desert that borders it, its economy, which isn't the greatest, is based on chemicals, glass manufacturing, and the potash which is produced nearby. Though its location is perfect for the Negev Institute for Arid Zone Research, tourism isn't booming. In fact, most Israelis, upon hearing you intend to spend half a day traveling to and about Be'er Sheva will ask "why?" It's a question worth thinking about.

ORIENTATION

Be'er Sheva is located at the northern edge of the **Negev**, about 89 kilometers southwest of Jerusalem, and has a population of around 114,000. The weather is hot, in summer it's very hot. And the dust from the desert coats the city in a fine layer of dirt. The central bus station is on Derekh Eilat, and Kenion HaNegev Mall is just across the street.

Other than this focal point, the main points of interest are west about 10 minutes walk. Just past the mall, Eilat intersects with many branching streets. HeHalutz and Herzl both branch to the left and both go in the correct general direction to get to the sights, hotels, and food. HeHalutz will take you past HaAtzma'ut, where the Negev Museum is, to the pedestrian mall (the midrahov). A right on the midrahov will take you to Derekh Hevron and the start of the walking tour of the city.

ARRIVALS & DEPARTURES

By Car

Next to the bus station is a mall, and under the mall is an enormous parking garage, free of charge.

By Bus

Egged Bus Station, *off Eilat Street, Tel. 07-629-4311*, is across from Tourist Information. To or from Jerusalem, the bus costs NIS 28 and takes close to two hours. To or from Arad, bus 384, 385, 386, and 388 leave every 15 minutes and cost NIS 15. There are also frequent buses to Tel Aviv, and buses to Eilat go nearly every hour.

Not many buses go all the way to the Dead Sea (most transfer in Arad), but on Saturday there's a special morning Egged bus to Ein Gedi via Arad and Masada.

GETTING AROUND TOWN

By Foot

Most of the spots you might want to see are easily accessible by foot. If drive in, ditch your car in the parking garage under the Mall near the bus station and walk the few blocks to the sights.

By City Bus

City buses traverse the sprawl of greater Be'er Sheva. The map sold by the Tourism Office includes a map of the bus routes and a description of their destinations. For information, call *Tel. 07-627-7381.*

WHERE TO STAY

DESERT INN, *north of the Old City, Tel. 07-642-4922, Fax 07-641-2772, charges $63-$88 a single and $85-$116 a double, breakfast included.*

Their 164 rooms all come with bath, air conditioning, and phone. A four-star hotel, and Be'er Sheva's best, they've got a swimming pool and tennis courts. To get there, drive or bus north up Ha'Atzma'ut.

BET YATSIV, *Ha'Atzma'ut, Tel. 07-627-7444, Fax 07-627-5735, charges NIS 140 for singles, NIS 198 a double, and NIS 70 for good dorm beds.*

North of the Old City past Assaf Simhoni Street (take bus 13 from the bus station), the guest house has 76 rooms and the hostel has 22, all complete with heat and air conditioning. There's a pleasant, garden, no curfew, and in summer there's a pool for adults and another for toddlers.

HOTEL HANEGEV, *26 Ha'Atzma'ut, Tel. 07-627-7026, at the corner of Trumpeldor, charges $25-$45, no credit cards accepted.*

There are 16 rooms varying in quality and price. The least appealing, across the hall from the bathroom, costs $25, and a drab room with shower and air conditioning is $35 ($40 with breakfast). In the "new" wing the rooms are somewhat better. $45 gets you a room with air conditioning, toilet, and shower, while $45 takes the prize with bath and TV.

HOTEL AVIV, *40 Mordei Hagetaot, Tel. 07-627-8059, charges $27 a single, and a double is $37, plus $3 for breakfast.*

There are 21 reasonably clean rooms, each with shower and toilet, TV, air conditioning, and pink phone. Some rooms have small balconies and look okay, but the establishment seems to have more than its share of sleazy, questionable sorts hanging around.

HOTEL ARAVA, *37 Ha'Histadrut, Tel. 07-627-8792, charges $20-$25 a single, $30-$35 a double, breakfast not included.*

The entrance is next to the jewelry store, the 27 rooms come with shower and toilet, and are basic and clean. The location is handy (just off the midrahov) and next to a cafe, but the staff isn't the friendliest.

BET YAZIV YOUTH HOSTEL, *79 HaAtzma'ut, past the Bedouin School, Tel. 07-627-7444, Fax 07-627-5735, costs NIS 82 per dorm bed (four to a room), breakfast included. Visa/Mastercard accepted.*

There's a swimming pool open July-August, and dinner and lunch are available for NIS 45 each. The rooms are clean and tidy, with a small desk, phone, radio, fan, shower, and toilet. City buses 12 and 13 stop by here every 45 minutes or so.

WHERE TO EAT

PAPA MICHEL, *95 HaHistadrut, Tel. 07-627-7298,* open 12-12 daily, is a quality place for a sit-down meal. With appetizers for NIS 10, vegetarian dishes NIS 10-25, couscous NIS 40, and grilled meats and fish NIS-50, they serve cocktails, have a decent wine list, and accept visa/ mastercard. The room is attractive, with linen table clothes and wicker lamps, and the restaurant is a very pleasant shift from the grodiness of downtown Be'er Sheva.

Kenion Ha-Negev, *HaNessi'im, Tel. 07-628-1222,* the shopping mall next to the central bus station, has a large **SUPERMARKET** (open Sunday-Thursday 9am-10pm) with a very respectable baklava section. Downstairs is an enormous **FOOD PLAZA**, with all sorts of different stalls and fast food restaurants. There's a **BURGER RANCH**, plus stands with burekas, pizza, falafel, shwarma, etc. Especially good is the salad bar with stuffed pitas for NIS 6 and gigantic lufahs for NIS 9.

There's a good **BAKERY**, *40 Mordei Hagetaot,* next to Hotel Aviv.

And there's tasty cheap **ICE CREAM**, *corner of HaHistadrut and HaAtzma'ut.*

Smilansky Street, *via HaHistadrut or HeHaluz,* has lots of cafes, restaurants, and pubs.

SEEING THE SIGHTS

The city of Be'er Sheva has invested in painting a walking tour that loops around the main sights, such as they are. If you want to see every structure relating to Be'er Sheva history, they are numbered and labeled; it's fairly easy to follow the path and take in all the hot spots.

Abraham's Well–Be'er Avraham–is at number 1 Hevron Street. Supposedly the source of the city's name, here you can see the gouges the ropes have made in the rock over the years, as well as the scoop-wheel structure built in the late 1800s and operated by camel in the pursuit of water. Number 2 marks the spot on the Pedestrian Mall where the **first Jewish grain mill** in the Negev once stood.

After you calm down from that excitement, proceed up the midrahov and turn right on HaHistradrut to #3, the **home of Sheik Brich Abu-Medin**, appointed by the British to be Be'er Sheva's first mayor. A left on HaAtzma'ut takes you to #4, the home of the Araf Al-Araf, the district ruler. Just past this is #6, the **Governor's House**, *Tel. 07-628-0256,* now a part of #5, the **Negev Museum**, *60 HaAtzma'ut, Tel. 628-2056.* It chronicles the region's history and houses the **Archaeology Wing**, has been 'temporarily' closed for reconstruction for years, but currently hopes to reopen in 1998. It's housed in what looks to be a great building, a Turkish Mosque built in 1906. The **Art Wing** of the museum is in what used to be the

Governor's Residence (also built in 1906); it's open Sunday-Thursday 10am-5pm, Friday and Saturday 10am-1pm, and costs NIS 5 for adults, NIS 3 for students. At a rate of a shekel a minute (less for students), you need about five minutes to take it all in. The most interesting modern art display by far was the room with many white pillows, on some of which lay loaves of bread, entitled "The Nimitz Sanatorium" by Michael Rapaport and Roman Baembaer.

The northern loop of the walking tour turns right on Assaf Simhoni from HaAtzma'ut, taking you to #7, the **Be'eri School**, built by the British in the 40s. Turn left on Rambam to see the # 8-10, the old **Turkish Railway Station**, the **station manager's home**, and the **water tower**. Today, the station structures are used as an art gallery. Back on the path, cut across the **British Army WWI cemetery** (#11) to return to HaAtzma'ut, and turn left.

On the corner with Hativat HaNegev is #12, the **old Bedouin School** (soon to become a part of the Negev Museum). Continue down HaAtzma'ut to Herzl across from the Museum and turn right by #13, **Allenby Garden** (Gan Allenby), a patch of land in fairly sad shape just now. Right nearby is #14, **Bet Hasaraya**, built by the Turks as the government center, and now used by the army. Follow Herzl all the way to **Gan HaNassi** (HaNassi Garden) then cut across to see #15, **Bet HaNegbi**, the home of the first military ruler following Be'er Sheva's liberation.

Also nearby is Smilansky Street, filled with pubs, restaurants, cafes, and galleries. From HaHistadrut, turn south on Anielewicz to where it intersects with HeHaluz to see #16, the **Youth Art Center**. Built in the 30s, it was the city's first high school in 1953. A left on HeHaluz and a right on HaAvot takes you to #17, the **Mission House** (Bet HaMisi'on). One of the first houses of the modern city, the house and its surrounding stone wall were built in 1903. A right on Trumpeldor and a left on HaPalmah lead you to the artists' colony (#18) of **Shuk Hilman**, and then back to where you started at Abraham's Well.

The **Bedouin Market** (on Thursdays only) is in a new location by the intersection of Exel and Yehud Ha Levi, near the Sports Center, north of the center, but it's the same old colorful weekly market that opened in 1905. A little more touristic (with camel rides and such), it still serves the needs of the Bedouin community. It gets going around 6am, and the earlier you go the better. In the afternoon it's hot, and it becomes more of a tourist trap than a genuine market.

Shuk Hilman, the new artists' market, starts at the intersection of Palmach and Bet-Eshel, about a block from Abraham's Well (and number 18 on the walking tour).

Zoological Garden, *Be'er Sheva-Hatzerim Road, Tel. 07-641-4777*, is open Sunday-Thursday 9am-5pm, Friday 9am-1pm, and Saturday 10am-

3:30pm, and costs NIS 10 an adult, and NIS 15 a child (kids under two admitted free). Started by a couple of teachers as a modest collection of animals for their students, they now have a fair collection, including a good bunch of snakes, and a darkroom for seeing nocturnal animals.

Ben Gurion University, *Ben Gurion Boulevard, Tel. 07-646-1111*, was established in 1965 as the Negev Institute of Higher Education, became Negev University in 1969, and honored Ben Gurion after his death in 1973 by being renamed yet again. It now instructs over 8,000 students. Call ahead to arrange a tour of the campus.

Founded by David Ben Gurion in 1957 as the Institute for Negev Research, the **Institutes for Applied Research**, *HaShalom, Tel. 07-646-1901*, researches living conditions in the desert. An exhibition of their discoveries (in the fields of food preservation, cosmetics, industrial, and agricultural products) is on display.

NIGHTLIFE & ENTERTAINMENT

Form is a popular disco/pub in *Qiryat Yehudit*. Otherwise, there are a number of **pubs** on *Smilansky Street* to check out.

For more cultured fare, call the **Be'er Sheva Theater**, *Tel. 07-627-8111*, or the **Israel Symphonieta**, *Tel. 07-623-1616*, to see what's scheduled.

In early July Be'er Sheva hosts the **International Harmonica and Accordian Festival**. If you're a fan of these instruments, Be'er Sheva is a unique setting for the music.

SHOPPING

The big **Kanion HaNegev Mall**, *HaNessi'im, Tel. 07-628-1222*, next to the central bus station has all the shops you'll ever need, including a Steimatzky Book Store.

For Bedouin crafts, try the **Bedouin Market** in town on Thursdays or the **Bedouin Heritage Center**, *Rahat*, for its Saturday market or its shop, open daily–see *Excursions & Day Trips*, below, for more details.

EXCURSIONS & DAY TRIPS

Go north along Route 40 to Route 31 to get to the **Joe Alon Center**, the **Bedouin Culture Museum**, *Kibbutz Lahav, Tel. 07-991-8597*. Open Saturday-Thursday 9am-5pm, Friday 9am-2:30pm, and costing NIS 12 for adults, NIS 10 for students, the museum explains the desert culture and demonstrates crafts such as weaving and baking. There is also an archaeological display of the cave culture since Mishnaic and Talmudic times, featuring caves from Chalcolithic, Israelite, Hellenistic, Roman, and Byzantine days (4000 BCE-640 CE). Bus 369 to Tel Aviv passes the intersection turn-off, but it's an eight kilometer hike in from there. Bus 42 goes directly to the kibbutz, but only once a day, so check Egged's schedule.

Bedouins' Heritage Center at Rahat, *Route 264, Tel. 07-991-8263, Fax 07-991-0303*, is north a bit from Be'er Sheva. The Center is in the middle of the Bedouin town of Rahat in the Northern Negev, near Kibbutz Shuval. In the past, the tribe of Al Hoseil was led here by Suleiman the Great. In the present, the Center provides examples of Bedouin culture, offering refreshments in a typical Bedouin tent, and demonstrating traditional skills and handicrafts such as rug-weaving and pita bread baking. There are performances of the Debka Dance to traditional music, and a Bazaar selling Bedouin clothing, jewelry, spices, and food. In addition, there are camel and donkey rides, and on Saturdays they hold their Bedouin Market selling a colorful melee of animals, fruit, vegetables, and clothes.

Air Force Museum, *Be'er Sheva-Hatzerim Road, Tel. 07-990-6855*, is west of the city. Open Sunday-Thursday 8am-5pm, Friday 8am-1pm, costing NIS 18 per adult, NIS 10 a child, the museum promotes the bravery of the air force and displays a variety of planes.

Mitzpeh Bet Eshel, *southeast on the road to Dimona, Tel. 07-627-7890*, is now a youth education center. It was founded in 1943 as one of three mitzpim in reaction to the "White Paper" which forbade the purchase of Negev land. The mitzpim were forts with watch towers, serving as observation posts and security houses. You can arrange a guided tour if you call in advance.

Nevatim Synagogue, *further along the road to Dimona, Tel. 07-627-7277*, is not only an impressive and unusual synagogue, the settlement of Nevatim has an unusual history to match. It was one of 11 spots settled in 1946 on the night after Yom Kippur, but was abandoned once the war was over. It remained bereft of permanent occupants until 1955, when immigrants from the Cochin province of India moved in, along with as many bits from the synagogue in Cochin as they were able to bring. To see the synagogue, call and make arrangements in advance. There is an exhibit describing the history of the settlement, and you can visit the moshav greenhouses as well.

HaNegev-Palmach Brigade Memorial, *northeast on the road to Omer*, was designed by Dani Karavan. The structure starkly overlooks the city in memory of the settlers who defended the Negev during the War of Independence.

Tel Be'er Sheva National Park, *further a bit on the Omer road, Tel. 07-646-7286*, is open daily from 9am-5pm, admission free. This is the excavated site of the Biblical Be'er Sheva of Judean Kingdom (900s BCE) days. There are gates, water systems, guard rooms, and more. There is also a little restaurant, Bedouin Museum, and Bedouin crafts shop. By bus, take the Egged bus to Tel-es-Sab, a nearby Bedouin village, and ask the driver where to get off. The bus does this route infrequently, however, so find out when the last bus returns lest you be stranded.

THE BIBLICAL HISTORY OF BE'ER SHEVA

According to the Old Testament, Be'er Sheva was where the Patriarch **Abraham** *lived; it was also the southernmost town in ancient Israel, and the site of a Canaanite cult. It was in the wilderness of Be'er Sheva that Abraham sent his slave woman Hagar and son Ishmael to wander (Genesis 21:9). It was also here that Abraham made a pact with the Philistine king Abimelech (Genesis 21:22-34) in which Abraham gave Abimelech seven ewes, saying "'You are to accept these seven ewes from me as proof that I dug this well.' Hence that place was called Beer-sheba, for there the two of them swore an oath."*

The name 'Be'er Sheva' is interpreted to mean 'the well of seven,' or 'well of the oath.' Wells in the desert figure prominently for survival and symbolism, and when later in life Abraham moved northeast to Hebron, the Philistines were said to have filled up the well with earth, and Abraham's son Isaac had to dig it out again (Genesis 26:18). After some spats, Abimelech (probably son of the previous one) again swore an oath of peace over a well with Isaac (Genesis 26:33), reconfirming the name of Beersheba.

In later years the settlement by the well was given to the tribe of Simeon (Joshua 19:2) as the southernmost town in ancient Israel, as demonstrated by the expression 'from Dan to Beersheba' (Judges 20:1 and Samuel 3:20, to name a few) which referred to the whole of Israel. Samuel (the prophet and last of the Judges) set his sons Joel and Abijah as judges in Be'er Sheva (I Samuel 8:2), but they "subverted justice" and didn't follow in his footsteps. The prophet Amos warned against the rise of the Canaanite cult in Be'er Sheva (Amos 8:14), and the Bible mentions Be'er Sheva again when the Jews returning from Babylon reestablish a settlement (Nehemiah 11:27-30).

Fifty-eight kilometers southwest lies **Shivta** (**Subeita**), a remarkable excavation in the middle of desert nowhere land. Open Saturday-Thursday 8am-5pm, Friday 8am-4pm, and closing one hour earlier in winter, the site costs NIS 10 for adults, NIS 6 for students. This is the ruined site of Shivta, a Nabataean city founded in the first century BCE. In its heyday in the fourth century Shivta had a population of 7,000 and was the largest town in the Negev, conveniently located on the caravan route between Egypt and Anatolia, but it was abandoned in the 900s CE.

Many Nabataean houses have been preserved and restored, along with a double water reservoir and tiled streets. There are also two early Christian churches from the 300s CE and a Byzantine church built in the 500s. It's difficult to get here, however, without a car. You can take bus 44 toward Nizzana, get off at Horvot Shivta and then walk/hitch 8.5 kilometers, but don't count on the hitching.

If you do this, take plenty of water and make sure not to miss the last bus back.

PRACTICAL INFORMATION
- **Fire Department**, *Tel. 07-627-9691*, or *Tel. 102* in emergencies.
- **First Aid** (Magen David Adom), *Tel. 07-627-8333*, or *Tel. 101* in emergencies.
- **Municipal "Moked" hotline**, *Tel. 07-646-3777*.
- **Police**, *Herzl*, *Tel. 07 616-2714*, or *Tel. 100* in emergencies.
- **Post office** and **telecommunications center**, *corner of HaNaessi'im and Nordau*, is just north of the bus station. There is another branch, *corner of Histadrut and Hadassa*.
- **Soroka Medical Center**, *Tel. 07-640-0111*.
- **Tourist Information Office**, *6 Ben-Zvi, Tel./Fax 07-623-4613*, is opposite the bus station. They are open Sunday-Thursday 8am-4pm or 5pm, sell detailed maps of Be'er Sheva for NIS 7, and have information about guided tours.

KIBBUTZ SDE BOKER

Established in 1952 by ambitious settlers wanting to raise cows in the desert, the name **Sde Boker** means *Ranchers' Field* in Hebrew. Now, in addition to cattle, the kibbutz raises olives, fruit, wheat, and corn, and is considered a desert success.

It's best known, however, not for its productivity but because **David Ben Gurion** chose to retire here when he stepped down from being Israel's first prime minister in 1953. After little more than a year out to pasture, he returned to another term as prime minister, and came back to Sde Boker in 1963, where he remained with his wife till his death 10 years later.

ORIENTATION
In the middle of the Negev desert, roughly half-way between Mitzpe Ramon and Be'er Sheva, Sde Boker is a fine place to appreciate the verdant wonders of desert irrigation, visit the Sde Boker campus of Ben Gurion University, get your fill of Ben Gurion memorabilia, and explore the desert by hiking the **Ein Avdat Nature Reserve** in nearby Zin Canyon.

ARRIVALS & DEPARTURES

There are three separate turn-offs for Sde Boker: the first (coming from Be'er Sheva) is the main entrance to the kibbutz, the next is to Ben Gurion's Home (now a museum), and the last is for the university campus, the Ben Gurion graves, and Ein Avdat. Whether traveling by car or by bus (the Be'er Sheva-Mitzpe Ramon bus travels this route every hour or so until 9pm or 10pm), know where you're going before choosing your exit.

WHERE TO STAY

SPNI HOSTEL, *edge of Zin Canyon, Tel. 07-653-2828, Fax 07-653-2721.*

Often full with youth groups, the hostel sometimes has dorm beds available, for students only, for NIS 83. Doubles (for students and others) are NIS 185, and family rooms are NIS 240. There's a kitchen available, and a pleasant palm-shaded verandah.

SDE BOKER GUEST INN, *Zin Canyon, Tel. 07-659-6711, 8am-4pm in the office, Tel. 07-653-2933, at home–contact Shosh at least a day ahead.*

The Guest Inn is a roomy place, with singles for $55 and doubles for $70. Included in the price is an enormous common room with great canyon views, and a much-appreciated pool.

WHERE TO EAT

SDE BOKER INN, *right next to the Ben Gurion House, Tel. 07-656-0379,* is open Sunday-Thursday 8am-4pm, Friday 8am-3pm, Saturday 8:30am-3pm. They serve full meals for around NIS 30.

There's also a **supermarket** and **cafeteria** open Sunday-Thursday 8am-7pm, Friday 8am-2pm near the Ein Avdat Nature Reserve.

SEEING THE SIGHTS

Ben Gurions' hut, *Tel. 07-655-8444, Fax 07-656-0320,* only slightly larger than the homes of their kibbutz neighbors, has been preserved as a museum. It's open Sunday-Thursday 8am-3pm, Friday 8am-2pm, Saturday 9am-2:30pm, and admission is free.

The kibbutz also has a small **zoo**, not far from Ben Gurions' home. Feeding time is around 2pm.

Ben Gurions' graves are near the Zin rim, with views into the beauty of the canyon.

Ben Gurion University Sde Boker Campus includes the Jacob Blaustein Institute for Desert Research, the Blaustein International Center for Desert Studies, and the Ben Gurion Research Institute. The focus is clear, and the work ground-breaking. Tours of the campus can be arranged.

EXCURSIONS & DAY TRIPS

Ein Avdat Nature Reserve, *Zin Canyon, Tel. 07-655-5684*, is a desert Garden of Eden for hikers, open daily 8am-4pm, and costing NIS 12 for adults, NIS 6 for children, or get a combination ticket for Ein Avdat and the Avdat ruins for NIS 19 per adult, NIS 10 per child. Lower and upper parking lots aid access for drivers, and trails run between the two. The entrance is through the Ben Gurion Institute. If you don't have a car, take bus 60 toward Mitzpe Ramon and ask the driver to let you out at the Ein Avdat trailhead. The trail is well-marked and maintained, with ladders and footholds. Signs near the entrance point out a three-four hour route and a one-two hour route, both of which take you past waterfalls, pools, caves, and Byzantine fortress ruins.

Eleven kilometers south of Sde Boker are the preserved **Avdat ruins** of a third century BCE Nabatean city. Open daily 8am-5pm, admission to this site on the hill is NIS 16 for adults, NIS 7 for children, or get a combination ticket for Ein Avdat and the Avdat ruins for NIS 19 per adult, NIS 10 per child. Named after the Nabatean god-king Obodas II (30-9 BCE), the town was situated some 50 kilometers south of Be'er Sheva on the old caravan route from the Nabatean capital of Petra to the Mediterranean port at Gaza, and may have served as a base for raids on other caravans. Coins and inscriptions show Avdat was flourishing in the second and first centuries BCE, and finds indicate links with Egypt, Greece, and Asia Minor.

Avdat was really booming under Aretasa IV (9BCE-40CE), son of Obodas. He's the one who built the retaining walls of the castle hill. In 106 CE the Romans incorporated the Nabateans into the Roman Empire, and Avdat was thriving again during the third century CE. In the fifth and sixth centuries, Avdat became popular with Byzantine monks–almost all the buildings on the castle hill are from this period. The Persians conquered in 614, 20 years later Avdat was taken by the Muslims, and in the 10th century was abandoned for good. The remains of canals, cisterns, and dams attest to the Nabateans' great irrigation skills. Nabatean burial chambers have been excavated, as well as a Byzantine bath house and dwelling house. There's also a Byzantine high wall, street, monastery, baptistry, two churches, and a watchtower.

Bus 60 from Be'er Sheva to Sde Boker stops here (make sure the bus driver understands you want the Avdat archaeological site, not Ein Avdat the oasis). It's a 15 minute hike from the road to the ruins. There's drinking water and bathrooms across from the ticket booth, and a **gas station** and **restaurant** near the bus stop.

PRACTICAL INFORMATION

• **Post office**, *near Ein Avdat Nature Reserve, the supermarket and cafeteria*, is open Sunday-Thursday 9-11am and 1-2pm, Friday 9-11am.
• **SPNI Field School**, *Tel. 07-653-2828, Fax 07-653-2721*, is open Sunday-Thursday 8am-6:30pm, Friday 8-11:30am and can answer your questions about hiking routes (they sell detailed maps, though they are in Hebrew only), and they know all about the local plants and animals as well. There's also an audio video show on Ben Gurion's life for NIS 6 (NIS 4 for students and children). They lead guided hikes (NIS 400 a day) but it must be arranged ahead of time.

MITZPE RAMON

Mitzpe Ramon (*Ramon Observation Point*) looks out over **Makhtesh Ramon** (*Ramon Crater*) in the heart of the Negev. Happened upon by government explorers after Israel declared statehood in 1948, and used as a stop-over point on trips to Eilat in the days before a direct route was built from the Dead Sea, Mitzpe Ramon is now a growing desert town of 8,000 on a plateau some 900 meters above sea level, which keeps its climate air conditioned by mountain breezes.

If you want to get to know the desert, this is a fine expedition launching site. The **Ramon Crater**, 40 kilometers long, nine kilometers wide, and 400 meters deep, is the largest crater in the world, and it has remarkable geological formations going back thousands of years, remnants of ancient cultures, and fossils from the dinosaur age. The National Geological Park is an excellent place for hiking, rappelling, and jeep tours, as well as being a quiet away-from-it-all, holiday-making, sunset-watching haven.

ORIENTATION

Mitzpe Ramon is located 160 kilometers from Eilat and 190 kilometers from Tel Aviv, Mitzpe Ramon is high in the mountains of the desert, giving it an unusually hospitable climate. The air is desert dry, but the summer evenings are cooled by mountain breezes.

ARRIVALS & DEPARTURES

By Bus

Bus 60 runs to Be'er Sheva every hour or so from 6:30am-10pm, costing NIS 21. Bus 392 goes to Eilat every couple of hours from 8:20am-7:30pm for NIS 32. There are two bus stops, one on Ben Gurion Street next to a cafeteria, and the other is near the youth hostel.

Ramon Transports, *Tel 07-658-8626*, arranges private transportation to and from Mitzpe Ramon.

GETTING AROUND TOWN

It's a small town, easy to walk around and get to know.

WHERE TO STAY

RAMON INN, *1 Ein Akev, Tel. 07-658-8822, Fax 07-658-8151, or in the US, Tel. 800/552-0141, has suites for two to six people, costing $80-$330, depending on the season, including Israeli buffet breakfast and 15% service charge.*

Another hotel in the Isrotel chain (the company that owns so many of the up-scale hotels in Eilat, they offer 96 apartments with kitchenette, TV, and phone. This used to be an apartment complex for Russian immigrants, but four years ago the whole place was renovated into a beautiful hotel with all the amenities (except an elevator–let them know in advance if you need first floor accommodations). The lobby is lovely, with gorgeous picture frame windows, plants, and a big fire place lit every evening.

There's a self-service laundromat as well, and a dining room with exceptional food. They employ Mitzpe Ramon housewives as chefs, and they do a buffet of their specialties, including home-made bread, couscous, and other local oriental specialties. The hotel also has a swimming pool, organizes jeep tours of the crater (about $22 per person), and offers massages in your room for NIS 90. The apartments are very nice (they sleep up to six), the hotel has a warm, friendly feel, and families are welcome. Busiest in the spring and autumn, it's an appealing place to stay year round.

MITZPE RAMON YOUTH HOSTEL, *near the Visitors' Center, Tel. 07-658-8443, Fax 07-658-8074, has dorm beds (six per room) for NIS 60, breakfast included. For private rooms, the rates are NIS 130 a single, NIS 180 a double, NIS 60 per additional person, visa and mastercard accepted.*

The dorms are separated by gender. Both dorms and private rooms are very clean, with wood furniture and cheery colors, roomy and comfortable, with private toilet and shower. There's a snack shop and dining room, and reception is open 7am-11pm. There's a disco as well, but only by group reservation and rental (it costs NIS 300 a night). The only drawback is that the hostel is frequently taken over by large youth groups, and it can get fairly noisy with crowds of kids running about.

CHEZ ALEXIS, *7 Ein Saharonim, Tel. 07-658-8258, has a small hostel with five rooms at NIS 75 per adult, NIS 70 per child, reservations appreciated.*

Chex Alexis is a charming alternative. The rooms have two-six beds and their own toilets. There's a large, fully equipped kitchen to share, a dining room, TV living room, and fire place. They've a pay phone, a nice patio, and a garden as well. It's not deluxe, but it's most pleasant. Not far from the center of town, call them and they'll pick you up.

NOF RAMON HOTEL, *7 Nahal Meishar, Tel. 07-658-8255, charges NIS 140 a double, a triple is NIS 170, and a quad is NIS 220.*
The hotel rents rooms and apartments. They have 18 rooms, all with toilets, some with extra couches to pull out for kids. This small hotel is clean and friendly but a bit tatty, with no frills, and exposed wires. The rooms are adequate, and there's a shared room with fridge and burners.
SUCCAH BAMIDBAR, *seven kilometers west of town, Tel. 07-658-6280, has seven remote huts for NIS 75-100 a night and tents with cushions for NIS 20.*
It's name means Tabernacle in the Desert, and it's open daily for tea from 11am-noon and 4-6pm, and serves vegetarian meals as well.
TZAIL MIDBAR, *outside of town, Tel./Fax 07-658-6229, they charge NIS 50 per person, breakfast included.*
Their name means Desert Shade, and along with tents and mattresses for camping, they provide showers and toilets, Bedouin-style atmosphere and light refreshments, though you can arrange for full board, including pre-packaged meals for trips, as well. Head north along the main road, past the visitors' center, near the gas station.
BE'EROT CAMPSITE, *16 kilometers east of town, has Bedouin-style tents for NIS 16. Make arrangements in advance with SPNI at the Visitor Center, Tel. 07-658-8691.*
There's running water and toilets, but no showers. There's also a kiosk that sells drinks and firewood.

WHERE TO EAT

RAMON INN CAFÉ, *1 Ein Akev, Tel. 07-658-8822, Fax 07-658-8151*, has unusually good, home-cooked food. See description of hotel.
THE TEA HOUSE, *Nof Ramon Hotel, 7 Nahal Meishar, Tel. 07-658-8255*, is open 5pm-midnight, and serves vegetarian meals at reasonable prices. Soups are NIS 10, salads NIS 12-15, and vegetable pies NIS 15.
HA-TZUKIT RESTAURANT, *near the Visitor Center, Tel. 07-658-6079*, is open daily 8am-6pm. They are an air conditioned self-service place with sandwiches for NIS8-10 and meals from NIS 19-24.

SEEING THE SIGHTS

Ramon Crater (*Makhtesh Ramon*) in **Ramon Nature Reserve** is why people come out of their way to this desert town. The crater, the largest in the world, was formed by deep erosion of weak spots along the Har haNegev ridge. The progressing erosion has revealed layers of rock to interest geologists and curious tourists alike. Just because it's desert doesn't mean it all looks alike.
There are canyons and creeks in addition to the wide open desert; there are ibex and wolves, and over 1,200 types of plants in this 250,000

acre park. There are also archaeological sites from Canaanite, Judean, Nabatean, and Byzantine cultures still being restored, and a research center for geology, botany, zoology, and archaeology is being constructed nearby.

The **Visitor Center**, *Tel. 07-658-8691, Fax 07-658-8620*, is a combination of science museum and information site, and it's open Saturday-Thursday (and holidays) 9am-5pm, Fridays and holiday eves 9am-4pm. Admission to the Visitor Center costs NIS 15 per adult, NIS 8 for youth/ soldiers/police, and NIS 12 for seniors. A combo ticket for the Center and Hai Ramon costs NIS 17 for adults, NIS 11 for youth/soldiers/police, and NIS 15 for seniors. There's also a Natureland Pass that's still being worked out. The Center's main focus is the geology of craters, but the displays aren't that well done. There are nicely photographed pictures of places nearby, labeled neatly with their names. Upstairs is an observation circle from which you can see a panoramic view of the crater; it's quite an amazing sight. This is a popular destination for school field trips, and is frequently over-run by groups of kids.

The Visitor Center staff is very good at suggesting hiking or driving routes to take in the Crater first-hand, and they can show you how to get to popular destinations like the **Carpentry Shop**, **Ein Saharonim**, and **Arden Stream**. The only map they have is in Hebrew, but still it shows the area, and the staff will trace out your route on it. There's a 15 minute audio video program reminiscent of eighth grade science films, a bit condescending and repetitive. Makes one yearn for spit balls.

Hai Ramon, *right next door, Tel. 07-658-8755*, is a living desert museum displaying indigenous flora and fauna, open Sunday-Thursday 8am-3pm, Friday 8am-1pm, Saturday 9am-4pm. Admission for just for Hai Ramon is NIS 6 an adult, and NIS 5 for youth/soldiers/seniors, but you can get a combo ticket (see above) for both Hai Ramon and the Visitor Center. There's a wonderful garden walk, with six landscape and habitat types labeled and described, and all the plants labeled as well. Outside in the garden are glorious *Fragona Glutinosa* and *Echiochiloa Fruticosum* , while inside rodents, lizards and insects sit about in cages. There are free tours Saturdays and holidays at 12:30pm, and the office has information pamphlets in English you can borrow as you walk around.

Desert Sculpture Park (*Pi-ssul Midbari*) is on the outskirts of the crater. You can tour the park by car or on foot, but a guide pamphlet (available at the "Amunit" gift shop by the Visitor Center) makes a difference.

Alpaca Farm, *off the southern end of Ben Gurion Boulevard, Tel. 07-658-8047*, is just what it sounds like, and it's open every day of the year, 8:30am-6:30pm, charging NIS 16 for adults, NIS 12 for children, seniors, students, and soldiers. You can visit and feed the big-eyed beasts of burden, and the llamas and kangaroos as well. Their gift shop sells alpaca wool items, and they offer alpaca rides along the crater's edge. Take care, however, the alpaca are full of messy fluids they are all too willing to share with you, spitting and exuding mucus all over the place.

Mitzpe Planetarium, *part of the Tel Aviv University, Tel. 07-658-8133*, can be arranged by calling in advance.

NIGHTLIFE & ENTERTAINMENT

Mitzpe Ramon is a small town without much night action. Visitors typically wear themselves out during the day and go to bed early for another day in the Crater.

Matnas music and culture center, *73 Ben Gurion, Tel. 07-658-8442*, has Israeli folk dancing Sunday evenings at 8pm for NIS 9 and shows first-run American movies Saturday and Monday nights at 8:30 (8pm in winter).

S. Rubin Cultural Center, *Tel. 07-658-8346*, has details on the films shown in Town Hall.

For the adventurous, there's a **bar**, *Nahal Tziah 16*, just below the water tower, complete with pool tables and seedy clientele.

SHOPPING

"Amunit" gift shop by the Visitor Center sells camping supplies. **Alpaca Farm** sells alpaca wool items.

DAY TRIPS/RECREATION

It's best to come with a car, drive to some places and walk from there. Four-wheel drive is only necessary for some spots.

Keren Kayemet (Jewish National Fund) **Grove**, *entrance to Mitzpe Ramon*, has tables and running water for a **desert picnic**.

Shu'alei Shimshon (Samson's Foxes), *Tel./Fax 07-658-8868*, guides tours by jeep. They also have package tours including Bedouin hospitality.

Ramon Tours, *Tel. 07-658-8623*, organizes tours from all around Israel if you phone in advance.

Tzail Midbar Desert Tourism Center, *Tel. 07-658-6229*, guides trips by camel or jeep. They also lead rapelling trips and walking tours.

Municipal Swimming Pool, *off David Ben Gurion Boulevard, Tel. 07-658-8815*, is open in summer.

PRACTICAL INFORMATION

The Mitzpe Ramon office, *Jerusalem, Tel. 02-538-7471*, can give up-to-date information on Visitor Center prices and times, as well as about the new Natureland Pass.

• **Gas stations**: **Paz-Avdat**, *Tel. 07-655-6851*, is open 24 hours daily. **Mitzpe Ramon**, *Tel. 07-658-8158*, is open Monday-Thursday 5:30am-9:30pm, Saturday 8am-6pm, and has a restaurant and snack bar as well.
• **Moked** (**municipal hot-line**): *Tel. 07-658-8569* or *Tel. 07-658-8333*.
• **First Aid** (Magen David Adom): *Tel. 07-658-6058*, or *Tel. 101* for emergencies.
• **Police**: *Tel. 07-658-8444*, or *Tel. 100* in emergencies.
• **Pharmacy**: *Tel. 07-658-6112*.
• **Mitzpe Ramon Local Council**: *Tel. 07-658-8561*.

EILAT

Israel's southernmost city, and its only port on the Red Sea, **Eilat** is all tourist center and resort playground. Founded for its port potential, its main import is mineral oil; in fact it was Egypt's blockade of the Gulf of Eilat on May 22, 1967, that triggered the Six Day War.

Though this is not what draws the hordes, Eilat did figure in Biblical history. In Deuteronomy 2:8 Eilat is mentioned along with the town of Ezion-geber, King Solomon (961-922 BCE) used Eilat as a shipyard and trading port, and in 773-736 BCE, Eilat was captured from the Edomites by King Azariah of Judah and enlarged (2 Kings 14:21-23). The Romans had a port here named *Aila* or *Aelana*. After them came the Crusaders under King Baldwin I in 1116 CE, followed Salah al-Din in 1170 CE, then the Crusaders again, and the Mamluks, and the Turks. After WWI Eilat became part of the British Mandate, and in 1949 it joined the State of Israel.

And now Eilat is Israel's premier sun and sea recreation hot spot and desert trek launching pad, a relatively secular town where hundreds of thousands of Israelis (and Europeans, and Japanese) come yearly to toss cares to the desert winds and revel in the joys of merry-making, not daunted at all by the shadows cast by three somewhat intimidating Arab neighbors.

In fact, its proximity with Jordan and Egypt, destinations now available to those with Israeli passports and passport stamps, makes Eilat even more popular as a convenient passageway to these destinations, as well as a recuperation station for those returning from arduous jaunts in the Sinai or further afield.

BEST OF EILAT

BEST HOTELS

• *ORCHID HOTEL, across from Coral Beach, Tel. 07-636-0360, Fax 07-637-5323. Cost: $187-$231 for singles, and $209-$286 for doubles, depending on the season, breakfast included. This place is a bit of paradise, with great charm and elegance, loads of flowers, room for kids, and easy access to Coral Beach.*

• *RED SEA HOTEL, HaTmarim, Tel. 07-637-2171, Fax 07-637-4605. Cost: $60-$90 a single and $65-$105 a double, depending on the season, breakfast included. The Red Sea is a family-run hotel with a friendly atmosphere and a pool .*

• *BEIT HA'ARAVA, 106 Almogim, Tel. 07-637-1052, Fax 07-637-1052, is at the corner of Hativat Golami. A dorm bed costs NIS 30 in winter, NIS 50 in summer, and private doubles are NIS 120 in winter, NIS 200 in summer, price negotiable. With a pleasant cafe, laundry services, snorkel masks, foosball games, a garden barbecue and terrace, and a warm welcome for families and students, the owner cares about this place and stays involved in the upkeep.*

BEST FOOD & DRINK

• *NARGILA, HaTmarim, by the central bus station, Tel. 07-637-6101. They serve large portions of tasty and reasonably priced Yemenite food.*

• *MAI THAI, Yotam Road near the New Tourist Center, Tel. 07-637-0104. They offer delicious, spicy Thai-Chinese cuisine. It's not cheap, but some dishes are exceptionally good.*

BEST SIGHTS

• *CORAL WORLD, on Coral Beach, a little south of the city, Tel. 07-637-6666, Fax 07-637-3193. This is much more than your average aquarium, and the underwater observatory is exceptional.*

ORIENTATION

Five kilometers west of Jordan's gulf city **Aqaba** and ten kilometers north of **Taba** on the border with Egypt, Eilat lies on the Red Sea's Gulf of Eilat. Eilat is a real holiday whoopee town, hemmed in as it is by the hostile desert elements of the Negev to the north and the Sinai to the west, and the somewhat, though decreasingly hostile, borders of Egypt and Jordan, and Saudi Arabia looming large to the south. All this has spawned a town that has grown up hedonistic in its attempts to deal with the heat, both natural and political.

The resorts' busiest times are during Passover and Sukkot (holidays in the spring and fall), when scads of Israelis flood the city, frenetically intent on relaxing. The energy can be fun, but it's not the best time to come. Hotel rates soar, and thievery is more pronounced. The winter is slower, and not a bad time to visit (rates are lower, and the weather is warmer than elsewhere in Israel), and the autumn and spring (when not in holiday crush) are lovely.

Summer gets very, very hot, but that's when most of us have time off. You come to Eilat to enjoy, anyway, so if the heat forces you to take afternoon siestas and cool down with evening libations, it could be worse. The weather also affects the businesses. Many offices (banks, the post office, pharmacies, etc.) have morning and late afternoon-evening hours, but are shut during the heat of the day.

Eilat's a medium sized city, with a population of around 26,000, but there are only a few areas regularly visited by tourists. There is **City Center**, where you'll find the central bus station and many of the cheaper hotels and hostels. The main street here is **Sederot HaTmarim**, which runs northwest-southeast and is home to the bus station, many banks, and a number of shopping centers. Most of the hostels are just minutes from HaTmarim. Head down toward the water and you'll hit a big intersection. To the northeast is **Derekh Ha'Arava**, which flanks Ha'Arava Park near Eilat's irritatingly centrally located airport, and has a number of hotels and hostels on it.

To the southwest, the boulevard is called **Derekh Mizrayim** on some maps and Derekh Ha'Arava on others; following it will take you down past Central Park (in which is Eilat's Tourist Information Center), past the New Tourist Center and its cluster of hotels, to the beach. From that point, you can walk north and east along the beach on Pa'Ame HaShalom (the beach front **Promenade**) to the ritzy tourist development of **North Beach**, with its luxury hotels, restaurants, nightspots, and beaches. Or, stay on Derekh Ha'Arava and head south toward **Coral Beach** and its resort hotels.

In general, the way establishments are numbered doesn't make a lot of sense. A street number can help, but cross streets and landmarks are more useful when looking for a specific address.

ARRIVALS & DEPARTURES
International
For details on crossing the Egyptian border at Taba and the Jordan border at Arava, see Chapter 6, *Planning Your Trip*, Getting To Israel section.

By Air

The **Airport**, *intersection of HaTmarim and Ha'Arava Tel. 07-637-3553*, hosts **Arkia Airlines**, *Tel. 07-638-4888 or toll-free Tel. 180-800-4888*, which has frequent flights to and from Tel Aviv and Jerusalem for $80 one way, and Haifa for $95. **El Al**, *Tel. 07-633-1515*, also frequents this airport.

By Bus

The **central bus station**, *HaTmarim, Tel. 07-636-5711*, has a luggage drop (NIS 6 per bag), and you can reserve tickets here two days in advance (four days in high season). Bus 394 goes to **Tel Aviv** for NIS 54, runs 5am-5pm, and takes five hours. Bus 444 goes to **Jerusalem** via the **Dead Sea** for NIS 52, leaving Sunday-Friday 7am, 9am, 2pm, 5pm, and midnight (Friday's last two buses are 1:30pm and 3:30pm), and Saturday there are two buses at noon and 3:45pm. Bus 392 also goes to **Jerusalem** for NIS 45, leaves at 7:45am and 9am and transfers in **Beersheva**. Bus 392 also goes to **Mitzpe Ramon**, takes two-three hours, and costs NIS 31.50.

The 991 goes to **Haifa** for NIS 61.50. For **Timna**, take a Beersheva or Mitzpe Ramon bus. It costs NIS 9.50 and takes one hour.

GETTING AROUND TOWN

By City Bus

The #15 runs down HaTmarim and Ha'Arava, through the North Beach hotel area, south toward Coral Beach, and on to Taba and the border. Shuttling between all the main sights, it runs every 20 or so minutes Sunday-Thursday 7am-9pm, Saturday 5pm-9pm, and costs NIS 4.

By Ferry

Coral World also offers **Superticket**, a deal that gets you a cruise on the Coral Pearl from Eilat Marina to Coral World, entrance to the park, a dive in the Yellow Submarine, and a return cruise to Eilat Marina. The offer comes in every combination of the above, depending on your interests and wallet. The Coral Pearl departs from Eilat Marina at 10am, noon, and 2pm, and from Coral World at 10:45am, 12:45pm, and 2:45pm.

By Car

A rental car is handy in Eilat, not so much for the city itself, but for added convenience in getting to Coral Beach, and the further Nature Reserve areas. It really depends on how much moving about you plan to do. You can rent from **Hertz**, *Red Canyon Center, Tel. 07-637-6682*, from **Eurodollar**, *HaTmarim near Red Sea Hotel, Tel. 07-637-1813*, and in *Shalom Center*: **Budget**, *Tel. 07-637-1063*, **Europcar**, *Tel. 07-637-4014*, **Eldan**, *Tel. 07-637-4027*, **Reliable**, *Tel. 07-637-4126*, and **Thrifty**, *Tel. 07-637-2511*.

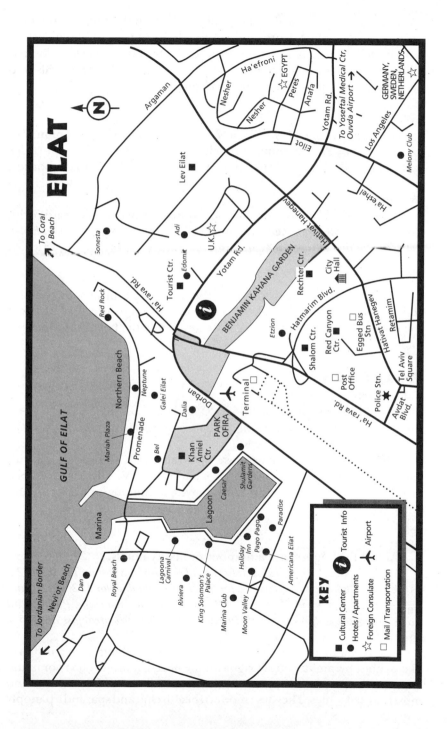

Rates and special deals change all the time, so flip through the Eilat This Week pamphlet from the Tourist Information office and shop around (off-season rates average around $200-$280 per week, unlimited mileage, insurance not included). At present you can't take rentals into Egypt or Jordan, but this may be changing as well.

By Taxi

Arava, *Tel. 07-637-4141*, **Taba**, *Tel. 07-633-3339*, **King Solomon**, *Tel. 07-633-2424*, or **Yael Daroma**, inter-city only, *Tel. 07-637-2279*. City rides cost around NIS 15; NIS 20 to Coral World, and NIS 20-30 to the border.

By Bicycle

A bicycle is a fine option for local transport between Coral World, Coral Beach, and Eilat. **Red Sea Sports Club**, *near the King Solomon Hotel, Tel. 07-637-9685*, is open 8:30am-5pm daily and rents cycles for $18 a day.

By Foot

Going about the city is certainly the most economical choice, and if you are mostly going to hang out by the beach and nearby facilities, feet will take you where you want to go. Be aware that the heat gets intense in mid-day.

WHERE TO STAY

Taba Beach

EILAT PRINCESS, *Tel. 07-636-5555, Fax 07-637-6333, $234-$444 a single and $258-$468, depending on grade of room and season, breakfast included.*

The Princess is a large expanse of royalty, with 420 rooms, all with bath, air conditioning, phone, fridge, and cable TV. The hotel offers a health club (with fees), tennis courts, gym, swimming pool, disco, and synagogue.

Across the Lagoon

Across the Lagoon are a number of luxury hotels:

ROYAL BEACH HOTEL, *HaYam, Tel. 07-636-8888 or Tel. 177-022-6404, Fax 07-636-8811, has singles for $201-$379, doubles for $226-$420, and regular suites run $354-$542, while the Royal, Honeymoon and Presidential suites are priced $383-$1159, all including Israeli buffet breakfast and 15% service charge.*

The Royal Beach is Isrotel's deluxe model. Looking from a distance like a cubist pyramid, and set right on the beach, it offers 363 rooms and suites whose prices reflect their luxury tone. All rooms face the sea, and most have balconies. They've a modern health club and spa, and a panoply of restaurants and shops. The Vista Restaurant is especially pleasant, with its palm trees and terrace overlooking the sea.

There is a private beach with chairs and umbrellas, and guests are welcome to use the Sport Hotel facilities. For kids, there are activities and puppet shows, and for those over 18, there's the Three Monkey's Pub in traditional English style, and the nightly Galaxy Disco with full flashing lights extravaganza.

KING SOLOMON'S PALACE, *on the lagoon a little bit north, Tel. 07-633-4111, Fax 07-633-4189, is about 200 meters from the Isrotel beach. They're priced by season, with singles ranging $155-$309 and doubles $156-$383, Israeli buffet breakfast and 15% service charge included.*

Despite their 419 rooms, the hotel is frequently booked up, attesting to its continuing popularity. King Solomon's Palace sports a pool ringed by palm trees, a health and fitness club, and a Kiddo Club for the children. For adults, they've the Sheba Disco for late night partying under laser lights. This used to be the classiest of Istrotel's line until the Royal Beach usurped that spot. It's still a swell place, with bridges decorating the pool, and oodles of yellow lounge chairs.

LAGOONA HOTEL, *North up Antibes and on the Lagoon, Tel. 07-636-5555, Fax 07-636-6699, has singles for $109-$271, and doubles $128-$313, including Israeli buffet breakfast and 15% service charge.*

The Lagoona is less opulent but more relaxing than some of Isrotel's chain. Their 256 rooms are priced identically to the Sport's and the rooms are pleasant, with attractive art work on the walls. The Lagoona has a central pool and a caring staff, and seems popular with British pensioners.

SPORT HOTEL, *Further east and across the street from the Royal Beach, Tel. 07-633-3333, Fax 07-633-2765, their singles are $109-$271, and doubles are $128-$313, including Israeli buffet breakfast and 15% service charge.*

The Sport lives up to its name in its facilities and focus. It's 327 rooms are priced more moderately than other Isrotel hotels. Right by the beach, the Sport provides squash, tennis, swimming, a health and fitness spa, Jacuzzi and sauna, open 9am-9pm, and costing NIS 55 a day full access (or lesser amounts for specific sports). The staff is less attentive than at the more luxury-minded hotels, and the atmosphere is younger and more energetic. They do, however, have a children's kindergarten to entertain the kids while the parents are off sporting.

RIVIERA APARTMENT HOTEL, *across the street from King Solomon's Palace, Tel. 07-636-8818, Fax 07-633-3939, charges $96-$116 a double, $115-$134 for four people, and $144-$164 for five, and a ground floor apartment with pool access for $174, including 15% service, but not the breakfast, available in the cafeteria for $9 per person.*

Catering to families with more moderate budgets, and nature hikers who want an Eilat base, each of the 172 apartments have fully equipped kitchenettes, but some have more rooms than others. The hotel has a mini-market aimed at self-catering families. For kids, there is a children's club open 10am-1pm and 3-5pm, as well as a video game room, ping-pong, and billiards. There is convenient parking, and the staff is especially friendly and caring.

North Beach Hotels

These are all in the same vicinity, between the lagoon and the beach, near Ofira Park, the Khan Center (airline and tour agency hub), and the Promenade.

RADISSON MORIAH PLAZA, *Tel. 07-636-1111, Fax 07-633-4158, charges $220-$250 a single and $265-$290 a double, depending on the season, breakfast included.*

This is a very pleasant place, run by Isrotel. Their 330 rooms all come with the standard comforts, some with balconies overlooking the sea. The hotel is family oriented, with two pools (one heated in winter) and a gym, a kids' club for morning and afternoon activities, and a Snoopy Disco (also for the kids) for evening fun. For adults, there's lobby entertainment (singers, etc.) in the evenings, a bridge play room, and a nightclub on weekends. Moriah also has a beach with lounge chairs for their guests.

NEPTUNE HOTEL, *Tel. 07-636-9369 or Tel. 177-022-3131, Fax 07-633-4389, costs $128-$236 for singles, $172-$279 for doubles, depending on the season, breakfast included.*

Closer to the beach, the Neptune has 278 rooms with air conditioning, phone, cable TV, and bath. Expensive and unfriendly, they do have a swimming pool, health club, and private beach.

GALEI EILAT HOTEL, *Tel. 07-636-7444, Fax 07-633-0627, has singles for $92-$158 and doubles for $131-$199, depending on the season, breakfast included.*

There are 107 rooms here. Only seven have a sea view–the rest look over the city–but all have little balconies, air conditioning, phone, and cable TV. The rooms are fine, with large bathrooms and vases of fresh flowers. It's a family kind of place, and they provide daily activity programs that feature such events as morning aerobics by Neptune's pool, cocktail demonstration workshops in Neptune's lobby, and personal beauty care in Neptune's health club. Affiliated with the Neptune Hotel, guests can use the Neptune beach, pool, etc.

THE NEW CAESAR HOTEL, *Tel. 07-633-3111 or Tel. 177-022-3536, Fax 07-633-3492, has single rooms for $110 and doubles are $152 in winter, more in summer, breakfast included.*

Located across from the Khan Center, this is a great place. Its stunning marble lobby and verandah greet you with a spacious, airy feel that sets a luxurious tone despite the relatively moderate prices. The rooms are pleasant, almost all have small balconies, and many can accommodate families of up to five. The hotel has a nice pool and tennis courts, while on the weekend there's a disco. In the winter, the Caesar is popular with pensioners and families looking for a quiet visit, but in the summer it attracts all types of holiday-seekers.

LA COQUILLE, *Tel. 07-637-0031, Fax 07-637-0032, charges $70-$140 a single, and $100-$140 a double, by season, breakfast included.*

An apartment hotel with 15 rooms, the suites all have air conditioning, bath, phone, cable TV, and kitchenette.

DALIA HOTEL, *Tel. 07-633-4004, Fax 07-633-4072, charges $45-$65 a single, $65-$90 a double, depending on the season, breakfast included.*

In the same cluster as La Coquiller, it has 47 comfortable and proper but somewhat plain rooms. Most of the rooms have baths (the others have showers), and all have phones and TV. They also have a small pool and a friendly aura.

SHULAMIT GARDENS, *Tel. 07-633-3999, Fax 07-633-4140, is further up the road from Caesar.*

At press time they were closed for renovations, so call first.

Across the Marina

Across the Marina is another set of hotels, all a bit removed from the action, and a little inconvenient when you want to get to and from the Promenade and City Center. It's a good 10-15 minute walk to the beach.

CROWNE PLAZA HOLIDAY INN, *Tel. 07-636-7777, Fax 07-633-0831, charges $195-$385 for a single and $220-$410 a double, by season, including breakfast but not the 15% service charge.*

The Holiday Inn offers 266 rooms, most with balconies. They've a nice pool and terrace, a tennis court, jacuzzi, and ping-pong room, but the beach is a good walk.

MARINA CLUB, *Tel. 07-633-4191, Fax 07-633-4206, has 131 suites, all with air conditioning, phone, cable TV, bath, and kitchenette, for $119-$285, depending on season and type of suite, meals not included.*

The hotel has a pool (heated in winter), disco, mini market, and children's club.

PARADISE EILAT, *Tel. 07-630-4444, Fax 07-633-2348, has 247 rooms at $112-$177 a single, $140-$219 a double, breakfast included.*

The rooms all have bath, cable TV, phone, and air conditioning. The hotel is fully equipped with swimming pool, disco, and a children's playground.

THE AMERICANA INN EILAT, *Tel. 07-633-3777, Fax 07-633-4174, charges $70-$100 a single, $90-$120 a double.*

A less grand hotel than others in this area, the 130 rooms have the usual air conditioning, bath, phone, and cable TV, and kitchenettes on request; the hotel has a swimming pool, children's playground, gym, and disco.

South/Coral Beach Hotels
ORCHID HOTEL, *across from Coral Beach, Tel. 07-636-0360, Fax 07-637-5323, charges $187-$231 for singles, and $209-$286 for doubles, depending on the season, breakfast included.*

The Orchid is a real gem. The two-story cottages (136 of them), with walls of woven bamboo from Thailand and Thai-style pointed roofs, are truly lovely. Up on a hill, they have privacy and great views of the water, and are well-constructed, with balconies, big bathrooms, and lofts for the children. There's real attention to detail here–welcome fruit baskets in the cottages, beautiful landscaping, and flowers everywhere. The Orchid motor cart can take you and your luggage to your hut, there's a Jungle Kindergarten for the kids, and a health club and swimming pool as well. The Siam Diving Club is also on the premises, with equipment rentals, courses, and organized dives. One of the few hotels in this price range that give you your money's worth of charm, beauty, peace, and recreation.

CLUB IN, *Tel. 07-638-5555, Fax 07-638-5533, rents 168 villas that accommodate up to four and cost $100-$200, depending on the season, no meals included.*

The air conditioned villas are all equipped with shower, kitchenette, phone, and cable TV, while the main facility has a swimming pool (heated in winter), gym, nightclub, and children's playground.

RED SEA SPORTS CLUB HOTEL, *Tel. 07-638-2222, Fax 07-638-2200, $105-$140 a single and $140-$190 a double, by season, breakfast included.*

The Red Sea has 86 rooms, all with air conditioning, phone, cable TV, and bath, and the hotel has a swimming pool and a sports facility.

THE REEF, *Tel. 07-636-4444, Fax 07-636-4488, has 79 rooms with all the usual amenities for $88-$135 a single and $110-$170 a double, depending on season, breakfast included.*

It's a nice place, with a swimming pool (heated in winter).

PRIMA CARLTON EILAT, *Tel. 07-633-3555, Fax 07-633-4088, $73-$104 a single and $94-$135 a double, depending on the season, breakfast included.*

The Carlton Coral Sea has 144 rooms with air conditioning, phone, and cable TV. The hotel has a swimming pool, tennis court, children's playground, and babysitting.

EILAT FIELD SCHOOL AND STUDY CENTER, *Tel. 07-637-2021, Fax 07-637-1771, charges NIS 245 for a double.*

They have basic rooms that sleep five-to-seven people. It's usually full of Israeli school kids, and the guided group tours are led in Hebrew. If you pre-arrange, guides are available to lead tours for NIS 500 a day.

Downtown Hotels

RED SEA HOTEL, *HaTmarim, Tel. 07-637-2171, Fax 07-637-4605, costs $60-$90 a single and $65-105 a double, depending on the season, breakfast included.*

This is one of the first hotels in Eilat, with 41 nice little rooms, some with balcony, all with air conditioning, phone, TV, and bath. It's a family hotel with a friendly staff, tile walls in the hall, a pool (closed annually in February for maintenance), and a nightclub upstairs that opens at 11pm. The rooms can accommodate two-four people, and families are welcome. It's conveniently located next to a supermarket and pharmacy, and there are rate discounts if you stay longer than a week.

ETZION HOTEL, *1 HaTmarim, Tel. 07-637-4131, or Tel. 177-022-2070, Fax 07-637-0002, has 97 rooms, costing $60-$70 a single and $80-$90 a double, breakfast included.*

Rooms come with TV, bath, air conditioning, and phone. The bathrooms are clean but small, the hotel has a musty smell and no decor to speak of, and the rooms aren't dirty but don't exactly sparkle, either. It's an adequate sleep option with no real appeal.

Tsofit District

Southwest of Derekh Yotam, this area has some hotels near the New Tourist Center and others near the southern portion of the beach Promenade.

LEV EILAT, *southwestern end of Hativat HaNegev, Tel./Fax 07-637-6895, charges NIS 400-500 suites accommodating up to five people.*

The Lev Eilat has one hundred holiday apartments. The suites are equipped with air conditioning, phone, cable TV, bath, and kitchenette. The hotel also has a sports facility, swimming pool, and tennis courts.

SUN SUITES, *southwestern end of Ha'Arava, Tel. 07-637-6222, Fax 07-637-5888, is near the Promenade, charging $85-$230 a single, $120-$295, depending on season and size of suite.*

The Sun Suites offer 300 resort suites with air conditioning, cable TV, phone, bath and fridge. The hotel has a health club, gym, swimming pool, disco, and synagogue.

RED ROCK HOTEL, *off Pa'Ame HaShalom, Tel. 07-637-3171, Fax 07-637-1530, near the beach, costs $85-$118 a single, and $110-$148 a double, depending on the season, breakfast included.*

The Red Rock has 110 rooms with air conditioning, cable TV, phone and bath. They've two swimming pools (indoor and out), a disco, and a nice beach.

EDOMIT, *Yotam, Tel. 07-637-9511, Fax 07-637-9738, is next to the Mai Tai Restaurant, near the New Tourist Center, costing $77-$100 a single and $105-$130 a double, by season, breakfast included.*

The 85 rooms have air conditioning, bath, radio, and direct-dial phone. There's parking, baby-sitting and car rental services, room service, and vegetarian-dairy dinners. The tall building features views of the sea from each room.

ADI HOTEL, *17 Zofit, off Topaz, Tel. 07-637-6151, Fax 07-637-6154, costs $50-$60 a single, $70-$80 a double, breakfast included.*

The Adi has 32 rooms with bath, air conditioning, and phone. It's a small place, with parking, a bar and a TV room, baby-sitting available.

OFARIM, *116/2 Ofarim, Tel. 07-637-6289, costs NIS 150 a room.*

A hostel no longer, Ofarim offers private rooms with air conditioning, shower, and toilet.

RED MOUNTAIN HOTEL, *Hativat HaNegev, Tel. 07-637-4936, Fax 07-637-4263,* is temporarily closed while renovating from a hostel to a hotel. Call for new rates.

Hostels & Apartments

There are new hostels opening all the time, and places that offer rooms for rent, as well. Touts generally swarm around arriving buses, and the competition between them can get ferocious (I've seen them actually come to blows over a prospective roomer's business). Look at their places before promising anything, or take a card and visit them in your own time. The Tourist Information office keeps an up-dated list of all hostels and establishments that rent rooms.

EILAT'S YOUTH HOSTEL & GUEST HOUSE, *next to the Sun Hotel on Ha'Arava, Tel. 07-637-2358, Fax 07-637-5835, is near the New Tourist Center. Dorm beds cost $18.50, (non members $20), private rooms are NIS 163, and breakfast is included.*

The air conditioning rooms, while not fancy, are colorful and clean, and the dining room has wonderful views of the harbor. There are 370 beds as well as family rooms (two-six beds per room with private bath). The facility has a safe for valuables, car rental, TV rental, and refrigerator rental, laundry services, a TV room and a disco.

NATHAN'S WHITE HOUSE, *131/1 Retamim, Tel. 07-637-6572, has dorm beds for NIS 30-45 in winter, NIS 50-65 in summer, and private rooms for NIS 100-150.*

They've eight rooms, with six dorm beds to a room. There's a kitchen, a TV and video lounge, and often a party vacationing Israeli soldiers.

MOTEL HASHALOM, *Hativat HaNegev, Tel. 07-637-6544, has dorm beds for NIS 50 and private rooms (two twins pushed together) for NIS 200-250.*

In business for 13 years, each dorm room has eight dorm beds, private toilet, and shower. Lockers are NIS 10. The place is fairly clean, though there've been some cockroach sightings.

CORINNE HOSTEL, *127/1 Retamim, Tel 07-637-1472, has dorm beds that cost NIS 50, private rooms are NIS 150, and keys are available for NIS 5.*

They've air conditioned rooms with bath, and four-ten beds per room. To get to Retamim, go up HaTmarim from the bus station and take your second right.

BEIT HA'ARAVA, *106 Almogim, Tel. 07-637-1052, Fax 07-637-1052, is at the corner of Hativat Golami. A dorm bed costs NIS 30 in winter, NIS 50 in summer, and private doubles are NIS 120 in winter, NIS 200 in summer, price negotiable.*

There are 23 air conditioned and desert cooler rooms of four-six beds each. There's also a thatched tent crammed with mattresses at NIS 25 per head. There's a cafe open 8am-midnight serving nicely prepared food, laundry service for NIS 12, lockers available for NIS 5, and snorkel/masks for rent for NIS 17. Students and families are welcome, credit cards are accepted, and private parking is provided. In addition, there are video and foosball games, a garden barbecue and terrace, and special discounts for students, soldiers, and long-term stays. The owner cares about this place, and stays involved in the upkeep and care.

THE HOME, *108/2 Almogim, Tel. 07-637-2403, is next door to Beit Ha'Arava, but the gate is on Ofarim. Dorm beds (10-12 a room) go for NIS 43 and outdoor mattresses are NIS 27, breakfast included.*

A somewhat dilapidated establishment with a lot of long-termers, it's comfortable in a casual, college-dorm sloppy sort of way.

SUNSET HOSTEL, *130/1 Retamim, Tel. 07-637-3817, charges 40 NIS per bed.*

This hostel has claustrophobic dorms (no private rooms) with 10 bunks and a host of backpackers jam-packed in. Outside is a tent-like, shack-like structure at NIS 25 a mattress. They've a big safe but no lockers. No drugs, no booze, but also no air, no space.

SPRING HOSTEL, *126 Ofarim Lane, Tel. 07-637-4660, Fax 07-637-1543, has dorm beds (three bunks per room) for NIS 30, and private rooms (with one bunk and two twin beds for up to four people) costing NIS 180-240, visa accepted.*

Opposite Tnuva, on the corner of Agmonim, there are 26 rooms with shower, toilet, and air conditioning. It's a very clean place, with a porch cafe, snooker table, kitchen, plastic tables, and bougainvillea all around.

TABA HOSTEL, *Hativat HaNegev, Tel. 07-637-3405, Fax 07-637-1435, offers dorm beds costing NIS 25 and private rooms for NIS 120.*

Around the corner from the central bus station on Hativat HaNegev, the first right off HaTmarim, there are lockers available for NIS 7 a day, one locker token per use. It's a young crowd, with music going and a youthful terrace lounge. The manager is not Mr. Friendly, and can turn nasty.

SHLOMO DAVID APARTMENTS, *429/4 behind the Dekel Shopping Center, Tel. 07-637-5052, has apartments to let.*

These apartments have air conditioned rooms and shared kitchen privileges. They advertise clean sheets, prices to be arranged.

Nearby Kibbutz

YE'ELIM DESERT HOLIDAY CAMP, *38 kilometers north of Eilat, Tel. 07-637-4362, Fax 07-635-7734, is just near Kibbutz Yotvata and the Hai Bar Nature Reserve. They have tent space for NIS 30, and 25 air conditioned wooden lodges for $71-$84 a single, and $98-$126 a double.*

They've a swimming pool, free for guests and NIS 10 for visitors, as well as a cafeteria serving the well-known Yotvata dairy. And the lodges are all outfitted with kitchenette, private toilet and shower, plus a small garden.

Camping

THE CAROLINA, *across from Almog (Coral) Beach, Tel. 07-637-1911, has camping south of the city. There are campsites for NIS 33 per person and bungalows for NIS 60 per person.*

The 'bungalows' are tent-shaped structures with flimsy double mattresses, electricity, and air conditioning. Toilets and showers are available for NIS 4, as are lockers. Beyond that, there are a lot of picnic tables and bungalows crowded together, without much else to look at.

TIMNA PARK, *25 kilometers north of Eilat, Tel. 07-635-6215, Fax 07-635-6217, is in the Nature Reserve.*

The park has a campground on a man-made lake in the Nature Reserve. To camp there you must call or fax in advance and make arrangements.

WHERE TO EAT

The stretch of **HaTmarim** near the bus station is full of shops offering falafel, pizza, and other fast food. For inexpensive, tasty sit down meals, the Yemenite restaurants are worth trying. The other main location that's full of restaurants and food stands is the **Wharf** and **Promenade**. All the big hotels there have restaurants, and there are many independent eateries as well.

MAI THAI, *Yotam Road, Tel. 07-637-0104*, near the New Tourist Center and open 1-3:30pm, 7pm-midnight, has tasty Thai Chinese fare.

The fish soup is delicious and very spicy, and the duck curry is also exceptionally good. Soups are about NIS 13, main dishes average NIS 36, and an all-inclusive dinner costs NIS 52-65.

MAMAN RED SEA FISH RESTAURANT, *behind the Moriah Hotel, Tel. 07-637-1958*, has been around a long time and has a good reputation. Open 9am-1am, they cook up fish and meat Italian style.

AU BISTROT, *3 Eilot Street, Tel. 07-637-4333*, off HaTmarim, is open 7pm-11pm serving French cuisine.

TANDOORI RESTAURANT, *King Solomon's Warf near Yacht Pub, Tel. 07-633-3879*, provides a panoply of quality curries, tandoori meat, and nicely spiced vegetarian dishes for NIS 18-40.

FISHERMAN HOUSE, *next to Coral Beach, Tel. 07-637-9830*, is a self-service, all-you-can-eat, cafeteria with salads, fish, potatoes, and such truck. Of moderate quality, they provide quantity for NIS 25.

NARGILA, *HaTmarim, Tel. 07-637-6101*, right by the central bus station, offers large portions of tasty and reasonably priced Yemenite food. Open 11am-5am, you can eat well for NIS 15. The hummus with fuul and egg is well prepared and the pita is served warm. The decor is a bit off, but the music is good and the volume not deafening. It's a fine local eatery, and they take credit cards.

HA KEREM RESTAURANT, *HaTmarim, Tel. 07-6374-77*, corner of Eilat, is open noon-3pm and 6-10pm, and serves good Yemenite food. Compared to Nargila, the food is more authentic and a tad cheaper, but the attention to detail is missing. Not a touristed spot, the decor features oil cloth covered tables, cheap chairs, and walls plastered with pictures of the proud owner with his arm around various celebrities and guests.

HARD LUCK CAFE, *15 Almogim near Agmonim, Tel. 07-637-2788*, overflows with music, beer, and bare-chested travelers hanging out. They dish up cheap fish and chips, pasta, and schnitzel to their hungry but not overly picky clientele.

TUNISIAN RESTAURANT, *just up from the Taba Hostel on Hativat HaNegev*, though closed at the moment, might be worth trying for a couscous change of pace.

THE FAMILY BAKERY, *112 HaTmarim*, sells good burekas and more, and is open 24 hours a day.

BEN & JERRY'S, *near King Solomon's Wharf*, and **DR. LEK**, *at the end of the Promenade near Durban beach*, dish up cooling ice cream to top off your meal.

For a picnic on the beach, there are a few supermarkets to pick from. The **Supermarket**, *Eilat and HaTmarim*, is open Sunday-Thursday 7:30am-7:30pm, Friday 7:30am-2pm; **SuperKolbo Supermarket**, *Rekhter Center*, is open Saturday-Thursday 7am-11pm; and **Shekem Supermarket**, *Red*

Canyon Center, is open Sunday-Thursday 8:30am-8:30pm, Friday 8:30am-2:30pm.

SEEING THE SIGHTS
Coral World
Coral World, *a little south of the city, Tel.* 07-637-6666, Fax 07-637-3193, with its Underwater Observatory and Yellow Submarine, is well worth visiting. On Coral Beach and open Saturday-Thursday from 8:30am-4:30pm in winter, 8:30am-5pm in summer, and 8:30am-3pm on Friday, Coral World is a fantastic introduction into the complex ecosystem of the coral reef, with stunning views of fish to be had without sticking your head under the water. It costs NIS 44 an adult, NIS 35 for seniors, NIS 29 a child, and no special student reduction.

Special times to visit: 11:30am is feeding time in the Marine Aquarium, 1pm in the Reef Tank, 1:30pm for the turtles, and Monday, Wednesday, Saturday at 1:40pm the sharks are fed.

The **Marine Aquarium** is impressively designed, and the rental electronic guide (NIS 13) adds greatly to the experience. You get to look at Blacktipped Reef Sharks, Slingjaw Wrasses, the dreaded poisonous Turkeyfish, and many more with recorded words of wisdom a code punch away on the fish phone. If you begin to tire, the Shark pool and Coral Reef tank are better than the others. Leave time and energy for the Underwater Observatory, a windowed room six meters below sea level, where you can see the underwater world without having to breathe through a rubber tube. There's also a more traditional observatory (24 meters up) from which you can see Israel, Jordan, Saudi Arabia, Egypt, and the Red Sea.

The **Yellow Submarine** takes you 60 meters down for a unique view of the Red Sea from the bottom up (children younger than four not allowed). Open Monday-Saturday from 9am, the dive takes about an hour, and you need to be there 30 minutes in advance. It costs NIS 200 an adult and NIS 115 a child (including Coral World entrance). Morning is better for a visit, before the afternoon winds kick up, and to leave you the extra time you're going to find you want once you're here.

Coral World also offers **Superticket**, a deal that gets you a cruise on the Coral Pearl from Eilat Marina to Coral World, entrance to the park, a dive in the Yellow Submarine, and a return cruise to Eilat Marina for NIS 210 per adult, and NIS 120 per child. The offer comes in every combination of the above, depending on your interests and wallet. The Coral Pearl departs from Eilat Marina at 10am, noon, and 2pm, and from Coral World at 10:45am, 12:45pm, and 2:45pm.

Other Sights
The Ostrich Farm, *four kilometers south of Eilat, Tel. 07-637-2405, Fax 07-637-3213*, is by the entrance to Wadi Shlomo. There are ostriches, donkeys, goats, and camels to see, and tours by donkey-pulled chariots to experience. They also have jeep tours and desert quad runners–a rugged tractor-like vehicle.

Kadurit, *HaArava at the northern entrance to the city, Tel. 07-633-3301*, is open Sunday-Thursday 8am-7pm, and Friday-Saturday 8am-2pm. There's a gem museum with precious stones (featuring the Eilat Stone), and a video telling "The Story of the Diamond." They provide free shuttle service to entice you there; call for details.

NIGHTLIFE & ENTERTAINMENT

The pubs and discos are as salient a feature of Eilat's night scene as the beaches and coral reefs are during the day. Often full of Israelis celebrating the conclusion of their military duty and equally happy Europeans on holiday, spirits of all kinds flow readily after the sun goes down, though the night action doesn't really start to heat up till after 11pm.

Pubs
The Yacht Pub, *King Solomon's Wharf, Tel. 07-633-4111*, is a very popular drink spot, always full of merry-makers downing beer. They have happy hour 9-10pm with drinks two for the price of one. Later on a live band plays oldies while people drink, talk, and dance.

Teddy's Pub, *across from Shulamit Gardens Hotel, 07-634-0612*, is Tudor in style and Israeli in popularity. They have live jazz and blues on Fridays, Israeli rock on Saturdays, and open at 7pm.

Three Monkeys' Pub, *The Royal Beach Hotel across the Lagoon, Tel. 07-636-8888*, features another British-sort mahogany and draft beer kind of place.

The Underground, *New Tourist Center, Tel. 07-637-0239*, is a cheap place to drink. Open 9am-5am, they feature live bands on Friday nights. It's a popular hang-out for students and backpackers.

Hard Luck Cafe, *15 Almogim near Agmonim, Tel. 07-637-2788*, serves cheap beer and food to reveling travelers.

Siam Pub, *The Orchid Hotel, across from Coral Beach, 07-634-0101*, is a pleasant pub set in the attractive Thai bamboo style of the hotel.

Ya'eni Pub, *Ostrich Farm, near Coral Beach, Tel. 07-637-2405*, open Monday-Saturday 7pm-dawn, does a Light Show on the hills surrounding the farm.

Dolphin Reef Pub, *further south by Dolphin Reef, Tel. 07-637-1846*, is open 10am-whenever. There's cheap beer nightly and dancing on the beach Monday and Thursday nights and Friday afternoons. It's a popular spot, with a cover of NIS 20.

Discos
Sheba Disco, *King Solomon's Palace, Tel. 07-633-4111*, is a swank place with laser lights and video walls.

Spiral, *Red Sea Tower in the marina, Tel. 07-637-6640*, is a two-story flashy affair with lots of lights and action. It's open 10pm-5am, with covers from NIS 20-30 (one beer or soft drink included), and the name is pronounced *Speeral*.

There are plenty of other discos to try as well, such as the **Americana**, *Tel. 07-633-3777*, **Cafe Royal**, *Tel. 07-636-3444*, **Club In**, *Tel. 07-637-5132*, **Cotton Club**, *Dalia Hotel, Tel. 07-633-4004*, **Hamarteff**, *Etzion Hotel, Tel. 07-637-4131*, and **Neptune**, *Tel. 07-633-4333*.

Other Fun
Luna Park Miniland, near the Eilat Marina on North Beach Promenade, Tel. 07-637-6095, Fax 07-637-4226, is open Monday-Saturday 6pm-midnight, and on Saturdays and holidays, 10am-1pm as well. Great for kids, it's a night-time amusement park with lots of rides. Nearby and also popular with kids is **Volcania, the Miniature City**, *Tel. 07-637-7702, Fax 07-633-4924*. With houses, mountains lakes, ships and electric trains, you can test your ability to handle remote-controlled ships or elaborate trucks.

Night in the Desert, *four kilometers south of the city, Tel. 07-367-3565*, is at the Ostrich Farm in Wadi Shlomo, across from Coral Beach. In winter only, they simulate their version of the Bedouin Evening. It's a Wednesday evening event from 7-10pm, costs $45 and adult, $30 a child, providing shuttle service to and fro. The evening includes a Bedouin dinner in a Bedouin tent, serving meat, rice, pita, tea/coffee, and beer/wine/soda. You also get a belly dance show, desert stories, and a light show. Call to book and to arrange pick-up (they stop at Royal Beach, Riviera, Paradise, Khan Center, Red Rock, Taba Border, Princess, Orchid, and Red Sea Sports Hotel), and dress comfortably for sitting on cushions all evening. They're also open during the day for some Bedouin hospitality of tea or coffee (pay as you like, NIS 1-3), camel rides, and conversation about rug-making and Bedouin culture.

Kibbutz Eilot, *Tel. 07-637-5468*, puts on a Saturday evening of **Israeli Folklore**. They prepare an Israeli buffet dinner and perform Israeli folk dances, with music, costumes and the works.

Music Festivals
In late August, Eilat hosts an annual four-day **Red Sea Jazz Festival**. There's also a week-long **Hebrew Rock Music Festival** on Eilat Beach the

week preceding Passover. Check with Tourist Information for the exact dates.

SHOPPING

There are plenty of Shopping Centers in Eilat. **Red Canyon Center** is just down the street (toward the water) from the central bus station on HaTmarim. Even closer to the water, at the intersection of HaTmarim and Ha'Arava, is the **Shalom Center.** There are a lot of shops along the **Promenade.**

The **New Tourist Center** on Derekh Yotam also yet another place to shop. In addition, there's a **flea market** every Tuesday in City Center.

EXCURSIONS & DAY TRIPS

Coral Island, 12 kilometers south in Egyptian territory, has the ruins of a Crusader castle from the 12th century CE. Many of the local hotels, such as the Orchid, take groups there on diving trips.

Nahal-Hakevtovot, to the southwest, is a group of rock walls with drawings and Hebrew, Aramaic and Greek writing, dated at around 2000 years old.

Timna Park

Timna Park, *25 kilometers north of Eilat, Tel. 07-635-6215, Fax 07-635-6217,* is open daily 7:30am to sunset, and costs NIS 14-21 to enter. The copper mines of Timna were closed in 1976 because they'd stopped being economically feasible, but the ore, which sometimes occurs in the form of semi-precious green malachite, is still in popular demand as the Eilat Stone.

Nearby are the so-called **copper mines of King Solomon,** remnants of ancient copper mines from the third millennium BCE, the 13/12th century BCE, the 10th century BCE, and the Byzantine period in 324-640 CE. Timna Valley spreads over 60 square kilometers and is full of colorful sandstone formations, carved into mushrooms and arches by years of wind and water. They're both beautiful and of geological interest.

There are several archaeological sites here, including Solomon's Pillars and the copper mines. **King Solomon's Pillars** are two natural sandstone columns side by side rising 165 feet high. An Egyptian temple from the late Bronze Age (1600-1200 BCE) stands beside the columns, and there are wall paintings of animals from ancient times. There are sign-posted trails to all the sites, as well as rest facilities, a campground (available only by prior arrangement, so call or fax ahead), and a restaurant on the man-made Timna Lake. Bring some bottled water for the hike–it gets searing hot in the desert.

Getting there: Guided tours are available at the site, and there are plenty of everything-included tours leaving from Eilat as well. **Timna Park Express**, *Tel. 07-637-4741*, runs daily tours from Eilat, leaving 8am, returning late afternoon, and costing $42 an adult and $32 a child, lunch included. They pick up and drop off at hotels, but you need to call and make a booking. There is also a transport bus from **ETI** for NIS 50. It leaves around 8:30am (when a group of 10 has formed) from near the tourist information office.

Other Day Trips

Hai-Bar Yotvata Wildlife Reserve, *35 kilometers north of Eilat, Tel. 07-637-6018*, is one-half kilometer east of the Kibbutz Sarar Junction. Stop in the Visitors' Center, open daily 8:30am-3pm, before touring the reserve. The admission fee is NIS 26 for adults, NIS 13 for children. There are two-hour guided tours leaving at 9am, 10am, 11am, noon, and 1:30pm, and entrance is by Reserve vehicles only.

The wildlife park is designed to repopulate the area with animals that roamed during Biblical times, many of which are now rare. While there, you can also visit the Carnivore Center (open 8:30am-3pm) with such desert fauna as caracals (a desert lynx) and wolves. They also have a day/night inversion room to observe activities of nocturnal animals.

Chanoch Camel Safari, *leaving from the lobby of Sport Hotel in North Beach, Tel. 07-637-4741*, leads half-day camel excursions for $40 per person. The morning tour is from 9am-1pm, and the afternoon tour is 4-8pm in summer, 2-6pm in winter. Wear long pants, ones you don't mind getting a bit saturated with that certain camel something.

Texas Ranch, *Tel. 07-637-6663 by day, 07-637-8638 by night*, also does half-day camel safaris. The morning trip is 9am-1pm, and the afternoon one is 3-7pm. You get a light Bedouin meal and a ride through Wadi Shlomo and Wadi Zfahot. Again, long pants are essential.

Camel Riders, *Tel. 07-637-3218*, is another option, leading two-day caravans along smugglers' routes.

Solomon's Chariot, *Tel. 07-637-2405*, offers donkey wagon rides for NIS 55 per person.

Guided Tours of Negev Sights & the Sinai

Egged Tours, *Tel. 07-636-5122, Fax 07-636-5130*, is open 8am-6pm.

Johnny Desert Tours, *Bridge House near Moriah Hotel, Tel. 07-631-6215, Fax 631-6217*, operates Jeep tours.

Avi Desert Tours, *Tel./Fax 07-633-8090 or Tel. 05-039-4149*.

Neot Hakikar, *Tel. 07-632-6281, Fax 07-632-6297*, leads a variety of tours in the nearby Sinai, ranging from one-seven days. See *Sinai* section for more details.

BABY, LET ME TAKE YOU ON A SEA CRUISE!

There's a swarm of yachts, motor and sail, waiting to take you on a Red Sea cruise for NIS 90 per person. The Holiday Charter, in the Marina Tel. 07-633-1717, Fax 07-633-3351, is open daily 8am-8pm and can arrange a reservation on the vessel of your choice. You can also contact some yacht companies directly. Choose from the Eilat, Tel. 07-637-9165, Yamanga, Tel. 05-262-9837, and Zino Star, Tel. 07-633-5115.

For parachute ships, there are the Manta Sport and Paracraft, Tel. 07-633-1717.

SPORTS & RECREATION

Most of the beaches in Eilat charge an entrance fee, but the **Northern Beach** and **Southern Beach** are free. The **central town beach** costs NIS 8 for use of their windbreak and lounge chairs. In the summer there is a wagon that stores your valuables for NIS 5 because people often have stuff stolen when they're swimming. There is also a nice beach open to the public just past the Red Rock Hotel, near the Navy.

Isrotel Beach, *in front of the Royal Beach Hotel*, is stocked with deck chairs and Isrotel personnel.

Coral Beach, *south of the city, Tel. 07-637-6829*, or **Almog Beach** as it's known in Hebrew, is a 1.2 kilometer stretch of reef that's part of the Nature Reserve. It costs NIS 15 an adult, NIS 8 for youth, it's open daily 9am-6pm (entrance till 5pm), except days before holidays, when it shuts at 1pm. The safe, enclosed facilities include toilets, hot showers, lockers, and snorkel equipment rental, but it's not a declared bathing beach, and has no lifeguard. The world's most northerly coral reef, and the only one in Israel, the clarity of the water here is equally good for snorkelers and the health of the reef. With snorkel and mask (bring your own or rent them here), you get good views of a variety of coral, large starfish who feed on the coral, and zillions of vibrantly colorful reef fish.

There are also the usual attendant dangers of spiny sea urchins and stone fish (and lion fish, but they tend to come out in the evening) to be very wary of. *Recommended precautions*: wear some form of footgear (old sneakers or fins); avoid touching things (coral, etc.) under water; swim as much as possible when in the water to minimize foot contact with the coral or what appears to be sand (but could be a variety of camouflaged creatures); cross the reef by the routes marked by floats and ropes; don't walk on the reef (it's bad for you and the reef); and wear sun screen.

Dolphin Reef, *southern beach of Eilat, Tel. 07-637-1846, Fax 07-637-5921*, open daily 9am-9pm, offers a unique opportunity to observe, mingle with, and swim with the dolphins for NIS 29 per adult, NIS 22 per child. There's a private beach with umbrellas and beach chairs, and observation points from which to watch the dolphin training sessions at 10am, noon, 2pm, and 4pm. There are also films about dolphins, whales, and sea lions. To swim with the dolphins and trainers, make reservations in advance. They have a Diving Center with equipment rental and courses, a restaurant, and a pub (open 5pm till late). Dolphin Reef is about three kilometers south of Eilat, and bus 15 from the town center or North Beach hotel cluster provides frequent transport.

Red Rock Beach, *North Beach, Tel. 07-637-2088*, has water sports like pedal boats, kayaks, motor boats, and banana boats available, NIS 70 per half hour, NIS 20 per person.

Airodium, *behind the Riviera Hotel, Tel. 07-637-2745, Fax 07-633-1676*, lets you fly without a parachute. In one hour you get taught the basic theory, suit up, and hurl yourself into the padded abyss. Suitable for the Daedalus-minded, ages eight and up, it's open daily 10am-1pm and 5-10pm in summer, 10am-6pm in winter, and costs NIS 120 per person.

Attractions House, *Tel. 07-631-6359*, open 8:30am-9pm, bills itself as a sailing observatory. What it is a triple-layer motor boat with an underwater observation deck and panoramic windows, a middle deck with a snack bar and shade, and an upper observation deck for sunbathing and vista-viewing. It departs from the Holiday Inn Wharf and costs NIS 50 an adult and NIS 35 a child. Call for reservations and schedules.

There are also a number of **glass-bottomed boats** that tour the coral reefs leaving from the port area near Opening Bridge. For information on their daily cruises, call *Tel. 07-631-6359*.

Eilat has many **scuba diving** clubs and schools. A representative example is **Siam Divers**, *Hotel Orchid across from Coral Beach, Tel. 07-636-0363, Fax 07-637-1033*. This is a relatively new club with top-of-the-line equipment, open daily 8am-5pm. They offer a wide variety of dives for every level of experience. Siam Divers rents all types of equipment, starting at $3.50 for a mask and snorkel. They also sponsor Swimming with the Dolphins in the Sinai for $100 per person.

Snuba, *Coral Nature Reserve, Tel. 07-637-2722, Fax 07-637-6767*, is a unique scuba diving opportunity in that you need no experience and no time-and-money consuming instruction. The air tanks remain on the boat, allowing you to dive in pairs (accompanied by an instructor) to a depth of six meters for an hour. For ages 10 and older. Costing NIS 110 for an hour and a half, they're open 9am-5pm, 3pm in winter.

Red Sea Sports Club, *King's Wharf next to King Solomon's Palace, Tel. 07-637-6569*, is Israel's leading diving club. They do more, however, than just dives. They have bare boat charters, deep sea fishing, daily cruises, and diving safaris to the Sinai. They also offer desert safaris, camel and horseback rides, pedal boats and motor boats, kayaks, parasailing, and water skiing. They rent mountain bikes by the day or week as well. There are plenty of other diving clubs as well. To shop around, call **Aqua Sport**, *Tel. 07-633-4404*, **Coral Reserve, Coral Beach, Dolphin Reef**, *Tel. 07-637-1846*, **Lucky Divers**, *Tel. 07-633-5990*, **Manta Red Sea Sport Club**, *Tel. 07-637-6569*, and **King Solomon's Wharf**, *Tel. 07-637-9685*.

Eilat Nature Reserve, *northwest of Eilat, Tel. 07-637-3988*, is a wonderland of desert habitat and dry, rugged mountains of the lunar landscape variety, stretching for miles. It's stunning, and cooler, in the early morning light. Bus 392 takes you to the trail heads (ask the driver where to get off) for hikes to Ein Netafim, Mount Shlomo, or HaCanyon Ha'Adom (Red Canyon).

Ein Netafim, *Valley of the Moon Road*, is a small spring at the foot of a 30 meter waterfall. The only year-round source of water, it's an important watering hole for the reserve's ibex, hyrax, and birds. A sand track leads to it from Valley of the Moon road. From the car park it takes about 10 minutes to walk there. From there you can carry on to the lookout above **Valley of the Moon**, and Amram's Pillars (four pillars sculpted by the elements to resemble the columns of a Greek temple).

Red Canyon, *northern edge of Valley of the Moon, Tel. 07-637-4233*, is one of the most beautiful canyons near Eilat. It's about 600 meters long, one-three meters wide, up to ten meters deep, and completely carved out of red Nubian sandstone. A path leads to the canyon, ascends at the southern bank, and returns to the parking lot. You can get good Nature Reserve Authority hikers' maps from the tourist information office. Spending a day hiking the hills and bluffs of the desert is very rewarding, but you need to follow all precautions–the desert elements don't joke around. Take plenty of water, something to cover your head, sunscreen, and more water.

Bird Sanctuary, *offices in the City Center Mall opposite the central bus station, Tel. 07-637-4276*, is open Sunday-Thursday 9am-1pm and 5-7pm. Israel is the only land bridge between Africa, Asia, and Europe, and as such it's quite a popular rest stop for migrating birds that winter in Africa but breed in Europe and Asia. In spring and autumn, more than two million birds take advantage of the Eilat mountain air currents to stop or refuel. There are viewing stations, walking trails in the reserve, and jeep tours run by the center. IBCE (International Bird Watching Center in Eilat) works on conservation, research, and migration surveys. They also lead half or full day birding tours, visits to ringing stations, and run the annual **Spring Migration Festival** in late March.

JNF Planting Center, *in the Bird Center, Tel. 07-637-4276*, provides an alternative way for you to interact with Eilat by planting a tree with your own hands.

Nature's Way, *Eilat's Shalom Center, Tel. 07-637-0648 or Tel. 05-032-8070, Fax 07-637-2608*, is not a laxative but an Ecology Hikes company. For $35 an adult and $28 a child (lunch of homemade cheese, pita, and vegetables included), they lead morning desert tours (easy, moderate, and hard), picking you up at 8:00am and returning around 1:30pm.

Monday morning's hike, ranked easy to moderate, goes to Netafim Spring and Wadi. Monday's evening hike, an easy one leaving 3:30pm, returning after sunset, and costing $25, goes 278 meters up Mount Tsfahot to see the sunset from the summit.

Wednesday's Mount Shlomo trip is hard and not recommended for children; it goes 705 meters up to the summit and descends by Dry Falls Wadi. The twilight predator feeding tour, (oddly titled the "family tour," perhaps because there's no hiking on this one), leaves at 5pm, returns at 9:30pm, and takes you (and your gore-minded family) to see hyenas and leopards devour their meals.

And Thursday's moderate-to-easy hike in Gishron Canyon takes you through 500 million years of geological history. For the day hikes, bring two bottles of water per person, as well as comfortable shoes, a hat, and sunscreen.

PRACTICAL INFORMATION

- **Airport**, *intersection of HaTmarim and Ha'Arava, Tel. 07-636-3838.*
- **Book shop**, Eilat Street, and **Steimatzky branches**, *bus station* and *Shalom Center*.
- **Central bus station**, *HaTmarim, Tel. 07-636-5111*, is a convenient landmark as well as the public transportation hub.
- **Egyptian Consulate**, *68 Ha'Efroni, Tel. 07-637-6882*, from the bus station, go up HaTmarim, left on Eilat, right by the Mor Center on Anafa, and the third left is Ha'Efroni. The consulate is at the end of the street under the Egyptian flag. The visa office is open Sunday-Thursday 9-11am and 1-1:30pm, Friday 9-10am and 11am-12pm. The morning hours are for submitting your applications and the afternoon time slots are for visa pick-up. Visas will be free of charge until May 1998, and thereafter may be $15 for US citizens. You can get one at a consulate or at the border.
- **Films**, *Eilat Cinema, Tel. 07-637-3178.*
- **Fire**, *Tel. 102* in emergencies, *Tel. 07-637-2222* otherwise.
- **First Aid**, *HaTmarim, Tel. 101* for emergencies, *Tel. 07-637-2333* otherwise. There are Magen David Adom (first aid) stations on some beaches as well.

- **Hospital:** Yoseftal Hospital, *Derekh Yotam, Tel. 07-635-8011.*
- **Laundromats: Chikita,** *15 Almogim Street,* is open Sunday-Friday 9am-9pm and costs NIS 18 to wash and dry; **Kviskal,** *Razin Center, HaTmarim, Tel. 07-637-4838;* **Nikita,** *shop #23 in Mor Center,* is open daily 9am-9pm and costs NIS 18 to wash and dry; **Yael's Laundry,** *Sdel Boneh Center, Ha'Arava, Tel. 07-637-3443.*
- **Medical Centers: Clalit,** *Tel. 177-022-3430,* **INS Care Medical Center,** *Tel. 07-633-4445,* **Leumit,** *Tel. 07-637-2451,* and **Maccabee,** *Tel. 07-635-5222.*
- **Nature Reserves Authority,** *Coral Beach, Tel. 07-637-6829,* is open 9am-5pm and can provide information, maps, and advice about hikes, coral reefs, and bird-watching.
- **News in English: TV,** Ch. 1 daily at 6:15pm, and **Israel Radio** (AM) on 575, 1170, 1305 kHz (news summary at 7am and 5pm, news and features at 1pm, and news headlines at 1:20pm).
- **Pharmacies: Avigdor,** *bottom floor of New Tourist Center, Tel. 07-637-2374,* open Sunday-Thursday 10am-1pm and 5-10pm, Friday 10am-1pm and 7-8pm, Saturday 11am-1pm and 8-10pm; **Eilat Pharmacy,** *25/4 Eilat, Tel. 07-637-4665,* is open Sunday-Thursday 8am-1:30pm and 4-8pm, Friday 8:15-am-2pm; **Michlin Pharmacy,** *Rekhter Center, Tel. 07-637-2434,* is open Sunday-Thursday 8:30am-2pm and 4:30-8pm, Friday 8am-2pm.
- **Police:** *Avdat, at the eastern end of Hativat HaNegev, Tel. 100* in emergencies or *Tel. 07-636-2444* otherwise, has a lost-and-found for packs "gone missing" from the beach.
- **Post office,** *Red Canyon Center, Tel. 07-637-8878,* just down HaTmarim from the bus station, has Western Union and Poste Restante and is open Sunday-Tuesday, Thursday 8:30am-12pm and 4-6pm, Wednesday 8am-1pm, and Friday 8am-12pm.
- **Telephone service: Starcom Gold,** *main floor of the New Tourist Center, Tel. 07-637-2237,* has international rates that are cheaper than public or post office options, and they're open Sunday-Thursday 9am-midnight, Friday 9am-5pm, Saturday 8am-1am.
- **Tourist Information Office,** *corner of Yotam and Ha'Arava, Tel. 07-637-2111,* in the **New Tourist Center** is open Sunday-Thursday 8am-9pm, Friday 8am-3pm, Saturday 10am-2pm. Parking there is no problem. It's a great center, one of the best and most helpful in Israel, with maps, brochures, coupons, and computer printouts. **Municipal Tourist Information Office,** *Tourist Center, 07-637-4233,* is open Sunday-Thursday 8am-6pm, Friday 8am-1pm, and has maps. The **Reservation and Information Center,** *Durban, Tel. 07-637-4741,* is open 24 hours but should not be confused with Tourist Information. They will

help you reserve a room in keeping with your budget, it's not the place for maps, etc.

• **Tour groups: Egged Tours,** *Tel. 07-636-5122,* **Galilee Tours,** *Tel. 07-633-5131,* **Johnny Tours,** *Tel. 07-631-6215,* **Neot Hakikar,** *Tel. 07-632-6281,* **Peltours,** *Tel. 07-637-6184,* **Riva Tours,** *Tel. 07-637-1495,* **SPNI,** *Tel. 07-628-6824,* **United Tours,** *Tel. 07-637-1740,* and **Uni Tours,** *Tel. 07-631-6253.*

• **UK Consulate,** *Dizahav, above the New Tourist Center, Tel. 07-634-0810.*

20. PALESTINIAN AUTHORITY - THE WEST BANK & GAZA

The tourist situation in most of the **West Bank** has been changing dramatically as Israel and the Palestinians hammer out treaties and agreements. PLO chief Yasser Arafat and Israeli Foreign Minister Shimon Peres negotiated through the summer of 1995, interrupted from time to time by terrorist attacks aimed at derailing the peace process, to iron out the kinks involved in Israel's returning the West Bank land. They hoped to reach a full accord in September 1995, leaving aside unresolved issues such as control over holy sites, water rights and the status of Hebron (where 450 Jewish settlers live among 80,000 Palestinians).

In August 1995, Israel was committed to pulling out of six of the seven main West Bank towns over a few months, giving the **Palestinian Authority** (PA) control over many of the West Bank's one million Palestinian residents. The Palestinians would control only 18 percent of West Bank territory in the first stage. There would then be three more withdrawals (one every six months) starting after Palestinian elections were held. Israel would release Palestinian prisoners in three stages.

In September 1995, Rabin and Arafat signed the 300 page **Interim Agreement** (also known as **Oslo II**) on the West Bank and Gaza Strip, establishing guidelines on everything from Palestinian elections and Israeli redeployment to security, water, and prisoner release. Much of what was agreed upon has taken place: in January 1996, Palestinian Council elections were held and Yasser Arafat was elected *Ra'ees* (head) of the Authority; the IDF (Israeli Defense Force) evacuated most West Bank cities (with Hebron the notable exception); in April 1996, the Palestinian National Charter was amended to remove the articles that called for the destruction of Israel; and in May 1996 Israel and the PA began permanent status negotiations on the touchy subjects of Jerusalem, settlements, and refugees.

Yitzhak Rabin's Death

But between the signing of the Interim Agreement and the implementations, Yitzhak Rabin was killed. On November 4, 1995, 25-year-old Yigal Amir assassinated Israel's Prime Minister Yitzhak Rabin at a peace rally in Tel Aviv. Over one million Israelis (both Arabs and Jews) paid respects to Rabin at his funeral, and nearly 80 world leaders (including representatives from six Arab states and President Clinton) attended the Jerusalem funeral. Right-wing Amir shot Rabin to derail the peace talks, and though the talks haven't entirely disintegrated, it's come pretty close.

Acting Prime Minister Shimon Peres called for early elections, but by the time the elections were held in May 1996, three Hamas bombs caused 57 deaths plus a political backlash; the moderates who'd turned from Likud to Labor after Rabin was murdered renewed their conservative sympathies and peace process distrust. **Benjamin Netanyahu**, the Likud party candidate, defeated Shimon Peres by a razor-thin majority of 50.4%. Netanyahu vowed to continue the peace process, but he's had anything but a light touch. For more details, see Chapter 5, *A Short History*.

Despite the frustration, poverty, and anger, many Palestinians welcome visitors into their homes with traditional hospitality, offering conversation as intense and thick as the coffee that accompanies it. Visitors to the West Bank, however, would do well to dress modestly in deference to the residents' values and norms.

While loads of tourists visit Bethlehem and a smaller number go to Jericho as well, many of the sites in the West Bank are on the US Embassy's "Stay Away" list, due to their hostility and violence potential. **Hebron** is one of the touchiest spots in Israel, and **Gaza Strip** is not considered safe either. By all means contact the embassy for an update on the situation before venturing far afield, and *carry your passport at all times*.

In the next few years, however if progress continues, it is likely that more hotels and restaurants will be appearing in the Palestinian Authority areas, since the desire to share in the Holy Land tourism windfall is one of the incentives driving the peace process.

ORIENTATION

Most of the Palestinian Authority cities are clustered near Jerusalem. **Bethlehem** is just south of Jerusalem, 10 kilometers along the Bethlehem road, and south of that is **Hebron**, some 35 kilometers from Jerusalem. **Ramallah** is just a few kilometers to the north, and further north is **Nablus**, a good 48 kilometers from Jerusalem. East of Jerusalem is **Bethany**, and further on is **Jericho**, 39 kilometers east of Jerusalem and near the Allenby Bridge crossing.

Gaza Strip, however, is not part of the West Bank. It stretches about 40 kilometers along the Mediterranean coast, from south of Ashkelon to the Sinai border of Egypt.

ARRIVALS & DEPARTURES

By Car

You can take a rental car into the Palestinian Authority, but Israeli plates will attract some stares and maybe even glares. Renting from an Arab rental agency in East Jerusalem is one way around the problem. For now, all you need is your passport to cross into Palestinian areas, but this may change. Get the most recent embassy update before driving there.

By Bus

When Israel hasn't sealed its borders in reaction to a terrorist event, the Arab buses from the East Jerusalem stations ply the routes to the nearby Palestinian cities. There is one station on **Suleiman** between Damascus and Herod's Gates for southern routes and another on **Nablus** serving northern routes.

When the political situation allows, the 22 goes every 15 minutes or so to **Bethlehem** for NIS 2.5 from the Suleiman Station. The 23 goes to **Hebron** for NIS 7, the 28 goes to **Jericho** for NIS 5, and the 36 goes to **Bethany** for NIS 2. From the Nablus Station, take the 18 to **Ramallah** for NIS 3 and the Tamimi Company 23 to **Nablus** for NIS 6.

By Sherut

Sheruts (share taxis) line up across from the Damascus Gate in Jerusalem, and shout out their destinations to passersby. There are loads to Bethlehem, but you can find sheruts to other places as well. They're a cheap (NIS 2 to Bethlehem, NIS 9 to Nablus), comfortable, and friendly means of transport. And more reliable than the buses.

By Taxi

You can always pay a private cab to take you where you want to go, but don't expect them to be as inexpensive as the sheruts.

Getting Around

A city like Bethlehem is easy to see by foot, but the sights in Jericho are more spread out, so you'll want a taxi (for NIS 60 or so to see the sights, but make the deal before you set out) or rental car to get from place to place, or you can rent a bicycle there (for NIS 2 an hour). The other option is to take an organized tour including Bethlehem and Jericho, and leave the transport to them.

WHERE TO STAY

Bethlehem

Your dollars and shekels will go farthest in Bethlehem, and they want your business.

PARADISE BETHLEHEM, *Manger Square, Tel. 02-674-4542, Fax 02-674-4544, charges $53 a single and $72 a double, breakfast included.*

Is this really paradise? No, but it's not bad–there are 99 rooms, some with bath and some with shower, and all with phone.

THE BETHLEHEM STAR, *Al'Baten, Tel. 02-674-3249, Fax 02-674-1494, costs $35 a single and $55 a double most of the year, breakfast included, but $65 a single and $150 a double during Christmas and Easter.*

The Bethlehem Star has 72 rooms, half with bath and half with shower. The rooms all have heat and phones, with TVs by request.

HANDAL, *Abdul Nasser, Tel./Fax 02-674-4888, charges $25 a single and $40 a double, breakfast included, and the rates go up a few dollars in high season. Name may have changed*

There are 42 rooms here, most with baths, and a few have showers. Rooms also have heat, phones, balconies, and TVs by request.

THE PALACE HOTEL, *Manger Street right by the Church of the Nativity, Tel. 02-674-2798, 02-674-4100, Fax 02-674-1562, has 27 rooms for NIS 80 a single and NIS 100 a double, breakfast included, prices negotiable.*

The Palace has a lovely stone courtyard. The rooms are okay, brown and not exciting; the facade is definitely grander than the interior.

CASA NOVA, *off Manger Square to the left of the Basilica of the Nativity, Tel. 02-674-3981, Fax 02-674-3982, costs $20, breakfast included–with other meal plans are available. Reserve up to a year in advance for Christmas. Telephone number may have changed.*

The Casa Nova has marble and stained glass, but is for pilgrims only.

Jericho

NEW JERICHO PENSION, *Jerusalem Road, Tel. 02-992-2215, is across from the New Jericho mosque. Singles are $13-$15 and doubles are $20.*

Near city center, their rooms feature wooden beds and good mattresses, while the common room has a TV and radio.

HISHAM'S PALACE HOTEL, *Ein as-Sultan Street, Tel. 02-992-2156, charges NIS 40 for singles without bath, and NIS 100 a single with bath, NIS 80 for doubles.*

Hisham's is downtown near city center, and sports a porch. The rooms have balconies and fans, but not the most modern facilities. It's a shabby place.

Ramallah
   AL-WIHDEH HOTEL, *26 Main Street, Tel. 995-6452, provides rooms for NIS80-150.*
   Near the center of town, all rooms come with private bathroom, TV, and telephone.
   And other hotels are under construction.

   Check with the **Palestinian Tourist Office** in Bethlehem for the latest scoop and to see if the Jericho YMCA is open. Do the same for **Ramallah, Hebron,** and the **Gaza Strip**, depending on the political climate when you visit.
   Beit Sahour, *a village near Jerusalem, Tel. 02-674-3921,* is setting up a B&B program–a call will tell you if it's started yet.

WHERE TO EAT
Bethlehem
   Manger Square is chock-a-block with restaurants serving the standard Arabic foods, or head up the winding streets and visit one of the smaller stalls and bakeries.

Jericho
   Small restaurants near the center of town serve big plates of falafel, rice, sauce and salad for NIS 10, and good Arabic coffee plus a glass of cold water for NIS 1.5.

SEEING THE SIGHTS
Bethlehem
   Its name means House of Bread in Hebrew (*Beit Lehem*) and House of Meat in Arabic (*Beit Lahm*) but it's really a place of churches, though it's inhabited half and half by Muslims and Christians alike. It's easy to visit from Jerusalem on your own if you don't want to do the tour. You get hassled less by souvenir hawkers if you don't pile out of a tour bus, and you get to wander the narrow streets and the market as well.
   This is where Rachel died, where shepherd David was found, and, most famous of all, where Jesus was born to Mary in a manger. The *intifada* affected Bethlehem as it did all of the West Bank, but it's come back with a bang; tourism is booming, and Christmas in the square is a thronged event once more (see description in Jerusalem chapter).
   The main church here is the **Church of the Nativity**, shared by Greek Orthodox, Armenian, and Catholics alike, open daily 6:30am-7pm in summer and 7am-6pm in winter. Sponsored by Constantine in 326 CE at Helena's prompting, restored by Justinian, and spared Persian destruc-

tion (thanks perhaps to the mosaic of the Three Kings in Oriental dress), this is the oldest continuously used church in the world. The entrance is off Manger Square, and there are 12 rules for visitors, including: no headdresses, and no animals. It's a beautiful church, with a faint smell of incense.

The **Grotto of the Nativity** is part of a natural cave, and it's divided among three denominations, with Greek Orthodox dominating. There are Crusader mosaics on the walls, old religious graffiti on the columns, and a star with the Latin inscription *Hic De Virgine Maria Jesus Christus Natus Est* (Here, of the Virgin Mary, Jesus Christ was Born) marking the sacred spot.

Then there's the **Roman Catholic Church of Saint Catherine**, *Tel. 02-674-2425*. It was built in the late 1800's and is nice enough, though it's nowhere near as impressive as the Grotto of the Nativity. The walls have fine wood carvings of the 14 Stations of the Cross, and the first room, the **Chapel of Saint Joseph**, is where Joseph is said to have had his vision prompting them to flee to Egypt in order to escape Herod's violent ways. Below in the **Chapel of the Innocents** is the burial cave of less fortunate children murdered by Herod. The Franciscan Fathers hold a procession daily, and the church is open daily 5:30am-noon and 2-8pm.

Near the Basilica down Milk Grotto Street is **Milk Grotto Church**, *Tel. 02-674-2425*. This cellar is believed to be the cave where Mary, Joseph, and Jesus hid from Herod before taking off to Egypt for a while. The cave rock was once a milky white (hence the name), but it's been darkened by time and smoke. There's another milk connection, however, beyond rock coloring. A few drops of Mary's milk is said to have dropped while she was nursing Jesus, whitewashing the rocks and causing women ever since to come here to pray for fertility. Open daily 8-11am and 2-5pm, you may need to ring the bell for a monk to let you in.

On Star Street about 500 meters north of Manger Square is the **Well of David**, *Tel. 02-674-2477*. Open daily 8am-noon and 2-5pm, the restored cisterns are believed to be the very same from which David was offered water while he was fighting the Philistines, whereupon he turned and made an offering to God.

Between Bethlehem and Jerusalem on Nablus Road is **Rachel's Tomb**, *Tel. 02-678-7507*. Open Sunday-Thursday 8am-5pm, Friday 8am-2pm, it's a sacred site for Jews, and synagogues have been built up and torn down here through the ages. Rachel died in Bethlehem giving birth to Benjamin, and despite her sad story the tomb is viewed as the place to come to pray for a child or a healthy pregnancy. It's a 20 minute walk from the Basilica, but the tour buses just pass on by and point at it out the window.

The market, *up the hill from Manger Square*, is wonderful and colorful. There are clothes and plastic wash tubs, live chickens and trays of sweets, mounds of fresh produce, stalls of shoes, and another world from Jerusalem.

Bethlehem Museum, *Paul VI, Tel. 02-674-2589*, just a few blocks down from the market has Palestinian crafts and traditional costumes, and is open Monday-Wednesday, Friday, and Saturday 8am-5pm.

Near Bethlehem

Just four kilometers from Jerusalem, **Bethany** is where **Lazarus** (and his sisters Mary and Martha) lived. There's a **Franciscan Church**, *Tel. 02-627-1706*, to mark where Jesus slept, and it has some impressive mosaics depicting the Last Supper and Lazarus rising from the dead. Earlier shrines, one built in the fourth century, have been excavated nearby, and there's part of an abbey built in 1143 by Queen Melisende to the south of the church. It's open 8-11:30am and 2-6pm in summer, 8-11:30am and 2-5pm in winter.

Greek Orthodox Church is built above the **Tomb of Lazarus**. Open daily 8am-7pm, a donation of NIS 2 is expected by the caretakers showing you to the tomb. Farther up the main road is the **Greek Orthodox Convent** with its silver domes, built over the rock Jesus sat on while waiting for Martha from Jericho. To see the rock, ring the bell. Dress modestly.

Shepherd's Field is just past the village of Beit Sahur (see below) to the east of Bethlehem. The **Field of Ruth** is where the biblical Book of Ruth is supposedly set, and Shepherd's Field is where the angel pronounced the birth of Jesus to those out with their flocks (Luke 2:9-11). There's a 6th century **Byzantine basilica**, *Tel. 02-674-3135*, with a **Greek Orthodox monastery**, the **Holy Cave** dating from 350 CE with mosaic crosses in the floor, and a small cave with human bones. Down the road is the **Franciscan Shepherd's Field** with its own monastery from 400 CE and a collection of ancient shepherd cooking pots and coins, open daily 8-11am and 2-5pm.

The ruins of **Herodian** are 10 kilometers southeast of Bethlehem, up in the Judean Hills on a pointy peak. Back when King Herod was waxing fearful about assassination, he had this hideout constructed with watch towers (four) and huge double walls. Within was a sumptuous palace with baths and gardens. Rebels from the Jewish revolts took advantage of Herod's solid construction, and holed up there for a while. Open daily 8am-5pm and costing NIS 12 (NIS 6 for students), you can get there from Bethlehem by taxi (about NIS 30-40 round trip).

Less accessible but more remarkable than Herodian is **Mar Saba Monastery**, carved into a canyon above the Kidron River. This is where

Saint Saba took to asceticism in 478 CE, and his spirit lives in the tourism restrictions. Women are forbidden to enter and must make do with an outside view, while men must wear pants and long-sleeved shirts to go inside. Open daily 7-11am and 1:30-5pm, you'll need a private taxi from Bethlehem to get here.

Jericho
The Palestinian Tourism literature says "Since the dawn of history, Jericho has been the bride of the Jordan Valley whose wedding is still going on." Whatever, precisely, this means, it's a beautiful oasis town with lots of green. There are orchards and oranges, graceful palms and Arabs in headdress herding goats.

Tel Jericho (also known as **Tel as-Sultan**) has a piece of the old **city wall** (the one that came tumbling down) dating back to 2,600 BCE. You can see it from the main road, where people stop to snap pictures of it, or trek closer to see the excavated remains of 23 cities built one on top of another. There's also a seven meter **Neolithic tower** going back to 7,000 BCE.

Ein as-Sultan, the spring of Elisha, is Jericho's water source just across from the Tel. Water gushes at 1,000 gallons a minute and irrigates the wadi.

Mount of Temptation, *three kilometers northwest of town*, is where Jesus is said to have fasted for 40 days and nights. There's a Greek Orthodox monastery 350 meters up in the cliff, lots of caves, and the climb takes about half an hour.

Hisham's Palace at Khirbet al-Mafjar is one of few well-preserved examples of eighth century Islamic architecture (some of the finer finds are on display at the Rockefeller Museum in Jerusalem). There's also a small pottery museum on the site. The best find, still on location, is the beautiful and undamaged mosaic.

Saint John's Monastery, four kilometers east of Jericho and nearing the Allenby Bridge, is where Jesus was baptized. One of the most beautiful monasteries, however, is the Greek Orthodox **Monastery of Saint George of Koziba**. It's set in the truly stunning Wadi Kelt, one of the most popular hiking destinations when local tension was less evident. It's a four hour path through Wadi Kelt to Saint George Monastery, the caves below look beautiful, and the view of Saint George Monastery, carved out of canyon rock, is magnificent.

The sheer rock walls of the wadi stretch 35 kilometers between Jericho and Jerusalem, and three springs feed the oasis. It's worth taking a look from the road even if the hike isn't possible (check with the embassy for an assessment of the situation).

Ramallah

Up in the hills, some 900 meters above sea level, **Ramallah** is just 16 kilometers north of Jerusalem. Before 1967 this was a prosperous town, a cool summer holiday spot for wealthy Arabs. Relatively liberal, the people are friendly and construction is booming.

The **market** by the bus station is open Saturday-Thursday till 3pm and Friday till noon. There's also the **Silvana Chocolate Company**, *Tel. 02-995-2467*, just 1.5 kilometers down from Manara Square on Jaffa Street, open for tours and tastes Monday-Saturday 7:30am-4pm.

Beitin (also known as **Bethel**) is five kilometers northeast on the road to Nablus. It's supposed to be where Jacob slept and dreamt of a ladder going up to heaven. Jacob woke up, built an altar, and named the place Beit El (House of God) according to Genesis 28:12-19. There's a Jewish settlement nearby named Beit El, with a *tefillin* factory. This was the site of more settler unrest (a Palestinian was killed) in August '95 in protest against the Palestinian-Israeli accords, and it's not recommended as a safe destination.

Birzeit is the home of **Birzeit University**, the West Bank's largest (with around 2,500 students). Twelve kilometers northwest of Ramallah, the university has been a center of young and vocal protest to Israeli occupation, and was shut down from '88-'92. The old campus is next to the last bus stop, while the new campus is two kilometers out of town.

Nablus

Not counting East Jerusalem, **Nablus** is the largest city in the West Bank, home to a large Muslim community and a small Samaritan community of around 500–two thirds of the world's total Samaritan population. Founded by Titus in 72 CE as Flavia Neapolis, it was built near the old city of Shekhem. After Solomon died in 922, Jeroboam (who had earlier rebelled unsuccessfully against Solomon and fled to Egypt to escape punishment) returned to rule the ten northern tribes in the Kingdom of Israel from the new northern capital of Shekhem from 922-901 BCE.

Shekhem was built up to rival Jerusalem, and while it never quite managed the feat, it housed many kings and was a religious center till the Babylonians swept in around 587 BCE. Since then Crusaders, earthquakes (there was a nasty one in 1927), the British Mandate, the Israeli occupation, and the intifada have consumed Nablus, and it's now trying to get on its feet again.

Nablus has a busy **market**, full of fresh fruit and big pans of sweets.

Jacob's Well, *three kilometers to the east, Tel. 09-837-5123*, is a famous pilgrim site, but there's not much there now. It's supposed to be where Jacob pitched his tents, is now enclosed in a subterranean Greek Orthodox shrine, *and is open daily 8am-noon and 2-5pm*. Nearby is the **Tomb of Joseph** where it is believed Joseph's bones (which had been carried out of Egypt) were buried as per Joshua 24:32. It was a Muslim shrine and now it's a Jewish shrine, but it's still just a tomb, *open daily 6am-10pm and modest dress required*.

Mount Gerizim, *to the southeast*, has some swell views of Shomron Valley. The Samaritans believe it's the place where Abraham bound Isaac in sacrificial preparations and also where the original 10 Commandment tablets are buried. This is where the Samaritans perform their bloody paschal lamb sacrifice before audiences of Jerusalem and Tel Aviv gawkers. It's a hefty hike up the mountain, but taxis can be hired for around NIS 15.

Sabastiya, *11 kilometers northwest*, is the site of the Israelite, Hellenistic, and Roman ruins of **Shomron** (Samaria). Despite all the history that took place here there's not that much to see. There's a Roman theater ruin and the Israelite and Hellenistic acropolis walls, and column bases of the Temple of Augustus. Untended and free (for now), there are service taxis from Nablus to the base of the hill for around NIS 3.

Hebron

In Hebrew, *Hevron* means friend, and the Arabic name for the city (*Al khalil ar-Rahman*) means compassionate friend, all a bit ironic given the thick veil of hostility that shrouds the place. It's been important in Jewish lore ever since Abraham chose Hebron for his family cemetery. All the matriarchs and patriarchs of Judaism (except Rachel, whose tomb is near Bethlehem) are said to be buried here in the **Cave of Makhpela**, a very holy and revered site for Jews and Muslims alike.

It's also claimed that Adam and Eve were buried there, and that was why Abraham chose it. And the biblical references continue with Moses who sent scouts to Canaan, only to have them come back telling tales of the giants of Hebron. Herod built a synagogue to worship there, transformed by the Byzantines into a church, made over by the Muslims into a mosque, and back to a church again by a new wave of Crusaders. The Mamluks added some minarets as they changed it back to a mosque, and the Israelis, who were only allowed to stand outside and pray in 1929, have reinstituted a synagogue. This prayer house battle is indicative of the Hebron temperament, and while Muslims and Jews both pray in the same structure over the same holy cave, the hostilities are such that it's unlikely you'll be getting to see it.

The history of settlements and stubbornness, killings and massacres are as endemic to the place as the worship wars. In 1925 a Russian yeshiva was set up. Angry Arabs responded violently in the 1929 riots. Israel captured it in 1967, and a number of settlements were begun. In February

1994, an American Jew named **Baruch Goldstein** massacred a number of Palestinians as they prayed in the mosque, and it's not gotten much friendlier since then. The embassy security officer said Hebron was still tense and certain strike dates and anniversaries were observed, such as the 23rd, anniversary of the Baruch Goldstein massacre, as well as the 9th and 17th. There's still a lot of bitterness over Baruch Goldstein, and attempts to glorify him and turn him into a martyr have intensified things.

Add to the stew the fact that Israel is turning the West Bank over to the Palestinians, and that the settlers now in Hebron refuse to leave, and you get a sense why they can't all just get along over there. While the governments try to work out a deal, the individuals clash and spar with predictable frequency and intensity. Check with the consulate before attempting a visit here.

Gaza City

More than 200,000 people live in this stressed, economically depressed city. A port city that's been fought over and invaded since Biblical times, it is not a safe place for tourists to visit right now, though this may change.

The **intifada** (*uprising*) began here in 1987 over Palestinian deaths caused by a traffic accident, and spread like a brush fire through the crowded and unsanitary refugee camps. The uprisings have been the angriest here and the Israeli crackdowns the harshest, so it's not surprising that the PLO and Hamas, the Islamic militant branch of the Muslim Brotherhood, have such strong followings here. Yasser Arafat has made this his home base as he leads the PLO in negotiations with Israel for autonomous Palestinian rule.

In 570 CE, a Christian pilgrim described it as "a splendid and beautiful city, its men most honest, liberal in every respect and friendly to pilgrims." That was then. For now, Gaza Strip is still under curfew from 8pm-4am, and daytime curfews as well after any major disturbances.

If things open up, places to see include **Tel Gaza** (Tel Harube), the partly excavated site of ancient Gaza. There's a **Byzantine church** with an excavated **mosaic** showing animals listening to music, and the **Greek Orthodox Church of Saint Porphurous** in Gaza's oldest Zaitoun Quarter. The **Great Mosque**, also known as the **Mosque of Omar**, and at the end of Omar al-Mukhtar in the center of Gaza City, is in a 12th century Norman church dedicated to John the Baptist.

SHOPPING

Shops on the way to **Bethlehem** contain ridiculously priced religious shlock, with a little Bethlehem bubbled snow shaker going for $7! In

Bethlehem there are tourist souvenirs on the square, with astonishingly garish, bloodied crucifixes of olive wood and mother of pearl for $150.
Tamimi Ceramics, *Tel. 02-992-0358, Fax 02-992-9253*, sells hand-crafted ceramics in Hebron.

SPORTS & RECREATION

SPNI, *13 Helene Ha'Malka, Jerusalem, Tel. 02-624-4605*, offers a popular Wadi Kelt hike.

Bicycles, *in Jericho*, can be rented from a shop just off the central square and east of the municipal buildings for NIS 2 an hour.

EXCURSIONS & DAY TRIPS

The Alternative Tourism Program in **Beit Sahour**, Tel. *02-674-3921*, is setting up a program to offer a Palestinian experience in lieu of (or along side) the normal sight-seeing trip. Beit Sahour, a small Palestinian village just outside of Jerusalem, would organize things so you could visit and see the town, meet the people, and even volunteer in the community.

They have lectures on topics such as Christian-Islamic Coexistence, Liberation Theology, and the ever popular Taxation. For more info, call Dr. Majed Nassar at the Medical Clinic or Mr. Ghassan Andoni at the Palestinian Center for Rapprochement at the numbers above.

Deir Hanna, up north in the Bet Netofa Valley in Central Galilee and 20 kilometers northwest of the Golani junction, is a small Palestinian village with archaeological remains of its Crusader and Turkish past. In the 17th century, Said al-Omar (Daher al-Omar's brother) used this place as his military base against the Turks, and there are Citadel ruins from this time.

PRACTICAL INFORMATION

- **B'Tselem**, *43 Emek Rafaim, West Jerusalem, Tel. 02-561-7271,* is the Israeli Information Center for Human Rights in the Occupied Territories.
- **Currency**: The **New Israeli Shekel** (NIS) is the most common currency, but US dollars and Jordanian dinars are also generally accepted. There are plenty of money changers around, and there are the banks, as well.
- **Gaza Center for Rights and Law**, *Imam building on Omar al-Mukhtar, Gaza, Tel. 07-686-6287.*
- **Jerusalem Media and Communication Center**, *18 Nashashibi, Sheikh Jarrah, East Jerusalem, Tel. 02-581-9776.*
- **Medical Services**: see Jerusalem.
- **Newspaper**: *The Jerusalem Times*, the independent Palestinian English weekly, is available in the shuk inside the Damascus Gate, and in hotels in East Jerusalem.

- **Palestinian Authority Tourism Office**, *Manger Square, Bethlehem, Tel. 02-674-1581, Fax 02-674-3753*. They're open Monday-Saturday 8am-4pm and provide maps of Bethlehem as well as updated information on the rest of the West Bank.
- **Palestine Human Rights Information Center**, *12 Masa'udi, East Jerusalem, Tel. 02-628-7076*.
- **Police** in **Bethlehem**: *Manger Square, Tel. 02-674-8222;* in **Jericho**, *Tel. 02-992-2521*.
- **Post office** in **Bethlehem**: *next to the tourist office, Tel. 02-674-2668*. It's open Monday-Wednesday, Friday and Saturday 8am-2:30pm, and Thursday 8am-12:30pm, and they have a poste restante section.

21. JORDAN

Jordan is a very different experience from Israel, and wonderful in different ways. There's plenty to see and do there, but as the usual travel problems boil down to time and money, the problem is rarely whether you want to go there, but how to fit in a visit to Jordan, given that you've ended up with less time and/or money than you'd planned on.

The easiest, most hassle-free way to see Jordan is to hop aboard one of the many Israeli tours that have proliferated with the peace process. One day, three days, five days, they deal with the border crossings, transportation, and arrangements. You just shell out the money and sit back, knowing you'll get to see **Petra** and **Jerash**.

Or you can go it alone, for less money, more adventure, and more uncertainty as to whether you'll actually make it to all the places you want to see. Budget tours (you get to the Jordanian side of the border on your own) cost around $160-$185 for two days (one night) and $285-$360 for four days (three nights), compared to a two-day budget trip on your own for $67, and about $110 for four days. Or, alternatively, you can travel to Amman and sign up there with a Jordanian tour of all the major sights for about $140. Your choice, your call, depending mostly on how your situation and preferences tip the scales of time, money, convenience, and experience.

For those opting to travel independent of a tour, there are lots of places to stay for all sorts of tastes and budgets. Listed here are some of the best in different budget categories, but as the tourism industry begins to reap the rewards of recent peace treaties with Israel, more hotels are being built in Petra. As for Amman, more than enough hotels exist already, anxiously awaiting the tourist dollar.

History

Village life in Jordan dates from at least 8000 BCE. Hebrew states developed on the hills west of the Jordan River, while the small states of Edom, Gilead, Moab, and Ammon were settled east of the Jordan River.

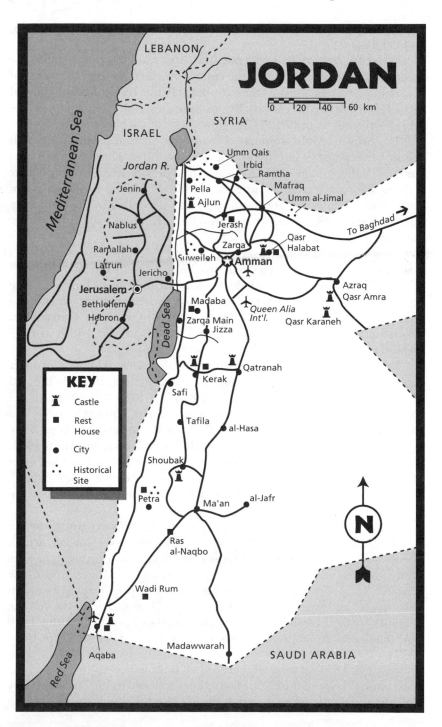

The area was frequently invaded by the Assyrians, Egyptians, Babylonians, and Persians.

In the 4th century BCE, the northern area was incorporated into the kingdom of the Seleucids, but the south was ruled by the Arab tribe of Nabataeans, who established their capital at Petra. The Romans displaced the Seleucids in the 1st century BC, but they weren't able to get past the Petra fortifications until 106 CE.

The Muslim Arabs dominated from the 7th century until the 16th century, except for an interlude of Crusader control. The Ottoman Turks conquered the area in 1517, and after the Turkish defeat in World War I, the territory of Jordan became part of the short-lived Syrian kingdom under Faisal I (later king of Iraq). After Faisal's defeat by French forces in 1920, **Transjordan** was incorporated into Britain's League of Nations' mandate of Palestine.

Transjordan was treated separately from Palestine, however, and its residents were assured that it would not be affected by the establishment of a Jewish homeland. **Abdullah**, Faisal's brother, was chosen to rule Transjordan in 1921. He cooperated closely with the British, who helped create the Arab League. In 1928 a treaty with Britain made Transjordan a constitutional monarchy, and a second treaty with the British in 1946 created the Hashemite Kingdom of Transjordan.

Transjordan opposed the partition of Palestine and joined the other Arab League nations in fighting the new Israeli state in 1948. By the end of the war it occupied a section of West Bank territory designated for the Arabs in the United Nations partition plan. The country's name was changed to Jordan in 1949, and in 1950 it formally annexed the West Bank territory, including Old Jerusalem. Abdullah was assassinated in 1951, and a year later his son Talal was forced to abdicate in favor of Talal's son **Hussein I**. Hussein established greater independence from Britain, especially after 1956, but his relations with the other Arab countries were somewhat strained.

In the **Six Day War** of June 1967, Jordan's forces were routed by the Israelis, who then occupied the West Bank territories. Jordan, which already had many Palestinian refugees, received a new influx. Guerrilla groups among the refugees challenged Hussein's authority and made Jordan a target for Israeli attacks. In 1970 civil war erupted between government and guerrilla forces, but by 1971 Hussein had destroyed the guerrilla bases. Like other Arab states, Jordan condemned the 1979 Egyptian-Israeli peace treaty, breaking diplomatic ties with Egypt from 1979 to 1984.

In 1988, Hussein formally severed all links between Jordan and the West Bank in favor of the PLO. Martial law (imposed in 1967) was virtually abolished in 1991, when a new national charter lifted an old ban on political parties, and multiparty legislative elections were held on November 8, 1993.

Many Jordanians supported the August 1990 Iraqi invasion of Kuwait, and Jordan refused to join the US-led anti-Iraq alliance in the 1991 Persian Gulf War, although Hussein openly broke with Iraq in 1993. Hussein supported the September 1993 Israeli-PLO accord on Palestinian self-rule, and Jordan ended its state of war with Israel on July 25, 1994. The two nations signed a formal peace treaty on Oct. 26, 1994, causing various reactions among the citizens, some of whom are hurrying across the borders to visit previously off-limit sites and others who are clinging to old hatreds.

CURRENCY QUESTIONS?

The Jordanian dinar (JD) is worth about $1.11. Smaller denominations are fils, and there are 1000 fils to the dinar. 10 fils equals a piaster (pt), however, and prices may be labeled or referred to either way, so a gooey pastry may cost 500 fils, or alternately, 50 piasters.

ARRIVALS & DEPARTURES

On Your Own

There are three border crossings between Jordan and Israel. See the *Getting To Israel* section in Chapter 6 for all the times, departure taxes, and other details.

By Tour from Israel

ABC-BTC, *1 Hasoreg, 2nd floor (off Jaffa near Shlomzion), Tel. 02-623-3990, Fax 02-625-7827*, and open Sunday-Thursday 9am-7pm, Friday 9am-1pm offer two-day Petra trips (starting from the Jordan side of the Arava border) for $339 and three-day trips for $439, with a single supplement of $36 a night.

Mazada, *Jerusalem, Tel. 02-623-5777, Fax 02-625-5454, Tel Aviv, Tel. 03-544-4454, Fax 03-546-1928, and Haifa, Tel. 04-862-4440, Fax 04-862-4464*, offers coach service to Amman ($35 one way and $55 round trip) from Tel Aviv, Jerusalem, or Haifa, as well as excursions in Jordan for $160 for a full day.

Neot Hakikar, *Khan Amiel Center, Eilat, Tel. 07-632-6281 Fax 07-632-6297 and 67 Ben Yehuda, Tel Aviv, Tel. 03-520-5858, Fax 03-522-1020*, does two-day Petra trips for $169, leaving from Eilat but not including the Petra entrance fee, and a two-day Spice Route hiking and camel-riding trip from Petra to the Mediterranean Sea for $134.

Galilee Tours, *Jerusalem, Hillel Street, Tel. 02-625-8666*, has more upscale trips leaving from Tel Aviv and Jerusalem. A three-day tour, leaving Thursdays, costs $330 or $390 (for two or three star hotels), and the two-day trip, departing Mondays, is $325 or $350 (with single supplements $27-$39 a night).

ORIENTATION

The Jordan River crossing near Beit She'an lands you near **Irbid** in the north of Jordan. Further north from there is the castle at **Umm Quis**, and to the south is the castle of **Ajlun**. Heading further south in the direction of Amman is the preserved Roman city **Jerash**. Southeast of Jerash is Jordan's capital **Amman**, which is where you'll find yourself if you take the Allenby Bridge crossing.

Southwest of Amman is **Madaba** and **Mount Nebo**, east of Amman are the desert castles **Qasr Amra**, **Qasr Karraneh**, and **Qasr Hallabat**. Way south of Amman, past the castles at **Qairanah**, **Kerak**, and **Shoubak**, is **Petra**. From Petra, **Wadi Rum** is south some more, and **Aqaba** is at the southern point of Jordan, across the Gulf of Aqaba from Israel's Eilat and Egypt's Sinai Peninsula.

GETTING AROUND JORDAN

By Air

Royal Jordanian Airlines operates regular flights between Amman and Aqaba for $85 roundtrip, $42 one way. **Queen Alia International Airport**, *35 kilometers south of Amman, Tel 08-53-333* has buses to and from Abduli bus station, leaving every 30 minutes or so, round the clock, for JD1. There are no *service* to the airport, but there are private taxis, costing JD10.

By Bus

Buses from Amman's **Wa'ahid** station go west and south, while buses from **Abduli** go north and west. There are also minibuses that rev and rock and seem like they're about to go but don't actually get started till they have a full load.

To get to **Petra**, for example, you take the bus (or minibus or service taxi) from Wa'ahid station to Ma'in for JD 3.5 and transfer from there to a Petra-bound minibus for 500 fils (don't believe the taxi drivers swearing that all the buses have left for the day, but they'll take you for . . .). Start the journey early, however, as buses do peter out in the afternoon.

Buses from Amman up north are very cheap, just 450 fils to **Ajlun** and 270 fils to **Jerash**.

JETT Bus, *Jordan Express Tours, Al-Malek al-Hussein Street, Tel. 06-664-146, Fax 06-605-005*, is less than half a mile from the Abduli bus station.

It's a little more expensive, more reliable, and less frequent than other travel options. Buses leave five times daily to **Aqaba** (JD4). The JETT from Amman to **Petra** is JD8.5 (it leaves 6:30am, returns at 6-7am and 3pm, and tickets should be bought days in advance), but they also have a tour bus that includes guide, lunch, horse ride, and round trip transport for JD26.5 (plus Petra entrance). The JETT to the **King Hussein/Allenby Bridge**, departing at 6:30am, is JD6, and there's a JETT to **Cairo**, leaving 7:30am and taking close to 24 hours, for JD48.

By Service Taxi

Pronounced "serveese" with the second syllable stressed, these taxis take you all over for very, very little money. The problem is the routes aren't marked and the tourist office won't make a service taxi route map because, as they put it, they'd prefer to attract the kind of tourists with money to spend. The best thing to do is stay at a hotel with helpful staff who'll be willing to direct you to the right corner. Once there, you stand in the orderly queue and wait your taxi turn.

An average ride, say from the Al-Husseini mosque to the Ministry of Tourism costs 90 fils (or about 13¢) instead of a JD2 taxi ride. Jordanians round up, however–it's considered rude to make exact change.

Jordanian women sometimes pass up their turn in favor of the next service so they don't have to be squeezed in among a car of men–not a bad idea for a lone woman traveler. Women always ride in back, even if they're the first in, but for men it's polite to sit next to the driver if that seat's free.

By Taxi

You can hire them in the street to go anywhere in Jordan, but make sure a price is negotiated before you set out, don't pay in advance, and if you're a woman traveling alone, take a bus instead. If there are any problems make sure to report them; the police take that sort of thing very seriously.

By Car

Hertz, Budget, Avis, and Reliable **rentals** are all readily available in Jordan, so long as you have an international license and major credit card. They cost around JD23-35 a day with unlimited mileage and full insurance, + 7% tax.

Or, you can hire a **guided** (chauffeured) **car** for JD40 for six hours plus JD10 with air conditioning.

AMMAN

High on a steppe at 2,692 feet above sea level, **Amman** lies in a narrow valley with the newer sections built on the surrounding slopes to the nearby plateau. The hills, and the white stones that construct the city, help give a spacious feeling to this city of over 1 million. A commercial as well as administrative center, Amman exports phosphates mined nearby at El Hasa and manufactures textiles and leather goods.

Amman may have been settled as early as the 17th century BCE; it was the biblical city Rabbah (Ammon), and the main city and capital of the Ammonites. As the ancient Greek city Philadelphia, southernmost of the ten cities of the Decapolis, it prospered under the leadership of Ptolemy II Philadelphus (reigning 285-246 BCE) and later under the Roman Empire. The city assumed its current name in the seventh century. It was a small town until it became the capital of Transjordan in 1921, but it now has a population of 1,300,300, about one-third of whom are Palestinians.

Ruins of Ammonite tombs, a Roman theater seating 6,000, an odeon (a small, roofed theater), a citadel, and an acropolis remain, although many of the city's ancient buildings have been destroyed by earthquakes, and Amman was further damaged during the civil fighting between Palestinian guerrillas and the Jordanian Army in 1970 and 1971.

ORIENTATION

Amman, the capital and largest city of Jordan, is located about 40 kilometers northeast of the Dead Sea. There's the Old City near Al Husseini in the east where the working class live, the New City to the west with the richer neighborhoods, and lots of mountains, each like its own city. Amman now sprawls over 19 hills (far more territory than its original seven), making it a complicated city to get to know. It's broken up into *jebels* (hills), and the eight numbered traffic circles (*duwwar*) heading westward are commonly used for directions, addresses, and landmarks.

The **downtown district (Al Balad)** is where the cheap hotels and restaurants are, the money changers, and the commercial district with its suk and gold market. Main streets here such as **King Faisal** and **King Talal** branch off from **Al Husseini Mosque**, and **Prince Mohammed** and **King Hussein** branch off of them. Not far off the northeast is the **Roman Amphitheater** and piazza.

Northwest of the Jebel al Amman slopes is the posh district of **Shmeisani**, home to nice residences and luxury hotels, embassies and Jordanian ministry offices. The **Abduli bus station** and blue-domed **Abduli mosque** (both excellent as landmarks or direction references if you're in a taxi) are on the northern slopes of Jebel al Weibdeh, and there are some quiet neighborhoods and pleasant hotels there, as well as a busy falafel center around the bus depot on main street **King Hussein**.

Khalid Ibn Al Walid runs northwest on Jebel Al Hussein to the **Gamal Abdul Nasser Square**, where Shmeisani starts, across from the Ministry of the Interior. And **Zahran** is another major thoroughfare heading northwest from **second circle**, past the US Embassy and the Inter Continental Hotel to the Ministry of Information at **third circle**, where it veers west. Hussein Bin Ali Street continues north from third circle ending in Shmeisani Junction.

WHERE TO STAY

INTER-CONTINENTAL, *between 2nd and 3rd circle, Tel. 06-641-361, Fax 06-645-217, has singles for JD130, doubles for JD140, and suites that start at JD345.*

With its five star comfort and service, the Inter-Con has been an Amman standby since 1963. The rooms are roomy and pleasant, with a balcony, a nice big desk, phone, TV, etc. Tennis courts, bar, disco (not during Ramadan), and pool available. With restaurants ranging from Indian to Arabic, they have car rentals, tour agencies, and good maps of Amman.

EL YASSMIN, *3rd circle Jebel Amman, Tel. 06-643-216, Fax 06-643-219, suites only (10 of them) for JD120 regular and JD140 executive.*

Also top notch. Recently renovated, El Yassmin is lovely, with artful tiles, ornate chandeliers, and a business center with secretarial services. The rooms are beautiful, and all have cable TV, phone, air conditioning. The coffee shop has marble tables and flowers, and in the summer the garden terrace is open. Fewer services than the Inter-Con, but it's quiet and the staff is eager to please.

THE JERUSALEM HOTEL, *Tel. 06-607-121, Fax 06-689-328, has rooms for JD75 a single, JD90 a double, and JD140-330 (plus 20%) for suites.*

This is a great, opulent sort of place, with 125 rooms. Bell boys walk around in pristine white shirts and red fezzes, and the rooms, along with the standard cable TV, phone, minibar, and tiled bath, have textured walls and rich oriental colors. There's a belly dancer nightclub, a billiard room, and a health club with sauna as well.

AL QASR GARDEN, *Abdilhamd Sharif Street, Shmeisani, Tel. 06-689-671, Fax 06-689-673, is a three-star hotel with 33 rooms for JD40 a single and JD55 a double, plus 20%.*

With restaurant, room service, business center, etc., the rooms all have phone, minibar, and cable TV, plus a pleasant atmosphere and flowery drapes.

CARAVAN HOTEL, *Police College Road, Jebel al-Weibdehm, Tel. 06-661-195, Fax 661-196, has singles for JD18 and doubles for JD24, breakfast included, and prices subject to negotiation when tourism is down, with 10% off to Open Road Guide users.*

Owned by the Canary Hotel people and of the same high quality, the 27 rooms all have bathrooms, cable TV, and phones that can handle international calls. Located in a residential area near the center of the city, they are also near King Abduli Mosque, the Greek Orthodox Church, and a Copt Church. The staff is happy and able to help with information, tour arrangements, you name it. The rooms are nice, with blue polka dot chandeliers and all, but the real piece de resistance is the antique phone switchboard in the dining room.

DOVE HOTEL, *Qurtubah Street (off Zahran between 4th and 5th circles), Tel. 06-697-601, Fax 06-674-676, charges JD18 a single and JD24 a double, (discounted 10% on presentation of Open Road guide), breakfast included and Visa/Mastercard accepted.*

In the high society residential neighborhood near the embassies. Owned by the Canary and Caravan people, they have 27 cheery rooms, with wood beds, phone and TV, and an enormous toilet with bidet. There's a lift that works, and the bar/restaurant has an interesting collection of taxidermy.

CANARY HOTEL, *Karmely Street, Jebel al-Weibdeh, Tel. 06-638-353, Fax 06-654-353, is off Lulliat Ash Sharia near Abduli station. They charge JD16 a single and JD24 a double (prices negotiable, big breakfasts included, credit cards accepted).*

The Canary is that Amman rarity – a hotel on a quiet street that is centrally located. There are 22 rooms, fairly nice with phone, chairs, wardrobe, TV, and big bath (or shower). There are nice details like a lovely floor mosaic at the entrance, and the staff is very helpful. Show your Open Road guide and get 10% off!

NEFERTITI, *26 Al-Jahiz, Al Shmeisani, Tel. 06-603-865, has singles for JD11.55 while doubles are JD14.85.*

The Nefertiti is an anomaly. It's a reasonably priced hotel hiding out in fancy hotel land, just across from the Ambassador and down the street from Al Qasr in Al Shmeisani. They've 21 rooms which are clean and adequate with phone, bathroom, and desk. Some rooms have terraces, and the hotel has a small restaurant.

NEW PARK HOTEL, *King Hussein (opposite the Court), Tel. 06-648-145, Fax 06-648-145, charges JD10 a single, JD14 a double, and JD18 a triple (all plus 10%), visa and mastercard.*

One of the best in this price category, they've been in business for more than 25 years. They have 35 rooms, each with TV, nice wood trim and big green curtains, phone, desk, little balcony, better than usual beds, and big clean bathrooms.

JERUSALEM JEWEL HOTEL, *across from Abduli bus station, next to Zalatino Sweets, 4th floor of a big building, Tel. 06-613-970, Fax 06-619-933, has 18 rooms costing JD10 a single and JD12 a double (plus 10%), no credit cards accepted.*

The rooms are perfectly adequate, with phone, toilet, and shower.

PALACE HOTEL, *King Faisal, Tel. 06-624-327, has singles for JD7, doubles are JD13.*

One and a half blocks from the mosque, it's a tiny step up in class from Cliff Hotel. The Palace has 38 rooms and is an okay place. The rooms all have their own phone and bath, and there's a working elevator.

LORD'S HOTEL, *King Hussein, Tel. 06-654-167, is just up a bit and across the street from Al Qud's. Singles are JD7 and cute (but with shared toilets) and doubles are JD12.*

A bit cleaner than the King Faisal hotels. Rooms have their own shower and toilet, fan and hot water. It's not a bad deal if you want a little nicer than Cliff's.

CLIFF HOTEL, *Prince Mohammed, Downtown, Tel. 06-624-273, Fax 06-638-078, has single rooms costing JD6, doubles are JD8, and triples are JD9, the summer roof beds are JD2, the hot shower is 500 fils.*

The budget best. Abu Suleiman runs the place, and he is one of the sweetest, most helpful old men around. There are 19 rooms, each with big creaky bed, wardrobe, table, and sink, and some with fans. It's kept fairly clean though the place retains a bit of dive ambiance. Right in the center of things, it's convenient, noisy, and very popular, so reservations come in handy. Abu Suleiman's help is priceless, as he'll take the time to explain how to get around Amman, which service taxi to take where, and how to find it.

There are tons of other cheap hotels in the neighborhood on Faisal if the Cliff is full and you need a room.

BAGDAD GRAND, *King Faisal, Tel. 06-625-433, is not bad, with singles for JD5 and doubles for JD6.*

There are Asian toilets, but the rooms are fairly clean, the beds all have thick comforters in winter, and some rooms have balconies. The staff if friendly though their English is so-so.

WHERE TO EAT

AL QUDS RESTAURANT, *Al-Malek al-Hussein Street, Tel. 06-630-168,* downtown, is good quality. You can get a bowl of spinach, beans, lamb, and rice and other authentic Jordanian plates for JD1.5 -JD2.2. Just up King Hussein past the yellow awning of the sweets shop, it's very popular with locals.

For falafel and shwarma, go to **King Talal** (take a left off King Faisal).

The **alley** *across from Cliff Hotel* has cheap (250 fils), simple, good food such as *um subanah* with hummus, fuul, tehina, chili, and olive oil.

In front of the **Roman Amphitheater** is an outdoor restaurant/coffee shop, just next to the green and with a full view of the theater.

SEEING THE SIGHTS

Most travelers don't stay in Amman longer than it takes to get a good meal and find the bus to somewhere else, but if you spend some time here there are neighborhoods to wander around, the **Citadel** to see, and a hill with ruins of the **Temple of Hercules**. The **Archaeological Museum**, *Tel. 06-638-795*, is up there, with finds from ancient sites across Jordan. Open Monday, Wednesday, Thursday, Saturday 9am-5pm, Friday 10am-4pm, it costs JD2. At the foot of the Citadel, is the old **Roman amphitheater**, open 9am-5:30pm, free of charge, and with guards who are willing to show you around and "tell you everything" for JD3.

Off the amphitheater is the **Traditional Jewels and Costumes Museum**, *Tel. 06-651-760*, open Wednesday-Monday 8am-5pm (9am-4pm during Ramadan) and costing JD1. It has great mosaics from Jerash and Madaba as well as tribal clothing, jewelry, and Bedouin stones (plus explanations of their charms). On the other side of the amphitheater is the **Folklore Museum**, *Tel. 06-651-742*, costing JD1. It's got a Bedouin tent, camels, and the like but though they charge the same, it's less interesting the Traditional Jewels and Costumes.

SHOPPING

The **gold market** (*souq dahab*) downtown is quite a scene, whether you're shopping for jewelry or not. Gleaming yellow metal, mostly 18k-21k, is displayed in some 50-60 shops all selling the same stuff. Appreciated for its status, ornamental, and monetary values, gold is big business in Jordan. And unlike anywhere else in Jordan, the wares have fixed prices, based solely on weight. There are also lots of **spice** and **herb** stores with aromatic bins of oriental powders and leaves. Saffron is a good buy, as are mixes special to the region.

EXCURSIONS & DAY TRIPS

Just 51 kilometers and an hour's drive north of Amman, **Jerash** (formerly Gerasa) is one of the best preserved Roman outposts in the world, open daily 7:30am until dark and JD2 is the entrance fee. Known as the Pompeii of the East for its amazing state of preservation, the triple-arched gateway that greets your arrival was built to honor Emperor Hadrian's arrival in 129 CE. You could spend a half day, a full day, or more (depending on your Archaeological interest) exploring the remains of settlements from the Bronze and Iron Ages, Hellenistic, Roman, Byzantine, Umayyad, and Abbasid periods. The Colonnades Street is renowned, the Cathedral Gate and South Theater are impressive, and there's much more to see as well. There used to be nightly **sound and light shows** in the summer, but the **Jerash Festival of Culture and Arts** is still held each July. Their **Visitors Information Center**, *400 meters north of the Triumphal Arch, 04-451-272*, lies west of the main road and is open daily 8am-6:30pm in summer and 8am-5pm in winter.

The **Decapolis**, meaning ten cities in Greek, referred to the ten Graeco-Roman cities in Northern Jordan, Syria, and Palestine. Jerash was one, and **Pella** was another. While not as impressive as Jerash, it's one of the more important Archaeological sites to be discovered in Jordan. Most of the finds date from the Roman, Byzantine, and Islamic periods (300s-1500s CE), but there are remains from settlements are far back as Neolithic and Mesolithic (10,000-3,000 BCE) as well, and excavations are still going on. Further north, **Umm Qais** (which used to be Gadara) is another archaeological site. The **Ottoman Governor's house** has been restored and opened as a museum, and the views (on a clear day) take in the Jordan Valley, Sea of Galilee, and Golan Heights.

Abila is northeast and more rural, with Byzantine churches, Roman temples, and early mosques among olive groves and wheat fields. Another Decapolis city is **Umm el Jimal**, full of black basalt remains of houses, churches, and Roman barracks. Closer to Amman is **Iraz el Amir**, a site dating back to the second century BCE where you can visit a restored Hellenistic villa.

The Bible's Medeba is today's **Madaba**, a small town just 30 kilometers south of Amman. There are a number of ruins in this ancient town, but it's the **Greek Orthodox Church of Saint George** and its earliest surviving mosaic map of the Holy Land (done around 560 CE) that people come here to see. Ten kilometers west is **Mount Nebo**. From Nebo's hilly slopes you can see Jerusalem's spires (on a clear day, that is), but people don't come for the views, they come because it's here that Moses is believed to be buried. Within a 1933 Franciscan building lie the ruins of the 4th and 6th century church and its beautiful mosaics. Southeast of Madaba (about 30 kilometers) is **Umm er Rasas**, a walled settlement with a Byzantine tower used by early monks seeking solitude. Archaeologists there have uncovered the amazing mosaic floor of the **Church of Saint Stephen**, done in the Umayyad era, with Jordanian, Palestinian, and Egyptian city plans.

Less than 40 kilometers south of Madaba is **Mukawir**, which used to be Machaerus. This fortress, built by Herod the Great and passed on to his son Herod Antipas, is where John the Baptist was imprisoned and where his bloody head was later presented to Salome after her many-veiled dance.

Jordan's **desert castles**, a collection of forts, towers, and caravan inns, dot the arid steppes of eastern Jordan and the central hills, but no two are alike. The medieval **Kerak** and **Shobak** castles along the King's Highway are 12th century Crusader fortresses with the lofty views the Crusaders prized. **Habees** and **Wu'eira**, also Crusader castle ruins, are down by Nabataean Petra.

Up north, **Ajlun castle** (Qal'at Al-Rabad), 23 kilometers west of Jerash is a wonderful example of 12th century Arab/Islamic military architecture. Saladin's retort to Belvoir, he used it for his base against the Crusaders in his successful 1189 campaign to drive them from Jordan. Now it's a rocky old maze of steps, rooms, and paths, and for JD1 from 8am-7pm in summer and 8am-5pm in winter you're welcome to get lost in the stony twists and turns and to see the view of the green stubbled hills from the top. Service taxis (minibuses) ply the steep uphill grade for 50 fils, and taxis will take you one way for 500 fils.

Qasr Amra baths stand out among the desert plains with its zodiac dome and fresco art, while **Qasr Kharanah** juts up imposingly ominous. **Qasr Hallabat** was a Roman fort that was turned by the Umayyad sultans into a residential palace, and **Qasr Mushatta** (never quite completed) sprawls out with vaulted brick. The Roman/Medieval Islamic fort at **Azraq** is known for its black basalt, and the **Al Sayad Hotel**, *06-647-611*, there has a fine restaurant and garden, while **Qasr Tuba**, made of fire-baked brick, looms massive but unfinished.

And by the **Dead Sea**, spas offer the same sort of treatments and fun as the Dead Sea spas on the Israeli side.

PRACTICAL INFORMATION

- **American Culture Center**, *American Embassy building, Tel. 06-820-101, Fax 06-813-759*, is open Sunday-Thursday 8am-4pm.
- **Bookstores**: **University Bookstore**, *Jebel al Weibdeh near Khalaf Circle, Tel. 06-636-339*, has English books on Jordanian archaeology. The **Marriot** and **Intercontinental** also have book stores with a few English books.
- **Car Rentals**: **Avis**, *Tel. 06-699-420, Fax 06-819-779*; **Budget**, *Tel. 06-698-131, Fax 06-673-312*; **Reliable**, *Tel. 06-819-676*.
- **Currency**: **Al Churuk** (an area about 50 meters from the Cliff Hotel) is good for money changers who will give better deals than the banks, though you need to be wary with the calculations because they may well try to swindle you.

- **Department of Antiquity**, *on Zahran a little past the Third Circle, Tel. 06-644-482*, has a library, and maps highlighting archaeological sites, and they're open Saturday-Thursday 8am-2pm.
- **Egyptian Embassy**, *Zahran Street between second and third circles, Tel. 06-605-175*, just down from the US Embassy, is open Saturday-Thursday 9am-3pm.
- **Holidays**: during **Ramadan** offices and museums generally open an hour later and close an hour earlier. Tourist restaurants (like those in big hotels) are open during the day, but local restaurants don't open for business till dusk. Also, it's against the law for Jordanians to break Ramadan in public, so you need to be sensitive with your eating and drinking and not be ostentatious about it. It's legal for you, as visitor, to eat and drink, but it's hard on them. **November 14th** is the King's Birthday, and there is much celebration and hoopla.
- **Hospitals: Hussein Medical Center**, *Mecca Street, Tel. 06-813-832*; **Shmeisani Hospital**, *Shmeisani, Tel. 06-607-431*.
- **Medical Emergencies**: *call Tel. 06-621-111*, or for **ambulances** specifically *call Tel. 193*. American citizens can call the **24 hour embassy hotline**, *Tel. 06-820-101*, for police or ambulance help.
- **The Ministry of Tourism**, *Zahran Street near the third circle, Tel. 06-642-311, 06-648-465*, is open Saturday-Thursday 8am-2pm. You can get a map of Jordan from them, but they were out of Amman maps when I visited and seemed doubtful about ordering more, and if they do, they're going to start charging for them. Friendlier and more convenient is the desk at the Inter Continental, a good place for information and maps. There's also a Tourist Office in the airport.
- **Pharmacies: As-Salam**, *downtown, Tel. 06-636-730*, **Firas**, *near Abduli bus station, Tel. 06-661-912*, and **Deema**, *near Wahadat, Tel 06-787-040*. **Jacob's Pharmacy**, *near third circle, Tel. 06-644-945*, is open every day, 24 hours a day.
- **Police**: *call Tel. 192* or *Tel. 06-621-111*.
- **Post Office**, *Prince Mohammed Street, Tel. Tel. 121 for information*, is open Saturday-Thursday 8am-7pm, Friday 8am-4pm, and has a poste restante.
- **Telephones**: Jordan's code is *962*, Petra's and Aqaba's code is *3*, and Amman's area code is *6* (put a 0 before the area code if dialing from within Jordan, and remove the prefix entirely if calling from within that city).
- **Tourist Agencies**: In **Amman**, **Bisharat Tours**, *Hotel Inter-Continental, Tel. 06-641-350, Fax 06-659-330*, arranges any type of guided tour you may want–they're trustworthy, and exceptionally helpful.
- **US Embassy**, *off Zahran Street between second and third circles, Tel. 06-820-101, Fax 06-813-759*, is just down from the Egypt Embassy. It's open

Sunday-Thursday 8am-4pm and closed all Jordanian and most American holidays.

PETRA

Petra, located in a mountain basin 262 kilometers south of Amman, was the capital of the ancient Arabic kingdom of Nabataea from the fourth century BCE to the second century CE. Walled in by towering rocks except for a deep, narrow cleft (called a *siq*) and, in the Nabataean period, one of the few locations in the vicinity with an ample supply of pure water, it was a major city on the caravan trade route from southern Arabia. Petra was subject to strong Hellenistic cultural influence. It was conquered by Trajan in CE 106 and became part of the Roman province of Arabia. Subsequently declining in economic importance, Petra was forgotten until its ruins were identified in 1812 by the Swiss explorer Johann Ludwig Burckhardt. Petra is now a major Archaeological and tourist site, famous for its temples and tombs cut from surrounding cliffs.

So much hype surrounds Petra, the famed "rose-red city half as old as time," it's easy to fear a let-down, yet the place actually exceeds expectations. It truly is amazing and wonderful and all that the glossy brochures say.

ORIENTATION

Wadi Mussa, the closest town to Petra, is a few kilometers away. This is where the minibuses arrive and leave from, and where most of the hotels are clustered. They generally provide transport to and from Petra, however, and there is a grocery store, a few restaurants, and the other joys of a small Jordanian town.

ARRIVALS & DEPARTURES

From Petra to **Wadi Rum** there's a minibus at 6:30am for JD2, but in winter there aren't always enough passengers to warrant it, in which case taxis will take you for JD15-20. From Petra to **Aqaba** is JD3.

The JETT from **Amman** to Petra is JD8.5 (it leaves 6:30am and reservations are a good idea, returns at 6-7am and 3pm), but they also have a tour bus that includes guide, lunch, horse ride, and transport for JD26.5 (plus Petra entrance).

WHERE TO STAY

There's no camping allowed in Petra any more, and when you climb into some of the higher caves and see the rubbish left behind you understand why. Bedouins may offer lodging in their village ("do you need to spend the night with a Bedouin?) for JD5 or less, negotiable. There are a few hotels more than these but they aren't worth your time or money.

TAYBET ZAMAN, *up in the hills, just six miles from Petra, Tel. 03-215-0111, Fax 03-215-0101, offers singles for JD100 and doubles for JD120.*

The most remarkable hotel in all of Jordan, there are 100 rooms in this unique restored village (opened June '94). If you can afford the rates for a night in paradise, stay here be all means, because it's like no other hotel you've ever seen. And if you want more, the suites (King Hussein stayed here for his birthday) are JD380, with copper and weavings on the walls, cushions and rugs over the stone floor. The lobby greets you with cold stone walls and arches, warm colorful Bedouin rugs, brass wall sconces, bubbling hookahs, and assorted touches of class. You've entered another world.

This was a 200-year-old Arabic sandstone village that had fallen on hard times, and was at Queen Noor's behest, renovated and restored. They did a superb job; it manages to retain the aura of the traditional village it was while at the same time exude immaculate luxury, with all the modern conveniences surreptitiously included. The rooms keep the traditional styles, shapes, and colors, while TVs and phones lurk in niches, available but not intrusive. The tile tubs are recessed in the bathrooms, and hair blowers hang from pristine white plaster walls.

And as if the cobbled village paths and restored rooms weren't enough, there's the Turkish bath. Marble sitting rooms, stone lintels, and colored glass skylights imbue the steamy rooms with Oriental ambiance. The swimming pool's finished, and the gym's up and running, and the bar is cozy, tasteful and just dim enough. The main restaurant, Sahtain, is breathtakingly beautiful, and the food isn't too shoddy either. There's free shuttle service to and from Petra, but beware the tricky fogs of winter. It shrouds Taybet Zaman in extra beauty, but it makes driving treacherous.

PETRA FORUM HOTEL, *overlooking Petra, Tel. 03-215-6266, Fax 03-215-6977, singles are JD80, doubles are JD 90, and triples are JD115, all plus 20%.*

A big modern structure with 148 rooms, a nice pool overlooking the mountains, and standard rooms with everything in good shape, this is the hotel of choice for overnighting tours, and the parking lot is frequently packed full of buses.

THE PETRA HOTEL AND REST HOUSE, *Tel. 03-215-6014, Fax 03-215-6686, charges JD30-40 a single and JD60-72 a double, including half board and tax, all credit cards accepted.*

There are 69 rooms that are very, very clean and modern with lovely big balcony terraces overlooking Petra, and a fridge, sofa, and bathroom.

There's an old wing, and a new wing, and you're as close to Petra's entrance as you can get. The corridors are long, clean and pink, and the cave bar outside is open at night.

EL GEE, *Wadi Mussa, Tel. 03-215-6701, Fax 03-215-6701, costs JD25 a single, JD35 a double, breakfast included. They usually give student discounts.* Relatively new, they have 14 pleasant rooms. Right in town with a Petra view and colorful Bedouin weave stair runners, the rooms all have TVs and clean bathrooms.

AL-RASHID, *downtown, Wadi Mussa, Tel. 03-215-6800, Fax 03-215-6801, charges JD8 a single and JD10 a double, breakfast included, plus 10%.* The Al-Rashid has 14 rooms. The entrance is grotty but the rooms are cheery and clean, there's free transport to Petra, and the staff is friendly.

AL-ANBAT HOTEL, *Wadi Mussa, Tel. 03-215-6265, Fax 03-215-6888, provides singles for JD 7 and doubles for JD10, breakfast included, and they offer half board for an extra 4JD each. In summer there's camping for JD2, for students there's a dorm for JD4.*

Rooms are basic, with toilet, heat, and hot shower. Lovely carpets everywhere, and the rooms are spiffed up but there are flaws. There are shiny new pink toilets, for example, but the seat may be missing. Still and all, it's a notch better than Mussa Spring. They show *Indiana Jones* and *Lawrence of Arabia* movies nightly, and offer free transport to Petra.

MUSSA SPRING HOTEL, *Wadi Mussa, Tel. 03-215-6310, Fax 03-215-6910, charges JD5 a single, JD 8 a double (16 with bath), JD 4 for a dorm bed, and camping in summer is JD2.*

Mussa Spring was one of the first budget hotels here, and is the arch competitor of Al-Anbat. They both go for the same low-budget traveler, and both claim the other is the copy-cat. They offer free transport to Petra at 6-7am and return at 5pm, and buffet for JD3. The private rooms are clean with facilities, table and wardrobe, the dorms are okay. They show movies at night, and cater to a young crowd.

PENSION ATWAYZI, *Wadi Mussa, Tel. 03-215-6423, charges just JD4 per person (but no one will be turned away for lack of money).*

Run by Atif Abbas Mohammed Atwayzi, this is the cheapest lodging in town. Up a hill, this is a friendly if disorganized hostel. Some rooms have beds, some have cushions, and there's a room for couples. There's a washing machine for you to use, as well. Look for the Pension Atwayzi sign, or call Atwayzi and he'll pick you up.

WHERE TO EAT

Aside from half board at your hotel or hotel buffets, there are some restaurants in Wadi Mussa.

WADI PETRA TOURIST RESTAURANT, *next to Obelisk Circle, Wadi Mussa, Tel. 03-215-6749*, is open 8am-midnight and the prices are reasonable. Breakfasts are JD.3-1.5, and entrees are JD1.5-3.5. There's a wide variety of dishes and it's a festive place.

FLOWER RESTAURANT *on the roundabout, Wadi Mussa,* is also popular, and it has cheaper than usual prices.

SEEING THE SIGHTS

Walking down the sheer, narrow walls of the siq, you dodge Bedouins and the horses and camels they keep trying to get you to ride ("You get on the horse and then I'll get on behind you and take the ropes and then you can forget everything" was one of the best lines). But exiting the canyon into the bright plaza facing **The Treasury** (*el Khazneh*), is really special. Nearly 140 feet high and 90 feet wide, it's all carved right out of the side of the mountain. The **Monastery** up the steps after the amphitheater is also impressive.

And from the **Urn Tombs** you get a wonderful view of the whole shebang. Back down one flight, the colors in the **Nabataean Tombs** are outstanding, with reds and blacks and yellow stripes and swirls. The tradesmen and hotel owners of the town get a bit tedious with their disgust over how few days you're planning on staying, but the fact is you could easily spend a number of days wandering about the temples and tombs, theaters and baths, reservoirs, and red dusty rocky trails up among the mountains without seeing it all or getting bored.

The government thinks so too, and as incentive to get you to stay longer, their outrageously expensive entrance fee (JD20 for one day) is JD25 for two days, and just JD30 for three days (children under 12 are JD12.5 for one day, half price for more). The site is open daily 7am-4pm in winter, 6am-6pm in summer, and the gate closes at 7pm. They usually have maps to distribute, but if they're out you can buy one from the kiosk.

NIGHTLIFE & ENTERTAINMENT

There are movies at the **Mussa Spring** and the **Al-Anbat**, and bars at the larger hotels.

SHOPPING

There are a zillion stands selling little bottles filled with multi-colored Petra sands in a variety of designs.

SPORTS & RECREATION

Hiking in Petra is the main sport. Take plenty of water, and prepare for sore calves.

You can hire a guide for a two-hour tour for JD8, and for a whole day it's JD9. To go by **horse**, it's JD5 for the guide, JD7 for the horse and another for the guide's horse as well, so if there are two of you, it'll cost you JD26 all told. And if you're tired and don't feel like straddling Silver or Indiana Jones (the two most popular horse names) you can get in a **horse-pulled cart** for JD14 (or JD8 per person, for two).

You can also arrange (or be talked into) a **camel ride** for JD1 or so.

You can see Wadi Rum from a hot air balloon, an interesting alternative to the usual jeep or camel. Call **Balloons Over Jordan**, *Tel. 06-685-123, or in Amman, Tel. 03-316-335*, for bookings and info.

EXCURSIONS & DAY TRIPS

Not far from Petra (a mere 15 minute drive) is the 8,000-year-old excavated Stone Age villages of **Beidha** and **Basta**. While it's interesting to know that people lived there that long ago, the sites themselves aren't really that spectacular.

And then there's **Wadi Rum**. This evocative stretch of desert is where much of *Lawrence of Arabia* was filmed (for this reason the movie is shown nearly nightly at hostels in Wadi Mussa, along with *Indiana Jones and the Temple of Doom* for its ride down the Petra *siq*), and it's also where T. E. Lawrence based himself during the Arab Revolt. It's certainly a beautiful spot, and some find it downright religious (while others find it a bit out of the way and maybe a waste of time).

Weathered sandstone mountains rise out of white and pink desert sands, offering sheer cliffs for climbers, mountain trails to trek, and open landscape ripe for jeep or Land Rover exploration (bring enough gas). The Bedouin tribes who've lived there for generations will be happy to put you up overnight in their tents, but expect to pay around JD5 or so. There's a **police station** there as well, supplied with the traditional camel mounts.

PRACTICAL INFORMATION

In the same office complex where you purchase your Petra entrance tickets there's an **Arab bank** and a **souvenir shop** with rather expensive mementos.

There's also a **police office** across the way.

AQABA

Aqaba, Jordan's only port, is now a city of 46,000. Settled in ancient times, Aqaba experienced rapid growth in the 1980s when it became the leading port for Iraqi imports. Aqaba's economy was devastated by the 1990-91 Persian Gulf War crisis, when ships headed there were delayed or rerouted by Allied navies, and it still hasn't quite recovered.

Yes, there's a museum at the house of Sharif Hussein bin Ali, great grandfather of King Hussein, and yes, **Aqaba Castle** was built by the Mamluk Sultan Qansawh el Ghawri at the beginning of the 16th century, and there's even an archaeological excavation of old Aqaba dating back to Roman times at Ayla, but the finest treasures are to be seen under water through a snorkel mask. If you aren't an underwater enthusiast, chances are Aqaba won't thrill you, and it may not even if you do love to swim.

Some claim the tourist industry has had a relaxing effect on the Jordanian character, making Aqaba locals more tolerant and accepting of Western dress (or lack thereof). True, tourism has made an impact, but not necessarily a laudable one. The beach town dress code of shorts and bathing suits has upped the slime factor to far beyond anything you'll experience elsewhere in Jordan, where most people are kind and generous, and respect is a national virtue. But not in Aqaba. Here practice has led to expectation, and many hungry wolf locals look at foreign woman (even ones dressed exceedingly modestly) with bikini eyes. Take care, if you happen to be female, in Aqaba.

ORIENTATION

Aqaba is at the southern tip of Jordan on the Gulf of Aqaba, an arm of the Red Sea. It borders Israel to the west, Saudi Arabia to the south, and Egypt's Sinai just across the Gulf.

In Aqaba, directions go by landmark rather than by street names. The post office and the **Corniche** strand along the sea are the main navigational aids. Most of the tourist-oriented hotels and shops are along the Corniche, the road running along the Gulf of Aqaba coast, while the town center's mosque, post office, and **Haya Traffic Circle** form the hub of downtown restaurants, hospital, pharmacy, bank, cheap dives, and such.

ARRIVALS & DEPARTURES

By Air

Royal Jordanian Airlines, *Holiday Hotel International, Tel. 03-314-477*, operates regular flights between Amman and Aqaba for JD44 roundtrip, JD22 one way.

By Bus

To get to Petra it costs JD3. The **JETT** office, *Tel. 03-315-222*, is on the Corniche a bit past the Miramar, and you can buy a ticket for ferry and bus to Cairo for $45.

By Ferry

For ferries to Egypt and information on the Eilat border, see *Getting To Israel* in Chapter 6.

GETTING AROUND TOWN

There's by foot, there's taxi, and there's minibus depending on your destination, your stamina, and your wallet.

WHERE TO STAY

There are lots of hotels in Aqaba, but few of them are places you'd care to spend the night. Tourism has really been stuck in a bad rut for some years, and one unfortunate result is that hotels don't have the funds to do the maintenance and upkeep they need, so the seams show more and more, making it increasingly difficult to attract the tourists, and so it goes.

The hotels below are somewhat better than the Aqaba average:

THE AQABA GULF, *on the Corniche to the north of town, Tel. 03-316-636, Fax 03-318-246, they charge $70 a single and $90 a double, all plus 20%, but off-season bargaining is productive.*

Aqaba's only hotel with a four-star rating, they've 154 rooms. Though the sea views are fine, the rooms comfortable, and the beach handy, it hasn't the charm or touches of elegance you'll find at the Alcazar for less.

THE ALCAZAR HOTEL, *Tel. 03-314-131, Fax 03-314-133, has singles for JD40 and doubles JD55, including buffet breakfast and tax (but rates are negotiable, depending on the season).*

Far and away the nicest and best of the Aqaba hotels. A palm tree garden with red bougainvillea-draped entrance welcomes you, and the lobby is done in traditional Arabic design with tiles and key-shaped arches. There's a lovely outside terrace with Bedouin *dewan* (hubble bubble area) and good Arabic tea and coffee served by guys in fancy dress. The 132 rooms are nice and big, all have little balconies, bathroom with shower, etc., but they're all different, with varying decors and personalities.

They've a pool, and access to the Aqua Marina Beach free of charge, though they're working on opening their own private section of South Beach. They offer a five-day PADI course ($350 including everything), and lead diving tours. They also have a Beni Hana-style Teppanyaki Restaurant and the coziest snooker bar (The Dolphin Pub) in Aqaba. For guests and members only–they regulate the traffic to minimize the local sleaze factor. There are lots of other 3-star hotels in the same area between downtown and the beach, but none come close to comparing in quality, and their prices are the same or higher.

AL-SHUALA HOTEL, *Raghadan Street, Tel. 03-315-153, Fax 03-315-160, charges JD20 a single and JD28 a double (plus 10%, breakfast included).*

A fine mid-range option, there are 60 rooms, an elevator, and the rooms (with phone, TV, air conditioning, and fridge) have balconies facing the sea. And the bathrooms are clean, though the hallway carpets are a bilious green. It's in town center, a block up from the Corniche, not far from Qasr Al Nile.

THE PALM BEACH HOTEL, *on the Corniche (its main attraction), Tel. 03-313-551, Fax 03-313-551, has single suites for JD22, doubles for JD26 and triples for JD28.5 (plus 10%, and no credit cards accepted).*

The rooms are cheery with big beds and white walls, phone, TV, and fridge ,and the bathrooms are clean enough. It's definitely not first class, but if being right on the beach (they have a small private one) is important to you, this is an option.

NAIROUKH HOTEL I, *next to the Red Sea Hotel, Tel. 03-319-284, Fax 03-319-285, charges JD12 a single and JD18 a double.*

Not a bad choice. There are 20 rooms, all with bathroom, TV, phone, minibar, and air conditioning, and breakfast is JD2 extra. The hotel provides a minibus to the beach and the airport, discount vouchers to Aqaba Hotel Beach (1 dinar off JD2.5). The rooms are clean, with festive red trim on white formica furniture, and there's the all-important view of the sea as well. The hall carpets are grotty, but it is a budget place, and the staff is friendly and helpful.

RED SEA HOTEL, *one block back from the main street, near the post office, Tel/Fax 03-312-156, offers rooms from JD5-12, depending on style of toilet and whether the room has air conditioning or a TV.*

The Red Sea features 31 rooms managed by a great old man in a red dish towel turban. All rooms have windows with sea views, and the more expensive one come with TV and phone, nice beds, and big bathrooms. The rooms are plain, with shower and Arabic style toilet, but the prices are hard to beat.

JORDAN FLOWERS HOTEL, *next door to Jerusalem Hotel, Tel. 03-314-377, charges JD6 for singles and JD8 for doubles with ceiling fans, JD10 for singles, JD12 for doubles with air conditioning, and has no dorm rooms.*

In quality it's on a par with Jerusalem Hotel.

JERUSALEM HOTEL, *town center, Tel. 03-314-815, has singles for JD5, doubles for JD7, and dorm beds for JD1, but it varies depending on how hard times are.*

The rooms are pretty scungy, and some look over the sea.

NATIONAL TOURISTIC CAMP, *south of the city, Tel. 03-316-750, charges JD1 to camp.*

This is the only place for camping. People also come here to swim for JD.500. There's a cafeteria, shower, sun shelters, and toilet facilities, but no snorkel equipment rentals.

WHERE TO EAT

For good cheap **falafel** (10 fils a piece) and **shwarma** (250 fils) go to the stalls behind the post office.

ALI BABA, *down from the Shuala Hotel, across from the Mosque, Tel. 03-313-901*, is where everyone directs you to go, but the prices are high and some locals say it's a rip off. It's open 7am-midnight or 1am, and is usually packed.

ATA ALI, *next to Ali Baba, Tel. 03-315-200*, is popular for desserts and sweets. There's seating outside or upstairs, and the gooey treats are pretty good.

SEEING THE SIGHTS

Aqaba Museum is *down by the Aqaba Castle*, which was built by the Mamluk Sultan Qansawh el Ghawri at the beginning of the 16th century. Open Wednesday-Monday 8am-1pm and 3-5pm with JD1 admission.

The archaeological excavation of old Aqaba dating back to Roman times is at **Ayla**, *near the Miramar Hotel*.

NIGHTLIFE & ENTERTAINMENT

The big hotels have bars, discos, and belly dancing. If you're bored day or night in Aqaba you could go to the **Bedouin Tent** across from the Holiday Hotel on the Corniche. Here they serve Arabic coffee or mint tea for JD1. You can smoke the sheesha pipe, have your picture taken while wearing Bedouin garb, visit the pen of goats and pigeons, and listen to their night music.

Or better yet, go to the **Dolphin Pub** in the Alcazar and play a game of snooker. The Jordanians, however, are more apt to hang out at Ata Ali and linger over dessert.

SPORTS & RECREATION

The **public beach**, free and fairly clean, is near the Ayla excavations and the Miramar Hotel.

Aqaba offers lots of opportunities for **snorkeling** and **scuba diving** in the Gulf of Aqaba. The water is clear, the fish are brilliant, and there's nothing much else to do.

Sea Star, *Alcazar Hotel, Tel. 03-314-131, Fax 03-314-133*, teaches five-day PADI and BS-AC certified diving courses for $350, including everything. If you are already certified they rent equipment and lead a number of great dives.

AquaMarina Hotel Diving Club, *Tel. 03-316-250, Fax 03-314-271*, rents diving equipment, runs diving tours, teaches a PADI course, takes you snorkeling from their boat, and has a variety of other water activities such as water skiing, kayaking, and wind surfing. They also lead trips to Wadi Rum for JD38.5.

There's good snorkeling on the **South Coast** from Aqaba. You can go by taxi or minibus from in front of the castle for 200-300 fils.

Royal Diving Center, *South Beach, Tel. 03-317-035*, is a scuba and snorkel center. They have four-day scuba courses for JD150 (plus JD15 for the certificate). They offer beach dives for JD10, and snorkel equipment plus entry to their beach costs JD5. They're on the **Yemeniyyeh Reef**, purportedly one of the best for coral reefs and fish colonies around.

Marine Science Station, *South Beach, Tel. 03-315-145*, has an aquarium and is open Saturday-Wednesday 8am-5pm and it costs JD1 to enter. Taxis here cost JD3.

Royal Yacht Club, *Tel. 03-312-900*, is open daily 9am-1pm.

Aqaba has a **Royal Horse Riding Club**, *Kings Boulevard, Tel. 03-318-100*, is open 9am-5pm daily, and costs JD4 per half hour.

EXCURSIONS & DAY TRIPS

You can go to **Wadi Rum** from Aqaba—Aquamarine, *Tel. 03-316-250*, also leads trip to Wadi Rum for JD38.5. See the excursions from Petra section for more. There are also lots of trips (organized by the many Aqaba hotels) to **Pharoah's Island**, *Jaziret Far'aun* in Arabic. It's in the Gulf of Aqaba, seven kilometers offshore and eight kilometers from Taba, takes 45 minutes by boat, and features swimming, snorkeling, diving, and the ruins of a Saladin citadel and mosque. **Aquamarine Hotel**, *Tel. 03-316-250*, operates full-day trips there for JD20.

PRACTICAL INFORMATION

• **Aqaba Visitor's Center**, *in the castle and museum complex by the water, Tel. 03-313-363*, is open daily 8am-2pm, and has maps.
• **Book Stores**: **Yamani Bookshop** and **Redwan Library**, *across from the post office, Tel. 03-313-704*, are right next to each other. Both have books and newspapers in English.
• **Currency**: **American Express**, *downhill from the post office on your first left, Tel. 03-313-757*, changes money and holds mail for anyone. Banks will change money, of course, with a JD5 commission on traveler's checks, but there are also some money change kiosks around. There's **Kamal**, *Tel. 03-312-361*, **Freh**, *Tel. 03-314-844*, **Kabariti**, *Tel. 03-314-895*, **Al-Janoub**, *Tel. 03-315-692*, and **Gulf**, *Tel. 03-312-313*.
• **Emergency Medical Help**: *Tel. 193*.
• **Fire Department**: *Tel. 03-314-222*.
• **Holidays**: during **Ramadan** offices and museums generally open an hour later and close an hour earlier. Tourist restaurants (like those in big hotels) are open during the day, but local restaurants don't open for business till dusk. Also, it's against the law for Jordanians to break

Ramadan in public, so you need to be sensitive with your eating and drinking and not be ostentatious about it. It's legal for you, as visitor, to eat and drink, but it's hard on them. **November 14th** is the King's Birthday, and there is much celebration and hoopla. Aqaba has lots of special water contests on that day.

• **Medical: Princess Haya Hospital**, *near the post office, Tel. 03-314-111*, is a fine hospital, and it's fully equipped with a decompression chamber for divers.

• **Pharmacies: Al-Khayat**, *Tel. 03-312-091*, **Nader**, *Tel. 03-315-522*, **Zahi**, *Tel. 03-316-455*, **Aqaba**, *Tel. 03-312-237*, **Tbaileh**, *Tel. 03-315-050*, **Jerusalem**, *Tel. 03-314-454*, and **Al-Ahateh**, *Tel. 03-315-322*.

• **Police:** *Tel. 03-313-411.*

• **Telephones**: Jordan's code is 962, Petra's and Aqaba's code is 3, and Amman's area code is 6 (put a 0 before the area code if dialing from within Jordan).

• **Tourist Agencies: House of Travel and Tourism**, *Municipality Square*, can arrange ferry tickets to Egypt (as can other places in Aqaba, but they're very nice here). It's in the complex of stores on Corniche just near the Gulf Hotel.

22. SINAI

Sinai is part of the Syrian-African Rift. Two-thirds of the Sinai is a great plateau sloping down to the Mediterranean Sea, but it becomes ruggedly mountainous to the south. It may not sound like a place you'd want to wander for 40 days, let alone Moses' 40 years, but there is a special beauty to the desert that grows on you, and its beaches are stunning. The most celebrated mountain is Sinai (**Jubal Mussa**) on whose 7,500 foot summit Moses is said to have received the Ten Commandments. Now it receives travelers, as do the beach resorts on the east Red Sea (Gulf of Aqaba) coast.

At its height, the ancient Egyptian empire encompassed northern and western Sinai. Despite the inhospitable terrain and climate, the peninsula has been of great strategic importance as an invasion route and was a major battleground of the Arab-Israeli Wars. As a result of the 1967 war Sinai came under Israeli occupation, but under the terms of the Egyptian-Israeli peace treaty in 1979 most of it was restored to Egypt in April 1982 (though the resort of **Taba** wasn't returned until 1989). Bedouins used to follow their traditional nomadic ways here, but now, more and more, they're shifting to tourism to boost their economy.

ORIENTATION

The Sinai is a triangular desert peninsula that forms a land bridge between Africa and Asia in northeast Egypt, and its name comes from the ancient religious cult of the moon-god *Sin*. Bordered by the **Gulf of Suez** on the southwest, the **Red Sea** on the south, the **Gulf of Aqaba** on the southeast, and the **Mediterranean Sea** on the north, its 60,714 square kilometers has mountains, beaches, and endless vistas of scrubby, rocky terrain.

Taba (on the Gulf of Aqaba arm of the Red Sea) is on the border with Israel's Eilat on the northeast side of the Sinai peninsula. Down the coast 75 kilometers is **Nuweibe**, and further southwest another 89 kilometers is the beach town of **Dahab**. **Santa Katherina Village** is inland about 110

SINAI BY TOUR OR ON YOUR OWN

There are many advantages to a packaged tour of the Sinai, but the biggest boon by far is transportation. If you just want to laze or snorkel by the sea, take the bus and relax. But if you want to see Santa Katherina, climb Mount Sinai, tour the Nawamis burial sites, hike the Colored Canyon, and snorkel at the Blue Hole, and you don't have a couple weeks to do it in, a tour makes sense.

You give up your autonomy, of course, and a lot of money to boot. But once the payment is made, it's done with. Lodgings, food, and transport are all provided without your having to muck about with it or pay again and again. You're guided by people who know a lot about the land, the Bedouin, and the history. There is the patronizing air of the holiday camp ("now it's time to rest, now it's time for lunch, don't forget to drink more water") to contend with, and you are part of a group, a situation that can be wonderful or horrendous depending on who happens to be along. You could meet some really great people, or you could be stuck with duds.

If you do decide to go with a group, choose the four-day tour. It takes that long to slow down, to get to the isolated parts where you tell stories and camp out under the stars, and to let the peace and beauty of the desert sink in.

kilometers from Nuweibe on the only road that transverses the southern section of the triangle.

ARRIVALS & DEPARTURES

To enter the Sinai from Israel, your passport must be valid for at least another six months, and your Israeli visa must still be in effect for the time you'll be in the Sinai. Egyptian visas are currently available at the border, free of charge; you can get an automatic Sinai visa good for up to 14 days, or a full one month Egypt visa. The charge for an Egyptian visa may revert to $15 in May 1988, but visas will still be available at the border, or you can get it at a consulate in advance.

If you're sharing your passport with someone who entered Israel with you (like a child), you must leave together too, even if just for one day. And, if you don't want an Israeli stamp in your passport you can ask at passport control.

By Bus

From Eilat, **Taba**, *Tel. 07-6373-110*, a few kilometers and a short NIS 3.9 bus ride south of Eilat, is the point of entry into the Sinai, and it's open

24 hours a day, every day of the year save Yom Kippur and Eid al-Adha. From Israel there's a departure tax of NIS 59 followed by a $6 or E£18 Egyptian border tax (unless you're just going to the Taba Hilton, in which case you need only present your passport). Coming into Israel from Egypt the only tax to deal with is the Egyptian departure tax of E£21.

Private cars are allowed to cross the border, but not rentals. There's a bank at the border to change money, but it's rates are a bit steep. Change elsewhere if the opportunity comes up. Otherwise, the border ordeal consists of many passport showings, form fillings, lines and schleps from one bus to another. Pay strict attention to the Egyptian customs, and declare everything, or you could face a hassle getting those precious items back out of Egypt. Allow three hours for the whole process, though you could strike it lucky and breeze on through. Noon-1pm is a very busy time there, and you could wait quite a while for your Israeli security interview and baggage x-ray check.

There is bus transport from **Taba** into the Sinai and on to **Cairo** (six-seven hours) with the East Delta Company for E£70 at 2pm. Coming back, the 8am from Cairo costs E£45, the 7:30am is E£51, the 10pm costs E£78, and the 11pm is E£70.

Buses leave from **Taba** to **Dahab** at 3pm for E£15, trip two and a half hours. To **Nuweiba**, they leave at 3pm for E£12, trip one a half hours. Buses go to **Sharm el Sheikh** at 3pm for E£25, trip four hours, and they theoretically leave for **Santa Katherina** at 9:30am, but don't bet your water bottle on it.

To **Cairo** from **Dahab** the East Delta bus leaves daily at 8am, noon, and 9:30pm for E£45-E£75 (trip seven hours), to **Nuweibe** at 10:30am and 6:30pm for E£10 (trip one and a half hours), and to **Santa Katherina** at 9:30am for E£10 (trip one hour).

From **Nuweibe** to **Cairo** there are buses at 3pm for E£55, taking seven hours, to **Dahab** it's E£7, leaving at 7am and 4pm and taking one and a half hours, and to **Taba** buses leave at 6am and noon for E£7, one hour. Buses go to **Sharm el-Sheikh** at 7am and 4pm for E£10.

To get to **Santa Katherina** by bus, you need to get to the nearby village of **Milga** and take a taxi (E£3 per person when full) to the monastery from there. To get to Milga, buses leave from (and to) Cairo and Taba.

Warning: all bus schedules and times may (and probably will) fluctuate wildly. Make a plan, but don't have too much riding on it.

By Ferry

For a full description of all the details and horrors entailed in a ferry crossing between the Sinai (from Nuweibe) and Jordan (in Aqaba), see the Getting To Israel section in the *Planning Your Trip* chapter.

GETTING AROUND SINAI

Getting around the Sinai isn't easy. You must depend on fairly unreliable and inconvenient buses, or take a tour. Within the actually towns, such as they are, of Dahab, Nuweibe, and Taba, it's easy enough to get around by foot from hotel to beach and back.

WHERE TO STAY

Taba

TABA HILTON HOTEL, *Taba Beach, Tel. 530-140 Fax 530-301, has 326 rooms that cost $144-$160 a single and $192-$233 a double. Call Tel. 800/ 445-8667 in the US for reservations or information.*

The Taba Hilton is a deluxe facility with all the trappings of a plus oasis. All rooms come with air conditioning, phone, private bath, mini-bar, and windows that open, while the hotel offers three restaurants, room service, fitness center, pool, sauna, diving center, and its own private Red Sea beach. They even have their own casino, and provide complimentary shuttles to and from the border.

SALAH EL DEEN HOTEL, *Nuweibe Road, Tel. 530-340, Fax 530-343 has 62 rooms for $52 a single and $64 a double.*

Salah El Deen provides less expensive Taba accommodations in a clean, albeit not luxury, setting.

Nuweibe

NUWEIBE HILTON CORAL RESORT, *Tel. 520-320/1, Fax 520-327, has 200 rooms for $115-$152 a single and $142-$179 a double. Call Tel. 800/ 445-8667 in the US for reservations or information.*

Rooms have air conditioning, heat, direct phone lines, TV, and hairdryers in this well equipped four star resort. There are two outdoor pools (heated in winter), tennis courts, horseback riding, and squash.

HELNAN NUWEIBE HOTEL, *Nuweibe City, Tel. 500-402, Fax 500-407, has 130 rooms for $58 a single and $80 a double, and beach huts for $13.*

The bungalows are air conditioned, with TV and direct-dial phones, and the hotel has a private beach, a diving center, and even a disco.

EL SAYADEEN TOURISTIC VILLAGE, *south of the port, Tel. 520-340, has 99 rooms for $30 a single and $45 a double.*

The rooms here are all air conditioned with private baths. And the hotel sports a pool, a beach, and a decent restaurant.

EL SALAM TOURISTIC VILLAGE, *northern of Tarabin, Tel. 500-440, has 63 rooms and 26 caravans for $28 a single and $35 a double.*

It's roomy enough, with air conditioning and perks like TV and refrigerators, restaurants, swimming pools, and a private beach, but it's out in the middle of nowhere.

BAWAKI BEACH HOTEL, *Tel. 500-470, Fax 352-6123, 18 kilometers north of Nuweibe. Their 36 rooms cost $60 a single and $80 a double.*

SALLY LAND TOURIST VILLAGE, *Taba-Nuweibe Road, Tel. 530-380, Fax 530-381, has 68 rooms for E£95 a single and E£85 a double.*

EL WAHA TOURISTIC VILLAGE, *half a kilometer south of the Helnan, Nuweibe City, Tel./Fax 500-421, has 38 air conditioned rooms for E£44 a single and E£56 a double, and large tents with mattresses for E£10.*

You can also sleep out on their beach for E£4 a sleeping bag (provided by them).

The nearby Bedouin village of Tarabin has a clutter of cheap beach camps. It's a 30 minute walk north along the beach, or a E£10 taxi. There's **MOON LAND**, **CAMP DAVID**, **RED SEA CAMP**, and plenty more. They typically have bamboo huts for E£7 and tents for E£4, no mosquito protection and no ventilation included. Hotels come and go with the desert wind in Nuweibe, though some attain permanent fixture status.

Dahab

LAGUNA VILLAGE HOTEL, *between Dahab and Asilah, near the Dyarna, Tel. 640-350, Fax 640-351, has 45 rooms for $50-$70 a single and $95-$120 a double, breakfast included.*

This resort place has dome-shaped, air conditioned rooms, sea views, and a private beach. They also have a nice restaurant (no alcohol served), and a dive club.

GANET SINAI HOTEL, *Dahab City, Tel. 640-440, Fax 640-441, has 51 rooms for E£145 a single and E£200 a double, buffet breakfast included.*

All the rooms have air conditioning, TVs, and sea views. They've also got a windsurfing center and a private beach (no coral).

NOVOTEL HOLIDAY VILLAGE, *Dahab Bay, Tel. 640-301, Fax 640-302, charges E£110 a single and E£170 a double, breakfast included.*

This four-star resort has prime location on the bay, especially if you want to learn to windsurf. They've a nice beach, a dive club, inexpensive bungalows as well.

DYARNA DAHAB HOTEL, *between Dahab and Asilah, Tel. 640-120, Fax 640-122, has 42 rooms for E£40-60 a single and E£80-100 a double.*

The hotel features a private beach, with coral reef. They also have a pool and satellite TV.

The Bedouin Village has scads of **camps** featuring stifling nights in a concrete huts with a mattress and bare bulbs. It costs E£5 for a mattress on the ground, E£6 for a concrete bed, and E£10 for the luxury of a wooden one. There are also private doubles for around E£20. Bamboo huts are cooler than the concrete, but also less secure. There are close to 50 of them, and factors such as hot showers (which some sport) and strong gusts of wind (to reduce the mosquitoes) are worth considering.

Santa Katherina

ST. CATHERINE TOURIST VILLAGE, *half a kilometer from the monastery, Tel. 770-456, Fax 770-456, has 100 rooms for $85-$96 a single and $100-$121 a double, breakfast and dinner included.*

Right on the main road, their air conditioned apartments are quite comfortable, especially considering the rough setting.

DANIELA VILLAGE, *Saint Catherine's Village, Tel. 771-409, Fax 360-7750, has 54 rooms costing $38 a single and $48 a double.*

The rooms are all air conditioned, with private bath, and Daniela sports a restaurant, cafeteria, and bar.

MORGAN LAND VILLAGE, *Nuweiba Road, Tel. 02-356-2437, Fax 02-356-4104, has 92 rooms for $33-$36 and doubles for $36-$42.*

They're not far from Zeitona Camp, and their office is in Cairo (hence the Cairo prefix).

EL SALAM HOTEL, *near the Saint Catherine Airport, Tel. 771-409, Fax 247-6535, has 35 rooms for E£34 a single and E£87 a double.*

The rooms are all adequate, with private bath. They're 10 kilometers from Santa Katherina monastery, and are equipped with a restaurant and bar.

ALFAIROZ HOTEL, *behind the tourist village, Tel. 770-221, has tents for E£8, lots for your own tent for E£5, cramped dorm rooms for E£12 per mattress, singles with bath for E£55, and doubles for E£65.*

If you walk from the village towards the monastery, take your first left to find the hotel. It's not so close to the monastery, but it's blessed with a remarkable view of the mountains.

ZEITONA CAMP, *Nuweiba Road, 771-409, Fax 247-6535, has 50 rooms costing E£7-35 per person and doubles costing E£10-42, depending on whether you stay in tents, stone huts, or private rooms.*

Five kilometers from the monastery road and not far from Morgan Land Village, they've got communal showers and a restaurant.

MONASTERY YOUTH HOSTEL, *right fork just before the monastery, Tel. 770-945, has dorm beds costing E£35 per bed in the seven-eight bed room or E£40 in the rooms with three-four beds, all rooms with bath, all meals included.*

The rooms are all clean, though the larger rooms are a bit crowded. The reception office is across from the gift shop through the door marked "manager." And the location is magnificent.

GREEN LODGE, *10 kilometers east of the monastery, near the road to Wadi Feiran, Tel. 770-314, has dorm rooms (five beds) inside for E£21 a bed, two-person tents outside for E£11, Bedouin breakfasts for E£5, and lunch or dinner for E£12. Their office is in Cairo, 21 Mokhtar Said Street, Heliopolis, Tel. 02-291-1490, Fax 02-290-4534, but the local office is in Milga next to the post office.*

This is a charming Bedouin rest stop for meals, story-telling, and if you can convince them, night-time dancing. It's a nice place, with good staff and engaging atmosphere. The tents come with mattresses, blankets, and electricity, there are cushions in the courtyard for after your Mount Sinai hike, and fires in the winter. They'll provide transport between the Green Lodge and their Milga office, and to the monastery as well.

WHERE TO EAT

If you go by tour then the food is all arranged by them, but if you go on your own, your hotels (or other hotels) are the most likely food sources. **Dahab** has a few café and restaurant spots in town that cater to young travelers, **Nuweibe** has a an ever growing (and changing) cafe scene, and there are usually snack stands by the beaches as well.

SEEING THE SIGHTS

Taba

The most northerly resort on the Sinai's Red Sea Coast (go any further north and you're in Israel), it's positioned such that you can easily see Jordan, Saudi Arabia, and Israel. The beaches are beautiful and it's got a slower, more relaxed feel than nearby Eilat. There are lovely quiet bays and coves, and the Taba Hilton provides got plenty of comfy cafe's and terraces.

Nuweibe

A dive resort and seamy port town all rolled into one, this is where the ferries dock from Jordan amid a jumble of customs and luggage, but they also have a holiday village of sorts set up for the snorkel and dive trade, and a burgeoning cafe scene. **Tarabin**, the Bedouin village that caters to budget travelers, is one and a half kilometers north of the city, but Nuweibe's beach is nicer.

The favored activities here center on the beach, and folks pass the days lounging, snorkeling, diving, and sunbathing. However, you can also use Nuweibe as a base for desert exploration. People take camel or jeep safaris, hike in **Colored Canyon**, visit the desert oasis of **Ain Umm Ahmed** or **Ain Furtuga**. **Ain Khoudra** and **Bayer al-Sabreyer** are further oases in **Wadi Khoudra**, two days by camel and en route to Santa Katherina's. See *Sports & Recreation* for details.

And then there's the **Dolphin** who lost her mate in a tragic tale of mistaken identity (he was caught in a fishing net and shot for a shark). Abdullah, the deaf fisherman, consoled her in her grief, and they've been fast friends since. She lives near the fishing village of Sayadeen, Maagana Bay (now known as Dolphin Beach), and Abdullah claims swimming with her caused him to hear again. His dolphin seems to have recovered a bit from the tragedy, and in the spring of 1997 she gave birth to a baby dolphin (who looks nothing like Abdullah). Swimming with dolphin and child is now one of Nuweibe's chief attractions. It's a quick E£5 taxi ride or 20-minute walk south of Nuweibe Port. The beach is open until 6pm, and Bedouin opportunists will charge you E£12 for a dolphin swim, and another E£12 for fins, mask, and snorkel.

Dahab
The town of **Dahab** (*Gold* in Arabic) is much further south along the Red Sea coast, 89 kilometers from Nuweibe. It's more pleasant than Nuweibe, and near the famed **Blue Hole** dive spot. It has a hippyish kind of reputation. There are plenty of tie-died shirts and dreadlocked heads grooving down the streets, and boutiques full of baggy cotton pants and colorfully woven backpacks. There's room for all kinds here, but it is a bit like Katmandu on the Red Sea.

There are two bus stops. The first lets you off at the Bus Stop Cafeteria near the what used to be the Pullman Hotel resort and is now the Novotel Holiday Village, and a taxi from here to the Bedouin Village (which is now really another tourist village) costs about E£5. The second bus stop is the East Delta Bus Company office in town.

The **Blue Hole**, 80 meters deep and 15 meters from the shore, is a lovely spot for snorkeling, diving, and disappearing. Several divers a year head out through a passage 60 meters deep, become euphorically disoriented, and are never heard from again. There's a nice shaded spot to rest in, a snack bar that also rents snorkel equipment, and lots of little Bedouin girls selling hand-woven bracelets.

Near Dahab is **Colored Canyon**, an amazing and worthwhile place to hike. You need to get there by jeep, and it costs about E£55 per person for a group of six. There are also **camel trips** to **Wadi Gnay** (E£20) and **Nabq** (E£35-50).

Santa Katherina's
This beautiful monastery, about one kilometer from the small town of **Milga**, is open Monday-Thursday and Saturday 9am-noon, but closed all orthodox holidays. It's truly picturesque, but if you've spent hours and hours to get here you may end up feeling a bit let down.

Built by Emperor Justinian in the sixth century to shelter Christian monks, the Monastery houses the **Chapel of the Burning Bush**, the **Mosaic of the Transfiguration of Christ**, and a **library** containing early Christian manuscripts. Christian hermits lived in caves here in the second century, believing it to be the site of the Burning Bush and looking to escape persecution, and Saint Helena (Emperor Constantine's mother) had a small chapel built here. Justinian wanted a basilica on top of Mount Sinai, in part for the grandeur, but also in part because mountain passes were like today's toll roads, and he who controlled the pass earned a pocketful of traveler revenue.

Stephanos, Justinian's architect, claimed the peak was too narrow and built the Church of the Transformation in the valley instead, next to Saint Helena's chapel. Justinian wasn't pleased and ordered Stephanos be put to death, a sentence Stephanos eluded. He spent the rest of his days in the safety of a monastery, attained sainthood, and his old bones are on display in the ossuary.

One of the oldest unrestored examples of Byzantine architecture in the world, the monastery is more than just an architectural treasure. The chapel rooms are full of fourth century icons, though the mosaic of Christ is extremely difficult to see. Not so, the **ossuary**. It's around the back, and fascinating in a ghoulish sort of way. The bones of all the former residents are piled high, and a monk well on his way to joining the heap guards skeletally by the entrance. There's also a well with good, sweet water, but drink at your own risk: tradition has it that if you drink you'll get married within three years (though this doesn't seem to apply to the monks).

Beyond the monastery, monks built a staircase of rocks with 3,750 steps leading to the summit of **Mount Sinai** (*Gabal Mussa*, literally Mount Moses). It rises 7,495 feet above the desert and is an arduous but rewarding climb. Not only is it the revered site where Moses received the Ten Commandments, the views from the top are absolutely stunning. The site is considered holy by Christians, and for Muslims doubly so since Mohammed's horse is believed to have stopped here on his flying journey. It's not holy for Jews, however, since there's no proof this is where Moses actually received the tablets.

The steps, called the **Steps of Repentance** (for the monk who built them, not the traveler who climbs them), are fairly steep and take about two hours to climb. In the winter they can be slippery with snow, and you can twist your ankle in any season, so wear hiking boots if you have them, and bring plenty of water. There is also a camel path, however, that takes two-three hours by foot and less time by one of the camel-and-guide teams ready to tote you for $10. To start, walk up the hill to the monastery, bear left at the fork, keep on to the back of the monastery, and 100 meters further along the path you'll come to a fork with a sign telling which way the steps and which way the camel path. Near the top are a couple of tea huts offering hot and cold refreshments, but at the summit it's just you, the vista, and a small 1937 chapel over Byzantine church ruins, on the spot where Moses is believed to have come face to face with God.

Common sense dictates you avoid the climb in the heat of the day, though this isn't always possible. If you're starting off in the afternoon, take a flashlight because the path can be rather treacherous in the dark, and take a sweater against the evening chill. It's lovely in the morning, though the sunset it spectacular too.

Mount Catherine (*Gabal Katherina*) is six kilometers south of Mount Sinai, and at 8,666 feet it's the tallest mountain in Egypt. The path to the summit is less traveled than Mount Sinai but very beautiful, and takes about five-six hours from the village. Up top there's a chapel with water.
Shopping

Bedouin children sometimes come selling colorfully **braided thingamabobs**. You can wear it as a bracelet or anklet, attach it to your backpack for decoration, braid it into your hair for the hippy look, or give them to friends as a souvenir and let them figure out what to do with them. They're very pretty, don't cost much (an Egyptian pound or two) and help the local economy.

Dahab's streets are lines with shops selling **kilims** (rugs with some very beautiful designs, but bargain seriously for them), **jewelry**, **Dahab pants** (cotton, colorful, and draw-stringed), and **colorful backpacks**.

DON'T MISS THE CAMEL RACES!

*About mid-January, the **Valley of Zalqa** in the middle of the Sinai hosts the annual camel races. About three hours drive from Nuweibe or Santa Katherina, all the local tribes gather there the night before to barbecue and sing and boast about their camels. The next day some 60-100 camels race 30 miles for glory and a prize.*

SPORTS & RECREATION

The resort towns along the coast are popular because the coral reefs are so magnificent and the snorkeling/scuba diving so good. You can see the brilliant Red Sea fish in the Coral World Aquarium in Eilat, or you can swim the warm waters yourself and be amazed.

You can rent snorkel equipment all over, or bring your own. Clear swim goggles work alright in a pinch, but a mask that fits well a true joy.

Nisima, *Mazbat, southern end of town, Tel. 640-320, Fax 640-321*, is a cleanly white-washed dive center in **Dahab**. They leaded guided day and night dives ($45) and five-ten day packages ($175-$400), including all equipment and transportation, for certificated divers. They also offer diving courses. For the basic five-day PADI course it's $270, the Advances Open Water (PADI) two-day and Open Water II (NAUI) three-day courses are $190, the four-day Rescue course is $255, and the ten-day Dive Master course costs $500 (plus $30-$40 for certificates). You can rent equipment for snorkeling ($3 for mask and snorkel, $2 for fins) and scuba

---

UNDERWATER PRECAUTIONS

Avoid touching the **coral**, *beautiful as it is, because it can cause some nasty cuts that take a long time to heal.* **Sea Urchins** *look like round black porcupines, and you don't want to step on them. The barbed spines can go right through sea booties, not to mention skin, and taking them out is no fun.* **Stonefish** *are less evident, more dangerous, and camouflaged to look like rocks. If you step on one you'll either die or wish that you would.*

Lionfish *have feathery manes that look quite pretty but pack a paralyzing sting, and* **moray eels** *should be avoided as well. For snorkeling it's a good idea to wear plastic booties, sneakers, or fins, and an even better idea to float as much and as soon as possible and make contact with objects as little as possible. There are also the occasional* **sharks**, *so avoid swimming if you're oozing any blood.*

---

diving as well. **Club Red**, *next to Mohammed Aly Camp, southern end of Dahab, Tel./Fax 640-380*, has nice facilities and hotel rooms too, with PADI certification courses for $280-$300, and guided dives for $40-$55.

Other places in **Dahab** are the **Canyon Dive Club**, *a few kilometers north of the village at the Canyon, Tel. 640-043, Fax 640-3015*, **Inmo Diving Center**, *Mashrabat, Tel. 640-370, is the oldest in Dahab*, **Sinai Dive Club**, *Novotel Holiday Village, Tel. 640-301, Fax 640-302*, **Fantesea**, *northern end of town by the Lighthouse, Tel. 640-483, Fax 640-043, email: fdc@intouch.com*, **Lagouna Dive Center**, *Lagouna Village, Tel. 640-356, Fax 640-355*.

In **Nuweibe**, there's **Diving Camp Nuweibe**, *Helnan Nuweibe Hotel, Tel./Fax 500*, and **Aqua Sport**, *Coral Hilton Resort, Tel. 520-320, Fax 520-327*.

EXCURSIONS & DAY TRIPS
SINAI EXPLORATION FROM NUWEIBE

Nuweibe is a good jumping-off point for trips to nearby Colored Canyon, or to the oases Ain Umm Ahmed, Ain Furuga, Ain Khoudra, and Bayar al-Sabreyer. **Explore Sinai**, *Nuweibe City Mall, Tel. 500-141, Fax 500-140*, and **Tarabin Survival Safari**, *by Moon Land Camp, Tarabin, Tel. 500-299*. They charge about E£50-65 a person for **camel safaris** and E£45 per person for **jeep trips**.

Desert forays need a special permit, and your guide will take care of it for you. Camel permits are E£2 per day and jeep tour permits are E£10 per person per day, but these costs are usually included in the initial price. Also included in the price is the food, but not necessarily the water. Bring a lot of your own.

PRACTICAL INFORMATION

• **Currency**: You can change money into Egyptian Pounds in the Sinai, but the rates are much worse than in Cairo. If you have options, change money before you enter the Sinai. There's a **National Bank of Egypt** in **Dahab**, open daily 8:30am-2pm and 6-9pm in summer, 9am-1pm and 5-8pm in winter. **Nuweibe's National Bank** is open 8:30am-noon and 6-8pm, and **Milga's Bank Misr** is open Sunday-Thursday 8:30am-2pm and 6-9pm, Friday 9am-noon and 6-9pm, and Saturday 10am-1:30pm and 6-9pm.

• **English newspapers** and **books** can be found in **Nuweibe's newsstand**.

• **Hospital**: **Milga hospital**, *opposite the bus station on the square next to the tourist police*; *Tel.* 470-368, is open 24 hours; **Dahab Polyclinic**, *above the Ghazala supermarket, southern end of village, Tel 640-104*, is open 24 hours; **Nuweibe hospital**, *Tel. 500-303*, is open 24 hours.

• **Police**: **Dahab**, *Tel.* 640-215, **Nuweibe's tourist police**, *Tel. 502-424*, open 24 hours, and **Milga's station** is on top of the hill past the phone office, but your first stop should be the **Milga tourist police**, *on the square, opposite the bus station*.

• **Post offices**: **Dahab's**, with poste restante, is open Saturday-Thursday 8am-3pm, **Nuweibe's** is open 8am-2pm and has poste restante, and there's a post office in **Milga** as well, open 8am-3pm.

• **Prohibitions**: nude sunbathing is illegal, as is smoking hash (regardless of how many people want to sell you the stuff).

• **Supermarkets**: **Dahab** has one and it's open daily 8am-10pm, while **Nuweibe's supermarket** and **bakery** are open daily 8am-4pm and 6-10:30pm. **Milga** has a **supermarket**, *on the square*, that's open 6am-10pm, and their **bakery**, *opposite the mosque*, has fresh pitas.

• **Telephone area code** for Dahab, Taba, and Saint Catherine is *062* and for Nuweibe is *086*. **Dahab** has a **telephone office**, open 24 hours, from which you can place calls in Egypt or abroad (through Cairo's international operator). **Nuweibe's** telephone office is open 24 hours too, **Milga** also has a 24 hour international phone and telegraph office.

• **Tours**: **Neot Hakikar**, *Khan Amiel Center, Eilat, Tel. 07-632-6281, Fax 07-632-6297, and 67 Ben Yehuda, Tel Aviv, Tel. 03-520-5858, Fax 03-522-1020*, specializes in Sinai tours and has done for many years. They've got 1-day Santa Katherina trips for $55, 1-night sunrise on Mt. Sinai trips for $69, 2-day Sinai trips for $125-$165, a 2-day camel safari for $140, and a 4-day jeep and hike trip for $290. **Johnny Dessert Tours** *(07-376-777, Fax 07-372-608) the Shalom Center (2nd floor) in Eilat* has one-day Santa Katherina Monastery tours for $58 per person and two-day tours to Santa Katherina and Mount Sinai for $125 (including lodging and meals), border tax not included.

• **Weather**: Desert weather is inhospitable and extreme. Summer afternoons sizzle, winter nights can be very, very cold, and mosquitoes plague coastal towns in the spring and summer – mosquito nets come in handy.

23. CAIRO

It starts before you even get there. **Cairo**. The name itself conjures up images rich in imagery and fantasy, melding pyramids and crowded streets, elegant Arabic decor and teeming poor masses of people, the gateway to Africa.

Then you get there and you're aswamp with it all, up to your nose in smells of foods, spices, dust, and garbage, up to your ears with honking, belching cars, up to your eyes with just everything. Typically, the traveler establishes a relationship with the city. Heady love at first sight, where all you want to do is roam the streets, chat with the friendly Cairenes, eat the fantastic food, and absorb it all. Then there's the spat, where you've just had it, had enough with all the noise, the filth, the whole rotten pace, and you want out. So you head off for a day trip or more, see some of Egypt that isn't Cairo, and begin to miss that great cafe, that particular restaurant, even the site of hundreds of men clad in immaculate white jalabiyia (Egyptian robes) crossing intersections flooded with moving traffic. And it starts all over again.

About 2,000 years ago the Romans built a fortress called Babylon on the site of present-day Cairo, and in 640 CE Arabs established a military camp here called al-Fustat. It wasn't much of a city, though, till 969, when the Fatimid dynasty made Cairo its capital. Saladin ruled from 1169-93, the Mamluks reigned in the 13th-15th centuries, and the city kept on growing. Its population is estimated to have reached half a million during the mid-14th century, the height of its medieval prosperity. Then the city began a long decline, the result of plagues, a Mongol attack and, finally, Turkish conquest in 1517. It didn't recover until the 19th century, when, under **Mohammed Ali** (who ruled from 1805-49), Egypt became virtually independent of Ottoman Turkey.

Modern Cairo dates from the mid-19th century when the Egyptian ruler, **Ismail Pasha**, began European-style construction projects. From 1882 to 1922 Egypt was under British control. Then, since independence, Cairo has been expanding and expanding some more, so that Cairo's population is around 6,335,000, with more than 8 million in the metropolitan area (compared to the 56 million who live in Egypt). Not surprisingly, Cairo is extremely overcrowded, and its grand old buildings aren't enough to meet the needs of its rapidly increasing population.

Modern Cairo

Streets and traffic really shape your day in Cairo. Maps are all very helpful with the street names written in English, but the streets themselves are less obliging, rarely bothering with English street signs. People are friendly, however, and it doesn't take long to find someone who will tell you the name of the street you're on or point you (or lead you) to where you want to go. The dirt in the air is a different matter. It's so filthy that when you blow your nose your handkerchief comes away black. On the other hand, no need to apply mousse or hair spray – a walk down the Cairo streets acts as a natural hair styler.

The people in Cairo also make a big difference to your visit. While the values quickly become apparent (if you see a crowd on a street, chances are they are ogling the wares in a shoe store), folks are more cosmopolitan than elsewhere in Egypt. Most possess a lively sense of humor, and the men are much less on the make than in some other more provincial tourist sites like Luxor, for example, or Aswan. But despite the Coptic community and the urban (and urbane) tone of the city, it would be well to remember that Egypt is a Muslim country, and with the fundamentalists on the rise, so you should dress and act with Muslim sensibilities in mind, especially if you're female.

To visit from Israel, there are some of the same issues that come up for a Jordan trip. How much time do you have left, how much money do you have to spare, and how much hassle do you want to put up with to remain independent of group tours? There are tours leaving from Israel that take care of all the details from start to finish (see Practical Information), or you can make your own way there and look into guided day trips from Cairo to the pyramids, for example, or do it all on your own.

ORIENTATION

Cairo (*al-Qahirah* in Arabic) is the capital of Egypt and the largest city in Africa. Located in North Africa on the eastern bank of the **Nile River**, about 160 kilometers south of the Mediterranean Sea, eleven bridges link the banks with Cairo's islands, **Zamalek** and **Roda**. Metropolitan Cairo is made up of Cairo proper, the vast sprawl of **Old City** and **New City** districts east of the Nile, and **Giza**, the various neighborhoods on the west bank of the Nile.

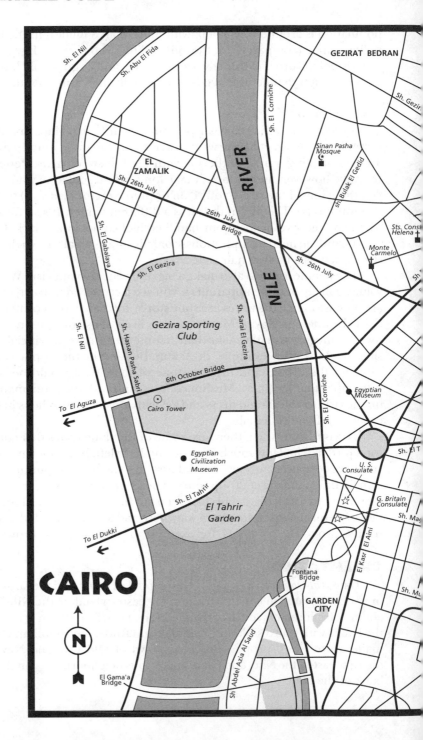

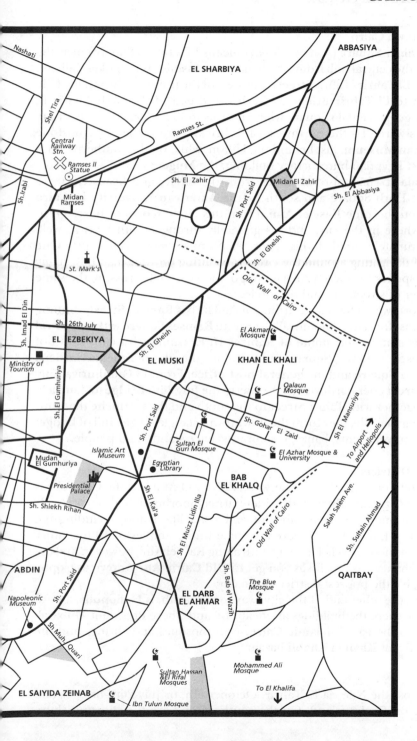

Downtown Cairo
   Tahrir Square (*Midan et-Tahrir* means Liberation Square) near the Nile is the central hub from which many confusing street spokes flail out. **Sharia El Tahrir** (Tahrir Street) runs west of the traffic circle past the **Nile Hilton** to **El Tahrir Bridge** to **Gezira**, and east of the circle Sharia El Tahrir goes to **Falaki Square** where it turns to **El Bustan** before continuing eastward. To the northwest of Tahrir Square is the big sandstone **Egyptian Museum**, just behind the Hilton, while on the southern end is the vast Egyptian bureaucracy building, the **Mugamma**.
   Tala'at Harb also emanates from the circle, and heads north to Tala'at Harb Square and south by the **American University in Cairo** (AUC) to become **Kasr el Aini**. From this circle scores of buses go to everywhere in the city, and it's generally thronged with taxis as well. Unfortunately, amid all this chaos, what's missing are street signs. One way of navigating around the circle is counting on your map how many street spokes to where you want to go, then carefully crossing the same number of streets around the circle.
   Northwest a few blocks from Tala'at Harb is **Ramses Street**, running northeast from the museum all the way to **Ramses Square** with its **central railway station** and **statue of Ramses II**. **El Gumhuriya** runs south of Ramses Sq. to **Opera Square**, and east along the edge of **Ezbekia Gardens** is **'Ataba Square** and the **general post office**. From El Gumhuriya, **July 26th Street** goes northwest all the way to the **July 26th Bridge** to Zamalek, and together with Tahrir Street to the south and the **Corniche** that runs all along the Nile, they form the downtown triangle tangle, full of budget hotels, travel agents, banks, restaurants, juice stands, and people.

Other Districts
   South of Tahrir Square between El Kasr el Aini and the Corniche is **Garden City**, an aptly named residential neighborhood that's surprisingly peaceful and calm. A number of embassies like it too, including the American Embassy, and there are some fine examples of 19th century mansions here as well. Further south along Kasr el Aini, however, and the tenor changes to squalid as you get to **Old Cairo**. Also known as Coptic Cairo, it's the poorest district in the city.
   On the other end of the city, way to the north, is **Heliopolis**, a posh suburb where the buildings are beautiful and where President Mubarak lives. To the east is **Islamic Cairo**, with mosques and shrines and the magnificent **Khan el Khalili** bazaar.

Giza
   Cross the Nile via El Tahrir, October 6th, or July 26th bridges and you're on **Gezira** island. On the southern end are the sporting clubs,

greens, and the Cairo Tower, while the northern end of the island is **Zamalek**, Cairo's poshest residential neighborhood with lots of embassies and expats. There are also a number of fancy hotels on the island. Carry on further west and you come to the water again, a narrow canal separating Gezira from the west bank neighborhoods of **Dokki**, and north of that, **Mohandiseen**.

Dokki, connected to Gezira by El Gala Bridge (a continuation of Tahrir bridge and street), also has a number of embassies and the Cairo Sheraton. Mohandiseen (Engineer's City) was built in the late 1950s by then President Nasser as a model neighborhood for engineers and journalists, and it's now a middle-class residential district.

Further north still is **Imbaba**, where a weekly **camel market** is held. To the south, past the Zoological Gardens and over the Giza Bridge, is **Giza Square** from whence starts Pyramids Road, running all the way to the **Pyramids**. Back in the Nile and south of Gezira is the island of **Roda**, the site of the Manial Palace Museum and also a Club Med.

ARRIVALS & DEPARTURES

See *Getting To Israel* in Chapter 6 for more details on border crossings, departure taxes, and the like.

You need a passport and visa to enter Egypt. If you're arriving by air you can get a 30-day tourist visa at the airport, and if you're entering the country by land or sea you can also get your 30-day visa there, or you could get it in advance. Visas are currently free for US citizens, but may revert to $15 in May 1998. You need proof of yellow fever and cholera immunizations if coming from an infected area, and anyone staying over 30 days needs proof of an AIDS test. You must register with the local authorities (through your hotel, local police, or central passport office) within seven days of arriving.

By Air

Egypt Air and **Royal Jordanian** fly between Egypt and Jordan (for around $180 one way Amman-Cairo), and **Air Sinai** and **El Al** fly between Egypt and Israel (for about E£473 one way, or $143). **ZAS** used to fly Egypt-Israel for much less. That seems to be a deal of the past, but it's worth looking into.

To get from the airport to downtown Cairo, take bus 422 to Tahrir Square Bus 400 goes to the airport form Tahrir Square and minibus 27 goes from the Mugamma stop.

By Bus

Any travel agent in Cairo can book you a bus to Jordan or Israel. **East Delta Company**, *Tel. 83-95-83*, goes through the **Sinai** to Israel Monday and Wednesday at 7am. Misr Travel has 5am buses and 3:30pm buses leaving from the Cairo Sheraton. To get to **Tel Aviv** costs E£110 (E£170 round trip) on the early bus and E£125 (round trip E£185) on the afternoon bus. BTC, in Jerusalem, also provides bus service to **Jerusalem** for $40 (round trip $60). The trip takes about 10 hours.

To get to **Eilat**, take the East Delta bus to **Taba**, leaving daily 7:30am for E£53, and at 10pm for E£78, taking seven and nine hours, respectively. There are also buses to **Taba** from the Abassiyya Station at 8am for E£45 and 11pm for E£70. And, there are supposed to be 9am buses to **Santa Katherina's**, costing E£35, taking eight hours.

From Cairo you can get to anywhere in Egypt by bus. Check with your embassy, however, about terrorist activity, as buses to Luxor and Aswan, for example, are prime targets and not safe for now.

By Train
Trains go all over Egypt with all level of comforts, from the plushest wagonlit to the hottest, dirtiest third class, with prices changing with the categories. Unfortunately, train travel to places like Luxor and Aswan (the places travelers generally want to train to) is the very means of locomotion that's been targeted by the terrorists, and it's not advised. Check with your embassy for updates on this situation.

GETTING AROUND TOWN
By Car
The drivers in Cairo are nuts, suicidal maniacs, and the big wonder is that more accidents don't happen. If you decide that driving is how you want to get around anyway, take care, and if you see an accident, don't stop. You, as a westerner, might get caught up in and become the victim of the hostility. The same holds true if you are involved in an accident (even if someone was injured). If you can drive your car, do so, and report it to the police immediately but from a safe distance.

There are car rental agencies all over Cairo and at all the big hotels, and a car costs around $48 a day, including insurance and 100 kilometers.

By Bus
Oh, the buses of Cairo. They are extraordinarily cheap (but then so are the taxis). They seem like an insurmountable hassle, but if you learn the Arabic numbers and don't mind asking a few people for help you can begin to learn your way around. **Tahrir Square** is one central bus locale, with two bus stations: The one in front of the Mugamma serves southern Islamic Cairo as well as Giza (and the pyramids) and points south, the bus depot in front of the Hilton does the North, with buses going to

Heliopolis, Zamalek and Mohandiseen. Buses from the **Arab League Building** go to Zamalek and Dokki.

There are also buses leaving from **'Ataba Square** (going to the Citadel, the Manial Palace, Giza, and Tahrir Square), from **Ramses Station** (going to Giza Square, the Citadel, and Tahrir) and from **Giza Square** (to the pyramids, airport, and Citadel). Bus fares are generally 10-25 piasters. You can catch buses mid-route but it's trickier as the buses are full, rarely come to a full stop, and you need to be pretty confident you're vying for the right one. People are usually very helpful about getting you to the right bus, and hotel and tourist office staff will write out your destinations in Arabic to help you on your way. But take care on the bus against pickpockets.

There are also Minibuses that ply some of the same routes. They are about 25-75 piasters a ride and more comfortable, but you'll need someone to direct you to the right one.

By Subway

Africa's first subway opened in Cairo in 1987. Subway (Metro) maps of Cairo include destinations and fares; an example is from Sadat to Nasser (a route, not a trip through history) which costs 40 piasters. It's a very clean, easy, civilized method of transport once you're familiar with the route. The line runs a single 40 kilometer route from Helwan in the south to Heliopolis in the north, and stops a few places in downtown.

The system is open 5:30am-1am in summer, closing at midnight in winter, and costing 30-80 piasters. Giant red "M"s mark the metro stations, most of which are unhelpfully named after presidents rather than locations. In downtown there's one at **Ramses Square** (Mubarak), **Orabi** and **Ramses** Streets (Orabi), **July 26th** and **Ramses** (Nasser), **Tahrir Square** (Sadat), **Mansur** and **Ismail Abaza** (Sa'ad Zaghloul), **Mansur** and **Ali Ibrahim** (Sayyida Zeinab), **Saleh Salem Road** (El Malik es-Saleh), and **Old Cairo** (Mar Girgis). Hold on to your ticket as you'll need it to exit, and make sure you're in when you hear the peeps sing out–the doors mean business when they close. Also good to know, the first compartment is always reserved for women, and the second car is reserved for women until 4pm.

A new line has been added to **Shubra**, and a project is underway to connect Cairo to the pyramids at **Giza** by metro – it ought to be finished by the year 2000.

By Taxi

It's a good idea to have your destination written out in Arabic to smooth out any sincere or self-serving misunderstandings. Any of the Tourist Office people will do this for you, as will most hotel staff. Though taxis are all equipped with meters, they are merely decorative, and the system of payment remains unchanged. You get in, do not discuss price, and pay the appropriate amount when you get out (E£3-4 in downtown, E£4 to Mohandiseen or the northern or southern cemeteries, E£7-10 to the pyramids, and E£8-10 to Heliopolis).

Once again, your hotel or tourist office helper can tell you the going rate. Just pay when you leave and you won't be challenged. Sometimes cabs will see you laden with luggage fresh off the bus and offer some outrageous fares, and it's up to you if you have the energy to drag yourself away from the depot sharks or if you don't care about the extra dollar and just want to get to your hotel. The black-and-white checkered taxis are the ones to hail. The Peugeot taxis don't even have meters to not use, and charge more.

There are also **taxi-vans**. They say "taxi" on the side but act like minibuses that go fixed routes. Shout your destination at them and if that's where they're going, they'll stop.

By Boat

River taxis are a pleasant alternative in negotiating Cairo. Boats run every 30 minutes or so from the Corniche in front of the television building (one kilometer north of Tahrir Square) to Old Cairo and cost 50 piasters.

By Foot

This is how you'll see your most amazing sights, have the most fun, get the worst headaches, and lose your last drop of patience. Downtown isn't all that big, and it doesn't take all that long to walk from one spot to another. But the streets are clogged with cars, buses, and taxis all blowing their horns.

Aside from the exhaust and noise pollution, the biggest challenge becomes how to cross the street. You get to a place like Tahrir Square which is really a big traffic circle with lots of intersections, and the flow of vehicles never stops. The time-honored way is to judge the current and wade out into and across it when you spy a fissure between cars. In practice, at first, this seems suicidal and impossible. The best way to accomplish street-crossing is to find a Cairene wanting to cross the same street and shadow him as he makes his practiced way across. I'm sure it happens, but I've never seen a pedestrian get hurt. New solutions are being installed, however, and at many of the major squares there are underground passageways as well.

WHERE TO STAY

Taxi drivers are full of lies about places being full or closed, but they happen to know a place you might like that just so happens to be owned by their uncles . . . so persist in being taken to the hotel of your choice.

NILE HILTON *Corniche El Nil on Tahrir Square, Tel. 578-0444, Fax 578-0475) costs $170-$220 a single, $190-$240 a double, and $600-$1900 for suites.*

The Nile Hilton is one of the main landmarks of Cairo. The lobby has lots of marble but not many seats. Facing the Nile, there's a wealth of greenery out front, and taxis and traffic as well. All the city side rooms have balconies, though few of the Nile side do. The hotel has a swimming pool and sauna, steam bath and massage, tennis courts, casino, bar, business center, and a multitude of restaurants. The rooms are nice (though not overwhelmingly so) but for central location, convenience, and services you can't do better.

THE SHERATON EL GEZIRAH, *Southern end of Gezirah Island, Tel. 341-1333, Fax 341-3640, has singles for $185-$210 and doubles for $210-$250, plus 19% service tax, no breakfast included.*

Scores high on service and views and low on charm, despite its distinctive tall, round tower. And it's expensive to boot.

HELNAN SHEPHEARD HOTEL, *Corniche El Nile in Garden City, Tel. 355-3800, Fax 355-7284. Singles cost $127, doubles are $155, and the sumptuous suites are $300, tax included.*

This is the best of the good hotels, combining class and style with comfort and service. From the bell boys in baggy oriental blue, the recessed hammered brass lights, to the elevators with wood and mirrors and no hotel ads, this is all that a Cairo hotel should be. The rooms are just as beautiful. Along with big beds and the usual amenities, brass and wood and key-hole arches decorate throughout, and rich tapestries line the walls. Breakfast isn't included, but they have a big buffet spread for E£24.25, or you can get an Egyptian breakfast with *fuul* for E£3-4. Afternoon tea is served for E£10-15 (with 17% tax) is a lovely setting.

MENA HOUSE OBEROI, *Great Pyramids, Giza, Tel. 383-3444, has singles for $130-194 and doubles for $160-240.*

This the place to be if you want to stay by the pyramids. A palace from the 19th century, T. E. Lawrence wrote some of his *7 Pillars of Wisdom* there, Faulkner stayed there, and a scene from James Bond's *The Spy Who Loved Me* was filmed there.

EL BORG HOTEL, *across the street from Opera Square on Gezira, Tel. 341-6827, Fax 341-7655, has singles for $50 and doubles for $70-120 (breakfast included, and lower rates often possible).*

Oriental carpets and palm trees in brass pots adorn the lobby, and the rooms have great balconies and views (some over the Nile and some over a garden). There's a funny, mothball smell in the hall, but it's a well-run place with a pool, disco, and nightclub.

WINDSOR HOTEL, *19 Alfi Bey, Tel. 915-810, Fax 921-621, has singles for E£67 and doubles for E£100, but show them your Open Road guide and they'll knock off 25% (all credit cards accepted).*

This is a wonderful hotel, full of old British Colonial touches, charm, and lots of history. There are 55 rooms and they're all different. From the ground level reception the old wood cage lift takes you up to where the classic old coffee shop and rooms are. Hard wood floors, big wood frame beds, old black phones, and huge bathrooms enjoy modern amenities such as air conditioning and TV. First built as a hammam for King Ismail in the late 1800s, it was used as the British Officer's Club for a while, since this was the best neighborhood in town till the big fire of '51 which trashed the first Shepheard Hotel and Opera House next door. Russian experts helping Nasser build the Aswan Dam stayed here, and the Michael Palin *Around the World in 80 Days* public TV series was filmed here in 1988.

The owners have taken care to retain the old classic charm, and the furniture are all colonial antiques. The Barrel Bar is a popular hang-out for foreigners, actors, and journalists, and during the day it's a peaceful place to eat, read, or write. The hotel, one of the oldest in Cairo, is family run with care. They'll help in all the day-to-day difficulties of getting around Cairo, and organize tours as well. It's the best you can find for the price in Cairo.

CARLTON HOTEL, *21 July 26th Street, Tel. 575-5022, Fax 575-5323, has singles for E£65 and doubles for E£85, big breakfast included.*

The Carlton is in a likable old building next to Cinema Rivoli. Both singles and doubles come with big beds, air conditioning, clean bathrooms, TV, old black phones, and breakfast. It's a great old structure with lovely marble floors and a few cockroaches, a sweet hotel in search of TLC and business.

THE LOTUS HOTEL, *12 Tala'at Harb, Tel. 575-0966, owned by the same folks who run the Windsor, is conveniently just across from the Felfela Cafeteria entrance. Singles are E£35-45 and doubles are E£50-70, depending on bath, shower, or neither. Credit cards accepted.*

Once you get past the grotty entrance it's pretty nice inside. The furniture's old but the feeling is warm and cozy.

GRESHAM HOTEL, *20 Tala'at Harb, Tel. 575-9043. Singles (no bath) cost E£25, singles with bath and air conditioning are E£50. Doubles are E£35 without bath, E£45 with bath and E£55 with air conditioning, breakfast and tax included and credit cards accepted.*

Not a bad mid-range choice. The lobby is done in Arabic style with cushions and pillows, and the rooms are very nice. Some have balconies and fireplaces, all have old world charm and faded grandeur.

ANGLO-SWISS, *14 Champollion, Tel. 575-1497, sports singles for E£25 and doubles for E£45-50.*

Another undeservedly popular cheap B&B. The circular staircase is swell but the rooms are shabby with peeling paint, and they've a lot of irritating pushy touts working for them, approaching you on the street to invite you in.

PENSION ROMA, *169 Mohammed Farid, Tel. 391-1088, has singles that cost E£22.75 (all without baths) and doubles that cost E£41.50 without baths and E£46 with bath.*

This is one of loveliest places to stay in Cairo. It doesn't cost much, but there's nothing cheap about the rooms or the staff. The shared baths are large and spotless, and the rooms are completely charming. With hardwood floors and Egyptian rugs, dark wood armoires with tall mirrors, night lamps and crisp, clean white linen, the rooms are full of old world touches. And the brothers who run the place are friendly, helpful, and funny. There's a slow-as-molasses grilled elevator that does in fact make it up to the 4th floor, and breakfast is included in the price of the room. You can (and should) call or write *(Pension Roma, 169 Mohammed Farid, Cairo)* for reservations.

ISMAILIA HOTEL, *1 Tahrir Square (8th floor, no lift), Tel. 356-3122, costs E£20 for singles and E£40-50 for doubles.*

Popular with students but it doesn't really shine. The rooms are clean but bare. It's humming with travelers but doesn't begin to compare to Pension Roma.

GARDEN CITY HOTEL, *23 Kamal Eldin Saleh Street in Garden City, Tel. 354-4969, Fax 354-4126, has singles without baths for E£21-27 and with baths for E£34, while doubles are E£29-36 without baths and E£43 with.*

This is in a lovely, serene location with very reasonable rates.

WHERE TO EAT

For street snacks, there are *hiwushi*, a spicy stuffed pie vender treat. There are also magnificent, refreshing, tasty fruit drink stands all over. Go easy on them, though. They use a little Cairo water with all the luscious fruits, and you'll need to let your innards get adjusted if you want to avoid a bad case of the runs.

Downtown

FELFELA, *15 Tala'at Harb, Tel. 392-2751*, is always a festive place for a meal, dependable for good food and an English menu. Felfela (meaning pepper) is slightly pricier than you'd pay for the same food elsewhere, but the wicker and wood, plants and waterfalls, and tables full of people (mostly fellow travelers) to watch make it worth the extra few cents.

Homemade soups are served in copper pots, and there are loads of fuul and falafel dishes, hummus and tehina, and sweet Om Ali as well. Open daily 9am-12:30am, a meal costs between E£10-20. The Tala'at Harb restaurant is the best known, but they also have a take-out counter (same food, cheaper prices) around the corner and branches in Giza, Ma'adi, Mohandesseen.

ABU TAREK, *32 Champolin about halfway down from the intersection with July 26th*, is one of the best kosheries in Cairo. It's a big, clean place with marble floor upstairs and down, is open 9-9 (except during Ramadan), and bowls cost E£1-2, depending on size. A **kosherie** is a restaurant specializing in a simple but splendid culinary treat. Made of lentils, macaroni, rice, grilled onions, and hot tomato sauce, these basic foods heaped together make a filling, tasty meal for pennies a bowl, and there's something great about a place that does just one dish and does it well. You can generally spot them by the bins of ingredients in the window.

Fatir is a special kind of Egyptian pizza, with a thin crust and choice of savory or sweet toppings. **FATATRI PIZZA EL TAHRIR**, *166 El Tahrir, Tel. 355-3596*, is a fine old place to try it out. A small costs E£6, a medium is E£8, and a large is E£10. The room is tiny, with just 5 marble tables, and a guy behind the counter twirling dough to papyrus-thin sheets. He folds it, adds a variety of goodies (veggies, egg, meat for a savory one) and sticks it in the oven. #1 pizza is salty spicy, with onion, tomato, camel feta, and something hot; #2 is sweet and delectable, with almonds, sweet gloppy stuff, and a filo dough crust dusted in confectioner's sugar. To get there from Tahrir Square, take the 3rd street to the left of the Mugamma (or the 1st to the left of Hotel Ismalia), go down half a block, and it's on your right.

ARABESQUE, *6 Kasr el Nil, Tel. 574-8677, Fax 574-8644*, open daily noon-4pm and 7:30-midnight, is a classic and classy oriental restaurant. Colored glass, amber lights, yellow linen, and lanterns cast the tone in this posh place. Hors d'oeuvres run E£7-30, salads are E£3-6, and main dishes are E£23-60. They cater mostly to tourists (about 80% of their business), but the lighting is good for a romantic dinner, just dim enough to hide the damage the Cairo streets have done to your face. If you want a splurge this place has the atmosphere to go with the food.

LA MUM TAKE AWAY, *Tala'at Harb*, has cheap oriental food, worth it if only for their menu featuring Brain Pane, a common Cairo condition. Sandwiches are E£1-1.5 and hot meals will cost you E£1-2.5.

ALI HASSAN AL HATY, *3 Halim Pasha Square, Tel. 591-6055*, in a passage between Alfy and 26th July near Mohammed Farid, is one of two restaurants with this name. This one, in business since 1920 and open noon-11pm, has a beautiful old dining room with high, high ceilings and crystal chandeliers, arch-shaped mirrors on the walls, red table clothes and excellent food. They've an English menu and main courses costing

E£8-15 and E£2-4 for smaller dishes. It has a long tradition as a good restaurant and it's where Cairenes go for a fine meal out.

EL HATY, *8 a&b July 26th, Tel. 391-8829*, is another fine restaurant off July 26th that's been in operation since 1932. King Farouk, Nasser and Sadat ate here, and so can you. Upstairs it's fancy and oriental, with hand-etched brass tables and real silver, stained glass windows and good oriental food. Salads cost E£2, soups are E£2-7, and main dishes cost E£20-23. Open 10am-1am daily and credit cards accepted. Downstairs is a cafeteria, open 12-12, with cheaper prices (E£2-17) a different menu, and the same standards for quality food.

THE IBIS ROOM, *the Nile Hilton*, is open 5am-11am and serves a huge morning buffet. The Continental is E£17.5, plus yogurt and cold meats is E£24, and with hot dish options too is E£30.

SUN COFFEE SHOP, *down an alley across from the Omayid Hotel on July 26th*, is a funky place. Open 6am-1am, there are tables inside and out, Egyptian scenes painted on all the walls, windows, and doors, nice old marble-topped tables, brass stands, and hubble bubbles, and aging cool hippy types sipping coffee and playing backgammon.

EL ABD PATISSERIE, *Tala'at Harb next to the Syrian Air office*, is a very popular place for ice cream (E£1.5 a scoop) and flaky pastries (E£1.8 for two). It's thronged at night.

Garden City

CASINO EL NILE, *across from the Semi Ramis Hotel, Garden City, Tel. 340-4655*, is a coffee patio over the Nile, with white wicker chairs, and yellow lamps at night. Open daily 7am-3am, they serve coffee and tea (E£3), salads (E£2), and grilled kabob, pigeon, chicken, etc. (E£30). It's a lovely place to sit, catch your breath, and watch the Nile flow by.

Khan el-Khalili

COFFEE SHOP NAGUIB MAHFOUZ, *5 El Badistante Lane, Tel. 903-788*, is two blocks west of El Hussein mosque. Supposedly a coffee spot favored by the Nobel prize winning author, they have music nightly and Lebanese cuisine for E£4-25.

FISHAWI'S, *four doors down from the El Hussein Hotel, Tel. 906-755*, has been serving great coffee and tea while providing a respite from the chaos of the market since 1752. Nicknamed Cafe des Miroirs, it's the best-known coffee hangout in the Egyptian market. Done up in 19th century European style, there are carved dark wooden thresholds, beautiful hammered brass and old marble tables and a lovely ancient carved bench to sit on, well worn by centuries of use. Coffee from little brass pots, tea in white enamel pots, sheesha smoke, and a perfect venue for people-watching make this as good a way of seeing Cairo as any, and much more relaxing.

SEEING THE SIGHTS

Students take note: you can get in for half-price at museums and sites.

Downtown

The **Egyptian Museum**, *behind the Nile Hilton on Tahrir Square*, costs E£10, and you should give yourself a minimum of 3 hours to wander around. Open daily 9am-4:45pm. They have slight organizational problems, but the old wooden cases with glass tops and endless, overwhelming, jumbled array of Pharaonic artifacts are delightful in their chaotic way, and the Cats Room is worth the search for it. The Mummy Room is now up and running, and the charge to visit the preserved, 5,000 year-old-man is an additional E£30 (E£15 for students).

Mugamma Building, *Tahrir Square*, is generally thought of as a landmark, but not a sight to see. Once inside its ominous facade, it's an interesting window on what bureaucracy can be, given its druthers. Like a vast ant farm, people hurry up and down the staircases in endless streams. Wander the stale halls and you'll see a multitude of rooms piled high with stacked dusty papers as ancient as the pyramids.

Cairo Synagogue, *Adly Street*, is a beautiful old building, and the caretaker will be only too happy to give you a personal tour.

Islamic Cairo

This is an overwhelming place in all ways. The smells and sights and sounds envelop you and as enormity of what there is to see sinks in. So figure your priorities, interests, and time, and see as much as appeals to you.

Al Azhar Mosque and **University**, *El-Hussein Square*, was founded in the 10th century by Shi'ite Fatimids, making Al Azhar the world's oldest university.

Across the street and 100 meters north is **Sayyidna el-Hussein**, revered by Muslims as the burial place of the skull of Hussein (Prophet Mohammed's grandson), and non-Muslims aren't allowed to enter. Behind Sayyidna el-Hussein is the 18th century **Musafirkhana Palace**. Open daily 9am-4pm, admission is E£3.

West from Sayyidna el-Hussein, all streets will lead you to the **Khan el-Khalili**, the most amazingly endless tourist shuk. The market here is crammed full of all the tourist souvenirs of Cairo. Everyone wants your business and your money and your time. Do you want souvenirs? This is probably the place to go for leather slippers, fezzes, brass and rugs and spices, leather floor cushions and *sheeshas*. The clamor and pressure may drive you away, but when you get home you may wish you'd gotten that brass coffee set, or maybe not. It's a colorful, noisy, wonderful place to wander around, whether you're shopping or not. And when you've had enough you can pop into Fishawi's (see *Where to Eat*) or cross over to **El Muski**, the Egyptian market, piled high with cotton and watermelons, slabs of granite and alleys of tin cooking utensils. It's much less touristed, friendlier, and a little quieter.

The area between Al Ashar Mosque and Bab el-Futuh on El Muizz is called **Bayn el-Qasrayn** ("between two palaces") and it's full of early Mamluk and Fatimid architecture.

North of there is the **Tomb and Madrasa of Malik es-Salih Ayyub** and its squarish minaret. Malik es-Salih Ayyub was the last of the Ayyubid Dynasty rulers, and husband to Shagarat ad-Durr who was one of the few women to be a legitimate ruler of Egypt (short-lived as it was), after Malik's death in 1249 and before her new husband began the Mamluk reign.

The **Mausoleum, Madrasa, and Hospital of Qalawun** is to the north. The complex is open daily 8am-5pm for E£3.

North of Qalawun, the **Mausoleum and Madrasa of En-Nasr Mohammed** is open 10am-8pm for free. Built in 1304 during Mamluk rule, the interior hasn't been preserved though the minaret still displays intricate carvings.

The **Mosque of Sultan Barquq** was built in 1386, a century after the Qalawun buildings, and is known for its painted timber roof, columns, and thin minaret. It's open daily 8am-8pm and costs E£3.

A short walk down Darb Kermez is **Qasr Bishtak**, what's left of a grand old palace from the 14th century. The **Mosque of El Aqmar**, meaning moonlit, is open 7:30am-9pm and is free. Another mosque, the **Mosque of Al-Muayid**, *Al Mu'ez in Gammaleya*, was built in 1474 above one of the city gates from 1091.

The **House of Gamal al-Din al-Dhahabi**, *Al-Ghoureya*, is an good example of 17th century Islamic architecture, and the **House of Al-Seheimi**, *Darb al-Asfar*, built in 1796, is another fine structure. It's open daily 10am-5pm and costs E£3. Nearby on El Gamaliya Street is **Baybars el-Gashankir**, built in 1310 and the oldest surviving example of a *khanqah* in Cairo.

Built in 1087 and successful in keeping medieval Cairo from being besieged, a few remains of the once vital and formidable **Fatimid walls** can still be seen. **Bab en-Nasr** at the top of El Gamaliya and **Bab el-Futuh** are two of the original rampart gates, and the walls once stretched around to **Bab Zuweila** on Darb el Ahmar to the southwest.

The Fatamid **El Hakim Mosque**, *off El Muizz*, was built between 990 and 1010 and is the second largest in Cairo. El Hakim, the Mad Caliph, was murdered after he announced his divinity and Ad-Darazi (his chief theologian) went off to Syria and founded the Druze sect. Open daily 8am-8pm, it costs E£6 to get in.

The **Citadel of Salah El-Din**, *eastern Cairo at the bottom of Mukattam Hill*, was built in the 13th century. One of the buildings in the complex is the **Mohammed Ali Mosque** (also called the Alabaster Mosque), which was built in 1830 and can be seen from most of Cairo. Another mosque in the complex is the small-domed **Mosque of Soliman Pasha**. Inside the Citadel is a **museum** with jewelry of Prince Farouk and a **Military Museum** as well, not to mention the **Police Museum** with fine examples of what marijuana looks like and police uniforms through the years. It costs E£8 to enter the Citadel and E£3 to enter the museum.

The **Mosque and Madrasah of Sultan Hassan**, *Salah El-Din Square*, built in the 14th century, is Cairo's largest mosque with the tallest minaret. Open Saturday-Thursday 9am-5pm, Friday 9-11am and 2-5pm, admission costs E£6.

The **Mosque of Ibn Tulon**, built in 879 CE and the third built in Egypt, is noted for its staircase that winds around the outside of the minaret, and its serene beauty. It's one of the most impressive in Cairo, is open 8am-6pm, and costs E£3.

Across the street is the **Rifa'a Mosque**. Built in 1912, its main claim to fame is its great size and the many tour groups it attracts. It's open Saturday-Friday 8-11am and 2-6pm, and costs E£6.

The **Blue Mosque**, *Tibbanah Street*, also called the mosque of Aqsunqur, was founded by Prince Aqsunqur Al-Nassery in 1347, and its name comes from the beautiful blue mosaics on the walls. Open daily 8am-6pm, it costs E£3 to enter.

The **Islamic Museum**, *Baab el-Khalq Square (intersection of Port Said, Muhammad Ali, and Ahmed Maher), Tel. 390-9930*, has one of the largest exhibits of Islamic art from all over the world, with many important Islamic artifacts, and it's housed in an enormous pink edifice. and is open Saturday-Thursday 9am-4pm and Friday 9-11:30am and 1:30-4pm. Usually uncrowded, it costs E£8.

Coptic Cairo

The **Coptic Museum**, *Misr al-Qadima, Old Cairo, Tel. 363-9742*, open 9am-4am in winter and 8am-1pm in summer, costs E£8 and contains thousands of historic relics from early Christianity. It shows the evolution of Coptic art and has exhibits on Hellenic, Nubian, and Islamic civilizations as well.

El Mu'allaqa Church, also called The **Hanging Church**, *next to the Coptic Museum, Old Cairo*, was constructed by the Romans in the 1st century BCE. Built in the 5th century, it sits on top of what was the **southern gate of the Fortress of Babylon**. It features a marble pulpit, a beautiful terrace, and a lot of icons.

Abou Serga Church (the Church of St. Sergius), *not far from El Mu'allaqa*, is supposed to be built over the cave where the Holy Family rested on their flight to Egypt. The church is dedicated to Sergius and Bacchus, two martyrs who died in the 4th century.

The **Church of the Virgin**, a basilica built in the 8th century, has three wooden altars inlaid with ivory and rare coins.

The **Church of Saint Barbara**, *to the east of the Fortress*, was built in the 5th century in honor of a Christian martyr.

A few meters south is the **Ben Ezra Synagogue**. It's gone from temple to Roman fortress to Christian church to 12th century synagogue.

Church of Saint George was built on the ruins of a much older church. Its three domes and Hall of Nuptials were built in the 13th century, but it was built on one of the towers of the Fortress.

The **Church of Saint Menas**, *Fumm Al-Khalig (mouth of the canal) near Old Cairo*, was built in the 6th century for Saint Menas.

The **Virgin Tree**, *Mattareyyah district*, is supposedly the tree under which the Holy Family rested during their Flight into Egypt.

Gezira

The **Cairo Tower** (Burg el Qahira), *near October 6th Bridge*, takes you straight up 187 meters for views all the way to the pyramids, especially nice at sunset. Open daily 8am-1am, it costs E£14 to take the elevator to the observation deck.

The **Mahmud Khalil Museum**, *1 Kafour St., Giza, Tel. 336-2376*, and has a superb collection of European and Islamic art as well as some fine Chinese jade. Open Saturday-Thursday 10am-6pm, admission is E£10.

Museum of Islamic Ceramics, *El Gezira Arts Center, 1 Sheikh Marfasy, Zamalek*, is across from the north end of the Gezira Sporting Club, hosts collections from the Ayyubid, Fatimid, and Mamluk eras.

The **Museum of Modern Art**, Gezira Street, near the Cairo Opera House, Tel. 341-6665, has Egyptian paintings from 1922 on. It's open Tuesday-Sunday 10am-1pm and 5-9pm, and admission is E£10.

The **Mukhtar Museum**, *Tahrir St., Zamalek, Tel. 340-2519*, is just before the Gala Bridge. It displays the works of sculptor Mahmoud Mukhtar (1891-1934), open Tuesday-Sunday 10am-1pm and 5-9pm for E£1.

Museum of Egyptian Civilization, *Tel. 340-6529*, shows Egypt's Pharaonic, Greek, Roman, Coptic, and Islamic periods. It's open daily 10am-2pm and costs E£1.

Dokki

The **Agricultural Museum**, *western end of the October 6 Bridge, Tel. 360-8682*, has a mummified Apis bull from the Serapium at Saqqara as well as agricultural exhibits. It's open Saturday-Thursday 10am-2pm, Friday 10am-noon, and costs E£1.

Roda

The **Manial Palace Museum**, *Salaya Street, Tel. 987-495*, is at the northern end of Roda Island next to the Cairo Youth Hostel. Built by Mohammed Ali in the 1800s, it's full of Islamic art and taxidermy treasures as well as the standard sumptuous palace rooms and decor. Open Saturday-Thursday 9am-4pm, Friday 9am-1pm and 2-4pm, it costs E£5.

On the other end of the island is the **Nilometer**, an 8th century device designed to measure the height of the river and used to predict the annual harvest yield. It's often locked but if you're persistent you can find the caretaker who'll take your E£3 and let you in.

Giza

West from Roda across El Gama'a Bridge is **Cairo University** and the beautiful **El Urman (Botanical) Gardens**. It's open daily 8:30am-5pm in summer, 8am-4pm in winter, and costs 50 piasters to get in plus another 50 for your camera.

Just south of the gardens is the **Cairo Zoo**. Open daily 8am-5pm, admission is 10 piaster and it's a rip-off at that.

Helwan

The **Wax Museum**, *across from the Ain Helwan metro station*, has the usual fine dramatic national scenes of executions, suicides, and heroes all rendered a bit ludicrous in cheesy wax likenesses. Open daily 9am-4pm, it costs E£1 to get in.

Heliopolis

Lots of fantastical architecture blending east and west in interesting combinations. It's worth strolling the avenues and looking at the various 19th century palaces.

Imbaba

North of Mohandiseen, there's a **camel market** (reputedly the largest in the country) every Friday from 5am-3pm, though the morning hours are best. It's quite a scene, and worth seeing.

Cities of the Dead

Northeast and south of the Citadel are hundreds of tombs and mausolea from the Mamluk era on, but not just the dead rest here. It also serves as a shanty town for the poor but living, making ghoulish use of all the grand old stone structures. The **Northern Cemetery** northeast of the Citadel has the finer and older monuments, while the **Southern Cemetery** is more crowded.

The tombs and mausolea are interesting and the necropoli are unique, but you're better off wandering in a small group than doing going solo.

NIGHTLIFE & ENTERTAINMENT

Coquillage, *Kasr el Nile Bridge near the Sheraton and New Opera Square, Tel. 340-6126*, this ornate and ritzy nightclub is open 10pm-4am and costs E£9-13 for the show. Also a restaurant, the entrees (all served with veggies and fries) cost E£25.

The **Cinema Rivoli**, *21 July 26th Street*, next to the Carlton Hotel, always has fascinating films advertised on their colorful posters.

The **Marriot Hotel**, *Zamalek, Tel. 340-8888*, has a swell roof top bar for views and drinks.

The **Zamalek** district for is the place for nightlife, discos, and snooty expatriates. For discos, your best bet is to go to the large hotels, all of which have them.

Miami Nightclub, *downtown*, has belly dancing in a dimly lit and entertaining venue.

Rida's Troupe, *Balloon Theater, En-Nil, Agouza, Tel. 247-7457*, is one of the best dance companies in Cairo, with fine Egyptian folk performances.

The **Goumhouriyya** The**ater**, *Tel. 919-956*, also has Arabic Music Troupe performances.

The **Cairo Puppet** The**ater**, *Azbakia Gardens near Opera Square, Tel. 910-954*, in performs nightly in Arabic, but you don't need English to understand.

Whirling dervishes, *Mausoleum of El Ghouri, El Muizz, Islamic Cairo*, are members of the Sufi sect of Islam. They can be seen doing their stuff Wednesday and Saturday at 9:30pm for free.

The **Opera House**, *Gezira*, has performances all year.

For a unique and bizarre daytime diversion, get a **Cairo pedicure**. Given the filth and dust that clogs the streets and coats your feet (if you're wearing sandals), swishing through the muck with painted toes is an experience not to be missed.

SHOPPING

See the *Khan El Khalili* entry in Islamic Cairo, and remember to bargain hard.

EXCURSIONS & DAY TRIPS
The Pyramids at Giza

The **Pyramids** are very big at the base, get very pointy at the top, and are surrounded by hideous tenement complexes, lots of sand, and men with horses and camels who say "hello, what country are you from, you are welcome, do you want camel, only 5 pounds, okay 2 pounds, both of you 1 pound, okay free, I don't want money from you, just ride 5 minutes."

Inside the pyramid the path is like a narrow ladder and incoming people stream up while others slither down, walking backwards. You go up, up, up to a small dark airless room with a sarcophagus, sweat gallons and, if female, may be subjected to numerous copped feel for the sight. But still, they are the pyramids, and they are impressive, and you can't see them (well, not these ones) anywhere else. Bring some water and a flashlight, as pyramid viewing is thirsty work and it's fairly dark inside.

The Pyramids at Giza and Saqqara, nine miles west of Cairo, are the most popular destination. After all, this is the reason many people come to Egypt in the first place. To get to Giza by bus from Tahrir Square take big bus 900 or 8 or minibus 82, or 83. Bus 30 goes from Ramses. It costs 35 piaster and takes an hour. To get to Saqqara there are share taxis from Giza Square that cost E£1. Entrance to the pyramids complex costs E£10 and to actually go inside the pyramids is another E£10. The Museum there costs E£10, as does the entrance to Saqqara, though it's 50% with a student card. The site is open daily 6:30am-8pm in summer, 7am-10pm in winter, and the pyramids are open daily 8am-5pm.

In the evening is the sound and light show, with different languages on different days. English presentations are Monday-Saturday, though it might be entertaining to hear the German show saying "Ich bin der Sphinkus" on Sunday. In summer the shows are at 8:30 and 9:30pm while in winter they're on at 6:30 and 7:30pm. Or, you may choose to go on one of the many available guided tours and limit the hassle somewhat. Ask you hotel person or check the *Practical Information* section for tour options.

The Egyptian pyramids were funerary monuments built for the pharaohs and their closest relatives. Most date from the Old Kingdom (c. 2686-2181 BCE) and are found on the west bank of the Nile, in a region approximately 100 kilometers long and situated south of the delta, between Hawara and Abu Ruwaysh. Pyramids developed from the Mastaba, a low, rectangular stone structure erected over a tomb.

The most elaborate example of the temple complex is found at **Giza**, where the 4th-dynasty pyramids of Kings Khufu (Cheops), Khafre (Chephren), and Menkaure (Mycerinus) lie in close proximity to each other. The pyramid of Khufu, erected c. 2500 BCE, is the largest in the world, measuring 756 feet on each side of its base and originally measuring 482 feet high. Beginning in the 10th century CE, the entire Giza complex served as a source of building materials for the construction of Cairo, and, as a result, all three pyramids were stripped of their original smooth outer facing of limestone. The temples have disappeared, with the exception of the extremely well preserved granite valley temple of Khafre.

Khufu, or **Cheops**, was the king of ancient Egypt around 2680 BCE who directed the construction of the Great Pyramid at Giza, the largest tomb-pyramid ever built. He was the son and successor of King Snefru, who founded the 4th dynasty (2613-2498). During his reign, Khufu mobilized nearly all of Egypt's male work force for his monumental building project. In 1954, remains of the 142 foot **funerary ship** of Khufu were discovered near the Great Pyramid and a second boat was found in 1987. An ivory statuette found in the temple at Abydos and thought to depict Khufu is in the Egyptian Museum in Cairo.

Khafre, also called **Chephren**, was the fourth king of the 4th dynasty (2613-2498 BCE) of ancient Egypt. The son of Khufu, he built the second of the three Great Pyramids and the **Great Sphinx** as well. A mythical creature that was frequently a subject of ancient Egyptian sculpture, the sphinx combined the body of an animal (usually a lion) with the head of a man, and was frequently shown lying down. Statues of sphinxes were often associated with Egyptian sanctuaries, as in the avenue of sphinxes connecting the temples of Luxor and Karnak in Thebes.

The most famous Egyptian sphinx is the one near the pyramid of Khafre at Giza. It measures 69 feet high and 243 feet long, and its face, now badly damaged, is believed to represent King Khafre himself. Originally built to guard the pyramid, the Great Sphinx was later worshipped as the god *Rahorakhty*, "Ra of the Two Horizons." Long one of Egypt's most celebrated monuments, it was disfigured by vandalism, and today is threatened by air pollution as well.

Menkaure, also called **Mycerinus**, ruled after Khafre from 2613-2494 BCE. The successor of Khafre, Menkaure built the third and smallest of the three Pyramids at Giza, which constitute the sole surviving example of the Seven Wonders Of The World.

The Pyramids at Saqqara

The easiest way to get here is on a tour, otherwise you'll have to hire a taxi. The sites are open 8am-5pm (8am-4pm in winter), and it costs E£10 to enter.

The oldest pyramid known, the **Step Pyramid** of King Zoser at Saqqara (2650 BCE), has a large *mastaba* as its nucleus and consists of six terraces of diminishing sizes, one built upon the other. It was surrounded by an elaborate complex of buildings, now partially restored, whose function related to the cult of the dead. Saqqara, or Sakkara, was the necropolis, or burial place, for the ancient Egyptian city of Memphis, containing remains from almost every period of Egypt's history. Among the most important monuments of the Old Kingdom is the **Step Pyramid**, erected about 2630 BCE by Imhotep for King Zoser of the 3d dynasty, and rising in six layers to a height of 200 feet. Its underground passages and chambers contained thousands of stone vessels as well as beautiful reliefs representing Zoser performing religious rites. The structures around this pyramid are translations into stone of earlier wattle-and-daub buildings, and as such they constitute an invaluable record of early Egyptian architecture.

To the northwest of this complex is the **Serapeum**, a vast subterranean passage dating from the New Kingdom, containing niches in which the Apis bulls were buried. Among the private tombs, those of the nobles of the 5th and 6th dynasties are noteworthy for their painted scenes of daily life. The best of these belong to the tomb of Tiy, a high court official of the 5th dynasty. The **Monastery of Saint Jeremiah**, founded by the Copts in the 5th century CE, includes two churches, a refectory, and various workshops.

North of Saqqara some six kilometers are the three pyramids of **Abu Sir**. The pyramids rising up out of the Eastern Desert here are not on the tourist bus route, which means you're limited to horse, camel, or foot for transport, but you're rewarded by pyramids all to yourself. There are also two pyramids in the funerary complex of **South Saqqara**, about four kilometers south. And there are a few ruins of the ancient city of **Memphis** near the Nile. The pyramids of **Dahshur** are just south of that. Located about 26 kilometers south of Cairo, Dahshur is the site of the first true (smooth-sided) Pyramids built by the kings of ancient Egypt (earlier pyramids had been built in step form). The two largest pyramids at Dahshur (each about 328 feet high) were built by King Snefru of the 4th dynasty (2613-2494 BCE).

The earlier of the two is called the **Bent Pyramid** because the angle of its sides was lowered due to structural problems halfway through construction. The other, known as the **Red (or North) Pyramid**, was built entirely at the lower angle used for the upper portion of the Bent Pyramid. Smaller pyramids were built at Dahshur during the Middle Kingdom period (2040-1786 BCE) as burial places for the 12th-dynasty kings Amenemhet II, Amenemhet III, and Sesostris III.

Luxor & Aswan

Unfortunately, people also really like to visit **Luxor** and **Aswan**, and this is not a good idea due to terrorist activity aimed at the government through attacks on Western tourists traveling to these places. So, the

Temple of Karnak in Luxor and **Abu Simbel** near Aswan are pretty much off limits until that situation resolves itself somewhat. Check with the embassy to keep tabs on any changes concerning the advisability of traveling to those regions.

PRACTICAL INFORMATION

- **Airlines: Air Sinai**, *Nile Hilton, Tel. 760-948*, is open daily 9am-5pm; **Egypt Air**, *Nile Hilton, Tel. 765-200; 6 Adly, Tel. 391-1256.* **ZAS Airlines**, *1 Tala'at Harb, Tel. 393-0425, Fax 393-0366.*
- **American Cultural Center**, *4 Ahmed Ragheb, Garden City, Tel. 354-9601 or Tel. 355-0532 for the library*, is across from the British Embassy. They're open Sunday-Friday 10am-4pm.
- **American Express**, *15 Kasr en-Nil, Tel. 574-7991*, is just off Tala'at Harb Square and is open daily 8:30am-6pm. They have a client letter service, a USA direct phone service, and change traveler checks as well. Other branches: *Cairo Airport, Nile Hilton, Marriot Hotel, Pullman Ma'adi, Mohandiseen at 4 Syria, Bus Travel Center at 72 Omar Ibn El Khattab in Heliopolis, and Giza at 21 Nile St.*
- **Banks**, scattered throughout the city, are closed Friday and Saturday.
- **British Council**, *192 En-Nil, Agouza, Tel. 345-3281*, is 1 block south of July 26th next to the Balloon Theater. They're open Monday-Saturday 9am-2:45pm, and the library, *Tel. 344-8445*, is open Monday-Wednesday 9am-2pm, Friday-Saturday 9am-3pm.
- **Car Rentals**: If you insist, there's **Avis**, *Tel. 354-8698*, **Europcar**, *Tel. 340-1152*, **Hertz**, *Tel. 347-4172*, **Max Rent-a-Car**, *Tel. 347-4712*, and **Budget**, *Tel. 340-0070.*
- **English Bookstores**: **Shorouk Bookshop**, *Tala'at Harb Square, Tel. 391-2480*, is open daily 9am-9pm; **AUC Bookstore**, *Hill House, American University in Cairo, 113 Kasr El 'Aini, Tel. 357-5377*, is open Sunday-Thursday 8:30am-4pm, Saturday 10am-3pm; **Anglo-Egyptian**, *165 Mohammed Farid, Tel. 391-4337*, is open Monday-Saturday 9am-1:30pm and 4:30-8pm; **Lehnert and Landroch**, *44 Sharif, Tel. 393-5324*, is open Monday-Friday 9:30am-1:30pm and 3:30-7:30pm, Saturday 9:30am-1:30pm; **Madbuli**, *Tala'at Harb Square, Tel. 575-6421*, is open daily 10am-10pm; and **L'Orientaliste**, *15 Kasr en-Nil, Tel. 575-3418*, is open Monday-Saturday 10am-7:30pm with lots of old books and maps and lithographs.
- **English newspapers and magazines**: lots of kiosks *along Tala'at Harb Square* sell them, as well as shops in all the major hotels.
- **Fire**: *125*
- **Hospitals: As-Salaam International Hospital**, *Corniche en-Nil, Ma'adi, Tel. 363-8050*, is well equipped; **Anglo-American Hospital**, *Botanical Garden Street, Gezira-Zamalek, Tel 340-6162*, is below the Cairo Tower;

for emergency care, call **Cairo Medical Center**, *Roxy Square, Heliopolis, Tel. 258-0566*. For an **ambulance**, call *123*.

• **Jordanian Embassy**, *6 El Goheina, Dokki, Tel. 348-5566*, is two blocks west of the Cairo Sheraton. The office is open Saturday-Thursday 9am-noon, and you'll need photos for a visa.

• **Lockers** are available in Ramses railway station for 40 piasters a day.

• **Ministry of Tourism**, *Misr Travel Tower, Tel. 282-8451*, is open Saturday-Thursday 8:30am-2:30pm.

• **Palestinian Office**, *23 En-Nahda, Dokki, Tel. 347-7567*.

• **Pharmacies**: **First Aid Pharmacy**, *corner of Ramses and July 26th, Tel. 743-69*, is open 24 hours; **Victoria Pharmacy**, *90 Kasr El 'Aini, Garden City, Tel. 354-8604*, is also open 24 hours.

• **Police**: *122* or *303-4122*.

• **Post Office**: The main branch, *55 Sarwat on 'Ataba Square, Tel. 391-2614*, is open Saturday-Thursday 8:30am-3pm. They have a poste restante section, but to sent Express Mail go around the corner on Bidek across from poste restante (open Saturday-Thursday 8am-7pm).

• **Supermarkets**: **Cash & Carry**, *64 Lebanon Square, Mohandiseen, Tel. 346-5350*; **Seoudi Market**, *25 Midan El Missaha, Dokki, Tel. 348-8440*; *15 Ahmad Hishmat, Zamalek, Tel. 334-0037*; and **Sunnyshine Supermarket**, *11 El Aziz Osman, Zamalek, Tel. 342-1121*.

Swimming Pools: **Fontana Hotel**, *Ramses Square, Tel. 922-145*, will let you swim in their pool for E£7, and the **Marriot** sells day passes for E£63, admitting you to pool, sauna, Jacuzzi, and gym. There are also sporting clubs: **Gezira Sporting Club**, *in front of the Marriot, Zamalek, Tel. 340-2272*, **Ma'adi Sporting Club**, *8 En-Nadi Square, Tel. 350-5504*, and **Heliopolis Sporting Club**, *117 El Merghany, Tel. 291-4800*.

• **Telegraph and Telex Office**, *'Ataba Square opposite the main post office*, is open 24 hours. There are also offices at *Tahrir Square, 26 Ramses, and Adly*.

• **Telephones**: **Directory Assistance** is 140, and the **Cairo area code** is 02. The main office of the **Telephone Office**, *Ramses, Tel. 340-1674*, is one block north of July 26th. There are other branches in Zamalek, *Tel. 340-1674*, at the Airport, *Tel. 247-5059*, Ma'adi, *Tel. 350-1122*, Tahrir Square, *Tel. 765-118*, and Alfy, *Tel. 907-314*. They're all open 24 hours. You can also make international phone calls and send **faxes** from most of the major hotels, for a surcharge.

• **Tourist Office**: The **Misr Travel Tower office**, Abbasiyya Square, Tel. 827-964, is open Saturday-Thursday 8:30am-3pm. Another branch, *5 Adly, Tel. 391-3454*, off Tala'at Harb to the right, is staffed by extremely lovely and helpful people with lots of maps, and is open 8:30-7pm. **Cairo International Airport**, *Tel. 667-475*, has a branch (open 24 hours), as does Giza, *Tel. 385-0259*, next to the Pyramids

Police station and in front of Menahouse Hotel, open Saturday-Thursday 8am-5pm.

- **Tourist Police**, *5 Adly, Tel. 126 or 391-944*, is right next to the tourist office branch. There's another branch at the Cairo International Airport, *Tel. 247-2548*, Giza , *Tel. 385-0259*, and in the Manial Palace Hotel.
- **Tours around Egypt: Misr Travel**, *1 Tala'at Harb, Tel. 393-0010, Fax 392-4440*, has half-day pyramid or Cairo trips for $55, full day Cairo trips for $120, and they lead tours to Luxor, Aswan, Mount Sinai and more as well. They can also be contacted in New York, *630 5th Ave, Suite 555, Tel. 212-582-9210, Fax 212-247-8142*; **BTC**, *2 Hasoreg, 2nd floor, off Jaffa near Shlomzion, Jerusalem, Tel. 02-233-990, Fax 02-257-827*, offers three-day tours in Cairo for $98, and a six-day tour of Cairo, Luxor, and Aswan for $205. **American Express**, *15 Kasr El Nil, Cairo, Tel. 574-7991*, has three-hour tours of Cairo (to Islamic Cairo or the Egyptian Museum and Hanging Church) and half-day pyramid tours as well. All prices subject to change.
- **Tours to Egypt: Mazada Tours**, *141 Ibn Givrol, Tel Aviv, Tel. 03-544-4454, Fax 03-546-1928*, and *24 Ben Sira, Jerusalem, Tel. 02-255-453, Fax 02-255-454*, offers both transport and tours to Egypt. Bus transport to Cairo costs $45 ($60 round trip). The tours all leave from and return to Israel; most tours go by bus transport but some go by plane instead. A four day tour of Cairo costs $79-$317 (depending on accommodation level), and two of the days are taken up with bus travel, while an 8-day tour of Cairo, Luxor, and Aswan costs $333-$790 ($770-$977 by plane). **Galilee Tours**, *42 Ben Yehuda, Tel Aviv, Tel. 03-546-6333, Fax 03-291-770*, and *3 Hillel, Jerusalem, Tel. 02-258-866, Fax 02-231-303*, has four-day tours to Cairo for $120-$289 (depending on hotel category) and eight-day trips for $341-$864. None of these prices include visa or departure taxes.
- **US Embassy**, *5 Latin America, Tel. 354-8211*, two blocks south of Tahrir Square, is open Sunday-Thursday 8am-4:30pm, but the American services department is only open 8am-noon. You can, however, call after hours in an emergency, or ask for the consular section in the afternoon for emergency passport or money problems. Lost or stolen passports can be replaced overnight for $65.

24. GLOSSARY

HEBREW - IVRIT

Many Hebrew words have a guttural throat-clearing sound not common in English, though the German and Scottish *ach* sound is pretty similar. Rendered in this book with a *kh*, it's sometimes written elsewhere with a *ch*. The Hebrew *r* is similar to the French *r*, and while there are subtle stresses, in general if you pronounce the words without any of the syllables emphasized it'll come out sounding right. Hebrew is read from right to left, but the numbers are read left to right.

USEFUL WORDS		NUMBERS	
hello, goodbye, peace	*shalom*	1	*ekhad*
yes	*ken*	2	*shtayeem*
no	*lo*	3	*shalosh*
good morning	*boker tov*	4	*arba*
good evening	*erev tov*	5	*khamesh*
good night	*liela tov*	6	*shesh*
see you later	*l'hitra'ot*	7	*sheva*
excuse me, sorry	*slikha*	8	*shmoneh*
wait, wait	*rega, rega*	9	*tisha*
thank you	*toda*	10	*esser*
you're welcome	*bevakasha*	11	*ekhad essray*
how are you	*ma shlomkha*	12	*shtaym essray*
fine, okay	*b'seder*	20	*essreem*
good	*tov*	21	*essreem v'ekhad*
not good	*lo tov*	30	*shlosheem*
excellent	*metzuyan*	50	*khamesheem*
I'm tired	*ani ayef*	100	*mayah*
where is?	*aifo*	200	*mahtayeem*
what	*mah*	300	*shloshmayoat*
when	*matai*	500	*khamayshmayoat*
why	*lama*	1000	*elef*

correct (right)	*nakhon*	3000	*shloshet alafeem*
my name is	*shmi*	5000	*khamayshet alafeem*
what's your name?	*eikh korim lekhah*		

GETTING AROUND

money	*kessef*	station	*takhana*
central bus station	*tahana merkazit*	bank	*bank*
stop here	*ahtsor kahn*	railway	*rahkehvet*
bus	*otoboos*	near	*karov*
straight	*yashar*	left	*smol*
right	*yamin*	road	*derekh*
boulevard, avenue	*sderot*	street	*rehov*
lane	*nateev*	square	*kikkar*
pedestrian walkway	*midrakha*	stairs	*madregot*
I'm going to...	*ani holekh l'...*		
which bus goes to...	*ehseh otoboos nosayah le...*		

DAYS & TIME

Sunday	*yom rishon*	Monday	*yom shaini*
Tuesday	*yom shlishi*	Wednesday	*yom revi'i*
Thursday	*yom hamishi*	Friday	*yom shishi*
Saturday	*Shabbat*	day	*yom*
week	*shavua*	month	*khodesh*
year	*shana*	today	*ha'yom*
yesterday	*etmol*	tomorrow	*mahar*
what time is it	*ma hasha'a*	minute	*daka*

FOOD & LODGING

hour, time	*sha'a*	to eat	*le'ehkhol*
six o'clock	*hasha'a shaysh*	to drink	*lishtot*
food	*okhel*	water	*mayim*
restaurant	*misahda*	menu	*tafreet*
breakfast	*ahrookhat boker*	dinner	*ahrookhat erev*
lunch	*ahrookhat tsohora'im*		
bread	*lekhem*	butter	*khema*
milk	*khalav*	cheese	*g'veena*
egg	*baytsa*	vegetables	*yehrakoht*
fruit	*payrot*	wine	*yahyin*
ice cream	*gleedah*	coffee	*kafeh*
tea	*teh*	waiter	*meltza*
waitress	*meltzarit*		

EMERGENCIES

hospital	*beit kholim*	doctor	*rofeh*
passport	*darkon*	airport	*s'deh te'ufa*
police	*mishtara*		

SHOPPING & SIGHTS

market	*shuk*	grocery store	*makolet*
what's this?	*ma zeh*	how much?	*kama zeh*
post office	*do'ar*	letter	*mikhtav*
envelopes	*ma'atafoth*	postcard	*glooya*
stamps	*boolim*	pharmacy	*beit merkakhat*
shop	*khanoot*	expensive	*yakar*
cheap	*zol*	bill	*kheshbon*
synagogue	*beit knesset*	change (money)	*odef*
church	*knaissia*	hotel	*mahlon*
museum	*muzaion*	hostel	*akhsaniya*
beach	*khof*	room	*kheder*
go away!	*tistalek*	toilet	*sherutim*

ARABIC - AL'ARABI

The language is read right to left, unlike the numbers which go left to right. The numerals, different from ours, are well worth learning for greater ease in the market or taking a bus. Generally speaking, an attempt to speak Arabic, no matter if you botch it up, will be warmly received in Arab markets or countries.

USEFUL WORDS

hello (informal)	*marhaba*
hello (formal)	*salaam aleikum*
response	*aleikum salaam*
yes	*aiwa*
no	*la*
thank you	*shukran*
you're welcome	*afwan*
excuse me, sorry	*'an iznak*
please	*min fadlak*
God willing	*inshallah*
praise God	*al hamdu lillah*
good morning	*sabah al-kheir*
response	*sabah an-nour*
good evening	*masa al-kheir*
response	*masa an-nour*

NUMBERS

0	*sifr*	٠
1	*waahid*	١
2	*tinein*	٢
3	*talaata*	٣
4	*arba'a*	٤
5	*khamsa*	٥
6	*sitta*	٦
7	*sab'a*	٧
8	*tamanya*	٨
9	*tis'a*	٩
10	*'ashara*	١٠
11	*hidash*	
12	*etnash*	
13	*talatash*	
20	*eshreen*	

goodbye	*ma' as-salaama*	21	*waahid we eshreen*
how are you	*keef helsack*	30	*talateen*
fine	*kwayyis*	100	*miya*
good	*meneh*	200	*mitein*
tired	*ana ta'baan*	1000	*ulaf*
very	*keteer*	4000	*arba'a ulaf*
wonderful (view)	*moodhesh*		
beautiful (people)	*jame'el, hiloo*		
ugly (people)	*mish hiloo*		
what's your name	*ismak eh*		
my name is	*ismi*		
pardon	*ahdesh hadah*		

GETTING AROUND

where	*feen*	I'm going to	*ana rayih*
left	*shemal*	right	*yemine*
straight	*dooree*	when	*eimta*
let's go	*yella*	street	*sharia*
station	*mahatta*	airport	*mataar*
square	*midan*	restaurant	*mat'am*
hotel	*funduq* or *otel*	room	*oda* or *ghurfa*

DAYS & TIME

Sunday	*yoam al-ahad*	Monday	*yoam al-itnein*
Tuesday	*yoam at-talat*	Wednesday	*yoam al-arba'a*
Thursday	*yoam al-khamees*	Friday	*yoam aj-jum'a*
Saturday	*yoam as-sabt*	day	*yoam*
week	*usbuu'*	month	*shaher*
year	*sana*	today	*al-yoam*
yesterday	*imbaareh*	tomorrow	*bukra*
hour, time	*saa'a*	what time is it	*es-saa'a kaam*

SHOPPING & SIGHTS

is there?	*fee*	is there no?	*mafeesh*
how much?	*addeish*	no way	*mish mumkin*
how about half?	*taakhud nuss*	money	*masaari*
change	*fraata*	I want	*biddee*
never mind	*ma'lish*	market	*souq*
post office	*maktab al-bareed*	museum	*mathaf*
church	*kineesa*	mosque	*masjad, jaame'*
what do you want?	*esh piduck*	go away!	*roh men hone*

EMERGENCIES

embassy	*safaarah*	police	*bolees*
hospital	*mustashfa*	doctor	*duktor*
passport	*basbor*		

INDEX

THINGS CHANGE!

Phone numbers, prices, addresses, quality of food, etc, all change. If you come across any new information, we'd appreciate hearing from you. No item is too small! Drop us an e-mail note at: Jopenroad@aol.com, or write us at:

Israel Guide
Open Road Publishing, P.O. Box 284
Cold Spring Harbor, NY 11724

TRAVEL NOTES